#2022 EDITION

THE SMART AIR FRYER COOKBOOK
FOR BEGINNERS

1000+

QUICK AND DELICIOUS IDEAS TO
EASILY FRY, BAKE, AND GRILL YOUR EVERYDAY MEALS,
INCLUDING RECIPES WITH
ONLY 5 INGREDIENTS OR LESS

KAREN STEVENS

Copyright ©2022 by **Karen Stevens**. All rights reserved.

This document is geared towards providing exact and reliable information in regard to the topic and issue covered.

From a Declaration of Principles which was accepted and approved equally by a Committee of the American Bar Association and a Committee of Publishers and Associations.

In no way is it legal to reproduce, duplicate, or transmit any part of this document in either electronic means or in printed format. All rights reserved.

The information provided herein is stated to be truthful and consistent, in that any liability, in terms of inattention or otherwise, by any usage or abuse of any policies, processes, or directions contained within is the solitary and utter responsibility of the recipient reader. Under no circumstances will any legal responsibility or blame be held against the publisher for any reparation, damages, or monetary loss due to the information herein, either directly or indirectly.

Respective authors own all copyrights not held by the publisher.

The information herein is offered for informational purposes solely and is universal as so. The presentation of the information is without contract or any type of guarantee assurance.

The trademarks that are used are without any consent, and the publication of the trademark is without permission or backing by the trademark owner. All trademarks and brands within this book are for clarifying purposes only and are owned by the owners themselves, not affiliated with this document.

All rights reserved by **KAREN STEVENS**

Table of Contents

INTRODUCTION 16
   1. The must-to-know 7 tips & tricks 16
   2. What's best to cook with an air fryer and what's not 17

CHAPTER 1 VEGGIES & SIDE DISHES 18
1. Easy melt cheesy mushrooms 18
2. Garlic stuffed mushrooms 18
3. Mixed cilantro and peppers 18
4. Goat cheese added to italian tomatoes 18
5. Zucchini bread 18
6. Japanese tempura 18
7. Stuffed spicy ricotta mushrooms 19
8. Mixture of kale and sprouts 19
9. Egg salad with vegetable 19
10. New broccoli puree 19
11. Yummy paprika leeks 19
12. Flavourful cranberry beans side salad 20
13. Cabbage with lemon 20
14. Fried green olives stuffed with pimiento .. 20
15. Delectable roasted cauliflower 20
16. Canapes made of cabbage 20
17. Cabbage cooked in butter 20
18. Healthy roasted eggplant 20
19. Roasted potatoes with a spicy twist 21
20. Delicious green beans 21
21. 23. Mix recipe for zucchini 21
22. Cauliflower dipped in buffalo sauce 21
23. Special potatoes and tomato sauce recipe .. 21
24. Mixed cranberries and broccoli 21
25. Cremini mushrooms with rice pilaf 21
26. Bacon fries with cheese 22
27. Chives, almond and broccoli 22
28. Eggplant meatballs with almond 22
29. Dill ravioli and nutmeg 22
30. Crispy rosemary potatoes 22
31. Crisp zucchini with parmesan 22
32. Rolls with veggies 23
33. Yummy mozzarella risotto 23
34. Delicious pumpkin rice dish 23
35. Simply baked potatoes 23
36. Buttered fennel 23
37. Mixed endives and rice 23
38. Pecorino parmesan on fried green beans .. 23
39. Air-fried cheesy broccoli with garlic 24
40. Celery puree 24
41. BBQ shrimps 24
42. Tomatoes and green beans recipe 24
43. Glazed tamarind and sweet potatoes 24
44. Spring onions and leeks 24
45. Mashed cauliflower 24
46. Amazing paprika asparagus 25
47. Sauté artichoke 25
48. Healthy potato casserole 25
49. Healthy zucchini latkes 25
50. Yummy scrambled eggs 25
51. Delicious chicken croquettes 25
52. Chips brussels sprout 26
53. Crispy tofu 26
54. Bite-size crispy cauliflower 26
55. Mozzarella eggplants and lime 26
56. Mixed zucchini and squash 26
57. Beefy meatballs 26
58. Delicious bacon and asparagus spears 26
59. Special squash noodles 27
60. Delicious zucchini nests 27
61. Tasty lemon fennel 27
62. Fried asparagus topped with goat cheese .. 27
63. Chicken BBQ pizza 27
64. Mixed balsamic cabbage 27
65. Shrimp with coconut 28
66. Brussels sprouts 28
67. Super fried agnolotti 28
68. Feta cheese and mediterranean tomatoes .. 28
69. Yummy portobello mushrooms 28
70. Tasty mix of turmeric kale 28
71. Creamy parmesan sauce with tomato bites .. 28
72. Healthy balsamic mustard greens 29
73. Spicy green beans 29
74. Mexican cauliflower fritters 29
75. Cheesy grilled cheese 29

76.	Mashed kale	29
77.	Chickpea taco and sweet potato	29
78.	Cauliflower rice and macadamia	30
79.	Tasty sweet-and-sour mixed veggies	30
80.	Flavourful lemon kale	30
81.	Amazing thyme mushroom pan	30
82.	Crispy and tasty pickles	30
83.	Parmesan croquettes and rainbow vegetable	30
84.	Yummy harissa broccoli spread	31
85.	Appetizing almond brussels sprouts	31
86.	Tasty crumbed beans	31
87.	Amazing pumpkin wedges	31
88.	Thin broccoli patties	31
89.	Mixed mung beans	31
90.	Delightful roasted cashews	32
91.	Appetizing kabocha fries	32
92.	Delectable coconut parmesan kale	32
93.	Flavorful roasted beet salad	32
94.	Mixed coconut mushrooms	32
95.	Avocado on sweet corn fritters	32
96.	Mixed rosemary olives	32
97.	Summer fritters- vegetable edition	32
98.	Vegetable bake rainbow cheese	33
99.	Healthy cabbage wedges	33
100.	Almonds, blue cheese and crispy wax beans	33
101.	Tasty winter vegetable braise	33
102.	Bake greek-style vegetable	33
103.	Creamy cauliflower and broccoli	34
104.	Tasty breaded mushrooms	34
105.	Avocados wrapped with bacon	34
106.	Mushrooms stuffed with mint-butter	34
107.	Delicious parmesan squash	34
108.	Crispy roasted broccoli	34
109.	Delicious Indian malai kofta	35
110.	Roasted tomatoes with feta, greek style	35
111.	Brussel sprout salad, american-style	35
112.	Crispy and delicious parmesan with sour cream and asparagus	35
113.	Chickpeas cooked in air-fryer with herbs	35
114.	Roasted and healthy vegetables	36
115.	Crispy sweet corn fritters	36
116.	Delicious mushroom cakes	36
117.	Cheesy spinach	36
118.	Shirataki noodles and fennel	36
119.	Tasty low-carb pita chips	36
120.	Parmesan artichoke hearts	37
121.	Awesome cheese sticks for everyone	37
122.	Veggie tots for kids	37
123.	Mixed mozzarella asparagus	37
124.	Mixed zucchinis and arugula	37
125.	Great-tasting smoked fish balls	37
126.	Green beans with butter	37
127.	Mushrooms stuffed with cheese	38
128.	Balsamic radishes	38
129.	Super jalapeno clouds	38
130.	Qui----healthy veggie fried balls	38
131.	Baked sweet potato	38
132.	Roasted red potatoes in duck fat	38
133.	1 gratin family vegetable	39
134.	Sprouts coconut celery	39
135.	Fried asparagus dipped in romesco sauce	39
136.	Yummy coconut risotto	39
137.	Bell pepper and tomato sauce recipe	39
138.	Mixed lemongrass rice	39
139.	Pancetta and plums bombs	40
140.	Lemony artichokes	40
141.	Fried onion and bell peppers	40
142.	Delicious smoked asparagus	40
143.	Cheesy sticks dipped in sweet thai sauce	40
144.	Dill corn	40
145.	Cheesy parmesan asparagus	40
146.	Chili rutabaga	41
147.	Cheesy parmesan cauliflower risotto	41

CHAPTER 1 SNACKS & APPETIZERS ... 42

148.	Coated prawns	42
149.	1. Roasted parsnip with maple syrup	42
150.	Dazzling pork meatballs	42
151.	Extra topped pita bread	42
152.	Crazy spicy nuts	42
153.	Crunchy cheddar & broccoli nuggets	42
154.	Roma tomatoes chips	43
155.	Delicious eggplant crisps	43
156.	Radish and sage chips	43
157.	Simply bacon and shrimp	43

#	Recipe	Page
158.	Zucchini spring rolls	43
159.	Broccoli golden nuggets	43
160.	Seasoned tofu with avocado	43
161.	Fabolous veggie fritters	44
162.	Spicy nutty nibble	44
163.	Tasty cauliflower popcorn	44
164.	Zucchini nibbles with mayonnaise	44
165.	Cheesy sticks with paprika	44
166.	Crispy cauliflower with herbs	45
167.	Vinegary hot sauce	45
168.	Spicy carrot and chives dressing	45
169.	Cauliflower tortillas	45
170.	Sriracha short ribs	45
171.	Spiced broccoli chips	45
172.	Super crispy broccoli fritters	45
173.	Fleshy beef cocktail wieners	46
174.	Brussels sprouts munch	46
175.	Cheesy bacon scoops	46
176.	Bacon-and cheddar kibble	46
177.	Sage-spiced chicken wings	46
178.	Pork and beef lavish meatball	46
179.	Fried cashew	47
180.	Superb chicken pillows	47
181.	Cheesy cauliflower bombs	47
182.	Spinach and parsley rolls	47
183.	Spicy pickle chips with Greek yogurt dip	47
184.	Onion rings	48
185.	Golden fried baby corn	48
186.	Cashew and cilantro sauce	48
187.	Sweet potato fingers	48
188.	Tasty roasted peanuts	48
189.	Fantasy of roasted vegetables	48
190.	Cheesy crisps	49
191.	Delicious feta cheese pastries	49
192.	Smart popcorn	49
193.	Cheesy mushrooms and herbs	49
194.	Savory and crunchy eggplant with Italian seasoning	49
195.	No stress cocktail franks	49
196.	Easy potato cloves	50
197.	Fried pepper fingers	50
198.	Spicy apple chips	50
199.	Fried tomatoes with parmesan cheese	50
200.	Yummy spiced sweet potato tots	50
201.	Coconut cookies with vanilla scent	50
202.	Carrots and rhubarb salad	50
203.	Creamy spinach sauce	51
204.	Minty pineapple kibbles	51
205.	Lemony tofu	51
206.	Famous pork chops by grandma	51
207.	Super cheesy jalapeno peppers	51
208.	Flaky pizza with bacon and sausage	52
209.	Cheddar quick sandwich	52
210.	Easy and scrumptious radish chips	52
211.	Mozzarella and pepperoni appetizer	52
212.	Cheddar and bacon tots	52
213.	Bacon and dark chocolate bites	52
214.	Fried avocado cloves	52
215.	Mexican cheesy muffins	52
216.	Fried polenta nuggets	53
217.	Lemony cauliflower with curry	53
218.	Nuts symphony	53
219.	Mayo cauliflower	53
220.	Avocado nuggets with spicy sauce	53
221.	Beef nibbles	53
222.	Pork and beef smokies in keto sauce	54
223.	Avocado wrappers	54
224.	Kalamata olives fritters	54
225.	Minty pork meatballs	54
226.	Tilapia fillets with ranch dressing	54
227.	Thousand herbs tomato	54
228.	Sweety mozzarella snack	55
229.	Shrimps and chives cakes	55
230.	Sausage wonton nibbles	55
231.	Ricotta and orange balls	55
232.	Brussels sprouts with balsamic vinegar	55
233.	Veggie cocktail with sausages	55
234.	Butter balls	55
235.	Cheesy smoked breadsticks	56
236.	Tantalizing bacon with avocado	56
237.	Garlicky green beans	56
238.	Chicken wings in pungent sauce	56
239.	Bite-size cheeseburgers	56
240.	Flavored pork loin	57
241.	Bacon and eggs with hot sauce	57
242.	Crispy bacon with Brussels sprouts	57

243. Appetizing kale chips 57
244. Mozzarella and parmesan cheese appetizer 57
245. Plain banana chips 57
246. Mushrooms with a veggie cream stuffing 57
247. Sandwich with vegetables 58
248. Shrimps wrapped with bacon 58
249. Crispy pork rinds 58
250. Onion sauce 58
251. Chicken drumettes in teriyaki sauce 58
252. Sesame okra 59
253. Pickle spears wrapped in bacon slices 59
254. Healthy bread with veggies 59
255. Lemony beans 59
256. Scallops and bacon skewers 59

CHAPTER 2 VEGETARIAN & VEGAN RECIPES 60

257. Broccoli stuffed with cheese and pepper 60
258. Healthy veggie rice 60
259. Sweet and spicy tofu 60
260. Delicious vegan calzone 60
261. Tofu ala italian 61
262. Stuffed eggplant with a twist 61
263. Glazed carrots 61
264. Veggies air-fried sushi 61
265. Drizzling onion 61
266. Eggplant potato and zucchini chips 61
267. Baked potato and parsnip 62
268. Cheesy pizza with a crust made of broccoli .. 62
269. Cheesy muffins 62
270. Braised vegetables with a twist 62
271. Cheesilicious brussel sprouts 62
272. French green beans and shallots 'n almonds 63
273. Vegetables and stuffed mushrooms 63
274. Delightful ratatouille 63
275. Crescent triangles spinach and feta 63
276. Healthy broccoli casserole 63
277. Sweet honey glazed carrots 63
278. Delightful sweet and sour brussel sprouts 64
279. Sweet hoisin-glazed bok choy 64
280. Pasta 'n cheese, baked portobello 64
281. Baked layered tortilla 64
282. Awesome vegetables recipe 64
283. Mayo and buttered carrot-zucchini 65
284. Crispy and tasty butternut squash fries 65
285. Shallots on a minty green beans 65
286. Grilled veggie with tandoori spice 65
287. Healthy stuffed eggplant 65
288. Vegetable frittata two-cheese 65
289. Mexican baked zucchini recipe 66
290. Herb and veggie cornish pasties 66
291. Refreshing zesty broccoli 66
292. Fried cauliflower 66
293. Baked vegetable with olives and cheese 66
294. Cauliflower asian-style 67
295. Sweet and sour tofu 67
296. Delicious and ultra-crispy tofu 67
297. Delicious roasted mushrooms in herb-garlic oil 67
298. Bell peppers and oatmeal 67
299. Sweet grilled 'n glazed strawberries 68
300. Delicious falafel with chickpeas 68
301. Chopped paprika brussels sprouts 68
302. Au gratin potatoes ala rosemary 68
303. Seasoned vegetables creole 68
304. Tofu with a twist 68
305. Yummy buttered rolls 69
306. Oatmeal with bell pepper 69
307. Healthy hearty carrots 69
308. Crispy and spicy asparagus with paprika-garlic sauce 69
309. Air fried skewered corn 69
310. Thailand's spicy veggie recipe 69
311. Crispy and delicious ham rolls 70
312. Delightful caviar eggplant 70
313. Balsamic sweet and sour brussel sprouts 70
314. Stylish roasted vegetables 70
315. Crunchy round eggplant 70
316. Crusted rice flour tofu 70
317. Crisp swiss cheese and eggplant 71
318. Open-faced flatbread vegan sandwich 71
319. Almond-apple special 71
320. Glazed parsnips 71
321. Rice casserole made of egg and cauliflower 71

322.	Delightful roast winter vegetable	71
323.	Cream cheese-pesto with stuffed mushrooms	71
324.	Stuffed cheese tomatoes	72
325.	Marinated pearl onions on a tofu bowl	72
326.	Kiddie zucchini fries	72
327.	Spiced bread rolls curry 'n coriander	72
328.	Salted garlic and roasted broccoli	72
329.	Crispy avocado fingers	73
330.	Tasty shawarma broccoli	73
331.	3 Mediterranean dill sauce on zucchini	73
332.	Specially sautéed spinach	73
333.	Amazing vegetable croquettes	73
334.	Delicious roasted pepper salad and goat cheese	73
335.	No-egg spinach quiche	74
336.	Onion rings with spicy sauce	74
337.	Air fried ravioli	74
338.	Rosemary vegetables	74
339.	Baked zucchini garlic-sour cream	74
340.	Tasty croissant rolls	75
341.	Original indian bhaji	75
342.	Yummy crispy tofu	75
343.	Sandwich tomato with feta and pesto	75
344.	Ribs and pineapple appetizer	75
345.	Healthy radish salad	75
346.	Special cauliflower and tofu	76
347.	Original baked banana recipe	76
348.	Flavored garlic-wine vegetables	76
349.	Battered crisped onion rings with almond flour	76
350.	Aloo tikka indian-style	76
351.	Cheesiest mushroom pizza	77
352.	Cheesy stuffed mushrooms	77
353.	Eggplants stuffed with salsa	77
354.	Cheesy balls made of mushroom and cauliflower	77
355.	Yummy potato pancakes	77
356.	Eggplants stuffed with more veggies	78
357.	Easy to prepare garden fresh veggie	78
358.	Pecorino parmesan and crispy green beans	78
359.	Tofu BBQ with green beans	78
360.	Monterey jack cheese on veggie fingers with	78
361.	Stuffed peppers greek-style	79
362.	Cauliflower tater tots twice-fried	79
363.	Potato chips with velveeta dip mediterranean-style	79
364.	Kid-loved vegetable fritters	79
365.	Crispy 'n savory spring rolls	79
366.	Healthy fritters made from ricotta cauliflower	80
367.	Battered wings with almond flour	80
368.	Crispiest tofu with paprika	80
369.	Delicious corn cakes	80
370.	Fresh green beans	80
371.	Easy and healthy chips	80
372.	Roasted barbecue almonds	80
373.	Sautéed spinach and bacon	81
374.	Italian-styled easy pasta chips	81
375.	Oatmeal with berries, baked	81
376.	Awesome roasted mushrooms	81
377.	Amazing air-fried falafel	81
378.	Tomatoes and cauli rice salad	81
379.	Pizza with mushroom 'n bell pepper	81
380.	Sweet hasselback potatoes	82
381.	Healthy granola with nuts and raisins	82
382.	Vegetable kabobs with peanut sauce dip	82
383.	Tasty stuffed tomato	82
384.	Tasty paneer cutlet	82
385.	Grilled mushrooms	82
386.	Balsamic vinaigrette added to radish and mozzarella salad	83
387.	Roasted rosemary	83
388.	Famous buffalo cauliflower	83
389.	Veggies and healthy air fried halloumi	83
390.	Fried okra with a twist	83
391.	Green beans and okra	84
392.	Spicy avocado spread on a corn on the cob	84
393.	Falafel with tzatziki mediterranean-style	84
394.	Roasted cashew nuts, spiced	84
395.	Flavourful celery croquettes dipped in chive mayo	84
396.	Spicy wasabi popcorn	84
397.	Mushrooms stuffed with bacon and cheese	85
398.	Marinara baked cheesy eggplant	85

399. Delicious vegetable salsa wraps 85
400. Polenta fries 85
401. Fast and easy to prep crispy cheese lings 85
402. Healthy roast peppers and potatoes 86
403. Cheesiest mushrooms 86
404. Great garlicy mushroom 86
405. Tasteful mushrooms with cheddar cheese ... 86
406. Spiced veggie burger with chives 'n thyme ... 86
407. Mediterranean skewers made of vegetable 86
408. Sweet potato balls Thailand-style 86
409. Delicious asparagus and mushroom fritters 87

CHAPTER 3 MEAT RECIPES 88

410. Kansas city's baby back rib recipe 88
411. Top round roast with herbs blend 88
412. Pork in garlic sauce 88
413. Peanut sauce with flavorsome pork chops ... 88
414. Loin chops with za'atar lamb 88
415. Short loin steak with grilled mayo 89
416. Potatoes with pork loin 89
417. Dill pickles with smoked brisket 89
418. Worcester meatloaf 89
419. Wine marinated flank steak 89
420. Pork roulade 89
421. Old-fashioned beef burgers 90
422. Beef jerky 90
423. Vegetables with hearty beef cubes 90
424. Buttered strip loin steak 90
425. Buttered garlic-celery with roast beef 90
426. Smoked pork 90
427. Cumin lamb kebabs, Sichuan and caraway ... 91
428. Hot paprika beef 91
429. Beef schnitzel 91
430. Hot bacon bites 91
431. Sage sauce recipe with pork chops 91
432. Meatball sausage 91
433. Ghee mushroom with beef mix 91
434. Cumin-paprika with beef brisket 92
435. 4 garlic pork in ginger and coconut sauce ... 92
436. Stuffed bell pepper 92
437. Brekky casserole and Monterey Jack sausage 92
438. Rhubarb and peppercorn lamb 92
439. Figs with grilled prosciutto 92
440. Coconut pork with green beans 93
441. Smoked bacon with peppery roasted potatoes 93
442. Steak in cascabel-garlic sauce 93
443. Herb meatballs 93
444. Moroccan style beef kebab 93
445. Balsamic-raspberry jam with pork 93
446. Filet mignon in herb-crust 94
447. Minty lamb chops 94
448. Salami rolls in homemade mustard and manchego 94
449. Corn dog bites 94
450. Thai meatballs 94
451. Mushroom casserole and cheesy meatball ... 94
452. Beef burgers, smoked style 95
453. Saucy beef fingers and tangy 95
454. Spicy chicken wings 95
455. Beef steaks with saucy lemony 95
456. Lamb with herbs crumbed rack 96
457. Southwest meaty pasta bake 96
458. Basil lamb with mustard chives 96
459. Cauliflower frittata and sausage 96
460. Tomato-olive salad on steak 96
461. Cheeseburgers with classic keto 97
462. Lamb steak with garlic lemon-wine 97
463. Buttered filet mignon 97
464. Omelet with kale and beef 97
465. Veggies and classic skirt steak strips 97
466. Garlic-mayo sauce and winter beef 97
467. Beef with zucchini sauté 97
468. Pork butt with herb-garlic sauce 98
469. Country fried steak 98
470. Biscuit brekky with eggs and bacon 98
471. Beef with spring onions 98
472. Lamb chops with roasted cilantro 98
473. Osso buco with lemon 98
474. Marinated pork chops marinate 99
475. Sweety pork belly 99
476. Honey mustard cheesy meatballs 99
477. Sweet pork chops with soy sauce 99
478. Nutmeg pork cutlets with parmesan 99

#	Title	Page
479.	Easy to do beef (beef, easy way)	99
480.	Classic beef stroganoff	100
481.	Chinese-style beef	100
482.	Honey and mustard ham	100
483.	Sesame and za'atar lamb chops	100
484.	Pork loin roast with herbs de Provence	100
485.	Herbed lamb leg	100
486.	Sirloin with curry, paprika and yogurt	101
487.	Stuffed pork roll	101
488.	Pork and cabbage	101
489.	Beef rump steaks with fresh herbs	101
490.	Oregano beef roast	101
491.	Rosemary lamb with mint flavor	101
492.	Sour & sweet glazed fried pork	102
493.	Pork with chili tomato	102
494.	Beef and tofu mix recipe	102
495.	Rubbed chicken tenderloin with paprika-cumin	102
496.	Cheesy and buttery sausage	102
497.	500. Sausages with lamb beef	102
498.	Chicken tenders with shaking tarragon	103
499.	Lemony lamb loin chops	103
500.	Chicken wings with ginger	103
501.	Kebabs with veggie and beef	103
502.	Pork riblets in tomato sauce	103
503.	Salted butter with chicken fillets	103
504.	Wrapped pork	104
505.	Peach mash on ribeye	104
506.	Rubbed chicken with curry-peanut butter	104
507.	Steak with Irish whisky	104
508.	Beef burgers Asian style	104
509.	Mustard turkey fingers with creole	105
510.	Super-hot chicken skin	105
511.	Crusts with chicken pizza	105
512.	Chicken wings and lemon pepper	105
513.	5 garlicky beef chops with mustard	105
514.	Ginger chicken tenders	105
515.	Scallion kabobs with chicken	105
516.	Cabbage salad, lettuce and beef	106
517.	Strips of buffalo chicken	106
518.	Chicken tenderloin that is air-fried	106
519.	Minty lamb mixture	106
520.	Easy crunch wrap for Thanksgiving	106
521.	Vegetables and Italian turkey sausage	107
522.	Spiced rack of lamb with saffron	107
523.	Beef sausage meatballs with Mexican chili	107
524.	Pork schnitzel with heavy cream	107
525.	Crunchy stuffed chicken breast	107
526.	Greek style chicken	108
527.	Egg frittata with salted meaty	108
528.	Turkey chimichurri	108
529.	Chicken and veggies roll	108
530.	Turkey ground mix	108
531.	Turkey nuggets with thyme	108
532.	Chicken tenders from India	109
533.	Chicken tenders from KFC	109
534.	Sweet turkey bake	109
535.	BBQ beastly drumsticks	109
536.	Prawn paste and chicken	109
537.	Yummy chicken fingers with fresh chives	109
538.	Shredded chicken Moroccan style	110
539.	Peppercorn duck with vanilla	110
540.	Chicken mix with bacon	110
541.	Traditional Asian chicken	110
542.	Okra chicken thighs with thyme	110
543.	Scrambled eggs and turkey bacon	110
544.	Turkey breast rolls	111
545.	Shallots with almond turkey	111
546.	Scallions mix with duck legs	111
547.	Enchilada bake with leftovers	111
548.	Orange beef	111
549.	Garlicky chicken	112
550.	Chicken glazed with agave mustard	112
551.	Pepperyturkey sandwiches	112
552.	Parmesan and lime with chicken tenders	112
553.	Broccoli brekky, cauliflower and eggs	112
554.	Chicken wings in sweet chili sauce	112
555.	Glazed and spicy chicken wings	113
556.	Chicken wings with garlic sausages	113
557.	Drumsticks with spicy and sweet chicken	113
558.	Cashew nuts and chicken	113
559.	Turkey breast with buttermilk	113
560.	Scallion kabobs and chicken	113
561.	Turkey burgers and vermouth bacon	114

#	Title	Page
562.	Chicken mix with cream cheese	114
563.	Buttered chicken thighs	114
564.	Chicken with marjoram	114
565.	Spicy and juicy chicken wings	114
566.	Chicken tenders with Worcestershire sauce	115
567.	Orange chicken with spicy honey	115
568.	Cheese and bacon-wrapped turkey	115
569.	Parsley breast duck	115
570.	Lemon asparagus and garlic turkey	115
571.	Oregano duck spread	116
572.	Spicy and crispy whole chicken	116
573.	Cauliflower and Ethiopian-style chicken	116
574.	Sweet 'n sour sauce and chicken BBQ	116
575.	Blackberry mix with duck	116
576.	Chicken tenders with tortilla chips crust	116
577.	Tasty chicken from Caribbean	117
578.	Simple and delicious chicken with mayonnaise and mustard	117
579.	Tetrazzini traditional chicken	117
580.	Chicken breasts bacon wrapped	117
581.	Chicken halves with oregano	117
582.	Drumsticks with lemon chicken and oregano	118
583.	Coleslaw and crispy turkey sandwich	118
584.	Teriyaki with traditional chicken	118
585.	Flavorful chicken fajitas	118
586.	Simple and delight chicken wings	118
587.	Walnut rice and duck	118
588.	Candy onion and Thai red duck	119
589.	Lime Dijon chicken drumsticks	119
590.	Miso-ginger with chicken meatballs	119
591.	Breakfast frittata with turkey	119
592.	Chicken drumsticks with sweet and spicy flavour	119
593.	Buttery chicken quesadilla	120
594.	Chicken mix with bleu cheese	120
595.	Colby turkey meatloaf for holiday	120
596.	Mongolian chicken	120
597.	Delicious strawberry turkey	120
598.	Chicken breasts in marinara sauce	120
599.	Chicken burgers with onion and garlic	121
600.	Juicy herbed drumsticks with mustard	121
601.	Chicken breasts with spinach	121
602.	Chicken wings with maple syrup	121
603.	Chicken breasts with cheddar and cream	121
604.	Simple chicken sliders	121
605.	Rice and veggies with chicken	122
606.	Special maple-glazed chicken	122
607.	Chicken wings with soy sauce and honey	122
608.	Manchego cheese and turkey meatballs	122
609.	Chili chicken barbecue with sweet lime	122
610.	Chinese-style turkey thighs sticks	122
611.	Spicy turkey meatloaf	123
612.	The finest pizza chicken	123
613.	Supreme Creole chicken tenders	123
614.	Coconut chicken fritters t dill	123
615.	Coconut meatballs with chicken	123
616.	Turnip with paprika chicken legs	124
617.	Cheese, black bean and baked rice	124
618.	Honey glazed turkey breast	124
619.	King buffalo chicken	124
620.	Lemon sauce with ginger chicken	125
621.	Shallot sauce with paprika turkey	125
622.	Coconut broccoli and turkey	125
623.	Italian seasoned whole chicken	125
624.	Maple mustard with turkey	125
625.	Middle Eastern tzatziki sauce and chicken BBQ	125
626.	Chicken tenders with Worcestershire sauce	126
627.	Pecorino parmesan and cauliflower chicken	126
628.	Coconut milk casserole and spinach-egg	126
629.	Carrots and chicken	126
630.	Pesto chicken with ginger	126
631.	Chicken wings with cheese	127
632.	Casserole with pizza spaghetti	127
633.	Smart chicken wings	127
634.	Dill chicken and parmesan	127
635.	Lemon-chicken breast with pepper flavor	127
636.	Battered thighs with lemon-butter	127
637.	Fried cheesy chicken	128
638.	Crunchy chicken legs	128
639.	Chinese style duck	128
640.	Paprika liver spread	128
641.	Spicy chicken in tomato sauce	128

642. Roasted tomatoes with Mediterranean chicken breasts 129
643. English muffins and eggs Benedict 129
644. Sweet curried chicken cutlets 129
645. Black olives and chicken sauce recipe 129
646. Chicken enchiladas 129
647. Asian chicken fillets with cheese and ginger 130
648. Veggie breakfast frittata 130
649. Old-fashioned chicken drumettes 130
650. Garlic and herbs chicken 130
651. Leftover turkey in mushroom sauce 130
652. Easy to cook turkey wings 130
653. The finest chicken burgers 131
654. Coconut milk with chicken pot pie 131
655. Battered chicken with almond flour coco-milk 131
656. Chicken casserole with broccoli-rice 131
657. Zaatar chicken 131
658. Quick and easy chicken drumsticks 132
659. Peanut sauce with Malaysian chicken satay 132
660. Veggie kabobs, pineapple and jerk chicken 132

CHAPTER 4 FISH RECIPES 133

661. Tilapia fillet, spicy and salty 133
662. Smooth salmon 133
663. Trout with shallots 133
664. Creamy breaded shrimp 133
665. Creole lemon salmon 133
666. Catfish nibbles 133
667. Superb shrimps with goat cheese 134
668. Buttery chives trout 134
669. Salmon fillets with broccoli 134
670. Saporous herbed trout 134
671. Lemony branzino with Creole 134
672. Bacalao Portuguese style 134
673. Garlicky salmon 135
674. Pollock with a mix of Kalamata olives and herbs 135
675. Summertime shrimp skewers 135
676. Slightly acid branzini fillets 135
677. Spiced coco-lime skewered shrimp 135
678. Flaky crab croquettes 135
679. Crab cakes in Dijon seasoning 136
680. Salmon in chili sauce 136
681. Burned halibut in brioche 136
682. Trouble-free salmon fillets 136
683. Creole cod fillets with avocado sauce 136
684. Fish packets 137
685. Creamed trout salad with mayonnaise 137
686. Peppery halibut fillets 137
687. Flaky cod fish nuggets 137
688. Cool breaded flounder 137
689. Pistachio incrusted salmon 137
690. Ham tilapia fillets 138
691. Greek-style roast fish 138
692. Herbed salmon 138
693. Tender tuna with herbs 138
694. Basil and paprika cod 138
695. Saucy catfish with ginger and garam masala 139
696. Halibut with lemony capers mix 139
697. Creole fish cakes with Swiss cheese 139
698. Strong cod fillets 139
699. Tasty and smooth fish fillets 139
700. Snapper fillets with nutty sauce 139
701. Browned branzino 140
702. Cod fillets Hong Kong style 140
703. Grilled shrimp 140
704. Yummy sockeye salmon fillets 140
705. Shrimp in rice flour coating 140
706. Definitive parmesan fish fillets 141
707. Mustard and parmesan cod 141
708. Shrimps with Monterey Jack cheese 141
709. Sunlight pollock fish 141
710. Glazed halibut steak 141
711. Lime-garlic shrimps 141
712. Basil paprika calamari 142
713. Delightful crab cakes 142
714. Butter paprika swordfish 142
715. Rosemary garlic prawns 142
716. Air fried fresh broiled tilapia 142
717. Mouthwatering tuna cakes 142
718. No-stress cat fish recipe 143
719. Cumin, thyme 'n oregano herbed shrimps 143
720. Fresh lobster tails with green olives 143

#	Title	Page
721.	Zesty salmon fillet	143
722.	Fantastic calamari	143
723.	Lively calamari salad	143
724.	Salmon with honey blackberry sauce	144
725.	Cod fennel platter	144
726.	Shrimps with black olives	144
727.	Fish fillets with sesame	144
728.	Zesty briny prawns	144
729.	White fish fillets	144
730.	Italian style shrimp	145
731.	Peppery shrimps	145
732.	Sea scallops mediterranean style	145
733.	White fish tots	145
734.	Superb fried cod fish	145
735.	Flounder in mascarpone sauce	145
736.	Italian-style mackerel	146
737.	Boneless paprika tilapia	146
738.	Garlic shrimps combination	146
739.	Haddock with rosemary and sesame seeds	146
740.	Milkfish bellies, filipino-style	146
741.	Marinated salmon	146
742.	Salmon with spinach	147
743.	7 creole shrimps	147
744.	Shrimps with lemon flavor	147
745.	Flounder fillets with worcestershire sauce	147
746.	Char and fennel	147
747.	Easy cod fillets with garlic and herbs	147
748.	Quick and easy salmon	148
749.	Haddock with herbs	148
750.	Fisherman's fish fingers	148
751.	Coconut crusted shrimps	148
752.	Crunchy cod sticks	148
753.	Chinese-style garlicky shrimp	148
754.	Buttery scallops with rosemary	149
755.	Japanese-style flounder with chives	149
756.	Fish fillets in pesto sauce	149
757.	Shrimps with pine nuts fusion	149
758.	Mouth-watering shrimps skewers	149
759.	Mahi mahi fillets with green beans	149
760.	Trout in nutty butter sauce	150
761.	Jumbo shrimp	150
762.	Amazing ginger cod	150
763.	Shrimps with parmesan	150
764.	Sesame seeds coated tuna	150
765.	Hake fillets with garlic sauce	151
766.	Fried shrimps with chili	151
767.	Indian famed fish curry	151
768.	Pleasant thyme catfish	151
769.	Sweety sea bass with lentils	151
770.	Beer cod filet	151
771.	Quick and easy scallops	152
772.	Linguine with grilled tuna	152
773.	Turmeric salmon with soy sauce	152
774.	Succulent crab cake burgers	152
775.	Pleasant baby octopus salad	152
776.	Sole fish and cauliflower nibbles	152
777.	Cod with spring onions	153
778.	Grilled shrimp with butter	153
779.	Tasty halibut steaks	153
780.	Crispy herbed calamari rings	153
781.	Haddock in creamy sauce	153
782.	Prawns and salmon pasta	153
783.	Grilled squids rings with kale	154
784.	Classic fish and chips	154
785.	Shrimps kebabs	154
786.	Louisiana-style shrimps	154
787.	Salmon with green beans	154
788.	Sea bass and olives combination	155
789.	Crispy pesto salmon fillets	155
790.	Shrimp and celery salad	155
791.	Lemony grilled halibut with tomatoes	155
792.	Ghee shrimps	155
793.	Buttered scallops	155
794.	Pecan crusted tilapia	155
795.	Pecan crusted tilapia	156
796.	Avocado sauce on creole cod fillets	156
797.	Chives trout in butter	156
798.	Yummy buttered scallops	156
799.	Juicy jumbo shrimp	156
800.	Butterflied prawns with garlic-sriracha	156
801.	Paprika tilapia	157
802.	Dijon mustard and parmesan crusted tilapia	157
803.	Summertime fish packets	157

804. LOVELY SEAFOOD PIE 157
805. CRAB CAKES 157
806. SHRIMPS WITH CELERY SALAD 158
807. HALIBUT STEAKS 158
808. TROUT WITH ZUCCHINIS AND TOMATO SALAD 158
809. MOUTH-WATERING SPICED COCO-LIME SKEWERED SHRIMP 158
810. FISH FILLETS WITH TARRAGON 158
811. STUFFED TUNA WITH CAPERS AND GREEK YOGURT 158
812. LEAN SALMON WITH CAULIFLOWER RICE 159
813. GRILLED FISH BURGERS 159
814. BOILED TILAPIA 159
815. PIQUANT SHRIMP KEBAB 159
816. GINGER COD 159
817. GRILLED SHRIMPS ON PESTO SAUCE 159
818. DELICIOUS CRAB CAKES 160
819. CREOLE VEGGIE-SHRIMP BAKE 160
820. SPRING ONIONS SALMON WITH TARRAGON 160
821. TILAPIA WITH COTTAGE CHEESE AND CAPER SAUCE 160

CHAPTER 5 DESSERTS RECIPES 161

822. ALMOND FLOUR CRACKERS 161
823. VANILLA PLUM CAKE 161
824. THE QUICKEST BANANA CAKE 161
825. OLD STYLE BUTTERMILK BISCUITS 161
826. PEANUT BUTTER AND CHOCOLATE FONDANTS ...161
827. NUTELLA PASTRIES 162
828. SPEEDY POUND CAKE 162
829. MOZZARELLA CHEESE COOKIES 162
830. APPLESAUCE BROWNIES 162
831. APPLE-TOFFEE WITH UPSIDE-DOWN CAKE 162
832. EASY PEACH PIE 163
833. MACADAMIA COOKIES 163
834. APPLE NUTTY PUDDING 163
835. PEANUT CRUMBLE 163
836. CUSTARD WITH A HINT OF NUTMEG 163
837. LEMON MUFFINS 164
838. GINGER AND CINNAMON PEAR FRITTERS 164
839. FIERY DARK CHOCOLATE CAKE 164
840. VANILLA-SCENTED CUSTARD 164
841. HAZELNUTS COBBLER 164
842. CAKE OF OTHER TIMES 165

843. COCONUT VANILLA COOKIES 165
844. STRAWBERRY AND PHILADELPHIA POP TARTS 165
845. TASTY PLUM BARS 165
846. CHEESECAKE WITH WHITE CHOCOLATE AND BERRIES 165
847. HAZELNUT BROWNIES 165
848. PEANUT BUTTER COOKIES 166
849. SOFT RICE PUDDING 166
850. FRITTERS WITH STRAWBERRIES 166
851. CLASSIC LEMON CURD 166
852. CHERRIES BARS 166
853. CHOCOLATE CASHEW CAKE 166
854. CLASSIC BANANA SPLIT 167
855. LEMON CAKE 167
856. QUICK AND EASY CHEESECAKE 167
857. RHUBARB PIE WITH NUTMEG FLAVOR 167
858. QUICK APPLE WEDGES WITH APRICOTS 167
859. CREAM CHEESE COOKIES 168
860. BEST FUDGY BROWNIES WITH RICOTTA CHEESE 168
861. NUTTY SWEETY MUFFINS 168
862. GRIDDLE CAKES WITH GREEK YOGURT ... 168
863. CHOCOLATE CAKE 168
864. HONEY AND BLUEBERRY PANCAKES 168
865. LEMONY RICOTTA CAKE 169
866. DARK CHOCOLATE CUPCAKES 169
867. WALNUTS AND DARK CHOCOLATE BROWNIES 169
868. RASPBERRIES AND AVOCADO CAKE 169
869. DELICIOUS COCONUT CREAM PIE 169
870. CINNAMON CAKE WITH CRANBERRIES ... 170
871. LEMON CAKE FOR BEGINNERS 170
872. COCONUTTY BARS WITH LEMON FLAVOR 170
873. SUPERB CHOCOLATE AND MERINGUE CAKE 170
874. VANILLA AND COCONUT OAT COOKIES ... 171
875. COCONUT AND WHITE CHOCOLATE COOKIES 171
876. APPLES STUFFED WITH OATS, MIELKE AND WALNUTS 171
877. SWEETY PEACH SKEWERS 171
878. EASY GHEE CAKE 171
879. SUCCULENT CHOCOLATE CAKE 171
880. VANILLA CUSTARD PEACHES 172
881. LAVA CHOCOLATE CAKE 172
882. COCONUT AND VANILLA COOKIES 172
883. OLD FASHION CRÈME BRULEE 172

884. Buttery doughnuts 172
885. Almond and coconut bars 173
886. Soft biscuits with buttermilk 173
887. Orange nuggets 173
888. Mascarpone cake with peppermint flavor 173
889. Pears clafouti 174
890. Vanilla cookies 174
891. Sweety coconut flour rolls 174
892. Coconut and cacao pudding 174
893. Sweet potato and heavy cream pie 174
894. Pecan streusel with mixed berries 175
895. Vanilla-scented mozzarella bombs 175
896. Nutmeg churros 175
897. 900. Coconut berry pudding 175
898. Ricotta dessert 175
899. Lemon and tangerine cake 175
900. Banana and chocolate brownie 176
901. Dark chocolate and cream cheese cheesecake 176
902. Old style churros 176
903. Cheat apple pie 176
904. Chocolate custard with heavy cream 176
905. Pecan cookies and puffy coconut 176
906. Strawberries and lemon stew 177
907. Cranberry bread pudding 177
908. 9 almond cheese cake with strawberries 177
909. Almond and coconut cookies with butter rum flavor 177
910. Dark chocolate and zucchini brownies 177
911. Simple angel food cake 178
912. Fast dark chocolate hot drink 178
913. Pecans cake 178
914. Dark chocolate brownies with avocado dough 178
915. Tejeringos spanish-style doughnut 178
916. Peaches and honey cake 178
917. Vanilla sauce apples 179
918. Buttery fritters 179
919. Cranberry brownies for°father's day 179
920. Lemon glazed pop-tarts 179

CHAPTER 6 MORE RECIPES 181

921. Ham and baked eggs on a veggie casserole 181
922. Spinach and eggs florentine 181
923. Chicken frittata, chive, and feta 181
924. Delicious and healthy celery and bacon cakes 181
925. Delicious chicken with tomato sauce 181
926. Western eggs recipe 182
927. Stuffed chicken rolls with cheese and chive 182
928. Fruit skewers greek style 182
929. Stuffed chicken with double cheese 182
930. Special potato and kale croquettes 182
931. Beef and tomato with baked eggs 183
932. Original pork rinds 183
933. Fontina, frittata and sausage, pepper 183
934. Deviled eggs farmer's breakfast 183
935. Cheesy and yummy broccoli 183
936. Manchego and cauliflower croquettes 183
937. Halibut and eggs keto rolls 184
938. Delicious roasted cherries 184
939. Apple fries country-style 184
940. Tasty paprika chicken 184
941. Melting bagel 'n' egg 184
942. Finger sage and lime wings 185
943. Baked eggs and bacon with quinoa 185
944. Eggs, swiss chard and ham 185
945. Cheesy mozzarella stick nachos 185
946. Parsley yogurt dip for green pea fritters .. 185
947. Avocado chicken sliders for dinner 186
948. Crispy wontons with asian-style sauce 186
949. Super sweet potato fries 186
950. Asparagus and spinach egg salad 186
951. Sweet chocolate doughnuts 186
952. Roasted garlic and sausage and decadent frittata 186
953. Peppery egg salad with a twist 187
954. Chicken and provolone cheese and za'atar eggs 187
955. Blueberries and honey with french toast 187
956. Goat cheese in a roasted green bean salad 187
957. Mushroom omelet philadelphia style 187
958. Stuffed chicken breasts with cheese and garlic 188
959. Tasty omelet with beef 188
960. Super cheesy mushroom balls 188

961. Egg muffins for breakfast 188
962. Curry turkey and Dijon cutlets 188
963. Sausage in a scrambled eggs 189
964. Cheesy parmesan broccoli fritters 189
965. Cheesy cheese and shrimp dip 189
966. Chicken creamed creole 189
967. Healthy vegetable burrito 189
968. Sausage and Swiss cheese with spicy eggs 190
969. Delicious baked hot fruit 190
970. Omelet with sausage, baked 190
971. Cheesy bacon rolls 190
972. Baked eggs masala-style 190
973. Pork meatloaf country-style 190
974. Italian sausage and winter baked eggs 191
975. Cornmeal pudding Jamaican style 191
976. Seafood casserole and breakfast eggs 191
977. Florentine baked eggs 191
978. Grilled pork chops with lemon 191
979. Meatloaf a la creole turkey 192
980. Bacon wrapped onion rings 192
981. Linguica sausage and baked eggs 192
982. Super english muffins 192
983. Savory crespelle italian style 192
984. Sweet small monkey rolls 193
985. Original pork chops 193
986. Omelet with special mushrooms and peppers 193
987. Healthy and zesty broccoli bites with hot dip 193
988. Kernel and sweet corn fritters 193
989. Chicken sausage with delectable frittata 194
990. Kale omelet with beef 194
991. Fried mushrooms for all 194
992. Delicious chicken with tamari sauce 194
993. Cheese and cauli rice with baked eggs 194
994. Creamy frittata with kale Italian-style 194
995. Caci cavallo with keto brioche 195
996. Turkey bacon, green onions and eggs 195
997. Cauliflower balls with cheese 195
998. Yummy omelet with smoked veggies and tofu 195
999. Fried rice with eggs Japanese style 196
1000. Cheesy risotto balls with a spicy twist 196
1001. Garlic-mayo sauce for potato 196
1002. Creamy asparagus and egg salad 196
1003. Cheesy carrot fries 196
1004. Original onion rings with mayo dip 197
1005. Amazing Greek revithokeftedes 197
1006. Potato wedges with a spicy twist 197
1007. Chicken and goat cheese in a spring frittata 197
1008. Cheesy cheese sticks with ketchup dip 197
1009. Ground meat omelet Filipino-style 198
1010. Cashew sauce for fingerling potatoes 198
1011. Salty pretzel crescents 198

CHAPTER 7 COOKING MEASUREMENTS & KITCHEN CONVERSION CHART 199

CHAPTER 8 AIR FRYER COOKING CHART 201

Introduction

If you have purchased your first air fryer, it may be difficult to figure out how to operate it effectively. The first and most important thing to remember is they are not for deep frying. The air fryer is the ideal kitchen appliance for frying, grilling, or baking a meal.

Air fryers, with their convection quality, are the ideal equipment for quick and simple cooking. Using any air fryer instead of a deep fryer results in far healthier fried dishes. Grilling and frying food takes less time and produces dishes with the perfect degree of crispiness every time. Baking goodies will take less time and produce half the mess.

Most air fryers feature baskets on the interior that house the various meals or ingredients, as well as a convection coil and fan that distributes heat evenly throughout the basket to cook your meal. Depending on the model of your air fryer, it is important to follow the recommendations or instructions particular to that device in order to get the best temperature for your meal without compromising the contents.

Also, after each usage, make sure you clean the air fryer well to remove any germs or residual smells from old food crumbs. Before you start using your air fryer, read the handbook to get precise instructions on how to care for it. In general, you should wipe out the basket and crumb tray after each usage. These trays may often be put immediately in the dishwasher.

I recommend cleaning out the inside of your air fryer at least once a week, or every five cooked meals. A lot of residue may accumulate on the edges of your air fryer and make its way into your other dishes. When cleaning the inside of your air fryer, make sure it is switched off and disconnected.

When cleaning the air fryer, make sure you don't use any harsh chemicals. Consider it like cleaning the interior of a microwave. Clean thoroughly with a medium-strength brush or cloth and a light soap or cleaner. To avoid any chemical reactions within the air fryer, I use a natural baking soda paste or an equal store-bought choice.

1. The must-to-know 7 tips & tricks

1) The first important tip for utilizing an air fryer is to have your favourite cooking oil available at all times. While there are certain exceptions, I suggest using a mild olive oil cooking spray. Cooking oil comes in a variety of brands and flavors, and having one on hand is vital for many air fryer dishes. Coating the air fryer basket with cooking oil prevents the item from getting stuck.

2) Another tip for utilizing your air fryer is to use the timer on the air fryer. Using the timer allows you to set the time for half of the total cook time to guarantee you are flipping the food at the correct moment.

3) It is vital to remember to insert a piece of parchment or foil in the air fryer when preparing a dish that requires a sauce or wet dredging. Without the parchment barrier, the sauce will seep through the basket and may jeopardize the integrity of your air fryer.

4) While foil and parchment are always handy, it's also a good idea to have extra cooking tools on available when using an air fryer. Baking cookies and egg muffins will be lot simpler using silicone muffin or cupcake molds. There are many other sorts of culinary equipment that might complement the air fryer; silicone cupcake molds and cannoli tubes are just two examples.

5) Make sure your air fryer is in a well-ventilated environment. Placing the air fryer against a wall or in a corner of the kitchen might create a fire danger. Make sure the air fryer is far enough away from the wall and provide adequate room for the airflow that exits from the device on all sides to protect your safety. Also, remember to disconnect your air fryer between usages to prevent short-circuiting it.

6) Many of the recipes in this cookbook may need making numerous batches. The air fryer cooks meals by circulating air through the basket, and if you layer or overcrowd the air fryer basket, the food will not cook through correctly. Use the other techniques provided and avoid overloading your air fryer to ensure a delicious, evenly-cooked food every time!

7) The last tip for using an air fryer is to have an internal temperature reader available. While you are not need to use one for these recipes, it is a good idea to check the internal temperature of any foods you are cooking in the air fryer to verify they are fully cooked. Here are some of the most typical items included in air fryer recipes, as well as the internal temperature required in the center:

Common air fryer foods	Internal Temperature
Chicken	165 °F
Turkey	165 °F
Beef	145 °F
Pork	145 °F
Bacon	150 °F
Fish	145 °F
Eggs	145 °F
Duck	165 °F
Beans	135 °F
Rice and Pasta	135 °F
Shellfish	145 °F
Tofu	165 °F
Mushrooms	165 °F
Root Vegetables	205 °F
Leafy Greens	40 °F
Peppers and Tomatoes	165 °F
Squash and Cucumbers	165 °F
Fruit	135 °F
Bread and Pastries	210 °F

Dairy	145 °F
Fritters	210 °F
Muffins	200 °F
Donuts	195 °F
Cookies	180 °F

2. What's best to cook with an air fryer and what's not

The air fryer is an extremely flexible cooking tool. I advocate getting an air fryer for yourself because of the health advantages, convenience of use, and creative recipes you may make. But what foods work best and worst in an air fryer?

Some things to attempt in the air fryer that provide consistently good results are:

Chicken. The ventilation of the air fryer will ensure the chicken is always cooked through and juicy.

Fish. The air fryer is a quick and easy way to cook flakey fish or fish steaks. You'll be able to enjoy juicy and tasty fish that's fully cooked every time.

Steak. If you want to regulate each dish you prepare in order to achieve the ideal steak every time, the air fryer will assist you. You can cook the ideal steak from rare to medium-rare to well-done using an internal temperature reading and the proper cooking time.

Bacon. Many of the recipes in this cookbook use bacon, and the air fryer is perfectly capable of producing deliciously crispy bacon every time! Always add a piece of foil in the basket to prevent the bacon grease from leaking through the holes in the basket, and you'll be OK.

Frozen foods. The air fryer reduces the influence of condensation from frozen meals on the contents. The air fryer will crisp up all of your frozen dinners, replacing mushy food.

Starchy vegetables. Potatoes, pumpkins, zucchini, and asparagus will all have a great bite to them when cooked in the air fryer. It's helpful to have an internal temperature reader for starchy veggies to ensure they're neither overcooked or undercooked.

Cookies. Whether you want crispy or chewy cookies, the air fryer will always give quick and excellent results. If you put a piece of parchment in the basket, you'll get excellent cookies every time.

Certain items should not be cooked in an air fryer. The items listed below are significantly more likely to compromise the integrity of your air fryer or entirely dissolve in the air fryer. The following are the worst foods to consume:

Pasta. Because there is no safe method to boil water in the air fryer, trying to cook pasta in the air fryer will fail. It is feasible, however, to crisp up previously cooked past

Rice. The same principles apply to rice as they do to pasta. The rice must be cooked in boiling water, and the air fryer does not support boiling liquids. However, several of the recipes in this book call for cooked rice, which should be done on the stovetop or in a rice cooker.

Popcorn. The kernels of popcorn are a horror! Cooking popcorn in the air fryer may cause popcorn kernels to get caught and damage the equipment. If the kernels fall through the perforations in the basket, your air fryer will be unable to cook the popcorn, and you risk destroying it or causing a kitchen fire.

Dehydrated fruit- Because the air fryer employs a convection cooking technique, putting dehydrated food in the air fryer might cause it to entirely disintegrate, making cleanup a pain. However, you may use an air fryer to transform fresh fruit (such as apples or apricots) into dried fruit, which is completely safe.

Soups and sauces- The air fryer cannot be used to boil sauces or soups. There are also openings in the air fryer basket, thus putting too much liquid in the air fryer can ruin its integrity. However, several of the recipes in this cookbook call for light sauces, so use parchment or foil to prevent any liquid from escaping through the holes in the basket.

Peanut oil- This also applies to heavier olive oils. When utilizing an air fryer, the oil has the potential to smoke, and peanut oil has a high smoke point that might possibly emit harmful smoke. There have also been some reports that peanut oil smoke poses health dangers, so approach it with care.

Chapter 1
Veggies & Side Dishes

1. Easy melt cheesy mushrooms
Servings: 2
Prep & Cooking Time: 20 Minutes
Ingredients:
- Salt & pepper for better taste
- 10 button mushroom caps
- 2 cups mozzarella cheese, minced
- 2 cups cheddar cheese, minced
- 3 tbsps. mixture of Italian herbs

Directions:
1. First, heat up your air fryer to 340°F.
2. In a bowl, mix oil, salt, pepper, and herbs to form a marinade. Add button mushrooms to the marinade and toss to coat well.
3. In a separate bowl, mix both kinds of cheese.
4. Stuff mushrooms with the cheese mixture.
5. Place in air fryer's cooking basket and cook for 15 minutes.

2. Garlic stuffed mushrooms
Servings: 4
Prep & Cooking Time: 25 Minutes
Ingredients:
- 6 small mushrooms
- 1 oz. onion, peeled and diced
- 1 tbsp. friendly bread crumbs
- 1 tbsp. olive oil
- 1 tsp. garlic, pureed
- 1 tsp. parsley
- Salt & pepper for better taste

Directions:
1. Combine the bread crumbs, oil, onion, parsley, salt, pepper and garlic in a bowl. Cut out the mushrooms' stalks and stuff each cap with the crumb mixture.
2. Set the air fryer to 350°F. Cook it for 10 minutes.
3. Serve with a side of mayo dip.

3. Mixed cilantro and peppers
Servings: 4
Prep & Cooking Time: 20 Minutes
Ingredients:
- 8 ounces mini bell peppers, halved
- 1 tbsp. olive oil
- 1 tbsp. cilantro, minced
- 8 ounces cream cheese, soft
- 1 cup cheddar cheese, shredded
- Salt & black pepper to the taste

Directions:
1. Find a baking dish that fits in your air fryer. Grease it with oil and place the bell peppers on top.
2. Combine all ingredients and whisk them thoroughly. Spread over the bell peppers evenly.
3. Introduce the dish in the air fryer and cook at 370°F for 20 minutes.
4. Divide the peppers between plates and serve as a side dish.

4. Goat cheese added to italian tomatoes
Servings: 4
Prep & Cooking Time: 20 Minutes
Ingredients:
- 6 ounces goat cheese, sliced
- 2 shallots, slimly sliced
- 2 Pantano Romanesco tomatoes, sliced into 1/2-inch slices
- 1 1/2 tbsps. extra-virgin olive oil
- 3/4 tsp. sea salt
- Fresh parsley, for garnish
- Fresh basil, minced

Directions:
1. First, heat up your air fryer to 380°F.
2. Now, pat each tomato slice dry using a paper towel. Sprinkle each slice with salt and minced basil. Top with a slice of goat cheese.
3. Top with the shallot slices; drizzle with olive oil. Add the prepared tomato and feta "bites" to the air fryer food basket.
4. Cook in the air fryer for about 1minutes. Lastly, adjust seasonings for better taste and serve garnished with fresh parsley leaves. Enjoy!

5. Zucchini bread
Servings: 12
Prep & Cooking Time: 40 Minutes
Ingredients:
- 2 cups almond flour
- 2 tsps. baking powder
- 3/4 cup swerve sweetener
- 1/2 cup coconut oil, melted
- 1 tsp. lemon juice
- 1 tsp. vanilla extract
- 3 eggs, whisked
- 1 cup zucchini, shredded
- 1 tbsp. lemon zest
- Cooking spray

Directions:
1. Mix all the ingredients in a large size bowl except the cooking spray and stir well.
2. Grease a loaf pan that fits the air fryer with the cooking spray, line with parchment paper and transfer the loaf mix inside.
3. Put the pan in the air fryer and cook at 330°F for 40 minutes.
4. Cool down, slice and serve.

6. Japanese tempura
Servings: 3
Prep & Cooking Time: 20 Minutes
Ingredients:
- 1 cup all-purpose flour
- Kosher salt and ground black pepper for better taste
- 1/2 tsp. paprika
- 2 eggs
- 3 tbsps. soda water

- 1 cup panko crumbs
- 2 tbsps. olive oil
- 1 cup green beans
- 1 onion, sliced into rings
- 1 zucchini, sliced into slices
- 2 tbsps. soy sauce
- 1 tbsp. mirin
- 1 tsp. dashi granules

Directions:
1. In an empty and shallow bowl, put the flour then add salt, black pepper, and paprika. In a separate bowl, whisk the eggs and soda water. In another shallow bowl, add panko crumbs to the olive oil.
2. Dip the vegetables in flour mixture, then in the egg mixture; lastly, roll over the panko mixture to coat evenly.
3. Set your air fryer at 400°F and cook it for 10 minutes, shaking the basket halfway through the cooking time. Work in slowly with each batch until the vegetables becomes crispy and turn golden brown.
4. Then, make the sauce by whisking the soy sauce, mirin, and dashi granules. Bon appétit!

7. Stuffed spicy ricotta mushrooms
Servings: 4
Prep & Cooking Time: 35 Minutes
Ingredients:
- 1/2 lb. small white mushrooms
- Ground black pepper and sea salt for better taste
- 2 tbsp. Ricotta cheese
- 1/2 tsp. ancho chili powder
- 1 tsp. paprika
- 4 tbsps. all-purpose flour
- 1 egg
- 1/2 cup fresh breadcrumbs

Directions:
1. Remove the stems from the mushroom caps and chop them; mix the minced mushrooms steams with the salt, black pepper, cheese, chili powder, and paprika.
2. Fill each mushroom caps with cheese.
3. Place the flour in a shallow bowl, and beat the egg in another bowl. Position the breadcrumbs in a third empty bowl.
4. Dip the mushrooms in the flour, then, dip in the egg mixture; finally, dredge in the breadcrumbs and press to adhere. Drizzle the stuffed mushrooms with cooking spray.
5. Cook in the preheated air fryer at 360°F for 18 minutes. Bon appétit!

8. Mixture of kale and sprouts
Servings: 8
Prep & Cooking Time: 15 Minutes
Ingredients:
- 1 lb. Brussels sprouts, trimmed
- 2 cups kale, torn
- 1 tbsp. olive oil
- Salt & black pepper to the taste
- 3 ounces mozzarella, shredded

Directions:
1. In a pan that fits the air fryer, stir all the ingredients except the mozzarella and toss.
2. Put the pan in the air fryer and cook at 380°F for minutes.
3. Serve in plates equally, add the cheese on top by sprinkling it and serve.

9. Egg salad with vegetable
Servings: 4
Prep & Cooking Time: 35 Minutes
Ingredients:
- 1/3 lbs. Brussels sprouts
- 1/2 cup radishes, sliced
- 1/2 cup mozzarella cheese, crumbled
- 1 red onion, minced
- 4 eggs, hardboiled and sliced

Dressing:
- 1/4 cup olive oil
- 2 tbsps. champagne vinegar
- 1 tsp. Dijon mustard
- Ground black pepper and sea salt for added taste

Directions:
1. First, heat up your air fryer to 380°F.
2. Add the Brussels sprouts and radishes to the cooking basket. In quick, short succession, add oil and cook for 15 minutes. Leave it for 15 minutes or until it cools down.
3. Toss the vegetables with cheese and red onion.
4. Combine all ingredients then add dressing. Toss to combine. Serve topped with the hard-boiled eggs. Bon appétit!

10. New broccoli puree
Servings: 4
Prep & Cooking Time: 20 Minutes
Ingredients:
- 20 ounces broccoli florets
- A drizzle of olive oil
- 4 tbsps. basil, minced
- 3 ounces butter, melted
- 1 garlic clove, minced
- A pinch of salt and black pepper

Directions:
1. In a bowl, add oil. Put the broccoli next along with pepper and salt. Mix well before putting in your air fryer's basket. Cook at 380°F for 20 minutes, cool the broccoli down and put it in a blender. Add the rest of the ingredients, pulse, divide the mash between plates and serve as a side dish.

11. Yummy paprika leeks
Servings: 3
Prep & Cooking Time: 8 Minutes
Ingredients:
- 2 big leeks, roughly sliced
- 1 egg, beaten
- 1/2 tsp. ground paprika
- 1/2 tsp. salt
- 1/2 tsp. ground turmeric
- 2 tbsps. almond flour
- Cooking spray

Directions:
1. Sprinkle the leek slices with ground paprika, salt, and ground turmeric. After this, dip every leek slice in the egg and coat in the almond flour.
2. Preheat the air fryer to 400f and put the leek bites inside.
3. Splash with oil, cook for 8 minutes. Shake after 4 minutes of cooking.

12. Flavourful cranberry beans side salad
Servings: 6
Prep & Cooking Time: 15 Minutes
Ingredients:
- 6 garlic cloves, minced
- 2 1/2 cups canned cranberry beans, drained
- 1 yellow onion, minced
- 2 celery ribs, minced
- 1/2 tsp. smoked paprika
- 1/2 tsp. red pepper flakes
- 3 tsps. basil, minced
- Salt & black pepper for better taste
- 25 ounces canned tomatoes, drained and minced
- 10 ounces kale, torn

Directions:
1. Drop all of the ingredients in your air fryer pan and mix it.
2. Place the pan in the fryer and cook at 370°F for 15 minutes.
3. Serve in plates equally as a side salad.

13. Cabbage with lemon
Servings: 4
Prep & Cooking Time: 25 Minutes
Ingredients:
- Whole green cabbage, cut and divided into large wedges
- 2 tbsp. olive oil
- 1 tbsp. cilantro, minced
- 1 tbsp. lemon juice
- A pinch of salt and black pepper

Directions:
1. First, heat up your air fryer at 370°F, add the cabbage wedges mixed with all the ingredients in the basket and cook for 25 minutes.
2. Serve it as a side dish and divide it among plates.

14. Fried green olives stuffed with pimiento
Servings: 4
Prep & Cooking Time: 15 Minutes
Ingredients:
- 1/4 cup flour
- 1/4 cup Parmesan cheese
- Salt & black pepper for better taste
- 1/2 cup panko breadcrumbs
- 1 egg, beaten
- 1 tsp. cayenne pepper

Directions:
1. Preheat the air fryer to 390°F. Put cooking oil by spraying it lightly to the air fryer basket.
2. In a mixing bowl, combine flour, cayenne pepper, salt, and black pepper. In another bowl, add the beaten egg. Place panko breadcrumbs with Parmesan cheese in a third bowl.
3. Drain and pat dry the olives using a paper towel. Dredge olives in flour, then in egg, and finally in the breadcrumbs. Drop into the air fryer cooking basket, spray them with cooking spray, and cook for 5 minutes, shake and continue cooking for another minutes. Allow to cool before serving.

15. Delectable roasted cauliflower
Servings: 4
Prep & Cooking Time: 12 Minutes
Ingredients:
- 1 big cauliflower head, divided into florets
- 1 lemon zest
- 3 tbsps. olive oil
- 2 tsp. lemon juice
- 1/2 tsp. Italian seasoning
- 1/2 tsp. garlic powder
- 1/4 tsp. pepper
- 1/4 tsp. salt

Directions:
1. Preheat the air fryer to 400°F.
2. In a mixing bowl, combine together olive oil, lemon juice, Italian seasoning, garlic powder, lemon zest, pepper, and salt.
3. Add cauliflower florets to the bowl and toss well.
4. Add cauliflower florets into the air fryer basket and cook for 12 minutes. Shake basket halfway through.
5. Serve and enjoy.

16. Canapes made of cabbage
Servings: 2
Prep & Cooking Time: 15 Minutes
Ingredients:
- 1 cube Amul cheese
- 1/2 carrot, cubed
- 1/4 onion, cubed
- 1/4 capsicum, cubed
- Fresh basil to garnish

Directions:
1. First, heat up your air fryer to 360°F. Using a bowl, mix onion, carrot, capsicum and cheese. Toss to coat every element evenly. Add cabbage rounds to the air fryer's cooking basket. Top with the veggie mixture and cook for 5 minutes. Once ready to be served, add a garnish of fresh basil.

17. Cabbage cooked in butter
Servings: 4
Prep & Cooking Time: 20 Minutes
Ingredients:
- 2 ounces butter, melted
- 1 green cabbage head, shredded
- 1 and 1/2 cups heavy cream
- 1/4 cup parsley, minced
- 1 tbsp. sweet paprika
- 1 tsp. lemon zest, shredded

Directions:
1. Heat up a pan that fits the air fryer with the butter, add the cabbage and sauté for 5 minutes.
2. Add the remaining ingredients, toss, put the pan in the air fryer and cook at 380°F for 15 minutes.
3. Serve in plates as a side dish.

18. Healthy roasted eggplant
Servings: 1
Prep & Cooking Time: 20 Minutes
Ingredients:
- 1 large eggplant
- 2 tbsps. olive oil
- 1/4 tsp. salt
- 1/2 tsp. garlic powder

Directions:
1. Prepare the eggplant by slicing off the top and bottom and cutting it into slices around a quarter-inch thick.
2. Apply olive oil to the slices with a brush, coating both sides. Season each side with sprinklings of salt and garlic powder.
3. Place the slices in the fryer and cook for fifteen minutes at 350°F.
4. Serve right away.

19. Roasted potatoes with a spicy twist
Servings: 2
Prep & Cooking Time: 15 Minutes
Ingredients:
- 4 potatoes, peeled and sliced into wedges
- 2 tbsps. olive oil
- Ground black pepper and sea salt for better taste
- 1 tsp. cayenne pepper
- 1/2 tsp. ancho chili powder

Directions:
1. Toss all ingredients in a mixing bowl until the potatoes are well covered.
2. Transfer them to the air fryer basket and cook at 400°F for 6 minutes; shake the basket and cook for a further 6 minutes.
3. Choose a sauce to dip it with and serve warm. Bon appétit!

20. Delicious green beans
Servings: 4
Prep & Cooking Time: 6 Minutes
Ingredients:
- 1 lb. green beans, trimmed
- Pepper
- Salt

Directions:
1. With a cooking spray, apply cooking oil to the air fryer basket.
2. Preheat the air fryer to 400°F.
3. Add green beans in air fryer basket and season with pepper and salt.
4. Cook green beans for 6 minutes. Turn halfway through.
5. Serve and enjoy.

21. 23. Mix recipe for zucchini
Servings: 6
Prep & Cooking Time: 24 Minutes
Ingredients:
- 6 zucchinis; halved and then sliced
- 3 garlic cloves; minced
- 2 oz. parmesan; shredded
- 3/4 cup heavy cream
- Salt & black pepper to the taste
- 1 tbsp. butter
- 1 tsp. oregano; dried
- 1/2 cup yellow onion; minced

Directions:
1. In your air fryer pan, add butter and wait for it to melt. Now add onion and stir it. Leave it for 2 minutes to cook.
2. Add garlic, zucchinis, oregano, salt, pepper and heavy cream, toss, introduce in your air fryer and cook at 350 °F, for 10 minutes.
3. Add parmesan; stir, divide among plates and serve.

22. Cauliflower dipped in buffalo sauce
Servings: 4
Prep & Cooking Time: 25 Minutes
Ingredients:
- 3 tbsps. buffalo hot sauce
- 1 egg white
- 1 cup panko breadcrumbs
- 1/2 tsp. salt
- 1/4 tsp. freshly ground black pepper
- A half of cauliflower, divided into florets
- Cooking spray

Directions:
1. In a mixing bowl, stir in butter, hot sauce, and egg white. Mix breadcrumbs with salt and pepper, in a separate bowl. Toss the florets in the hot sauce mixture until well-coated.
2. Toss the coated cauliflower in crumbs until coated, then transfer the coated florets to the air fryer. Spray with cooking spray. Cook for 18 minutes at 340°F. Cook in batches if needed.

23. Special potatoes and tomato sauce recipe
Servings: 4
Prep & Cooking Time: 26 Minutes
Ingredients:
- 2 lbs. potatoes; cubed
- 4 garlic cloves; minced
- 1 yellow onion; minced.
- 1 cup tomato sauce
- 1/2 tsp. oregano; dried
- 1/2 tsp. parsley; dried
- 2 tbsps. basil; minced
- 2 tbsps. olive oil

Directions:
1. In your air fryer pan, add oil and set it to medium heat. Now add onion and stir it. Leave it for 2 minutes to cook.
2. Add garlic, potatoes, parsley, tomato sauce and oregano; stir, introduce in your air fryer and cook at 370 °F and cook for 16 minutes. Add basil, toss every element, divide among plates and serve

24. Mixed cranberries and broccoli
Servings: 4
Prep & Cooking Time: 25 Minutes
Ingredients:
- 1 broccoli head, florets separated
- 2 shallots, minced
- A pinch of salt and black pepper
- 1/2 cup cranberries
- 1/2 cup almonds, minced
- 6 bacon slices, cooked and crumbled
- 3 tbsps. balsamic vinegar

Directions:
1. In a pan that fits the air fryer, combine the broccoli with the rest of the ingredients and toss. Put the pan in the air fryer and cook at 380°F for 25 minutes. Serve in plates equally.

25. Cremini mushrooms with rice pilaf
Servings: 6
Prep & Cooking Time: 30 Minutes
Ingredients:
- 4 cups heated vegetable stock
- 2 cups long-grain rice
- 1 onion, minced
- 2 garlic cloves, minced
- 2 cups cremini mushrooms, minced
- Salt & ground black pepper for better taste
- 1 tbsp. fresh minced parsley (as needed for taste)

Directions:
1. First, heat up your air fryer to 400°F.
2. Place a frying pan over medium heat. Add oil, onion, garlic, and rice; cook for 5 minutes. Pour the vegetable stock and mushrooms and whisk well. Season with salt and pepper for better taste.
3. Transfer to your air fryer's basket and cook for 20 minutes.
4. Serve sprinkled with fresh minced parsley.

26. Bacon fries with cheese
Servings: 4
Prep & Cooking Time: 25 Minutes
Ingredients:
- 5 slices bacon, minced
- 2 tbsps. vegetable oil
- 2 1/2 cups Cheddar cheese, shredded
- 3 ounces melted cream cheese
- Salt & pepper for better taste
- 1/4 cup chives, minced

Directions:
1. First, heat up your air fryer to 400°F.
2. Add bacon to air fryer's basket and cook for 4, shaking once; set aside. Add in potatoes and drizzle oil on top to coat. Cook for 15 minutes, shaking the basket every 5 minutes. Season with salt and pepper.
3. In a bowl, mix cheddar cheese and cream cheese. Pour over the potatoes and cook for 5 more minutes at 400°F. Sprinkle minced chives on top and serve.

27. Chives, almond and broccoli
Servings: 4
Prep & Cooking Time: 12 Minutes
Ingredients:
- 1 lb. broccoli florets
- 3 garlic cloves, minced
- A pinch of salt and black pepper
- 3 tbsp. coconut oil, melted
- 1/2 cup almonds, minced
- 1 tbsp. chives, minced
- 2 tbsps. red vinegar

Directions:
1. In a bowl, put some oil first. Add the broccoli, garlic and vinegar. Now toss the salt and pepper. Mix well.
2. Put the broccoli in your air fryer's basket and cook at 380°F for minutes.
3. Serve in plates equally and serve with almonds and chives sprinkled on top.

28. Eggplant meatballs with almond
Servings: 7
Prep & Cooking Time: 8 Minutes
Ingredients:
- 3 eggplants, peeled, boiled
- 1 egg, beaten
- 1 tsp. minced garlic
- 3 spring onions, minced
- 1/2 cup almond flour
- 1 tsp. chives
- 1/2 tsp. chili flakes
- 1/2 tsp. salt
- 1 tsp. sesame oil

Directions:
1. Chop the boiled eggplants and squeeze the juice from them.
2. After this, transfer the eggplants in the blender. Add egg, minced garlic, spring onions, almond flour, chives, chili flakes, and salt. Grind the mixture until it is homogenous and smooth.
3. After this, make the eggplant meatballs from the mixture with the help of the scooper.
4. Preheat the air fryer to 380°F.
5. Put the eggplant meatballs in the air fryer and sprinkle them with sesame oil. Cook the meatballs for 8 minutes.

29. Dill ravioli and nutmeg
Servings: 6
Prep & Cooking Time: 8 Minutes
Ingredients:
- 4 tbsps. almond flour
- 2 tbsps. coconut flour
- 1 tbsp. cornstarch
- 1/2 tsp. baking powder
- 1 egg, beaten
- 1 tbsp. water
- 1 tsp. white wine vinegar
- 4 tbsps. ricotta cheese
- 1/2 tsp. minced garlic
- 1/4 tsp. ground nutmeg
- 1/2 tsp. dried dill
- 1 egg yolk, whisked
- Cooking spray

Directions:
1. Make the dough: mix up almond flour, coconut flour, cornstarch, baking powder, egg, water, and white wine vinegar.
2. Use your fingers to knead the dough. It should become soft and doesn't sticky. Roll up the dough and cut it on the ravioli squares.
3. Make the ravioli filling: mix up dried ill, ground nutmeg, minced garlic, and ricotta cheese. Then fill the dough squats with ricotta cheese.
4. Top the cheese with another ravioli dough squares. Secure the edges. Brush the ravioli with egg yolk.
5. Preheat the air fryer to 375°F. Position the ravioli inside the air fryer basket in single layer.
6. Cook the meal for 4 minutes from each side or until they are light brown.

30. Crispy rosemary potatoes
Servings: 4
Prep & Cooking Time: 35 Minutes
Ingredients:
- 2 tbsps. olive oil
- 3 garlic cloves, shredded
- 1 tbsp. minced fresh rosemary
- 1 tsp. salt
- 1/4 tsp. freshly ground black pepper

Directions:
1. In a bowl, mix potatoes, olive oil, garlic, rosemary, salt, and pepper, until they are well-coated. Set the potatoes in the air fryer and cook on 360°F for 25 minutes, shaking twice during the cooking. Cook until crispy on the outside and tender on the inside.

31. Crisp zucchini with parmesan
Servings: 4
Prep & Cooking Time: 20 Minutes
Ingredients:
- 1 lb. zucchini, peeled and sliced
- 1 egg, lightly beaten
- 1 cup Parmesan cheese, preferably freshly shredded

Directions:
1. Dry the zucchini. Use kitchen towel as needed or just leave it to dry.
2. In a mixing dish, thoroughly combine the egg and cheese. Then, coat the zucchini slices with the breadcrumb mixture.
3. Set your air fryer at 400°F and cook it for 9 minutes, shaking the basket halfway through the cooking time.
4. Work in batches until the chips is golden brown. Bon appétit!

32. Rolls with veggies
Servings: 6
Prep & Cooking Time: 30 Minutes
Ingredients:
- 2 potatoes, mashed
- 1/4 cup peas
- 1/4 cup carrots, mashed
- 1 small cabbage, sliced
- 1/4 beans
- 2 tbsps. sweetcorn
- 1 small onion, minced
- 1 tsp. capsicum
- 1 tsp. coriander
- 2 tbsps. butter
- Ginger
- Garlic for better taste
- 1/2 tsp. masala powder
- 1/2 tsp. chili powder
- 1/2 cup bread crumbs
- 1 packet spring roll sheets
- 1/2 cup cornstarch slurry

Directions:
1. Boil all the vegetables in water over a low heat. Rinse and allow to dry.
2. Unroll the spring roll sheets and spoon equal amounts of vegetable onto the center of each one. Fold into spring rolls and coat each one with the slurry and bread crumbs.
3. Pre-heat the air fryer to 380°F. Cook the rolls for 10 minutes.
4. Serve with a side of boiled rice.

33. Yummy mozzarella risotto
Servings: 4
Prep & Cooking Time: 20 Minutes
Ingredients:
- 1 lb. white mushrooms, sliced
- 1/4 cup mozzarella, shredded
- 1 whole cauliflower, florets divided and riced
- 1 cup chicken stock
- 1 tbsp. thyme, minced
- 1 tsp. Italian seasoning
- A pinch of salt and black pepper
- 2 tbsps. olive oil

Directions:
1. Heat up a pan that fits the air fryer with the oil over medium heat, add the cauliflower rice and the mushrooms, toss and cook for a couple of minutes.
2. Add the rest of the ingredients except the thyme, toss, put the pan in the air fryer and cook at 360°F for 20 minutes.
3. Serve the risotto with thyme sprinkled on top, divide it equally

34. Delicious pumpkin rice dish
Servings: 4
Prep & Cooking Time: 35 Minutes
Ingredients:
- 12 oz. white rice
- 4 cups chicken stock
- 6 oz. pumpkin puree
- 2 tbsps. olive oil
- 1 small yellow onion; minced.
- 2 garlic cloves; minced
- 1/2 tsp. nutmeg
- 1 tsp. thyme; minced
- 1/2 tsp. ginger; shredded
- 1/2 tsp. cinnamon powder
- 1/2 tsp. allspice
- 4 oz. heavy cream

Directions:
1. Find a dish that fits your air fryer; mix oil with onion, garlic, rice, stock, pumpkin puree, nutmeg, thyme, ginger, cinnamon, allspice and cream; stir well,
2. place in your air fryer's basket and cook at 360 °F, for 30 minutes. Serve it as a side dish among all plates.

35. Simply baked potatoes
Servings: 4
Prep & Cooking Time: 45 Minutes
Ingredients:
- 2 tbsps. olive oil
- Salt & ground black pepper for better taste

Directions:
1. Rub potatoes with half tbsp of olive oil. To taste, sprinkle it with salt and pepper, the position it on the air fryer.
2. Cook for 40 minutes at 400°F. Let cool slightly, then make a slit on top. Use a fork to fluff the insides of the potatoes.
3. Fill the potato with cheese or garlic mayo.

36. Buttered fennel
Servings: 4
Prep & Cooking Time: 12 Minutes
Ingredients:
- 2 big fennel bulbs, sliced
- 2 tbsp. butter, melted
- Salt & black pepper to the taste
- 1/2 cup coconut cream

Directions:
1. In a pan that fits the air fryer, stir all the ingredients, toss, introduce in the machine and cook at 370°F for minutes.
2. Serve in plates as a side dish.

37. Mixed endives and rice
Servings: 4
Prep & Cooking Time: 20 Minutes
Ingredients:
- 2 chives, minced
- 3 garlic cloves, minced
- 1 tbsp. olive oil
- Salt & black pepper for better taste
- 1/2 cup white rice
- 1 cup veggie stock
- 1 tsp. chili sauce
- 4 endives, trimmed and shredded

Directions:
1. Take the oil and grease a pan that fits your air fryer.
2. Add all other ingredients and toss.
3. Place the pan in the air fryer. Set it to 500°F. Leave it for 20 minutes.
4. Divide every element between plates and serve as a side dish.

38. Pecorino parmesan on fried green beans
Servings: 3
Prep & Cooking Time: 15 Minutes
Ingredients:
- 2 tbsps. buttermilk
- 1 egg
- 4 tbsps. cornmeal
- 4 tbsps. tortilla chips, crushed
- 4 tbsps. Parmesan cheese, finely shredded

- Coarse salt black pepper (crushed) for better taste
- 1 tsp. smoked paprika
- 12 ounces green beans, trimmed

Directions:
1. In an empty bowl, combine the buttermilk and egg and whisk it.
2. In a separate bowl, combine the cornmeal, tortilla chips, Parmesan cheese, salt, black pepper, and paprika.
3. Dip the green beans in the egg mixture, then, in the cornmeal/cheese mixture. Place the green beans in the lightly greased cooking basket.
4. Cook in the preheated air fryer at 390°F for minutes. Give the basket a shake cook for another 3 minutes.
5. Taste, adjust the seasonings, and serve with the dipping sauce if desired. Bon appétit!

39. Air-fried cheesy broccoli with garlic
Servings: 2
Prep & Cooking Time: 25 Minutes
Ingredients:
- 1 egg white
- 1 garlic clove, shredded
- Salt & black pepper for better taste
- 1/2 lb. broccoli florets
- 1/3 cup shredded Parmesan cheese

Directions:
1. In a mixing bowl, combine all ingredients. Add salt. Add the black pepper for added taste.
2. Toss in broccoli to coat well. Cover the top with Parmesan cheese and toss to coat. Put the broccoli air fryer.
3. Arrange it in single layer with enough space in between broccolis. Cook for 20 minutes at 360°F. Put it on a plate and sprinkle Parmesan cheese on top of it.

40. Celery puree
Servings: 6
Prep & Cooking Time: 6 Minutes
Ingredients:
- 1-lb celery stalks, minced
- 1/2 cup spinach, minced
- 2 ounces Parmesan, shredded
- 1/4 cup chicken broth
- 1/2 tsp. cayenne pepper

Directions:
1. In the air fryer pan, mix celery stalk with minced spinach, chicken broth, and cayenne pepper. Blend the mixture until homogenous.
2. After this, top the puree with Parmesan.
3. Preheat the air fryer to 400°F.
4. Put the pan with puree in the air fryer basket and cook the meal for 6 minutes.

41. Bbq shrimps
Servings: 1
Prep & Cooking Time: 10 Minutes
Ingredients:
- 2 tsps. coconut oil, melted
- 1/4 tsp. smoked paprika
- 1 tsp. chili powder
- 1/4 tsp. cumin
- 1 cup raw shrimps

Directions:
1. Mix the melted coconut oil with the paprika, chili powder, and cumin. Place the s in a large bowl and drop the coconut oil over them, tossing them to cover them evenly.
2. Place the shrimps in the basket of your fryer and spread them out across the base.
3. Cook for six minutes at 380°F, giving the basket an occasional shake to make sure every slimg is cooked evenly.
4. Leave to cool and serve.

42. Tomatoes and green beans recipe
Servings: 4
Prep & Cooking Time: 25 Minutes
Ingredients:
- 1-pint cherry tomatoes
- 2 tbsps. olive oil
- 1 lb. green beans
- Salt & black pepper to the taste

Directions:
1. In a mixing bowl stir cherry tomatoes with green beans, olive oil, salt and pepper, toss, transfer to your air fryer and cook at 400 °F, for 15 minutes.
2. Serve in plates hot.

43. Glazed tamarind and sweet potatoes
Servings: 4
Prep & Cooking Time: 24 Minutes
Ingredients:
- 1/3 tsp. white pepper
- 1 tbsp. butter, melted
- 1/2 tsp. turmeric powder
- 5 garnet sweet potatoes, peeled and diced
- A few drops liquid Stevia
- 2 tsps. tamarind paste
- 1 1/2 tbsp. fresh lime juice
- 1 1/2 tsp. ground allspice

Directions:
1. In a mixing bowl, toss all ingredients until sweet potatoes are well coated.
2. Air-fry them at 335°F for 1minutes.
3. Pause the air fryer and toss again. Increase the temperature to 360°F and cook for an additional 10 minutes. Eat warm.

44. Spring onions and leeks
Servings: 4
Prep & Cooking Time: 6 Minutes
Ingredients:
- 1 cup spring onions, minced
- 3 leeks, sliced
- 2 ounces Parmesan, shredded
- 1 egg, beaten
- 1/2 tsp. ground black pepper
- 1 tsp. dried parsley

Directions:
1. Preheat the air fryer to 400°F. Combine all the ingredients inside and cook for 6 minutes.
2. Serve in plates equally and serve.

45. Mashed cauliflower
Servings: 4
Prep & Cooking Time: 20 Minutes
Ingredients:
- 2 lbs. cauliflower florets
- 1 tsp. olive oil
- 3 ounces parmesan, shredded
- 4 ounces butter, soft
- Juice of 1/2 lemon

- Zest of 1/2 lemon, shredded
- Salt & black pepper to the taste

Directions:
1. Preheated you air fryer at 380°F, add the basket inside, add the cauliflower, also add the oil, rub well and cook for 20 minutes.
2. Transfer the cauliflower to a bowl, mash well, add the rest of the ingredients, stir really well, serve in plates as a side dish.

46. Amazing paprika asparagus
Servings: 4
Prep & Cooking Time: 10 Minutes
Ingredients:
- 1 lb. asparagus, trimmed
- 3 tbsps. olive oil
- A pinch of salt and black pepper
- 1 tbsp. sweet paprika

Directions:
1. In a bowl, mix the asparagus with the rest of the ingredients and toss. Put the asparagus in your air fryer's basket and cook at 400°F for minutes.
2. Serve in plates equally.

47. Sauté artichoke
Servings: 4
Prep & Cooking Time: 10 Minutes
Ingredients:
- 4 artichoke hearts, minced
- 4 tsps. lemon juice
- 2 tsps. avocado oil
- 1/4 tsp. lemon zest, shredded

Directions:
1. Preheat the air fryer to 360°F.
2. Meanwhile, sprinkle the minced artichoke hearts with lemon juice, avocado oil, and lemon zest. Shake them well and leave for 15 minutes to marinate.
3. After this, put the artichoke hearts in the preheated air fryer and cook them for 8 minutes.
4. Shake them well and cook for an additional 2 minutes.

48. Healthy potato casserole
Servings: 4
Prep & Cooking Time: 55 Minutes
Ingredients:
- 3 lbs. sweet potatoes; scrubbed
- 1/4 cup milk
- 2 tbsp. white flour
- 1/4 tsp. allspice; ground
- 1/2 tsp. nutmeg; ground
- Salt to the taste

For the topping:
- 1/2 cup almond flour
- 1/2 cup walnuts; soaked, drained and ground
- 1/4 cup sugar
- 1 tsp. cinnamon powder
- 5 tbsps. butter
- 1/4 cup pecans; soaked, drained and ground
- 1/4 cup coconut; shredded
- 1 tbsp. chia seeds

Directions:
1. Place potatoes in your air fryer's basket, prick them with a fork and cook at
2. 360°F, for 30 minutes.
3. Meanwhile; in a bowl, mix almond flour with pecans, walnuts, 1/4 cup coconut, 1/4 cup sugar, chia seeds, 1 tsp. cinnamon and the butter and stir every element.
4. Transfer potatoes to a cutting board, cool them, peel and place them in a baking dish that fits your air fryer.
5. Add milk, flour, salt, nutmeg and allspice and stir
6. Add crumble mix you've made earlier on top; place dish in your air fryer's basket and cook at 400°F, for 8 minutes. Serve it as a side dish among all plates.

49. Healthy zucchini latkes
Servings: 6
Prep & Cooking Time: 12 Minutes
Ingredients:
- 7 ounces zucchini, shredded
- 1 egg, beaten
- 1 tsp. salt
- 2 spring onions, minced
- 2 tbsps. almond flour
- 1 tsp. avocado oil
- 1/2 tsp. ground black pepper

Directions:
1. In the mixing bowl mix up shredded zucchini, egg, salt, minced onion, almond flour, and ground black pepper.
2. With the help of the spoon make medium-sized latkes.
3. Preheat the air fryer to 390°F. Place the latkes in the air fryer in one layer and sprinkle with avocado oil.
4. Cook the side dish for 6 minutes on each side.

50. Yummy scrambled eggs
Servings: 2
Prep & Cooking Time: 15 Minutes
Ingredients:
- 2 tbsps. olive oil, melted
- 4 eggs, whisked
- 5 oz. fresh spinach, minced
- 1 medium-sized tomato, minced
- 1 tsp. fresh lemon juice
- 1/2 tsp. coarse salt
- 1/2 tsp. ground black pepper
- 1/2 cup of fresh basil, roughly minced

Directions:
1. Grease the air fryer baking pan with the oil, tilting it to spread the oil around. Pre-heat the fryer at 280°F.
2. Mix the remaining ingredients, apart from the basil leaves, whisking well until every element is completely combined.
3. Cook in the fryer for 8 - 12 minutes.
4. Make it look better by adding basil leaves on top. Add sour cream for better taste.

51. Delicious chicken croquettes
Servings: 4
Prep & Cooking Time: 20 Minutes
Ingredients:
- 1 egg, beaten
- Salt & pepper for better taste
- 1 cup oats, crumbled
- 1/2 tsp. garlic powder
- 1 tbsp. parsley

Directions:
1. Preheat air fryer to 360°F. Rub chicken with garlic, parsley, salt, and pepper.

2. In a mixing bowl, add beaten egg. In a separate bowl, add crumbled oats.
3. Form croquettes from the chicken mixture and dip in egg, and in oats until coated. Place the nuggets in your fryer's basket.
4. Cook for 15 minutes, shaking once.

52. Chips brussels sprout
Servings: 1
Prep & Cooking Time: 15 Minutes
Ingredients:
- 1 lb. Brussels sprouts
- 1 tbsp. coconut oil, melted
- 1 tbsp. unsalted butter, melted

Directions:
1. Divide the Brussels sprouts into two. Don't use loose leaves.
2. Add coconut oil to the Brussel sprouts. Position it in you air fryer.
3. Cook at 400°F for ten minutes, giving the basket a good shake throughout the cooking time to brown them up if desired.
4. Check if it is now caramelized. If it is, then it is cooked. If not, leave it for a few more minutes.
5. Remove them from the fryer and serve with a topping of melted butter before serving.

53. Crispy tofu
Servings: 4
Prep & Cooking Time: 30 Minutes
Ingredients:
- 1 block firm tofu, pressed and sliced into 1-inch cubes
- 1 tbsp arrowroot flour
- 2 tsps. grapeseed oil
- 1 tsp. vinegar
- 2 tbsps. soy sauce

Directions:
1. In a mixing bowl, toss tofu with oil, vinegar, and soy sauce and let sit for 5 minutes.
2. Toss marinated tofu with arrowroot flour.
3. With a cooking spray, apply cooking oil to the air fryer basket.
4. Add tofu in air fryer basket and cook for 20 minutes at 370°F. Shake basket halfway through.
5. Serve and enjoy.

54. Bite-size crispy cauliflower
Servings: 4
Prep & Cooking Time: 20 Minutes
Ingredients:
- 1 cup flour
- 1 cup milk
- 1 egg, beaten
- 1 head cauliflower, sliced into florets

Directions:
1. Preheat the air fryer to 390°F. Put cooking oil by spraying it lightly to the air fryer basket.
2. In a bowl, mix flour, milk, egg, and Italian seasoning. Coat the cauliflower in the mixture, then drain the excess liquid.
3. Place the florets in the air fryer cooking basket, spray them with cooking spray, and cook for 7 minutes, shake and continue cooking for another 5 minutes.
4. Allow to cool before serving.

55. Mozzarella eggplants and lime
Servings: 4
Prep & Cooking Time: 15 Minutes
Ingredients:
- 2 tbsps. olive oil
- 2 eggplants, roughly cubed
- 8 ounces mozzarella cheese, shredded
- 3 spring onions, minced
- Juice of 1 lime
- 2 tbsps. butter, melted
- 4 eggs, whisked

Directions:
1. Heat up a pan that fits the air fryer with the oil and the butter over medium-high heat, add the spring onions and the eggplants, stir and cook for 5 minutes. Add the eggs and lime juice and stir well. Sprinkle the cheese on top, introduce the pan in the fryer and cook at 380°F for minutes. Serve in plates as a side dish.

56. Mixed zucchini and squash
Servings: 4
Prep & Cooking Time: 12 Minutes
Ingredients:
- 10 ounces Kabocha squash
- 1/2 zucchini, minced
- 3 spring onions, minced
- 1 tsp. dried oregano
- 2 tsps. ghee
- 1 tsp. salt
- 1 tsp. ground turmeric

Directions:
1. Chop the squash into small cubes and sprinkle with salt and ground turmeric. Put the squash in the bowl, add zucchini, spring onions, dried oregano, and ghee. Shake the vegetables gently.
2. Preheat the air fryer to 400°F.
3. Put the vegetable mixture in the air fryer and cook for 8 minutes.
4. Shake the vegetables after 6 minutes of cooking to avoid burning.

57. Beefy meatballs
Servings: 3
Prep & Cooking Time: 25 Minutes
Ingredients:
- 1 small finger ginger, crushed
- 1 tbsp hot sauce
- 3 tbsps. vinegar
- 1 1/2 tsp. lemon juice
- 1/2 cup tomato ketchup, reduced sugar
- 2 tbsps. sugar
- 1/4 tsp. dry mustard
- Salt & pepper for better taste or as needed

Directions:
1. In a mixing bowl, add beef, ginger, hot sauce, vinegar, lemon juice, tomato ketchup, sugar, mustard, pepper, and salt, and mix well using a spoon. Shape 2-inch sized balls, with hands.
2. Add the balls to the fryer without overcrowding.
3. Cook at 370°F for 20 minutes, shaking once.
4. Serve with tomato dip.

58. Delicious bacon and asparagus spears
Servings: 4
Prep & Cooking Time: 25 Minutes
Ingredients:
- 4 bacon slices
- 1 tbsp. olive oil
- 1 tbsp. grapeseed oil

- 1 tbsp. brown sugar
- 1 garlic clove, crushed

Directions:
1. First, heat up your air fryer to 380°F. In a bowl, mix the oils, sugar and crushed garlic.
2. Separate the asparagus into 4 bunches (5 spears in bunch) and wrap each bunch with a bacon slice.
3. Coat the bunches with the sugar and oil mix.
4. Place the bunches in your air fryer's cooking basket and cook for 8 minutes.

59. Special squash noodles
Servings: 2
Prep & Cooking Time: 17 Minutes
Ingredients:
- 1 medium butternut squash, peel and spiralized
- 3 tbsps. cream
- 1/4 cup parmesan cheese
- 1 tsp. thyme, minced
- 1 tbsp sage, minced
- 1 tsp. garlic powder
- 2 tbsps. cream cheese

Directions:
1. Preheat the air fryer to 370°F.
2. In a bowl, mix the thyme, cream cheese, sage, parmesan, cream, and garlic powder.
3. Add noodles into the air fryer baking pan.
4. Place pan in the air fryer and cook for 15 minutes.
5. Spread cream cheese mixture over noodles and cook for 2-3 minutes more.
6. Serve and enjoy.

60. Delicious zucchini nests
Servings: 6
Prep & Cooking Time: 6 Minutes
Ingredients:
- 10 ounces zucchini, shredded
- 4 quail eggs
- 1 tbsp. coconut flour
- 1 ounce Parmesan, shredded
- 1/4 tsp. cayenne pepper
- 1 tsp. butter, melted

Directions:
1. Brush the muffin molds with butter. Then mix up cayenne pepper and shredded zucchini.
2. Put the vegetable mixture in the muffin molds and flatten it in the shape of the nests.
3. After this, crack the quail eggs in the nests and sprinkle with shredded Parmesan.
4. Preheat the air fryer to 390°F.
5. Put the muffin molds with nests in the air fryer basket and cook for 6 minutes.

61. Tasty lemon fennel
Servings: 4
Prep & Cooking Time: 15 Minutes
Ingredients:
- 1 lb. fennel, sliced into small wedges
- A pinch of salt and black pepper
- 3 tbsps. olive oil
- Salt & black pepper to the taste
- Juice of 1/2 lemon
- 2 tbsps. sunflower seeds

Directions:
1. In a bowl, mix the fennel wedges with all the ingredients except the sunflower seeds, put them in your air fryer's basket and cook at 400°F for 10 minutes.
2. Divide the fennel between plates, sprinkle the sunflower seeds on top, and serve as a side dish.

62. Fried asparagus topped with goat cheese
Servings: 3
Prep & Cooking Time: 15 Minutes
Ingredients:
- 1 bunch of asparagus, trimmed
- 1 tbsp. olive oil
- 1/2 tsp. kosher salt
- 1/4 tsp. grounded black pepper for better taste
- 1/2 tsp. dried dill weed
- 1/2 cup goat cheese, crumbled

Directions:
1. Place the asparagus spears in the lightly greased cooking basket. Toss or combine the asparagus with the olive oil, salt, black pepper, and dill.
2. Set your air fryer to 400°F. Cook it for 9 minutes.
3. Serve garnished with goat cheese. Bon appétit!

63. Chicken bbq pizza
Servings: 1
Prep & Cooking Time: 15 Minutes
Ingredients:
- Cooking spray
- 1/4 cup barbeque sauce
- 1/4 cup shredded mozzarella cheese
- 1/4 cup shredded Monterrey Jack cheese
- 2 tbsps. red onion, slimly sliced
- 1/2 chicken herby sausage
- Chopped cilantro or parsley, for garnish

Directions:
1. Spray naan's bread bottom with cooking spray and arrange it in the air fryer.
2. Brush well with barbeque sauce, sprinkle mozzarella cheese, Monterrey Jack cheese, and red onion on top.
3. Top with the sausage over and spray the crust with cooking spray.
4. Cook for 8 minutes in a preheated air fryer at 400°F.

64. Mixed balsamic cabbage
Servings: 4
Prep & Cooking Time: 15 Minutes
Ingredients:
- 6 cups green cabbage, shredded
- 6 radishes, sliced
- 1/2 cup celery leaves, minced
- 1/4 cup green onions, minced
- 2 tbsp. balsamic vinegar
- 1 tsp. lemon juice
- 3 tbsps. olive oil
- 1/2 tsp. hot paprika

Directions:
1. In your air fryer's pan, stir all the ingredients and toss well.
2. Introduce the pan in the fryer and cook at 380°F for 15 minutes.
3. Serve in plates as a side dish.

65. Shrimp with coconut
Servings: 5
Prep & Cooking Time: 30 Minutes
Ingredients:
- 3/4 cup shredded coconut
- 1 tbsp. maple syrup
- 1/2 cup breadcrumbs
- 1/3 cup cornstarch
- 1/2 cup milk

Directions:
1. Pour the cornstarch and shrimp in a zipper bag and shake vigorously to coat. Mix the syrup and milk in a bowl and set aside.
2. In a separate bowl, mix the breadcrumbs and shredded coconut. Open the zipper bag and remove shrimp while shaking off excess starch.
3. Dip shrimp in the milk mixture and then in the crumb mixture.
4. Drop into the fryer.
5. Cook 1minutes at 350°F, flipping once halfway through.
6. Cook until golden brown. Serve with a coconut-based dip.

66. Brussels sprouts
Servings: 2
Prep & Cooking Time: 10 Minutes
Ingredients:
- 2 cups Brussels sprouts, sliced
- 1 tbsp. balsamic vinegar
- 1 tbsp. olive oil
- 1/4 tsp. sea salt

Directions:
1. Add all ingredients into the large bowl and toss well.
2. Sprinkle cooking oil to the air fryer basket.
3. Transfer Brussels sprouts mixture into the air fryer basket.
4. Cook Brussels sprouts at 350°F for 10 minutes. Shake basket halfway through.
5. Serve and enjoy.

67. Super fried agnolotti
Servings: 6
Prep & Cooking Time: 25 Minutes
Ingredients:
- 1 cup flour
- Salt & black pepper
- 4 eggs, beaten
- 2 cups breadcrumbs
- Cooking spray

Directions:
1. Mix flour with salt and pepper. Dip pasta into the flour, then into the egg, and finally in the breadcrumbs.
2. Spray with oil and arrange in the air fryer in an even layer.
3. Set to 400°F and cook for 15 minutes, turning once halfway through cooking.
4. Cook until nice and golden. Serve with goat cheese.

68. Feta cheese and mediterranean tomatoes
Servings: 2
Prep & Cooking Time: 20 Minutes
Ingredients:
- 3 medium-sized tomatoes, sliced into four slices, pat dry
- 1 tsp. dried basil
- 1 tsp. dried oregano
- 1/4 tsp. dried peppers, crushed
- 1/2 tsps. sea salt
- 3 slices°Feta cheese

Directions:
1. With cooking oil, spritz the tomatoes and transfer them to the air fryer basket. Sprinkle with seasonings.
2. Cook at 350°F approximately 8 minutes turning them over halfway through the cooking time.
3. Top with the cheese and cook an additional 4 minutes. Bon appétit!

69. Yummy portobello mushrooms
Servings: 4
Prep & Cooking Time: 22 Minutes
Ingredients:
- 4 Portobello mushrooms; stems removed and minced.
- 10 basil leaves
- 1 cup baby spinach
- 3 garlic cloves; minced
- 1 cup almonds; roughly minced.
- 1 tbsp. parsley
- 1/4 cup olive oil
- 8 cherry tomatoes; halved
- Salt & black pepper to the taste

Directions:
1. In your food processor, mix basil with spinach, garlic, almonds, parsley, oil, salt, black pepper to the taste and mushroom stems and blend well
2. Stuff each mushroom with this mix, place them in your air fryer and cook at 350 °F, for 1minutes. Divide mushrooms on plates and serve.

70. Tasty mix of turmeric kale
Servings: 2
Prep & Cooking Time: 12 Minutes
Ingredients:
- 3 tbsps. butter, melted
- 2 cups kale leaves
- Salt & black pepper for better taste
- 1/2 cup yellow onion, minced
- 2 tsps. turmeric powder

Directions:
1. Position all ingredients in a pan that fits your air fryer and combine them well.
2. Put the pan in the fryer and cook at 360°F for 12 minutes.
3. Serve in plates equally.

71. Creamy parmesan sauce with tomato bites
Servings: 4
Prep & Cooking Time: 20 Minutes
Ingredients:
For the Sauce:
- 1/2 cup Parmigiano-Reggiano cheese, shredded
- 4 tbsps. pecans, minced
- 1 tsp. garlic puree
- 1/2 tsp. fine sea salt
- 1/3 cup extra-virgin olive oil

For the Tomato Bites:
- 2 large-sized Roma tomatoes, sliced into slim slices and pat them dry
- 8 ounces Halloumi cheese, sliced into slim slices
- 1/3 cup onions, sliced
- 1 tsp. dried basil
- 1/4 tsp. red pepper flakes, crushed
- and tsp. sea salt

Directions:
1. First, heat up your air fryer to 385°F.
2. Make the sauce by mixing all ingredients, except the extra-virgin olive oil, in your food processor.
3. While the machine is running, slowly and gradually drop in the olive oil; puree until every element is well-blended.
4. On top of each tomato slice, spread 1 tsp. of the sauce. Place a slice of Halloumi cheese on top of each tomato slice. Top with onion slices. Top it with sea salt, basil and red pepper.
5. Transfer the assembled bites to the air fryer cooking basket. Add a nonstick cooking spray and l cook for 13 minutes or more (as needed).
6. Arrange these bites on a nice platter, garnish with the remaining sauce and serve at room temperature. Bon appétit!

72. Healthy balsamic mustard greens
Servings: 4
Prep & Cooking Time: 12 Minutes
Ingredients:
- 1 bunch mustard greens, trimmed
- 2 tbsp. olive oil
- 1/2 cup chicken stock
- 2 tbsps. tomato puree
- 3 garlic cloves, minced
- Salt & black pepper for better taste
- 1 tbsp. balsamic vinegar

Directions:
1. Combine all ingredients in a pan that fits your air fryer and toss well.
2. Place the pan in the fryer and cook at 370°F for 12 minutes.
3. Divide every element between plates, serve, and enjoy!

73. Spicy green beans
Servings: 2
Prep & Cooking Time: 10 Minutes
Ingredients:
- 2 cups green beans
- and tsp. cayenne pepper
- and tsp. ground allspice
- 1/4 tsp. ground cinnamon
- 1/2 tsp. dried oregano
- 2 tbsps. olive oil
- 1/4 tsp. ground coriander
- 1/4 tsp. ground cumin
- 1/2 tsp. salt

Directions:
1. Put all ingredients in an empty large bowl and mix well.
2. With a cooking spray, apply cooking oil to the air fryer basket.
3. Add bowl mixture into the air fryer basket.
4. Cook at 370°F for 10 minutes. Shake basket halfway through
5. Serve and enjoy.

74. Mexican cauliflower fritters
Servings: 6
Prep & Cooking Time: 48 Minutes
Ingredients:
- 2 tsps. chili powder
- 1 1/2 tsps. kosher salt
- 1 tsp. dried marjoram, crushed
- 2 1/2 cups cauliflower, broken into florets
- 1 1/3 cups tortilla chip crumbs
- 1/2 tsp. crushed dried peppers
- 3 eggs, whisked
- 1 1/2 cups Queso cotija cheese, crumbled

Directions:
1. In the food processor place all the cauliflower florets until they're crumbled (it is the size of ricc). Then, combine the cauliflower "rice" with the other items.
2. Now, roll the cauliflower mixture into small balls; refrigerate for 30 minutes.
3. First, heat up your air fryer to 500°F and set the timer for 14 minutes; cook until the balls are browned and serve right away.

75. Cheesy grilled cheese
Servings: 2
Prep & Cooking Time: 25 Minutes
Ingredients:
- 4 slices bread
- 1/2 cup sharp cheddar cheese
- 1/4 cup butter, melted

Directions:
1. Pre-heat the air fryer at 360°F.
2. Put cheese and butter in separate bowls.
3. Apply the butter to each side of the bread slices with a brush.
4. Spread the cheese across two of the slices of bread and make two sandwiches. Transfer both to the fryer.
5. Cook for – 7 minutes or until a golden brown color is achieved and the cheese is melted.

76. Mashed kale
Servings: 4
Prep & Cooking Time: 20 Minutes
Ingredients:
- 1 cauliflower head, florets separated
- 4 tsps. butter, melted
- 4 garlic cloves, minced
- 3 cups kale, minced
- 2 chives, minced
- A pinch of salt and black pepper
- 1/3 cup coconut cream
- 1 tbsp. parsley, minced

Directions:
1. In a pan that fits the air fryer, combine the cauliflower with the butter, garlic, chives, salt, pepper and the cream, toss, introduce the pan in the machine and cook at 380°F for 20 minutes.
2. Mash the mix well, add the remaining ingredients, whisk, serve in plates equally.

77. Chickpea taco and sweet potato
Servings: 4
Prep & Cooking Time: 15 Minutes
Ingredients:
- 2 cups sweet potato puree
- 2 tbsps. butter, melted
- 14 ounces canned chickpeas, rinsed
- 1 cup Colby cheese, shredded
- 1 tsp. garlic powder
- 1 tsp. onion powder
- Freshly grounded black pepper and salt for better taste
- 8 corn tortillas
- 1/4 cup Pico de Gallo
- 2 tbsps. fresh coriander, minced

Directions:
1. Mix the sweet potatoes with the butter, chickpeas, cheese, garlic powder, onion powder, salt, black pepper.
2. Divide the sweet potato mixture between the tortillas. Bake in the preheated air fryer at 390°F for 7 minutes.
3. Garnish with Pico de Gallo and coriander. Bon appétit!

78. Cauliflower rice and macadamia
Servings: 4
Prep & Cooking Time: 8 Minutes
Ingredients:
- 9 ounce cauliflower
- 1 tbsp. butter
- 1 ounce macadamia nuts, grinded
- 3 tbsps. chicken broth

Directions:
1. Cut the cauliflower on the florets. Then grate the cauliflower with the help of the grater. Grease the air fryer pan with butter and put the cauliflower rice inside. Add grinded macadamia nuts and chicken broth. Gently stir the vegetable mixture. Cook the cauliflower rice at 365°F for 8 minutes. Stir the vegetables after 4 minutes of cooking.

79. Tasty sweet-and-sour mixed veggies
Servings: 4
Prep & Cooking Time: 25 Minutes
Ingredients:
- 1/2 lb. asparagus, sliced into 1 1/2-inch pieces
- 1/2 lb. broccoli, sliced into 1 1/2-inch pieces
- 1/2 lb. carrots, divided into 1 1/2-inch pieces
- 2 tbsps. peanut oil
- Some salt and white pepper for better taste
- 1/2 cup water
- 4 tbsp. raisins
- 2 tbsps. honey
- 2 tbsps. white wine vinegar

Directions:
1. Place the vegetables in a single layer in the lightly greased cooking basket. Sprinkle and cover the peanut oil on top of the vegetables.
2. Sprinkle with salt and white pepper.
3. Cook at 370°F for 15 minutes, shaking the basket halfway through the cooking time.
4. Add 1/2 cup of water to a saucepan; bring to a rapid boil and add the raisins, honey, and vinegar. Cook until the sauce thickens and reduce to half.
5. Spoon the sauce over the warm vegetables and serve immediately. Bon appétit!

80. Flavourful lemon kale
Servings: 4
Prep & Cooking Time: 15 Minutes
Ingredients:
- 10 cups kale, torn
- 2 tbsps. olive oil
- Salt & black pepper to the taste
- 2 tbsps. lemon zest, shredded
- 1 tbsp. lemon juice
- 1/3 cup pine nuts

Directions:
1. In a pan that fits the air fryer, stir all the ingredients, toss, introduce the pan in the machine and cook at 380°F for minutes.
2. Serve in plates as a side dish.

81. Amazing thyme mushroom pan
Servings: 2
Prep & Cooking Time: 8 Minutes
Ingredients:
- 1/2 lb. cremini mushrooms, sliced
- 1 cup coconut cream
- 1 tsp. avocado oil
- 1/4 tsp. minced garlic
- 1/2 tsp. dried oregano

Directions:
1. In the air fryer's pan, mix the mushrooms with the cream and the other ingredients, toss and cook at 380°F for 8 minutes.
2. Divide into bowls and serve.

82. Crispy and tasty pickles
Servings: 4
Prep & Cooking Time: 6 Minutes
Ingredients:
- 16 dill pickles, sliced
- 1 egg, lightly beaten
- 1/2 cup almond flour
- 3 tbsps. Parmesan cheese, shredded
- 1/2 cup pork rinds, crushed

Directions:
1. Take three bowls. Mix together pork rinds and cheese in the first bowl.
2. In a second bowl, add the egg.
3. Ready the almond flour on the last bowl.
4. Coat each pickle slice with almond flour then dip in egg and finally coat with pork and cheese mixture.
5. With a cooking spray, apply cooking oil to the air fryer basket.
6. Place coated pickles in the air fryer basket.
7. Cook pickles for 6 minutes at 380°F.
8. Serve and enjoy.

83. Parmesan croquettes and rainbow vegetable
Servings: 4
Prep & Cooking Time: 40 Minutes
Ingredients:
- 1 lb. potatoes, peeled
- 4 tbsps. milk
- 2 tbsps. butter
- Salt & black pepper for better taste
- 1/2 tsp. cayenne pepper
- 1/2 cup mushrooms, minced
- 1/4 cup broccoli, minced
- 1 carrot, shredded
- 1 clove garlic, minced
- 3 tbsps. chives, minced
- 2 tbsps. olive oil
- 1/2 cup all-purpose flour
- 2 eggs
- 1/2 cup panko bread crumbs
- 1/2 cup parmesan cheese, shredded

Directions:
1. In a large saucepan, boil the potatoes for 20 minutes. Leave the potatoes to dry and mash with the milk, salt, butter black pepper, and cayenne pepper.
2. Add the mushrooms, broccoli, carrots, garlic, chives, and olive oil; stir to combine well. Shape the mixture into patties.
3. In a shallow bowl, place the flour; beat the eggs in another bowl; in a third bowl, combine the breadcrumbs with the parmesan cheese.
4. Prepare your flour and egg, dip the patty on the flour first then to the egg, and then the breadcrumb mixture; press to adhere.
5. Cook in the preheated air fryer at 370°F for 16 minutes, shaking halfway through the cooking time. Bon appétit!
6.

84. Yummy harissa broccoli spread
Servings: 4
Prep & Cooking Time: 6 Minutes
Ingredients:
- 2 cups broccoli, minced
- 1 tsp. tahini
- 2 tbsps. sesame oil
- 1 tsp. salt
- 1 garlic clove
- 1 tsp. coconut oil, melted
- 1 tsp. harissa

Directions:
1. Preheat the air fryer to 400°F.
2. Put the broccoli and garlic clove in the air fryer basket and sprinkle with tsp. of sesame oil. Cook the vegetables for 6 minutes.
3. Then transfer the cooked broccoli and garlic in the blender and grind the ingredients until you get the smooth texture. Add salt, all remaining sesame oil, coconut oil, and harissa.
4. After this, add tahini and blend the mixture for 30 seconds more. Place the cooked hummus in the bowl.

85. Appetizing almond brussels sprouts
Servings: 4
Prep & Cooking Time: 20 Minutes
Ingredients:
- 8 ounces Brussels sprouts
- 2 tbsps. almonds, grinded
- 1 tsp. shredded coconut
- 2 egg whites
- 1/2 tsp. salt
- 1/2 tsp. white pepper
- Cooking spray

Directions:
1. Whisk the egg whites and add salt and white pepper. Then cut the Brussels sprouts into halves and put the egg white mixture.
2. Shake the vegetables well and then coat in the grinded almonds and shredded coconut. Preheat the air fryer to 380°F.
3. Place the Brussels sprouts in the air fryer basket and cook them for 15minutes. Shake the vegetables after 8 minutes of cooking.

86. Tasty crumbed beans
Servings: 4
Prep & Cooking Time: 10 Minutes
Ingredients:
- 1/2 cup flour
- 1 tsp. smoky chipotle powder
- 1/2 tsp. ground black pepper
- 1 tsp. sea salt flakes
- 2 eggs, beaten
- 1/2 cup crushed saltines
- 10 oz. wax beans

Directions:
1. Combine the flour, chipotle powder, black pepper, and salt in a bowl. Put the eggs in a second bowl. Place the crushed saltines in a third bowl.
2. Using cold water, wash and remove tough strings from the beans.
3. In the flour mixture, dip the beans until it is covered then dip it into the egg. Lastly cover them with the crushed saltines.
4. With a cooking spray, spritz the beans.
5. Air-fry at 360°F for 4 minutes. Give the cooking basket a good shake and continue to cook for 3 minutes. Serve hot.

87. Amazing pumpkin wedges
Servings: 3
Prep & Cooking Time: 30 Minutes
Ingredients:
- 1 tbsp. paprika
- 1 whole lime, squeezed
- 1 cup paleo dressing
- 1 tbsp balsamic vinegar
- Salt & pepper for better taste
- 1 tsp. turmeric

Directions:
1. First, heat up your air fryer to 360°F.
2. Add the pumpkin wedges in your air fryer's cooking basket, and cook for 20 minutes.
3. In a mixing bowl, mix lime juice, vinegar, turmeric, salt, pepper and paprika to form a marinade. Pour the marinade over pumpkin, and cook for 5 more minutes.

88. Thin broccoli patties
Servings: 4
Prep & Cooking Time: 8 Minutes
Ingredients:
- 1/2 tsp. onion powder
- 1 cup broccoli, shredded
- 1/2 tsp. salt
- 1/2 tsp. chili flakes
- 1 tsp. ground paprika
- 1 egg, beaten
- 1/4 cup coconut flour
- 1 tsp. chives, minced

Directions:
1. In the mixing bowl mix up onion powder, shredded broccoli, salt, chili flakes, ground paprika, and chives.
2. After this, add egg and stir the mixture with the help of the spoon. Add coconut flour and stir it well again.
3. Make the patties with the help of the fingertips.
4. Then preheat the air fryer to 385°F and put the patties in the air fryer basket.
5. Cook them for 4 minutes from each side.

89. Mixed mung beans
Servings: 3
Prep & Cooking Time: 16 Minutes
Ingredients:
- 1 cup mung beans
- 1/2 tsp. olive oil
- 1 tsp. coriander, ground
- 1/2 tsp. turmeric powder
- 1 cup veggie stock
- 1/2 cup red onion, minced
- 1/2 tsp. cumin seeds
- 3 tomatoes, minced
- 1/2 tsp. garam masala
- Salt & black pepper for better taste
- 1 tbsp. lemon juice
- 4 garlic cloves, minced

Directions:
1. Position all of the ingredients in the pan that fits your air fryer and toss.
2. Place the pan in the fryer and cook at 365°F for 16 minutes.
3. Divide the mix between plates and serve as a side dish.

90. Delightful roasted cashews
Servings: 12
Prep & Cooking Time: 20 Minutes
Ingredients:
- 3 tbsps. liquid smoke
- 2 tsp. salt
- 2 tbsps. molasses
- 2 cups cashews

Directions:
1. First, heat up your air fryer to 360°F.
2. In a mixing bowl, add salt, liquid, molasses, and cashews; toss to coat.
3. Place in your air fryer's cooking basket and cook for 15 minutes, shaking the basket every 5 minutes.

91. Appetizing kabocha fries
Servings: 2
Prep & Cooking Time: 11 Minutes
Ingredients:
- 6 ounces Kabocha squash, peeled
- 1/2 tsp. olive oil
- 1/2 tsp. salt

Directions:
1. Cut the Kabocha squash into the shape of the French fries and sprinkle with olive oil.
2. Preheat the air fryer to 390°F.
3. Put the Kabocha squash fries in the air fryer basket and cook them for 5 minutes. Then shake them well and cook for 6 minutes more.
4. Sprinkle the cooked Kabocha fries with salt and mix up well.

92. Delectable coconut parmesan kale
Servings: 4
Prep & Cooking Time: 15 Minutes
Ingredients:
- 2 lbs. kale, torn
- A pinch of salt and black pepper
- 2 tbsps. olive oil
- 2 garlic cloves, minced
- 1 and 1/2 cups coconut cream
- 1/2 tsp. nutmeg, ground
- 1/2 cup parmesan, shredded

Directions:
1. In a pan the size of your air fryer, mix the kale with the rest of the ingredients, toss, introduce the pan in the fryer and cook at 400°F for minutes.
2. Serve in plates equally and serve.

93. Flavorful roasted beet salad
Servings: 2
Prep & Cooking Time: 20 Minutes + Chilling Time
Ingredients:
- 2 medium-sized beets, peeled and divide it into wedges
- 2 tbsps. extra virgin olive oil
- 1 tbsp. balsamic vinegar
- 1 tsp. yellow mustard
- 1 garlic clove, minced
- 1/4 tsp. cumin powder
- Ground black pepper and sea salt for better taste
- 1 tbsp. fresh parsley leaves, roughly minced

Directions:
1. Place the beets in a single layer in the lightly greased cooking basket.
2. Cook at 370°F for 13 minutes, shaking the basket halfway through the cooking time.
3. Let it cool to room temperature; toss the beets with the remaining ingredients. Serve well chilled. Enjoy!

94. Mixed coconut mushrooms
Servings: 4
Prep & Cooking Time: 15 Minutes
Ingredients:
- 1 lb. brown mushrooms, sliced
- 1 lb. kale, torn
- Salt & black pepper to the taste
- 2 tbsps. olive oil
- 14 ounces coconut milk

Directions:
1. In your air fryer pan, mix the kale with the rest of the ingredients and toss.
2. Put the pan in the fryer, cook at 380°F for minutes, serve in plates equally.

95. Avocado on sweet corn fritters
Servings: 3
Prep & Cooking Time: 20 Minutes
Ingredients:
- 2 cups sweet corn kernels
- 1 small-sized onion, minced
- 1 garlic clove, minced
- 2 eggs, whisked
- 1 tsp. baking powder
- 2 tbsp. fresh cilantro, minced
- Ground black pepper and sea salt for better taste
- 1 avocado, peeled, pitted and diced
- 2 tbsps. sweet chili sauce

Directions:
1. In a mixing bowl, thoroughly combine the corn, onion, garlic, eggs, baking powder, cilantro, salt, and black pepper.
2. Shape the corn mixture into 6 patties and transfer them to the lightly greased air fryer basket.
3. Cook in the preheated air fry at 380°F for 8 minutes; turn them over and cook for 7 minutes longer.
4. Serve the fritters with the avocado and chili sauce.

96. Mixed rosemary olives
Servings: 4
Prep & Cooking Time: 15 Minutes
Ingredients:
- 2 cups black olives, pitted and halved
- A handful basil, minced
- 2 rosemary springs, minced
- 2 red bell peppers, sliced
- 12 ounces tomatoes, minced
- 4 garlic cloves, minced
- 2 tbsps. olive oil

Directions:
1. In a pan that fits the air fryer, combine the olives with the rest of the ingredients, toss, put the pan in the fryer and cook at 380°F for minutes.
2. Serve in plates equally.

97. Summer fritters- vegetable edition
Servings: 2
Prep & Cooking Time: 20 Minutes
Ingredients:
- 1 zucchini, shredded and squeezed

- 1 cup cauliflower florets, boiled
- 4 tbsp. Parmesan cheese, shredded
- 2 tbsps. fresh shallots, minced
- 1 tsp. fresh garlic, minced
- 1 tbsp. peanut oil
- Ground black pepper and sea salt for added taste
- 1 tsp. cayenne pepper

Directions:
1. In a mixing bowl, thoroughly combine all ingredients until everything is well incorporated.
2. Shape the mixture into patties. Spray the cooking basket with cooking oil.
3. Cook in the preheated air fryer at 355°F for 6 minutes. Do the same thing for the other side.
4. Serve immediately and enjoy!

98. Vegetable bake rainbow cheese

Servings: 4
Prep & Cooking Time: 50 Minutes
Ingredients:
- 1 lb. cauliflower, minced into small florets
- 2 tbsp. olive oil
- 1/2 tsp. dried peppers, crushed
- 1/2 tsp. freshly ground black pepper
- Salt for better taste
- 3 bell peppers, slimly sliced
- 1 serrano pepper, slimly sliced
- 2 medium-sized tomatoes, sliced
- 1 leek, slimly sliced
- 2 garlic cloves, minced
- 1 cup Monterey cheese, shredded

Directions:
1. Set your air fryer to 350°F.
2. Add cooking oil to your casserole dish.
3. In the casserole dish, lay the cauliflower evenly; drizzle 1 tbsp. of olive oil over the top. Then, add the red pepper, black pepper, and salt.
4. Add 2 bell peppers and 1/2 of the leeks. Add the tomatoes and the remaining 1 tbsp. of olive oil.
5. Add the remaining peppers, leeks, and minced garlic. Top with the cheese.
6. Using foil, cover the casserole, bake it for 32 minutes.
7. Take off the foil and increase the temperature to 400°F; leave it for 16 minutes. Bon appétit!

99. Healthy cabbage wedges

Servings: 6
Prep & Cooking Time: 14 Minutes
Ingredients:
- 1 small cabbage head, sliced into wedges
- 3 tbsps. olive oil
- 1/4 tsp. red chili flakes
- 1/2 tsp. cumin seeds
- 1 tsp. garlic powder
- 1 tsp. onion powder
- Pepper
- Salt

Directions:
1. With a cooking spray, apply cooking oil to the air fryer basket.
2. In a small bowl, mix together garlic powder, red chili flakes, cumin seeds, onion powder, pepper, and salt.
3. Coat cabbage wedges with oil and rub with garlic powder mixture.
4. Place cabbage wedges into the air fryer basket and cook at 360°F for 8 minutes.
5. Turn cabbage wedges to another side and cook for 6 minutes more.
6. Serve and enjoy.

100. Almonds, blue cheese and crispy wax beans

Servings: 3
Prep & Cooking Time: 15 Minutes
Ingredients:
- 1 lb. wax beans, cleaned
- 2 tbsps. peanut oil
- 4 tbsps. seasoned breadcrumbs
- Ground black pepper and sea salt for better taste
- 1/2 tsp. red pepper flakes, crushed
- 2 tbsps. almonds, sliced
- 1/3 cup blue cheese, crumbled

Directions:
1. Toss the wax beans with the peanut oil, breadcrumbs, salt, black pepper, and red pepper.
2. Place the wax beans in the lightly greased cooking basket.
3. Set your air fryer to 400°F and cook it for 5 minutes.
4. Shake the basket once or twice.
5. Add the almonds and cook for 3 minutes more or until lightly toasted.
6. Serve topped with blue cheese and enjoy!

101. Tasty winter vegetable braise

Servings: 2
Prep & Cooking Time: 25 Minutes
Ingredients:
- 4 potatoes, peeled and divided into 1-inch pieces
- 1 celery root, peeled and divided into 1-inch pieces
- 1 cup winter squash
- 2 tbsps. unsalted butter, melted
- 1/2 cup chicken broth
- 1/4 cup tomato sauce
- 1 tsp. parsley
- 1 tsp. rosemary
- 1 tsp. thyme

Directions:
1. First, heat up your air fryer to 370°F. Add all ingredients in a lightly greased casserole dish. Stir to combine well.
2. Bake in the preheated air fryer for 10 minutes. Gently stir the vegetables with a large spoon and increase temperature to 400°F; cook for 10 minutes more.
3. 1. Serve in individual bowls with a few drizzles of lemon juice. Bon appétit!

102. Bake greek-style vegetable

Servings: 4
Prep & Cooking Time: 35 Minutes
Ingredients:
- 1 eggplant, peeled and sliced
- 2 bell peppers, seeded and sliced
- 1 red onion, sliced
- 1 tsp. fresh garlic, minced
- 4 tbsps. olive oil
- 1 tsp. mustard
- 1 tsp. dried oregano
- 1 tsp. smoked paprika
- Salt & ground black pepper for better taste
- 1 tomato, sliced

- 6 ounces halloumi cheese, sliced lengthways

Directions:
1. Heat up first your air fryer to 370°F. Add a nonstick cooking spray to your baking pan.
2. Place the eggplant, peppers, onion, and garlic on the bottom of the baking pan. Add the olive oil, mustard, and spices. Transfer to the cooking basket and cook for 14 minutes.
3. Top with the tomatoes and cheese; increase the temperature to 360°F and cook for 5 minutes more until bubbling.
4. Leave it on a cooling rack for 10 minutes to cool down before serving.
5. Bon appétit!

103. Creamy cauliflower and broccoli
Servings: 4
Prep & Cooking Time: 20 Minutes
Ingredients:
- 15 ounces broccoli florets
- 10 ounces cauliflower florets
- 1 leek, minced
- 2 spring onions, minced
- Salt & black pepper to the taste
- 2 ounces butter, melted
- 2 tbsps. mustard
- 1 cup sour cream
- 5 ounces mozzarella cheese, shredded

Directions:
1. In a baking pan that fits the air fryer, add the butter and spread it well.
2. Except for mozzarella, add the broccoli, cauliflower and the rest of the ingredients then toss it.
3. Sprinkle the cheese on top, introduce the pan in the air fryer and cook at 380°F for 20 minutes.
4. Serve in plates as a side dish.

104. Tasty breaded mushrooms
Servings: 4
Prep & Cooking Time: 35 Minutes
Ingredients:
- 2 cups breadcrumbs
- 2 eggs, beaten
- Salt & pepper for better taste
- 2 cups Parmigiano Reggiano cheese, shredded

Directions:
1. Preheat air fryer to 360°F. Pour breadcrumbs in a bowl, add salt and pepper and mix well.
2. Pour cheese in a separate bowl. Dip each mushroom in the eggs, then in the crumbs, and then in the cheese.
3. Slide-out the fryer basket and add 6 to mushrooms. Cook for 20 minutes. Serve with cheese dip.

105. Avocados wrapped with bacon
Servings: 6
Prep & Cooking Time: 40 Minutes
Ingredients:
- 3 large avocados, sliced
- 1/3 tsp. salt
- 1/3 tsp. chili powder
- 1/3 tsp. cumin powder

Directions:
1. Stretch the bacon strips to elongate and cut in half to make 24 pieces. Wrap each bacon piece around a slice of avocado. Tuck the end of bacon into the wrap. Season with salt, chili and cumin.
2. Arrange wrapped pieces on the fryer and cook at 350°F for 8 minutes, flipping halfway through to cook evenly. Remove onto a wire rack and repeat the process for the remaining avocado pieces.

106. Mushrooms stuffed with mint-butter
Servings: 3
Prep & Cooking Time: 19 Minutes
Ingredients:
- 3 garlic cloves, minced
- 1 tsp. ground black pepper (add more) for better taste
- 1/3 cup seasoned breadcrumbs
- 1 1/2 tbsp. fresh mint, minced
- 1 tsp. salt, or more for better taste
- 1 1/2 tbsp. melted butter
- 14 medium-sized mushrooms, cleaned, stalks removed

Directions:
1. Mix all of the above ingredients, minus the mushrooms, in a mixing bowl to prepare the filling.
2. Then, stuff the mushrooms with the prepared filling.
3. Air-fry stuffed mushrooms at 365°F for about 12 minutes. Taste for doneness and serve at room temperature as a vegetarian appetizer.

107. Delicious parmesan squash
Servings: 4
Prep & Cooking Time: 25 Minutes
Ingredients:
- 1 medium spaghetti squash
- 2 ounces Mozzarella, shredded
- 1 ounce Parmesan, shredded
- 1 tsp. avocado oil
- 1/2 tsp. dried oregano
- 1/2 tsp. dried cilantro
- 1/2 tsp. ground nutmeg
- 2 tsps. butter

Directions:
1. Cut the spaghetti squash into halves and remove the seeds. Then sprinkle it with avocado oil, dried oregano, dried cilantro, and ground nutmeg.
2. Put some butter in every spaghetti squash half and transfer the vegetables in the air fryer.
3. Cook them for 15 minutes at 365°F. After this, fill the squash with Mozzarella and Parmesan and cook for 10 minutes more at the same temperature.

108. Crispy roasted broccoli
Servings: 4
Prep & Cooking Time: 7 Minutes
Ingredients:
- 4 cups broccoli florets
- 1/4 cup water
- 1 tbsp. olive oil
- 1/4 tsp. pepper
- and tsp. kosher salt

Directions:
1. Add broccoli, oil, pepper, and salt in a bowl and toss well.
2. Add 1/4 cup of water into the bottom of air fryer (under the basket).
3. Transfer broccoli into the air fryer basket and cook for 7 minutes at 400°F.
4. Serve and enjoy.

109. Delicious indian malai kofta

Servings: 4
Prep & Cooking Time: 40 Minutes
Ingredients:
- Veggie Balls:
- 1 lb. potatoes, peeled and diced
- 1/2 lb. cauliflower, broken into small florets
- 2 tbsps. olive oil
- 2 cloves garlic, minced
- 1 tbsp. Garam masala
- 1 cup chickpea flour
- Himalayan salt plus ground black pepper for added taste

Sauce:
- 1 tbsp. sesame oil
- 1/2 tsp. cumin seeds
- 2 cloves garlic, roughly minced
- 1 onion, minced
- 1 Kashmiri chili pepper, seeded (minced)
- 1 (1-inch piece ginger, minced
- 1 tsp. paprika
- 1 tsp. turmeric powder
- 2 ripe tomatoes, pureed
- 1/2 cup vegetable broth
- 1/4 full fat coconut milk

Directions:
1. First, heat up your air fryer to 400°F. Place the potato and cauliflower in a lightly greased cooking basket.
2. Cook for 15 minutes, shaking the basket halfway through the cooking time. Mash and combine the cauliflower and potatoes in a mixing bowl.
3. Add the remaining ingredients for the veggie balls and stir to combine well. Make small balls from the vegetable mixture, then place it in the cooking basket.
4. Cook in the preheated air fryer at 360°F for 15 minutes or until thoroughly cooked and crispy. Repeat steps 1-3.
5. Warm the sesame oil in a saucepan over medium heat and add the cumin seeds. Wait for the cumin seeds to turn brown. Now add the garlic, ginger, onions, chili pepper. Sauté for 2 to 3 minutes.
6. Add the paprika, turmeric powder, tomatoes, and broth; let it simmer, covered, for 4 to 5 minutes, stirring occasionally.
7. Add the coconut milk. Warm off; add the veggie balls and gently stir to combine. Bon appétit!

110. Roasted tomatoes with feta, greek style

Servings: 2
Prep & Cooking Time: 20 Minutes
Ingredients:
- 3 medium-sized tomatoes, sliced into four slices, pat dry
- 1 tsp. dried basil
- 1 tsp. dried oregano
- 1/4 tsp. red pepper flakes, crushed
- 1/2 tsp. sea salt
- 3 slices Feta cheese

Directions:
1. With cooking oil, spritz the tomatoes and transfer them to the air fryer basket. Sprinkle with seasonings.
2. Cook at 350°F approximately 8 minutes turning them over halfway through the cooking time.
3. Top with the cheese and cook an additional 4 minutes. Bon appétit!

111. Brussel sprout salad, american-style

Servings: 4
Prep & Cooking Time: 35 Minutes
Ingredients:
- 1 lb. Brussels sprouts
- 1 apple, cored and diced
- 1/2 cup mozzarella cheese, crumbled
- 1/2 cup pomegranate seeds
- 1 small-sized red onion, minced
- 4 eggs, hardboiled and sliced

Dressing:
- 1/4 cup olive oil
- 2 tbsps. champagne vinegar
- 1 tsp. Dijon mustard
- 1 tsp. honey
- Ground black pepper and sea salt for better taste

Directions:
1. Set your air fryer to 380°F.
2. Add the Brussels sprouts to the cooking basket. In quick, short succession, add oil and cook for 15 minutes. Let it cool to room temperature about 15 minutes.
3. Toss the Brussels sprouts with the apple, cheese, pomegranate seeds, and red onion.
4. For the dressing, just mix the ingredients. Serve topped with the hard-boiled eggs. Bon appétit!

112. Crispy and delicious parmesan with sour cream and asparagus

Servings: 4
Prep & Cooking Time: 20 Minutes
Ingredients:
- 2 eggs
- 1 tsp. Dijon mustard
- 1 cup Parmesan cheese, shredded
- 1 cup bread crumbs
- Ground black pepper and sea salt for better taste
- 18 asparagus spears, trimmed
- 1/2 cup sour cream

Directions:
1. First, heat up your air fryer to 400°F.
2. In a shallow bowl, whisk the eggs and mustard. In another shallow bowl, combine the Parmesan cheese, breadcrumbs, salt, and black pepper.
3. Dip the asparagus spears in the egg mixture, then in the parmesan mixture; press to adhere.
4. Cook for 5 minutes; work in three batches. Serve with sour cream on the side. Enjoy!

113. Chickpeas cooked in air-fryer with herbs

Servings: 4
Prep & Cooking Time: 20 Minutes
Ingredients:
- 2 tbsps. olive oil
- 1 tsp. dried rosemary
- 1/2 tsp. dried oregano
- 1/4 tsp. dried sage
- 1/4 tsp. salt

Directions:
1. In a bowl, mix together chickpeas, oil, rosemary, thyme, sage, and salt. Transfer them to the air fryer and spread in an even layer.
2. Cook minutes at 380°F, shaking once, halfway through cooking.

114. Roasted and healthy vegetables
Servings: 6
Prep & Cooking Time: 30 Minutes
Ingredients:
- 1 1/3 cup small parsnips
- 1 1/3 cup celery [3 – 4 stalks]
- 2 red onions
- 1 1/3 cup small butternut squash
- 1 tbsp. fresh thyme needles
- 1 tbsp. olive oil
- Salt & pepper for better taste

Directions:
1. Pre-heat the air fryer to 390°F.
2. Peel the parsnips and onions and cut them into cm cubes. Slice the onions into wedges.
3. Do not peel the butternut squash. Cut it in half, de-seed it, and cube.
4. Combine the cut vegetables with the thyme, olive oil, salt and pepper.
5. Put the vegetables in the basket and transfer the basket to the air fryer.
6. Cook for 20 minutes, stirring once throughout the cooking time, until the vegetables are nicely browned and cooked through.

115. Crispy sweet corn fritters
Servings: 4
Prep & Cooking Time: 20 Minutes
Ingredients:
- 1 medium-sized carrot, shredded
- 1 yellow onion, finely minced
- 4 oz. canned sweet corn kernels, drained
- 1 tsp. sea salt flakes
- 1 heaping tbsp. fresh cilantro, minced
- 1 medium-sized egg, whisked
- 2 tbsps. plain milk
- 1 cup of Parmesan cheese, shredded
- 1/4 cup flour
- 1/3 tsp. baking powder
- 1/3 tsp. sugar

Directions:
1. Place the shredded carrot in a colander and press down to squeeze out any excess moisture. Dry it with a paper towel.
2. Combine the carrots with the remaining ingredients.
3. Mold 1 tbsp. of the mixture into a ball and press it down with your hand or a spoon to flatten it. Do the same thing with the rest of the mixture.
4. With cooking spray., spritz the balls.
5. Arrange in the basket of your air fryer, taking care not to overlap any balls. Cook at 380°F for 8 to 11 minutes or until they're firm.
6. Serve warm.

116. Delicious mushroom cakes
Servings: 4
Prep & Cooking Time: 8 Minutes
Ingredients:
- 9 ounce mushrooms, finely minced
- 1/4 cup coconut flour
- 1 tsp. salt
- 1 egg, beaten
- 3 ounce Cheddar cheese, shredded
- 1 tsp. dried parsley
- 1/2 tsp. ground black pepper
- 1 tsp. sesame oil
- 1 ounce spring onion, minced

Directions:
1. In the mixing bowl mix up minced mushrooms, coconut flour, salt, egg, dried parsley, ground black pepper, and minced onion.
2. Stir the mixture until smooth and add Cheddar cheese. Stir it with the help of the fork, Preheat the air fryer to 385°F.
3. Position some baking paper in the air fryer pan. With the help of the spoon make the medium size patties and put them in the pan.
4. Sprinkle the patties with sesame oil and cook for 4 minutes on each side.

117. Cheesy spinach
Servings: 4
Prep & Cooking Time: 10 Minutes
Ingredients:
- 14 ounces spinach
- 1 tbsp. olive oil
- 2 eggs, whisked
- 2 tbsp. milk
- 3 ounces cottage cheese
- Salt & black pepper for better taste
- 1 yellow onion, minced

Directions:
1. In your air fryer's pan, heat up the oil over medium heat, add the onions, stir, and sauté for 2 minutes.
2. Add all other ingredients and toss.
3. Set the pan in the air fryer. Set the temperature to 390°F. Cook it for 8 minutes.
4. Divide the spinach between plates and serve as a side dish.

118. Shirataki noodles and fennel
Servings: 3
Prep & Cooking Time: 20 Minutes + Chilling Time
Ingredients:
- 1 fennel bulb, quartered
- Salt and white pepper for better taste
- 1 clove garlic, finely minced
- 1 green onion, slimly sliced
- 1 cup Chinese cabbage, shredded
- 2 tbsps. rice wine vinegar
- 2 tbsps. sesame oil
- 1 tsp. ginger, freshly shredded
- 1 tbsp. soy sauce
- 1 1/3 cups Shirataki noodles, boiled

Directions:
1. First, heat up your air fryer to 370°F.
2. Now, cook the fennel bulb in the lightly greased cooking basket for 15 minutes, shaking the basket once or twice.
3. Let it cool completely and toss with the remaining ingredients. Serve well chilled.

119. Tasty low-carb pita chips
Servings: 1
Prep & Cooking Time: 15 Minutes
Ingredients:
- 1 cup mozzarella cheese, shredded
- 1 egg
- 1/4 cup blanched finely ground flour
- 1/2 oz. pork rinds, finely ground

Directions:
1. Melt the mozzarella in the microwave. Add the egg, flour, and pork rinds and combine together to form a smooth paste. Microwave the cheese again if it begins to set.

2. Put the dough between two sheets of parchment paper and use a rolling pin to flatten it out into a rectangle. The thickness is up to you. With a sharp knife, cut into the dough to form triangles. It may be necessary to complete this step-in multiple batches.
3. Place the chips in the fryer and cook for five minutes at 360°F. Turn them over and cook on the other side for another five minutes, or until the chips are golden and firm.
4. Allow the chips to cool and harden further. They can be stored in an airtight container.

120. Parmesan artichoke hearts
Servings: 4
Prep & Cooking Time: 15 Minutes
Ingredients:
- 1 egg
- 1/4 cup flour
- 1/4 Parmesan cheese, shredded
- 1/3 cup panko breadcrumbs
- 1 tsp. garlic powder
- Salt & black pepper for better taste

Directions:
1. Preheat the air fryer to 390°F. Put cooking oil by spraying it lightly to the air fryer basket.
2. Pat dry the artichokes with paper towels and cut them into wedges. In an empty pan, combine the whisked egg white and salt. In another bowl, combine Parmesan cheese, breadcrumbs, and garlic powder. In a third drop the flour; mix with salt and pepper.
3. Dip the artichokes in the flour, followed by a dip in the egg, and finally coat with breadcrumb mixture. Place in your air fryer's cooking basket and cook for 10 minutes, flipping once. Let cool before serving.

121. Awesome cheese sticks for everyone
Servings: 6
Prep & Cooking Time: 15 Minutes
Ingredients:
- 12 sticks mozzarella cheese
- 1/4 cup flour
- 2 cups breadcrumbs
- 2 whole eggs
- 1/4 cup Parmesan cheese, shredded

Directions:
1. Preheat air fryer to 350°F.
2. Pour breadcrumbs in a bowl. Beat the eggs in a separate bowl. In a third bowl, mix Parmesan and flour.
3. Dip each cheese stick the in flour mixture, then in eggs and finally in breadcrumbs.
4. Put in air fryer's basket and cook for 7 minutes, turning once.

122. Veggie tots for kids
Servings: 4
Prep & Cooking Time: 20 Minutes
Ingredients:
- 1 zucchini, shredded
- 1 parsnip, shredded
- 1 carrot, shredded
- 1 onion, minced
- 1 garlic clove, minced
- 2 tbsps. ground flax seeds
- 2 eggs, whisked
- 1/2 cup tortilla chips, crushed
- 1/4 cup pork rinds
- Ground black pepper and sea salt for better taste

Directions:
1. First, heat up your air fryer to 400°F.
2. Then, in a mixing bowl, thoroughly combine all ingredients until every element is well combined. Form the mixture into tot shapes and place in the lightly greased cooking basket.
3. Bake for 9 to 12 minutes, flipping halfway through, until golden brown around the edges. Bon appétit!

123. Mixed mozzarella asparagus
Servings: 4
Prep & Cooking Time: 10 Minutes
Ingredients:
- 1 lb. asparagus, trimmed
- 2 tbsps. olive oil
- A pinch of salt and black pepper
- 2 cups mozzarella, shredded
- 1/2 cup balsamic vinegar
- 2 cups cherry tomatoes, halved

Directions:
1. In your air fryer's pan, except the mozzarella, mix the asparagus with the rest of the ingredients; toss it.
2. Put the pan in the air fryer and cook at 400°F for 10 minutes. Serve in plates equally.

124. Mixed zucchinis and arugula
Servings: 4
Prep & Cooking Time: 20 Minutes
Ingredients:
- 1 lb. zucchinis, sliced
- 1 tbsp. olive oil
- Salt and white pepper to the taste
- 4 ounces arugula leaves
- 1/4 cup chives, minced
- 1 cup walnuts, minced

Directions:
1. In a pan that fits the air fryer, stir all the ingredients except the arugula and walnuts, toss, put the pan in the machine and cook at 360°F for 20 minutes.
2. Transfer this to a salad bowl, add the arugula and the walnuts, toss and serve as a side salad.

125. Great-tasting smoked fish balls
Servings: 6
Prep & Cooking Time: 45 Minutes
Ingredients:
- 2 cups cooked rice
- 2 eggs, lightly beaten
- 1 cup shredded Grana Padano cheese
- 1/4 cup finely minced thyme
- Salt & pepper for better taste
- 1 cup panko crumbs
- Cooking spray

Directions:
1. In a mixing bowl, add fish, rice, eggs, Grana Padano cheese, thyme, salt and pepper into a bowl; stir to combine.
2. Shape the mixture into even-sized balls. Cover the balls with crumbs by rolling it in it then spray with oil.
3. Set the balls into the fryer and cook for 16 minutes at 400°F, until crispy.

126. Green beans with butter
Servings: 4
Prep & Cooking Time: 12 Minutes
Ingredients:

- 3/4 lb. green beans, cleaned
- 1 tbsp. balsamic vinegar
- 1/4 tsp. kosher salt
- 1/2 tsp. mixed peppercorns, freshly grounded
- 1 tbsp. butter
- 2 tbsp. toasted sesame seeds, to serve

Directions:
1. Set your air fryer to cook at 390°F.
2. Mix the green beans with all of the above ingredients, apart from the sesame seeds. Set the timer for 10 minutes.
3. Meanwhile, toast the sesame seeds in a small-sized nonstick skillet; make sure to stir continuously.
4. Serve sautéed green beans on a nice platter sprinkled with toasted sesame seeds. Bon appétit!

127. Mushrooms stuffed with cheese
Servings: 10
Prep & Cooking Time: 30 Minutes
Ingredients:
- Olive oil to brush the mushrooms
- 1 cup cooked brown rice
- 1 cup shredded Grana Padano cheese
- 1 tsp. dried mixed herbs
- Salt & black pepper

Directions:
1. Brush every mushroom with oil and set aside.
2. In a bowl, mix rice, cheese, herbs, salt and pepper.
3. Stuff the mushrooms with the mixture.
4. Set the mushrooms in the air fryer and cook for 25 minutes at 360°F.
5. Make sure the mushrooms cooked until golden and the cheese has melted. Serve with herbs.

128. Balsamic radishes
Servings: 4
Prep & Cooking Time: 15 Minutes
Ingredients:
- 2 bunches red radishes, halved
- 1 tbsp. olive oil
- 2 tbsps. balsamic vinegar
- 2 tbsps. parsley, minced
- Salt & black pepper to the taste

Directions:
1. In a bowl, mix the radishes with the remaining ingredients except the parsley, toss and put them in your air fryer's basket.
2. Cook at 400°F for minutes, serve in plates equally, add parsley on top by sprinkling it and serve as a side dish.

129. Super jalapeno clouds
Servings: 4
Prep & Cooking Time: 4 Minutes
Ingredients:
- 2 egg whites
- 1 jalapeno pepper
- 1 tsp. almond flour
- 1 ounce Jarlsberg cheese, shredded

Directions:
1. Whisk the egg whites until you get the strong peaks. After this, carefully mix up egg white peaks, almond flour, and Jarlsberg cheese.
2. Slice the jalapeno pepper on 4 slices.
3. Preheat the air fryer to 385°F.
4. Place baking paper to the air fryer basket. With the help of the spoon make the egg white clouds on the baking paper.
5. Top the clouds with sliced jalapeno.
6. Cook them for 4 minutes or until the clouds are light brown.

130. Qui----healthy veggie fried balls
Servings: 3
Prep & Cooking Time: 30 Minutes
Ingredients:
- 1/2 lb. sweet potatoes, shredded
- 1 cup carrots
- 1 cup corn
- 2 garlic cloves, minced
- 1 shallot, minced
- Ground black pepper and sea salt for better taste
- 2 tbsps. fresh parsley, minced
- 1 egg, well beaten
- 1/2 cup purpose flour
- 1/2 cup Parmesan cheese, shredded
- 1/2 cup dried bread flakes
- 1 tbsp. olive oil

Directions:
1. Mix the veggies, spices, egg, flour, and Parmesan cheese until every element is well incorporated.
2. Take 1 tbsp. of the veggie mixture and roll into a ball. Roll the balls onto the dried bread flakes. Brush the veggie balls with olive oil on all sides.
3. Cook in the preheated air fryer at 360°F for 15 minutes or until thoroughly cooked and crispy.
4. Do the same steps until all mixture is mixed up. Bon appétit!

131. Baked sweet potato
Servings: 3
Prep & Cooking Time: 35 Minutes
Ingredients:
- 1 stick butter, melted
- 1 lb. sweet potatoes, mashed
- 2 tbsps. honey
- 2 eggs, beaten
- 1/3 cup coconut milk
- 1/4 cup flour
- 1/2 cup fresh breadcrumbs

Directions:
1. First, heat up your air fryer to 325°F.
2. Drizzle your casserole dish with cooking oil.
3. In a mixing bowl, combine all ingredients, except for the breadcrumbs and 1 tbsp. of butter. Take the mixture with a spoon into the prepared casserole dish.
4. Top with the breadcrumbs and brush the top with the remaining 1 tbsp. of butter. Bake in the preheated air fryer for 30 minutes. Bon appétit!

132. Roasted red potatoes in duck fat
Servings: 4
Prep & Cooking Time: 20 Minutes
Ingredients:
- 1 tbsp garlic powder
- Salt & black pepper for better taste
- 2 tbsps. thyme, minced
- 3 tbsps. duck fat, melted

Directions:
1. Preheat the air fryer to 380°F. In a bowl, mix duck fat, garlic powder, salt, and pepper. Add the potatoes and shake to coat. Drop into the air fryer cooking basket and cook for 15 minutes, then shake and continue cooking for another 10 minutes. Serve warm sprinkled with thyme.

133. 1 gratin family vegetable
Servings: 4
Prep & Cooking Time: 35 Minutes
Ingredients:
- 1 lb. Chinese cabbage, roughly minced
- 2 bell peppers, seeded and sliced
- 1 jalapeno pepper, seeded and sliced
- 1 onion, thickly sliced
- 2 garlic cloves, sliced
- 1/2 stick butter
- 4 tbsps. all-purpose flour
- 1 cup milk
- 1 cup cream cheese
- Sea Salt & freshly ground black pepper for better taste
- 1/2 tsp. cayenne pepper
- 1 cup Monterey Jack cheese, shredded

Directions:
1. Warm a pan of salted water and bring to a boil. Leave the Chinese cabbage to boil for 2 to 3 minutes. Once done, put the cabbage to the cold water.
2. Place the Chinese cabbage in a lightly greased casserole dish. Add the peppers, onion, and garlic.
3. In a moderate heat melt the butter. Make a paste by adding flour slowly and cooking it for 2 minutes.
4. Slowly pour in the milk, stirring continuously until a thick sauce forms. Add the cream cheese. Add taste by putting with black pepper, salt and cayenne pepper. Place the mixture to the casserole dish.
5. Cover its top with shredded cheese, Monterey Jack. Bake at 390°F for 2 minutes. Serve hot.

134. Sprouts coconut celery
Servings: 4
Prep & Cooking Time: 12 Minutes
Ingredients:
- 1 celery stalks, roughly minced
- 1 cup coconut cream
- Salt & black pepper to the taste
- 1 tbsp. parsley, minced
- 1 tbsp. coconut oil, melted
- 1/2 lb. Brussels sprouts, halved

Directions:
1. Heat up a pan that fits the air fryer with the oil over medium heat, add the sprouts and celery, stir and cook for 2 minutes. Add the cream and the remaining ingredients, toss, put the pan in the air fryer and cook at 380°F for 10 minutes. Transfer to bowls and serve.

135. Fried asparagus dipped in romesco sauce
Servings: 4
Prep & Cooking Time: 30 Minutes
Ingredients:
- Salt & black pepper for better taste
- 1/2 cup almond flour
- 1 lb. asparagus spears, trimmed and washed
- 2 eggs
- 2 tomatoes, minced

Romesco Sauce
- 2 roasted peppers, minced
- 1/2 cup almond flour
- 1/2 tsp. garlic powder
- 1 tbsp. vinegar
- 2 slices toasted bread, torn into pieces
- 1/2 tsp. paprika
- 1 tsp. crushed red chili flakes
- 1 tbsp tomato purée
- 1/2 cup extra-virgin olive oil

Directions:
1. Preheat the air fryer to 390°F. Put cooking oil by spraying it lightly to the air fryer basket.
2. On a plate, combine panko breadcrumbs, salt, and pepper. In another shallow dish, whisk the eggs, season with salt and pepper.
3. In a third, plate pour the almond flour. Dip asparagus in the almond flour, followed by a dip in the eggs, and finally, coat with breadcrumbs. Place in your air fryer's cooking basket and cook for 10 minutes, turning once halfway.
4. In a food processor, position all sauce ingredients until a nice sauce is formed.
5. Serve asparagus with the romesco sauce.

136. Yummy coconut risotto
Servings: 4
Prep & Cooking Time: 20 Minutes
Ingredients:
- 2 cups cauliflower rice
- 1 cup coconut milk
- 2 tbsps. coconut oil, melted
- 1 tbsp. cilantro, minced
- 1 tbsp. olive oil
- 1 tsp. lime zest, shredded
- 2 tbsps. Parmesan, shredded

Directions:
1. Get a pan that is good for your air fryer, mix all the ingredients, stir, introduce in the fryer and cook at 360°F for 20 minutes. Serve in plates as a side dish.

137. Bell pepper and tomato sauce recipe
Servings: 4
Prep & Cooking Time: 25 Minutes
Ingredients:
- 2 red bell peppers; minced
- 2 garlic cloves; minced
- 2 tbsps. olive oil
- 1 tbsp. balsamic vinegar
- 1 lb. cherry tomatoes; halved
- 1 tsp. rosemary; dried
- 3 bay leaves
- Salt & black pepper to the taste

Directions:
1. In a bowl mix tomatoes with garlic, salt, black pepper, rosemary, bay leaves, half of the oil and half of the vinegar, toss to coat, introduce in your air fryer and roast them at 320 °F, for 20 minutes
2. Meanwhile; in your food processor, mix bell peppers with a pinch of sea salt, black pepper, the rest of the oil and the rest of the vinegar and blend very well.
3. Divide roasted tomatoes on plates, drizzle the bell peppers sauce over them and serve

138. Mixed lemongrass rice
Servings: 4
Prep & Cooking Time: 20 Minutes
Ingredients:
- 1/2 cup broccoli, shredded
- 1/2 cup cauliflower, shredded
- 1/4 tsp. lemongrass

- 1 tsp. ground turmeric
- 1/4 cup beef broth
- 1 tsp. butter
- 1/2 tsp. salt
- 3 ounces Cheddar cheese, shredded

Directions:
1. In the mixing bowl mix up shredded broccoli and cauliflower. Add lemongrass, turmeric, and salt. Then transfer the mixture in the air fryer baking pan and add beef broth. Add butter and top the keto rice with Cheddar cheese.
2. Preheat the air fryer to 365°F. Put the pan with "rice" in the air fryer and cook it for 10 minutes.

139. Pancetta and plums bombs
Servings: 10
Prep & Cooking Time: 25 Minutes
Ingredients:
- 2 tbsps. fresh rosemary, finely minced
- 1 cup almonds, minced into small pieces
- Salt & black pepper
- 15 dried plums, minced
- 15 pancetta slices

Directions:
1. Line baking paper on the air fryer basket.
2. In a mixing bowl, add cheese, rosemary, almonds, salt, pepper and plums; stir well. Roll into balls and wrap with a pancetta slice.
3. Set the bombs on the fryer and cook for 20 minutes at 400°F.
4. Let cool before removing them from the air fryer. Serve with toothpicks.

140. Lemony artichokes
Servings: 4
Prep & Cooking Time: 25 Minutes
Ingredients:
- 2 medium artichokes; trimmed and halved
- 2 tbsps. lemon juice
- Cooking spray
- Salt & black pepper to the taste

Directions:
1. Grease your air fryer with cooking spray, add artichokes; drizzle lemon juice and sprinkle salt and black pepper and cook them at 380°F, for 20 minutes.
2. Divide them on plates and serve as a side dish.

141. Fried onion and bell peppers
Servings: 3
Prep & Cooking Time: 25 Minutes
Ingredients:
- 6 bell peppers, sliced
- 1 tbsp. Italian seasoning
- 1 tbsp. olive oil
- 1 onion, sliced

Directions:
1. Add all ingredients into the large size mixing bowl and toss well.
2. Preheat the air fryer to 385°F.
3. Transfer bell pepper and onion mixture into the air fryer basket and cook for 15 minutes.
4. Toss well and cook for 20 minutes more.
5. Serve and enjoy.

142. Delicious smoked asparagus
Servings: 4
Prep & Cooking Time: 20 Minutes
Ingredients:
- 1 lb. asparagus stalks
- Salt & black pepper to the taste
- 1/4 cup olive oil+ 1 tsp.
- 1 tbsp. smoked paprika
- 2 tbsp. balsamic vinegar
- 1 tbsp. lime juice

Directions:
6. In a bowl, mix the asparagus with salt, pepper and tsp. oil, toss, transfer to your air fryer's basket and cook at 370°F for 20 minutes.
7. Meanwhile, in a bowl, mix all the other ingredients and whisk them well.
8. Divide the asparagus between plates, drizzle the balsamic vinaigrette all over and serve as a side dish.

143. Cheesy sticks dipped in sweet thai sauce
Servings: 4
Prep & Cooking Time: 20 Minutes +°Freezing Time
Ingredients:
- 2 cups breadcrumbs
- 3 eggs
- 1 cup sweet Thai sauce
- 4 tbsps. skimmed milk

Directions:
1. Pour crumbs in a bowl. Beat eggs into another bowl with milk. One after the other, dip sticks in the egg mixture, in the crumbs, then egg mixture again and then in the crumbs again. Freeze for hour.
2. Preheat air fryer to 380°F.
3. Set the sticks on the fryer. Cook for 5 minutes, flipping them halfway through cooking to brown evenly. Cook in batches.
4. Serve with a sweet Thai sauce.

144. Dill corn
Servings: 4
Prep & Cooking Time: 6 Minutes
Ingredients:
- 4 ears of corn
- Salt & black pepper for better taste
- 2 tbsps. butter, melted
- 2 tbsps. dill, minced

Directions:
1. In a mixing bowl, combine the salt, pepper, and the butter.
2. Rub the corn with the butter mixture, and then put it in your air fryer.
3. Cook at 360°F for 6 minutes.
4. Divide the corn between plates, sprinkle the dill on top, and serve.

145. Cheesy parmesan asparagus
Servings: 4
Prep & Cooking Time: 5 Minutes
Ingredients:
- 1 lb. asparagus, cut the ends
- 1/2 cup parmesan cheese, shredded
- 1 tbsp. fresh lemon juice
- 1 tsp. garlic powder
- 1 tbsp. olive oil
- 1/4 tsp. pepper
- 1/2 tsp. sea salt

Directions:
1. Set the air fryer to 390°F.
2. In a large bowl, add asparagus.
3. In a small basin, combine the pepper, olive oil, garlic powder, and salt.
4. Pour oil mixture over asparagus and toss well.
5. Spread asparagus into the air fryer basket and cook for minutes.
6. Pour lemon juice over cooked asparagus and sprinkle with shredded cheese.
7. Serve and enjoy.

146. Chili rutabaga
Servings: 4
Prep & Cooking Time: 20 Minutes
Ingredients:
- 15 ounces rutabaga, cut into fries
- 4 tbsps. olive oil
- 1 tsp. chili powder
- A pinch of salt and black pepper

Directions:
1. In a dish, add the rutabaga fries with all the other ingredients, toss and put them in your air fryer's basket. Cook at 400°F for 20 minutes, serve in plates as a side dish.

147. Cheesy parmesan cauliflower risotto
Servings: 4
Prep & Cooking Time: 18 Minutes
Ingredients:
- 1 cup cauliflower, shredded
- 4 ounces cremini mushrooms, sliced
- 2 ounces Parmesan, shredded
- 1 tsp. ground black pepper
- 1 tbsp. heavy cream
- 1/4 tsp. garlic powder
- 3 spring onions, diced
- 1 tbsp. olive oil
- 1/2 tsp. Italian seasonings

Directions:
1. Preheat the air fryer to 400F. Then sprinkle the air fryer basket with olive oil. Place the mushrooms inside and sprinkle them with ground black pepper. Cook them at 400°F for 4 minutes.
2. Then stir them well and add the spring onion.
3. Cook the vegetables for 4 minutes more. Then shake them well and sprinkle with garlic powder and Italian seasonings. Mix up well and transfer in the air fryer mold. Add heavy cream and shredded cauliflower.
4. Then add Parmesan and mix up. Position the mold in the air fryer and set it to 375°F. Then mix up risotto and transfer into the serving plates.

Chapter 1
Snacks & Appetizers

148. Coated prawns
Servings: 4
Prep & Cooking Time: 8 Minutes
Ingredients:
- 1 egg
- 1/2 lb. nacho chips, crushed
- 18 prawns, peeled and emptied

Directions:
1. In a shallow dish, crack the egg, and beat well.
2. Put the crushed nacho chips in another dish.
3. Now, dip the prawn into beaten egg and then, coat with the nacho chips.
4. Preheat your air fryer to 355°F.
5. Place the prawns in an air fryer basket in a single layer.
6. air fry for about 8 minutes.
7. Serve hot.

149. 1. Roasted parsnip with maple syrup
Servings: 5
Prep & Cooking Time: 55 Minutes
Ingredients:
- 2 lbs. parsnips [about 6 large parsnips]
- 2 tbsps. maple syrup
- 1 tbsp. coconut oil
- 1 tbsp. parsley, dried flakes

Directions:
1. Melt the duck fat or coconut oil in your air fryer for 2 minutes at 320°F.
2. Rinse the parsnips to clean them and dry them. Chop into 1-inch cubes. Transfer to the fryer.
3. Cook the parsnip cubes in the fat/oil for 35 minutes, tossing them regularly.
4. Season the parsnips with parsley and maple syrup and allow to cook for another 5 minutes or longer to achieve a soft texture throughout. Serve straightaway.

150. Dazzling pork meatballs
Servings: 8
Prep & Cooking Time: 20 Minutes
Ingredients:
- 1/2 tsp. fine sea salt
- 1 cup Parmesan cheese, shredded
- 3 cloves garlic, minced
- 1 1/2 lbs. ground pork
- 1/2 cup chives, finely minced
- 2 eggs, well whisked
- 1/3 tsp. cumin powder
- 2/3 tsp. ground black pepper, or more to taste
- 2 tsp. basil

Directions:
1. Simply stir all the ingredients in a large-sized mixing bowl.
2. Shape into bite-sized balls; cook the meatballs in the air fryer for 18 minutes at 345°F. Serve with some tangy sauce such as marinara sauce if desired. Bon appétit!

151. Extra topped pita bread
Servings: 4
Prep & Cooking Time: 6 Minutes
Ingredients:
- 1 pita bread
- 1/4 cup mozzarella cheese
- 7 slices pepperoni
- 1/4 cup sausage
- 1 tbsp. yellow onion, sliced slimly
- 1 tbsp. pizza sauce
- 1 drizzle extra-virgin olive oil
- 1/2 tsp. fresh garlic, minced

Directions:
1. Preheat the air fryer to 350°F and grease an air fryer basket.
2. Spread pizza sauce on the pita bread and add sausages, pepperoni, onions, garlic and cheese.
3. Drizzle with olive oil and place it in the air fryer basket.
4. Cook for about 6 minutes and dish out to serve warm.

152. Crazy spicy nuts
Servings: 8
Prep & Cooking Time: 15 Minutes
Ingredients:
- 2 cup mixed nuts
- 1 tsp. chipotle chili powder
- 1 tsp. ground cumin
- 1 tbsp. butter, melted
- 1 tsp. pepper
- 1 tsp. salt

Directions:
1. In a bowl, mix all the ingredients, coating the nuts well.
2. Set your air fryer to 350°F and allow to heat for 5 minutes.
3. Place the mixed nuts in the fryer basket and roast for 4 minutes, shaking the basket halfway through the cooking time.

153. Crunchy cheddar & broccoli nuggets
Servings: 4
Prep & Cooking Time: 15 Minutes
Ingredients:
- 1/4 cup almond flour
- 2 egg whites
- 2 cups broccoli florets, cooked until soft
- 1 cup cheddar cheese, shredded
- 1/8 tsp. salt

Directions:
1. Preheat the air fryer to 325°F.
2. Spray air fryer basket with cooking spray.
3. Add cooked broccoli into the bowl and using a masher mash broccoli into small pieces.
4. Add remaining ingredients to the bowl and mix well to combine.
5. Make small nuggets from broccoli mixture and place into the air fryer basket.

6. Cook broccoli nuggets for 15 minutes. Turn halfway through.
7. Serve and enjoy.

154. Roma tomatoes chips
Servings: 4
Prep & Cooking Time: 20 Minutes
Ingredients:
- 4 Roma tomatoes, sliced
- 2 tbsp. olive oil
- Sea salt and white pepper, to taste
- 1 tsp. Italian seasoning mix
- 4 tbsp. Parmesan cheese, shredded

Directions:
1. Heat the fryer to 340°F. Generously grease the air fryer basket with nonstick cooking oil.
2. Toss the sliced tomatoes with the remaining ingredients. Transfer them to the cooking basket without overlapping.
3. Cook for about 5 minutes.
4. Shake the cooking basket and cook an additional 5 minutes. Work in batches.
5. Serve with Mediterranean aioli for dipping, if desired. Bon appétit!

155. Delicious eggplant crisps
Servings: 4
Prep & Cooking Time: 45 Minutes
Ingredients:
- 1 eggplant, peeled and slimly sliced
- Salt
- 1/2 cup almond meal
- 1/4 cup canola oil
- 1/2 cup water
- 1 tsp. garlic powder
- 1/2 tsp. dried dill weed
- 1/2 tsp. ground black pepper, to taste

Directions:
1. Salt the eggplant slices and let them stay for about 30 minutes. Squeeze the eggplant slices and rinse them under cold running water.
2. Toss the eggplant slices with the other ingredients. Cook at 390°F for 13 minutes, working in batches.
3. Serve with a sauce for dipping. Bon appétit!

156. Radish and sage chips
Servings: 6
Prep & Cooking Time: 35 Minutes
Ingredients:
- 2 cups radishes, sliced
- 1/2 tsp. sage
- 2 tsp. avocado oil
- 1/2 tsp. salt

Directions:
1. In the mixing bowl mix up radishes, sage, avocado oil, and salt. Preheat the air fryer to 320°F. Put the sliced radishes in the air fryer basket and cook it for 35 minutes. Shake the vegetables every few minutes.

157. Simply bacon and shrimp
Servings: 10
Prep & Cooking Time: 45 Minutes
Ingredients:
- 1/2 tsp. ground black pepper
- 1 tsp. paprika
- 1 tsp. chili powder
- 1/2 tsp. red pepper flakes, crushed
- 1 tbsp. salt
- 1 tbsp. shallot powder
- 1/4 tsp. cumin powder
- 1 1/4 lbs. slim bacon slices
- 1 1/4 lbs. shrimp, peeled and emptied

Directions:
1. Toss the shrimps with all the seasoning until they are coated well.
2. Next, wrap a slice of bacon around the shrimps, securing with a toothpick; repeat with the remaining ingredients; chill for 30 minutes.
3. Air-fry them at 280°F for 7 to 8 minutes, working in batches. Serve with cocktail sticks if desired. Enjoy!

158. Zucchini spring rolls
Servings: 2 – 4
Prep & Cooking Time: 15 Minutes
Ingredients:
- 3 zucchinis, sliced slimly lengthwise
- 1 tbsp. olive oil
- 1 cup goat cheese
- 1/4 tsp. black pepper

Directions:
1. Preheat your air fryer to 390°F.
2. Coat each zucchini strip with a light brushing of olive oil.
3. Combine the sea salt, black pepper and goat cheese.
4. Scoop a small, equal amount of the goat cheese onto the center of each strip of zucchini. Roll up the strips and secure with a toothpick.
5. Transfer to the air fryer and cook for minutes until the cheese is warm and the zucchini slightly crispy. If desired, add some tomato sauce on top.

159. Broccoli golden nuggets
Servings: 4
Prep & Cooking Time: 25 Minutes
Ingredients:
- 1 lb. broccoli, minced
- 1/2 cup almond flour
- 1/4 cup ground flaxseed
- 1/2 tsp. garlic powder
- 1 tsp. salt

Directions:
1. Add broccoli into the microwave-safe bowl and microwave for 3 minutes.
2. Transfer steamed broccoli into the food processor and process until it looks like rice.
3. Transfer broccoli to a large size mixing bowl.
4. Add remaining ingredients into the bowl and mix until well combined.
5. Spray air fryer basket with cooking spray.
6. Make small tots from broccoli mixture and place into the air fryer basket.
7. Cook broccoli tots for 12 minutes at 3°F.
8. Serve and enjoy.

160. Seasoned tofu with avocado
Servings: 2
Prep & Cooking Time: 7 Minutes
Ingredients:
- 1/2 tsp. ground coriander
- 1 tbsp. avocado oil
- 1 tsp. lemon juice
- 1/2 tsp. chili flakes
- 6 ounces tofu

Directions:
1. In the shallow bowl mix up ground coriander, avocado oil, lemon juice, and chili flakes. Chop the tofu into cubes and sprinkle with coriander mixture. Shake the tofu. After this, preheat the air fryer to 400°F and put the tofu cubes in it. Cook the tofu for 4 minutes. Then flip the tofu on another side and cook for 3 minutes more.

161. Fabolous veggie fritters
Servings: 4
Prep & Cooking Time: 15 Minutes
Ingredients:
- 1 cup bell peppers, emptied and minced
- 1 tsp. sea salt flakes
- 1 tsp. cumin
- 1/4 tsp. paprika
- 1/2 cup shallots, minced
- 2 cloves garlic, minced
- 1 1/2 tbsp. fresh minced cilantro
- 1 egg, whisked
- 3/4 cup Cheddar cheese, shredded
- 1/4 cup cooked quinoa
- 1/4 cup flour

Directions:
1. Whisk all the ingredients well into a medium bowl.
2. Divide the mixture into equal portions and shape each one into a ball. Use your palm to flatten each ball very slightly to form patties.
3. Lightly coat the patties with a cooking spray.
4. Put the patties in your air fryer cooking basket, taking care not to overlap them.
5. Cook at 340°F for 10 minutes, turning them over halfway through.

162. Spicy nutty nibble
Servings: 5
Prep & Cooking Time: 30 Minutes
Ingredients:
- 2 tbsp. Cajun seasoning
- 1/2 cup butter, melted
- 2 cups peanut
- 2 cups mini wheat slim crackers
- 2 cups mini pretzels
- 2 tsp. salt
- 1 tsp. cayenne pepper
- 4 cups plain popcorn
- 1 tsp. paprika
- 1 tsp. garlic
- 1/2 tsp. thyme
- 1/2 tsp. oregano
- 1 tsp. black pepper
- 1/2 tsp. onion powder

Directions:
1. Pre-heat the air fryer to 370°F.
2. In a mixing bowl, combine the Cajun spice with the melted butter.
3. In a separate bowl, stir together the peanuts, crackers, popcorn and pretzels. Coat the snacks with the butter mixture.
4. Drop into the fryer and fry for 8 - 10 minutes, shaking the basket frequently during the cooking time. You will have to complete this step in two batches.
5. Put the snack mix on a cookie sheet and leave to cool.
6. The snacks can be kept in an airtight container for up to one week.

163. Tasty cauliflower popcorn
Servings: 4
Prep & Cooking Time: 11 Minutes
Ingredients:
- 1 cup cauliflower florets
- 1 tsp. ground turmeric
- 2 eggs, beaten
- 2 tbsp. almond flour
- 1 tsp. salt
- Cooking spray

Directions:
1. Cut the cauliflower florets into tiny pieces and season with salt and turmeric.
2. Dip the vegetables in the eggs and coat in the almond flour. Preheat the air fryer to 400°F.
3. Place the cauliflower popcorn in the air fryer in one layer and cook for 7 minutes. Give a good shake to the vegetables and cook them for 4 minutes more.

164. Zucchini nibbles with mayonnaise
Servings: 2
Prep & Cooking Time: 20 Minutes
Ingredients:
- 1 zucchini, sliced into strips
- 2 tbsp. mayonnaise
- 1/4 cup tortilla chips, crushed
- 1/4 cup Parmesan cheese, shredded
- Sea salt and black pepper, at your convenience
- 1 tbsp. garlic powder
- 1/2 tsp. red pepper flakes

Directions:
1. Coat the zucchini with mayonnaise.
2. Mix the crushed tortilla chips, cheese and spices in a shallow dish.
3. Then, coat the zucchini sticks with the cheese/chips mixture.
4. Cook in the preheated air fryer at 290°F for 12 minutes, shaking the basket halfway through the cooking time.
5. Work in batches until the sticks are crispy and golden brown. Bon appétit!

165. Cheesy sticks with paprika
Servings: 6
Prep & Cooking Time: 30 Minutes
Ingredients:
- 1 cup all-purpose flour
- Sea salt & ground black pepper, to taste
- 1/4 tsp. smoked paprika
- 1/2 tsp. celery seeds
- 4 ounces mature Cheddar, cold, freshly shredded
- 1 stick butter

Directions:
1. Warm your fryer to 330°F. Line the air fryer basket with parchment paper.
2. In a mixing bowl, thoroughly combine the flour, salt, black pepper, paprika, and celery seeds.
3. Then, combine the cheese and butter in the bowl of a stand mixer. Slowly stir in the flour mixture and mix to combine well.
4. Then, pack the dough into a cookie press fitted with a star disk. Pipe the long ribbons of dough across the parchment paper. Then cut into six-inch lengths.
5. Bake in the preheated air fryer for 1 minute.
6. Repeat with the remaining dough.
7. Let the cheese straws cool on a rack.
8. You can store them between sheets of parchment in an airtight container. Bon appétit!

166. Crispy cauliflower with herbs
Servings: 2
Prep & Cooking Time: 20 Minutes
Ingredients:
- 3 cups cauliflower florets
- 2 tbsp. sesame oil
- 1 tsp. onion powder
- 1 tsp. garlic powder
- 1 tsp. thyme
- 1 tsp. paprika
- 1 tsp. sage
- 1 tsp. rosemary
- Sea salt & ground black pepper to taste

Directions:
1. Preheat the air fryer to 400°°F.
2. Toss the cauliflower with the remaining ingredients; toss to coat well.
3. Cook for 12 minutes, shaking the cooking basket halfway through the cooking time. They will crisp up as they cool. Bon appétit!

167. Vinegary hot sauce
Servings: 6
Prep & Cooking Time: 5 Minutes
Ingredients:
- 12 ounces hot peppers, minced
- 1 1/2 cups white wine vinegar
- Pepper
- Salt

Directions:
1. Add all ingredients into the air fryer baking dish and stir well.
2. Put in the dish in the air fryer and cook at 380°F for 5 minutes.
3. Transfer pepper mixture into the blender and blend until smooth.
4. Serve and enjoy.

168. Spicy carrot and chives dressing
Servings: 6
Prep & Cooking Time: 15 Minutes
Ingredients:
- 2 cups carrots, shredded
- 1/4 tsp. cayenne pepper
- 4 tbsp butter, melted
- 1 tbsp chives, minced
- Salt & pepper

Directions:
1. Add all ingredients into the air fryer baking dish and stir until well combined.
2. Put the dish into the air fryer and cook at 380°F for 15 minutes.
3. Transfer cook carrot mixture into the blender and blend until smooth.
4. Serve and enjoy.

169. Cauliflower tortillas
Servings: 4
Prep & Cooking Time: 30 Minutes
Ingredients:
- 1 large head of cauliflower divided into florets.
- 4 large eggs
- 2 garlic cloves (minced)
- 1 1/2 tsp. herbs (whatever your favorite is - basil, oregano, thyme)
- 1/2 tsp. salt

Directions:
1. Preheat your fryer to 375°F.
2. Put parchment paper on two baking sheets.
3. In a food processor, break down the cauliflower into rice.
4. Add 1/4 cup water and the riced cauliflower to a saucepan.
5. Cook on a medium high heat until tender for 10 minutes. Drain.
6. Dry with a clean kitchen towel.
7. Mix the cauliflower, eggs, garlic, herbs and salt.
8. Make 4 slim circles on the parchment paper.
9. Bake for 20 minutes, until dry.

170. Sriracha short ribs
Servings: 4
Prep & Cooking Time: 35 Minutes
Ingredients:
- 1 lb. meaty short ribs
- 1/2 rice vinegar
- 2 tbsps. soy sauce
- 1 tbsp. Sriracha sauce
- 2 garlic cloves, minced
- 1 tbsp. daenjang (soybean paste)
- 1 tsp. kochukaru (chili pepper flakes)
- Sea salt & ground black pepper, to taste
- 1 tbsp. sesame oil
- 1/4 cup green onions, roughly minced

Directions:
1. Place the short ribs, vinegar, soy sauce, Sriracha, garlic, and spices in Ziploc bag; let it marinate overnight.
2. Rub the sides and bottom of the air fryer basket with sesame oil. Discard the marinade and transfer the ribs to the prepared cooking basket.
3. Cook the marinated ribs in the preheated air fryer at 355°F for 17 minutes. Turn the ribs over, brush with the reserved marinade, and cook an additional 15 minutes.
4. Garnish with green onions. Bon appétit!

171. Spiced broccoli chips
Servings: 4
Prep & Cooking Time: 15 Minutes
Ingredients:
- 3/4 lb. broccoli florets
- 1/2 tsp. onion powder
- 1 tsp. granulated garlic
- 1/2 tsp. cayenne pepper
- Sea salt & ground black pepper, to taste
- 2 tbsp. sesame oil
- 4 tbsp. parmesan cheese, preferably freshly shredded

Spicy Dip:
- 1/4 cup mayonnaise
- 1/4 cup Greek yogurt
- 1/4 tsp. Dijon mustard
- 1 tsp. hot sauce

Directions:
1. Warm the air fryer to 400°F.
2. Boil the broccoli in salted water until al dente, about 3 to 4 minutes. Drain well and transfer to the lightly greased air fryer basket.
3. Add the onion powder, garlic, cayenne pepper, salt, black pepper, sesame oil, and Parmesan cheese.
4. Cook for 6 minutes, tossing once halfway through.
5. Meanwhile, mix all of the spicy dip ingredients. Serve broccoli fries with chilled dipping sauce. Bon appétit!

172. Super crispy broccoli fritters
Servings: 4
Prep & Cooking Time: 15 Minutes
Ingredients:
- 1 lb. broccoli florets

- 1/2 tsp. onion powder
- 1 tsp. granulated garlic
- 1/2 tsp. cayenne pepper
- Sea salt & ground black pepper, to taste
- 2 tbsps. grapeseed oil
- 4 tbsps. Parmesan cheese, preferably freshly shredded

Directions:
1. Warm your air fryer to 400°F.
2. Boil the broccoli in the water, about 3 to 4 minutes. Drain well and transfer to the lightly greased air fryer basket.
3. Add the onion powder, garlic, cayenne pepper, salt, black pepper, and grapeseed oil.
4. Cook for 6 minutes, tossing halfway through the cooking time. Bon appétit!

173. Fleshy beef cocktail wieners

Servings: 6
Prep & Cooking Time: 20 Minutes
Ingredients:
- 1 lb. beef cocktail wieners
- 10 ounces barbecue sauce, no sugar added

Directions:
1. Warm your air fryer to 380°F.
2. Prick holes into your sausages using a fork and transfer them to the baking pan.
3. Cook for 1 minute. Spoon the barbecue sauce into the pan and cook an additional 2 minutes.
4. Serve with toothpicks. Bon appétit!

174. Brussels sprouts munch

Servings: 4
Prep & Cooking Time: 20 Minutes
Ingredients:
- 3/4 lb. Brussels sprouts
- 1 tsp. kosher salt
- 1 tbsp. lemon zest
- Non-stick cooking spray
- 1 cup feta cheese, cubed

Directions:
1. Firstly, peel the Brussels sprouts using a small paring knife.
2. Toss the leaves with salt and lemon zest; spritz them with a cooking spray, coating all sides.
3. Bake at 380°F for 8 minutes; shake the cooking basket halfway through the cooking time and cook for 7 more minutes.
4. Make sure to work in batches so every element can cook evenly. Taste and adjust the seasonings. Serve with feta cheese. Bon appétit!

175. Cheesy bacon scoops

Servings: 4
Prep & Cooking Time: 22 Minutes
Ingredients:
- 1/3 cup Swiss cheese, shredded
- 1/3 tsp. fine sea salt
- 1/3 tsp. baking powder
- 1/3 cup chives, finely minced
- 1/2 tbsp. fresh basil, finely minced
- 1 zucchini, trimmed and shredded
- 1/2 tsp. freshly grounded black pepper
- 1 tsp. Mexican oregano
- 1 cup bacon, minced
- 1/4 cup almond meal
- 1/4 cup coconut flour
- 2 small eggs, lightly beaten
- 1 cup Cotija cheese, shredded

Directions:
1. Mix all ingredients, except for Cotija cheese, until every element is well combined.
2. Then, gently flatten each ball. Spritz the cakes with a nonstick cooking oil.
3. Bake your cakes for 1 minute at 305°F; work with batches. Serve warm with tomato ketchup and mayonnaise.

176. Bacon-and cheddar kibble

Servings: 6
Prep & Cooking Time: 8 Minutes
Ingredients:
- 1 lb. slim bacon slices
- 1 lb. cheddar cheese, cut into 1-inch rectangular pieces
- 1 cup all-purpose flour
- 3 eggs
- 1 cup breadcrumbs
- 1 tbsp. olive oil
- Salt, to taste

Directions:
1. Preheat the air fryer to 390°F and grease an air fryer basket.
2. Wrap 1 piece of cheddar cheese with bacon slices, covering completely.
3. Repeat with the remaining cheese and bacon slices.
4. Set the croquettes in a baking dish and freeze for about 10 minutes.
5. Place flour in a shallow dish.
6. Whisk the eggs in a second dish.
7. Mix together oil, breadcrumbs and salt in a third shallow dish.
8. Coat the croquettes evenly in flour and dip in the eggs.
9. Dredge in the breadcrumbs mixture and place the croquettes in an air fryer basket.
10. Cook for about 8 minutes and dish out to serve warm.

177. Sage-spiced chicken wings

Servings: 4
Prep & Cooking Time: 1 Hour 10 Minutes
Ingredients:
- 1/3 cup almond flour
- 1/3 cup buttermilk
- 1 1/2 lbs. chicken wings
- 1 tbsp. tamari sauce
- 1/3 tsp. fresh sage
- 1 tsp. mustard seeds
- 1/2 tsp. garlic paste
- 1/2 tsp. freshly ground mixed peppercorns
- 1/2 tsp. seasoned salt
- 2 tsp. fresh basil

Directions:
1. Place the seasonings along with the garlic paste, chicken wings, buttermilk, and tamari sauce in a large-sized mixing dish. Let it soak about 55 minutes; drain the wings.
2. Dredge the wings in the almond flour and transfer them to the air fryer cooking basket.
3. Air-fry for 16 minutes at 5°F. Serve on a nice platter with a dressing on the side. Bon appétit!

178. Pork and beef lavish meatball

Servings: 6
Prep & Cooking Time: 20 Minutes
Ingredients:
- 1/2 lb. ground pork
- 1/2 lb. ground beef

- 1 tsp. dried onion flakes
- 1 tsp. fresh garlic, minced
- 1 tsp. dried parsley flakes
- Salt & black pepper, to taste
- 1 red pepper, 1-inch pieces
- 1 cup pearl onions
- 1/2 cup barbecue sauce

Directions:
1. Mix the ground meat with the onion flakes, garlic, parsley flakes, salt, and black pepper. Shape the mixture into inch balls.
2. Thread the meatballs, pearl onions, and peppers alternately onto skewers.
3. Microwave the barbecue sauce for 10 seconds.
4. Cook in the preheated air fryer at 380°F for 5 minutes.
5. Flip the skewers halfway through cooking.
6. Brush with the sauce and cook for a further 5 minutes. Work in batches.
7. Serve with the remaining barbecue sauce and enjoy!

179. Fried cashew
Servings: 4
Prep & Cooking Time: 5 Minutes
Ingredients:
- 4 ounces cashews
- 1 tsp. ranch seasoning
- 1 tsp. walnut oil

Directions:
1. Preheat the air fryer to 375°F. Mix up cashews with ranch seasoning and walnut oil and put in the preheated air fryer.
2. Cook the cashews for 4 minutes. Then shake well and cook for 1 minute more.

180. Superb chicken pillows
Servings: 4
Prep & Cooking Time: 20 Minutes
Ingredients:
- 1 tsp. olive oil
- 1 cup ground chicken
- 1 (8-ounces) can Pillsbury Crescent Roll dough
- Sea salt & ground black pepper, to taste
- 1 tsp. onion powder
- 1/2 tsp. garlic powder
- 4 tbsp. tomato paste
- 4 ounces cream cheese, at room temperature
- 2 tbsp. butter, melted

Directions:
1. In a pan over medium-high heat warm the olive oil. Then, cook the ground chicken until browned or about 4 minutes.
2. Unroll the crescent dough. roll out the dough using a rolling pin; cut into 8 pieces.
3. Place the browned chicken, salt, black pepper, onion powder, garlic powder, tomato paste, and cheese in the center of each piece.
4. Fold each corner over the filling using wet hands. Press together to cover the filling entirely and seal the edges.
5. Now, spritz the bottom of the air fryer basket with cooking oil. Lay the chicken pillows in a single layer in the cooking basket. Drizzle the melted butter all over chicken pillows.
6. Bake at 370°F for minutes or until golden brown. Work in batches. Bon appétit!

181. Cheesy cauliflower bombs
Servings: 4
Prep & Cooking Time: 25 Minutes

Ingredients:
- 1/2 lb. cauliflower
- 2 ounces Ricotta cheese
- 1/3 cup Swiss cheese
- 1 egg
- 1 tbsp. Italian seasoning mix
- Sweet and Sour Sauce:
- 1 red bell pepper, jarred
- 1 clove garlic, minced
- 1 tsp. sherry vinegar
- 1 tbsp. tomato puree
- 2 tbsps. olive oil
- Salt & black pepper, to taste

Directions:
1. Blanch the cauliflower in salted boiling water about 3 to 4 minutes until al dente. Drain well and pulse in a food processor.
2. Add the remaining ingredients for the cauliflower bombs; mix to combine well.
3. Bake in the preheated air fryer at 385°F for 16 minutes, shaking halfway through the cooking time.
4. In the meantime, pulse all ingredients for the sauce in your food processor until combined. Season to taste. Serve the cauliflower bombs with the Sweet and Sour Sauce on the side. Bon appétit!

182. Spinach and parsley rolls
Servings: 6
Prep & Cooking Time: 4 Minutes
Ingredients:
- 1 (16-ounces) package frozen spinach, thawed
- 1 red onion, minced
- 1 cup fresh parsley, minced
- 1 cup fresh mint leaves, minced
- 1 egg
- 1 cup feta cheese, crumbled
- 1/2 cup Parmesan cheese, shredded
- 1/4 tsp. ground cardamom
- Salt and grounded black pepper, to taste
- 1 package frozen filo dough, thawed
- 2 tbsp. olive oil

Directions:
1. Put all the listed ingredients except filo dough and oil in a food processor and pulse until smooth.
2. Place one filo sheet on the cutting board and cut into three rectangular strips.
3. Brush each strip with the oil.
4. Add about one tsp. of spinach mixture along with the short side of a strip.
5. Roll the dough to secure the filling.
6. Repeat the same process with the rest of the filo sheets and spinach mixture.
7. Preheat the air fryer to 355°F.
8. Grease an air fryer basket.
9. Place rolls into the prepared basket in a single layer.
10. Air fry for about 4 minutes.
11. Enjoy!

183. Spicy pickle chips with greek yogurt dip
Servings: 5
Prep & Cooking Time: 20 Minutes
Ingredients:
- 1/2 cup cornmeal
- 1/2 cup all-purpose flour
- 1 tsp. cayenne pepper
- 1/2 tsp. shallot powder

- 1 tsp. garlic powder
- 1/2 tsp. porcini powder
- Salt & ground black pepper, to taste
- 2 eggs
- 2 cups pickle chips, pat dry with kitchen towels

Greek yogurt dip:
- 1/2 cup Greek yogurt
- 1 clove garlic, minced
- 1/4 tsp. ground black pepper
- 1 tbsp. fresh chives, minced

Directions:
1. In a bowl, whisk the cornmeal and flour; add the seasonings and mix to combine well.
2. Beat the eggs in a different mixing bowl.
3. Dredge the pickle chips in the flour mixture, then, in the egg mixture. Press the pickle chips into the flour mixture again, coating evenly.
4. Warm the air fryer at 400°F for 5 minutes; shake the basket and cook for 5 minutes more. Work in batches.
5. Meanwhile, mix all the sauce ingredients until well combined. Serve the fried pickles with the Greek yogurt dip and enjoy.

184. Onion rings
Servings: 4
Prep & Cooking Time: 10 Minutes
Ingredients:
- 1 large onion, cut into rings
- 1 1/4 cups all-purpose flour
- 1 cup milk
- 1 egg
- 3/4 cup dry bread crumbs
- Salt, to taste

Directions:
1. Preheat the air fryer to 360°F and grease the air fryer basket.
2. Mix together flour and salt in a dish.
3. Whisk egg with milk in a second dish until well mixed.
4. Place the breadcrumbs in a third dish.
5. Coat the onion rings with the flour mixture and dip into the egg mixture.
6. Lastly dredge in the breadcrumbs and transfer the onion rings in the air fryer basket.
7. Cook for about 10 minutes and dish out to serve warm.

185. Golden fried baby corn
Servings: 4
Prep & Cooking Time: 20 Minutes
Ingredients:
- 8 oz. baby corns, boiled
- 1 cup plain flour
- 1 tsp. garlic powder
- 1/2 tsp. carom seeds
- 1/4 tsp. chili powder
- Pinch of baking powder
- Salt to taste

Directions:
1. In a mixing bowl, combine the flour, chili powder, garlic powder, baking powder, salt and carom seed. Add in a little water to create a batter-like consistency.
2. Coat each baby corn in the batter.
3. Pre-heat the air fryer at 350°F.
4. Cover the air fryer basket with aluminum foil before laying the coated baby corns on top of the foil.
5. Cook for 10 minutes.

186. Cashew and cilantro sauce
Servings: 6
Prep & Cooking Time: 8 Minutes
Ingredients:
- 1/2 cup cashews, soaked in water for 4 hours and drained
- 3 tbsp. cilantro, minced
- 2 garlic cloves, minced
- 1 tsp. lime juice
- A pinch of salt and black pepper
- 2 tbsp. almond milk

Directions:
1. In a blender, stir all the ingredients, pulse well and transfer to a ramekin.
2. Put the ramekin in your air fryer's basket and cook at 350°F for 8 minutes. Serve as a party dip.

187. Sweet potato fingers
Servings: 2
Prep & Cooking Time: 30 Minutes
Ingredients:
- 2 sweet potatoes, diced into 1-inch cubes
- 1 tsp. red chili flakes
- 2 tsp. cinnamon
- 2 tbsp. olive oil
- 2 tbsp. honey
- 1/2 cup fresh parsley, minced

Directions:
1. Pre-heat the air fryer at 350°F.
2. Drop the ingredients in a mixing bowl and stir well to coat the sweet potato cubes entirely.
3. Put the sweet potato mixture into the air fryer basket and cook for 15 minutes.

188. Tasty roasted peanuts
Servings: 10
Prep & Cooking Time: 14 Minutes
Ingredients:
- 2 1/2 cups raw peanuts
- 1 tbsp. olive oil
- Salt, as required

Directions:
1. Set the temperature of air fryer to 320°F.
2. Add the peanuts in an air fryer basket in a single layer.
3. Air fry for about 9 minutes, tossing twice.
4. Remove the peanuts from air fryer basket and transfer into a bowl.
5. Add the oil, and salt and toss to coat well.
6. Return the nuts mixture into air fryer basket.
7. Air fry for about 5 minutes.
8. Serve the heated nuts in a glass or steel dish.

189. Fantasy of roasted vegetables
Servings: 4
Prep & Cooking Time: 45 Minutes
Ingredients:
- 3.5 oz. radishes
- 1/2 tsp. parsley
- 3.5 oz. celeriac
- 1 yellow carrot
- 1 orange carrot
- 1 red onion
- 3.5 oz. pumpkin

- 3.5 oz. parsnips
- Salt to taste
- Epaulette pepper to taste
- 1 tbsp. olive oil
- 4 cloves garlic, unpeeled

Directions:
1. Peel and slice up all the vegetables into 2- to 3-cm pieces.
2. Pre-heat your air fryer to 390°F.
3. Pour in the oil and allow it to warm before placing the vegetables in the fryer, followed by the garlic, salt and pepper.
4. Roast for 18 – 20 minutes.
5. Top with parsley and serve warm with rice if desired.

190. Cheesy crisps
Servings: 4
Prep & Cooking Time: 15 Minutes
Ingredients:
- 1/2 cup Parmesan cheese, shredded
- 1 cup Cheddar cheese, shredded
- 1 tsp. Italian seasoning
- 1/2 cup marinara sauce

Directions:
1. Start by preheating your air fryer to 350°F. Place a piece of parchment paper in the cooking basket.
2. Mix the cheese with the Italian seasoning.
3. Add about 1 tbsp. of the cheese mixture (per crisp to the basket, making sure they are not touching. Bake for 6 minutes or until browned at your convenience.
4. Work in batches and place them on a large tray to cool slightly. Serve with the marinara sauce. Bon appétit!

191. Delicious feta cheese pastries
Servings: 6
Prep & Cooking Time: 5 Minutes
Ingredients:
- 1 egg yolk
- 4 ounces feta cheese, crumbled
- 1 scallion, finely minced
- 2 tbsp. fresh parsley, finely minced
- Salt & ground black pepper, as needed
- 2 frozen filo pastry sheets, thawed
- 2 tbsp. olive oil

Directions:
1. In a mixing bowl, whisk well the egg yolk.
2. Add in the feta cheese, scallion, parsley, salt, and black pepper. Mix well.
3. Cut each filo pastry sheet in three strips.
4. Add about 1 tsp. of feta mixture on the underside of a strip.
5. Fold the tip of sheet over the filling in a zigzag manner to form a triangle.
6. Repeat with the remaining strips and fillings.
7. Heat the air fryer to 390°F.
8. Coat each pastry evenly with oil.
9. Place the pastries in an air fryer basket in a single layer.
10. Air fry for about 3 minutes, then air fryer for about 2 minutes on 360°F.
11. Serve.

192. Smart popcorn
Servings: 4
Prep & Cooking Time: 20 Minutes
Ingredients:
- 2 tbsp. dried corn kernels
- 1 tsp. safflower oil
- Kosher salt, to taste
- 1 tsp. red pepper flakes, crushed

Directions:
1. Add the dried corn kernels to the air fryer basket; brush with safflower oil.
2. Cook at 395°F for 15 minutes, shaking the basket every 5 minutes.
3. Sprinkle with salt and red pepper flakes. Bon appétit!

193. Cheesy mushrooms and herbs
Servings: 6
Prep & Cooking Time: 5 Minutes
Ingredients:
- 1 tbsp. butter
- 9 ounce mushrooms, cut stems
- 1 tsp. dried parsley
- 1 tsp. dried dill
- 6 ounce Swiss cheese, shredded
- 1/4 tsp. salt

Directions:
1. Finely chop mushrooms stem and add to bowl.
2. In a large bowl, add parsley, dill, cheese, butter, and salt.
3. Preheat oven to 400°F.
4. Stuff mushroom caps with bowl mixture and place in air fryer basket.
5. Cook mushrooms for 5 minutes.
6. Enjoy.

194. Savory and crunchy eggplant with italian seasoning
Servings: 4
Prep & Cooking Time: 20 Minutes
Ingredients:
- 1 eggplant, cut into 1-inch pieces
- 1/2 tsp. Italian seasoning
- 1 tsp. paprika
- 1/2 tsp. red pepper
- 1 tsp. garlic powder
- 2 tbsp olive oil

Directions:
1. Add all ingredients into the large size mixing bowl and toss well.
2. Transfer eggplant mixture into the air fryer basket.
3. Cook at 385°F for 20 minutes. Shake basket halfway through.
4. Serve and enjoy.

195. No stress cocktail franks
Servings: 4
Prep & Cooking Time: 45 Minutes
Ingredients:
- 1x 12-oz. package cocktail franks
- 1x 8-oz. can crescent rolls

Directions:
1. Drain the cocktail franks and dry with paper towels.
2. Unroll the crescent rolls and slice the dough into rectangular strips, roughly 1" by 1.5".
3. Wrap the franks in the strips with the ends poking out. Leave in the freezer for 5 minutes.
4. Pre-heat the air fryer to 330°F.
5. Take the franks out of the freezer and put them in the cooking basket. Cook for 6 – 8 minutes.
6. Reduce the heat to 390°F and cook for another 3 minutes or until a golden-brown color is achieved.

196. Easy potato cloves
Servings: 4
Prep & Cooking Time: 30 Minutes
Ingredients:
- 4 medium potatoes, cut into wedges
- 1 tbsp. Creole
- 1 tbsp. olive oil
- Pepper to taste
- Salt to taste

Directions:
1. Put the potato wedges into the air fryer basket and pour in the olive oil.
2. Cook wedges at 370°F for 15 minutes, shaking the basket twice throughout the cooking time.
3. Put the cooked wedges in a bowl and coat them with the Creole, pepper, and salt. Serve warm.

197. Fried pepper fingers
Servings: 4
Prep & Cooking Time: 20 Minutes
Ingredients:
- 1 egg, beaten
- 1/2 cup Parmesan, shredded
- 1 tsp. sea salt
- 1/2 tsp. red pepper flakes, crushed
- 3/4 lb. bell peppers, emptied and cut to 1/4-inch strips
- 2 tbsp. grapeseed oil

Directions:
1. In a medium size bowl, combine together the egg, Parmesan, salt, and red pepper flakes; mix to combine well.
2. Dip bell peppers into the batter and transfer them to the cooking basket. Brush with the grapeseed oil.
3. Cook in the preheated air fryer at 320°F for 4 minutes. Shake the basket and cook for a further 3 minutes. Work in batches.
4. Taste, adjust the seasonings and serve. Bon appétit!

198. Spicy apple chips
Servings: 2
Prep & Cooking Time: 16 Minutes
Ingredients:
- 1 apple, peeled, cored and slimly sliced
- 1 tbsp. sugar
- 1/2 tsp. ground cinnamon
- A pinch of ground cardamom
- A pinch of ground ginger
- A pinch of salt

Directions:
1. Preheat air fryer to 390°F.
2. In a mixing bowl, add all the ingredients and toss to coat well.
3. Set the apple slices in an air fryer basket in a single layer in 2 batches.
4. Air fry for about 7-8 minutes, flipping once halfway through.
5. Serve.

199. Fried tomatoes with parmesan cheese
Servings: 2
Prep & Cooking Time: 10 Minutes
Ingredients:
- 2 medium green tomatoes
- 1 egg
- 1/4 cup blanched finely ground flour
- 1/3 cup parmesan cheese, shredded

Directions:
1. Slice the tomatoes about a half-inch thick.
2. Beat the eggs in a small bowl. In a different bowl, combine together the flour and parmesan cheese.
3. Dredge the tomato slices in egg, then dip them into the flour-cheese mixture to coat. Place each slice into the fryer basket. They may need to be cooked in multiple batches.
4. Cook at 300°F for seven minutes, turning them halfway through the cooking time, and then serve warm.

200. Yummy spiced sweet potato tots
Servings: 24
Prep & Cooking Time: 31 Minutes
Ingredients:
- 2 sweet potatoes, peeled
- 1/2 tsp. Cajun seasoning
- Salt

Directions:
1. Add water in large pot and bring to boil.
2. Add sweet potatoes in pot and boil for several minutes until soft.
3. Drain well.
4. Grate the boiled sweet potatoes into a large bowl using a shredder.
5. Add Cajun seasoning and salt to the shredded sweet potatoes and mix until well combined.
6. Spray air fryer basket with cooking spray.
7. Make small tots of the sweet potato mixture and place in air fryer basket.
8. Cook at 400°F for 8 minutes. Turn tots to another side and cook for 8 minutes more.
9. Serve and enjoy.

201. Coconut cookies with vanilla scent
Servings: 8
Prep & Cooking Time: 12 Minutes
Ingredients:
- 2 1/4 ounces caster sugar
- 3 1/2 ounces butter
- 1 small egg
- 1 tsp. vanilla extract
- 5 ounces self-rising flour
- 1 1/4 ounces white chocolate, minced
- 3 tbsp. desiccated coconut

Directions:
1. In a large size bowl, mix the butter with the sugar and whisk until fluffy and light.
2. Add the egg, and vanilla extract and whisk until well combined.
3. Now, add the flour, and chocolate and mix well.
4. In a shallow bowl, place the coconut.
5. With your hands, make small balls from the mixture and roll evenly into the coconut.
6. Put the balls into an ungreased baking sheet about 1- inch apart and gently, press each ball.
7. Preheat your air fryer to 355°F.
8. Place baking sheet into the air fryer basket.
9. Air fry for about 8 minutes and then, another 4 minutes at 320°F.
10. Remove from air fryer and place the baking sheet onto a wire rack to cool for about 5 minutes.
11. Now, invert the cookies onto wire rack to cool completely before serving.
12. Serve.

202. Carrots and rhubarb salad
Servings: 4
Prep & Cooking Time: 35 Minutes
Ingredients:
- 1 lb. heritage carrots
- 1 lb. rhubarb

- 1 medium orange
- 1/2 cup walnuts, halved
- 2 tsps. walnut oil
- 1/2 tsp. sugar or a few drops of sugar extract

Directions:
1. Rinse the carrots to wash. Dry and chop them into 1-inch pieces.
2. Transfer them to the air fryer basket and drizzle over the walnut oil.
3. Cook at 320°F for about 20 minutes.
4. In the meantime, wash the rhubarb and chop it into 1/2-inch pieces.
5. Coarsely dice the walnuts.
6. Wash the orange and grate its skin into a small bowl. Peel the rest of the orange and cut it up into wedges.
7. Place the rhubarb, walnuts and sugar in the fryer and allow to cook for an additional 5 minutes.
8. Add in 2 tbsp. of the orange zest, along with the orange wedges. Serve immediately.

203. Creamy spinach sauce
Servings: 8
Prep & Cooking Time: 40 Minutes
Ingredients:
- 8 ounces cream cheese, softened
- 1/4 tsp. garlic powder
- 1/2 cup onion, minced
- 1/3 cup water chestnuts, drained and minced
- 1 cup mayonnaise
- 1 cup parmesan cheese, shredded
- 1 1/4 cup frozen spinach, thawed and squeezed
- 1/2 tsp. pepper

Directions:
1. Grease the air fryer baking pan with cooking spray.
2. Use a bowl to combine all ingredients. Mix well.
3. Pour the mixture in the baking pan and place it in the air fryer basket.
4. Cook at 300°F for 35- minutes. After 20 minutes of cooking stir dip.
5. Serve and enjoy.

204. Minty pineapple kibbles
Servings: 4
Prep & Cooking Time: 10 Minutes
Ingredients:
- 1/2 of pineapple, cut into long 1-2 inch thick sticks
- 1/4 cup desiccated coconut
- 1 tbsp. fresh mint leaves, minced
- 1 green chili, minced
- 1 cup vanilla yogurt
- 1 tbsp. honey

Directions:
1. Preheat the air fryer to 390°F and grease an air fryer basket.
2. Place the coconut in a shallow dish.
3. Dip pineapple sticks in the honey and then dredge in the coconut.
4. Transfer the pineapple sticks in the air fryer basket and cook for about 10 minutes.
5. For yogurt dip:
6. Mix together mint, chili and vanilla yogurt in a bowl.
7. Serve these pineapple sticks with yogurt dip.

205. Lemony tofu
Servings: 4
Prep & Cooking Time: 15 Minutes
Ingredients:
- 1 lb. tofu, drained and pressed
- 1 tbsp. arrowroot powder
- 1 tbsp. tamari

For sauce:
- 2 tsps. arrowroot powder
- 2 tbsps. erythritol
- 1/2 cup water
- 1/3 cup lemon juice
- 1 tsp. lemon zest

Directions:
1. Cut tofu into cubes. Add tofu and tamari into the zip-lock bag and shake well.
2. Add 1 tbsp. arrowroot into the bag and shake well to coat the tofu. Set aside for 15 minutes.
3. In a bowl, combine together all sauce ingredients and set aside.
4. Spray air fryer basket with cooking spray.
5. Add tofu into the air fryer basket and cook at 390°F for 10 minutes. Shake halfway through.
6. Add cooked tofu and sauce mixture into the pan and cook over medium-high heat for 3-5 minutes.
7. Serve and enjoy.

206. Famous pork chops by grandma
Servings: 4
Prep & Cooking Time: 1 Hour 12 Minutes
Ingredients:
- 3 eggs, well-beaten
- 1 1/2 cups crushed butter crackers
- 2 tsps. mustard powder
- 1 1/2 tbsps. olive oil
- 1/2 tbsps. soy sauce
- 2 tbsps. Worcestershire sauce
- 1/2 tsp. dried rosemary
- 4 large-sized pork chops
- 1/2 tsp. dried oregano
- 2 tsps. cumin seeds
- Salt & grounded black pepper, to taste
- 1 tsp. red pepper flakes, crushed

Directions:
1. Add the pork chops along with olive oil, soy sauce, Worcestershire sauce, and seasonings to a resealable plastic bag. Allow pork chops to marinate for 50 minutes in your refrigerator.
2. Next step, dip the pork chops into the beaten eggs; then, coat the pork chops with the butter crackers on both sides.
3. Cook in the air fryer for 18 minutes at 405°F, turning once. Bon appétit!

207. Super cheesy jalapeno peppers
Servings: 5
Prep & Cooking Time: 5 Minutes
Ingredients:
- 10 fresh jalapeno peppers, cut in half and remove seeds
- 2 bacon slices, cooked and crumbled
- 1/4 cup cheddar cheese, shredded
- 6 ounce cream cheese, softened

Directions:
1. In a mixing bowl, combine together bacon, cream cheese, and cheddar cheese.
2. Stuff each jalapeno half with bacon cheese mixture.
3. Spray air fryer basket with cooking spray.
4. Place stuffed jalapeno halved in air fryer basket and cook at 370°F for 5 minutes.
5. Serve and enjoy.

208. Flaky pizza with bacon and sausage
Servings: 1
Prep & Cooking Time: 15 Minutes
Ingredients:
- 1/2 cup mozzarella cheese, shredded
- 2 slices sugar-free bacon, cooked and crumbled
- 1/4 cup ground sausage, cooked
- 7 slices pepperoni
- 1 tbsp. parmesan cheese, shredded

Directions:
1. Spread the mozzarella across the bottom of a six-inch cake pan. Throw on the bacon, sausage, and pepperoni, then add a sprinkle of the parmesan cheese on top. Place the pan inside your air fryer.
2. Cook at 400°F for five minutes. The cheese is ready once it turns brown in color and gets bubbly.
3. Remove the pan from the fryer and serve.

209. Cheddar quick sandwich
Servings: 2
Prep & Cooking Time: 5 Minutes
Ingredients:
- 4 white bread slices
- 1/2 cup melted butter, softened
- 1/2 cup cheddar cheese, shredded
- 1 tbsp. mayonnaise

Directions:
1. Preheat the air fryer to 355°F and grease an air fryer basket.
2. Spread the mayonnaise and melted butter over one side of each bread slice.
3. Sprinkle the cheddar cheese over the buttered side of the 2 slices.
4. Cover with the remaining slices of bread and transfer into the air fryer basket.
5. Cook for a few minutes and dish out to serve warm.

210. Easy and scrumptious radish chips
Servings: 12
Prep & Cooking Time: 15 Minutes
Ingredients:
- 1 lb. radishes, wash and slice into chips
- 2 tbsp. olive oil
- 1/4 tsp. pepper
- 1 tsp. salt

Directions:
1. Preheat the air fryer to 375°F.
2. Toss all the ingredients in a medium mixing bowl and toss well.
3. Add radish slices into the air fryer basket and cook for 15 minutes. Shake basket 2-times while cooking.
4. Serve and enjoy.

211. Mozzarella and pepperoni appetizer
Servings: 10
Prep & Cooking Time: 3 Minutes
Ingredients:
- 10 Mozzarella cheese slices
- 10 pepperoni slices

Directions:
1. Preheat the air fryer to 400°F.
2. Line the air fryer pan with baking paper and put Mozzarella in it in one layer.
3. After this, place the pan in the air fryer basket and cook the cheese for 3 minutes or until it is melted. After this, remove the cheese from the air fryer and cool it to room temperature. Then remove the melted cheese from the baking paper and put the pepperoni slices on it.
4. Fold the cheese in the shape of turnovers.

212. Cheddar and bacon tots
Servings: 6
Prep & Cooking Time: 8 Minutes
Ingredients:
- 1 lb. slim bacon slices
- 1 lb. sharp cheddar cheese block, cut into 1-inch rectangular pieces
- 1 cup all-purpose flour
- 3 eggs
- 1 cup breadcrumbs
- Salt, as required
- 1/4 cup olive oil

Directions:
1. Wrap 2 bacon slices around piece of cheddar cheese, covering completely.
2. Repeat with the remaining bacon and cheese pieces.
3. Set the croquettes in a baking dish and freeze for about 5 minutes.
4. Add the flour in a shallow dish.
5. In a second dish, crack the eggs and beat well.
6. Use another small bowl to mix together the breadcrumbs, oil, and salt.
7. Coat the croquettes with flour, then dip into beaten eggs and finally, evenly coat with the breadcrumbs mixture.
8. Heat the fryer to 380°F.
9. Set the croquettes in an air fryer basket in a single layer.
10. Air fry for about 7-8 minutes.
11. Serve hot.

213. Bacon and dark chocolate bites
Servings: 4
Prep & Cooking Time: 10 Minutes
Ingredients:
- 4 bacon slices, halved
- 1 cup dark chocolate, melted
- A pinch of pink salt

Directions:
1. Dip each bacon slice in some chocolate, sprinkle pink salt over them, put them in your air fryer's basket and cook at 350°F for 10 minutes. Serve as a snack.

214. Fried avocado cloves
Servings: 4
Prep & Cooking Time: 8 Minutes
Ingredients:
- 4 avocados, peeled, pitted and cut into wedges
- 1 egg, whisked
- 1 and 1/2 cups almond meal
- A pinch of salt and black pepper
- Cooking spray

Directions:
1. Put the egg in a bowl, and the almond meal in another. Season avocado wedges with salt and pepper, coat them in egg and then in meal almond. Set the avocado bites in your air fryer's basket, grease them with cooking spray and cook at 400°F for 8 minutes. Serve as a snack right away.

215. Mexican cheesy muffins
Servings: 4
Prep & Cooking Time: 15 Minutes
Ingredients:
- 1 cup ground beef
- 1 tsp. taco seasonings
- 2 ounce Mexican blend cheese, shredded
- 1 tsp. keto tomato sauce
- Cooking spray

Directions:
1. Preheat the air fryer to 375°F.
2. Meanwhile, in the mixing bowl mix up ground beef and taco seasonings.
3. Spray the muffin molds with cooking spray. Then transfer the ground beef mixture in the muffin molds and top them with cheese and tomato sauce.
4. Transfer the muffin molds in the preheated air fryer and cook them for 10 minutes.

216. Fried polenta nuggets
Servings: 4
Prep & Cooking Time: 6 Minutes
Ingredients:
- 2 1/2 cups cooked polenta
- Salt, as required
- 1/4 cup Parmesan cheese, shredded

Directions:
1. Add the polenta evenly into a greased baking dish and with the back of a spoon, smooth the top surface.
2. Cover the baking dish and refrigerate for about 1 hour or until set.
3. Remove from the refrigerator and cut down the polenta into the desired size slices.
4. Preheat your air fryer to 350°F.
5. Set the temperature of air fryer to 350°F. Grease a baking dish.
6. Set the polenta sticks into the prepared baking dish in a single layer and sprinkle with salt.
7. Place the baking dish into an air fryer basket.
8. Air fry for about 5-6 minutes.
9. Top with the cheese and serve.

217. Lemony cauliflower with curry
Servings: 2
Prep & Cooking Time: 30 Minutes
Ingredients:
- 1/2 lemon, squeezed
- 1 head cauliflower
- 1/2 tbsp. olive oil
- 1 tsp. curry powder
- Sea salt to taste
- Ground black pepper to taste

Directions:
1. Wash the cauliflower. Cut out the leaves and core.
2. Chop the cauliflower into equally-sized florets.
3. Using the oil, grease the air fryer basket and allow it to warm up for about 2 minutes at 120°F.
4. In a bowl, mix together the fresh lemon juice and curry powder. Add in the cauliflower florets. Sprinkle in the pepper and salt and mix again, coating the florets well.
5. Transfer to the fryer, cook for 20 minutes, and serve warm.

218. Nuts symphony
Servings: 3
Prep & Cooking Time: 14 Minutes
Ingredients:
- 1/2 cup raw peanuts
- 1/2 cup raw almonds
- 1/2 cup raw cashew nuts
- 1/2 cup raisins
- 1/2 cup pecans
- 1 tbsp. olive oil
- Salt, to taste

Directions:
1. Preheat the air fryer to 320°F and grease an air fryer basket.
2. Place the nuts in the air fryer basket and cook for about 9 minutes, tossing twice in between.
3. Remove the nuts from the air fryer basket and transfer into a bowl.
4. Drizzle with olive oil and salt and toss to coat well.
5. Return the nuts mixture into the air fryer basket and cook for about minutes.
6. Serve and serve warm.

219. Mayo cauliflower
Servings: 4
Prep & Cooking Time: 30 Minutes
Ingredients:
- 4 cups bite-sized cauliflower florets
- 1 cup friendly bread crumbs, mixed with 1 tsp. salt
- 1/4 cup melted butter [vegan/other]
- 1/4 cup buffalo sauce [vegan/other]
- Mayo [vegan/other] or creamy dressing for dipping

Directions:
1. In a mixing bowl, combine the butter and buffalo sauce to create a creamy paste.
2. Completely cover each floret with the sauce.
3. Coat the florets with the bread crumb mixture. Cook the florets in the air fryer for approximately 15 minutes at 350°F, shaking the basket occasionally.
4. Serve with a raw vegetable salad, mayo or creamy dressing.

220. Avocado nuggets with spicy sauce
Servings: 3
Prep & Cooking Time: 20 Minutes
Ingredients:
- 2 tbsp. fresh lime juice
- 1 avocado, pitted, peeled, and sliced
- Pink Himalayan salt and ground white pepper, to taste
- 1/4 cup flour
- 1 egg
- 1/2 cup breadcrumbs
- 1 chipotle chili in adobo sauce
- 1/4 cup light mayonnaise
- 1/4 cup plain Greek yogurt

Directions:
1. Drizzle lime juice all over the avocado slices and set aside.
2. Then, set up your breading station. Mix the salt, pepper, and all-purpose flour in a shallow dish. In a separate dish, whisk the egg.
3. Finally, place your breadcrumbs in a third dish.
4. Start by dredging the avocado slices in the flour mixture; then, dip them into the egg. Press the avocado slices into the breadcrumbs, coating evenly.
5. Cook in the preheating air fryer at 380°F for 11 minutes, shaking the cooking basket halfway through the cooking time.
6. Meanwhile, blend the chipotle chili, mayo, and Greek yogurt in your food processor until the sauce is creamy and uniform.
7. Serve the warm avocado slices with the sauce on the side. Enjoy!

221. Beef nibbles
Servings: 2
Prep & Cooking Time: 15 Minutes
Ingredients:
- 1 tsp. cayenne pepper
- 8 ounce beef loin, minced
- 1 tbsp. coconut flour
- 1 tsp. nut oil
- 1/4 tsp. salt
- 1 tsp. white wine vinegar

Directions:
1. Sprinkle the beef with white wine vinegar and salt. Then sprinkle it with cayenne pepper and coconut flour.
2. Shake the meat well and transfer in the air fryer. Sprinkle it with nut oil and cook at 365°F for 15 minutes.
3. Shake the minced beef every 5 minutes to avoid burning.

222. Pork and beef smokies in keto sauce
Servings: 10
Prep & Cooking Time: 10 Minutes
Ingredients:
- 12 ounces pork and beef smokies
- 3 ounces bacon, sliced
- 1 tsp. keto tomato sauce
- 1 tsp. stevia
- 1 tsp. avocado oil
- 1/2 tsp. cayenne pepper

Directions:
1. Sprinkle the smokies with cayenne pepper and tomato sauce. Then sprinkle them with stevia and olive oil.
2. After this, wrap every smokie in the bacon and secure it with the toothpick.
3. Preheat the air fryer to 400°F. Place the bacon smokies in the air fryer and cook them for 10 minutes.
4. Shake them gently during cooking to avoid burning.

223. Avocado wrappers
Servings: 5
Prep & Cooking Time: 20 Minutes
Ingredients:
- 10 egg wrappers
- 3 avocados, peeled and pitted
- 1 tomato, diced
- Salt and pepper, to taste

Directions:
1. Pre-heat your air fryer to 350°F.
2. Put the tomato and avocados in a bowl. Sprinkle on some salt and pepper and mash together with a fork until a smooth consistency is achieved.
3. Spoon equal amounts of the mixture onto the wrappers. Roll the wrappers around the filling, enclosing them entirely.
4. Transfer the rolls to a lined baking dish and cook for 5 minutes.

224. Kalamata olives fritters
Servings: 6
Prep & Cooking Time: 12 Minutes
Ingredients:
- Cooking spray
- 1/2 cup parsley, minced
- 1 egg
- 1/2 cup almond flour
- Salt & black pepper to the taste
- 3 spring onions, minced
- 1/2 cup kalamata olives, pitted and minced
- 3 zucchinis, shredded

Directions:
1. Blend all the ingredients into a bowl, stir well, and shape medium fritters out of this mixture.
2. Place the fritters in your air fryer's basket, grease them with cooking spray and cook at 380°F for 6 minutes on each side.
3. Serve them as an appetizer.

225. Minty pork meatballs
Servings: 4
Prep & Cooking Time: 10 Minutes
Ingredients:
- 2 eggs, lightly beaten
- 2 tbsp capers
- 1/2 lb. ground pork
- 3 garlic cloves, minced
- 2 tbsps. fresh mint, minced
- 1/2 tbsp cilantro, minced
- 2 tsp. red pepper flakes, crushed
- 1 1/2 tbsps. butter, melted
- 1 tsp. kosher salt

Directions:
1. Preheat the air fryer to 395°F.
2. Mix, in a bowl, all ingredients until well combined.
3. Spray air fryer basket with cooking spray.
4. Make small balls from meat mixture and place into the air fryer basket.
5. Cook meatballs for 10 minutes. Shake basket halfway through.
6. Serve and enjoy.

226. Tilapia fillets with ranch dressing
Servings: 2
Prep & Cooking Time: 13 Minutes
Ingredients:
- 1/4 cup panko breadcrumbs
- 1 egg beaten
- 2 tilapia fillets

Garnish:
- Herbs and chilies
- 1/2 packet ranch dressing mix powder
- 1 1/4 tbsp. vegetable oil

Directions:
1. Preheat the air fryer to 350°F and grease an air fryer basket.
2. Mix ranch dressing with panko breadcrumbs in a bowl.
3. Whisk eggs in a shallow bowl and dip the fish fillet in the eggs.
4. Dredge in the breadcrumbs and transfer into the air fryer basket.
5. Cook for about 13 minutes and garnish with chilies and herbs to serve.

227. Thousand herbs tomato
Servings: 2
Prep & Cooking Time: 30 Minutes
Ingredients:
- 2 large tomatoes, washed and cut into halves
- Herbs, such as oregano, basil, thyme, rosemary, sage to taste
- Cooking spray
- Pepper to taste
- Parmesan, shredded [optional]
- Parsley, minced [optional]

Directions:
1. Spritz both sides of each tomato half with a small amount of cooking spray.
2. Coat the tomatoes with a light sprinkling of pepper and the herbs of your choice.
3. Place the tomatoes in the basket, cut-side-up. Cook at 280°F for 20 minutes, or longer if necessary.
4. Serve hot, at room temperature, or chilled as a refreshing summer snack. Optionally, you can garnish them with shredded Parmesan and minced parsley before serving.

228. Sweety mozzarella snack
Servings: 8
Prep & Cooking Time: 5 Minutes
Ingredients:
- 2 cups mozzarella, shredded
- 3/4 cup almond flour
- 2 tsp. psyllium husk powder
- 1/4 tsp. sweet paprika

Directions:
1. Put the mozzarella in a bowl, melt it in the microwave for 2 minutes, add all the other ingredients quickly and stir really until you obtain a dough.
2. Form 2 balls of dough, roll them on 2 baking sheets and cut into triangles. Set the tortillas in your air fryer's basket and bake at 370°F for 5 minutes.
3. Transfer to bowls and serve as a snack.

229. Shrimps and chives cakes
Servings: 4
Prep & Cooking Time: 5 Minutes
Ingredients:
- 10 ounces shrimps, minced
- 1 egg, beaten
- 1 tsp. dill, minced
- 1 tsp. Psyllium husk
- 2 tbsp. almond flour
- 1 tsp. olive oil
- 1 tsp. chives

Directions:
1. In the mixing bowl mix up shrimps, egg, dill, Psyllium husk, almond flour, and chives.
2. When the mixture is homogenous, make 4 cakes.
3. Preheat the air fryer to 400°F.
4. Put the cakes in the air fryer and sprinkle with olive oil. Cook the meal for 5 minutes.

230. Sausage wonton nibbles
Servings: 5
Prep & Cooking Time: 20 Minutes
Ingredients:
- 1/2 lb. ground sausage
- 2 tbsps. chives, minced
- 1 garlic clove, minced
- 1/2 tbsp. fish sauce
- 1 tsp. Sriracha sauce
- 20 wonton wrappers
- 1 egg, whisked with 1 tbsp. water

Directions:
1. In a medium size bowl, combine the chives, ground sausage, fish sauce, garlic, fish sauce, and Sriracha.
2. Divide the mixture between the wonton wrappers. Dip your fingers in the egg wash
3. Fold the wonton in half. Bring up the 2 ends of the wonton and use the egg wash to stick them together. Pinch the edges and coat each wonton with the egg wash.
4. Place the folded wontons in the lightly greased cooking basket. Let it cook at 360°F for 10 minutes.
5. Work in batches and serve warm. Bon appétit!

231. Ricotta and orange balls
Servings: 2 – 4
Prep & Cooking Time: 25 Minutes
Ingredients:
- 2 cups ricotta, shredded
- 2 eggs, separated
- 2 tbsp. chives, finely minced
- 2 tbsp. fresh basil, finely minced
- 4 tbsp. flour
- 1/4 tsp. salt to taste
- 1/4 tsp. pepper powder to taste
- 1 tsp. orange zest, shredded
- For coating
- 1/4 cup friendly bread crumbs
- 1 tbsp. vegetable oil

Directions:
1. Pre-heat your air fryer at 390°F.
2. In a mixing bowl, combine the yolks, flour, salt, pepper, chives and orange zest. Throw in the ricotta and incorporate with your hands.
3. Mold equal amounts of the mixture into balls.
4. Mix the oil with the bread crumbs until a crumbly consistency is achieved.
5. Coat the balls in the bread crumbs and transfer each one to the fryer's basket.
6. Put the basket in the fryer. Air fry for 8 minutes or until a golden brown color is achieved.
7. Serve with a sauce of your choosing, such as ketchup.

232. Brussels sprouts with balsamic vinegar
Servings: 2
Prep & Cooking Time: 15 Minutes
Ingredients:
- 2 cups Brussels sprouts, sliced in half
- 1 tbsp. balsamic vinegar
- 1 tbsp. olive oil
- 1/4 tsp. salt

Directions:
1. Mix all the ingredients in a small bowl, make sure to cover the Brussels sprouts well.
2. Place the sprouts in the air fryer basket and air fry at 400°F for 10 minutes, shaking the basket at the halfway point.

233. Veggie cocktail with sausages
Servings: 4
Prep & Cooking Time: 25 Minutes
Ingredients:
- 16 cocktail sausages, halved
- 16 pearl onions
- 1 red bell pepper, cut into 1 1/2-inch pieces
- Salt and grounded black pepper, to taste
- 1/2 cup tomato chili sauce

Directions:
1. Thread the cocktail sausages, pearl onions, and peppers alternately onto skewers. Sprinkle with salt and black pepper.
2. Cook in the preheated air fryer at 380°F for 15 minutes, turning the skewers over once or twice to ensure even cooking.
3. Serve with the tomato chili sauce on the side. Enjoy!

234. Butter balls
Servings: 50 Treats
Prep & Cooking Time: 25 Minutes
Ingredients:
- 1/2 cup unsweetened applesauce
- 1 cup peanut butter
- 2 cup oats
- 1 cup flour
- 1 tsp. baking powder

Directions:
1. Combine the applesauce and peanut butter in a bowl to create a smooth consistency.
2. Pour in the oats, flour and baking powder. Continue mixing to form a soft dough.
3. Shape a half-tsp. of dough into a ball and continue with the rest of the dough.
4. Pre-heat the air fryer to 350°F.
5. Use the oil to grease the bottom of the basket.
6. Place the poppers in the fryer and cook for 8 minutes, flipping the balls at the halfway point. You may need to cook the poppers in batches.
7. Let the poppers cool and serve immediately or keep in an airtight container for up to 2 weeks.

235. Cheesy smoked breadsticks
Servings: 6
Prep & Cooking Time: 30 Minutes
Ingredients:
- 1/2 cup almond meal
- Sea salt & ground black pepper, to taste
- 1/4 tsp. smoked paprika
- 1/2 tsp. celery seeds
- 6 ounces mature Cheddar, cold, freshly shredded
- 2 tbsp. cream cheese
- 2 tbsp. cold butter

Directions:
1. Preheat your fryer to 355°F.
2. Place some parchment paper over the fryer basket.
3. In a mixing bowl, thoroughly combine the almond meal, salt, black pepper, paprika, and celery seeds.
4. Then, combine the cheese and butter in the bowl of a stand mixer. Slowly stir in the almond meal mixture and mix to combine well.
5. Then, pack the batter into a cookie press fitted with a star disk. Pipe the long ribbons of dough across the parchment paper. Then cut into six-inch lengths.
6. Bake in the preheated air fryer for 1minutes.
7. Repeat with the remaining dough. Let the cheese straws cool on a rack. Bon appétit

236. Tantalizing bacon with avocado
Servings: 5
Prep & Cooking Time: 10 Minutes
Ingredients:
- 2 tsp. chili powder
- 2 avocados, pitted and cut into 10 pieces
- 1 tsp. salt
- 1/2 tsp. garlic powder
- 1 tsp. ground black pepper
- 5 slices bacon, cut into halves

Directions:
1. Lay the bacon rashers on a clean surface; then, place one piece of avocado slice on each bacon slice. Add the salt, black pepper, chili powder, and garlic powder.
2. Then, wrap the bacon slice around the avocado and repeat with the remaining rolls; secure them with a cocktail sticks or toothpicks.
3. Preheat your air fryer to 390°F; cook in the preheated air fryer for 5 minutes and serve with your favorite sauce for dipping.

237. Garlicky green beans
Servings: 4
Prep & Cooking Time: 10 Minutes
Ingredients:
- 1 lb. green beans, trimmed
- 1 cup butter
- 2 cloves garlic, minced
- 1 cup toasted pine nuts

Directions:
1. Boil a pot of water.
2. Put the green beans and cook until tender (about 5 minutes).
3. Heat the butter in a large skillet over a high heat. Add the garlic and pine nuts and sauté for 2 minutes or until the pine nuts are lightly browned.
4. Transfer the green beans to the skillet and turn until coated. Serve!

238. Chicken wings in pungent sauce
Servings: 6
Prep & Cooking Time: 20 Minutes
Ingredients:
For the Sauce:
- 1 tbsp. yellow mustard
- 1 tbsp. white wine vinegar
- 1 tbsp. olive oil
- 1/4 cup ketchup, no sugar added
- 1 garlic clove, minced
- Salt & ground black pepper, at your convenience
- 1/8 tsp. ground allspice
- 1/4 cup water

For the wings:
- 2 lbs. chicken wings
- 1/4 tsp. celery salt
- 1/4 cup habanero hot sauce
- Chopped fresh parsley, or garnish

Directions:
1. In a sauté pan that is preheated over a medium-high flame, place all the ingredients for the sauce and bring it to a boil. Then, reduce the temperature and simmer until it has thickened.
2. Meanwhile, heat the fryer to 400°F; cook the chicken wings for 6 minutes; flip them over and cook for additional 6 minutes. Season them with celery salt.
3. Serve with the prepared sauce and habanero hot sauce, garnished with fresh parsley leaves. Bon appétit!

239. Bite-size cheeseburgers
Servings: 4
Prep & Cooking Time: 20 Minutes
Ingredients:
- 1 tbsp. Dijon mustard
- 2 tbsps. minced chives
- 1 lb. ground beef
- 1 1/2 tsps. minced green garlic
- 1/2 tsp. cumin
- Salt & ground black pepper, to savor
- 12 cherry tomatoes
- 12 cubes cheddar cheese

Directions:
1. In a large-sized mixing dish, place the mustard, ground beef, cumin, chives, garlic, salt, and pepper; mix with your hands or a spatula so that every element is evenly coated.
2. Form into meatballs and cook them in the preheated air fryer for 15 minutes at 375°F. Air-fry until they are cooked in the middle.
3. Thread cherry tomatoes, mini burgers and cheese on cocktail sticks. Bon appétit!

240. Flavored pork loin
Servings: 4
Prep & Cooking Time: 12 Minutes
Ingredients:
- 2 eggs, beaten
- 4 tbsps. flax meal
- 1/2 tsp. chili powder
- 1/4 tsp. ground cumin
- 8 ounce pork loin
- 1 tsp. grapeseed oil

Directions:
1. Cut the pork loin into the sticks and sprinkle with chili powder and cumin powder.
2. Then dip the pork sticks in the eggs and coat in the flax meal. Place the meat in the air fryer and sprinkle with grapeseed oil.
3. Cook the snack at 400°F for 6 minutes. Then flip the pork sticks on another side and cook for 6 minutes more.

241. Bacon and eggs with hot sauce
Servings: 3
Prep & Cooking Time: 25 Minutes
Ingredients:
- 6 eggs
- 6 slices bacon
- 2 tbsp. mayonnaise
- 1 tsp. hot sauce
- 1/2 tsp. Worcestershire sauce
- 2 tbsp. scallions, minced
- 1 tbsp. pickle relish
- Salt & ground black pepper, to taste
- 1 tsp. smoked paprika

Directions:
1. Place the eggs onto the pan, and place it the air fryer
2. Cook at 280°F for 15 minutes.
3. Transfer them to an ice-cold water bath to stop the cooking. Peel the eggs under cold running water; slice them into halves.
4. Cook the bacon at 400°F for 3 minutes; flip the bacon over and cook an additional 3 minutes; chop the bacon and reserve.
5. Mash the egg yolks with the mayo, hot sauce, Worcestershire sauce, scallions, pickle relish, salt, and black pepper; add the reserved bacon and spoon the yolk mixture into the egg whites.
6. Garnish with smoked paprika. Bon appétit!

242. Crispy bacon with brussels sprouts
Servings: 2
Prep & Cooking Time: 45 Minutes
Ingredients:
- 24 ounce Brussels sprouts
- 1/4 cup fish sauce
- 1/4 cup bacon grease
- 6 strips bacon
- Pepper to taste

Directions:
1. De-stem and quarter the brussels sprouts.
2. Mix them with the bacon grease and fish sauce.
3. Slice the bacon into small strips and cook.
4. Add the bacon and pepper to the sprouts.
5. Spread onto a greased pan and cook at 400°F/230°C for 35 minutes.
6. Stir every 5 minute or so.
7. Broil for a few more minutes and serve.

243. Appetizing kale chips
Servings: 4
Prep & Cooking Time: 5 Minutes
Ingredients:
- 2 1/2 tbsp. olive oil
- 1 1/2 tsp. garlic powder
- 2/3 cup of kale, minced
- 2 tbsp. lemon juice
- 1 1/2 tsp. seasoned salt

Directions:
1. Toss your kale with the other ingredients.
2. Cook at 195°F for 4 to 5 minutes, tossing kale halfway through.
3. Serve with your favorite dipping sauce.

244. Mozzarella and parmesan cheese appetizer
Servings: 4
Prep & Cooking Time: 60 Minutes
Ingredients:
- 6 x 1-oz. mozzarella string cheese sticks
- 1 tsp. dried parsley
- 1/2 oz. pork rinds, finely ground
- 1/2 cup parmesan cheese, shredded
- 2 eggs

Directions:
1. Halve the mozzarella sticks and freeze for forty-five minutes. Optionally you can leave them longer and place in a Ziploc bag to prevent them from becoming freezer burned.
2. In a small bowl, combine the dried parsley, pork rinds, and parmesan cheese.
3. In a different bowl, beat the eggs with a fork.
4. Take a frozen mozzarella stick and dip it into the eggs, then into the pork rind mixture, making sure to coat it all over. Proceed with the rest of the cheese sticks, placing each coated stick in the basket of your air fryer.
5. Cook at 400°F for ten minutes, until they are golden brown.
6. Serve hot, with some homemade marinara sauce if desired.

245. Plain banana chips
Servings: 8
Prep & Cooking Time: 10 Minutes
Ingredients:
- 2 raw bananas, peeled and sliced
- 2 tbsp. olive oil
- Salt & black pepper, to taste

Directions:
1. Preheat the air fryer to 355°F and grease an air fryer basket.
2. Drizzle banana slices evenly with olive oil and arrange in the air fryer basket.
3. Cook for about 10 minutes and season with salt and black pepper.
4. Serve and serve warm.

246. Mushrooms with a veggie cream stuffing
Servings: 12
Prep & Cooking Time: 8 Minutes
Ingredients:
- 24 ounce mushrooms, cut stems
- 1/2 cup sour cream
- 1 cup cheddar cheese, shredded
- 1 small carrot, diced
- 1/2 bell pepper, diced
- 1/2 onion, diced
- 2 bacon slices, diced

Directions:
1. Chop mushroom stems finely.
2. Grease your pan with cooking spray. Heat it over medium heat.
3. Add minced mushrooms, bacon, carrot, onion, and bell pepper into the pan and cook until tender.
4. Remove pan from heat. Add cheese and sour cream into the cooked vegetables and stir well.
5. Stuff vegetable mixture into the mushroom cap and place into the air fryer basket.
6. Cook mushrooms at 350°F for 8 minutes.
7. Serve and enjoy.

247. Sandwich with vegetables
Servings: 2
Prep & Cooking Time: 25 Minutes
Ingredients:
Barbecue Sauce:
- 1 tsp. olive oil
- 1 garlic clove, minced
- 1/4 of onion, minced
- 1/2 cup water
- 1/2 tbsp. sugar
- 1/2 tbsp. Worcestershire sauce
- 1/4 tsp. mustard powder
- 1 1/2 tbsp. tomato ketchup
- Salt & ground black pepper, as needed

For Sandwich:
- 2 tbsp. butter, softened
- 1 cup sweet corn kernels
- 1 roasted red bell pepper, minced
- 4 bread slices, trimmed and cut horizontally

Directions:
1. For barbecue sauce: in a medium skillet, heat the oil over medium heat and sauté the garlic, and onion for about 3-5 minutes.
2. Stir in the remaining ingredients and bring to a boil over high heat.
3. Turn down the heat to medium and continue to cook for 8-10 minutes, or until the desired thickness is reached.
4. For the sandwich: in a skillet, melt the butter on medium heat and stir fry the corn for about 1-2 minutes.
5. In a bowl, mix together the barbecue sauce, corn, and bell pepper.
6. Spread the corn mixture on one side of 2 bread slices.
7. Top with the remaining slices.
8. Warm air fryer to 355°Fahrenheit.
9. Place the sandwiches in an air fryer basket in a single layer.
10. Air fry for about 5-6 minutes.
11. Serve.

248. Shrimps wrapped with bacon
Servings: 6
Prep & Cooking Time: 7 Minutes
Ingredients:
- 1 lb. bacon, sliced slimly
- 1 lb. shrimp, peeled and emptied
- Salt, to taste

Directions:
1. Preheat the air fryer to 390°F and grease an air fryer basket.
2. Wrap 1 shrimp with a bacon slices, covering completely.
3. Repeat the process using the remaining shrimp and bacon slices.
4. Set the bacon wrapped shrimps in a baking dish and freeze for about 15 minutes.
5. Place the shrimps in an air fryer basket and cook for about 7 minutes.
6. Serve warm.

249. Crispy pork rinds
Servings: 3
Prep & Cooking Time: 10 Minutes
Ingredients:
- 6 ounces pork skins
- 1 tbsp. keto tomato sauce
- 1 tsp. olive oil

Directions:
1. Chop the pork skins into the rinds and sprinkle with the sauce and olive oil. Mix up well.
2. Warm your air fryer to 400°F. Place the pork skin rinds in the air fryer basket in one layer and cook for 5 5 minutes. Flip the rinds on another side after 5 minutes of cooking.

250. Onion sauce
Servings: 8
Prep & Cooking Time: 25 Minutes
Ingredients:
- 2 lbs. onion, minced
- 1 tsp. baking powder
- 6 tbsps. butter, softened
- Pepper
- Salt

Directions:
1. Let melt the butter in a pan over medium heat.
2. Add onion and baking powder and sauté for 5 minutes.
3. Transfer onion mixture into the air fryer baking dish.
4. Drop into the air fryer and cook at 370°F for 25 minutes.
5. Serve and enjoy.

251. Chicken drumettes in teriyaki sauce
Servings: 6
Prep & Cooking Time: 40 Minutes
Ingredients:
- 1 1/2 lbs. chicken drumettes
- Sea salt & grounded black pepper, to taste
- 2 tbsp. fresh chives, roughly minced
- Teriyaki Sauce:
- 1 tbsp. sesame oil
- 1/4 cup soy sauce
- 1/2 cup water
- 1/2 tsp. Five-spice powder
- 2 tbsps. rice wine vinegar
- 1/2 tsp. fresh ginger, shredded
- 2 cloves garlic, crushed

Directions:
1. Preheat your air fryer to 380°F.
2. Salt and pepper the chicken drumettes.
3. Cook for 15 minutes in the preheated air fryer.
4. Turn the chicken drumettes over and cook for 7 minutes more.
5. In a small pan, mix sesame oil, soy sauce, water five-spice powder, vinegar, ginger and garlic while the chicken drumettes roast. Stir occasionally for 5 minutes.
6. Slowly boil until the glaze thickens. After that, brush the glaze all over the chicken drumettes.
7. Air-fry for a further 6 minutes or until the surface is crispy. Serve topped with the remaining glaze and garnished with fresh chives. Bon appétit!

252. Sesame okra
Servings: 4
Prep & Cooking Time: 4 Minutes
Ingredients:
- 11 ounces okra, wash and chop
- 1 egg, lightly beaten
- 1 tsp. sesame seeds
- 1 tbsp. walnut oil
- 1/4 tsp. pepper
- 1/2 tsp. salt

Directions:
1. In a mixing bowl, whisk together egg, pepper, and salt.
2. Add okra into the whisked egg. Sprinkle with sesame seeds.
3. Preheat the air fryer to 400°F.
4. Stir okra well. Spray air fryer basket with cooking spray.
5. Place okra pieces into the air fryer basket and cook for 4 minutes.
6. Serve and enjoy.

253. Pickle spears wrapped in bacon slices
Servings: 4
Prep & Cooking Time: 20 Minutes
Ingredients:
- 4 dill pickle spears, sliced in half and quartered
- 8 bacon slices, halved
- 1 cup avocado mayonnaise

Directions:
1. Wrap each pickle spear in a bacon slice, and put them in your air fryer's basket and let it cook at 400°F for about 15 min.
2. Serve as a snack with the mayonnaise.

254. Healthy bread with veggies
Servings: 8
Prep & Cooking Time: 33 Minutes
Ingredients:
- 5 large potatoes, peeled
- 2 tbsp. vegetable oil, divided
- 2 small onions, finely minced
- 2 green chilies, seeded and minced
- 2 curry leaves
- 1/2 tsp. ground turmeric
- Salt, as required
- 8 bread slices, trimmed

Directions:
1. In the pan of a boiling water, add the potatoes and cook for about -20 minutes.
2. Drain the potatoes well and with a potato masher, mash the potatoes.
3. In a skillet, heat 1 tsp. of oil over a medium heat and sauté the onion for about 4-5 minutes.
4. Add the green chilies, curry leaves, and turmeric. Sauté for about 1 minute.
5. Add in the mashed potatoes, and salt and mix them well.
6. Once done, remove from the heat and set aside to cool completely.
7. Make 8 equal-sized oval-shaped patties from the mixture.
8. Wet the bread slices completely with water.
9. Using your hands, press each bread slice between your hands to remove the excess water.
10. Place 1 bread slice in your palm and place 1 patty in the center.
11. Roll the bread slice in a spindle shape and seal the edges to secure the filling.
12. Coat the roll with some oil.
13. Repeat with the remaining slices, filling and oil.
14. Heat your air fryer to 390°F. Grease the air fryer basket with cooking spray.
15. Add rolls into the prepared basket in a single layer.
16. Air fry for about 12-13 minutes.
17. Serve.

255. Lemony beans
Servings: 4
Prep & Cooking Time: 20 Minutes
Ingredients:
- 1 lemon, squeezed
- 1 lb. green beans, washed and destemmed
- 1/4 tsp. extra virgin olive oil
- Sea salt to taste
- Black pepper to taste

Directions:
1. Pre-heat the air fryer to 400°F.
2. Put the green beans in your air fryer basket and drizzle the lemon juice over them.
3. Sprinkle on the pepper and salt. Pour in the oil, and toss to coat the green beans well.
4. Cook for 10 – 12 minutes and serve warm.

256. Scallops and bacon skewers
Servings: 6
Prep & Cooking Time: 40 Minutes
Ingredients:
- 1 lb. sea scallops
- 1/2 cup almond milk
- 1 tbsp. vermouth
- Sea salt & ground black pepper, to taste
- 1/2 lb. bacon, diced
- 1 shallot, diced
- 1 tsp. garlic powder
- 1 tsp. paprika

Directions:
1. In a ceramic bowl, place the sea scallops, almond milk, vermouth, salt, and black pepper; let it marinate for 30 minutes.
2. Assemble the skewers alternating the scallops, bacon, and shallots. Sprinkle garlic powder and paprika all over the skewers.
3. Bake in the preheated air Fryer at 400°F for 6 minutes. Serve warm and enjoy!

Chapter 2
Vegetarian & Vegan Recipes

257. Broccoli stuffed with cheese and pepper
Servings: 4
Prep & Cooking Time: 20 Minutes
Ingredients:
- 4 eggs
- 2 bell peppers, medium, divided in half, remove seeds
- 1 tsp. dried sage
- 2.5 ounces cheddar cheese, shredded
- 7 ounces almond milk
- 1/4 cup baby broccoli florets
- 1/4 cup cherry tomatoes
- Pepper
- Salt

Directions:
1. Preheat the air fryer to 370°F.
2. In a mixing bowl, whisk together eggs, milk, broccoli, cherry tomatoes, sage, pepper, and salt.
3. With a cooking spray, apply cooking oil to the air fryer basket.
4. Place bell pepper halves into the air fryer basket.
5. Pour egg mixture into the bell pepper halves.
6. Sprinkle cheese on top of bell pepper and cook for 20 minutes.
7. Serve and enjoy.

258. Healthy veggie rice
Servings: 2
Prep & Cooking Time: 18 Minutes
Ingredients:
- 2 cups cooked white rice
- 1 large egg, lightly beaten
- 1/2 cup frozen peas, thawed
- 1/2 cup frozen carrots, thawed
- 1/2 tsp. sesame seeds, toasted
- 1 tbsp. vegetable oil
- 2 tsps. sesame oil, toasted and divided
- 1 tbsp. water
- Salt and ground white pepper, as required
- 1 tsp. soy sauce
- 1 tsp. Sriracha sauce

Directions:
1. Prepare the air fryer by setting it to 380 degree°F. Grease the pan with cooking oil.
2. Mix the rice, vegetable oil, white pepper, 1 tsp. of sesame oil, salt and water in a bowl.
3. Transfer the rice mixture into the air fryer basket and cook for about 12 minutes.
4. Pour the beaten egg over rice and cook for about minutes.
5. Add the peas and carrots. Cook for 2 more minutes.
6. Meanwhile, mix soy sauce, Sriracha sauce, sesame seeds and the remaining sesame oil in a bowl.
7. Serve the potato cubes onto serving plates and drizzle with sauce to serve.

259. Sweet and spicy tofu
Servings: 3
Prep & Cooking Time: 23 Minutes
Ingredients:
For Tofu:
- 1 (14-ounces) block firm tofu, pressed and cubed
- 1/2 cup arrowroot flour
- 1/2 tsp. sesame oil

For Sauce:
- 4 tbsps. low-sodium soy sauce
- 1 1/2 tbsp. rice vinegar
- 1 1/2 tbsp. chili sauce
- 1 tbsp. agave nectar
- 2 large garlic cloves, minced
- 1 tsp. fresh ginger, peeled and shredded
- 2 chives (green part), minced

Directions:
1. In a dish, combine the arrowroot flour, tofu, and sesame oil.
2. Set the temperature of air fryer to 360°F. Generously, grease an air fryer basket.
3. Arrange tofu pieces into the prepared air fryer basket in a single layer.
4. Air fry for about 20 minutes, shaking once halfway through.
5. As for the sauce: in a dish, combine all the ingredients. Leave the chives behind. Beat it until well combined.
6. Remove from air fryer and transfer the tofu into a skillet with sauce over medium heat and cook for about 3 minutes, stirring occasionally.
7. Garnish with chives and serve warm.

260. Delicious vegan calzone
Servings: 1
Prep & Cooking Time: 25 Minutes
Ingredients:
- 1 tsp. olive oil
- 1/2 small onion, minced
- 2 sweet peppers, seeded and sliced
- Sea salt for better taste
- 1/4 tsp. ground black pepper
- 1/4 tsp. dried oregano
- 4 ounces prepared Italian pizza dough
- 1/4 cup marinara sauce
- 2 ounces plant-based cheese Mozzarella-style, shredded

Directions:
1. Use nonstick pan, warm it and add oil. Once hot, cook the onion and peppers until tender and fragrant, about 5 minutes. Add salt, black pepper, and oregano.
2. Sprinkle some flour on a kitchen counter and roll out the pizza dough.
3. Spoon the marinara sauce over half of the dough; add the sautéed mixture and sprinkle with the vegan cheese. Now, gently fold over the dough to create a pocket; make sure to seal the edges.

4. Use a fork to poke the dough in a few spots. Add a few drizzles of olive oil and place in the lightly greased cooking basket.
5. Bake in the preheated air fryer at 330°F for 12 minutes, turning the calzones over halfway through the cooking time. Bon appétit!

261. Tofu ala italian
Servings: 2
Prep & Cooking Time: 30 Minutes
Ingredients:
- Black pepper for better taste
- 1 tbsp. vegetable broth
- 1 tbsp. soy sauce
- 1/3 tsp. dried oregano
- 1/3 tsp. garlic powder
- 1/3 tsp. dried basil
- 1/3 tsp. onion powder

Directions:
1. Cut the tofu squarely, at least 3 lengthwise. Line a side of the cutting board with paper towels, place the tofu on it and cover with paper towel. Use your hands to press the tofu gently until as much liquid has been extracted from it.
2. Remove the paper towels and use a knife to chop the tofu into 8 cubes; set aside. In another bowl, add the soy sauce, vegetable broth, oregano, basil, garlic powder, onion powder, and black pepper; mix well with a spoon.
3. Pour the spice mixture on the tofu, stir the tofu until well coated; set aside to marinate for 10 minutes. Preheat the air fryer to 380°F, and arrange the tofu in the fryer's basket, in a single layer; cook for 10 minutes, flipping it at the 6-minute mark.
4. Remove to a plate and serve with green salad.

262. Stuffed eggplant with a twist
Servings: 4
Prep & Cooking Time: 12 Minutes
Ingredients:
- 8 baby eggplants
- 4 tsps. olive oil, divided
- 3/4 tbsp. dry mango powder
- 3/4 tbsp. ground coriander
- 1/2 tsp. ground cumin
- 1/2 tsp. ground turmeric
- 1/2 tsp. garlic powder
- Salt for better taste

Directions:
1. Preheat the air fryer to 370°F before greasing the fryer basket with oil.
2. Make slits from the bottom of each eggplant leaving the stems intact.
3. Mix one tsp. of oil and spices in a bowl and fill each slit of eggplants with this mixture.
4. Brush the outer side of each eggplant with remaining oil and arrange in the air fryer basket.
5. Cook for about 12 minutes and dish out in a serving plate to serve warm.

263. Glazed carrots
Servings: 4
Prep & Cooking Time: 12 Minutes
Ingredients:
- 3 cups carrots, peeled and divided into large chunks
- 1 tbsp. olive oil
- 1 tbsp. honey
- Salt & black pepper for better taste

Directions:
1. Preheat the air fryer to 390°F before greasing the fryer basket with oil.
2. Mix all the ingredients in a bowl and toss to coat well.
3. Transfer into the air fryer basket and cook for about 12 minutes.
4. Serve and serve warm.

264. Veggies air-fried sushi
Servings: 4
Prep & Cooking Time: 60 Minutes
Ingredients:
- 4 nori sheets
- 1 carrot, sliced lengthways
- 1 red bell pepper, seeds removed, sliced
- 1 avocado, sliced
- 1 tbsp. olive oil mixed with
- 1 tbsp. rice wine vinegar
- 1 cup panko crumbs
- 2 tbsps. sesame seeds
- Serve it with soy sauce or wasabi. Add picked ginger as desired.

Directions:
1. Prepare a clean working board, a small bowl of lukewarm water and a sushi mat. Wet hands, and lay a nori sheet onto sushi mat and spread half cup sushi rice, leaving a half-inch of nori clear, so you can seal the roll.
2. Place carrot, pepper and avocado sideways to the rice. Roll sushi tightly and rub warm water along the clean nori strip to seal.
3. In a bowl, mix oil and rice vinegar. In another bowl, mix crumbs and sesame seeds. Roll each sushi log in the vinegar mixture and then straight to the sesame bowl to coat.
4. Arrange sushi onto air fryer and cook for 14 minutes at 360°F, turning once.
5. Slice and serve with soy sauce, pickled ginger and wasabi.

265. Drizzling onion
Servings: 4
Prep & Cooking Time: 20 Minutes
Ingredients:
- Olive oil as needed
- 1 tsp. cayenne pepper
- 1 tsp. garlic powder
- 2 cups flour
- 1 tbsp. pepper
- 1 tbsp. paprika
- 1 tbsp. salt
- 1/4 cup mayonnaise
- 1 tbsp. ketchup
- 1/4 cup mayonnaise
- 1/4 cup kefir

Directions:
1. In a mixing bowl, mix salt, pepper, paprika, flour, garlic powder, and cayenne pepper. Add mayonnaise, ketchup, kefir to the mixture and stir.
2. Coat the onions with prepared mixture and spray with oil.
3. First, heat up your air fryer to 360°F. Add the coated onions to the basket and cook for 15 minutes.

266. Eggplant potato and zucchini chips
Servings: 4
Prep & Cooking Time: 10 Minutes
Ingredients:
- 5 potatoes, divided strips
- 3 zucchinis, divided into strips
- 1/2 cup cornstarch

- 1/2 cup water
- 1/2 cup olive oil
- Salt to season

Directions:
1. Preheat air fryer to 390°F. In a mixing bowl, stir in cornstarch, water, salt, pepper, oil, eggplants, zucchini, and potatoes.
2. Place one-third of the veggie strips in the fryer's basket and cook them for 5 minutes, shaking once.
3. Once ready, transfer them to a platter. Serve warm.

267. Baked potato and parsnip
Servings: 8
Prep & Cooking Time: 30 Minutes
Ingredients:
- 3 tbsps. pine nuts
- 28 ounces parsnips, minced
- 1 3/4 ounces coarsely minced Parmesan cheese
- 6 3/4 ouncse crème fraiche
- 1 slice bread
- 2 tbsps. sage
- 4 tbsps. butter
- 4 tsps. mustard

Directions:
1. Preheat air fryer to 360°F. Put salted water in a pot over medium heat. Add potatoes and parsnips. Bring to a boil for 10 minutes.
2. In a bowl, mix mustard, crème fraiche, sage, salt and pepper. Leave the potatoes and parsnips to dry and mash with the milk, salt, butter, black pepper, and cayenne pepper.
3. Add mustard mixture, bread, cheese, and nuts to the mash and mix. Add the batter to your air fryer's basket and cook for 15 minutes, shaking once. Serve.

268. Cheesy pizza with a crust made of broccoli
Servings: 1
Prep & Cooking Time: 30 Minutes
Ingredients:
- 3 cups broccoli rice, steamed
- 1/2 cup parmesan cheese, shredded
- 1 egg
- 3 tbsps. low-carb Alfredo sauce
- 1/2 cup parmesan cheese, shredded

Directions:
1. Drain the broccoli rice and combine with the Parmesan cheese and egg in a bowl, mixing well.
2. Cut a piece of parchment paper roughly the size of the base of the fryer's basket. Spoon four equal-sized amounts of the broccoli mixture onto the paper and press each portion into the shape of a pizza crust. You may have to complete this part in two batches. Transfer the parchment to the fryer.
3. Cook at 280°F for five minutes. When the crust is firm, flip it over and cook for an additional two minutes.
4. Add the Alfredo sauce and mozzarella cheese on top of the crusts and cook for an additional seven minutes. The crusts are ready when the sauce and cheese have melted. Serve hot.

269. Cheesy muffins
Servings: 3
Prep & Cooking Time: 8 Minutes
Ingredients:
- 1 cup cheddar cheese, smoked and shredded
- 1 mashed avocado
- 1/4 cup ranch-style salad dressing
- 1 cup alfalfa sprouts
- 1 tomato, minced
- 1 sweet onion, minced
- 1/4 cup sesame seeds, toasted

Directions:
5. Set the muffins open-faced in the air fryer's basket. Spread the mashed avocado on each half of the muffin.
6. Place the halves close to each other. Cover the muffins with the sprouts, tomatoes, onion, dressing, sesame seeds and the cheese.
7. Cook for 7-8 minutes at 350°F.
8. Greek mayo sauce on Roasted peppers

Servings: 4
Prep & Cooking Time: 35 Minutes
Ingredients:
- 2 bell peppers, cut into strips
- 1 tsp. avocado oil
- 1/2 tsp. celery salt
- 1/4 tsp. dried peppers, crushed
- 1/2 cup mayonnaise
- 1 clove garlic, minced
- 1 tsp. lemon juice

Directions:
1. Toss the peppers with avocado oil, celery salt, and dried peppers.
2. Air-fry them at 380°F for 10 minutes. Shake the cooking basket and cook for 20 minutes more.
3. In the meantime, thoroughly combine the mayonnaise, garlic, and lemon juice.
4. When the peppers come out of the air fryer, check them for doneness. Serve with chilled mayonnaise sauce and enjoy!

270. Braised vegetables with a twist
Servings: 4
Prep & Cooking Time: 25 Minutes
Ingredients:
- 1 large-sized zucchini, sliced
- 1 Serrano pepper, emptied and slimly sliced
- 2 bell peppers, emptied and slimly sliced
- 1 celery stalk, cut into matchsticks
- 1/4 cup olive oil
- 1/2 tsp. porcini powder
- 1/4 tsp. mustard powder
- 1/2 tsp. cumin seeds
- 1 tbsp. garlic powder
- 1/2 tsp. fine sea salt
- 1/4 tsp. ground black pepper
- 1/2 cup tomato puree

Directions:
1. Place the sweet potatoes, zucchini, peppers, and the carrot into the air fryer cooking basket.
2. Spray it with olive oil and coat it over; cook in the preheated air fryer at 350°F for 15 minutes.
3. While the vegetables are cooking, prepare the sauce by thoroughly whisking the other ingredients, without the tomato ketchup. Lightly grease a baking dish that fits into your machine.
4. Once cook, put the cooked veggies in the baking dish. Add the sauce and toss to coat well.
5. Turn the air fryer to 390°F and cook the vegetables for more minutes. Bon appétit!

271. Cheesilicious brussel sprouts
Servings: 3
Prep & Cooking Time: 10 Minutes
Ingredients:
- 1 lb. Brussels sprouts, divide into halves
- 1/4 cup whole wheat breadcrumbs
- 1/4 cup Parmesan cheese, shredded

- 1 tbsp. balsamic vinegar
- 1 tbsp. extra-virgin olive oil
- Salt & black pepper for better taste

Directions:
1. Preheat the air fryer and set to 400°F before greasing the basket with oil.
2. Mix Brussel sprouts, vinegar, oil, salt, and black pepper in a bowl and toss to coat well.
3. Set the Brussel sprouts in the air fryer basket and cook for about 5 minutes.
4. Sprinkle with breadcrumbs and cheese and cook for about 5 more minutes.
5. Serve and serve warm.

272. French green beans and shallots 'n almonds
Servings: 4
Prep & Cooking Time: 10 Minutes
Ingredients:
- 1/4 cup slivered almonds, toasted
- 1/2 lb. shallots, peeled and divided into quarters
- 1/2 tsp. ground white pepper
- 1 1/2 lbs. French green beans, stems removed and blanched
- 1 tbsp. salt
- 2 tbsps. olive oil

Directions:
1. Preheat the air fryer to 400°F.
2. Mix all ingredients in a mixing bowl. Toss until well combined.
3. Place inside the air fryer basket and cook for 10 minutes or until lightly browned.

273. Vegetables and stuffed mushrooms
Servings: 3
Prep & Cooking Time: 15 Minutes
Ingredients:
- 1 tomato, diced
- 1 small red onion, diced
- 1 red bell pepper, diced
- 1/2 cup shredded mozzarella cheese
- 1/2 tsp. garlic powder
- 1/4 tsp. pepper
- 1/4 tsp. salt

Directions:
1. Preheat air fryer to 330°F.
2. Wash the mushrooms, remove the stems, and pat them dry. Coat with the olive oil.
3. Combine all remaining ingredients, except mozzarella, in a bowl.
4. Divide the filling between the mushrooms.
5. Top the mushrooms with mozzarella.
6. Drop into the air fryer and cook for 8 minutes.

274. Delightful ratatouille
Servings: 6
Prep & Cooking Time: 15 Minutes
Ingredients:
- 1 eggplant, diced
- 3 garlic cloves, minced
- 1 onion, diced
- 3 tomatoes, diced
- 2 bell peppers, diced
- 1 tbsp vinegar
- 1 1/2 tbsps. olive oil
- 2 tbsps. herb de Provence
- Pepper
- Salt

Directions:
1. Preheat the air fryer to 400°F.
2. Add all ingredients into the bowl and toss well and transfer into the air fryer baking dish.
3. Place dish into the air fryer and cook for 15 minutes. Stir halfway through.
4. Serve and enjoy.

275. Crescent triangles spinach and feta
Servings: 4
Prep & Cooking Time: 20 Minutes
Ingredients:
- 1 cup steamed spinach
- 1 cup crumbled feta cheese
- 1/4 tsp. garlic powder
- 1 tsp. minced oregano
- 1/4 tsp. salt

Directions:
1. Set the air fryer first to 350°F, and roll the dough onto a lightly floured flat surface.
2. Combine the feta, spinach, oregano, salt, and garlic powder together in a bowl. Divide the dough into.
3. Divide the spinach/feta mixture between the dough pieces. Fold the dough and secure with a fork. Place onto a lined baking dish, and then in the air fryer.
4. Cook for 1minutes, until lightly browned.

276. Healthy broccoli casserole
Servings: 8
Prep & Cooking Time: 30 Minutes
Ingredients:
- 2 lbs. broccoli florets
- 2 cups cheddar cheese, shredded
- 1/4 cup vegetable stock
- 1/2 cup heavy cream
- 2 garlic cloves, minced
- 4 ounces cream cheese
- 1 cup mozzarella cheese
- 3 tbsps. olive oil
- Pepper
- Salt

Directions:
1. Set the air fryer to 370°F.
2. Layer broccoli florets in an air fryer baking dish. Sprinkle olive oil and add pepper and salt for taste.
3. Cook broccoli in the air fryer for 15 minutes.
4. Meanwhile, combine together heavy cream, stock, garlic, cream cheese, mozzarella cheese, and 1 cup cheddar cheese in a medium saucepan over medium-low heat. Stir frequently.
5. Once broccoli is cooked then drop heavy cream mixture on top of broccoli and stir every element well.
6. Cover the top with cheddar cheese. Cook it for 12 more minutes.
7. Serve and enjoy.

277. Sweet honey glazed carrots
Servings: 4
Prep & Cooking Time: 12 Minutes
Ingredients:
- 3 cups carrots, peeled and cut into large chunks
- 1 tbsp. olive oil
- 1 tbsp. honey
- 1 tbsp. fresh thyme, finely minced
- Salt & ground black pepper, as required

Directions:
1. Set the temperature of air fryer to 390°F. Grease an air fryer basket.
2. In a bowl, mix well carrot, oil, honey, thyme, salt, and black pepper.
3. Arrange carrot chunks into the prepared air fryer basket in a single layer.
4. Air fry for about 12 minutes.
5. Remove from air fryer and transfer the carrot chunks onto serving plates.
6. Serve hot.

278. Delightful sweet and sour brussel sprouts
Servings: 2
Prep & Cooking Time: 10 Minutes
Ingredients:
- 2 cups Brussels sprouts, divided and halved lengthwise
- 1 tbsp. balsamic vinegar
- 1 tbsp. maple syrup
- Salt, as required

Directions:
1. Set the air fryer to 400°F before greasing the fryer basket with oil.
2. Mix all the ingredients in a bowl and toss to coat well.
3. Set the Brussel sprouts in the air fryer basket and cook for about 10 minutes, shaking once halfway through.
4. Serve in a bowl and serve warm.

279. Sweet hoisin-glazed bok choy
Servings: 4
Prep & Cooking Time: 10 Minutes
Ingredients:
- 1 lb. baby Bok choy, bottoms removed, leaves separated
- 2 garlic cloves, minced
- 1 tsp. onion powder
- 1/2 tsp. sage
- 2 tbsps. hoisin sauce
- 2 tbsps. sesame oil
- 1 tbsp. all-purpose flour

Directions:
1. Place the Bok choy, garlic, onion powder, and sage in the lightly greased air fryer basket.
2. Cook in the preheated air fryer at 350°F for 3 minutes.
3. In a small mixing dish, whisk the hoisin sauce, sesame oil, and flour. Drizzle the sauce over the Bok choy. Cook for a further minutes. Bon appétit!

280. Pasta 'n cheese, baked portobello
Servings: 4
Prep & Cooking Time: 30 Minutes
Ingredients:
- 1 cup milk
- 1 cup shredded mozzarella cheese
- 1 large clove garlic, minced
- 1 tbsp. vegetable oil
- 1/4 cup margarine
- 1/4 tsp. dried basil
- 1/4-lb. portobello mushrooms, slimly sliced
- 2 tbsps. all-purpose flour
- 2 tbsps. soy sauce
- 4-ounce penne pasta, cooked according to manufacturer's Directions for Cooking
- 5-ounces frozen minced spinach, thawed

Directions:
1. Lightly add oil to your air fryer's baking pan. For 2 minutes, heat on 360°F. Add mushrooms and cook for a minute. Transfer to a plate.
2. In same pan, melt margarine for a minute. Stir in basil, garlic, and flour. Cook for 3 minutes. Stir and cook for another minutes. Stir in half of milk slowly while whisking continuously. Cook for another 2 minutes. Mix well. Cook for another 2 minutes. Stir in remaining milk and cook for another 3 minutes.
3. Add cheese and mix well.
4. Stir in soy sauce, spinach, mushrooms, and pasta. Mix well. Top with remaining cheese.
5. Cook for 1 minute at 390°F until tops are lightly browned.
6. Serve and enjoy.

281. Baked layered tortilla
Servings: 6
Prep & Cooking Time: 30 Minutes
Ingredients:
- 1 (15 ounce) can black beans, washed and dried
- 1 cup salsa
- 1 cup salsa, divided
- 1/2 cup minced tomatoes
- 1/2 cup sour cream
- 2 (15 ounce) cans pinto beans, washed and dried
- 2 cloves garlic, minced
- 2 cups shredded reduced-fat Cheddar cheese
- 2 tbsp. minced fresh cilantro
- 7 (8 inch) flour tortillas

Directions:
1. Mash pinto beans in a large bowl and mix in garlic and salsa.
2. In another bowl whisk together tomatoes, black beans, cilantro, and 1/4 cup salsa.
3. Lightly grease baking pan of air fryer with cooking spray. Spread 1 tortilla, spread 3/4 cup pinto bean mixture evenly up to 1/2-inch away from the edge of tortilla, spread 1/4 cup cheese on top. Cover with another tortilla, spread 2/cup black bean mixture, and then 1/4 cup cheese. Repeat twice the layering process. Cover with the last tortilla, top with pinto bean mixture and then cheese.
4. Cover pan with foil.
5. Cook for 2minutes at 390°F, remove foil and cook for 5 minutes or until tops are lightly browned.
6. Serve and enjoy.

282. Awesome vegetables recipe
Servings: 4
Prep & Cooking Time: 35 Minutes
Ingredients:
- 1/2 lb. carrots, peeled and sliced
- 1 lb. yellow squash, sliced
- 1 lb. zucchini, sliced
- 1 tbsp. tarragon leaves, minced
- 6 tsp. olive oil, divided
- 1 tsp. kosher salt
- 1/2 tsp. ground white pepper

Directions:
1. Preheat the air fryer to 400°F before greasing the fryer basket with oil.
2. Mix tsp. olive oil and carrots in a bowl until combined.
3. Transfer into the air fryer basket and cook for about 5 minutes.
4. Meanwhile, mix remaining tsp. of olive oil, yellow squash, zucchini, salt and white pepper in a large bowl.
5. Transfer this veggie mixture into the air fryer basket with carrots.
6. Cook for about 30 minutes and dish out in a bowl.
7. Top with tarragon leaves and mix well to serve.

283. Mayo and buttered carrot-zucchini

Servings: 4
Prep & Cooking Time: 25 Minutes
Ingredients:
- 1 tbsp. shredded onion
- 2 tbsps. butter, melted
- 1/2-lb carrots, sliced
- 1-1/2 zucchinis, sliced
- 1/4 cup water
- 1/4 cup mayonnaise
- 1/4 tsp. prepared horseradish
- 1/4 tsp. salt
- 1/4 tsp. ground black pepper
- 1/4 cup Italian bread crumbs

Directions:
1. Lightly oil your air fryer's baking pan. Put in the carrots. Set it to 360 degree°F and cook it for 8 minutes. Put in the zucchini and for another 5 minutes, continue cooking.
2. Meanwhile, in a bowl whisk well pepper, salt, horseradish, onion, mayonnaise, and water. Pour into pan of veggies. Toss well to coat.
3. In a small bowl mix melted butter and bread crumbs. Sprinkle over veggies.
4. Cook for 10 minutes at 390°F until tops are lightly browned.
5. Serve and enjoy.

284. Crispy and tasty butternut squash fries

Servings: 4
Prep & Cooking Time: 25 Minutes
Ingredients:
- 1 cup all-purpose flour
- Salt & ground black pepper for better taste
- 3 tbsps. nutritional yeast flakes
- 1/2 cup almond milk
- 1/2 cup almond meal
- 1/2 cup bread crumbs
- 1 tbsp. herbs (oregano, basil, rosemary, minced)
- 1 lb. butternut squash, remove the skin and cut it in length size

Directions:
1. In a shallow bowl, combine the flour, salt, and black pepper. In another shallow dish, mix the nutritional yeast flakes with the almond milk until well combined.
2. Mix the almond meal, breadcrumbs, and herbs in a third shallow dish. Dredge the butternut squash in the flour mixture, shaking off the excess. Then, dip in the milk mixture; lastly, dredge in the breadcrumb mixture.
3. Spritz the butternut squash fries with cooking oil on all sides.
4. Cook in the preheated air fryer at 360°F approximately 12 minutes, turning them over halfway through the cooking time.
5. Serve with your favorite sauce for dipping. Bon appétit!

285. Shallots on a minty green beans

Servings: 6
Prep & Cooking Time: 25 Minutes
Ingredients:
- 1 tbsp. fresh mint, minced
- 1 tbsp. sesame seeds, toasted
- 1 tbsp. vegetable oil
- 1 tsp. soy sauce
- 1-lb. fresh green beans, trimmed
- 2 large shallots, sliced
- 2 tbsps. fresh basil, minced
- 2 tbsps. pine nuts

Directions:
1. Preheat the air fryer to 330°F.
2. Position the grill pan accessory inside the air fryer.
3. In a mixing bowl, combine the green beans, shallots, vegetable oil, and soy sauce.
4. Dump in the air fryer and cook for 25 minutes.
5. Once cooked, garnish with basil, mints, sesame seeds, and pine nuts.

286. Grilled veggie with tandoori spice

Servings: 6
Prep & Cooking Time: 20 Minutes
Ingredients:
- 1/2 head cauliflower, cut into florets
- 1/2 cup yogurt
- 1 carrot, peeled and shaved to and-inch thick
- 1 cup young ears of corn
- 1 handful sugar snap peas
- 1 small zucchini, divided into thick slices
- 1 yellow sweet pepper, seeded and minced
- 2 small onions, divided into wedges
- 2 tbsps. canola oil
- 2-inch fresh ginger, minced
- 3 tbsps. Tandoori spice blend
- 6 cloves of garlic, minced

Directions:
1. Preheat the air fryer to 330°F.
2. Position the grill pan accessory inside the air fryer.
3. In a Ziploc bag, put all ingredients and give a shake to season all vegetables.
4. Dump all ingredients on the grill pan and cook for 20 minutes.
5. Make sure to give the vegetables a shake halfway through the cooking time.

287. Healthy stuffed eggplant

Servings: 2
Prep & Cooking Time: 35 Minutes
Ingredients:
- Large eggplant
- 1/4 medium yellow onion, diced
- 2 tbsps. red bell pepper, diced
- 1 cup spinach
- 1/4 cup artichoke hearts, minced

Directions:
1. Cut the eggplant lengthwise into slices and spoon out the flesh, leaving a shell about a half-inch thick. Chop it up and set aside.
2. Set a skillet over a medium heat and spritz with cooking spray. Cook the onions for about three to five minutes to soften. Then add the pepper, spinach, artichokes, and the flesh of eggplant.
3. Fry for a further five minutes, then remove from the heat.
4. Scoop this mixture in equal parts into the eggplant shells and place each one in the fryer.
5. Cook for twenty minutes at 320°F until the eggplant shells are soft. Serve warm.

288. Vegetable frittata two-cheese

Servings: 2
Prep & Cooking Time: 35 Minutes
Ingredients:
- 1/3 cup sliced mushrooms
- 1 large zucchini, sliced with a 1-inch thickness
- 1 small red onion, sliced
- 1/4 cup minced chives
- 1/4 lb. asparagus, trimmed and sliced slimly

- 2 tsps. olive oil
- 4 eggs, grounded into a bowl
- 1/3 cup milk
- Salt & pepper for better taste
- 1/3 cup shredded Cheddar cheese
- 1/3 cup crumbled Feta cheese

Directions:
1. Preheat the air fryer to 380°F. Line a baking dish with parchment paper; set aside. In the egg bowl, add milk, salt, and pepper; beat evenly. Place a skillet over medium heat on a stovetop, and heat olive oil.
2. Add the asparagus, zucchini, onion, mushrooms, and baby spinach; stir-fry for 5 minutes.
3. Pour the veggies into the baking dish and top with the egg mixture. Sprinkle feta and cheddar cheese over and place in the air fryer. Cook for 15 minutes.
4. Remove the baking dish and garnish with fresh chives.

289. Mexican baked zucchini recipe
Servings: 4
Prep & Cooking Time: 30 Minutes
Ingredients:
- 1 tbsp. olive oil
- 1-1/2 lb. zucchini, cubed
- 1/2 cup minced onion
- 1/2 tsp. garlic salt
- 1/2 tsp. paprika
- 1/2 tsp. dried oregano
- 1/2 tsp. cayenne pepper for better taste
- 1/2 cup cooked long-grain rice
- 1/2 cup cooked pinto beans
- 1-1/4 cups salsa
- 3/4 cup shredded Cheddar cheese

Directions:
1. Take the air fryer's baking pan, grease it with olive oil. Add onions and zucchini and for 8 minutes, cook on 360°F. Halfway through cooking time, stir.
2. Season with cayenne, oregano, paprika, and garlic salt. Mix well.
3. Stir in salsa, beans, and rice. Cook for 5 minutes.
4. Stir in cheddar cheese and mix well.
5. Cover pan with foil.
6. Cook for 15 minutes at 390°F until bubbly.
7. Serve and enjoy.

290. Herb and veggie cornish pasties
Servings: 4
Prep & Cooking Time: 30 Minutes
Ingredients:
- 1/4 cup mushrooms, minced
- 3/4 cup cold coconut oil
- 1 1/2 cups plain flour
- 1 medium carrot, minced
- 1 medium potato, diced
- 1 onion, sliced
- 1 stick celery, minced
- 1 tbsp. nutritional yeast
- 1 tbsp. olive oil
- 1 tsp. oregano
- A pinch of salt
- Cold water for mixing the dough
- Salt and pepper for better taste

Directions:
1. Preheat the air fryer to 400°F.
2. Prepare the dough by mixing the flour, coconut oil, and salt in a bowl. Use a fork and press the flour to combine every element.
3. Gradually add a drop of water to the dough until you achieve a stiff consistency of the dough. Cover the dough with a cling film and let it rest for 30 minutes inside the fridge.
4. Roll the dough out and cut into squares. Set aside.
5. Warm olive oil over medium heat and sauté the onions for 2 minutes. Add the celery, carrots and potatoes. Continue stirring for 3 to 5 minutes before adding the mushrooms and oregano.
6. Season with salt and pepper for better taste. Add nutritional yeast last. Let it cool and set aside.
7. Drop a tbsp. of vegetable mixture on to the dough and seal the edges of the dough with water.
8. Place inside the air fryer basket and cook for 20 minutes or until the dough is crispy.

291. Refreshing zesty broccoli
Servings: 4
Prep & Cooking Time: 15 Minutes
Ingredients:
- 1 tbsp. butter
- 1 large whole broccoli, divide into small pieces
- 1 tbsp. white sesame seeds
- 2 tbsps. vegetable stock
- 1 tbsp. fresh lemon juice
- 3 garlic cloves, minced
- 1/2 tsp. fresh lemon zest, shredded finely
- 1/2 tsp. red pepper flakes, crushed

Directions:
1. Preheat the air fryer to 355°F and grease an air fryer pan.
2. Mix butter, vegetable stock and lemon juice in the air fryer pan.
3. Transfer into the air fryer and cook for about 2 minutes.
4. Stir in garlic and broccoli and cook for about 1 minutes.
5. Add sesame seeds, lemon zest and red pepper flakes and cook for minutes.
6. Serve and serve warm.

292. Fried cauliflower
Servings: 4
Prep & Cooking Time: 20 Minutes
Ingredients:
- 2 tbsps. olive oil
- 1/2 tsp. salt
- 1/4 tsp. freshly ground black pepper

Directions:
1. In a mixing bowl, toss cauliflower, oil, salt, and black pepper, until the florets are well-coated.
2. Set the florets in the air fryer and cook for 8 minutes at 360°F; work in batches if needed. Serve the crispy cauliflower in lettuce wraps with chicken, cheese or mushrooms.

293. Baked vegetable with olives and cheese
Servings: 3
Prep & Cooking Time: 25 Minutes
Ingredients:
- 1/2 lb. cauliflower, divided into 1-inch florets
- 1/4 lb. zucchini, divided into 1-inch chunks
- 1 red onion, sliced
- 2 bell peppers, divided into 1-inch chunks
- 2 tbsps. extra-virgin olive oil
- 1 cup dry white wine
- 1 tsp. dried rosemary
- Freshly grounded black pepper and sea salt and for better taste
- 1/2 tsp. dried basil

- 1/2 cup tomato, pureed
- 1/2 cup cheddar cheese, shredded
- 1 ounce Kalamata olives, pitted and halved

Directions:
1. Toss the vegetables with the olive oil, wine, rosemary, salt, black pepper, and basil until well coated.
2. Add the pureed tomatoes to a lightly greased baking dish; spread to cover the bottom of the baking dish.
3. Add the vegetables and top with shredded cheese. Scatter the Kalamata olives over the top.
4. Bake in the preheated air fryer at 390°F for 20 minutes, rotating the dish halfway through the cooking time. Serve warm and enjoy!

294. Cauliflower asian-style

Servings: 4
Prep & Cooking Time: 25 Minutes
Ingredients:
- 2 cups cauliflower, shredded
- 1 onion, peeled and finely minced
- 1 tbsp. sesame oil
- 1 tbsp. tamari sauce
- 1 tbsp. sake
- 2 cloves garlic, peeled and pressed
- 1 tbsp. ginger, freshly shredded
- 1 tbsp. fresh parsley, finely minced
- 1/4 cup of lime juice
- 2 tbsps. sesame seeds

Directions:
1. Combine the cauliflower, onion, sesame oil, tamari sauce, sake, garlic, and the ginger in a mixing dish; stir until every element's well incorporated.
2. Air-fry at 400°F for 1minutes.
3. Pause the air fryer. Add the parsley and lemon juice. Turn the machine to cook at 390°F; cook additional 10 minutes.
4. Meanwhile, toast the sesame seeds in a non-stick skillet; stir them constantly over a medium-low flame. Sprinkle over prepared cauliflower and serve warm.

295. Sweet and sour tofu

Servings: 3
Prep & Cooking Time: 25 Minutes
Ingredients:
- 2 tbsps. Shoyu sauce
- 16 ounces extra-firm tofu, drained, pressed and cubed
- 1/2 cup water
- 1/4 cup pineapple juice
- 2 garlic cloves, minced
- 1/2 tsp. fresh ginger, shredded
- 1 tsp. cayenne pepper
- 1/4 tsp. ground black pepper
- 1/2 tsp. salt
- 1 tsp. honey
- 1 tbsp. arrowroot powder

Directions:
1. Drizzle the Shoyu sauce all over the tofu cubes. Cook in the preheated air fryer at 380°F for 6 minutes; shake the basket and cook for a further 5 minutes.
2. Meanwhile, cook the remaining ingredients in a heavy skillet over medium heat for 10 minutes, until the sauce has slightly thickened.
3. Stir the fried tofu into the sauce and continue cooking for 4 minutes more or until the tofu is thoroughly heated.
4. Serve warm and enjoy!

296. Delicious and ultra-crispy tofu

Servings: 4
Prep & Cooking Time: 30 Minutes
Ingredients:
- 1 tsp. chicken bouillon granules
- 12-ounces extra-firm tofu, drained and cubed into 1-inch size
- 1 tsp. butter
- 2 tbsps. low-sodium soy sauce
- 2 tbsps. fish sauce
- 1 tsp. sesame oil

Directions:
1. Preheat the air fryer to 355°F before greasing the fryer basket with oil.
2. Mix soy sauce, fish sauce, sesame oil and chicken granules in a bowl and toss to coat well.
3. Stir in the tofu cubes and mix until well combined.
4. Keep aside to marinate for about 30 minutes and then transfer into air fryer basket.
5. Leave it for 30 minutes to cook. Every 10 minutes, give it a flip and serve warm.

297. Delicious roasted mushrooms in herb-garlic oil

Servings: 4
Prep & Cooking Time: 25 Minutes
Ingredients:
- 1/2 tsp. minced garlic
- 2 lbs. mushrooms
- 2 tsps. herbs de Provence
- 3 tbsp. coconut oil
- Salt & pepper for better taste

Directions:
1. Prepare air fryer by preheating it for five minutes.
2. Position all ingredients in a baking dish that is large enough for your air fryer.
3. Mix to combine.
4. Position the baking dish in the air fryer.
5. Cook for 2minutes at 350°F.

298. Bell peppers and oatmeal

Servings: 2
Prep & Cooking Time: 16 Minutes
Ingredients:
- 2 red bell peppers, large, divided into half, without seeds
- 2 cups cooked oatmeal
- 4 tbsps. canned red kidney beans, rinsed and drained
- 4 tbsps. coconut yogurt
- 1/4 tsp. ground cumin
- 1/4 tsp. smoked paprika
- Salt & ground black pepper, as required

Directions:
1. Set the temperature of air fryer to 355°F. Grease an air fryer basket.
2. Arrange bell peppers into the prepared air fryer basket, cut-side down.
3. Air fry for about 8 minutes.
4. Take it out of the air fryer and let it cool down.
5. Meanwhile, in a bowl, mix well oatmeal, beans, coconut yogurt, and spices.
6. Stuff each bell pepper half with the oatmeal mixture.
7. Now, set the air fryer to 355°F.
8. Arrange bell peppers into the air fryer basket and air fry for about minutes.
9. Remove from air fryer and transfer the bell peppers onto a platter.
10. Set aside to cool slightly.
11. Serve warm.

299. Sweet grilled 'n glazed strawberries
Servings: 2
Prep & Cooking Time: 20 Minutes
Ingredients:
- 1 tablespoon of honey
- 1 tablespoon of lemon zest
- 1 pound strawberries
- 3 tbsps. butter, melted
- Lemon, divided into wedges
- Kosher salt, just a pinch

Directions:
1. Put the strawberries in skewers.
2. Except for lemon wedges, mix all ingredients. Cover the strawberries with the mixture.
3. Position the skewer inside the air fryer.
4. Set the air fryer to 360°F then start cooking. Set it to 10 minutes. After about five minutes, use the honey mixture and brush it around the strawberries in skewers.
5. When serving, add lemon to taste.

300. Delicious falafel with chickpeas
Servings: 2
Prep & Cooking Time: 20 Minutes
Ingredients:
- 1 cup dried chickpeas, soaked overnight
- 1 small-sized onion, minced
- 2 cloves garlic, minced
- 2 tbsps. fresh cilantro leaves, minced
- 1 tbsp. flour
- 1/2 tsps. baking powder
- 1 tsp. cumin powder
- A pinch of ground cardamom
- Ground black pepper and sea salt for added taste

Directions:
1. Pulse all the ingredients in your food processor until the chickpeas are ground.
2. Form the falafel mixture into balls and place them in the lightly greased air fryer basket.
3. Cook at 330°F for about 15 minutes, shaking the basket occasionally to ensure even cooking.
4. Serve in pita bread with toppings of your choice. Enjoy!

301. Chopped paprika brussels sprouts
Servings: 2
Prep & Cooking Time: 20 Minutes
Ingredients:
- 10 Brussels sprouts
- 1 tsp. canola oil
- 1 tsp. coarse sea salt
- 1 tsp. paprika

Directions:
1. Toss all ingredients in the lightly greased air fryer basket.
2. Bake at 380°F for 15 minutes, shaking the basket halfway through the cooking time to ensure even cooking.
3. Serve and enjoy!

302. Au gratin potatoes ala rosemary
Servings: 4
Prep & Cooking Time: 45 Minutes
Ingredients:
- 2 lbs. potatoes
- 1/4 cup sunflower kernels, soaked overnight
- 1/2 cup almonds, soaked overnight
- 1 cup unsweetened almond milk
- 2 tbsp. nutritional yeast
- 1 tsp. shallot powder
- 2 fresh garlic cloves, minced
- 1/2 cup water
- Black pepper, ground, and kosher salt for added taste
- 1 tsp. cayenne pepper
- 1 tbsp. fresh rosemary

Directions:
1. Boil water in a large pan. Cook the whole potatoes for about 20 minutes. Leave the potatoes to dry, wait for it to cool down.
2. Peel your potatoes and slice into and-inch rounds.
3. Add the sunflower kernels, almonds, almond milk, nutritional yeast, shallot powder, and garlic to your food processor; blend until uniform, smooth, and creamy. Add the water and blend for a few seconds more.
4. Place 1/2 of the potatoes overlapping in a single layer in the lightly greased casserole dish. Spoon 1/2 of the sauce on top of the potatoes. Repeat the layers, ending with the sauce.
5. Top with salt, black pepper, cayenne pepper, and fresh rosemary. Bake in the preheated air fryer at 320°F for 20 minutes. Serve warm.

303. Seasoned vegetables creole
Servings: 5
Prep & Cooking Time: 15 Minutes
Ingredients:
- 1/4 cup honey
- 1/4 cup yellow mustard
- 1 large red bell pepper, sliced
- 1 tsp. black pepper
- 1 tsp. salt
- 2 large yellow squash, divided into 1/2 inch thick slices
- 2 medium zucchinis, divided into 1/2 inch thick slices
- 2 tsps. creole seasoning
- 2 tsps. smoked paprika
- 3 tbsps. olive oil

Directions:
1. Preheat the air fryer to 330°F.
2. Position the grill pan accessory inside the air fryer.
3. In a Ziploc bag, put the zucchini, squash, red bell pepper, olive oil, salt and pepper. Give a shake to season all vegetables.
4. Position it on a grill pan and let it cook for 15 minutes.
5. Meanwhile, prepare the sauce by combining the mustard, honey, paprika, and creole seasoning. Season with salt for added taste.
6. Serve the vegetables with the sauce.

304. Tofu with a twist
Servings: 3
Prep & Cooking Time: 13 Minutes
Ingredients:
- 1 (14-ounces) block extra-firm tofu, pressed and cut into 3/4-inch cubes
- 3 tsps. cornstarch
- 1 1/2 tbsps. avocado oil
- 1 1/2 tsps. paprika
- 1 tsp. onion powder
- 1 tsp. garlic powder
- Salt & black pepper for added taste

Directions:
1. Set the air fryer to 390°F before greasing the fryer basket with oil.
2. Mix the tofu, oil, cornstarch, and spices in a bowl and toss to coat well.

3. Set the tofu pieces in the air fryer basket and cook for about 1 minute, tossing twice in between.
4. Serve the tofu onto serving plates and serve warm.

305. Yummy buttered rolls
Servings: 12
Prep & Cooking Time: 30 Minutes
Ingredients:
- 1 cup milk
- 1 tbsp. coconut oil
- 1 tbsp. olive oil
- 3 cups plain flour
- 7 1/2 tbsp. unsalted butter
- 1 tsp. yeast
- Salt & ground black pepper, as required

Directions:
1. In a pan, add the milk, coconut oil, and olive oil and cook until lukewarm.
2. Remove from the heat and stir well.
3. In a large bowl, add the flour, butter, yeast, salt, black pepper, and milk mixture and mix until a dough forms.
4. With your hands, knead for about 5 minutes
5. With a damp cloth, cover the dough and set aside in a warm place for about minutes.
6. Again, with your hands, knead the dough for about 4-5 minutes
7. With a damp cloth, cover the dough and set aside in a warm place for about 30 minutes.
8. Place the dough onto a lightly floured surface.
9. Make 12 small balls from the dough mixture.
10. Set the temperature of air fryer to 360°F. Grease an air fryer basket.
11. Arrange rolls into the prepared air fryer basket in 2 batches in a single layer.
12. Air fry for about 15 minutes.
13. Once cooked, serve it immediately.

306. Oatmeal with bell pepper
Servings: 2
Prep & Cooking Time: 16 Minutes
Ingredients:
- 1 red bell pepper, large, without seed and divided into half
- 1 cup cooked oatmeal
- 2 tbsps. canned red kidney beans
- 2 tbsps. plain yogurt
- and tsp. ground cumin
- and tsp. smoked paprika
- Black pepper and salt for a more flavorful taste

Directions:
1. Preheat the air fryer to 355°F and grease an air fryer pan.
2. Put the bell peppers in the air fryer pan and cook for about 8 minutes.
3. Meanwhile, mix oatmeal with remaining ingredients in a bowl.
4. Stuff the oatmeal mixture in each pepper half and cook for about 8 minutes.
5. Serve in a bowl and serve warm.

307. Healthy hearty carrots
Servings: 4
Prep & Cooking Time: 25 Minutes
Ingredients:
- 2 shallots, minced
- 3 carrots, sliced
- Salt for added taste
- 1/4 cup yogurt
- 2 garlic cloves, minced
- 3 tbsps. parsley, minced

Directions:
1. Preheat air fryer to 370°F.
2. In a bowl, mix carrots, salt, garlic, shallots, parsley and yogurt. Sprinkle with oil.
3. Place the veggies in air fryer basket and cook for 20 minutes.
4. Serve with basil and garlic mayo.

308. Crispy and spicy asparagus with paprika-garlic sauce
Servings: 5
Prep & Cooking Time: 15 Minutes
Ingredients:
- 1/4 cup almond flour
- 1/2 tsp. garlic powder
- 1/2 tsp. smoked paprika
- 10 medium asparagus, trimmed
- 2 large eggs, beaten
- 2 tbsps. parsley, minced
- Salt & pepper for better taste

Directions:
1. Prepare air fryer by preheating it for five minutes.
2. In a mixing bowl, combine the parsley, garlic powder, almond flour, and smoked paprika. Season with salt and pepper for better taste.
3. Soak firs the asparagus in the beaten eggs and dredge in the almond flour mixture.
4. Drop into the air fryer basket. Close.
5. Cook for 1 minute at 350°F.

309. Air fried skewered corn
Servings: 2
Prep & Cooking Time: 25 Minutes
Ingredients:
- 1-lb. apricot, halved
- 2 ears of corn
- 2 medium green peppers, cut into large chunks
- 2 tsps. prepared mustard
- Salt & pepper to taste

Directions:
1. Preheat the air fryer to 330°F.
2. Position the grill pan accessory inside the air fryer.
3. On the double layer rack with the skewer accessories, skewer the corn, green peppers, and apricot. Season with pepper and salt for added taste.
4. Place skewered corn on the double layer rack and cook for 25 minutes.
5. Once cooked, brush with prepared mustard.

310. Thailand's spicy veggie recipe
Servings: 4
Prep & Cooking Time: 15 Minutes
Ingredients:
- 1 1/2 cups packed cilantro leaves
- 1 tbsp. black pepper
- 1 tbsp. chili garlic sauce
- 1/3 cup vegetable oil
- 2 lbs. vegetable of your choice, sliced into cubes
- 2 tbsps. fish sauce
- 8 cloves of garlic, minced

Directions:
1. Preheat the air fryer to 330°F.
2. Position the grill pan accessory inside the air fryer.

3. Place all ingredients in a mixing bowl and toss to coat all ingredients.
4. Put in the grill pan and cook for 15 minutes.

311. Crispy and delicious ham rolls
Servings: 3
Prep & Cooking Time: 17 Minutes
Ingredients:
- 3 packages Pepperidge farm rolls
- 1 tbsp softened butter
- 1 tsp. mustard seeds
- 1 tsp. poppy seeds
- 1 small minced onion

Directions:
1. Mix butter, mustard, onion and poppy seeds. On top of the rolls, spread the mixture. Cover with the minced ham.
2. Roll up and arrange them in the basket of the air fryer; cook at 350°F for 10 minutes.

312. Delightful caviar eggplant
Servings: 3
Prep & Cooking Time: 20 Minutes
Ingredients:
- 1/2 red onion, minced and blended
- 2 tbsps. balsamic vinegar
- 1 tbsp. olive oil
- Salt

Directions:
1. Set the eggplants in the basket and cook them for 15 minutes at 380°F. Remove them and let them cool. Then cut the eggplants in half, lengthwise, and empty their insides with a spoon.
2. Blend the onion in a blender. Put the inside of the eggplants in the blender and process every slimg.
3. Blend the other ingredients such as olive oil, vinegar, and salt. Serve cool with bread and tomato sauce or ketchup.

313. Balsamic sweet and sour brussel sprouts
Servings: 2
Prep & Cooking Time: 10 Minutes
Ingredients:
- 2 cups trimmed Brussels sprouts, divided lengthwise
- 1 tbsp. balsamic vinegar
- 1 tbsp. maple syrup
- Salt, as required

Directions:
1. Set the temperature of air fryer to 400°F. Grease an air fryer basket.
2. In a mixing bowl, add all the ingredients and toss to coat well.
3. Arrange Brussels sprouts into the prepared air fryer basket in a single layer.
4. Air fry for about 8-10 minutes, shaking once halfway through.
5. Remove from air fryer and transfer the Brussels sprouts onto serving plates.
6. Serve hot.

314. Stylish roasted vegetables
Servings: 4
Prep & Cooking Time: 25 Minutes
Ingredients:
- 1 ripe bell pepper, without seed and divided into 1/2-inch chunks
- 1 green bell pepper, seeded and cut into 1/2-inch chunks
- 1 yellow onion, quartered
- 1 ripe bell pepper, without seed and divided into 1/2-inch chunks
- 1 cup broccoli, broken into 1/2-inch florets
- 1/2 cup parsnip, trimmed and cut into 1/2-inch chunks
- 2 garlic cloves, minced
- Ground black pepper and Pink Himalayan salt for added taste
- 1/2 tsp. marjoram
- 1/2 tsp. dried oregano
- 1/4 cup dry white wine
- 1/4 cup vegetable broth
- 1/2 cup Kalamata olives, pitted and sliced

Directions:
1. Arrange your vegetables in a single layer in the baking pan in the order of the rainbow (red, orange, yellow, and green). Scatter the minced garlic around the vegetables.
2. Season with salt, black pepper, marjoram, and oregano. Drizzle the white wine and vegetable broth over the vegetables.
3. Roast in the preheated air fryer at 380°F for 15 minutes, rotating the pan once or twice.
4. Scatter the Kalamata olives all over your vegetables and serve warm. Bon appétit!

315. Crunchy round eggplant
Servings: 4
Prep & Cooking Time: 45 Minutes
Ingredients:
- 1 (1-lb.) eggplant, sliced
- 1/2 cup flax meal
- 1/2 cup rice flour
- Ground black pepper and sea salt for added taste
- 1 tsp. paprika
- 1 cup water
- 1 cup cornbread crumbs, crushed
- 1/2 cup vegan parmesan

Directions:
1. Toss the eggplant with tbsp. of salt and let it stand for 30 minutes. Drain and rinse well.
2. Mix the flax meal, rice flour, salt, black pepper, and paprika in a bowl. Add water and combine it well.
3. In another shallow bowl, mix the cornbread crumbs and vegan parmesan.
4. Dip the eggplant slices in the flour mixture, then in the crumb mixture; press to coat on all sides. Transfer to the lightly greased air fryer basket.
5. Set the air dryer to 370°F. Let it cook for 6 minutes. Cook the other side for 6 minutes as well.
6. Serve garnished with spicy ketchup if desired. Bon appétit!

316. Crusted rice flour tofu
Servings: 3
Prep & Cooking Time: 28 Minutes
Ingredients:
- 1 (14-ounces) block firm tofu, pressed and cubed into 1/2-inch size
- 2 tbsps. cornstarch
- 1/4 cup rice flour
- Salt & ground black pepper, as required
- 2 tbsps. olive oil

Directions:
1. In a bowl, mix together cornstarch, rice flour, salt, and black pepper.
2. Coat the tofu evenly with flour mixture.
3. Drizzle the tofu with oil.
4. Set the temperature of air fryer to 360°F. Grease an air fryer basket.
5. Arrange tofu cubes into the prepared air fryer basket in a single layer.

6. Air fry for about 14 minutes per side.
7. Remove from air fryer and transfer the tofu onto serving plates.
8. Serve warm.

317. Crisp swiss cheese and eggplant
Servings: 4
Prep & Cooking Time: 45 Minutes
Ingredients:
- 1/2 lb. eggplant, sliced
- 1/4 cup almond meal
- 2 tbsps. flaxseed meal
- Ground black pepper and coarse sea salt for added taste
- 1 tsp. paprika
- 1 cup Parmesan, freshly shredded

Directions:
1. Toss the eggplant with tbsp. of salt and let it stand for 30 minutes. Drain and rinse well.
2. Mix the almond meal, flaxseed meal, salt, black pepper, and paprika in a bowl. Add water and mix it well.
3. Then, place Parmesan in another shallow bowl.
4. Dip the eggplant slices in the almond meal mixture, then in parmesan; press to coat on all sides. Transfer to the lightly greased air fryer basket.
5. Set it to 370°F then let it cook for 6 minutes. Cook the other side for another 6 minutes.
6. Serve garnished with spicy ketchup if desired. Bon appétit!

318. Open-faced flatbread vegan sandwich
Servings: 4
Prep & Cooking Time: 25 Minutes
Ingredients:
- 1 can chickpeas, washed and dried
- 1 medium-sized head of cauliflower, divided into florets
- 1 tbsp. extra-virgin olive oil
- 2 ripe avocados, mashed
- 2 tbsps. lemon juice
- 4 flatbreads, toasted
- Salt and pepper for added taste

Directions:
1. Preheat the air fryer to 4250°F.
2. In a mixing bowl, combine the cauliflower, chickpeas, olive oil, and lemon juice. Season with pepper and salt for added taste.
3. Place inside the air fryer basket and cook for 25 minutes.
4. Once cooked, place on half of the flatbread and add avocado mash.
5. Season with pepper and salt for added taste.
6. Serve with hot sauce.

319. Almond-apple special
Servings: 4
Prep & Cooking Time: 15 Minutes
Ingredients:
- 1 1/2 ounces almonds
- 3/4 ounce raisins
- 2 tbsps. sugar

Directions:
1. Preheat air fryer to 360°F.
2. In a mixing bowl, mix sugar, almonds, and raisins.
3. Blend the mixture with a hand mixer.
4. Fill apples with almond mixture.
5. Place in air fryer's basket and cook for 10 minutes. Serve.

320. Glazed parsnips
Servings: 6
Prep & Cooking Time: 44 Minutes
Ingredients:
- 2 lbs. parsnips, peeled and cut into 1-inch chunks
- 1 tbsp. butter, melted
- 2 tbsps. maple syrup
- 1 tbsp. dried parsley flakes, crushed
- 1/4 tsp. red pepper flakes, crushed

Directions:
1. Set the air fryer to 355°F before greasing the fryer basket with oil.
2. Mix parsnips and butter in a bowl and toss to coat well.
3. Set the parsnips in the air fryer basket and cook for about 40 minutes.
4. Meanwhile, mix remaining ingredients in a large bowl.
5. Transfer this mixture into the air fryer basket and cook for about 4 more minutes.
6. Serve and serve warm.

321. Rice casserole made of egg and cauliflower
Servings: 4
Prep & Cooking Time: 15 Minutes
Ingredients:
- 2 tsps. olive oil
- 1 green bell pepper, minced
- 1 cup okra, minced
- 1/2 cup minced onion
- Black pepper and salt for added taste.
- 1 tbsp. soy sauce
- 2 eggs, beaten

Directions:
1. Preheat the air fryer to 380°F. Grease a baking dish with cooking spray.
2. Pulse cauliflower in your food processor until it becomes like small rice-like granules.
3. Add the rice to the baking dish and mix with bell pepper, okra, onion, soy sauce, salt, and pepper.
4. Pour over the beaten eggs and drizzle with olive oil.
5. Drop into the air fryer and cook for 1minutes. Serve warm.

322. Delightful roast winter vegetable
Servings: 2
Prep & Cooking Time: 30 Minutes
Ingredients:
- 1 cup minced butternut squash
- 2 small red onions, cut in wedges
- 1 cup minced celery
- 1 tbsp. minced fresh thyme
- Salt & pepper for added taste
- 2 tsps. olive oil

Directions:
1. Set the air fryer to 200°F, and in a dish, add turnip, squash, red onions, celery, thyme, pepper, salt, and olive oil; mix well.
2. Pour the vegetables into the fryer's basket and cook for 20 minutes, tossing once halfway through.

323. Cream cheese-pesto with stuffed mushrooms
Servings: 5
Prep & Cooking Time: 15 Minutes
Ingredients:
- 1/4 cup olive oil
- 1/2 cup cream cheese
- 1/2 cup pine nuts
- 1 cup basil leaves

- 1 tbsp. lemon juice, freshly squeezed
- 1-lb. cremini mushrooms, stalks removed
- Salt to taste

Directions:
1. Position all ingredients except the mushrooms in a food processor.
2. Pulse until fine.
3. Scoop the mixture and place on the side where the stalks were removed.
4. Place the mushrooms in the fryer basket.
5. Close and cook for 1 minute in a 350°F preheated air fryer.

324. Stuffed cheese tomatoes
Servings: 2
Prep & Cooking Time: 15 Minutes
Ingredients:
- 2 large tomatoes
- 1/2 cup broccoli, finely minced
- 1/2 cup cheddar cheese, shredded
- 1 tbsp. unsalted butter, melted
- 1/2 tsp. dried oregano, crushed

Directions:
1. Remove the top part of each tomato and remove the seeds and pulp.
2. In a bowl, mix together the minced broccoli and cheese.
3. Stuff each tomato evenly with broccoli mixture.
4. Set the temperature of air fryer to 355°F. Grease an air fryer basket.
5. Arrange tomatoes into the prepared air fryer basket.
6. Drizzle evenly with butter.
7. Air fry for about 12-15 minutes.
8. Remove from air fryer and transfer the tomatoes onto a platter.
9. Set aside to cool slightly.
10. Garnish with thyme and serve.

325. Marinated pearl onions on a tofu bowl
Servings: 4
Prep & Cooking Time: 1 Hour 20 Minutes
Ingredients:
- 16 ounces firm tofu, pressed and divided into 1-inch pieces
- 2 tbsps. vegan Worcestershire sauce
- 1 tbsp. white wine vinegar
- 1 tbsp. maple syrup
- 1/2 tsp. shallot powder
- 1/2 tsp. porcini powder
- 1/2 tsp. garlic powder
- 2 tbsps. peanut oil
- 1 cup pearl onions, peeled

Directions:
1. Place the tofu, Worcestershire sauce, vinegar, maple syrup, shallot powder, porcini powder, and garlic powder in a ceramic dish. Let it marinate in your refrigerator for hour.
2. Transfer the tofu to the lightly greased air fryer basket. Add the peanut oil and pearl onions; toss to combine.
3. Cook the tofu with the pearl onions in the preheated air fryer at 360°F for 6 minutes; pause and brush with the reserved marinade; cook for a further 5 minutes.
4. Serve immediately. Bon appétit!

326. Kiddie zucchini fries
Servings: 4
Prep & Cooking Time: 20 Minutes
Ingredients:
- 2 tbsps. olive oil
- 1/2 tsp. smoked cayenne pepper
- 1 large zucchini, peeled and divided into 1/4-inch long slices
- 1/2 tsp. shallot powder
- 1/3 tsp (or more depending on your palette) of freshly ground black pepper for added taste
- 3/4 tsp. garlic salt

Directions:
1. Firstly, heat up your air fryer to 360°F.
2. Then, add the zucchini to a mixing dish; toss them with the other ingredients.
3. Cook the zucchini fries approximately 14 minutes. Serve with a dipping sauce of choice.

327. Spiced bread rolls curry 'n coriander
Servings: 5
Prep & Cooking Time: 15 Minutes
Ingredients:
- 1/2 tsp. mustard seeds
- 1/2 tsp. turmeric
- 1 bunch coriander, minced
- 1 tbsp. olive oil
- 2 green chilies, seeded and minced
- 2 small onions, minced
- 2 sprigs, curry leaves
- 5 large potatoes, boiled
- 8 slices of vegan wheat bread, brown sides discarded
- Salt and pepper to taste

Directions:
1. In a mixing bowl, mash the potatoes. Season it with pepper and salt for added taste. Set aside.
2. Warm olive oil in a skillet over medium low flame and add the mustard seeds. Stir until the seeds sputter. Then add the onions and fry until translucent. Stir in the turmeric powder and curry leaves. Continue to cook for more minutes until fragrant. Remove from heat and add to the potatoes. Stir in the green chilies and coriander. This will be the filling.
3. Wet the bread and remove the excess water.
4. Place a tbsp. of the potato mixture in the middle of the bread and gently roll the bread in so that the potato filling is completely sealed inside the bread.
5. Brush with oil and place inside the air fryer.
6. Cook in a 400°F preheated air fryer for 15 minutes. Make sure to shake the air fryer basket gently halfway through the cooking time for even cooking.

328. Salted garlic and roasted broccoli
Servings: 6
Prep & Cooking Time: 15 Minutes
Ingredients:
- 1/2 tsp. black pepper
- 1/2 tsp. lemon juice.
- 1 clove of garlic, minced
- 1 tsp. salt
- 2 heads broccoli, cut into florets
- 2 tsps. extra virgin olive oil

Directions:
1. Place aluminum foil on the air fryer basket. Brush it lightly with oil.
2. Preheat the air fryer to 3750°F.
3. Combine all ingredients except the lemon juice in a mixing bowl and place inside the air fryer basket.

4. Cook for 15 minutes.
5. Serve with lemon juice.

329. Crispy avocado fingers
Servings: 4
Prep & Cooking Time: 10 Minutes
Ingredients:
- 1/2 cup panko breadcrumbs
- 1/2 tsp. salt
- 1 pitted Haas avocado, peeled and sliced
- Liquid from 1 can white beans or aquafaba

Directions:
1. Preheat the air fryer at 350°F.
2. In a shallow bowl, toss the breadcrumbs and salt until well combined.
3. Dredge the avocado slices first with the aquafaba then in the breadcrumb mixture.
4. Lay each avocado slices in a single layer in the air fryer basket.
5. Cook for 10 minutes and shake halfway through the cooking time.

330. Tasty shawarma broccoli
Servings: 4
Prep & Cooking Time: 25 Minutes
Ingredients:
- 1 lb. broccoli, steamed and drained
- 2 tbsps. canola oil
- 1 tsp. cayenne pepper
- 1 tsp. sea salt
- 1 tbsp. Shawarma spice blend

Directions:
1. Toss all ingredients in a mixing bowl.
2. Roast in the preheated air fryer at 380°F for 10 minutes, shaking the basket halfway through the cooking time.
3. Work in batches. Bon appétit!

331. 3 mediterranean dill sauce on zucchini
Servings: 4
Prep & Cooking Time: 1 Hour
Ingredients:
- 1 lb. zucchini, peeled and cubed
- 2 tbsps. melted butter
- 1 tsp. sea salt flakes
- 1 sprig rosemary, leaves only, crushed
- 2 sprigs thyme, leaves only, crushed
- 1/2 tsp. freshly grounded black peppercorns

For Mediterranean Dipping Sauce:
- 1/2 cup mascarpone cheese
- 1/3 cup yogurt
- 1 tbsp. fresh dill, minced
- 1 tbsp. olive oil

Directions:
1. Firstly, set your air fryer to cook at 350°F. Now, add the potato cubes to the bowl with cold water and soak them approximately for 35 minutes.
2. After that, dry the potato cubes using a paper towel.
3. In a mixing dish, thoroughly whisk the melted butter with sea salt flakes, rosemary, thyme, and freshly grounded peppercorns. Rub the potato cubes with this butter/spice mix.
4. Air-fry the potato cubes in the cooking basket for 18 to 20 minutes or until cooked through; make sure to shake the potatoes to cook them evenly.
5. Meanwhile, make the Mediterranean dipping sauce by mixing the remaining ingredients. Serve warm potatoes with Mediterranean sauce for dipping and enjoy!

332. Specially sautéed spinach
Servings: 2
Prep & Cooking Time: 9 Minutes
Ingredients:
- 1 small onion, minced
- 6 ounces fresh spinach
- 2 tbsps. olive oil
- 1 tsp. ginger, minced
- Black pepper and salt for a more flavorful taste

Directions:
1. Preheat the air fryer to 360°F and grease an air fryer pan.
2. Put olive oil, onions and ginger in the air fryer pan and place in the air fryer basket.
3. Cook for about 4 minutes and add spinach, salt, and black pepper.
4. Cook for about more minutes and dish out in a bowl to serve.

333. Amazing vegetable croquettes
Servings: 4
Prep & Cooking Time: 40 Minutes
Ingredients:
- 1/2 lb. broccoli
- 4 tbsps. milk
- 2 tbsps. butter
- Salt & black pepper, to taste
- 1/2 tsp. cayenne pepper
- 1/2 cup mushrooms, minced
- 1 bell pepper, minced
- 1 clove garlic, minced
- 3 tbsps. chives, minced
- 2 tbsps. olive oil
- 1/2 cup almond flour
- 1/4 cup coconut flour
- 2 eggs
- 1/2 cup Parmesan cheese, shredded

Directions:
1. In a large saucepan, boil the broccoli for 20 minutes. Drain the broccoli and mash with the milk, butter, salt, black pepper, and cayenne pepper.
2. Add the mushrooms, bell pepper, garlic, chives, and olive oil; stir to combine well. Shape the mixture into patties.
3. In a shallow bowl, place the flour; beat the eggs in another bowl; in a third bowl, place the parmesan cheese.
4. Each patty should be dipped into the flour till covered then to the whisked egg to coat it. Now roll it over on the parmesan cheese. Press it to stay firm.
5. Cook in the preheated air fryer at 370°F for 16 minutes, shaking halfway through the cooking time. Bon appétit!

334. Delicious roasted pepper salad and goat cheese
Servings: 4
Prep & Cooking Time: 20 Minutes + Chilling Time
Ingredients:
- 1 green bell pepper
- 1 red bell pepper
- 1 Serrano pepper
- 4 tbsps. olive oil
- 2 tbsp. cider vinegar
- 2 garlic cloves, peeled and pressed
- 1 tsp. cayenne pepper
- Sea salt, to taste
- 1/2 tsp. mixed peppercorns, freshly crushed
- 1/2 cup goat cheese, cubed
- 2 tbsp. fresh Italian parsley leaves, roughly minced

Directions:
1. First, heat up your air fryer to 400°F. Brush the air fryer basket lightly with cooking oil.
2. Then, roast the peppers for 5 minutes. Give the peppers a half turn; place them back in the cooking basket and roast for another 5 minutes.
3. Turn them one more time and roast until the skin is charred and soft or 5 more minutes. Peel the peppers and let them cool to room temperature.
4. In a small mixing dish, whisk the olive oil, vinegar, garlic, cayenne pepper, salt, and crushed peppercorns. Dress the salad and set aside.
5. Scatter goat cheese over the peppers and garnish with parsley. Bon appétit!

335. No-egg spinach quiche
Servings: 4
Prep & Cooking Time: 30 Minutes
Ingredients:
- 1/2 cup cold coconut oil
- 1/2 tbsp. dried dill
- 3/4 cup whole meal flour
- 1 onion, minced
- 1 package firm tofu, pressed to remove excess water then crumbled
- 1-lb. spinach, washed and minced
- 2 tbsps. cold water
- 2 tbsps. nutritional yeast
- 2 tbsps. olive oil
- 4 ounces mushrooms, sliced
- A pinch of salt
- A sprig of fresh parsley, minced
- Salt and pepper

Directions:
1. Preheat the air fryer to 3750°F.
2. Create the pastry by sifting the flour and salt together. Add the coconut oil until the flour crumbles. Gradually add water to bind the dough or until you form a stiff dough. Wrap with a cling film and leave inside the fridge to rest for 30 minutes.
3. Warm olive oil in a skillet over medium heat and sauté the onion for 1 minute.
4. Add the mushroom and tofu. Add the spinach, dried dill, and nutritional yeast. Season with pepper and salt for added taste. Throw in the parsley last. Set aside.
5. Roll the dough on a floured surface until you form a slim dough. Place the dough in a greased baking dish that fits inside the air fryer.
6. Pour the tofu mixture and cook for 30 minutes or until the pastry is crisp.

336. Onion rings with spicy sauce
Servings: 2
Prep & Cooking Time: 30 Minutes
Ingredients:
- 1 onion, sliced into rings
- 1/3 cup all-purpose flour
- 1/2 cup oat milk
- 1 tsp. curry powder
- 1 tsp. cayenne pepper
- Salt & ground black pepper, at your convenience
- 1/2 cup cornmeal
- 4 tbsps. vegan parmesan
- 1/4 cup spicy ketchup

Directions:
1. Place the onion rings in the bowl with cold water; let them soak approximately 20 minutes; drain the onion rings and pat dry using a kitchen towel.
2. In a shallow bowl, mix the flour, milk, curry powder, cayenne pepper, salt, and black pepper. Mix to combine well.
3. Mix the cornmeal and vegan parmesan in another shallow bowl. Dip the onion rings in the flour/milk mixture; then, dredge in the cornmeal mixture.
4. Spritz the air fryer basket with cooking spray; arrange the breaded onion rings in the air fryer basket.
5. Set the air fryer at 400°F and let it cook for 4 to minutes, turning them over halfway through the cooking time. Serve with spicy ketchup. Bon appétit!

337. Air fried ravioli
Servings: 6
Prep & Cooking Time: 15 Minutes
Ingredients:
- 2 cups Italian breadcrumbs
- 1/4 cup Parmesan cheese
- 1 cup buttermilk
- 1 tsp. olive oil
- 1/4 tsp. garlic powder

Directions:
1. Turn on and set the air fryer to 390°F, and in a small dish, combine the breadcrumbs, Parmesan cheese, garlic powder, and olive oil. Dip the ravioli in the buttermilk and then coat them with the breadcrumb mixture.
2. Use parchment paper, arrange the ravioli on top of it. Drop into the air fryer and cook for 5 minutes.
3. Serve the air-fried ravioli with marinara jar sauce.

338. Rosemary vegetables
Servings: 4
Prep & Cooking Time: 45 Minutes
Ingredients:
- 3/4 lb. cauliflower, steamed
- 1 onion, sliced
- 2 garlic cloves, minced
- 1 bell pepper, emptied and sliced
- 2 eggs, beaten
- 1 cup kefir
- Ground black pepper and Kosher salt for added taste
- 1 tsp. cayenne pepper
- 1 tbsp. fresh rosemary

Directions:
1. Place your vegetables in the lightly greased casserole dish. In a mixing dish, thoroughly combine the remaining ingredients.
2. Spoon the cream mixture on top of the vegetables.
3. Bake in the preheated air fryer at 365°F for 20 minutes. Serve warm.

339. Baked zucchini garlic-sour cream
Servings: 5
Prep & Cooking Time: 20 Minutes
Ingredients:
- 1 (8 ounce) package cream cheese, softened
- 1 cup kefir
- 1 zucchini, large, divided lengthwise
- 1 tbsp. minced garlic
- 1/4 cup shredded Parmesan cheese
- Paprika to taste

Directions:
1. Spray the baking pan with cooking oil.
2. Place zucchini slices in a single layer in pan.
3. In a bowl whisk well, remaining ingredients except for paprika. Spread on top of zucchini slices. Sprinkle paprika.
4. Cover pan with foil.
5. For 10 minutes, cook on 390°F.
6. Remove foil and cook for 10 minutes at 330°F.
7. Serve and enjoy.

340. Tasty croissant rolls
Servings: 8
Prep & Cooking Time: 6 Minutes
Ingredients:
- 1 (8-ounces) can croissant rolls
- 4 tbsps. butter, melted

Directions:
1. Set the temperature of air fryer to 320°F. Grease an air fryer basket.
2. Arrange croissant rolls into the prepared air fryer basket.
3. Air fry for about 4 minutes.
4. Flip the side and air fry for 1-2 more minutes.
5. Remove from the air fryer and transfer onto a platter.
6. Sprinkle with melted butter and don't let it cool down before consuming.

341. Original indian bhaji
Servings: 4
Prep & Cooking Time: 40 Minutes
Ingredients:
- 2 eggs, beaten
- 1/2 cup almond meal
- 1/2 cup coconut flour
- 1/2 tsp. baking powder
- 1 tsp. curry paste
- 1 tsp. cumin seed
- 1 tsp. minced fresh ginger root
- Salt & black pepper, at your convenience
- 2 red onions, minced
- 1 Indian green chili, pureed
- Non-stick cooking spray

Directions:
1. Whisk the eggs, almond meal, coconut flour and baking powder in a mixing dish to make a thick batter; add in the cold water if needed.
2. Add in curry paste, cumin seeds, ginger root, salt, and black pepper.
3. Now, add onions and chili pepper; mix until every element is well incorporated.
4. Shape the balls and slightly press them to make the patties. Shower the patties with cooking oil on every sides.
5. Place a sheet of aluminum foil in the air fryer food basket. Place the fritters on foil.
6. Then, air-fry them at 380°F for 15 minutes; flip them over, press the power button and cook for another 20 minutes. Serve right away!

342. Yummy crispy tofu
Servings: 4
Prep & Cooking Time: 55 Minutes
Ingredients:
- 16 ounces firm tofu, pressed and cubed
- 1 tbsp. vegan oyster sauce
- 1 tbsp. tamari sauce
- 1 tsp. cider vinegar
- 1 tsp. pure maple syrup
- 1 tsp. sriracha
- 1/2 tsp. shallot powder
- 1/2 tsp. porcini powder
- 1 tsp. garlic powder
- 1 tbsp. sesame oil
- 5 tbsps. cornstarch

Directions:
1. Toss the tofu with the oyster sauce, tamari sauce, vinegar, maple syrup, sriracha, shallot powder, porcini powder, garlic powder, and sesame oil. Let it marinate for 30 minutes.
2. Toss the marinated tofu with the cornstarch.
3. Cook at 370°F for 10 minutes; turn them over and cook for 12 minutes more. Bon appétit!

343. Sandwich tomato with feta and pesto
Servings: 2
Prep & Cooking Time: 60 Minutes
Ingredients:
- 1 (4- oz) block°Feta cheese
- 1 small red onion, slimly sliced
- 1 clove garlic
- Salt to taste
- 2 tsps. + 1/4 cup olive oil
- 1 1/2 tbsps. toasted pine nuts
- 1/4 cup minced parsley
- 1/4 cup shredded Parmesan cheese
- 1/4 cup minced basil

Directions:
1. Add basil, pine nuts, garlic and salt to a food processor. Process while adding the 1/4 cup of olive oil slowly. Once the oil is finished, pour the basil pesto into a bowl and refrigerate for 30 minutes.
2. Prepare the air fryer and set it to 390°F. Slice the feta cheese and tomato into 1/2 inch circular slices. Use a kitchen towel to pat the tomatoes dry. Remove the pesto from the fridge and use a tbsp. to spread some pesto on each slice of tomato. Top with a slice of feta cheese. Add the onion and remaining olive oil in a bowl and toss. Spoon on top of feta cheese.
3. Place the tomato in the fryer's basket and cook for 12 minutes. Remove to a platter, sprinkle lightly with salt and top with the remaining pesto. Serve with a side of rice or lean meat.

344. Ribs and pineapple appetizer
Servings: 4
Prep & Cooking Time: 30 Minutes
Ingredients:
- 7 ounces salad dressing
- 5 ounces can pineapple juice
- 2 cups water
- Garlic salt
- Salt and black pepper

Directions:
1. Add salt and pepper to the ribs before placing to the saucepan.
2. Pour water and cook the ribs for 10 minutes on high heat. Drain the ribs and arrange them in the fryer; sprinkle with garlic salt. Cook for 15 minutes at 390°F.
3. Prepare the sauce by combining the salad dressing and the pineapple juice.
4. Serve the ribs drizzled with the sauce.

345. Healthy radish salad
Servings: 4
Prep & Cooking Time: 30 Minutes

Ingredients:
- 1 1/2 lbs. radishes, trimmed and halved
- 1/2 lb. fresh mozzarella, sliced
- 6 cups fresh salad greens
- 3 tbsps. olive oil
- 1 tsp. honey
- 1 tbsp. balsamic vinegar
- Black pepper and salt for a more flavorful taste

Directions:
1. Set the air fryer to 350°F before greasing the fryer basket with oil.
2. Mix the radishes, salt, black pepper, and olive oil in a bowl and toss to coat well.
3. Set the radishes in the air fryer basket and cook for about 5 minutes, flipping twice in between.
4. Serve the radishes in a serving bowl and keep aside to cool.
5. Add mozzarella cheese and greens and mix well.
6. Mix honey, oil, vinegar, salt, and black pepper in a bowl and pour over the salad.
7. Toss to coat well and serve immediately.

346. Special cauliflower and tofu
Servings: 2
Prep & Cooking Time: 15 Minutes
Ingredients:
- 1/2 (14-ounces) block firm tofu, pressed and cubed
- 1/2 small head cauliflower, cut into florets
- 1 tbsp. canola oil
- 1 tbsp. nutritional yeast*
- 1/4 tsp. dried parsley
- 1 tsp. ground turmeric
- 1/4 tsp. paprika
- Salt & ground black pepper, as required

Directions:
1. In a bowl, mix well tofu, cauliflower and the remaining ingredients.
2. Set the temperature of air fryer to 390°F. Grease an air fryer basket.
3. Arrange tofu mixture into the prepared air fryer basket in a single layer.
4. Air fry for about 12-15 minutes, shaking once halfway through.
5. Remove from air fryer and transfer the tofu onto serving plates.
6. Serve hot.

347. Original baked banana recipe
Servings: 2
Prep & Cooking Time: 20 Minutes
Ingredients:
- 2 just-ripe bananas
- 2 tsps. lime juice
- 2 tbsps. honey
- 1/4 tsp. shredded nutmeg
- 1/2 tsp. ground cinnamon
- A pinch of salt

Directions:
1. Toss the banana with all ingredients until well coated. Transfer your bananas to the parchment-lined cooking basket.
2. Bake in the preheated air fryer at 370°F for 1 minute, turning them over halfway through the cooking time. Enjoy!

348. Flavored garlic-wine vegetables
Servings: 4
Prep & Cooking Time: 15 Minutes
Ingredients:
- 1/4 cup minced fresh basil
- 1 1/2 tbsp. honey1 tsp. Dijon mustard
- 1 cup baby Portobello mushrooms, minced
- 1 package frozen minced vegetables
- 1 red onion, sliced
- 1/3 cup olive oil
- 3 tbsps. red wine vinegar
- 4 cloves of garlic, minced
- Pepper and salt for added taste

Directions:
1. Preheat the air fryer to 330°F.
2. Position the grill pan accessory inside the air fryer.
3. In a Ziploc bag, combine the vegetables and season with salt, pepper, and garlic. Give a good shake to combine every element.
4. Dump on to the grill pan and cook for 15 minutes.
5. Meanwhile, combine the rest of the Ingredients on bowl and season with more salt and pepper.
6. Drizzle the grilled vegetables with the sauce.

349. Battered crisped onion rings with almond flour
Servings: 3
Prep & Cooking Time: 15 Minutes
Ingredients:
- 1/2 cup almond flour
- 3/4 cup coconut milk
- 1 big white onion, sliced into rings
- 1 egg, beaten
- 1 tbsp. baking powder
- 1 tbsp. smoked paprika
- Salt and pepper for added taste

Directions:
1. Prepare air fryer by preheating it for five minutes.
2. In a mixing bowl, mix the almond flour, baking powder, smoked paprika, salt and pepper.
3. In another bowl, combine the eggs and coconut milk.
4. Soak the onion slices into the egg mixture.
5. Dredge the onion slices in the almond flour mixture.
6. Drop into the air fryer basket.
7. Close and cook for 15 minutes at 3250°F.
8. Halfway through the cooking time, shake the fryer basket for even cooking.

350. Aloo tikka indian-style
Servings: 2
Prep & Cooking Time: 20 Minutes
Ingredients:
- 3 tbsps. lemon juice
- 1 bell pepper, sliced
- Pepper and salt for added taste
- 2 onions, minced
- 4 tbsps. fennel
- 5 tbsps., flour
- 2 tbsps. ginger-garlic paste
- 1/2 cup mint leaves, minced
- 2 cups cilantro, minced

Directions:
1. First, heat up your air fryer to 360°F.
2. In a bowl, mix cilantro, mint, fennel, ginger garlic paste, flour, salt and lemon juice. Blend to form a paste and add potato.
3. In another bowl, mix bell pepper, onions and fennel mixture. Blend the mixture until you have a thick mix.
4. Divide the mixture evenly into 5-6 cakes. Add the prepared potato cakes into your air fryer and cook for 15 minutes.
5. Serve with ketchup.

351. Cheesiest mushroom pizza
Servings: 2
Prep & Cooking Time: 6 Minutes
Ingredients:
- 2 Portobello mushroom caps, stemmed
- 2 tbsps. olive oil
- and tsp. dried Italian seasonings
- Salt, to taste
- 2 tbsps. canned tomatoes, minced
- 2 tbsps. mozzarella cheese, shredded
- 2 Kalamata olives, pitted and sliced
- 2 tbsps. Parmesan cheese, shredded freshly
- 1 tsp. dried peppers, crushed

Directions:
1. Set the temperature of air fryer to 320°F. Grease an air fryer basket.
2. With a spoon, scoop out the center of each mushroom cap.
3. Coat each mushroom cap with oil from both sides.
4. Sprinkle the inside of caps with Italian seasoning and salt.
5. Place the canned tomato evenly over both caps, followed by the olives and mozzarella cheese.
6. Arrange mushroom caps into the prepared air fryer basket.
7. Air fry for about 5-6 minutes.
8. Remove from air fryer and immediately sprinkle with the Parmesan cheese and dried peppers.
9. Serve.

352. Cheesy stuffed mushrooms
Servings: 4
Prep & Cooking Time: 8 Minutes
Ingredients:
- 4 fresh large mushrooms, stemmed and gills removed
- 4 ounces cream cheese, softened
- 1/4 cup Parmesan cheese, shredded
- 2 tbsps. white cheddar cheese, shredded
- 2 tbsps. sharp cheddar cheese, shredded
- 1 tsp. Worcestershire sauce
- 2 garlic cloves, minced
- Salt & ground black pepper, as required

Directions:
1. In a bowl, mix well cream cheese, Parmesan, cheddar cheeses, Worcestershire sauce, garlic, salt, and black pepper.
2. Set the temperature of air fryer to 370°F. Grease an air fryer basket.
3. Stuff each mushroom with the cheese mixture.
4. Arrange stuffed mushrooms into the prepared air fryer basket.
5. Air fry for about 8 minutes.
6. Remove from air fryer and transfer the mushrooms onto a platter.
7. Set aside to cool slightly.
8. Serve warm.

353. Eggplants stuffed with salsa
Servings: 2
Prep & Cooking Time: 25 Minutes
Ingredients:
- 1 large eggplant
- 8 cherry tomatoes, quartered
- 1/2 tbsps. fresh parsley
- 2 tsps. olive oil, divided
- 2 tsps. fresh lemon juice, divided
- 2 tbsps. tomato salsa
- Salt & black pepper, as required

Directions:
1. Set the air fryer to 390°F before greasing the fryer basket with oil.
2. Set the eggplant into the air fryer basket and cook for about 15 minutes.
3. Cut the eggplant in half lengthwise and drizzle evenly with one tsp. of oil.
4. Set the air fryer to 355°F and arrange the eggplant into the air fryer basket, cut-side up.
5. Cook for another 10 minutes and dish out in a bowl.
6. Scoop out the flesh from the eggplant and transfer into a bowl.
7. Stir in the tomatoes, salsa, parsley, salt, black pepper, remaining oil, and lemon juice.
8. Squeeze lemon juice on the eggplant halves and stuff with the salsa mixture to serve.

354. Cheesy balls made of mushroom and cauliflower
Servings: 4
Prep & Cooking Time: 50 Minutes
Ingredients:
- 3 tbsps. olive oil
- 1 small red onion, minced
- 3 cloves garlic, minced
- 3 cups cauliflower, minced
- 2 tbsps. chicken stock
- 1 cup breadcrumbs
- 1 cup Grana Padano cheese
- 1/4 cup coconut oil
- 2 sprigs minced fresh thyme
- Salt & pepper to taste

Directions:
1. Place a skillet over medium heat. Add olive oil, once heated, sauté garlic and onion, until translucent. Add the mushrooms and cauliflower and stir-fry for 5 minutes. Pour in the stock, thyme, and simmer until the cauliflower has absorbed the stock. Add Grana Padano cheese, pepper, and salt. Allow the mixture cool and make bite-size balls of the mixture. Refrigerate for 30 minutes to harden.
2. Preheat the air fryer to 350°F.
3. In a mixing bowl, add the breadcrumbs and coconut oil and mix well. Remove the mushroom balls from the refrigerator, stir the breadcrumb mixture again, and roll the balls in the breadcrumb mixture.
4. Place the balls in the air fryer's basket without overcrowding, and cook for 15 minutes, tossing every 5 minutes for an even cook.
5. Serve with sautéed zoodles and tomato sauce.

355. Yummy potato pancakes
Servings: 4
Prep & Cooking Time: 15 Minutes
Ingredients:
- 1 medium onion, minced
- 1 beaten egg
- 1/4 cup milk
- 2 tbsps. unsalted butter
- 1/2 tsp. garlic powder
- 1/4 tsp. salt
- 1/4 tsp. pepper
- 3 tbsps. flour
- Black pepper to taste

Directions:
1. First, heat up your air fryer to 390°F, and in a medium bowl, mix egg, potatoes, onion, milk, butter, pepper, garlic powder and salt; add flour and form batter.
2. Forms cakes about 1/4 cup of batter.

3. Place the cakes in the fryer's cooking basket and cook for 10 minutes.
4. Serve and enjoy!

356. Eggplants stuffed with more veggies
Servings: 5
Prep & Cooking Time: 14 Minutes
Ingredients:
- 10 small eggplants, halved lengthwise
- 1 onion, minced
- 1 tomato, minced
- 1/4 cup minced cottage cheese
- 1/2 seeded and minced red bell pepper
- 1 tbsp. fresh lime juice
- 1 tbsp. vegetable oil
- 1/2 tsp. garlic, minced
- Salt & ground black pepper, as required
- 2 tbsps. tomato paste

Directions:
1. Set the air fryer to 320°F before greasing the fryer basket with oil.
2. Cut a slice from one side of each eggplant lengthwise and scoop out the flesh in a bowl.
3. Drizzle the eggplants with lime juice and arrange in the air fryer basket.
4. Cook for about minutes and remove from the Air fryer.
5. Warm vegetable oil in a skillet over medium heat and add garlic and onion.
6. Sauté for about 2 minutes and stir in the eggplant flesh, tomato, salt, and black pepper.
7. Sauté for about 3 minutes and add cheese, bell pepper, tomato paste, and cilantro.
8. Cook for about 1 minute and stuff this mixture into the eggplants.
9. Close each eggplant with its cut part and set the air fryer to 360°F.
10. Arrange in the air fryer basket and cook for about 5 minutes.
11. Serve in a serving plate and serve warm.

357. Easy to prepare garden fresh veggie
Servings: 4
Prep & Cooking Time: 15 Minutes
Ingredients:
- 2 green bell peppers seeded and minced
- 1 eggplant, minced
- 1 zucchini, minced
- 3 tomatoes, minced
- 2 small onions, minced
- 2 garlic cloves, minced
- 2 tbsp. herbs de Provence
- 1 tbsp. olive oil
- 1 tbsp. balsamic vinegar
- Black pepper and salt for a more flavorful taste

Directions:
1. Set the air fryer to 355°F before greasing the fryer basket with oil.
2. Mix all the ingredients in a bowl and toss to coat well.
3. Transfer into the air fryer basket and cook for about 15 minutes.
4. Keep in the air fryer for about 5 minutes and dish out to serve warm.

358. Pecorino parmesan and crispy green beans
Servings: 3
Prep & Cooking Time: 15 Minutes
Ingredients:
- 2 tbsps. buttermilk
- 1 egg
- 4 tbsps. almond meal
- 4 tbsps. golden flaxseed meal
- 4 tbsps. Parmesan cheese, finely shredded
- Coarse salt and crushed black pepper for added taste
- 1 tsp. smoked paprika
- 6 ounces green beans, trimmed

Directions:
1. In an empty dish, combine the egg and buttermilk.
2. In a separate bowl, combine the almond meal, golden flaxseed meal, Parmesan cheese, salt, black pepper, and paprika.
3. Dip the green beans in the egg mixture, then, in the cheese mixture. Place the green beans in the lightly greased cooking basket.
4. Cook in the preheated air fryer at 390°F for minutes. Give the basket a shake cook for another 3 minutes.
5. Taste, adjust the seasonings, and serve with the dipping sauce if desired. Bon appétit!

359. Tofu bbq with green beans
Servings: 3
Prep & Cooking Time: 1 Hour
Ingredients:
- 12 ounces super firm tofu, pressed and cubed
- 1/4 cup ketchup
- 1 tbsp. white vinegar
- 1 tbsp. maple sugar
- 1 tbsp. mustard
- 1/4 tsp. ground black pepper
- 1/2 tsp. sea salt
- 1/4 tsp. smoked paprika
- 1/2 tsp. freshly shredded ginger
- 2 cloves garlic, minced
- 2 tbsps. olive oil
- 1 lb. green beans

Directions:
1. Toss the tofu with the ketchup, white vinegar, maple sugar, mustard, black pepper, sea salt, paprika, ginger, garlic, and olive oil. Let it marinate for 30 minutes.
2. Set the temperature to 360°F and leave it for 10 minutes; turn them over and cook for 1 minutes more. Reserve.
3. Place the green beans in the lightly greased air fryer basket. Set it to 400°F then roast it for 5 minutes. Bon appétit!

360. Monterey jack cheese on veggie fingers with
Servings: 4
Prep & Cooking Time: 20 Minutes
Ingredients:
- 10 ounces cauliflower
- 1/4 cup almond flour
- 1 1/2 tsps. soy sauce
- Salt & freshly ground black pepper for better taste
- 1 tsp. cayenne pepper
- 1 cup parmesan cheese, shredded
- 3/4 tsp. dried dill weed
- 1 tbsp. olive oil

Directions:
1. Firstly, pulse the cauliflower in your food processor; transfer them to a bowl and add 4 cup almond flour, soy sauce, salt, black pepper, and cayenne pepper.
2. Roll the mixture into veggie fingers shape. In another bowl, place shredded parmesan cheese and dried dill.
3. Now, coat the veggie fingers with the parmesan mixture, covering completely. Drizzle veggie fingers with olive oil.
4. Air-fry for 15 minutes at 350°F; turn them over once or twice during the cooking time. Eat with your favorite sauce. Enjoy!

361. Stuffed peppers greek-style
Servings: 4
Prep & Cooking Time: 20 Minutes
Ingredients:
- 2 cups cooked rice
- 1 onion, minced
- 1 tbsp. Greek seasoning
- 1/4 cup sliced kalamata olives
- 3/4 cup tomato sauce
- Black pepper and salt for a more flavorful taste
- 1 cup feta cheese, crumbled
- 2 tbsps. fresh dill, minced

Directions:
1. Preheat the air fryer to 360°F. Microwave the bell peppers for 2 minutes until soft.
2. In a mixing bowl, combine rice, onion, Greek seasoning, feta cheese, olives, tomato sauce, salt, and pepper.
3. Divide and arrange the mixture of bell peppers and place it on the greased baking dish. Drop into the air fryer and cook for 15 minutes.
4. When ready, remove to a serving plate, scatter with dill and serve.

362. Cauliflower tater tots twice-fried
Servings: 12
Prep & Cooking Time: 16 Minutes
Ingredients:
- 1/2 cup bread crumbs
- 1/2 cup nutritional yeast
- 1 flax egg (1 tbsp. 3 tbsp. desiccated coconuts
- 1 onion, minced
- 1 tsp. chives, minced
- 1 tsp. garlic, minced
- 1 tsp. oregano, minced
- 1 tsp. parsley, minced
- 1-lb. cauliflower, steamed and minced
- 3 tbsps. oats
- Flaxseed meal + 3 tbsp. water)
- Salt and pepper to taste

Directions:
1. Preheat the air fryer to 390°F.
2. Place the steamed cauliflower on a paper towel and ring to remove excess water.
3. Place in a mixing bowl and add the rest of the ingredients except the bread crumbs.
4. Mix until well combined and form balls using your hands.
5. Roll the tater tots on the bread crumbs and place in the air fryer basket.
6. Cook for minutes. Once done, increase the cooking temperature to 400°F and cook for another 10 minutes.

363. Potato chips with velveeta dip mediterranean-style
Servings: 4
Prep & Cooking Time: 1 Hour
Ingredients:
- 1 large potato, cut into an inch thick slices
- 1 tbsp. olive oil
- Sea salt, to taste
- 1/2 tsp. dried peppers, crushed
- 1 tsp. fresh rosemary
- 1/2 tsp. fresh sage
- 1/2 tsp. fresh basil

Dipping Sauce:
- 1/3 cup raw cashews
- 1 tbsp. tahini
- 1 1/2 tbsps. olive oil
- 1/4 cup raw almonds
- 1/4 tsp. prepared yellow mustard

Directions:
1. Keep the potatoes submerged in water for at least half an hour. Leave the potatoes to dry or use kitchen towel to dry it.
2. Toss with olive oil and seasonings.
3. Drop into the lightly greased cooking basket and cook at 370°F for 30 minutes. Work in batches.
4. Meanwhile, puree the sauce ingredients in your food processor until smooth. Serve the potato chips with the Velveeta sauce for dipping. Bon appétit!

364. Kid-loved vegetable fritters
Servings: 4
Prep & Cooking Time: 20 Minutes
Ingredients:
- 1 lb. broccoli florets
- 1 tbsp. ground flaxseeds
- 1 yellow onion, finely minced
- 1 sweet pepper, seeded and minced
- 1 carrot, shredded
- 2 garlic cloves, pressed
- 1 tsp. turmeric powder
- 1/2 tsp. ground cumin
- 1/2 cup all-purpose flour
- 1/2 cup cornmeal
- Ground black pepper and salt for a more flavorful taste
- 2 tbsps. olive oil

Directions:
1. Blanch the broccoli in salted boiling water until al dente, about 3 to 4 minutes. Drain well and transfer to a mixing bowl; mash the broccoli florets with the remaining ingredients.
2. Make patties out of the mixture. Put it in the air fryer basket with oil.
3. Set it to 400°F and cook it for 6 minutes, turning them over halfway through the cooking time; work in batches.
4. Serve warm with your favorite Vegenaise. Enjoy!

365. Crispy 'n savory spring rolls
Servings: 4
Prep & Cooking Time: 15 Minutes
Ingredients:
- 1/2 tsp. ginger, finely minced
- 1 celery stalk, minced
- 1 cup shiitake mushroom, sliced slimly
- 1 medium carrot, shredded
- 1 tbsp. soy sauce
- 1 tsp. maple sugar
- 1 tsp. corn starch + 2 tbsps. water
- 1 tsp. nutritional yeast
- 8 spring roll wrappers

Directions:
1. In a mixing bowl, mix together the celery stalk, carrots, ginger, maple sugar, soy sauce and nutritional yeast.
2. Get a tbsp. of the vegetable mixture and place at the center of the spring roll wrappers.
3. Roll and seal the edges of the wrapper with the cornstarch mixture.
4. Cook in a preheated air fryer to 400°F for 15 minutes or until the spring roll wrapper is crisp.

366. Healthy fritters made from ricotta cauliflower

Servings: 4
Prep & Cooking Time: 30 Minutes
Ingredients:
- 1 tbsp. olive oil
- 1/2 lb. cauliflower
- 1/2 cup Ricotta cheese
- 1/4 cup ground flaxseed meal
- 1/4 cup almond flour
- 1/2 tsp. baking powder
- 1/2 onion, minced
- 1 garlic clove, minced
- Sea salt & ground black pepper, at your convenience
- 1 cup parmesan cheese, shredded

Directions:
1. First, heat up your air fryer to 400°F.
2. Drizzle the olive oil all over the cauliflower. Place the cauliflower in the air fryer basket and cook approximately 15 minutes, shaking the basket periodically.
3. Then, mash the cauliflower and combine with the other ingredients. Form the mixture into patties.
4. Bake in the preheated air fryer at 380°F for 1 minute, flipping them halfway through the cooking time to ensure even cooking. Bon appétit!

367. Battered wings with almond flour

Servings: 4
Prep & Cooking Time: 25 Minutes
Ingredients:
- 1/4 cup butter, melted
- 3/4 cup almond flour
- 16 pieces chicken wings
- 2 tbsps. stevia powder
- 4 tbsps. minced garlic
- Salt & pepper to taste

Directions:
1. Prepare air fryer by preheating it for five minutes.
2. In a mixing bowl, combine the chicken wings, almond flour, stevia powder, and garlic. Season with salt and pepper for added taste.
3. Drop into the air fryer basket and cook for 25 minutes at 400°F.
4. Halfway through the cooking time, make sure that you give the fryer basket a shake.
5. Once ready, serve it with melted butter on top or around it.

368. Crispiest tofu with paprika

Servings: 4
Prep & Cooking Time: 15 Minutes
Ingredients:
- 1/4 cup cornstarch
- 1 piece tofu, dried and press to reduce water content, cut small cubes
- 1 tbsp. smoked paprika
- Pepper and salt for added taste

Directions:
1. Add aluminum foil to the air fryer basket, arrange it in line and put some oil.
2. Preheat the air fryer to 370°F.
3. Mix all ingredients in a bowl. Toss to combine.
4. Drop into the air fryer basket and cook for 12 minutes.

369. Delicious corn cakes

Servings: 8
Prep & Cooking Time: 25 Minutes
Ingredients:
- 2 eggs, lightly beaten
- 1/3 cup finely minced green onions
- 1/4 cup roughly minced parsley
- 1 cup flour
- 1/2 tsp. baking powder
- Salt & black pepper

Directions:
1. In a mixing bowl, add corn, eggs, parsley and green onions, and season with salt and pepper; mix well to combine.
2. Combine flour and baking powder and mix thoroughly.
3. Line the air fryer's basket with baking paper and spoon batter dollops, making sure they are separated by at least an inch. Cook for 5 minutes at 400°F, turning once halfway through.
4. Serve with sour cream.

370. Fresh green beans

Servings: 4
Prep & Cooking Time: 12 Minutes
Ingredients:
- 1 lb. green beans, washed and trimmed
- 1 tsp. butter, melted
- 1 tbsp. fresh lemon juice
- 1/4 tsp. garlic powder
- Salt and freshly ground pepper for better taste

Directions:
1. Preheat the air fryer to 400°F before greasing the fryer basket with oil.
2. Put all the ingredients in a large bowl and transfer into the air fryer basket.
3. Cook for about 8 minutes and dish out in a bowl to serve warm.

371. Easy and healthy chips

Servings: 2
Prep & Cooking Time: 10 Minutes
Ingredients:
- 1 bunch kale
- 1 tsp. garlic powder
- 2 tbsps. almond flour
- 2 tbsps. olive oil
- Salt & pepper to taste

Directions:
1. Prepare air fryer by preheating it for five minutes.
2. Combine all ingredients in a mixing dish, take the kale leaves and dip it into the mixture.
3. Place in a fryer basket and cook for 10 minutes until crispy.

372. Roasted barbecue almonds

Servings: 6
Prep & Cooking Time: 20 Minutes
Ingredients:
- 1 1/2 cups raw almonds
- Sea salt & ground black pepper for added taste
- 1/4 tsp. garlic powder
- 1/4 tsp. mustard powder
- 1/2 tsp. cumin powder
- 1/4 tsp. smoked paprika
- 1 tbsp. olive oil

Directions:
1. Toss all ingredients in a mixing bowl.
2. Line the air fryer basket with baking parchment. Put out the coated almonds in the basket in a single layer.
3. Roast at 300°F for 6 to 8 minutes, shaking the basket once or twice. Work in batches. Enjoy!

373. Sautéed spinach and bacon
Servings: 2
Prep & Cooking Time: 9 Minutes
Ingredients:
- 3 meatless bacon slices, minced
- 1 onion, minced
- 4-ounce fresh spinach
- 2 tbsps. olive oil
- 1 garlic clove, minced

Directions:
1. Preheat the air fryer to 340°F and grease an air fryer pan.
2. Put olive oil and garlic in the air fryer pan and place in the air fryer basket.
3. Cook for about 2 minutes and add bacon and onions.
4. Cook for about 3 minutes and stir in the spinach.
5. Cook for about 4 minutes and dish out in a bowl to serve.

374. Italian-styled easy pasta chips
Servings: 2
Prep & Cooking Time: 10 Minutes
Ingredients:
- 1/2 tsp. salt
- 1 1/2 tsps. Italian seasoning blend
- 1 tbsp. nutritional yeast
- 1 tbsp. olive oil
- 2 cups whole wheat bowtie pasta

Directions:
1. Place the baking dish accessory in the air fryer.
2. Give a good stir.
3. Put in in the air fryer and let it cook for 10 minutes. Set temperature to 00°F.

375. Oatmeal with berries, baked
Servings: 4
Prep & Cooking Time: 30 Minutes
Ingredients:
- 1 cup fresh strawberries
- 1/2 cup dried cranberries
- 1 1/2 cups rolled oats
- 1/2 tsp. baking powder
- A pinch of sea salt
- A pinch of shredded nutmeg
- 1/2 tsp. ground cinnamon
- 1/2 tsp. vanilla extract
- 4 tbsps. agave syrup
- 1 1/2 cups almond milk

Directions:
1. Spritz a baking pan with cooking spray.
2. Place 1/cup of strawberries on the bottom of the pan; place the cranberries over that.
3. In a mixing bowl, thoroughly combine the rolled oats, baking powder, salt, nutmeg, cinnamon, vanilla, agave syrup, and milk.
4. Pour the oatmeal mixtures over the fruits; allow it to soak for 15 minutes. Top with the remaining fruits.
5. Bake at 330°F for 12 minutes. Serve warm or at room temperature. Enjoy!

376. Awesome roasted mushrooms
Servings: 4
Prep & Cooking Time: 32 Minutes
Ingredients:
- 1 tbsp. butter
- 2 lbs. mushrooms, quartered
- 2 tbsps. white vermouth
- 2 tsps. herbs de Provence
- 1/2 tsp. garlic powder

Directions:
1. Preheat the air fryer to 320°F and grease an air fryer pan.
2. Mix herbs de Provence, garlic powder and butter in the air fryer pan and transfer into the air fryer basket.
3. Cook for about 2 minutes and stir in the mushrooms.
4. Cook for about 25 minutes and add white vermouth.
5. Cook for more minutes and dish out to serve warm.

377. Amazing air-fried falafel
Servings: 6
Prep & Cooking Time: 25 Minutes
Ingredients:
- 1/2 cup chickpea flour
- 1 cup fresh parsley, minced
- Juice of 1 lemon
- 4 garlic cloves, minced
- 1 onion, minced
- 2 tsps. ground cumin
- 2 tsps. ground coriander
- 1 tsp. chili powder
- Salt & black pepper

Directions:
1. In a blender, add chickpeas, flour, parsley, lemon juice, garlic, onion, cumin, coriander, chili, turmeric, salt and pepper, and blend until well-combined but not too battery; there should be some lumps.
2. Shape the mixture into balls and press them with hands, making sure they are still round.
3. Line it in the air fryer basket then spray some oil; work in batches if needed. Cook at 360°F for 14 minutes, turning once halfway through. They should be crunchy and golden.

378. Tomatoes and cauli rice salad
Servings: 4
Prep & Cooking Time: 25 Minutes
Ingredients:
- 1 lb. cauliflower rice
- 2 garlic cloves, pressed
- 1/3 cup coriander, minced
- 1 cup shallots, minced
- 4 ounces tomato, sliced
- A cup of arugula lettuce, divide into pieces
- 2 tbsps. white wine vinegar
- Sea salt & ground black pepper for added taste

Directions:
1. Put cauliflower rice into the air fryer basket. Cook at 375°F for 10 minutes. Shake the basket and continue to cook for 10 minutes more.
2. Transfer the prepared couscous to a nice salad bowl. Put in the remaining ingredients; Mix well to combine and enjoy!
3. Bon appétit!

379. Pizza with mushroom 'n bell pepper
Servings: 10
Prep & Cooking Time: 10 Minutes
Ingredients:
- 1/4 red bell pepper, minced
- 1 cup oyster mushrooms, minced
- 1 shallot, minced
- 1 vegan pizza dough
- 2 tbsps. parsley
- Salt and pepper

Directions:
1. Preheat the air fryer to 400°F.
2. Slice the pizza dough into squares. Set aside.
3. In a mixing bowl, mix together the oyster mushroom, shallot, bell pepper and parsley.
4. Season with salt and pepper for added taste.
5. Place the topping on top of the pizza squares.
6. Place inside the air fryer and cook for 10 minutes.

380. Sweet hasselback potatoes
Servings: 4
Prep & Cooking Time: 30 Minutes
Ingredients:
- 4 potatoes
- 2 tbsps. Parmesan cheese, shredded
- 1 tbsp. fresh chives, minced
- 2 tbsps. olive oil

Directions:
1. Set the air fryer to 355°F before greasing the fryer basket with oil.
2. Cut slits along each potato about 1/4-inch apart with a sharp knife, making sure slices should stay connected at the bottom.
3. Coat the potatoes with olive oil and arrange into the air fryer basket.
4. Cook for about 30 minutes and dish out in a platter.
5. Top with chives and Parmesan cheese to serve.

381. Healthy granola with nuts and raisins
Servings: 8
Prep & Cooking Time: 40 Minutes
Ingredients:
- 2 cups rolled oats
- 1/2 cup walnuts, minced
- 1/3 cup almonds minced
- 1/4 cup raisins
- 1/4 cup whole wheat pastry flour
- 1/2 tsp. cinnamon
- 1/4 tsp. nutmeg, preferably freshly shredded
- 1/2 tsp. salt
- 1/3 cup coconut oil, melted
- 1/3 cup agave nectar
- 1/2 tsp. coconut extract
- 1/2 tsp. vanilla extract

Directions:
1. Thoroughly combine all ingredients. Into the air fryer trays, spread the mixture. Spritz with cooking spray.
2. Bake at 370°F for 25 minutes; rotate the trays and bake 10 to 15 minutes more.
3. This granola can be stored in an airtight container for up to 2 weeks. Enjoy!

382. Vegetable kabobs with peanut sauce dip
Servings: 4
Prep & Cooking Time: 30 Minutes
Ingredients:
- 8 whole baby potatoes, diced into 1-inch pieces
- 2 bell peppers, diced into 1-inch pieces
- 8 pearl onions, halved
- 8 small button mushrooms, cleaned
- 2 tbsps. extra-virgin olive oil
- Ground black pepper and sea salt for better taste
- 1 tsp. dried peppers, crushed
- 1 tsp. dried rosemary, crushed
- 1/3 tsp. granulated garlic

Peanut Sauce:
- 2 tbsps. peanut butter
- 1 tbsp. balsamic vinegar
- 1 tbsp. soy sauce
- 1/2 tsp. garlic salt

Directions:
1. Soak the wooden skewers in water for 10 minutes.
2. Thread the vegetables on skewers; drizzle the olive oil all over the vegetable skewers; sprinkle with spices.
3. Set the air fryer at 400°F and cook it for a minute.
4. Meanwhile, in a small dish, whisk the peanut butter with the balsamic vinegar, soy sauce, and garlic salt. Serve your kabobs with the peanut sauce on the side. Enjoy!

383. Tasty stuffed tomato
Servings: 4
Prep & Cooking Time: 22 Minutes
Ingredients:
- 4 tomatoes, tops and seeds removed
- 1 carrot, peeled and minced
- 1 onion, minced
- 1 cup frozen peas, thawed
- 2 cups cold cooked rice
- 1 tsp. olive oil
- 1 garlic clove, minced
- 1 tbsp. soy sauce

Directions:
1. Preheat the air fryer to 355°F before greasing the fryer basket with oil.
2. Warm olive oil in a skillet on low heat and add carrots, onions, peas and garlic.
3. Cook for about 2 minutes and stir in the soy sauce and rice.
4. Stuff the rice mixture into the tomatoes and arrange into the air fryer basket.
5. Cook for about 20 minutes and dish out to serve warm.

384. Tasty paneer cutlet
Servings: 1
Prep & Cooking Time: 15 Minutes
Ingredients:
- 1 cup shredded cheese
- 1/2 tsp. chai masala
- 1 tsp. butter
- 1/2 tsp. garlic powder
- 1 small onion, finely minced
- 1/2 tsp. oregano
- 1/2 tsp. salt

Directions:
1. Set the air fryer first to 350°F, then add some oil.
2. Mix all ingredients in a bowl, until well incorporated.
3. Make cutlets out of the mixture and place them on the greased baking dish.
4. Place the baking dish in the air fryer and cook the cutlets for 10 minutes, until crispy.

385. Grilled mushrooms
Servings: 4
Prep & Cooking Time: 20 Minutes
Ingredients:
- 2 garlic cloves, finely minced
- 3 tbsps. minced fresh thyme and/or rosemary leaves
- Large pinch of crushed dried peppers
- 1 tsp. kosher salt, plus more to taste
- 6 chives, cut crosswise into 2-inch pieces

- 1-pint cherry tomatoes
- 1-pint cremini or button (other small mushrooms is also acceptable)
- 1/2 cup extra-virgin olive oil
- 1/2 tsp. of black pepper
- 1/4 cup Sherry vinegar or wine (red)

Directions:
1. In Ziploc bag, mix well black pepper, salt, dried peppers, thyme, vinegar, oil, and garlic. Add mushrooms, tomatoes, and chives. Mix well and let it marinate for half an hour.
2. Thread mushrooms, tomatoes, and chives. Reserve sauce for basting. Place on skewer rack in air fryer. If needed, cook in batches.
3. For 10 minutes, cook on 390°F. Halfway through cooking time, turnover skewers and baste with reserved sauce.
4. Serve and enjoy.

386. Balsamic vinaigrette added to radish and mozzarella salad

Servings: 4
Prep & Cooking Time: 30 Minutes
Ingredients:
- 1 1/2 lbs. radishes, trimmed and halved
- 1/2 lb. fresh mozzarella, sliced
- Freshly ground black pepper and salt for a more flavorful taste
- 3 tbsps. olive oil
- 1 tsp. honey
- 1 tbsp. balsamic vinegar

Directions:
1. Preheat the air fryer to 350°F before greasing the fryer basket with oil.
2. Mix radishes, salt, black pepper and tbsp. of olive oil in a bowl and toss to coat well.
3. Set the radishes in the air fryer basket and cook for about 5 minutes, flipping twice in between.
4. Serve in a bowl and top with the remaining ingredients to serve.

387. Roasted rosemary

Servings: 2
Prep & Cooking Time: 30 Minutes
Ingredients:
- 1 tbsp dried rosemary
- Cooking spray
- Salt to season

Directions:
1. Place the butternut squash on a cutting board and peel it; cut it in half and remove the seeds. Cut the pulp into wedges and season with salt.
2. Preheat air fryer to 350°F, spray the squash with cooking spray and sprinkle with rosemary.
3. Grease the fryer's basket with cooking spray and place the wedges inside.
4. Slide the fryer basket back in and cook for 20 minutes, flipping once halfway through.
5. Serve with maple syrup and goat cheese.

388. Famous buffalo cauliflower

Servings: 4
Prep & Cooking Time: 30 Minutes
Ingredients:
- 1 lb. cauliflower florets
- 1/2 cup all-purpose flour
- 1/2 cup rice flour
- Sea salt & grounded black pepper for added taste
- 1/2 tsp. cayenne pepper
- 1/2 tsp. chili powder
- 1/2 cup soy milk
- 2 tbsps. soy sauce
- 2 tbsps. tahini
- 1 tsp. vegetable oil
- 2 cloves garlic, minced
- 6 scotch bonnet peppers, seeded and sliced
- 1 small-sized onion, minced
- 1/2 tsp. salt
- 1 cup water
- 2 tbsps. white vinegar
- 1 tbsp. granulated sugar

Directions:
1. Rinse the cauliflower florets and pat them dry. Cover the air fryer basket with cooking oil.
2. In a mixing bowl, combine the all-purpose flour and rice flour; add the salt, black pepper, cayenne pepper, and chili powder.
3. Add the soy milk, soy sauce, and tahini. Stir until a thick batter is formed. Cover cauliflower florets with batter by dipping it.
4. Cook the cauliflower at 370°F for 16 minutes, turning them over halfway through the cooking time.
5. Set it to medium-high heat then heat the vegetable oil; then, sauté the garlic, peppers, and onion for a minute or so or until they are fragrant.
6. Add the remaining ingredients and bring the mixture to a rapid boil. Continue cooking in a reduced heat to allow it to simmer, leave it for 10 minutes or until the sauce is reduced to half.
7. Pour the sauce over the prepared cauliflower and serve. Bon appétit!

389. Veggies and healthy air fried halloumi

Servings: 2
Prep & Cooking Time: 15 Minutes
Ingredients:
- 2 zucchinis, cut into even chunks
- 1 large carrot, cut into chunks
- Peel an eggplant (large), divided into chunks
- 2 tsp. olive oil
- 1 tsp. dried mixed herbs
- Salt & black pepper

Directions:
1. In a mixing bowl, add halloumi, zucchini, carrot, eggplant, olive oil, herbs, salt and pepper. Sprinkle with oil, salt and pepper.
2. Arrange halloumi and veggies on the air fryer basket and drizzle with olive oil.
3. Cook for 10 minutes at 340°F, shaking once. Sprinkle with mixed herbs to serve.

390. Fried okra with a twist

Servings: 4
Prep & Cooking Time: 15 Minutes
Ingredients:
- 3 tbsps. sour cream
- 2 tbsps. flour
- 2 tbsps. semolina
- 1/2 tsp. red chili powder
- Salt & black pepper for added taste

Directions:
1. Preheat the air fryer to 400°F. Add oil to the air fryer basket using a cooking spray.
2. In a mixing bowl, pour sour cream. In a separate bowl, mix flour, semolina, chili powder, salt, and pepper.
3. Dip okra in the sour cream, followed by a dip in the flour mixture.

4. Place in your air fryer's basket and cook for 5 minutes. Slide out the basket and shake.
5. Cook for 5 more minutes. Allow to cool and serve.

391. Green beans and okra
Servings: 2
Prep & Cooking Time: 20 Minutes
Ingredients:
- 1/2 (10-ounces) bag frozen cut okra
- 1/2 (10-ounces) bag frozen cut green beans
- 1/4 cup nutritional yeast
- 3 tbsps. balsamic vinegar
- Black pepper and salt for a more flavorful taste

Directions:
1. Preheat the air fryer to 400°F before greasing the fryer basket with oil.
2. Mix the okra, green beans, nutritional yeast, vinegar, salt, and black pepper in a bowl and toss to coat well.
3. Set the okra mixture into the air fryer basket and cook for about 20 minutes.
4. Serve in a serving dish and serve warm.

392. Spicy avocado spread on a corn on the cob
Servings: 4
Prep & Cooking Time: 15 Minutes
Ingredients:
- 4 corn cobs
- 1 avocado, pitted, peeled and mashed
- 1 clove garlic, pressed
- 1 tbsp. fresh lime juice
- 1 tbsp. soy sauce
- 4 tsps. nutritional yeast
- 1/2 tsp. cayenne pepper
- 1/2 tsp. dried dill
- Ground black pepper and sea salt for added taste
- 1 tsp. hot sauce
- 2 heaping tbsps. fresh cilantro leaves, roughly minced

Directions:
1. Shower the corn with cooking spray. Cook at 390°F for 6 minutes, turning them over halfway through the cooking time.
2. In the meantime, mix the avocado, lime juice, soy sauce, nutritional yeast, cayenne pepper, dill, salt, black pepper, and hot sauce.
3. Spread the avocado mixture all over the corn on the cob. Garnish with fresh cilantro leaves. Bon appétit!

393. Falafel with tzatziki mediterranean-style
Servings: 4
Prep & Cooking Time: 30 Minutes
Ingredients:
For the Falafel:
- 2 cups cauliflower, shredded
- 1/4 tsp. baking powder
- 1/3 cup warm water
- 1/2 tsp. salt
- 1 tbsp. coriander leaves, finely minced
- 2 tbsps. fresh lemon juice

Vegan Tzatziki:
- 1 cup plain Greek yogurt
- 2 tbsps. lime juice, freshly squeezed
- 1/4 tsp. of black pepper to taste
- 1/3 tsp. sea salt flakes
- 2 tbsps. extra-virgin olive oil
- 2 tbsps. minced fresh dill
- 1 clove garlic, pressed
- 1/2 fresh cucumber, shredded

Directions:
1. In a mixing bowl, thoroughly stir all the ingredients for the falafel. Allow the mixture to stay for several minutes.
2. Now, air-fry at 390°F for 15 minutes; make sure to flip them over halfway through the cooking time.
3. To make Greek tzatziki, blend all ingredients in your food processor.
4. Serve warm falafel with chilled tzatziki. Enjoy!

394. Roasted cashew nuts, spiced
Servings: 4
Prep & Cooking Time: 20 Minutes
Ingredients:
- 1 cup whole cashews
- 1 tsp. olive oil
- Salt & ground black pepper, for added taste
- 1/2 tsp. smoked paprika
- 1/2 tsp. ancho chili powder

Directions:
1. Toss all ingredients in the mixing bowl.
2. Line the air fryer basket with baking parchment. Put out the spiced cashews in the basket in a single layer form.
3. Roast at 370°F for 6 to 8 minutes, shaking the basket once or twice. Work in batches. Enjoy!

395. Flavourful celery croquettes dipped in chive mayo
Servings: 4
Prep & Cooking Time: 15 Minutes
Ingredients:
- 2 medium-sized celery stalks, trimmed and shredded
- 1/2 cup of leek, finely minced
- 1 tbsp. garlic paste
- 1/4 tsp. freshly grounded black pepper
- 1 tsp. fine sea salt
- 1 tbsp. fresh dill, finely minced
- 1 egg, lightly whisked
- 1/4 cup almond flour
- 1/2 cup parmesan cheese, freshly shredded
- 1/4 tsp. baking powder
- 2 tbsps. fresh chives, minced
- 4 tbsps. mayonnaise

Directions:
1. Place the celery on a paper towel and squeeze them to remove excess liquid.
2. Combine the vegetables with the other ingredients, except the chives and mayo. Shape the balls using 1 tbsp. of the vegetable mixture.
3. Then, gently flatten each ball with your palm or a wide spatula. Shower the croquettes with oil that is a non - stick.
4. Air-fry the vegetable croquettes in a single layer for 6 minutes at 360°F.
5. Meanwhile, mix fresh chives and mayonnaise. Serve warm croquettes with chive mayo. Bon appétit!

396. Spicy wasabi popcorn
Servings: 2
Prep & Cooking Time: 30 Minutes
Ingredients:
- 1/2 tsp. brown sugar
- 1 tsp. salt

- 1/2 tsp. wasabi powder, sifted
- 1 tbsp. avocado oil
- 3 tbsps. popcorn kernels

Directions:
1. Add the dried corn kernels to the air fryer basket; toss with the remaining ingredients.
2. Cook at 395°F for 15 minutes, shaking the basket every 5 minutes. Work in two batches.
3. Taste, adjust the seasonings and serve immediately. Bon appétit!

397. Mushrooms stuffed with bacon and cheese
Servings: 4
Prep & Cooking Time: 20 Minutes
Ingredients:
- 1 clove garlic, minced
- Salt and pepper for added taste
- 4 slices bacon, minced
- 1/4 cup shredded Cheddar cheese
- 1 tbsp. olive oil
- 1 tbsp. minced parsley

Directions:
1. Preheat air fryer to 390°F. In a mixing bowl, add oil, bacon, cheddar cheese, parsley, salt, pepper, and garlic. Mix well with a spoon.
2. Cut the stalks of the mushroom off and fill each cup with the bacon mixture.
3. Press the bacon mixture into the caps.
4. Place the stuffed mushrooms in the fryer's basket and cook at 390°F for 8 minutes.
5. Once golden and crispy, plate them and serve with a green salad.

398. Marinara baked cheesy eggplant
Servings: 3
Prep & Cooking Time: 45 Minutes
Ingredients:
- 1 clove garlic, sliced
- 1 large eggplants
- 1 tbsp. olive oil
- 1 tbsp. olive oil
- 1/2 pinch salt, or as needed
- 1/4 cup and 2 tbsp. dry bread crumbs
- 1/4 cup and 2 tbsp. ricotta cheese
- 1/4 cup shredded Parmesan cheese
- 1/4 cup shredded Parmesan cheese
- 1/4 cup water (add more) as needed
- 1/4 tsp. red pepper flakes
- 1-1/2 cups prepared marinara sauce
- 1-1/2 tsps. olive oil
- 2 tbsp. shredded pepper jack cheese
- Salt & freshly ground black pepper for better taste

Directions:
1. Cut eggplant crosswise in 5 pieces. Peel and chop two pieces into 1/2-inch cubes.
2. With 1 tbsp. olive oil, lightly grease your air fryer's pan. For 5 minutes, heat oil at 390°F. Add half eggplant strips and cook for minutes per side. Transfer to a plate.
3. Add 1 1/2 tsp. olive oil and add garlic. Cook for a minute. Add minced eggplants. Season with pepper flakes and salt. Cook for 4 minutes. Lower heat to 300°F and continue cooking eggplants until soft, around 8 minutes more.
4. Stir in water and marinara sauce. Cook for 7 minutes until heated through. Stirring every now and then. Transfer to a bowl.
5. In a bowl, whisk well pepper, salt, pepper jack cheese, Parmesan cheese, and ricotta. Spread cheese evenly on top of the eggplant strips. Fold it into half.
6. Lay folded eggplant in baking pan. Pour marinara sauce on top.
7. In a small bowl whisk well olive oil, and bread crumbs. Sprinkle all over sauce.
8. Cook for 15 minutes at 390°F until tops are lightly browned.
9. Serve and enjoy.

399. Delicious vegetable salsa wraps
Servings: 4
Prep & Cooking Time: 15 Minutes
Ingredients:
- 1 cup red onion, sliced
- 1 zucchini, minced
- 1 poblano pepper, emptied and finely minced
- 1 head lettuce
- 1/2 cup salsa (homemade or store-bought)
- 8 ounces mozzarella cheese

Directions:
1. First, heat up your air fryer to 390°F.
2. Cook red onion, zucchini, and poblano pepper until they are tender and fragrant or about 7 minutes.
3. Divide the sautéed mixture among lettuce leaves; spoon the salsa over the top. Finish off with mozzarella cheese. Wrap lettuce leaves around the filling. Enjoy!

400. Polenta fries
Servings: 4
Prep & Cooking Time: 80 Minutes
Ingredients:
- 2 cups milk
- 1 cup instant polenta
- Salt & black pepper
- Cooking spray
- Fresh thyme, minced

Directions:
1. Line a tray with paper. Combine milk and water in a dish and let it simmer. Keep whisking as you pour in the polenta. Continue to whisk until polenta thickens and bubbles; season to taste.
2. Add polenta into the lined tray and spread out. Refrigerate for 45 minutes.
3. Slice the cold, set polenta into batons and spray with oil.
4. Arrange polenta chips into the air fryer basket and cook for 16 minutes at 380°F, turning once halfway through.
5. Make sure the fries are golden and crispy.

401. Fast and easy to prep crispy cheese lings
Servings: 4
Prep & Cooking Time: 15 Minutes
Ingredients:
- 1 cup all-purpose flour
- 1 tbsp. butter
- 1 tbsp. baking powder
- 1/4 tsp. chili powder
- 1/4 tsp. salt, to taste
- 2 tbsps. water

Directions:
1. In an empty bowl, combine the flour and baking powder.
2. Add in chili powder, salt, butter, cheese and 2 tbsp of water. Make a stiff dough.
3. Knead the dough for a while and sprinkle about a tbsp. of flour on the table.
4. Roll the dough and make a 1/2-inch thickness roll with a rolling pin.

5. Cut into shapes.
6. Cook for 6 minutes at 370°F.

402. Healthy roast peppers and potatoes
Servings: 4
Prep & Cooking Time: 30 Minutes
Ingredients:
- 1 lb. russet potatoes, divide into an inch
- 2 bell peppers, seeded and divided into 1-inch pieces
- 2 tbsps. olive oil
- 1 tsp. dried rosemary
- 1 tsp. dried basil
- 1 tsp. dried oregano
- 1 tsp. dried parsley flakes
- Ground black pepper and sea salt for added taste
- 1/2 tsp. smoked paprika

Directions:
1. Toss all ingredients in the air fryer basket.
2. Roast at 400°F for 15 minutes, tossing the basket occasionally. Work in batches.
3. Serve warm and enjoy!

403. Cheesiest mushrooms
Servings: 4
Prep & Cooking Time: 8 Minutes
Ingredients:
- 6-ounce button mushrooms, stemmed
- 2 tbsps. mozzarella cheese, shredded
- 2 tbsps. cheddar cheese, shredded
- 2 tbsps. olive oil
- 2 tbsps. Italian dried mixed herbs
- Freshly ground black pepper and salt for a more flavorful taste
- 1 tsp. dried dill

Directions:
1. Set the air fryer to 355°F before greasing the fryer basket with oil.
2. Mix mushrooms, Italian dried mixed herbs, oil, salt and black pepper in a bowl and toss to coat well.
3. Set the mushrooms in the air fryer basket and top with mozzarella cheese and cheddar cheese.
4. Cook for about 8 minutes and sprinkle with dried dill to serve.

404. Great garlicy mushroom
Servings: 3
Prep & Cooking Time: 25 Minutes
Ingredients:
- 2 tbsps. vermouth
- 1/2 tsp. garlic powder
- 1 tbsp. olive oil
- 2 tsp. herbs
- 1 tbsp. duck fat

Directions:
1. First, heat up your air fryer to 350°F, add duck fat, garlic powder and herbs in a blender, and process.
2. Pour the mixture over the mushrooms and cover with vermouth.
3. Place the mushrooms in the cooking basket and cook for 15 minutes.
4. Top with more vermouth and cook for 5 more minutes.

405. Tasteful mushrooms with cheddar cheese
Servings: 4
Prep & Cooking Time: 22 Minutes
Ingredients:
- 2 cups mushrooms, sliced
- 2 tbsps. cheddar cheese, shredded
- 1 tbsp. fresh chives, minced
- 2 tbsps. olive oil

Directions:
1. Preheat the air fryer to 355°F before greasing the fryer basket with oil.
2. Coat the mushrooms with olive oil and arrange into the air fryer basket.
3. Cook for about 20 minutes and dish out in a platter.
4. Top with chives and cheddar cheese and cook for 2 more minutes.
5. Serve warm.

406. Spiced veggie burger with chives 'n thyme
Servings: 8
Prep & Cooking Time: 15 Minutes
Ingredients:
- 1/4 cup desiccated coconut
- 1/2 cup oats
- 1/2 lb. cauliflower, steamed and diced
- 1 cup bread crumbs
- 1 flax egg (1 flaxseed egg + 3 tbsp. water)
- 1 tsps. mustard powder
- 2 tsps. chives
- 2 tsps. coconut oil melted
- 2 tsps. garlic, minced
- 2 tsps. parsley
- 2 tsps. thyme
- 3 tbsps. plain flour
- Salt and pepper for added taste

Directions:
1. Preheat the air fryer to 390°F.
2. Place the cauliflower in a tea towel and ring out excess water. Place in a mixing bowl and add all ingredients except the bread crumbs. Mix well until well combined.
3. Form 8 burger patties with the mixture using your hands.
4. Roll the patties in bread crumbs and place in the air fryer basket. Put a space in between rolls.
5. Cook for 10 to 1minutes or until the patties are crisp.

407. Mediterranean skewers made of vegetable
Servings: 4
Prep & Cooking Time: 30 Minutes
Ingredients:
- Zucchini, medium size, two pieces, divided into pieces, 1-inch long
- red bell peppers, two pieces, divided into pieces, 1-inch long
- 1 red bell pepper, divided into 1-inch pieces
- Red onion, divided into pieces, 1-inch long
- 2 tbsps. olive oil
- Sea salt for better taste
- 1/2 tsp. black pepper, preferably freshly grounded
- 1/2 tsp. dried peppers

Directions:
1. Soak the wooden skewers in water for 20 minutes.
2. Thread the vegetables on skewers; drizzle olive oil all over the vegetable skewers; sprinkle with spices.
3. Place it in the air fryer.
4. Set it to 400°F and set timer to a minute. Serve warm and enjoy!

408. Sweet potato balls thailand-style
Servings: 4
Prep & Cooking Time: 50 Minutes
Ingredients:
- 1 lb. sweet potatoes
- 1 cup brown sugar

- 1 tbsp. orange juice
- 2 tsps. orange zest
- 1/2 tsp. ground cinnamon
- 1/4 tsp. ground cloves
- 1/2 cup almond meal
- 1 tsp. baking powder
- 1 cup shredded coconut

Directions:
1. Bake the sweet potatoes at 380°F for 30 to 35 minutes until tender; peel and mash them.
2. Add the brown sugar, orange juice, orange zest, ground cinnamon, cloves, almond meal, and baking powder; mix to combine well.
3. Roll the balls in the shredded coconut.
4. Bake in the preheated air fryer at 360°F for 15 minutes or until thoroughly cooked and crispy.
5. Apply the same steps on the remaining ingredients. Enjoy!

409. Delicious asparagus and mushroom fritters

Servings: 4
Prep & Cooking Time: 15 Minutes
Ingredients:
- 1 lb. asparagus spears
- 1 tbsp. canola oil
- 1 tsp. paprika
- Sea Salt & freshly ground black pepper for better taste
- 1 tsp. garlic powder
- 3 tbsps. chives, minced
- 1 cup button mushrooms, minced
- 1/2 cup fresh breadcrumbs
- 1 tbsp. flaxseeds, soaked in 2 tbsps. of water
- 4 tbsps. sun-dried tomato hummus

Directions:
1. Place the asparagus spears in the lightly greased cooking basket. Toss and add the asparagus with the canola oil, paprika, black pepper and salt.
2. For 5 minutes, cook it in an air fryer at 400°F. Chop the asparagus spears and add the garlic powder, chives, mushrooms, breadcrumbs, and vegan "egg."
3. Mix until every element is well incorporated and form the asparagus mixture into patties.
4. Cook in the preheated air fryer at 360°F for 5 minutes, flipping halfway through the cooking time. Serve with sun-dried tomato hummus. Bon appétit!

Chapter 3
Meat Recipes

410. Kansas city's baby back rib recipe
Servings: 2
Prep & Cooking Time: 50 Minutes
Ingredients:
- 1/4 cup white wine vinegar
- 1/4 cup molasses
- 1/4 tsp. cayenne pepper
- 1 cup ketchup
- 1 tbsp. brown sugar
- 1 tbsp. liquid smoke seasoning, hickory
- 1 tbsp. Worcestershire sauce
- 1 tsp. dry mustard
- 1-lb. pork ribs, small
- 2 cloves of garlic
- Salt & pepper to taste

Directions:
1. Mix all ingredients in a Ziploc bag and refrigerate for at least 2 hours.
2. Preheat the air fryer to 390°F°Fahrenheit.
3. Insert the air fryer's grill pan attachment.
4. Grill meat for 25 minutes per batch.
5. Flip the meat halfway through the cooking time.
6. Pour the marinade in a saucepan and allow to simmer until the sauce thickens.
7. Pour glaze over the meat before serving.

411. Top round roast with herbs blend
Servings: 10
Prep & Cooking Time: 1 Hour
Ingredients:
- 1 tsp. dry mustard
- 2 tsps. dried rosemary
- 3 tbsps. olive oil
- 4 lbs. beef top round roast
- 4 tsps. dried oregano
- 4 tsps. dried oregano
- Salt & pepper to taste

Directions:
1. Preheat the air fryer for 5 minutes.
2. Place all ingredients in a baking dish that will fit in the air fryer.
3. Place the dish in the air fryer and cook for 1 hour at 50°F.

412. Pork in garlic sauce
Servings: 4
Prep & Cooking Time: 25 Minutes
Ingredients:
- 1 lb. pork tenderloin, sliced
- A pinch of salt and black pepper
- 4 tbsps. butter, melted
- 2 tsps. garlic, minced
- 1 tsp. sweet paprika

Directions:
1. Heat up a pan that fits the air fryer with the butter over medium heat, add all the ingredients except the pork medallions, whisk well and simmer for 4-5 minutes.
2. Add the pork, toss, put the pan in your air fryer and cook at 380°F for 20 minutes.
3. Divide between plates and serve with a side salad.

413. Peanut sauce with flavorsome pork chops
Servings: 4
Prep & Cooking Time: 12 Minutes
Ingredients:
- 1 lb. pork chops, cubed into 1-inch size
- 1 shallot, minced finely
- 3/4 cup ground peanuts
- 3/4 cup coconut milk

For Pork:
- 1 tsp. fresh ginger, minced
- 1 garlic clove, minced
- 2 tbsps. soy sauce
- 1 tbsp. olive oil
- 1 tsp. hot pepper sauce

For Peanut Sauce:
- 1 tbsp. olive oil
- 1 garlic clove, minced
- 1 tsp. ground coriander
- 1 tbsp. olive oil
- 1 tsp. hot pepper sauce

Directions:
1. Preheat the air fryer to 390°F and grease an air fryer basket.
2. For Pork:
3. Mix all the ingredients in a bowl and keep aside for about 5 minutes.
4. Set the chops in the air fryer basket and cook for about 12 minutes, flipping once in between.
5. For Peanut Sauce:
6. In a medium pan, heat the olive oil, then add the shallot and garlic.
7. Sauté for about 3 minutes and stir in coriander.
8. Sauté for about 1 minute and add rest of the ingredients.
9. Cook for about 5 minutes and transfer over the pork chops to serve.

414. Loin chops with za'atar lamb
Servings: 4
Prep & Cooking Time: 30 Minutes
Ingredients:
- 8 (3 1/2-ounces) bone-in lamb loin chops, trimmed
- 3 garlic cloves, crushed
- 1 tbsp. fresh lemon juice
- 1 tsp. olive oil
- 1 tbsp. Za'ataro
- Salt & black pepper, to taste

Directions:
1. Preheat the air fryer to 400°F and grease an air fryer basket.
2. Mix the garlic, lemon juice, oil, Za'atar, salt, and black pepper in a large bowl.
3. Coat the chops generously with the herb mixture and arrange the chops in the air fryer basket.
4. Cook for about 15 minutes, flipping twice in between and dish out the lamb chops to serve warm.

415. Short loin steak with grilled mayo
Servings: 4
Prep & Cooking Time: 20 Minutes
Ingredients:
- 1 cup mayonnaise
- 1 tbsp. fresh rosemary, finely minced
- 2 tbsp. Worcestershire sauce
- Sea salt, to taste
- 1/2 tsp. ground black pepper
- 1 tsp. smoked paprika
- 1 tsp. garlic, minced
- 1 1/2 lbs. short loin steak

Directions:
1. Combine the mayonnaise, rosemary, Worcestershire sauce, salt, pepper, paprika, and garlic; mix to combine well.
2. Now, brush the mayonnaise mixture over both sides of the steak. Lower the steak onto the grill pan.
3. Grill in the preheated air fryer at 400°F for 8 minutes. Turn the steaks over and grill an additional 7 minutes.
4. Check for doneness with a meat thermometer.
5. Serve warm and enjoy!

416. Potatoes with pork loin
Servings: 5
Prep & Cooking Time: 25 Minutes
Ingredients:
- 2 lbs. pork loin
- 1 tsp. fresh parsley, minced
- 3 large red potatoes, minced
- 3 tbsps. olive oil, divided
- Salt & ground black pepper, as required
- 1/2 tsp. garlic powder
- 1/2 tsp. red pepper flakes, crushed

Directions:
1. Preheat the air fryer to 325°F and grease an air fryer pan.
2. Rub the pork loin evenly with 1 1/2 tbsp. olive oil, parsley, salt, and black pepper.
3. Mix the potatoes, remaining oil, garlic powder, red pepper flakes, salt, and black pepper in a bowl.
4. Set the pork loin in the air fryer basket and place potato pieces on sides.
5. Cook for about 2 minutes and dish out in a bowl.
6. Cut into desired size slices and serve alongside potatoes.

417. Dill pickles with smoked brisket
Servings: 6
Prep & Cooking Time: 1 Hour
Ingredients:
- 1/4 tsp. liquid smoke
- 1 cup dill pickles
- 3 lbs. flat-cut brisket
- Salt & pepper to taste

Directions:
1. Preheat the air fryer to 390°F
2. Season the brisket with liquid smoke, salt, and pepper, and put it on the grill pan; let it cook in the fryer for about 30 minutes per batch.
3. Flip the meat halfway through cooking time for even grilling.
4. Serve with dill pickles.

418. Worcester meatloaf
Servings: 4
Prep & Cooking Time: 35 Minutes
Ingredients:
- 1 large onion, peeled and diced
- 2 kgs. minced beef
- 1 tsp. Worcester sauce
- 3 tbsps. tomato ketchup
- 1 tbsp. basil
- 1 tbsp. oregano
- 1 tbsp. mixed herbs
- 1 tbsp. friendly bread crumbs
- Salt-and-pepper to taste

Directions:
1. In a wide bowl, mix the mince with the herbs, Worcester sauce, onion and tomato ketchup, incorporating every component well.
2. Pour in the breadcrumbs and give it another stir.
3. Transfer the mixture to a small dish and cook for 25 minutes in the air fryer at 380°F.

419. Wine marinated flank steak
Servings: 4
Prep & Cooking Time: 20 Minutes + Marinating Time
Ingredients:
- 1 1/2 lbs. flank steak
- 1/2 cup red wine
- 1/2 cup white wine vinegar
- 2 tbsps. soy sauce
- Salt, to taste
- 1/2 tsp. ground black pepper
- 1/2 tsp. red pepper flakes, crushed
- 1/2 tsp. dried basil
- 1 tsp. thyme

Directions:
1. Preheat the air fryer to 400°F
2. Add all ingredients to a large ceramic bowl. Cover and let it marinate for 3 hours in your refrigerator.
3. Transfer the flank steak to the air fryer basket that is previously greased with nonstick cooking oil.
4. Cook in the preheated air fryer for 12 minutes, flipping over halfway through the cooking time. Bon appétit!

420. Pork roulade
Servings: 2
Prep & Cooking Time: 17 Minutes
Ingredients:
- 2 pork chops
- 1 tsp. German mustard
- 1 tsp. chives, diced
- 1 pickled cucumber, diced
- 1 tsp. almond butter
- 1/2 tsp. ground black pepper
- 1 tsp. olive oil

Directions:
1. Beat the pork chops gently with the help of the kitchen hammer and place them on the chopping board overlap.
2. Then rub the meat with ground black pepper and German mustard.

3. Top it with chives, diced pickled cucumber, and almond butter.
4. Roll the meat into the roulade and secure it with the kitchen thread.
5. Then sprinkle the roulade with olive oil.
6. Preheat the air fryer to 390°F.
7. Put the roulade in the air fryer and cook it for 15 minutes.
8. Slice the cooked roulade.

421. Old-fashioned beef burgers
Servings: 6
Prep & Cooking Time: 12 Minutes
Ingredients:
- 2 lbs. ground beef
- 12 cheddar cheese slices
- 12 dinner rolls
- 6 tbsps. tomato ketchup
- Salt & black pepper, to taste

Directions:
1. Preheat the air fryer to 390°F and grease an air fryer basket.
2. Mix the beef, salt and black pepper in a bowl.
3. Make small equal-sized patties from the beef mixture and arrange half of patties in the air fryer basket.
4. Cook for about 12 minutes and top each patty with 1 cheese slice.
5. Set the patties between rolls and drizzle with ketchup.
6. Repeat with the remaining batch and dish out to serve warm.

422. Beef jerky
Servings: 3
Prep & Cooking Time: 1 Hour
Ingredients:
- 1 lb. bottom round beef, cut into slim strips
- 1/2 cup dark brown sugar
- 1/2 cup soy sauce
- 1/4 cup Worcestershire sauce
- 1 tbsp. chili pepper sauce
- 1 tbsp. hickory liquid smoke
- 1 tsp. garlic powder
- 1 tsp. onion powder
- 1 tsp. cayenne pepper
- 1/2 tsp. smoked paprika
- 1/2 tsp. ground black pepper

Directions:
1. Preheat the air fryer to 0°F and grease an air fryer basket.
2. Mix the brown sugar, all sauces, liquid smoke, and spices in a bowl.
3. Coat the beef strips with this marinade generously and marinate overnight.
4. Put half of the beef strips in the air fryer basket in a single layer.
5. Arrange a cooking rack over the strips and layer with the remaining beef strips.
6. Cook for about 1 hour and dish out to serve.

423. Vegetables with hearty beef cubes
Servings: 4
Prep & Cooking Time: 20 Minutes + Marinating Time
Ingredients:
- 1 lb. top round steak, cubed
- 2 tbsp. olive oil
- 1 tbsp. white wine vinegar
- 1 tsp. fine sea salt
- 1/2 tsp. ground black pepper
- 1 tsp. shallot powder
- 3/4 tsp. smoked cayenne pepper
- 1/2 tsp. garlic powder
- 1/4 tsp. ground cumin
- 1/4 lb. broccoli, cut into florets
- 1/4 lb. mushrooms, sliced
- 1 tsp. dried basil
- 1 tsp. celery seeds

Directions:
1. Firstly, marinate the beef with olive oil, vinegar, salt, black pepper, shallot powder, cayenne pepper, garlic powder, and cumin. Toss to coat well and let it stay for at least 3 hours.
2. Place the beef cubes in the air fryer cooking basket; cook at 365°F for 1 minute. Pause the machine, check the cubes for doneness and transfer them to a bowl.
3. Now, clean the cooking basket and place the vegetables in; sprinkle them with basil and celery seeds; toss to coat.
4. Set the temperature to 400°F; cook for 5 to 6 minutes or until the vegetables are warmed through.
5. Serve with reserved meat cubes. Bon appétit!

424. Buttered strip loin steak
Servings: 2
Prep & Cooking Time: 12 Minutes
Ingredients:
- 2 (7-ounces) striploin steak
- 1 1/2 tbsps. butter, softened
- Salt & black pepper, to taste

Directions:
1. Preheat the air fryer to 390°F and grease an air fryer basket.
2. Rub the steak generously with salt and black pepper and coat with butter.
3. Transfer the steak in the air fryer basket and cook for about 12 minutes, flipping once in between.
4. Serve the steak and cut into desired size slices to serve.

425. Buttered garlic-celery with roast beef
Servings: 8
Prep & Cooking Time: 1 Hour
Ingredients:
- 1 bulb of garlic, peeled and crushed
- 1 tbsp. butter
- 2 medium onions, minced
- 2 lbs. topside of beef
- 2 sticks of celery, sliced
- 3 tbsp. olive oil
- 1/4 cup fresh herbs of your choice
- Salt & pepper to taste

Directions:
1. Preheat the air fryer for 5 minutes.
2. Place all the ingredients in your air fryer pan and give a good stir.
3. Place the dish in the air fryer and bake for 1 hour at 300°F.

426. Smoked pork
Servings: 5
Prep & Cooking Time: 45 Minutes
Ingredients:
- 1-lb. pork shoulder
- 1 tbsp. liquid smoke
- 1 tbsp. olive oil
- 1 tsp. salt

Directions:
1. Preheat the air fryer to 390°F
2. Mix up liquid smoke, salt, and olive oil in the shallow bowl. Then carefully brush the pork shoulder with the liquid smoke mixture from each side.

3. Make the small cuts in the meat. Put the pork shoulder in the air fryer basket and cook the meat for 10 minutes.
4. Flip the meat on another side and cook it for 10 minutes more. Let the cooked pork shoulder rest for 10-15 minutes.
5. Shred it with the help of 2 forks.

427. Cumin lamb kebabs, sichuan and caraway
Servings: 3
Prep & Cooking Time: 1 Hour
Ingredients:
- 1 1/2 lbs. lamb shoulder, bones removed and cut into pieces
- 1 tbsp. Sichuan peppercorns
- 1 tsp. sugar
- 2 tbsps. cumin seeds, toasted
- 2 tsps. caraway seeds, toasted
- 2 tsps. crushed red pepper flakes
- Salt & pepper to taste

Directions:
1. Place all ingredients in a bowl and allow the meat to marinate for 30 minutes in the fridge.
2. Preheat the air fryer to 390°F.
3. Place the meat in the grill for 15 minutes per batch.
4. Flip the meat every 8 minutes for even grilling.

428. Hot paprika beef
Servings: 4
Prep & Cooking Time: 20 Minutes
Ingredients:
- 1 tbsp. hot paprika
- 4 beef steaks
- Salt & black pepper to the taste
- 1 tbsp. butter, melted

Directions:
1. In a bowl, mix the beef with the rest of the ingredients, rub well, transfer the steaks to your air fryer's basket and cook at 390°F for 15 minutes on each side.
2. Divide the steaks between plates and serve with a side salad.

429. Beef schnitzel
Servings: 1
Prep & Cooking Time: 30 Minutes
Ingredients:
- 1 egg
- 1 slim beef schnitzel
- 3 tbsps. friendly bread crumbs
- 2 tbsps. olive oil
- 1 parsley, roughly minced
- 1/2 lemon, cut in wedges

Directions:
1. Pre-heat your air fryer to the 360°F.
2. In a mixing bowl combine the olive oil with the bread crumbs and olive oil to form a loose, crumbly mixture.
3. Beat the egg with a whisk.
4. Coat the schnitzel first in the egg and then in the bread crumbs, ensuring to cover it fully.
5. Place the schnitzel in the air fryer and cook for 12 – 14 minutes. Garnish the schnitzel with the lemon wedges and parsley before serving.

430. Hot bacon bites
Servings: 4
Prep & Cooking Time: 10 Minutes
Ingredients:
- 4 bacon strips, cut into small pieces
- 1/2 cup pork rinds, crushed
- 1/4 cup hot sauce

Directions:
1. Add bacon pieces in a bowl.
2. Add hot sauce and toss well.
3. Add crushed pork rinds and toss until bacon pieces are well coated.
4. Transfer bacon pieces in air fryer basket and cook at 350°F for 10 minutes.
5. Serve and enjoy.

431. Sage sauce recipe with pork chops
Servings: 2
Prep & Cooking Time: 25 Minutes
Ingredients:
- 2 pork chops
- 1 shallot; sliced
- 1 handful sage; minced
- Salt & black pepper to the taste
- 1 tbsp. olive oil
- 2 tbsps. butter
- 1 tsp. lemon juice

Directions:
1. Use salt and pepper to season the pork with salt and pepper to taste, and brush with the oil, put in your air fryer and cook at 370 °F, for 20 minutes; flipping them halfway.
2. Meanwhile heat up a pan with the butter over medium heat, add shallot; stir and cook for minutes.
3. Add sage and lemon juice; stir well, cook for a few more minutes and take off heat.
4. Divide pork chops on plates, drizzle sage sauce all over and serve.

432. Meatball sausage
Servings: 4
Prep & Cooking Time: 15 Minutes
Ingredients:
- 3 1/2-ounce sausage, casing removed
- 1/2 medium onion, minced finely
- 1 tsp. fresh sage, minced finely
- 3 tbsps. Italian breadcrumbs
- 1/2 tsp. garlic, minced
- Salt & black pepper, to taste

Directions:
1. Preheat the air fryer to 355°F and grease the air fryer basket.
2. Combine all the ingredients in a bowl until well mixed.
3. Shape the mixture into equal-sized balls and arrange the balls in the air fryer basket.
4. Cook for about 15 minutes and dish out to serve warm.

433. Ghee mushroom with beef mix
Servings: 4
Prep & Cooking Time: 25 Minutes
Ingredients:
- 4 beef steaks
- 1 tbsp. olive oil
- A pinch of salt and black pepper
- 2 tbsps. ghee, melted
- 2 garlic cloves, minced
- 5 cups wild mushrooms, sliced
- 1 tbsp. parsley, minced

Directions:
1. Heat up a pan that fits the air fryer with the oil over medium-high heat, add the steaks and sear them for 2 minutes on each side.

2. Add the rest of the ingredients, toss, transfer the pan to your air fryer and cook at 380°F for 20 minutes.
3. Divide between plates and serve.

434. Cumin-paprika with beef brisket
Servings: 12
Prep & Cooking Time: 2 Hours
Ingredients:
- 1/4 tsp. cayenne pepper
- 1 1/2 tbsps. paprika
- 1 tsp. garlic powder
- 1 tsp. ground cumin
- 1 tsp. onion powder
- 2 tsps. dry mustard
- 2 tsps. ground black pepper
- 2 tsps. salt
- 5 lbs. brisket roast
- 5 tbsps. olive oil

Directions:
1. Preheat the air fryer to 350°F.
2. Mix all the ingredients in a Ziploc bag and refrigerate for at least 2 hours.
3. Place the meat in a baking dish large enough to fit in the air fryer.
4. Place in the air fryer and for 2 hours.

435. 4 garlic pork in ginger and coconut sauce
Servings: 4
Prep & Cooking Time: 35 Minutes
Ingredients:
- 1 lb. pork tenderloin, cut into strips
- 1 garlic clove, minced
- A pinch of salt and black pepper
- 1 tbsp. ginger, shredded
- 3 tbsps. coconut aminos
- 2 tbsps. coconut oil, melted

Directions:
1. Heat up a pan that fits the air fryer with the oil over medium-high heat, add the meat and brown for 3 minutes.
2. Add the rest of the ingredients, cook for 2 minutes more, put the pan in the fryer and cook at 380°F for 30 minutes.
3. Divide between plates and serve with a side salad.

436. Stuffed bell pepper
Servings: 4
Prep & Cooking Time: 25 Minutes
Ingredients:
- 4 bell peppers, cut top of bell pepper
- 16 oz. ground beef
- 2/3 cup cheese, shredded
- 1/2 cup rice, cooked
- 1 tsp. basil, dried
- 1/2 tsp. chili powder
- 1 tsp. black pepper
- 1 tsp. garlic salt
- 2 tsp. Worcestershire sauce
- 8 oz. tomato sauce
- 2 garlic cloves, minced
- 1 small onion, minced

Directions:
1. Slightly grease your frying pan with cooking spray and fry the onion and garlic over a medium heat.
2. Stir in the beef, basil, chili powder, black pepper, and garlic salt, combining every element well. Allow to cook until the beef is nicely browned, before taking the pan off the heat.
3. Add in half of the cheese, the rice, Worcestershire sauce, and tomato sauce and stir to combine.
4. Spoon equal amounts of the beef mixture into the four bell peppers, filling them entirely.
5. Pre-heat the air fryer at 400°F.
6. Lightly grease your air fryer basket with oil.
7. Put the stuffed bell peppers in the basket and allow to cook for 11 minutes.
8. Put the remaining cheese on top of each bell pepper with remaining cheese and cook for a further 2 minutes.
9. When the cheese is melted and the bell peppers are piping hot, serve immediately.

437. Brekky casserole and monterey jack sausage
Servings: 2
Prep & Cooking Time: 20 Minutes
Ingredients:
- 1/2 cup shredded Cheddar-Monterey Jack cheese blend
- 1 green onion, minced
- 1 pinch cayenne pepper
- 1/4 lb. breakfast sausage
- 2 tbsps. red bell pepper, diced
- 4 eggs

Directions:
1. Lightly grease your fryer baking pan with cooking spray.
2. Add sausage and for 8 minutes, cook on 390°F. Halfway through, crumble sausage and stir well.
3. Meanwhile, whisk eggs in a bowl and stir in bell pepper, green onion, and cayenne.
4. Remove basket and toss the mixture a bit. Evenly spread cheese and transfer eggs on top.
5. Cook for another 12 minutes at 330°F or until eggs are set to desired doneness.
6. Serve and enjoy.

438. Rhubarb and peppercorn lamb
Servings: 4
Prep & Cooking Time: 30 Minutes
Ingredients:
- 1 and 1/2 lbs. lamb ribs
- A pinch of salt and black pepper
- 1 tbsp. black peppercorns, ground
- 1 tbsp. white peppercorns, ground
- 1 tbsp. cumin seeds, ground
- 1 tbsp. coriander seeds, ground
- 4 rhubarb stalks, minced
- 1/4 cup balsamic vinegar
- 2 tbsps. olive oil

Directions:
1. Heat the oil in a pan (that can suit your air fryer) over medium heat, add the lamb and brown for 2 minutes.
2. Add the rest of the ingredients, toss, bring to a simmer for 2 minutes and take off the heat.
3. Put the pan in the fryer and cook at 380°F for 25 minutes. Divide every element into bowls and serve.

439. Figs with grilled prosciutto
Servings: 2
Prep & Cooking Time: 8 Minutes
Ingredients:
- 2 whole figs, sliced in quarters
- 8 prosciutto slices

- Pepper and salt to taste

Directions:
1. Wrap a prosciutto slice around one slice of fid and then thread into skewer. Repeat process for remaining ingredients. Place on skewer rack in air fryer.
2. For 8 minutes, cook on 390°F. Halfway through cooking time, turn over skewers.
3. Serve and enjoy.

440. Coconut pork with green beans
Servings: 4
Prep & Cooking Time: 25 Minutes
Ingredients:
- 4 pork chops
- 2 tbsps. coconut oil, melted
- 2 garlic cloves, minced
- A pinch of salt and black pepper
- 1/2 lb. green beans, trimmed and halved
- 2 tbsps. keto tomato sauce

Directions:
1. Heat up a pan that fits the air fryer with the oil over medium heat, add the pork chops and brown for 5 minutes.
2. Add the rest of the ingredients, put the pan in the machine and cook at 390°F for 20 minutes.
3. Divide every element between plates and serve

441. Smoked bacon with peppery roasted potatoes
Servings: 2
Prep & Cooking Time: 15 Minutes
Ingredients:
- 5 small rashers smoked bacon
- 1/3 tsp. garlic powder
- 1 tsp. sea salt
- 2 tsp. paprika
- 1/3 tsp. ground black pepper
- 1 bell pepper, seeded and sliced
- 1 tsp. mustard
- 2 habanero peppers, halved

Directions:
1. Simply toss all the ingredients in a mixing dish; then, transfer them to your air fryer's basket.
2. Air-fry at 375°F for 10 minutes. Serve warm.

442. Steak in cascabel-garlic sauce
Servings: 4
Prep & Cooking Time: 20 Minutes
Ingredients:
- 2 tsps. brown mustard
- 2 tbsps. mayonnaise
- 1 1/2 lbs. beef flank steak, trimmed and cubed
- 2 tsps. minced cascabel
- 1/2 cup chives, finely minced
- 1/3 cup Crème fraîche
- 2 tsps. cumin seeds
- 3 cloves garlic, pressed
- Pink peppercorns to taste, freshly grounded
- 1 tsps. fine table salt
- 1/3 tsp. black pepper, preferably freshly ground

Directions:
3. Firstly, fry the cumin seeds just about minute or until they pop.
4. After that, season your beef flank steak with fine table salt, black pepper and the fried cumin seeds; arrange the seasoned beef cubes on the bottom of your baking dish that fits in the air fryer.
5. Throw in the minced cascabel, garlic, and chives; air-fry approximately 8 minutes at 400°F.
6. Once the beef cubes start to tender, add your favorite mayo, Crème fraîche, freshly grounded pink peppercorns and mustard; air-fry 7 minutes longer. Serve over hot wild rice. Bon appétit!

443. Herb meatballs
Servings: 4
Prep & Cooking Time: 20 Minutes
Ingredients:
- 1 clove of garlic, minced
- 1 egg, beaten
- 1 tbsp. breadcrumbs or flour
- 1 tsp. dried mixed herbs
- 1-lb. lean ground beef

Directions:
1. Place all ingredients in a mixing bowl and mix together using your hands.
2. Form small balls using your hands and set aside in the fridge to set.
3. Preheat the air fryer to 380°F.
4. Place the meatballs in the air fryer basket and cook for 20 minutes.
5. Halfway through the cooking time, give the meatballs a shake to cook evenly.

444. Moroccan style beef kebab
Servings: 4
Prep & Cooking Time: 30 Minutes
Ingredients:
- 1/2 cup leeks, minced
- 2 garlic cloves, smashed
- 2 lbs. ground chuck
- Salt, to taste
- 1/4 tsp. ground black pepper, or more to taste
- 1 tsp. cayenne pepper
- 1/2 tsp. ground sumac
- 3 saffron threads
- 2 tbsp. loosely packed fresh continental parsley leaves
- 4 tbsps. tahini sauce
- 4 ounces baby arugula
- 1 tomato, cut into slices

Directions:
1. In a mixing bowl, mix the minced leeks, garlic, ground chuck, and spices; knead with your hands until every element is well incorporated.
2. Now, mound the beef mixture around a wooden skewer into a pointed-ended sausage.
3. Cook in the preheated air fryer at 370°F for 25 minutes.
4. Serve your kebab with the tahini sauce baby arugula and tomato. Enjoy!

445. Balsamic-raspberry jam with pork
Servings: 4
Prep & Cooking Time: 30 Minutes
Ingredients:
- 1/4 cup all-purpose flour
- 1/4 cup milk
- 1 cup minced pecans
- 1 cup panko breadcrumbs
- 2 large eggs, beaten
- 2 tbsps. raspberry jam
- 2 tbsps. sugar
- 2/3 cup balsamic vinegar

- 4 smoked pork chops
- Salt & pepper to taste

Directions:
1. Preheat the air fryer to 330°F.
2. Use salt and pepper to season the pork.
3. In a mixing bowl, whisk together eggs and milk. Set aside.
4. Dip the pork chops in flour then in the egg mixture before dredging in the panko mixed with pecans.
5. Drop into the air fryer and cook for 30 minutes.
6. Meanwhile, prepare the sauce by putting in the saucepan the remaining ingredients. Season with salt and pepper.
7. Drizzle the pork chops with the sauce once cooked.

446. Filet mignon in herb-crust
Servings: 4
Prep & Cooking Time: 20 Minutes
Ingredients:
- 1 lb. filet mignon
- Sea salt & ground black pepper, at your convenience
- 1/2 tsp. cayenne pepper
- 1 tsp. dried basil
- 1 tsp. dried rosemary
- 1 tsp. dried oregano
- 1 tbsp. sesame oil
- 1 small-sized egg, well-whisked
- 1/2 cup parmesan cheese, shredded

Directions:
1. Preheat the fryer to 400°F
2. Season the filet mignon with salt, black pepper, cayenne pepper, basil, rosemary, and thyme. Brush with sesame oil.
3. Put the egg in a shallow plate. Now, place the parmesan cheese in another plate.
4. Coat the filet mignon with the egg; then, lay it into the parmesan cheese.
5. Cook for about 10-13 minutes or until golden.
6. Serve with mixed salad leaves and enjoy!

447. Minty lamb chops
Servings: 4
Prep & Cooking Time: 8 Minutes
Ingredients:
- 2 tbsps. fresh mint leaves, minced
- 4 (6-ounce) lamb chops
- 2 carrots, peeled and cubed
- 1 parsnip, peeled and cubed
- 1 fennel bulb, cubed
- 1 garlic clove, minced
- 2 tbsps. dried rosemary
- 3 tbsps. olive oil
- Salt & black pepper, to taste

Directions:
1. Preheat your air fryer to 390°F and grease an air fryer basket.
2. Mix herbs, garlic and oil in a large bowl and coat chops generously with this mixture.
3. Marinate in the refrigerator for about hours.
4. Soak the vegetables in a large pan of water for about 15 minutes.
5. Set the chops in the air fryer basket and cook for about 2 minutes.
6. Remove the chops and place the vegetables in the air fryer basket.
7. Top with the chops and cook for about 6 minutes.
8. Serve and serve warm.

448. Salami rolls in homemade mustard and manchego
Servings: 4
Prep & Cooking Time: 10 Minutes
Ingredients:
- 7 ounces Manchego cheese, shredded
- 2/3 lb. pork salami, minced
- 7 ounces canned crescent rolls
- For the Mustard Spread:
- 1 tbsp. sour cream
- 1/3 tsp. garlic powder
- 1/3 cup mayonnaise
- 2 1/2 tbsps. spicy brown mustard
- Salt, to taste

Directions:
1. Preheat your air fryer to 350°F.
2. Now, form the crescent rolls into "sheets".
3. Place the minced Manchego and pork salami in the middle of each dough sheet.
4. Shape the dough into the rolls; bake the rolls for 8 minutes. Then, decrease the temperature and bake at 290°F for 5 more minutes.
5. Meanwhile, mix all the ingredients for the mustard spread.
6. Set the warm rolls on a platter and serve with the mustard spread on the side. Enjoy!

449. Corn dog bites
Servings: 2
Prep & Cooking Time: 10 Minutes
Ingredients:
- 1/2 cup all-purpose flour
- 1 1/2 cup crushed cornflakes
- 2 large beef hot dogs, cut in half crosswise
- 2 large eggs, beaten
- Salt & pepper to taste

Directions:
1. Preheat the air fryer to 330°F.
2. Skewer the hot dogs using the metal skewers included in the double layer rack accessory.
3. In a mixing bowl, combine the eggs and flour to form a batter.
4. Season with salt and pepper to taste. Add water if too dry.
5. Dip the skewered hot dogs in the batter and dredge in cornflakes.
6. Place on the double layer rack accessory and cook for 10 minutes.

450. Thai meatballs
Servings: 4
Prep & Cooking Time: 20 Minutes
Ingredients:
- 1 lb. ground beef
- 1 tsp. red Thai curry paste
- 1/2 lime, rind and juice
- 1 tsp. Chinese spice
- 2 tsps. lemongrass, finely minced
- 1 tbsp. sesame oil

Directions:
1. Thoroughly combine all ingredients in a mixing dish.
2. Shape into meatballs and place them into the air fryer cooking basket.
3. Cook at 380°F for 10 minutes; pause the machine and cook for a further 5 minutes, or until cooked through.
4. Serve accompanied by the dipping sauce. Bon appétit!

451. Mushroom casserole and cheesy meatball
Servings: 4
Prep & Cooking Time: 41 Minutes

Ingredients:
- 2 tbsps. Italian breadcrumbs
- 10 ounces lean ground pork
- 1 1/2 cups mushrooms, sliced
- 3 carrots, peeled and shredded
- 1 tsp. saffron
- 2 tsps. cumin seeds
- 1/3 cup Monterey Jack cheese, preferably freshly shredded
- 1/3 cup cream
- 2 medium-sized leeks, finely minced
- 1/tsp. dried dill weed
- 2 small-sized eggs
- 1/2 tsp. cumin
- 1/2 tsp. fine sea salt
- Freshly ground black pepper, to taste

Directions:
1. Begin by preheating the air fryer to 400°F.
2. Mix all the ingredients (unless carrots, mushrooms, and Monterey cheese) in a bowl. Shape the mixture into mini meatballs.
3. In an air fryer baking dish, toss the carrots and mushrooms with the cream; cook for 2 minutes in the preheated air fryer.
4. Pause the machine and place the reserved meatballs in a single layer on top of the carrot/mushroom mixture.
5. Top with the shredded Monterey Jack cheese;
6. Bake for 9 minutes longer. Serve warm.

452. Beef burgers, smoked style
Servings: 4
Prep & Cooking Time: 20 Minutes
Ingredients:
- 1 1/4 lbs. lean ground beef
- 1 tbsp. soy sauce
- 1 tsp. Dijon mustard
- A few dashes of liquid smoke
- 1 tsp. shallot powder
- 1 clove garlic, minced
- 1/2 tsp. cumin powder
- 1/4 cup chives, minced
- 1/3 tsp. sea salt flakes
- 1/3 tsp. freshly grounded mixed peppercorns
- 1 tsp. celery seeds
- 1 tsp. parsley flakes

Directions:
1. Mix all the listed ingredients in a mixing bowl; knead until every element is well incorporated.
2. Shape the mixture into four patties. Next, make a shallow dip in the center of each patty to prevent them puffing up during air-frying.
3. Spritz the patties on all sides using a non-stick cooking spray. Cook approximately 12 minutes at 400°F.
4. Check for doneness – an instant read thermometer should read 160°F. Bon appétit!

453. Saucy beef fingers and tangy
Servings: 4
Prep & Cooking Time: 20 Minutes + Marinating Time
Ingredients:
- 1 1/2 lbs. sirloin steak
- 1/4 cup red wine
- 1/4 cup fresh lime juice
- 1 tsp. garlic powder
- 1 tsp. shallot powder
- 1 tsp. celery seeds
- 1 tsp. mustard seeds
- Salt & ground black pepper, to taste
- 1 tsp. red pepper flakes
- 2 eggs, lightly whisked
- 1 cup Parmesan cheese
- 1 tsp. paprika

Directions:
1. Place the steak, red wine, lime juice, garlic powder, shallot powder, celery seeds, mustard seeds, salt, black pepper, and red pepper in a large ceramic bowl; let it marinate for 3 hours.
2. Tenderize the cube steak by lbing with a mallet; cut into 1-inch strips.
3. In a shallow bowl, whisk the eggs. In another bowl, mix the parmesan cheese and paprika.
4. Dip the beef pieces into the whisked eggs and coat on all sides. Now, dredge the beef pieces in the Parmesan mixture.
5. Cook at 400°F for 14 minutes, flipping halfway through the cooking time.
6. Meanwhile, make the sauce by heating the reserved marinade in a saucepan over medium heat; let it simmer until thoroughly warmed.
7. Serve the steak fingers with the sauce on the side. Enjoy!

454. Spicy chicken wings
Servings: 6
Prep & Cooking Time: 25 Minutes
Ingredients:
- 3 cloves garlic, peeled and halved
- 2 tbsp. habanero hot sauce
- 1/2 tbsp. soy sauce
- 1 1/2 lbs. chicken wings
- 1 tsp. garlic salt
- 1 tsp. smoked cayenne pepper
- 1 tsp. freshly ground black pepper, or to taste

Directions:
1. Rub the chicken wings with the garlic. Then, season them with the salt, black pepper, and the smoked cayenne pepper.
2. Transfer the chicken wings to the food basket; add the soy sauce, habanero hot sauce, and honey; toss to coat on all sides.
3. Air-fry the chicken wings at 385°F for 16 minutes or until warmed through.

455. Beef steaks with saucy lemony
Servings: 2
Prep & Cooking Time: 25 Minutes
Ingredients:
- 1 lb. beef steaks
- 4 tbsps. white wine
- 2 tsps. crushed coriander seeds
- 1/2 tsp. cumin seeds
- 1/3 cup beef broth
- 2 tbsps. lemon zest, shredded
- 2 tbsps. canola oil
- 1/2 lemon, cut into wedges
- Salt & freshly ground black pepper, to taste

Directions:
1. Warm the oil in a saucepan over a moderate flame. Then, cook the garlic for minute, or until just fragrant.
2. Remove the pan from the heat; add the beef broth, wine, lemon zest, coriander seeds, fennel, salt flakes, and freshly ground black. Pour the mixture into a baking dish.
3. Add beef steaks to the baking dish; toss to coat well. Now, tuck the lemon wedges among the beef steaks.
4. Bake for 18 minutes at 335°F. Serve warm.

456. Lamb with herbs crumbed rack
Servings: 5
Prep & Cooking Time: 30 Minutes
Ingredients:
- 1 tbsp. butter, melted
- 1 garlic clove, finely minced
- 13/4 lb. rack of lamb
- Salt & ground black pepper, as required
- 1 egg
- 1/2 cup panko breadcrumbs
- 1 tbsp. fresh thyme, minced
- 1 tbsp. fresh rosemary, minced

Directions:
1. Combine the butter, garlic, salt, and black pepper in a mixing bowl.
2. Evenly coat the rack of lamb with the garlic mixture.
3. In a shallow dish, beat the egg.
4. Combine the breadcrumbs and herbs in a separate bowl.
5. Coat the rack of lamb with the breadcrumbs mixture after dipping it in the beaten egg. Set the temperature of air fryer to 212°F. Grease an air fryer basket.
6. Place rack of lamb into the prepared air fryer basket.
7. Air fry for about 25 minutes and then 5 more minutes at 390°F.
8. Remove from air fryer and place the rack of lamb onto a cutting board for about 5 minutes
9. Cut the rack of lamb into individual chops with a sharp knife and serve.

457. Southwest meaty pasta bake
Servings: 6
Prep & Cooking Time: 45 Minutes
Ingredients:
- 1 can (14-1/2 ounces each) diced tomatoes, undrained
- 1 cup shredded Monterey Jack cheese
- 1 cup elbow macaroni (follow manufacturer's directions for cooking)
- 1 jalapeno pepper, seeded and minced
- 1 large onion, minced
- 1 tsp. chili powder
- 1 tsp. salt
- 1/2 can (16 ounces) kidney beans, rinsed and drained
- 1/2 can (4 ounces) minced green chilies, drained
- 1/2 can (6 ounces) tomato paste
- 1/2 tsp. ground cumin
- 1/2 tsp. pepper
- 1-lb. ground beef
- 2 garlic cloves, minced

Directions:
1. Grease your air frier baking pan with oil or cooking spray. Add, garlic, ground beef, and onion, and cook on 360°F for 30 minutes. Halfway through cooking time, stir and crumble beef.
2. Mix in diced tomatoes, kidney beans, tomato paste, green chilies, salt, chili powder, cumin, and pepper. Mix well. Cook for another 10 minutes.
3. Stir in macaroni and mix well. Top with jalapenos and cheese.
4. Cover pan with foil.
5. Cook for 1minutes at 390°F, remove foil and continue cooking for another 10 minutes until tops are lightly browned.
6. Serve and enjoy.

458. Basil lamb with mustard chives
Servings: 4
Prep & Cooking Time: 30 Minutes
Ingredients:
- 8 lamb cutlets
- A pinch of salt and black pepper
- A drizzle of olive oil
- 2 garlic cloves, minced
- 1/4 cup mustard
- 1 tbsp. chives, minced
- 1 tbsp. basil, minced
- 1 tbsp. oregano, minced
- 1 tbsp. mint minced

Directions:
1. In a deep plate, mix the lamb with the rest of the ingredients and rub well.
2. Put the cutlets in your air fryer's basket and cook at 380°F for 20 minutes on each side.
3. Divide between plates and serve with a side salad.

459. Cauliflower frittata and sausage
Servings: 3
Prep & Cooking Time: 30 Minutes
Ingredients:
- 1-lb. hot pork sausage, diced
- 1/2 cup shredded Cheddar cheese
- 1 tsp. salt
- 1/2 cup milk
- 1 small cauliflower, riced
- 3 large eggs
- 1/2 (3 1/5 cup) package frozen hash brown potatoes, thawed
- 1/2 tsp. black pepper, grounded

Directions:
1. Grease your air frier baking pan with oil. And add diced sausage and cook for 20 minutes on 360°F.
2. Add hash brown and riced cauliflower. Cook for another 5 minutes.
3. Meanwhile, whisk well eggs, salt, pepper, and milk.
4. Remove basket and toss the mixture a bit. Evenly spread cheese and transfer eggs.
5. Cook for another 12 minutes or until set
6. Serve and enjoy.

460. Tomato-olive salad on steak
Servings: 5
Prep & Cooking Time: 50 Minutes
Ingredients:
- 1/4 cup extra virgin olive oil
- 1/4 tsp. cayenne pepper
- 1/2 cup green olives, pitted and sliced
- 1 cup red onion, minced
- 1 tbsp. oil
- 1 tsp. paprika
- 2 1/2 lbs. flank
- 2 lbs. cherry tomatoes, halved
- 2 tbsps. Sherry vinegar
- Salt & pepper to taste

Directions:
1. Heat up the air fryer to 390°F.
2. Season the steak with salt, pepper, paprika, and cayenne pepper. Brush with oil
3. Place on the grill pan and cook for 45 minutes.
4. Meanwhile, prepare the salad by mixing the remaining ingredients.
5. Serve the beef with salad.

461. Cheeseburgers with classic keto
Servings: 4
Prep & Cooking Time: 15 Minutes
Ingredients:
- 1 1/2 lbs. ground chuck
- 1 envelope onion soup mix
- Salt & ground black pepper, to taste
- 1 tsp. paprika
- 4 slices Monterey-Jack cheese

Directions:
1. In a mixing dish, thoroughly combine ground chuck, onion soup mix, salt, black pepper, and paprika.
2. Then, set your air fryer to cook at 385°F. Shape the mixture into 4 patties. Air-fry them for 10 minutes.
3. Next step, place the slices of cheese on the top of the warm burgers. Air-fry for one minute more.
4. Serve with mustard and pickled salad of choice. Bon appétit!

462. Lamb steak with garlic lemon-wine
Servings: 4
Prep & Cooking Time: 1 Hour And 30 Minutes
Ingredients:
- 1/4 cup olive oil
- 1/2 cup dry white wine
- 1 tbsp. brown sugar
- 2 lbs. lamb steak, lbed
- 2 tbsps. lemon juice
- 3 tbsps. ancho chili powder
- 8 cloves of garlic, minced
- Salt & pepper to taste

Directions:
1. Place all ingredients in bowl and marinate the meat in the fridge for at least 30 minutes.
2. Heat up your air fryer to 390°F.
3. Place the grill pan in the air fryer, and grill the meat for 20 minutes per batch.
4. Meanwhile, transfer the marinade in a saucepan and allow to simmer for 10 minutes until the sauce thickens.

463. Buttered filet mignon
Servings: 4
Prep & Cooking Time: 14 Minutes
Ingredients:
- 2 (6-ounces) filet mignon steaks
- 1 tbsp. butter, softened
- Salt & black pepper, to taste

Directions:
1. Preheat the air fryer to 390°F and grease an air fryer basket.
2. Rub the steak generously with salt and black pepper and coat with butter.
3. Set the steaks in the air fryer basket and cook for about 14 minutes.
4. Serve the steaks and cut into desired size slices to serve.

464. Omelet with kale and beef
Servings: 4
Prep & Cooking Time: 20 Minutes
Ingredients:
- Cooking spray
- 1/2 lb. leftover beef, coarsely minced
- 2 garlic cloves, pressed
- 1 cup kale, torn into pieces and wilted
- 1 tomato, minced
- 1/4 tsp. sugar
- 4 eggs, beaten
- 4 tbsps. heavy cream
- 1/2 tsp. turmeric powder
- Salt & ground black pepper to taste
- tsp. ground allspice

Directions:
1. Grease four ramekins with cooking spray.
2. Place equal amounts of each of the ingredients into each ramekin and mix well.
3. Air-fry at 380°F for 16 minutes, or longer if necessary. Serve immediately.

465. Veggies and classic skirt steak strips
Servings: 4
Prep & Cooking Time: 17 Minutes
Ingredients:
- 1 (12-ounce) skirt steak, cut into slim strips
- 1/2 lb. fresh mushrooms, quartered
- 6-ounce snow peas
- 1 onion, cut into half rings
- 1/4 cup olive oil, divided
- 2 tbsps. soy sauce
- 2 tbsps. honey
- Salt & black pepper, to taste

Directions:
1. Preheat the air fryer to 390°F and grease an air fryer basket.
2. Mix tbsp. of oil, soy sauce and honey in a bowl and coat steak strips with this marinade.
3. Put vegetables, remaining oil, salt and black pepper in another bowl and toss well.
4. Transfer the steak strips and vegetables in the air fryer basket and cook for about 17 minutes.
5. Serve and serve warm.

466. Garlic-mayo sauce and winter beef
Servings: 4
Prep & Cooking Time: 1 Hour 22 Minutes
Ingredients:
- 1 1/2 lbs. beef, cubed
- 1/2 cup full fat kefir
- 1/2 cup white wine
- 2 tsps. dried rosemary
- 1 1/2 tbsps. herb vinegar
- 1 tsp. sweet paprika
- 3 cloves garlic, minced
- 2 tbsps. extra-virgin olive oil
- 2 tsps. dried basil
- 1 tbsp. mayonnaise
- Salt & ground black pepper, to taste

Directions:
1. In a large-sized mixing bowl, whisk together the oil, wine, and beef. Now, stir in the seasonings and herb vinegar. Cover and marinate at least 50 minutes.
2. Then, preheat your air fryer to 375°F. Roast the marinated beef for about 18 minutes, turning halfway through.
3. Meanwhile, make the sauce by mixing the kefir with the mayonnaise and garlic. Serve the warm beef with the garlic sauce and enjoy!

467. Beef with zucchini sauté
Servings: 4
Prep & Cooking Time: 25 Minutes
Ingredients:
- 1 lb. beef meat, cut into slim strips

- 1 zucchini, roughly cubed
- 2 tbsps. coconut aminos
- 2 garlic cloves, minced
- 1/4 cup cilantro, minced
- 2 tbsps. avocado oil

Directions:
1. Heat up the oil in a pan (large enough to suit your air fryer) over medium heat.
2. Add the meat and brown for 5 minutes.
3. Add the rest of the ingredients, toss, and put the pan in the fryer; let it cook at 380°F for 20 minutes.
4. Divide every element into bowls and serve.

468. Pork butt with herb-garlic sauce
Servings: 4
Prep & Cooking Time: 35 Minutes + Marinating Time
Ingredients:
- 1 lb. pork butt, cut into pieces 2-inches long
- 1 tsp. golden flaxseed meal
- 1 egg white, well whisked
- Salt & ground black pepper, to taste
- 1 tbsp. olive oil
- 1 tbsp. coconut aminos
- 1 tsp. lemon juice, preferably freshly squeezed

For the Coriander-Garlic Sauce:
- 3 garlic cloves, peeled
- 1/3 cup fresh parsley leaves
- 1/3 cup fresh coriander leaves
- 1/2 tbsp. salt
- 1 tsp. lemon juice
- 1/3 cup extra-virgin olive oil

Directions:
1. Combine the pork strips with the flaxseed meal, egg white, salt, pepper, olive oil, coconut aminos, and lemon juice. Cover and refrigerate for 30 to 45 minutes.
2. After that, spritz the pork strips with a nonstick cooking spray.
3. Set your air fryer to cook at 360°F. Press the power button and air-fry for 15 minutes; pause the machine, shake the basket and cook for 15 more minutes.
4. Meanwhile, puree the garlic in a food processor until finely minced. Now, puree the parsley, coriander, salt, and lemon juice. With the machine running, carefully transfer in the olive oil.
5. Serve the pork with well-chilled sauce with and enjoy!

469. Country fried steak
Servings: 2
Prep & Cooking Time: 25 Minutes
Ingredients:
- 1 cup flour
- 1 cup panko bread crumbs
- 1 tsp. garlic powder
- 1 tsp. onion powder
- 2 cups milk
- 2 tbsps. flour
- 3 eggs, beaten
- 6 ounces ground sausage meat
- 6 ounces sirloin steak, pounded slim
- Salt & pepper to taste

Directions:
1. Preheat the air fryer to 330°F.
2. Salt and pepper the meat to taste.
3. Dip the steak in egg and dredge in flour mixture (comprised of flour, bread crumbs, onion powder, and garlic powder).
4. Drop into the air fryer and cook for 25 minutes.
5. Meanwhile, place the sausage meat in a saucepan and allow the fat to render. Pour in the flour to form a roux and add milk. Season with salt and pepper to taste. Keep stirring until the sauce thickens.
6. Serve the steak with the milk gravy

470. Biscuit brekky with eggs and bacon
Servings: 4
Prep & Cooking Time: 28 Minutes
Ingredients:
- 1/4 cup milk
- 1/2 of 16-ounces refrigerated breakfast biscuits
- 1 cup shredded extra sharp cheddar cheese
- 4 chives, minced
- 5 eggs
- 8 slices cooked center cut bacon

Directions:
1. In baking pan cook bacon for 8 minutes at 360°F or until crisped. Remove bacon and discard excess fat.
2. Evenly spread biscuits on bottom. For 5 minutes, cook at same temperature.
3. Meanwhile, whisk eggs, milk, and chives.
4. Remove basket, evenly layer bacon on top of biscuit, sprinkle cheese on top, and transfer eggs.
5. Cook for another 1minutes or until eggs are set.
6. Serve and enjoy.

471. Beef with spring onions
Servings: 2
Prep & Cooking Time: 15 Minutes
Ingredients:
- 2 cups corned beef, cooked and shredded
- 2 garlic cloves, minced
- 1 lb. radishes, quartered
- 2 spring onions, minced
- A pinch of salt and black pepper

Directions:
1. In a pan combine the beef with the rest of the ingredients, toss, put the pan in the fryer and cook at 390°F for 15 minutes.
2. Divide every element into bowls and serve.

472. Lamb chops with roasted cilantro
Servings: 6
Prep & Cooking Time: 24 Minutes
Ingredients:
- 12 lamb chops
- A pinch of salt and black pepper
- 1/2 cup cilantro, minced
- 1 green chili pepper, minced
- 1 garlic clove, minced
- Juice of 1 lime
- 3 tbsp. olive oil

Directions:
1. In a bowl, mix the lamb chops with the rest of the ingredients and rub well.
2. Put the chops in your air fryer's basket and cook at 400°F for 20 minutes on each side.
3. Divide between plates and serve.

473. Osso buco with lemon
Servings: 4
Prep & Cooking Time: 40 Minutes
Ingredients:
- 3 spring onions, minced
- 1 garlic clove, diced

- 1 ounce celery, minced
- 1-lb. veal shank, boneless, minced
- 1/2 tsp. salt
- 1/2 tsp. ground black pepper
- 1 tbsp. ghee
- 1 tbsp. keto tomato sauce
- 2 tbsps. water
- 1/2 tsp. dried oregano
- 1 tsp. lemon juice
- 1 tsp. grapeseed oil

Directions:
1. Preheat the air fryer to 370°F.
2. In the mixing bowl mix up spring onions, garlic, celery, salt, ground black pepper, ghee, tomato sauce, water, dried oregano, lemon juice, and grapeseed oil.
3. Add the veal shank and mix up the ingredients carefully. Then cover the mixture with foil and transfer in the air fryer.
4. Cook Osso Bucco for 40 minutes.
5. Cool the cooked meal to the room temperature.

474. Marinated pork chops marinate
Servings: 4
Prep & Cooking Time: 25 Minutes
Ingredients:
- 2 tbsps. honey
- 2 tbsps. minced garlic
- 4 pork chops
- 4 tbsps. mustard
- Salt & pepper to taste

Directions:
1. Preheat the air fryer to 330°F.
2. Place the air fryer basket.
3. Season the pork chops with the rest of the Ingredients.
4. Place inside the basket.
5. Cook for 20 to 2minutes until golden.

475. Sweety pork belly
Servings: 6
Prep & Cooking Time: 55 Minutes
Ingredients:
- 1-lb. pork belly
- 1 tsp. Splenda
- 1 tsp. salt
- 1 tsp. white pepper
- 1 tsp. butter, softened
- 1/2 tsp. onion powder

Directions:
1. Sprinkle the pork belly with salt, white pepper, and onion powder.
2. Then preheat the air fryer to 385°F. P
3. ut the pork belly in the air fryer and cook it for 45 minutes.
4. Turn the pork belly on another side and spread it with butter. After this, top the pork belly with Splenda and cook it at 400F for 50minutes.

476. Honey mustard cheesy meatballs
Servings: 8
Prep & Cooking Time: 15 Minutes
Ingredients:
- 2 onions, minced
- 1 lb. ground beef
- 4 tbsps. fresh basil, minced
- 2 tbsps. cheddar cheese, shredded
- 2 tsps. garlic paste

- 2 tsps. honey
- Salt & black pepper, to taste
- 2 tsps. mustard

Directions:
1. Preheat the air fryer to 385°F and grease an air fryer basket.
2. Whisk all the ingredients in a wide bowl until well mixed.
3. Shape the mixture into equal-sized balls gently and arrange the meatballs in the air fryer basket.
4. Cook for about 15 minutes and dish out to serve warm.

477. Sweet pork chops with soy sauce
Servings: 4
Prep & Cooking Time: 16 Minutes
Ingredients:
- 6 pork loin chops
- Salt & black pepper, to taste
- 2 garlic cloves, minced
- 2 tbsps. honey
- 2 tbsps. soy sauce
- 1 tbsp. balsamic vinegar
- 1/4 tsp. ground ginger

Directions:
1. Preheat the air fryer to 355°F and grease a baking tray.
2. Season the chops with a little salt and black pepper.
3. Mix rest of the ingredients in a large bowl and add chops.
4. Coat with marinade generously and cover to refrigerate for about 8 hours.
5. Set the chops in a baking tray and transfer into the Air fryer.
6. Cook for about 1minutes, flipping once in between and dish out to serve warm.

478. Nutmeg pork cutlets with parmesan
Servings: 3
Prep & Cooking Time: 11 Minutes
Ingredients:
- 3 pork cutlets (3 ounce each cutlet)
- 2 ounces Parmesan, shredded
- 1 tbsp. almond flour
- 1/2 tsp. chili powder
- 1/4 tsp. ground nutmeg
- 1 tsp. sesame oil
- 1 tsp. lemon juice
- 1 egg, beaten

Directions:
1. In the mixing bowl mix up Parmesan, almond flour, chili powder, and ground nutmeg.
2. In a separated bowl mix up lemon juice and egg. After this, dip the pork cutlets in the egg mixture and then coat in the Parmesan mixture. Sprinkle every coated cutlet with sesame oil.
3. Preheat the air fryer to 400°F. Place the pork cutlets in the air fryer basket and cook them for 6 minutes.
4. Then carefully flip them on another side and cook for 5 minutes more.

479. Easy to do beef (beef, easy way)
Servings: 1
Prep & Cooking Time: 25 Minutes
Ingredients:
- 1 slim beef schnitzel
- 1 egg, beaten
- 1/2 cup friendly bread crumbs
- 2 tbsps. olive oil
- Pepper and salt to taste

Directions:
1. Pre-heat the air fryer to 350°F.
2. In a deep plate, blend the bread crumbs, oil, pepper, and salt.
3. In a second bowl, place the beaten egg.
4. Dredge the schnitzel in the egg before rolling it in the bread crumbs.
5. Put the coated schnitzel in the fryer basket and air fry for 12 minutes.

480. Classic beef stroganoff
Servings: 4
Prep & Cooking Time: 20 Minutes + Marinating Time
Ingredients:
- 1 1/3 lbs. beef sirloin steak, cut in strips
- 1/4 cup balsamic vinegar
- 1 tbsp. brown mustard
- 1 tbsp. butter
- 1 cup beef broth
- 1 cup leek, minced
- 2 cloves garlic, crushed
- 1 tsp. cayenne pepper
- Sea salt flakes and crushed red pepper, to taste
- 1 cup sour cream
- 2 1/2 tbsps. tomato paste

Directions:
1. Place the beef along with the balsamic vinegar and the mustard in a mixing dish; cover and marinate in your refrigerator for about hour.
2. Butter the inside of a baking dish and put the beef into the dish.
3. Add the broth, leeks and garlic. Cook at 400°F for 8 minutes. Pause the machine and add the cayenne pepper, salt, red pepper, sour cream and tomato paste; cook for additional 7 minutes.
4. Bon appétit!

481. Chinese-style beef
Servings: 4
Prep & Cooking Time: 19 Minutes
Ingredients:
- Cooked rice noodles
- 1/3 lb. beef tenderloin, cut into strips
- 1/2 tsp. balsamic vinegar
- 1/2 cup corn meal mix
- 1 cup buttermilk
- 1/3 tsp. ground black pepper, or to taste
- 1 1/2 cups plain flour
- Seven spice powder
- 1/2 tsp. ground cinnamon
- 1 tsp. hot paprika
- 1/3 tsp. salt

Directions:
1. Grab three mixing bowls. Combine the corn meal mix, 3/4 cup flour, and seven spice powder in the first mixing bowl.
2. Whisk the buttermilk and balsamic vinegar in the second bowl. Add the remaining 3/4 cup flour to the third shallow bowl.
3. Sprinkle the beef strips with black pepper, salt, ground cinnamon, and hot paprika. Coat each strip with the remaining flour; then, dip them in the buttermilk mixture; lastly, cover them with the spiced cornmeal mixture.
4. Cook in the air fryer baking tray for about 12 minutes at 365°F or until ready. Serve over the hot rice noodles. Bon appétit!

482. Honey and mustard ham
Servings: 4
Prep & Cooking Time: 40 Minutes
Ingredients:
- 1 lb. (101/2 ounce) ham joint
- 2 tbsps. French mustard
- 2 tbsps. honey

Directions:
1. Preheat the air fryer to 320°F and grease an air fryer pan.
2. Blend all the ingredients in a mixing bowl except ham.
3. Keep ham joint for about 10 minutes at room temperature and place in the air fryer pan.
4. Top with half of the mixture and transfer into the Air fryer.
5. Cook for about 1 minutes and flip the side.
6. Coat with the remaining mixture and cook for about 25 minutes.
7. Serve in a platter and serve warm.

483. Sesame and za'atar lamb chops
Servings: 6
Prep & Cooking Time: 11 Minutes
Ingredients:
- 6 lamb chops (3 ounce each lamb chop)
- 1 tbsp. walnut oil
- 1 tbsp. Za'atar seasonings

Directions:
1. Rub the lamb chops with Za'atar seasonings and sprinkle with walnut oil. Preheat the air fryer to 400°F. Then arrange the lamb chops in the air fryer in one layer and cook them for 5 minutes.
2. Flip the pork chops on another side and cook them for 6 minutes more.

484. Pork loin roast with herbs de provence
Servings: 4
Prep & Cooking Time: 35 Minutes
Ingredients:
- 4 lbs. pork loin
- A pinch of garlic salt
- A pinch of herbs de Provence

Directions:
1. Preheat the air fryer to 330°F.
2. Season pork with the garlic salt and herbs,
3. Drop into the air fryer grill pan.
4. Cook for 30 to 35 minutes.

485. Herbed lamb leg
Servings: 5
Prep & Cooking Time: 75 Minutes
Ingredients:
- 2 lbs. bone-in leg of lamb
- 2 tbsps. olive oil
- Salt & ground black pepper, as required
- 2 fresh rosemary sprigs
- 2 fresh thyme sprigs

Directions:
1. Coat the leg of lamb with oil and sprinkle with salt and black pepper.
2. Wrap the leg of lamb with herb sprigs.
3. Set the temperature of air fryer to 400°F. Grease an air fryer basket.
4. Place leg of lamb into the prepared air fryer basket.
5. Air fry for about 7 minutes.
6. Remove from air fryer and transfer the leg of lamb onto a platter.
7. Wrap the leg of lamb in foil for approximately 10 minutes before slicing.
8. Cut the leg of lamb into desired size pieces and serve.

486. Sirloin with curry, paprika and yogurt
Servings: 3
Prep & Cooking Time: 25 Minutes
Ingredients:
- 1/4 cup mint, minced
- 1/2 cup low-fat yogurt
- 1 1/2 lbs. boneless beef top loin steak
- 2 tsps. curry powder
- 2 tsps. paprika
- 3 tbsps. lemon juice
- 6 cloves of garlic, minced
- Salt & pepper to taste

Directions:
1. Blend all ingredients, except the green onions, in a Ziploc bag and refrigerate for at least 2 hours.
2. Preheat the air fryer to 390°Fahrenheit.
3. Insert the air fryer's grill pan attachment.
4. Cook for 25 to 30 minutes on the grill.
5. For even grilling, flip the steaks halfway during the cooking period.

487. Stuffed pork roll
Servings: 4
Prep & Cooking Time: 15 Minutes
Ingredients:
- 1 scallion, minced
- 1/4 cup sun-dried tomatoes, minced finely
- 2 tbsp. fresh parsley, minced
- 4 (6-ounce) pork cutlets, lbed slightly
- Salt & black pepper, to taste
- 2 tsps. paprika
- 1/2 tbsp. olive oil

Directions:
1. Preheat the air fryer to 390°F and grease an air fryer basket.
2. Mix scallion, tomatoes, parsley, salt and black pepper in a large bowl.
3. Coat the cutlets with tomato mixture and roll each cutlet.
4. Secure the cutlets with cocktail sticks and rub with paprika, salt and black pepper.
5. Coat evenly with oil and transfer into the air fryer basket.
6. Cook for about 15 minutes, flipping once in between and dish out to serve warm.

488. Pork and cabbage
Servings: 6
Prep & Cooking Time: 35 Minutes
Ingredients:
- 2 1/2 lbs. pork stew meat, cubed
- 2 tsps. olive oil
- 2 bay leaves
- 3 garlic cloves, minced
- 4 carrots, minced
- 1 red cabbage head, shredded
- Salt & black pepper to taste
- 1/2 cup tomato sauce

Directions:
1. Heat the oil in a pan (that suit your air fryer) over medium heat, and add the meat, and brown it for 5 minutes.
2. Add all remaining ingredients and toss.
3. Place the pan in the fryer and cook at 360°F for 30 minutes.
4. Divide the mix between plates and serve.

489. Beef rump steaks with fresh herbs
Servings: 4
Prep & Cooking Time: 40 Minutes
Ingredients:
- 2 heaping tbsp. fresh parsley, roughly minced
- 1 lb. beef rump steaks
- 2 heaping tbsp. fresh chives, roughly minced
- Salt & black pepper (or mixed peppercorns), to savor

For the Sauce:
- 1/4 cup rice vinegar
- 1 tbsp. fresh ginger, shredded
- 1 1/2 tbsps. mirin
- 3 garlic cloves, minced
- 2 tbsps. rice bran oil
- 1/3 cup soy sauce
- A few drops of liquid Stevia

Directions:
1. Firstly, steam the beef rump steaks for 8 minutes (use the method of steaming that you prefer).
2. Season the meat well with salt and black pepper; scatter the minced parsley and chives over the top.
3. Roast the beef rump steaks in an air fryer basket for 20 minutes at 345°F, turning halfway through.
4. While the beef is cooking, combine the ingredients for the teriyaki sauce in a sauté pan. Allow it to simmer, over low heat, until it has thickened.
5. Toss the beef with the teriyaki sauce until it is well covered and serve. Enjoy!

490. Oregano beef roast
Servings: 4
Prep & Cooking Time: 30 Minutes
Ingredients:
- 1 lb. beef roast, trimmed
- 1/2 tsp. oregano, dried
- 1/4 tsp. garlic powder
- Salt & black pepper, to taste
- 1/2 tsp. turmeric powder
- 1 tbsp. olive oil

Directions:
1. In a bowl, mix the roast with the rest of the ingredients, and rub well.
2. Put the roast in the air fryer's basket and cook at 390°F for 30 minutes.
3. Slice the roast, divide it between plates and serve with a side salad.

491. Rosemary lamb with mint flavor
Servings: 2
Prep & Cooking Time: 1 hour and 15 minutes
Ingredients:
- 1/2 ounce leg of lamb, boneless
- 1 tsp. dried rosemary
- 1/2 tsp. dried mint
- 1 garlic clove, diced
- 1/2 tsp. salt
- 1/4 tsp. ground black pepper
- 1 tsp. white wine vinegar
- 1 tbsp. olive oil

Directions:
1. In the mixing bowl mix up dried rosemary, mint, diced garlic, salt, ground black pepper, white wine vinegar, and olive oil.
2. Rub the leg of lamb with the spice mixture and leave for 30 minutes to marinate.
3. After this, preheat the air fryer to 400°F.
4. Put the leg of lamb in the air fryer and sprinkle with all remaining spice mixture. Cook the meal for 15 minutes. Then flip the meat on another side and cook it for 15 minutes more.

492. Sour & sweet glazed fried pork
Servings: 4
Prep & Cooking Time: 30 Minutes
Ingredients:
- 1/4 cup rice wine vinegar
- 1/4 tsp. Chinese five spice powder
- 1 cup potato starch
- 1 green onion, minced
- 2 large eggs, beaten
- 2 lbs. pork chops cut into chunks
- 2 tbsps. cornstarch + 3 tbsp. water
- 5 tbsps. brown sugar
- Salt & pepper to taste

Directions:
1. Preheat the air fryer to 390°F.
2. Season the pork chops to taste with salt and pepper.
3. Dip the pork chops in egg. Set aside.
4. In a mixing bowl, combine the potato starch and Chinese five spice powder.
5. Dredge the pork chops in the flour mixture.
6. Place in the double layer rack and cook for 30 minutes.
7. Meanwhile, place the vinegar and brown sugar in a saucepan. Season with salt and pepper to taste. Stir in the cornstarch slurry and allow to simmer until thick.
8. Serve the pork chops with the sauce and garnish with green onions.

493. Pork with chili tomato
Servings: 3
Prep & Cooking Time: 15 Minutes
Ingredients:
- 12 ounce pork tenderloin
- 1 tbsp. grain mustard
- 1 tbsp. swerve sweetener
- 1 tbsp. keto tomato sauce
- 1 tsp. chili pepper, grinded
- 1/4 tsp. garlic powder
- 1 tbsp. olive oil

Directions:
1. In the mixing bowl mix up grain mustard, swerve sweetener, tomato sauce, chili pepper, garlic powder, and olive oil.
2. Rub the pork tenderloin with mustard mixture generously and leave for 5- minutes to marinate.
3. Meanwhile, preheat the air fryer to 370°F.
4. Put the marinated pork tenderloin in the air fryer baking pan. Then insert the baking pan in the preheated air fryer and cook the meat for 15 minutes.
5. Cool the cooked meat to the room temperature and slice it into the servings.

494. Beef and tofu mix recipe
Servings: 6
Prep & Cooking Time: 30 Minutes
Ingredients:
- 1 cup beef stock
- 2 lbs. beef steak, cut into slim strips and browned
- Salt & black pepper to taste
- 1 yellow onion, slimly sliced
- 12 ounces extra firm tofu, cubed
- 1 chili pepper, sliced
- 1 scallion, minced

Directions:
1. Mix all of the ingredients in a pan that fits your air fryer; toss well.
2. Place the pan in the fryer and cook at 380°F for 30 minutes.
3. Divide between plates and serve.

495. Rubbed chicken tenderloin with paprika-cumin
Servings: 6
Prep & Cooking Time: 25 Minutes
Ingredients:
- 1/4 cup coconut flour
- 1/4 cup olive oil
- 1/2 tsp. garlic powder
- 1/2 tsp. ground cumin
- 1/2 tsp. onion powder
- 1/2 tsp. smoked paprika
- 1-lb. chicken tenderloins
- Salt & pepper to taste

Directions:
1. Preheat the air fryer for 5 minutes.
2. Soak the chicken tenderloins in olive oil.
3. Mix the rest of the ingredients and stir using your hands to combine every element.
4. Place the chicken pieces in the air fryer basket.
5. Cook for 2 minutes at 350°F.

496. Cheesy and buttery sausage
Servings: 4
Prep & Cooking Time: 30 Minutes
Ingredients:
- 1/2 cup uncooked grits
- 1/4-lb. ground pork sausage
- 1-1/2 cups water
- 2 tbsps. butter, divided
- 2 tbsps. milk
- 3 eggs
- 3/4 cup Cheddar cheese, shredded
- Salt and pepper to taste

Directions:
1. Bring water to a boil in a big saucepan. Stir in grits and simmer until liquid is absorbed, around 5 minutes. Stir in 1/4 cup cheese and tbsp butter. Mix well until thoroughly incorporated.
2. Grease your air frier baking pan with oil or cooking spray.
3. Add pork sausage and for 5 minutes, cook on 365°F. Crumble sausage and discard excess fat.
4. Transfer grits into pan of sausage.
5. In a mixing bowl whisk well, milk and eggs and transfer into pan. Mix well.
6. Dot the top with butter and sprinkle cheese. Season with pepper and salt.
7. Cook until tops are browned, around 20 minutes.
8. Serve and enjoy.

497. 500. Sausages with lamb beef
Servings: 4
Prep & Cooking Time: 10 Minutes
Ingredients:
- 4 sausage links
- 12 ounce ground lamb
- 1 tsp. minced garlic
- 1/2 tsp. onion powder
- 1 tsp. dried parsley
- 1/2 tsp. salt
- 1 tsp. ghee

- 1/2 tsp. ground ginger
- 1 tbsp. sesame oil

Directions:
1. In the mixing bowl mix up ground lamb, minced garlic, onion powder, dried parsley, salt, and ground ginger.
2. Then fill the sausage links with the ground lamb mixture. Secure the ends of the sausages.
3. Brush the air fryer basket with sesame oil from inside and put the sausages. Then sprinkle the sausages with ghee. Cook the lamb sausages for 8 minutes at 400°F.
4. Flip them on another side after 5 minutes of cooking.

498. Chicken tenders with shaking tarragon
Servings: 2
Prep & Cooking Time: 15 Minutes
Ingredients:
- Salt & pepper to taste
- 1/2 cup dried tarragon
- 1 tbsp. butter

Directions:
1. Preheat air fryer to 390°F. Lay a 12 inch cut of foil on a flat surface. Place the chicken on the foil, sprinkle the tarragon on both, and share the butter onto both breasts. Sprinkle with salt and pepper.
2. Loosely wrap the foil around the breasts to enable airflow. Place the wrapped chicken in the basket and cook for 1 minute.
3. Remove the chicken and carefully unwrap the foil.
4. Serve with the sauce extract and steamed veggies.

499. Lemony lamb loin chops
Servings: 4
Prep & Cooking Time: 30 Minutes
Ingredients:
- 2 tbsps. Dijon mustard
- 1 tbsp. fresh lemon juice
- 1/2 tsp. olive oil
- 1 tsp. dried tarragon
- Salt & ground black pepper, as required
- 8 (4-ounces) lamb loin chops

Directions:
1. In a large bowl, mix together the mustard, lemon juice, oil, tarragon, salt, and black pepper.
2. Add chops and generously coat with the mixture.
3. Set the temperature of air fryer to 400°F. Grease an air fryer basket.
4. Arrange chops into the prepared air fryer basket in a single layer in 2 batches.
5. Air fry for about 1minutes, flipping once halfway through.
6. Remove the chops from air fryer and transfer onto serving plates.
7. Serve hot.

500. Chicken wings with ginger
Servings: 4
Prep & Cooking Time: 25 Minutes
Ingredients:
- 1 tbsp. olive oil
- 1 tbsp. grapeseed oil
- 4 tbsps. honey
- 3 tbsps. light soy sauce
- 2 crushed garlic clove
- 1 small knob fresh ginger, shredded
- 2 tbsps. sesame seeds, toasted

Directions:
1. Add all ingredients in a freezer bag, except sesame.
2. Seal up and massage until the drumsticks are coated well.
3. Preheat air fryer to 400°F. Place the drumsticks in the cooking basket and cook for minutes. Flip and cook for 10 more minutes.
4. Sprinkle with some sesame and coriander seeds.

501. Kebabs with veggie and beef
Servings: 4
Prep & Cooking Time: 12 Minutes
Ingredients:
- 1/4 cup soy sauce
- 1/4 cup olive oil
- 1 tbsp. garlic, minced
- 1 tsp. brown sugar
- 1/2 tsp. ground cumin
- Salt & ground black pepper, as required
- 1 lb. sirloin steak, cut into-inch chunks
- 8 ounces baby Bella mushrooms, stems removed
- 1 large bell pepper, seeded and cut into 1-inch pieces
- 1 red onion, cut into 1-inch pieces

Directions:
1. In a bowl, mix together the soy sauce, oil, garlic, brown sugar, cumin, salt, and black pepper.
2. Add the steak cubes and generously coat with marinade.
3. Refrigerate to marinate for about 5 minutes.
4. Thread the steak cubes, mushrooms, bell pepper, and onion onto metal skewers.
5. Set the temperature of air fryer to 390°F. Grease an air fryer basket.
6. Arrange skewers into the prepared air fryer basket.
7. Air fry for about 10-12 minutes, flipping once halfway through.
8. Remove from air fryer and transfer the kebabs onto a platter.
9. Serve hot.

502. Pork riblets in tomato sauce
Servings: 4
Prep & Cooking Time: 40 Minutes
Ingredients:
- 1-lb. pork riblets
- 2 tbsps. stevia
- 1/2 tsp. ground paprika
- 1/2 tsp. chili powder
- 1 tsp. yellow mustard
- 2 tbsps. white wine vinegar
- 1 tsp. keto tomato sauce
- 1/4 cup of water
- 1 tsp. salt

Directions:
1. In the mixing bowl mix up Erythritol, ground paprika, chili powder, yellow mustard, white wine vinegar, tomato sauce, and water. Add salt. Whisk the mixture until homogenous.
2. Put the pork riblets in the homogenous mixture and mix up well. Leave the meat for 20 minutes in this sauce.
3. After this, preheat the air fryer to 355°F. Put the pork riblets in the air fryer and cook them for 40 minutes.
4. Flip the pork ribs on another side after 20 minutes of cooking.

503. Salted butter with chicken fillets
Servings: 3
Prep & Cooking Time: 30 Minutes
Ingredients:
- 8 pieces of chicken fillet [approximately 3 x 1 x 1-inch dimensions]
- 1 egg
- 1 oz. salted butter, melted
- 1 cup friendly bread crumbs
- 1 tsp. garlic powder

- 1/2 cup parmesan cheese
- 1 tsp. Italian herbs

Directions:
1. Cover the chicken pieces in the whisked egg, melted butter, garlic powder, and Italian herbs. Allow to marinate for about 5 minutes.
2. In a bowl, mix together the Panko bread crumbs and parmesan. Use this mixture to coat the marinated chicken.
3. Put the aluminum foil in your air fryer basket.
4. Set the fryer to 390°F and briefly allow to warm. Line the basket with aluminum foil.
5. Place 4 pieces of the chicken in the basket. Cook for 6 minutes until golden brown. Don't turn the chicken over.
6. Repeat with the rest of the chicken pieces.
7. Serve the chicken fillets hot.

504. Wrapped pork
Servings: 2
Prep & Cooking Time: 16 Minutes
Ingredients:
- 8 ounces pork tenderloin
- 4 bacon slices
- 1/2 tsp. salt
- 1 tsp. olive oil
- 1/2 tsp. chili powder

Directions:
1. Sprinkle the pork tenderloin with salt and chili powder. Then wrap it in the bacon slices and sprinkle with olive oil. Secure the bacon with toothpicks if needed.
2. Preheat the air fryer to 375°F. Put the wrapped pork tenderloin in the air fryer and cook it for 7 minutes. After this, carefully flip the meat on another side and cook it for 9 minutes more.
3. When the meat is cooked, remove the toothpicks from it (if the toothpicks were used) and slice the meat.

505. Peach mash on ribeye
Servings: 2
Prep & Cooking Time: 45 Minutes
Ingredients:
- 1/4 cup balsamic vinegar
- 1 cup peach puree
- 1 tbsp. paprika
- 1 tsp. thyme
- 1-lb. T-bone steak
- 2 tsps. lemon pepper seasoning
- Salt & pepper to taste

Directions:
4. Place all ingredients in a Ziploc bag and allow to marinate in the fridge for at least 2 hours.
5. Preheat the air fryer to 390°F.
6. Place the grill pan accessory in the air fryer.
7. Grill for 20 minutes and flip the meat halfway through the cooking time.

506. Rubbed chicken with curry-peanut butter
Servings: 3
Prep & Cooking Time: 12 Minutes
Ingredients:
- 1/2-lb. boneless and skinless chicken thigh meat, cut into 2-inch chunks
- 1 medium bell pepper, seeded and cut into chunks
- 1 tbsp. lime juice
- 1 tbsp. Thai curry paste
- 1 tsp. salt

- 2/3 cup oat milk
- 3 tbsp. peanut butter

Directions:
1. In a shallow dish, mix well all ingredients except for chicken and bell pepper.
2. Transfer half of the sauce in a small bowl for basting.
3. Add chicken to dish and toss well to coat. Marinate in the ref for 3 hours.
4. Thread bell pepper and chicken pieces in skewers. Place on skewer rack in air fryer.
5. For 12 minutes, cook on 360°F. Halfway through cooking time, turnover skewers and baste with sauce. If needed, cook in batches.
6. Serve and enjoy.

507. Steak with irish whisky
Servings: 6
Prep & Cooking Time: 25 Minutes + Marinating Time
Ingredients:
- 2 lbs. sirloin steaks
- 1 ½ tbsps. tamari sauce
- 1/3 tsp. cayenne pepper
- 1/3 tsp. ground ginger
- 2 garlic cloves, slimly sliced
- 2 tbsps. Irish whiskey
- 2 tbsps. olive oil
- Fine sea salt, to taste

Directions:
1. Firstly, add all the ingredients, minus the olive oil and the steak, to a resealable plastic bag.
2. Throw in the steak and let it marinate for a couple of hours. After that, drizzle the sirloin steaks with tbsp. olive oil.
3. Roast for approximately 22 minutes at 5°F, turning it halfway through the time. Bon appétit!

508. Beef burgers asian style
Servings: 4
Prep & Cooking Time: 20 Minutes
Ingredients:
- 3/4 lb. lean ground beef
- 1 tbsp. soy sauce
- 1 tsp. Dijon mustard
- Few dashes of liquid smoke
- 1 tsp. shallot powder
- 1 clove garlic, minced
- 1/2 tsp. cumin powder
- 1/4 cup chives, minced
- 1/3 tsp. sea salt flakes
- 1/3 tsp. freshly grounded mixed peppercorns
- 1 tsp. celery seeds
- 1 tsp. parsley flakes

Directions:
1. Mix together all of the ingredients in a bowl using your hands, combining every element well.
2. Take four equal amounts of the mixture and mold each one into a patty.
3. Use the back of a spoon to create a shallow dip in the center of each patty. This will prevent them from puffing up during the cooking process.
4. Lightly coat all sides of the patties with cooking spray.
5. Place each one in the air fryer and cook for roughly 12 minutes at 360°F.
6. Test with a meat thermometer – the patties are ready once they have reached 1°F. Serve them on top of butter rolls with any sauces and toppings you desire.

509. Mustard turkey fingers with creole
Servings: 4
Prep & Cooking Time: 20 Minutes
Ingredients:
- 1/2 cup cornmeal mix
- 1/2 cup all-purpose flour
- 1 1/2 tbsp. Creole seasoning
- 1 1/2 tbsp. whole-grain mustard
- 1 1/2 cups buttermilk
- 1 tsp. soy sauce
- 3/4 lb. turkey tenderloins, cut into finger-sized strips
- Salt & ground black pepper, at your convenience

Directions:
1. Grab three bowls. Combine the cornmeal, flour, and Creole seasoning in the first bowl. Mix the whole-grain mustard, buttermilk and soy sauce in the second one.
2. Season the turkey fingers with the salt and black pepper. Now, dip each strip into the buttermilk mix; after that, cover them with the cornmeal mixture on all sides.
3. Transfer the prepared turkey fingers to the air fryer baking pan and cook for 15 minutes at 370°F. Serve with hot tomato ketchup and enjoy!

510. Super-hot chicken skin
Servings: 4
Prep & Cooking Time: 30 Minutes
Ingredients:
- 1/2 tsp. chili paste
- 8 ounce chicken skin
- 1 tsp. sesame oil
- 1/2 tsp. chili powder
- 1/2 tsp. salt

Directions:
1. In the shallow bowl mix up chili paste, sesame oil, chili powder, and salt. Then brush the chicken skin with chili mixture well and leave for 5 minutes to marinate.
2. Meanwhile, preheat the air fryer to 365°F. Put the marinated chicken skin in the air fryer and cook it for 20 minutes.
3. When the time is finished, flip the chicken skin on another side and cook it for 10 minutes more or until the chicken skin is crunchy.

511. Crusts with chicken pizza
Servings: 1
Prep & Cooking Time: 35 Minutes
Ingredients:
- 1/2 cup mozzarella, shredded
- 1/4 cup parmesan cheese, shredded
- 1 lb. ground chicken

Directions:
1. Whisk all of the ingredients in a bowl, and then spread the mixture out, dividing it into four parts of equal size.
2. Cut a sheet of parchment paper into four circles, roughly six inches in diameter, and put some of the chicken mixture onto the center of each piece, flattening the mixture to fill out the circle.
3. Cook either one or two circles at a time at 250°F for 25 minutes.
4. Halfway through, turn the crust over to cook on the other side. Keep each batch warm while you move onto the next one.
5. Once all the crusts are cooked, top with cheese and the toppings of your choice. If desired, cook the topped crusts for an additional five minutes.
6. Serve hot!

512. Chicken wings and lemon pepper
Servings: 4
Prep & Cooking Time: 16 Minutes
Ingredients:
- 1 lb. chicken wings
- 1 tsp. lemon pepper
- 1 tbsp. olive oil
- 1 tsp. salt

Directions:
1. Add chicken wings into the large size mixing bowl.
2. Add remaining ingredients over chicken and toss well to coat.
3. Place chicken wings in the air fryer basket.
4. Cook chicken wings for 8 minutes at 400°F.
5. Turn chicken wings to another side and cook for 8 minutes more.
6. Serve and enjoy.

513. 5 garlicky beef chops with mustard
Servings: 3
Prep & Cooking Time: 35 Minutes
Ingredients:
- 1 1/2 tsps. English mustard
- 3 boneless beef chops
- 1/3 tsp. garlic pepper
- 2 tsps. oregano, dried
- 2 tbsps. vegetable oil
- 1 1/2 tbsps. fresh coriander, minced
- 1/2 tsp. onion powder
- 1/2 tsp. basil, dried
- Grated rind of 1/2 small-sized lime
- 1/2 tsp. fine sea salt

Directions:
1. Firstly, make the rub for the beef chops by mixing all the ingredients, except the chops and the new potatoes.
2. Now, evenly spread the beef chops with the English mustard rub.
3. Then, arrange the new potatoes in the bottom of the air fryer cooking basket. Top them with the prepared beef chops.
4. Roast for about 27 minutes at 365°F, turning halfway through. Serve on individual plates with a keto salad on the side, if desired.

514. Ginger chicken tenders
Servings: 4
Prep & Cooking Time: 30 Minutes
Ingredients:
- 1 lb. chicken tenders
- 1 tsp. ginger, minced
- 4 garlic cloves, minced
- 2 tbsp. walnut oil
- 6 tbsp. pineapple juice
- 2 tbsp. soy sauce
- 1/2 tsp. pepper

Directions:
1. Pour all the ingredients in a large bowl, except for the chicken, and combine well.
2. Thread the chicken onto skewers and coat with the seasonings. Allow to marinate for hours.
3. Pre-heat the air fryer to 360°F.
4. Put the marinated chicken in fryer basket and cook for 18 minutes. Serve hot.

515. Scallion kabobs with chicken
Servings: 4
Prep & Cooking Time: 24 Minutes
Ingredients:
- 1/4 cup light soy sauce

- 1 tbsp. mirin
- 1 tsp. garlic salt
- 1 tsp. sugar
- 4 (4-ounces) skinless, boneless chicken thighs, cubed into 1-inch size
- 5 chives, cut into 1-inch pieces lengthwise

Directions:
1. In a baking dish, mix together the soy sauce, mirin, garlic salt, and sugar.
2. Thread chicken and chives onto pre-soaked wooden skewers.
3. Place skewers into the baking dish and generously coat with marinade.
4. Cover and refrigerate for about 3 hours.
5. Set the temperature of air fryer to 3°F. Grease an air fryer basket.
6. Arrange skewers into the prepared air fryer basket in 2 batches in a single layer.
7. Air fry for about 10-12 minutes.
8. Once done, remove from air fryer and transfer the chicken skewers onto a platter.
9. Serve hot.

516. Cabbage salad, lettuce and beef
Servings: 4
Prep & Cooking Time: 25 Minutes
Ingredients:
- 1 lb. beef, cubed
- 1/4 cup coconut aminos
- 1 tbsp. coconut oil, melted
- 6 ounces iceberg lettuce, shredded
- 2 tbsps. cilantro, minced
- 2 tbsps. chives, minced
- 1 zucchini, shredded
- 1/2 green cabbage head, shredded
- 2 tbsps. almonds, sliced
- 1 tbsp. sesame seeds
- 1/2 tbsp. white vinegar
- A pinch of salt and black pepper

Directions:
1. Heat up a pan that fits the air fryer with the oil over medium-high heat, add the meat and brown for 5 minutes. Add the aminos, zucchini, cabbage, salt and pepper, toss, put the pan in the fryer and cook at 370°F for 20 minutes.
2. Cool the mix down, transfer to a salad bowl, add the rest of the ingredients, toss well and serve.

517. Strips of buffalo chicken
Servings: 1
Prep & Cooking Time: 30 Minutes
Ingredients:
- 1/4 cup hot sauce
- 1 lb. boneless skinless chicken tenders
- 1 tsp. garlic powder
- 1 1/2 oz. pork rinds, finely ground
- 1 tsp. chili powder

Directions:
1. Toss the hot sauce and chicken tenders together in a bowl, ensuring the chicken is completely coated.
2. In another bowl, combine the garlic powder, ground pork rinds, and chili powder. Use this mixture to coat the tenders, covering them well. Place the chicken into your fryer, taking care not to layer pieces on top of one another.
3. Cook the chicken at 385°F for twenty minutes until cooked all the way through and golden. Serve warm with your favorite dips and sides.

518. Chicken tenderloin that is air-fried
Servings: 8
Prep & Cooking Time: 15 Minutes
Ingredients:
- 1/2 cup almond flour
- 1 egg, beaten
- 2 tbsp. coconut oil
- 8 chicken tenderloins
- Salt & pepper to taste

Directions:
1. Preheat the air fryer for 5 minutes.
2. Use salt & pepper to season the chicken tenderloin.
3. Soak in beaten eggs then dredge in almond flour.
4. Drop into the air fryer and brush with coconut oil.
5. Cook for 1minutes at 370°F
6. Halfway through the cooking time, give the fryer basket a shake to cook evenly.

519. Minty lamb mixture
Servings: 4
Prep & Cooking Time: 24 Minutes
Ingredients:
- 8 lamb chops
- A pinch of salt and black pepper
- 1 cup mint, minced
- 1 garlic clove, minced
- Juice of 1 lemon
- 2 tbsps. olive oil

Directions:
1. In a blender, stir all the ingredients except the lamb and pulse well.
2. Rub lamb chops with the mint sauce, put them in your air fryer's basket and cook at 400°F for 20 minutes on each side.
3. Divide every slimg between plates and serve.

520. Easy crunch wrap for thanksgiving
Servings: 4
Prep & Cooking Time: 1 Hour 15 Minutes
Ingredients:
- 2 tbsp. sesame oil
- 1 lb. turkey breasts
- 1 tbsp. taco seasoning
- 2 onions, sliced
- 2 bell peppers, sliced
- 1 habanero pepper, sliced
- 8 corn tortillas, approx. 7-8-inch diameter
- 1/2 cup queso quesadilla
- 1 cup Manchego cheese, shredded
- 1 1/2 cups tortilla chips
- 1/2 cup mayonnaise
- 2 tbsps. lemon juice
- 1 tsp. yellow mustard
- 1 1/2 cup pickled jalapenos, minced
- 1/4 tsp. dried dill weed
- 1/2 tsp. Mexican oregano

Directions:
1. Preheat your air fryer to 400°F.
2. Drizzle the sesame oil all over the turkey breasts and cook it for 30 minutes, flipping them over halfway through.
3. Let them rest for 7 minutes; then, slice the turkey breast into strips, add the taco seasoning, and set aside.
4. Place the onions and peppers in the cooking basket.
5. Let it cook in the preheated air fryer at 400°F for 1minute and set aside.

6. Spritz the base of a baking pan with cooking oil. Divide the roasted turkey, pepper mixture and cheese between the tortillas. Top with tortilla chips.
7. Fold over your tortillas, then, arrange them in the baking pan. Drizzle the remaining 1 tbsp. of sesame oil over each tortilla. Bake at 380°F for 24 minutes.
8. Meantime, to prepare the sauce, combine the mayonnaise, lemon juice, mustard, jalapeño, dill, and oregano in a mixing bowl.
9. Serve with the warm tortillas. Enjoy!

521. Vegetables and italian turkey sausage
Servings: 4
Prep & Cooking Time: 40 Minutes
Ingredients:
- 1 onion, cut into wedges
- 2 carrots, trimmed and sliced
- 1 parsnip, trimmed and sliced
- 2 potatoes, peeled and diced
- 1 tsp. dried oregano
- 1/2 tsp. dried marjoram
- 1 tsp. dried basil
- 1/2 tsp. celery seeds
- Sea salt & ground black pepper, to taste
- 1 tbsp. melted butter
- 3/4 lb. sweet Italian turkey sausage

Directions:
1. Mix the vegetables with all seasonings and melted butter. Set the vegetables on the bottom of the air fryer cooking basket. Lower the sausage onto the top of the vegetables.
2. Roast at 360°F for 33 to 37 minutes or until the sausages are no longer pink. Work in batches as needed, shaking halfway through the roasting time. Bon appétit!

522. Spiced rack of lamb with saffron
Servings: 4
Prep & Cooking Time: 1 Hour And 10 Minutes
Ingredients:
- 1/2 tsp. crumbled saffron threads
- 1 cup plain Greek yogurt
- 1 tsp. lemon zest
- 2 cloves of garlic, minced
- 2 racks of lamb, rib bones frenched
- 2 tbsps. olive oil
- Salt & pepper to taste

Directions:
1. Preheat the air fryer to 390°F.
2. Place the grill pan accessory in the air fryer.
3. Season the lamb meat with salt and pepper to taste. Set aside.
4. In a mixing bowl, combine the rest of ingredients.
5. Brush the mixture onto the lamb.
6. Place on the grill pan and cook for 1 hour and 10 minutes.

523. Beef sausage meatballs with mexican chili
Servings: 4
Prep & Cooking Time: 25 Minutes
Ingredients:
- 1 cup green onion, finely minced
- 1/2 tsp. parsley flakes
- 2 tsps. onion flakes
- 1 lb. chili sausage, crumbled
- 2 tbsps. flaxseed meal
- 3 cloves garlic, finely minced
- 1 tsp. Mexican oregano
- 1 tbsp. poblano pepper, minced
- Fine sea salt and ground black pepper, to taste
- 1/2 tbsp. fresh minced sage

Directions:
1. Mix all ingredients in a bowl until the mixture has a uniform consistency.
2. Roll into bite-sized balls and transfer them to a baking dish.
3. Cook in the preheated air fryer at 5°F for 18 minutes. Serve on wooden sticks and enjoy!

524. Pork schnitzel with heavy cream
Servings: 2
Prep & Cooking Time: 10 Minutes
Ingredients:
- 8 ounces pork cutlets (4 ounce each cutlet)
- 1 tsp. sunflower oil
- 1 egg, beaten
- 1 tbsp. heavy cream
- 1/2 cup coconut flour
- 1/2 tsp. ground black pepper
- 1/2 tsp. salt

Directions:
1. Beat the pork cutlets with the help of the kitchen hammer and sprinkle them with ground black pepper and salt.
2. After this, mix up egg and heavy cream. Dip the pork cutlets in the egg mixture and then coat in the coconut flour.
3. Repeat the same steps one more time. Then preheat the air fryer to 400°F.
4. Sprinkle the pork cutlets with sunflower oil and put them in the air fryer.
5. Cook the schnitzels for 5 minutes from each side.

525. Crunchy stuffed chicken breast
Servings: 2
Prep & Cooking Time: 45 Minutes
Ingredients:
- 1 medium eggplant, halved lengthwise
- 1/4 cup pomegranate seeds
- 2 (4-ounce) chicken breasts, skinless and boneless
- 2 egg whites
- 1/4 cup breadcrumbs
- Salt, to taste
- Freshly ground black pepper, to taste
- 1/2 tbsp. olive oil

Directions:
1. Preheat the air fryer to 390°F and grease an air fryer basket.
2. Season the eggplant halves with some salt and keep aside for about 5 minutes.
3. Set the eggplant halves in the air fryer basket, cut side up and cook for about 20 minutes.
4. Serve and scoop out the flesh from each eggplant half.
5. Put the eggplant pulp and a pinch of salt and black pepper in the food processor and pulse until a puree is formed.
6. Serve the eggplant puree into a bowl and stir in the pomegranate seeds.
7. Cut the chicken breasts lengthwise to make a pocket and stuff in the eggplant mixture.
8. Whisk together egg whites, a pinch of salt and black pepper in a shallow dish.
9. Mix breadcrumbs, thyme and olive oil in another dish.
10. Dip the chicken breasts in the egg white mixture and then coat with flour.
11. Set the air fryer to 355°F and transfer the chicken breasts into the Air fryer.
12. Cook for about 25 minutes and dish out to serve warm.

526. Greek style chicken
Servings: 4
Prep & Cooking Time: 24 Minutes
Ingredients:
- 2 lbs. chicken tenders
- 1 cup cherry tomatoes
- 2 tbsps. olive oil
- 3 dill sprigs
- 1 large zucchini
- For topping:
- 2 tbsps. feta cheese, crumbled
- 1 tbsp fresh dill, minced
- 1 tbsp. olive oil
- 1 tbsp. fresh lemon juice

Directions:
1. Preheat the air fryer to 370°F.
2. Spray air fryer basket with cooking spray.
3. Add chicken, zucchini, dill, and tomatoes into the air fryer basket.
4. Drizzle with olive oil and season with salt.
5. Cook chicken for 2 minutes.
6. Meanwhile, in a small bowl, stir together all topping ingredients.
7. Place chicken on the serving plate then top with veggies and discard dill sprigs.
8. Sprinkle topping mixture on top of chicken and vegetables.
9. Serve and enjoy.

527. Egg frittata with salted meaty
Servings: 3
Prep & Cooking Time: 20 Minutes
Ingredients:
- 1/2 lb. ground beef
- 1 onion, minced
- 3 cloves of garlic, minced
- 3 eggs, beaten
- 3 tbsps. olive oil
- Salt & pepper to taste

Directions:
1. Arm the oil in a skillet under medium heat.
2. Sauté the garlic and onion until fragrant.
3. Add the ground beef and sauté for 5 minutes or until lightly golden. Set aside.
4. Preheat the air fryer for 5 minutes.
5. In a mixing bowl, combine the rest of the ingredients
6. Place the sautéed beef in a baking dish that will fit in the air fryer chamber.
7. Pour over the egg mixture.
8. Cook for 20 minutes at 320°F.

528. Turkey chimichurri
Servings: 1
Prep & Cooking Time: 70 Minutes
Ingredients:
- 1 lb. turkey breast
- 1/2 cup chimichurri sauce
- 1/2 cup butter
- 1/4 cup parmesan cheese, shredded
- 1/4 tsp. garlic powder

Directions:
1. Spread the chimichurri sauce in the turkey breast, then refrigerate in an airtight container for at least a half hour.
2. In the meantime, prepare the herbed butter. Mix together the butter, parmesan, and garlic powder, using a hand mixer if desired (this will make it extra creamy)
3. Preheat your fryer at 250°F and put the rack inside.
4. Remove the turkey from the refrigerator and set it aside to come to room temperature for roughly 20 minutes while the fryer warms.
5. Place the turkey in the fryer and cook for 20 minutes. Cook for another twenty minutes on the opposite side.
6. Serve with the herbed butter.

529. Chicken and veggies roll
Servings: 3
Prep & Cooking Time: 6 Minutes
Ingredients:
- 1 lb. ground chicken
- 1 tbsp. fresh lemon juice
- 1/4 cup almond flour
- 2 green onion, minced
- 1 egg, lightly beaten
- 1/3 cup fresh parsley, minced
- 3 garlic cloves
- 4 ounces onion, minced
- 1/4 tsp. turmeric powder
- 1/2 tsp. pepper

Directions:
1. Use a food processor, to blend all the ingredients until thoroughly incorporated.
2. Transfer chicken mixture to the bowl and place in the refrigerator for 1 hour.
3. Divide mixture into the 6 equal portions and roll around the soaked wooden skewers.
4. Spray air fryer basket with cooking spray.
5. Place skewers into the air fryer basket and cooks at 400°F for 6 minutes.
6. Serve and enjoy.

530. Turkey ground mix
Servings: 4
Prep & Cooking Time: 25 Minutes
Ingredients:
- 1 s. turkey meat, ground
- A pinch of salt and black pepper
- 2 tbsp. olive oil
- 2 tsps. parsley flakes
- 1 lb. green beans, trimmed and halved
- 2 tsps. garlic powder

Directions:
1. Heat up a pan that fits the air fryer with the oil over medium-high heat, add the meat and brown it for 5 minutes.
2. Add the remaining ingredients, toss, put the pan in the machine and cook at 370°F for 20 minutes.
3. Divide between plates and serve.

531. Turkey nuggets with thyme
Servings: 2
Prep & Cooking Time: 15 Minutes
Ingredients:
- 1 egg, beaten
- 1 cup breadcrumbs
- 1 tbsp. dried oregano
- 1/2 tbsp. dried parsley
- 1 cup turkey, grounded
- Salt and pepper, to taste

Directions:
1. Preheat air fryer to 350°F. In a bowl, mix ground turkey, thyme, oregano, parsley, salt and pepper.

2. Shape the mixture into balls.
3. Grease, with cooking spray, the air fryer basket.
4. Put the nuggets in the air fryer basket and let them cook for 10 minutes, shaking once.

532. Chicken tenders from india
Servings: 4
Prep & Cooking Time: 15 Minutes
Ingredients:
- 1 lb. chicken tenders, cut in half
- 1/4 cup parsley, minced
- 1/2 tbsp. garlic, minced
- 1/2 tbsp. ginger, minced
- 1/4 cup yogurt
- 3/4 tsp. paprika
- 1 tsp. garam masala
- 1 tsp. turmeric
- 1/2 tsp. cayenne pepper
- 1 tsp. salt

Directions:
1. Preheat the air fryer to 350°F.
2. Pour all the ingredients into a wide bowl and mix well. Place in refrigerator for 30 minutes.
3. Spray air fryer basket with cooking spray.
4. Add marinated chicken into the air fryer basket and cook for about 10-12 minutes.
5. Turn the chicken over and cook for another 4-5 minutes.
6. Serve and enjoy.

533. Chicken tenders from kfc
Servings: 4
Prep & Cooking Time: 25 Minutes
Ingredients:
For Breading
- 2 whole eggs, beaten
- 1/2 cup seasoned breadcrumbs
- 1/2 cup all-purpose flour
- 1 tbsp. black pepper
- 2 tbsps. olive oil

Directions:
1. Preheat your air fryer to 330°F. Add breadcrumbs, eggs and flour in three separate bowls. Mix breadcrumbs with oil and season with salt and pepper. Dredge the tenders into flour, eggs and crumbs.
2. Add chicken in the air fryer and cook for 10 minutes. Increase to 390°F, and cook for 5 more minutes.

534. Sweet turkey bake
Servings: 3
Prep & Cooking Time: 50 Minutes
Ingredients:
- Salt & pepper to season
- 1/4 cup chicken soup cream
- 1/4 cup mayonnaise
- 2 tbsp lemon juice
- 1/4 cup almonds, minced
- 1/4 cup breadcrumbs
- 2 tbsps. scallions, minced
- 2 tbsps. pimentos, minced
- 2 boiled eggs, minced
- 1/2 cup diced celery
- Cooking spray

Directions:
1. Warm your air fryer to 390°F.
2. Place the turkey breasts on a clean flat surface and season with salt and pepper. Grease with cooking spray and place in the fryer's basket; cook for 10 minutes.
3. Remove turkey back onto the chopping board, let cool, and cut into dices. In a mixing bowl, add celery, eggs, pimentos, scallions, almonds, lemon juice, mayonnaise, diced turkey, and chicken soup cream and mix well.
4. Grease a casserole dish with cooking spray, scoop the turkey mixture into the bowl, sprinkle the breadcrumbs on it, and spray with cooking spray.
5. Put the dish in the fryer basket, and bake the ingredients at 390°F for 30 minutes. Remove and serve with a side of steamed asparagus.

535. Bbq beastly drumsticks
Servings: 4
Prep & Cooking Time: 45 Minutes
Ingredients:
- 4 chicken drumsticks
- 1/2 tbsp. mustard
- 1 clove garlic, crushed
- 1 tsp. chili powder
- 2 tsp. sugar
- 1 tbsp. olive oil
- Freshly ground black pepper

Directions:
1. Pre-heat the air fryer to 390°F.
2. Mix together the garlic, sugar, mustard, a pinch of salt, freshly ground pepper, chili powder and oil.
3. Massage this mixture into the drumsticks and leave to marinate for a minimum of 20 minutes.
4. Put the drumsticks in the fryer basket and cook for 10 minutes.
5. Bring the temperature down to 300°F and continue to cook the drumsticks for a further 10 minutes. When cooked through, serve with bread and corn salad.

536. Prawn paste and chicken
Servings: 2
Prep & Cooking Time: 30 Minutes
Ingredients:
- 2 tbsp corn flour
- 1/2 tbsp. wine
- 1 tbsp. shrimp paste
- 1 tbsp. ginger
- 1/2 tbsp. olive oil

Directions:
1. Warm your air fryer to 355°F.
2. In a bowl, mix oil, ginger, and wine. Cover the chicken wings with the prepared marinade and top with flour.
3. Add the floured chicken to shrimp paste and coat it.
4. Place the chicken in your air fryer's cooking basket and cook for 20 minutes, until crispy on the outside.

537. Yummy chicken fingers with fresh chives
Servings: 2
Prep & Cooking Time: 8 Minutes
Ingredients:
- 3 tbsps. Parmesan cheese
- 1/4 tbsp. fresh chives, minced
- 1/3 cup breadcrumbs
- 1 egg white
- 2 tbsp plum sauce, optional
- 1/2 tbsp. fresh thyme, minced
- 1 tbsp. water

Directions:
1. Preheat air fryer to 360°F.
2. Mix chives, Parmesan cheese, thyme, and breadcrumbs. In another bowl, whisk the egg white mix the water.
3. Dip the chicken strips into the egg mixture and the breadcrumb mixture.
4. Place the strips in the air fryer basket and cook for 15 minutes.
5. Serve with plum sauce.

538. Shredded chicken moroccan style
Servings: 2
Prep & Cooking Time: 25 Minutes
Ingredients:
- 1/2 lb. shredded chicken
- 1 cup broth
- 1 carrot
- 1 broccoli, minced
- Pinch of cinnamon
- Pinch of cumin
- Pinch of red pepper
- Pinch of sea salt

Directions:
1. In a mixing bowl, cover the shredded chicken with cumin, red pepper, sea salt and cinnamon.
2. Chop up the carrots into small pieces. Put the carrot and broccoli into the bowl with the chicken.
3. Add the broth and stir every element well. Set aside for about 5 minutes.
4. Transfer to the air fryer. Cook for about 15 minutes at 390°F. Serve hot.

539. Peppercorn duck with vanilla
Servings: 4
Prep & Cooking Time: 30 Minutes
Ingredients:
- 4 duck legs, skin on
- Juice of 1/2 lemon
- 1 tsp. cinnamon powder
- 1 tsp. vanilla extract
- 10 peppercorns, crushed
- 1 tbsp. balsamic vinegar
- 1 tbsp. olive oil
- A pinch of salt and black pepper

Directions:
1. Warm the oil, in a pan, over medium-high heat, add the duck legs and sear them for 3 minutes on each side.
2. Transfer to a pan that fits the air fryer, add the remaining ingredients, toss, put the pan in the air fryer and cook at 380°F for 22 minutes.
3. Divide duck legs and cooking juices between plates and serve.

540. Chicken mix with bacon
Servings: 2
Prep & Cooking Time: 25 Minutes
Ingredients:
- 2 chicken legs
- 4 ounce bacon, sliced
- 1/2 tsp. salt
- 1/2 tsp. ground black pepper
- 1 tsp. sesame oil

Directions:
1. Sprinkle the chicken legs with salt and ground black pepper and wrap in the sliced bacon. After this, preheat the air fryer to 385°F.
2. Put the chicken legs in the air fryer and sprinkle with sesame oil.
3. Cook the bacon chicken legs for 25 minutes.

541. Traditional asian chicken
Servings: 3
Prep & Cooking Time: 25 Minutes
Ingredients:
- 1 tbsp. cilantro leaves, minced
- Salt & black pepper, to taste
- 1 tbsp. roasted peanuts, minced
- 1/2 tbsp white wine vinegar
- 1 garlic clove, minced
- 1/2 tbsp. chili sauce
- 1 ginger, minced
- 1 1/2 tbsp. soy sauce
- 2 1/2 tbsp. honey

Directions:
1. Preheat your air fryer to 360°F.
2. Wash chicken wingettes thoroughly; season with salt and pepper.
3. In a bowl, mix ginger, garlic, chili sauce, honey, soy sauce, cilantro, and vinegar. Cover chicken with honey sauce.
4. Place the prepared chicken to your air fryer's cooking basket and cook for 20 minutes. Serve sprinkled with peanuts.

542. Okra chicken thighs with thyme
Servings: 4
Prep & Cooking Time: 30 Minutes
Ingredients:
- 4 chicken thighs, bone-in and skinless
- A pinch of salt and black pepper
- 1 cup okra
- 1/2 cup butter, melted
- Zest of 1 lemon, shredded
- 4 garlic cloves, minced
- 1 tbsp. thyme, minced
- 1 tbsp. parsley, minced

Directions:
1. Warm half of the butter in a pan over medium heat.
2. Add the chicken thighs and brown them for 2-3 minutes on each side.
3. Add the rest of the butter, the okra and all the remaining ingredients, toss, put the pan in the air fryer and cook at 370°F for 20 minutes.
4. Divide between plates and serve.

543. Scrambled eggs and turkey bacon
Servings: 4
Prep & Cooking Time: 25 Minutes
Ingredients:
- 1/2 lb. turkey bacon
- 4 eggs
- 1/3 cup milk
- 2 tbsps. yogurt
- 1/2 tsp. sea salt
- 1 bell pepper, finely minced
- 2 green onions, finely minced
- 1/2 cup Colby cheese, shredded

Directions:
1. Place the turkey bacon in the cooking basket.
2. Cook at 360°F for 9 to 11 minutes. Work in batches. Reserve the fried bacon.
3. In a mixing bowl, thoroughly whisk the eggs with milk and yogurt. Add salt, bell pepper, and green onions.
4. Brush the sides and bottom of the baking pan with the reserved 1 tsp. of bacon grease.

5. Pour the egg mixture into the baking pan. Cook at 360°F about 5 minutes. Top with shredded Colby cheese and cook for 5 to 6 minutes more.
6. Serve the scrambled eggs with the reserved bacon and enjoy!

544. Turkey breast rolls
Servings: 3
Prep & Cooking Time: 40 Minutes
Ingredients:
- 1 lb. turkey breast fillet
- 1 garlic clove, crushed
- 1 1/2 tsp. ground cumin
- 1 tsp. ground cinnamon
- 1/2 tsp. red chili powder
- Salt, to taste
- 2 tbsp. olive oil
- 3 tbsp. fresh parsley, finely minced
- 1 small red onion, finely minced

Directions:
1. Place the turkey fillet on a cutting board.
2. Carefully, cut horizontally along the length about 1/3 of way from the top, stopping about 1/4-inch from the edge.
3. Open this part to have a long piece of fillet.
4. In a bowl, mix together the garlic, spices, and oil.
5. In a small cup, reserve about 1 tbsp. of oil mixture.
6. In the remaining oil mixture, add the parsley, and onion and mix well.
7. Set the temperature of air fryer to 355°F. Grease an air fryer basket.
8. Coat the open side of fillet with onion mixture.
9. Roll the fillet tightly from the short side.
10. With a kitchen string, tie the roll at 1-11/2-inch intervals.
11. Coat the outer side of roll with the reserved oil mixture.
12. Arrange roll into the prepared air fryer basket.
13. Air fry for about 40 minutes.
14. Remove from air fryer and place the turkey roll onto a cutting board for about 5-10 minutes before slicing.
15. With a sharp knife, cut the turkey roll into desired size slices and serve.

545. Shallots with almond turkey
Servings: 2
Prep & Cooking Time: 25 Minutes
Ingredients:
- 1 big turkey breast, skinless, boneless and halved
- 1/3 cup almonds, minced
- Salt & black pepper to the taste
- 2 tbsp. olive oil
- 1 tbsp. sweet paprika
- 2 shallots, minced

Directions:
1. In a pan that fits the air fryer, combine the turkey with all the other ingredients, toss, put the pan in the machine and cook at 370°F for 25 minutes. Divide every element between plates and serve.

546. Scallions mix with duck legs
Servings: 2
Prep & Cooking Time: 16 Minutes
Ingredients:
- 2 duck legs
- 1 tsp. olive oil
- 1/2 tsp. ground cumin
- 1 tsp. salt
- 1 tbsp. chives, minced

Directions:
1. In the shallow bowl mix up ground cumin and salt. Then rub the duck legs with the spice mixture. After this, mix up the chives and olive oil. Sprinkle the duck legs with the chives mix. Preheat the air fryer to 385°F. Put the duck legs in the air fryer and cook them for 8 minutes. Then flip the duck legs on another side and cook for 8 minutes.

547. Enchilada bake with leftovers
Servings: 3
Prep & Cooking Time: 45 Minutes
Ingredients:
- 1 egg
- 1/2 (2/3 cup) can black beans, drained
- 1/2 (2/3 cup) can tomato sauce
- 1/2 (1/3 cup) package cornbread mix
- 1/2 cup shredded Mexican-style cheese blend, or more to taste
- 1/2 envelope taco seasoning mix
- 1/2-lb. chicken breast tenderloins
- 1-1/2 tsps. vegetable oil
- 2 tbsp. cream cheese
- 2 tbsp. water
- 2-1/4 tsps. chili powder
- 3 tbsps. milk

Directions:
1. Lightly coat an air fryer baking pan with vegetable oil.
2. Cook the chicken for about 5 minutes per side at 350°F.
3. Stir in chili powder, taco seasoning mix, water, and tomato sauce. Cook for 10 minutes, while stirring and turning chicken halfway through cooking time.
4. Remove chicken from pan and shred with two forks. Return to pan and stir in cream cheese and black beans. Mix well.
5. Top with Mexican cheese.
6. In a mixing bowl, whisk well egg and milk. Add corn bread mix and mix well. Pour over chicken.
7. Cover pan with foil.
8. Cook for another 15 minutes.
9. Remove the foil and let it cook for 8-10 minutes more or until topping is lightly browned.
10. Let it rest for 5 minutes.
11. Serve and enjoy.

548. Orange beef
Servings: 4
Prep & Cooking Time: 25 Minutes
Ingredients:
- 1/4 lime
- 2 tbsps. orange juice
- 1 tsp. dried cilantro
- 1 chili pepper, minced
- 1 tbsp. sesame oil
- 1 tbsp. white wine vinegar
- 1/2 tsp. chili paste
- 1/2 tsp. ground cumin
- 1/2 tsp. salt
- 1-lb. beef skirt steak

Directions:
1. Chop the lime roughly and put it in the blender. Add orange juice, dried cilantro, chili pepper, sesame oil, white wine vinegar, chili paste, ground cumin, and salt. Blend the mixture until smooth.
2. Cut the skirt steak on 4 servings. Then brush every steak with blended lime mixture and leave for minutes to marinate.
3. Meanwhile, preheat the air fryer to 400°F.

4. Put the steaks in the air fryer in one layer and cook them for 7 minutes. Flip the meat on another side and cook it for 7 minutes more.

549. Garlicky chicken
Servings: 4
Prep & Cooking Time: 14 Minutes
Ingredients:
- 4 chives, minced
- 2 tsp. sesame seeds, toasted
- 1 lb. chicken tenders
- Wooden skewers, as required
- 1 tbsp. fresh ginger, shredded finely
- 4 garlic cloves, minced
- 1/2 cup pineapple juice
- 1/2 cup soy sauce
- 1/4 cup sesame oil
- Pinch of black pepper

Directions:
1. Preheat the air fryer to 390°F and grease an air fryer basket.
2. Mix all the ingredients in a large baking dish except chicken.
3. Thread chicken onto skewer and transfer the skewers on the baking dish.
4. Coat evenly with marinade and cover to refrigerate for about 3 hours.
5. Transfer half of the chicken skewers into the air fryer basket and cook for about 7 minutes.
6. Repeat with the remaining skewers and dish out to serve warm.

550. Chicken glazed with agave mustard
Servings: 4
Prep & Cooking Time: 30 Minutes
Ingredients:
- 1 tbsp. avocado oil
- 2 lbs. chicken breasts, boneless, skin-on
- 1 tbsp. Jamaican Jerk Rub
- 1/2 tsp. salt
- 3 tbsps. agave syrup
- 1 tbsp. mustard
- 2 tbsps. chives, minced

Directions:
1. Heat up your air fryer to 380°F
2. Drizzle the avocado oil all over the chicken breast. Then, rub the chicken breast with the Jamaican Jerk rub.
3. Cook for around 15 minutes in a preheated air fryer. Cook for an additional 8 minutes on the other side.
4. While the chicken breasts are roasting, combine the salt, agave syrup, and mustard in a pan over medium heat. Let it simmer until the glaze thickens.
5. After that, brush the glaze all over the chicken breast. Air-fry for a further 6 minutes or until the surface is crispy. Serve garnished with fresh chives. Bon appétit!

551. Pepperyturkey sandwiches
Servings: 4
Prep & Cooking Time: 25 Minutes
Ingredients:
- 1 cup leftover turkey, cut into bite-sized chunks
- 2 bell peppers, emptied and minced
- 1 Serrano pepper, emptied and minced
- 1 leek, sliced
- 1/2 cup sour cream
- 1 tsp. hot paprika
- 3/4 tsp. kosher salt
- 1/2 tsp. ground black pepper
- 1 heaping tbsp. fresh cilantro, minced
- A few dashes of Tabasco sauce
- 4 hamburger buns

Directions:
1. Toss all ingredients, without the hamburger buns, in an air fryer baking pan; toss until every slimg is well coated.
2. Now, roast it for 20 minutes at 385°F. Serve on hamburger buns; add some extra sour cream and Dijon mustard if desired. Bon appétit!

552. Parmesan and lime with chicken tenders
Servings: 6
Prep & Cooking Time: 20 Minutes
Ingredients:
- 1 lime
- 2 lbs. chicken tenderloins, cut up
- 1/2 cup pork rinds, crushed
- 1/2 cup Parmesan cheese, shredded
- 1 tbsp. olive oil
- Sea salt & ground black pepper, to taste
- 1 tsp. cayenne pepper
- 1/3 tsp. ground cumin
- 1 tsp. chili powder
- 1 egg

Directions:
1. Drizzle the lime juice over the chicken all over.
2. Grease the cooking basket with a nonstick cooking spray.
3. In a mixing bowl, thoroughly combine the pork rinds, Parmesan, olive oil, salt, black pepper, cayenne pepper, cumin, and chili powder.
4. In another shallow bowl, whisk the egg until well beaten.
5. Dip the chicken tenders in the egg, then in pork rind mixture.
6. Transfer the breaded chicken to the prepared cooking basket. Cook in the preheated air fryer at 380°F for 12 minutes.
7. Halfway through the cooking time, flip them over.
8. Serve immediately.

553. Broccoli brekky, cauliflower and eggs
Servings: 3
Prep & Cooking Time: 20 Minutes
Ingredients:
- 1/2 cup milk
- 1/2 cup shredded Cheddar cheese
- 1 cup broccoli, cut into little bits or riced
- 1 cup cauliflower, riced
- 1 tsp. salt
- 1/2 tsp. ground black pepper
- 1/2-lb. hot pork sausage, diced
- 3 large eggs

Directions:
1. Slightly grease the air fryer baking tray with cooking spray, and cook the pork sausage for 5 minutes at 360°F.
2. Remove basket and toss the mixture a bit.
3. Stir in riced cauliflower and broccoli. Cook for another 5 minutes.
4. Meanwhile, whisk well eggs, salt, pepper, and milk. Stir in cheese.
5. Remove basket and transfer in egg mixture.
6. Cook for another 10 minutes.
7. Serve and enjoy.

554. Chicken wings in sweet chili sauce
Servings: 4
Prep & Cooking Time: 20 Minutes

Ingredients:
- 1 tsp. garlic powder
- 1 tbsp. tamarind powder
- 1/4 cup sweet chili sauce

Directions:
1. Preheat your fryer to 390°F.
2. Slightly grease your air fryer basket with cooking spray.
3. Rub the chicken wings with tamarind and garlic powders. Spray with cooking spray and place in the cooking basket.
4. Cook for 6 minutes, Slide out the fryer basket and cover with sweet chili sauce; cook for 8 more minutes. Serve cooled.

555. Glazed and spicy chicken wings
Servings: 4
Prep & Cooking Time: 19 Minutes
Ingredients:
- 8 chicken wings
- 2 tbsp. all-purpose flour
- 1 tsp. garlic, minced finely
- 1 tbsp. fresh lemon juice
- 1 tbsp. soy sauce
- 1/2 tsp. dried oregano, crushed
- Salt & ground black pepper, to taste

Directions:
1. Preheat the air fryer to 355°F and grease an air fryer basket.
2. Mix all the ingredients except wings in a large bowl.
3. Coat wings generously with the marinade and refrigerate for about 2 hours.
4. Remove the chicken wings from marinade and sprinkle with flour evenly.
5. Transfer the wings in the air fryer tray and cook for about 6 minutes, flipping once in between.
6. Serve the chicken wings in a platter and serve warm.

556. Chicken wings with garlic sausages
Servings: 4
Prep & Cooking Time: 10 Minutes
Ingredients:
- 1 garlic clove, diced
- 1 spring onion, minced
- 1 cup ground chicken
- 1/2 tsp. salt
- 1/2 tsp. ground black pepper
- 4 sausage links
- 1 tsp. olive oil

Directions:
1. In the mixing bowl, mix up a diced garlic clove, onion, ground chicken, salt, and ground black pepper. Then fill the sausage links with the ground chicken mixture.
2. Cut every sausage into halves and secure the endings.
3. Preheat the air fryer to
4. Brush the sausages with olive oil and put it in the air fryer. Cook them for 10 minutes, and then flip the sausages on another side and cook for 5 minutes more.
5. Increase the cooking time to 390°F and cook for 8 minutes for faster results.

557. Drumsticks with spicy and sweet chicken
Servings: 4
Prep & Cooking Time: 20 Minutes
Ingredients:
- 1 garlic clove, crushed
- 1 tbsp. mustard
- 2 tsp. brown sugar
- 1 tsp. cayenne pepper
- 1 tsp. red chili powder
- Salt & ground black pepper, as required
- 1 tbsp. vegetable oil
- 4 (6-ounces) chicken drumsticks

Directions:
1. In a bowl, mix together garlic, mustard, brown sugar, oil, and spices
2. Rub the chicken drumsticks with marinade and refrigerate to marinate for about -30 minutes.
3. Set the temperature of air fryer to 380°F. Grease an air fryer basket.
4. Arrange drumsticks into the prepared air fryer basket in a single layer.
5. air fry for about 10 minutes and then 10 more minutes at 300°F.
6. Remove from air fryer and transfer the chicken drumsticks onto a platter.
7. Serve hot.

558. Cashew nuts and chicken
Servings: 4
Prep & Cooking Time: 30 Minutes
Ingredients:
- 2 tbsp soy sauce
- 1 tbsp corn flour
- 2 1/2 cups onion cubes
- 1 carrot, minced
- 1/3 cup cashew nuts, fried
- 1 capsicum, cut
- 2 tbsps. garlic, crushed
- Salt and white pepper to taste

Directions:
1. Marinate the chicken cubes in mixed with white pepper, salt, soy sauce, and corn flour. Set aside for 25 minutes.
2. Preheat the air fryer to 380°F and put in the marinated chicken. Add garlic, onion, capsicum, the carrot and fry for 5-6 minutes.
3. Roll it in the cashew nuts before serving.

559. Turkey breast with buttermilk
Servings: 8
Prep & Cooking Time: 20 Minutes
Ingredients:
- 3/4 cup brine from a can of olives
- 3 1/2s. boneless, skinless turkey breast
- 2 fresh thyme sprigs
- 1 fresh rosemary sprig
- 1/2 cup buttermilk

Directions:
1. Preheat the air fryer to 350°F and grease an air fryer basket.
2. Mix olive brine and buttermilk in a bowl until well combined.
3. Place the turkey breast, buttermilk mixture and herb sprigs in a resealable plastic bag.
4. Seal the bag and refrigerate for about 12 hours.
5. Remove the turkey breast from bag and arrange the turkey breast into the air fryer basket.
6. Cook for about 20 minutes, flipping once in between.
7. Serve the turkey breast onto a cutting board and cut into desired size slices to serve.

560. Scallion kabobs and chicken
Servings: 4
Prep & Cooking Time: 24 Minutes

Ingredients:
- 4 (4-ounces) skinless, boneless chicken thighs, cubed into 1-inch size
- 2 bell peppers, cut into 1-inch pieces lengthwise
- Wooden skewers, presoaked
- 1/4 cup light soy sauce
- 1 tbsp. mirin
- 1 tsp. garlic salt
- 1 tsp. sugar

Directions:
1. Preheat the air fryer to 355°F and grease an air fryer pan.
2. Mix the soy sauce, mirin, garlic salt, and sugar in a large baking dish.
3. Thread chicken and bell peppers onto presoaked wooden skewers.
4. Coat the skewers generously with marinade and refrigerate for about 3 hours.
5. Transfer the skewers in the air fryer pan in a single layer and cook for about 12 minutes.
6. Serve in a platter and serve warm.

561. Turkey burgers and vermouth bacon

Servings: 4
Prep & Cooking Time: 30 Minutes
Ingredients:
- 2 tbsp. vermouth
- 1 tbsp. honey
- 2 strips Canadian bacon, sliced
- 1 lb. ground turkey
- 1/2 shallot, minced
- 2 garlic cloves, minced
- 2 tbsps. fish sauce
- Sea salt & ground black pepper, to taste
- 1 tsp. red pepper flakes
- 4 soft hamburger rolls
- 4 tbsps. tomato ketchup
- 4 tbsps. mayonnaise
- 4 (1-ounce slices Cheddar cheese
- 4 lettuce leaves

Directions:
1. Heat up your air fryer to 400°F
2. Whisk the vermouth and honey in a mixing bowl; brush the Canadian bacon with the vermouth mixture.
3. Cook for minutes. Flip the bacon over and cook an additional 3 minutes.
4. Then, thoroughly combine the ground turkey, shallots, garlic, fish sauce, salt, black pepper, and red pepper. Form the meat mixture into burger patties.
5. Bake in the preheated air fryer at 370°F for 10 minutes. Flip them over and cook another 10 minutes.
6. Spread the ketchup and mayonnaise on the inside of the hamburger rolls and place the burgers on the rolls; top with bacon, cheese and lettuce; serve immediately.

562. Chicken mix with cream cheese

Servings: 4
Prep & Cooking Time: 16 Minutes
Ingredients:
- 1-lb. chicken wings
- 1/4 cup cream cheese
- 1 tbsp. white wine vinegar
- 1 tsp. Truvia
- 1/2 tsp. smoked paprika
- 1/2 tsp. ground nutmeg
- 1 tsp. avocado oil

Directions:
1. In the mixing bowl mix up cream cheese, Truvia, white wine vinegar, smoked paprika, and ground nutmeg.
2. Then add the chicken wings and coat them in the cream cheese mixture well.
3. Leave the chicken winds in the cream cheese mixture for -15 minutes to marinate.
4. Meanwhile, preheat the air fryer to 380°F.
5. Put the chicken wings in the air fryer and cook them for 8 minutes.
6. Flip the chicken wings and brush with cream cheese marinade.
7. Cook the chicken wings for 8 minutes more.

563. Buttered chicken thighs

Servings: 4
Prep & Cooking Time: 4 Hours 45 Minutes
Ingredients:
- 2 cups buttermilk
- 3 tsp. salt
- 1 tsp. cayenne pepper
- 1 tbsp. paprika
- 1 1/2 lbs. chicken thighs
- 2 tsps. black pepper
- 2 cups flour
- 1 tbsp. garlic powder
- 1 tbsp. baking powder

Directions:
1. Put the chicken thighs in a large bowl.
2. In a separate bowl, combine the buttermilk, salt, cayenne, and black pepper.
3. Coat the thighs with the buttermilk mixture. Place a sheet of aluminum foil over the bowl and set in the refrigerator for 4 hours.
4. Pre-heat your air fryer to 360°F.
5. Combine together the flour, baking powder, and paprika in a shallow bowl. Cover a baking dish with a layer of parchment paper.
6. Coat the chicken thighs in the flour mixture and bake in the fryer for 10 minutes. Turn the thighs over and air fry for another 8 minutes. You will have to do this in two batches.

564. Chicken with marjoram

Servings: 2
Prep & Cooking Time: 1 Hr.
Ingredients:
- 2 skinless, boneless small chicken breasts
- 2 tbsp. butter
- 1 tsp. sea salt
- 1/2 tsp. red pepper flakes, crushed
- 2 tsp. marjoram
- 1/4 tsp. lemon pepper

Directions:
1. In a mixing bowl, coat the chicken breasts with all of the other ingredients.
2. Set aside to marinate for 30 – 60 minutes.
3. Pre-heat your air fryer to 390°F.
4. Cook for 20 minutes, turning halfway through cooking time.
5. Check for doneness using an instant-read thermometer. Serve over jasmine rice.

565. Spicy and juicy chicken wings

Servings: 4
Prep & Cooking Time: 25 Minutes
Ingredients:
- 2 lbs. chicken wings

- 12 ounce hot sauce
- 1 tsp. Worcestershire sauce
- 1 tsp. Tabasco
- 6 tbsps. butter, melted

Directions:
1. Spray air fryer basket with cooking spray.
2. Put the chicken wings in your air fryer basket and cook at 380°F for 20 minutes. Shake basket after every 5 minutes.
3. Meanwhile, in a bowl, mix together hot sauce, Worcestershire sauce, and butter. Set aside.
4. Add chicken wings into the sauce and toss well.
5. Serve and enjoy.

566. Chicken tenders with worcestershire sauce
Servings: 3
Prep & Cooking Time: 30 Minutes
Ingredients:
- 2 (6-ounces) boneless, skinless chicken breasts, cut into tenders
- 3/4 cup buttermilk
- 1 1/2 tsp. Worcestershire sauce, divided
- 1/2 tsp. smoked paprika, divided
- Salt & ground black pepper, as required
- 1/2 cup all-purpose flour
- 1 1/2 cups panko breadcrumbs
- 1/4 cup Parmesan cheese, finely shredded
- 2 tbsp. butter, melted
- 2 large eggs

Directions:
1. In a large bowl, mix together buttermilk, 3/4 tsp. of Worcestershire sauce, 1/4 tsp. of paprika, salt, and black pepper.
2. Add in the chicken tenders and refrigerate overnight.
3. In another bowl, mix together the flour, remaining paprika, salt, and black pepper.
4. Place the remaining Worcestershire sauce and eggs in a third bowl and beat until well combined.
5. Mix well the panko, Parmesan, and butter in a fourth bowl.
6. Remove the chicken tenders from bowl and discard the buttermilk.
7. Coat the chicken tenders with flour mixture, then dip into egg mixture and finally coat with the panko mixture.
8. Preheat your fryer to 400°F, and grease the air fryer basket.
9. Arrange chicken tenders into the prepared air fryer basket in 2 batches in a single layer.
10. Air fry for about 13-15 minutes, flipping once halfway through.
11. Remove from air fryer and transfer the chicken tenders onto a platter.
12. Serve hot.

567. Orange chicken with spicy honey
Servings: 4
Prep & Cooking Time: 20 Minutes
Ingredients:
- 1 cup coconut, shredded
- 3/4 cup breadcrumbs
- 2 whole eggs, beaten
- 1/2 cup flour
- 1/2 tsp. pepper
- Salt to taste
- 1/2 cup orange marmalade
- 1 tbsp red pepper flakes
- 1/4 cup honey
- 3 tbsp Dijon mustard

Directions:
1. Preheat air fryer to 400°F. In a wide deep plate, combine flour, coconut, salt, and pepper.
2. In another plate, add the beaten eggs.
3. Place breadcrumbs in a bowl. Dredge chicken in egg mix, flour and finally in the breadcrumbs.
4. Place the chicken in the air fryer cooking basket and bake for 15 minutes.
5. In a separate bowl, mix honey, orange marmalade, mustard and pepper flakes. Cover chicken with marmalade mixture and fry for 5 more minutes.

568. Cheese and bacon-wrapped turkey
Servings: 12
Prep & Cooking Time: 20 Minutes
Ingredients:
- 1 1/2 small sized turkey breast, chop into 12 pieces
- 12 slim slices Asiago cheese
- Paprika, to taste
- Salt & ground black pepper, to savor
- 12 rashers bacon

Directions:
1. Lay out the bacon rashers; place slice of Asiago cheese on each bacon piece.
2. Top with turkey, season with paprika, salt, and pepper, and roll them up; secure with a cocktail stick.
3. Air-fry at 250°F for 13 minutes. Bon appétit!

569. Parsley breast duck
Servings: 4
Prep & Cooking Time: 25 Minutes
Ingredients:
- 4 duck breast fillets, boneless, skin-on and scored
- 2 tbsp. olive oil
- 2 tbsp. parsley, minced
- Salt & black pepper to the taste
- 1 cup chicken stock
- 1 tsp. balsamic vinegar

Directions:
1. Heat the oil over medium heat, in a pan that fit into the fryer, add the duck breasts skin side down and cook for 5 minutes.
2. Add the rest of the ingredients, toss, put the pan in the fryer and cook at 380°F for 20 minutes.
3. Divide every element between plates and serve

570. Lemon asparagus and garlic turkey
Servings: 4
Prep & Cooking Time: 25 Minutes
Ingredients:
- 1 lb. turkey breast tenderloins, cut into strips
- 1 lb. asparagus, trimmed and cut into medium pieces
- A pinch of salt and black pepper
- 1 tbsp. lemon juice
- 1 tsp. coconut aminos
- 2 tbsps. olive oil
- 2 garlic cloves, minced
- 1/4 cup chicken stock

Directions:
1. Heat up a pan that fits the air fryer with the oil over medium-high heat, add the meat and brown for 2 minutes on each side.
2. Add the rest of the ingredients, toss, put the pan in the machine and cook at 380°F for 20 minutes.
3. Divide every element between plates and serve

571. Oregano duck spread
Servings: 6
Prep & Cooking Time: 40 Minutes
Ingredients:
- 1/2 cup butter, softened
- 12 ounce duck liver
- 1 tbsp. sesame oil
- 1 tsp. salt
- 1 tbsp. dried oregano
- 1/2 onion, peeled

Directions:
1. Preheat the air fryer to 395°F.
2. Chop the onion. Put the duck liver in the air fryer, add onion, and cook the ingredients for 5 minutes.
3. Transfer the duck pate in the food processor and process it for 2-3 minutes or until the liver is smooth (it depends on the food processor power). Then add onion and blend the mixture for 2 minutes more.
4. Transfer the liver mixture into the bowl. After this, add oregano, salt, sesame oil, and butter. Stir the duck liver with the help of the spoon and transfer it in the bowl. Refrigerate the pate for 10-20 minutes before serving.

572. Spicy and crispy whole chicken
Servings: 8
Prep & Cooking Time: 60 Minutes
Ingredients:
- 5 lbs. chicken, wash and remove giblets
- 1/2 tsp. onion powder
- 1/2 tsp. pepper
- 1 tsp. paprika
- 1 tsp. dried oregano
- 1 tsp. dried basil
- 1 1/2 tsps. salt

Directions:
1. Preheat the air fryer to 360°F.
2. Mix together all spices and rub over chicken.
3. Place chicken into the air fryer basket. Make sure the chicken breast side down.
4. Cook chicken for 30 minutes then turn to another side and cook for 30 minutes more.
5. Slice and serve.

573. Cauliflower and ethiopian-style chicken
Servings: 6
Prep & Cooking Time: 30 Minutes
Ingredients:
- 2 handful fresh Italian parsleys, roughly minced
- 1/2 cup fresh minced chives
- 2 sprigs thyme
- 6 chicken drumsticks
- 1 1/2 small-sized head cauliflower, broken into large-sized florets

For the Berbere Spice Rub Mix:
- 2 tsps. mustard powder
- 1/3 tsp. porcini powder
- 1 1/2 tsp. berbere spice
- 1/3 tsp. sweet paprika
- 1/2 tsp. shallot powder
- 1 tsp. granulated garlic
- 1 tsp. freshly grounded pink peppercorns
- 1/2 tsp. sea salt

Directions:
1. Simply combine all items for the berbere spice rub mix. After that, coat the chicken drumsticks with this rub mix on all sides. Transfer them to the baking dish.
2. Now, lower the cauliflower onto the chicken drumsticks. Add thyme, chives and Italian parsley and spritz every element with a pan spray. Transfer the baking dish to the preheated air fryer.
3. Next step, set the timer for 28 minutes; roast at 385°F, turning occasionally. Bon appétit!

574. Sweet 'n sour sauce and chicken bbq
Servings: 6
Prep & Cooking Time: 40 Minutes
Ingredients:
- 1/4 cup minced garlic
- 1/4 cup tomato paste
- 3/4 cup minced onion
- 3/4 cup sugar
- 1 cup soy sauce
- 1 cup water
- 1 cup white vinegar
- 6 chicken drumsticks
- Salt & pepper to taste

Directions:
1. Place all ingredients in a Ziploc bag
2. Allow to marinate for at least hours in the fridge.
3. Preheat the air fryer to 380°F.
4. Insert the air fryer's grill pan attachment.
5. Cook the chicken for 40 minutes on a grill.
6. For even cooking, flip the chicken every 10 minutes.
7. Meantime, transfer the marinade in a saucepan and heat over medium flame until the sauce thickens.
8. Before serving the chicken, brush with the glaze.

575. Blackberry mix with duck
Servings: 4
Prep & Cooking Time: 25 Minutes
Ingredients:
- 4 duck breasts, boneless and skin scored
- A pinch of salt and black pepper
- 2 tbsps. olive oil
- 1 and 1/2 cups chicken stock
- 2 spring onions, minced
- 4 garlic cloves, minced
- 1 and 1/2 cups blackberries, pureed
- 2 tbsps. butter, melted

Directions:
1. Heat up a pan that fits the air fryer with the oil and the butter over medium-high heat, add the duck breasts skin side down and sear for 5 minutes.
2. Add the remaining ingredients, toss, put the pan in the air fryer and cook at 370°F for 20 minutes.
3. Divide the duck and sauce between plates and serve.

576. Chicken tenders with tortilla chips crust
Servings: 4
Prep & Cooking Time: 25 Minutes
Ingredients:
- 1 1/2 lbs. chicken tenderloins
- 2 tbsps. peanut oil
- 1/2 cup tortilla chips, crushed
- Sea salt & ground black pepper, to taste
- 1/2 tsp. garlic powder
- 1 tsp. red pepper flakes

- 2 tbsps. peanuts, roasted and roughly minced

Directions:
1. Preheat the air fryer to 370°F
2. Brush the chicken tenderloins with peanut oil on all sides.
3. In a mixing bowl, thoroughly combine the crushed chips, salt, black pepper, garlic powder, and red pepper flakes.
4. Dredge the chicken in the breading, shaking off any residual coating.
5. Lay the chicken tenderloins into the cooking basket.
6. Cook for about 10 to 12 minutes or until it is no longer pink in the center. Work in batches; an instant-read thermometer should read at least 165°F.
7. Serve garnished with roasted peanuts. Bon appétit!

577. Tasty chicken from caribbean

Servings: 8
Prep & Cooking Time: 10 Minutes
Ingredients:
- 3 lbs. chicken thigh, skinless and boneless
- 1 tbsp. coriander powder
- 3 tbsps. coconut oil, melted
- 1/2 tsp. ground nutmeg
- 1/2 tsp. ground ginger
- 1 tbsp. cayenne
- 1 tbsp. cinnamon
- Pepper
- Salt

Directions:
8. In a deep platter, mix together the spices and rub all over the chicken.
9. Spray air fryer basket with cooking spray.
10. Place the chicken in your fryer basket and cook at 360°F for 10 minutes.
11. Serve and enjoy.

578. Simple and delicious chicken with mayonnaise and mustard

Servings: 2
Prep & Cooking Time: 30 Minutes
Ingredients:
- 1/4 cup slivered s
- 2x 6-oz. boneless skinless chicken breasts
- 2 tbsp. mayonnaise
- 1 tbsp. Dijon mustard

Directions:
1. Pulse the s in a food processor until they are finely minced. Spread the s on a plate and set aside.
2. Cut each chicken breast in half lengthwise.
3. Mix the mayonnaise and mustard together and then spread evenly on top of the chicken slices.
4. Place the chicken into the plate of minced s to coat completely, laying each coated slice into the basket of your fryer.
5. Cook for 2 minutes at 350°F until golden. Test the temperature, making sure the chicken has reached 165°F. Serve hot.

579. Tetrazzini traditional chicken

Servings: 4
Prep & Cooking Time: 55 Minutes
Ingredients:
- 10 ounces noodles, cooked
- 2 tbsp. olive oil
- 1 lb. chicken breast
- Sea salt and pepper, to taste
- 1 onion, sliced
- 2 garlic cloves, minced
- 1 can cream of chicken soup
- 1 can cream of mushroom soup
- 1 cup kefir
- 1/2 cup mozzarella cheese, shredded

Directions:
1. Bring a big saucepan of lightly salted water to a boil over high heat.
2. Cook your noodles for 7 minutes or until al dente; drain and reserve, keeping warm.
3. Preheat your fryer to 370°F. Brush the cooking basket with 1 tsp. of olive oil.
4. Sprinkle the chicken breasts with salt and pepper.
5. Cook for 25 minutes or until the chicken breasts are slightly browned.
6. Add the onion, garlic, chicken soup, mushroom soup, and kefir.
7. Cook for 12 minutes.
8. Top with mozzarella and cook an additional minutes until it is bubbling. Serve warm.

580. Chicken breasts bacon wrapped

Servings: 4
Prep & Cooking Time: 23 Minutes
Ingredients:
- 6-7 Fresh basil leaves
- 2 tbsp. water
- 2 (8-ounces) chicken breasts, cut each breast in half horizontally
- 12 bacon strips
- 2 tbsp. fish sauce
- 1 tbsp. palm sugar
- Salt & ground black pepper, as required
- 1 ½ tsp. honey

Directions:
1. Preheat the air fryer to 365°F and grease an air fryer basket.
2. Cook the palm sugar in a small heavy-bottomed pan over medium-low heat for about 3 minutes until caramelized.
3. Stir in the basil, fish sauce and water and dish out in a bowl.
4. Season each chicken breast with salt and black pepper and coat with the palm sugar mixture.
5. Refrigerate to marinate for about 6 hours and wrap each chicken piece with 3 bacon strips.
6. Dip into the honey and arrange into the air fryer basket.
7. Cook for about 20 minutes, flipping once in between.
8. Serve in a platter and serve warm.
9. Refrigerate to marinate for about 4-6 hours.

581. Chicken halves with oregano

Servings: 4
Prep & Cooking Time: 45 Minutes
Ingredients:
- 16 ounce whole chicken
- 1 tbsp. dried oregano
- 1 tsp. ground cumin
- 1 tsp. salt
- 1 tbsp. avocado oil

Directions:
1. Cut the chicken into halves and sprinkle it with dried oregano, cumin, and salt.
2. Then brush the chicken halves with avocado oil.
3. Preheat the air fryer to 365°F.
4. Put the chicken halves in the air fryer and cook them for 20 minutes. Then flip the chicken halves on another side and cook them for 20 minutes more.

582. Drumsticks with lemon chicken and oregano
Servings: 4
Prep & Cooking Time: 20 Minutes
Ingredients:
- 4 chicken drumsticks, with skin, bone-in
- 1 tsp. dried cilantro
- 1/2 tsp. dried oregano
- 1/2 tsp. salt
- 1 tsp. lemon juice
- 1 tsp. butter, softened
- 2 garlic cloves, diced

Directions:
1. Preheat the air fryer to 380°F.
2. In the mixing bowl mix up dried cilantro, oregano, and salt. Then fill the chicken drumstick's skin with a cilantro mixture.
3. Add butter and diced garlic. Sprinkle the chicken with lemon juice.
4. Place the chicken drumsticks in the air fryer and let them cook for 20 minutes.

583. Coleslaw and crispy turkey sandwich
Servings: 4
Prep & Cooking Time: 20 Minutes
Ingredients:
- 1 lb. turkey fillets
- 1/2 cup milk
- 1 cup flour
- 1 tsp. paprika
- Salt & black pepper to taste
- 1/2 tsp. garlic powder
- 4 hamburger buns
- 1 cup coleslaw

Directions:
1. Preheat the air fryer to 350°F.
2. In a bowl, whisk eggs and milk. In another bowl, combine flour, paprika, garlic, turkey, salt, and pepper.
3. Dip the turkey in the egg mixture and then coat in flour mixture.
4. Spray with cooking spray the air fryer basket and put in the turkey. Cook for 7 minutes. Slide out the basket and flip; cook for another 5 minutes until golden brown.
5. Serve on buns with coleslaw.

584. Teriyaki with traditional chicken
Servings: 4
Prep & Cooking Time: 50 Minutes
Ingredients:
- 1 1/2 lbs. chicken breast, halved
- 1 tbsp. lemon juice
- 2 tbsps. Mirin
- 1/4 cup milk
- 2 tbsps. soy sauce
- 1 tbsp. olive oil
- 1 tsp. ginger, peeled and shredded
- 2 garlic cloves, minced
- 1/2 tsp. salt
- 1/2 tsp. ground black pepper
- 1 tsp. cornstarch

Directions:
1. In a large ceramic dish, place the chicken, olive oil, lemon juice, milk, Mirin, soy sauce, garlic, and ginger. Mix well, and let marinate the mixture for 30 minutes in your refrigerator.
2. Spritz the sides and bottom of the cooking basket with a nonstick cooking spray. Set the chicken in the cooking basket and cook at 370°F for 10 minutes.
3. Turn the chicken over, brush with the leftover marinade, and cook for another 4 minutes.
4. Taste for doneness, season with salt and pepper to taste, and set aside.
5. Combine the cornstarch and 1 tablespoon of water. Cook for 3 to 5 minutes in a hot pan over medium heat with the marinade. Stir in the cornstarch slurry and continue to simmer until the sauce thickens.
6. Spoon the saved chicken into the sauce and serve immediately.

585. Flavorful chicken fajitas
Servings: 4
Prep & Cooking Time: 15 Minutes
Ingredients:
- 4 chicken breasts
- 1 onion, sliced
- 1 bell pepper, sliced
- 1 1/2 tbsp. fajita seasoning
- 2 tbsps. olive oil
- 3/4 cup cheddar cheese, shredded

Directions:
1. Preheat the air fryer at 380°F.
2. Coat chicken with oil and rub with seasoning.
3. Place chicken into the air fryer baking dish and top with bell peppers and onion.
4. Cook for 15 minutes.
5. Top with shredded cheese and cook for 1-2 minutes until cheese is melted.
6. Serve and enjoy.

586. Simple and delight chicken wings
Servings: 4
Prep & Cooking Time: 55 Minutes
Ingredients:
- 3 lbs. bone-in chicken wings
- 3/4 cup flour
- 1 tbsp. old bay seasoning
- 4 tbsps. butter
- Couple fresh lemons

Directions:
1. In a mixing bowl, combine the all-purpose flour and Old Bay seasoning.
2. Toss the chicken wings with the mixture to coat each one well.
3. Pre-heat the air fryer to 375°F.
4. Give the wings a shake to shed any excess flour and place each one in the air fryer. You may have to do this in multiple batches, so as to not overlap any.
5. Cook for 30 – 40 minutes, shaking the basket frequently, until the wings are cooked through and crispy.
6. In the meantime, melt the butter in a frying pan over a low heat. Squeeze one or two lemons and add the juice to the pan. Mix well.
7. Serve the wings topped with the sauce.

587. Walnut rice and duck
Servings: 4
Prep & Cooking Time: 20 Minutes
Ingredients:
- 2 ounces mushrooms, sliced
- 2 tbsps. olive oil
- 2 cups cauliflower florets, riced
- 1/2 cup walnuts, toasted and minced
- 2 cups chicken stock
- A pinch of salt and black pepper
- 1/2 cup parsley, minced

- 2 lbs. duck breasts, boneless and skin scored

Directions:
1. Heat up a pan that fits the air fryer with the oil over medium-high heat, add the duck breasts skin side down and brown for 4 minutes.
2. Add the mushrooms, cauliflower, salt and pepper, and cook for minute more.
3. Add the stock, introduce the pan in the air fryer and cook at 380°F for 15 minutes.
4. Divide the mix between plates, sprinkle the parsley and walnuts on top and serve.

588. Candy onion and thai red duck

Servings: 4
Prep & Cooking Time: 25 Minutes
Ingredients:
- 1 1/2 s. duck breasts, skin removed
- 1 tsp. kosher salt
- 1/2 tsp. cayenne pepper
- 1/3 tsp. black pepper
- 1/2 tsp. smoked paprika
- 1 tbsp. Thai red curry paste
- 1 cup candy onions, halved
- 1/4 small pack coriander, minced

Directions:
1. Put the duck breasts between 2 foil sheets; then, use a rolling pin to bash the duck until they are inch thick.
2. Preheat your air fryer to 390°F.
3. Rub the duck breasts with salt, cayenne pepper, black pepper, paprika, and red curry paste. Place the duck breast in the cooking basket.
4. Cook for 11 to 12 minutes. Top with candy onions and cook for another 10 to 11 minutes.
5. Serve garnished with coriander and enjoy!

589. Lime dijon chicken drumsticks

Servings: 6
Prep & Cooking Time: 20 Minutes
Ingredients:
- 8 chicken drumsticks
- 1 lime juice
- 1 lime zest
- Kosher salt to taste
- 1 tbsp. light mayonnaise
- 3/4 tsp. black pepper
- 1 clove garlic, crushed
- 3 tbsps. Dijon mustard
- 1 tsp. dried parsley

Directions:
1. Pre-heat the air fryer to 375°F.
2. Remove the chicken skin and sprinkle the chicken with the salt.
3. In a bowl, mix the Dijon mustard with the lime juice, before stirring in the lime zest, pepper, parsley and garlic.
4. Cover the chicken with the lime mixture. Allow it to marinate for roughly 10 - 15 minutes.
5. Drizzle some oil in the bottom of your air fryer. Transfer the chicken drumsticks inside and cook for minutes.
6. Give the basket a shake and fry for an additional 5 minutes.
7. Serve immediately, with a side of mayo.

590. Miso-ginger with chicken meatballs

Servings: 4
Prep & Cooking Time: 10 Minutes
Ingredients:

- 1 1/2 tsp. white miso paste
- 1 large egg
- 1 tsp. finely shredded ginger
- 1/4 cup panko (Japanese breadcrumbs), or fresh breadcrumbs
- 1/4 tsp. kosher salt
- 2 tbsp. sliced chives
- 2 tsp. low-sodium soy sauce
- 3/4-lb. ground chicken

Directions:
1. In a medium bowl, whisk well soy sauce, miso paste, and ginger. Set aside.
2. In a large bowl, mix well with hands ground chicken, large egg, chives, and salt. Add panko and half of the sauce. Mix well.
3. Evenly divide into 12 balls. Thread into 4 skewers equally.
4. Place on skewer rack.
5. Cook for 2 minutes at 390°F. Baste with remaining sauce, turnover and cook for another 2 minutes. Baste with sauce on more time and cook for another minute.
6. Serve and enjoy.

591. Breakfast frittata with turkey

Servings: 4
Prep & Cooking Time: 50 Minutes
Ingredients:
- 1 tbsp. olive oil
- 1 lb. turkey breasts, slices
- 6 large-sized eggs
- 3 tbsps. Greek yogurt
- 3 tbsps. Cottage cheese, crumbled
- 1/4 tsp. ground black pepper
- 1/4 tsp. red pepper flakes, crushed
- Pink Himalayan salt, to taste
- 1 red bell pepper, seeded and sliced

Directions:
1. Grease the cooking basket with olive oil. Add the turkey and cook in the preheated air fryer at 350°F for 30 minutes, flipping them over halfway through. Cut into bite-sized strips and reserve.
2. Now, beat the eggs with Greek yogurt, cheese, black pepper, red pepper, and salt. Add the bell peppers to a baking pan that is previously lightly greased with a cooking spray.
3. Add the turkey strips; transfer the egg mixture over all ingredients.
4. Bake in the preheated air fryer at 360°F for 15 minutes. Serve right away!

592. Chicken drumsticks with sweet and spicy flavour

Servings: 4
Prep & Cooking Time: 20 Minutes
Ingredients:
- 4 (6-ounces) chicken drumsticks
- 1 garlic clove, crushed
- 1 tbsp. mustard
- 2 tsp. brown sugar
- 1 tsp. cayenne pepper
- 1 tsp. red chili powder
- Salt & ground black pepper, as required
- 1 tbsp. vegetable oil

Directions:
1. Preheat the air fryer to 375°F and grease an air fryer basket.
2. Mix garlic, mustard, brown sugar, oil, and spices in a bowl.
3. Rub the chicken drumsticks with marinade and refrigerate for about 5 minutes.

4. Set the drumsticks into the air fryer basket in a single layer and cook for about 10 minutes.
5. Set the air fryer to 300°F and cook for 10 more minutes.
6. Serve the chicken drumsticks onto a platter and serve warm.

593. Buttery chicken quesadilla
Servings: 2
Prep & Cooking Time: 10 Minutes
Ingredients:
- 2 low carb tortillas
- 7 ounce chicken breast, skinless, boneless, boiled
- 1 tbsp. cream cheese
- 1 tsp. butter, melted
- 1 tsp. minced garlic
- 1 tsp. fresh dill, minced
- 1/2 tsp. salt
- 2 ounces Monterey Jack cheese, shredded
- Cooking spray

Directions:
1. With a fork and knife, shred the chicken breast and put it in a bowl.
2. Add cream cheese, butter, minced garlic, dill, and salt. Add shredded Monterey jack cheese and stir the shredded chicken.
3. Then put tortilla in the air fryer baking pan. Top it with the shredded chicken mixture and cover with the second corn tortilla.
4. Cook for about 5 minutes at 400°F.

594. Chicken mix with bleu cheese
Servings: 4
Prep & Cooking Time: 20 Minutes
Ingredients:
- 1 lb. chicken breasts, skinless, boneless and cut into slim strips
- 1 small yellow onion, sliced
- 1/2 cup buffalo sauce
- 1/2 cup chicken stock
- 1/4 cup bleu cheese, crumbled

Directions:
1. Mix the chicken with the onions, buffalo sauce, and the stock.
2. Toss every element and then place the pan in the fryer; cook at 370°F for 15 minutes.
3. Sprinkle the cheese on top, divide every element between plates, and serve.

595. Colby turkey meatloaf for holiday
Servings: 6
Prep & Cooking Time: 50 Minutes
Ingredients:
- 1 lb. turkey mince
- 1/2 cup chives, finely minced
- 2 garlic cloves, finely minced
- 1 tsp. dried oregano
- 1/2 tsp. dried basil
- 3/4 cup Colby cheese, shredded
- 3/4 cup crushed saltines
- 1 tbsp. tamari sauce
- Salt & black pepper, at your convenience
- 1/4 cup roasted red pepper tomato sauce
- 1 tsp. brown sugar
- 3/4 tbsp. olive oil
- 1 medium-sized egg, well beaten

Directions:
1. In a nonstick skillet, that is preheated over a moderate heat, sauté the turkey mince, chives, garlic, thyme, and basil until just tender and fragrant.
2. Then set your air fryer to cook at 360°F. Combine sautéed mixture with the cheese, saltines and tamari sauce; then form the mixture into a loaf shape.
3. Mix the remaining items and transfer them over the meatloaf. Cook in the air fryer baking pan for 45 to 47 minutes. Eat warm.

596. Mongolian chicken
Servings: 5
Prep & Cooking Time: 15 Minutes
Ingredients:
- 8 ounces flour
- 8 ounces breadcrumbs
- 3 beaten eggs
- 4 tbsp canola oil
- Salt & pepper to taste
- 2 tbsps. sesame seeds
- 2 tbsps. red pepper paste
- 1 tbsp. white wine vinegar
- 2 tbsps. honey
- 1 tbsp. soy sauce
- Sesame seeds, to serve

Directions:
1. Preheat your fryer to 355°F.
2. Separate the chicken wings into winglets and drumettes.
3. In a bowl, mix salt, oil and pepper.
4. Coat the chicken with beaten eggs followed by breadcrumbs and flour.
5. Grease the fryer basket with some oil and transfer the chicken into it. Let it cook for about 15 minutes
6. Mix red pepper paste, white wine vinegar, soy sauce, honey and 1/4 cup of water in a saucepan and bring to a boil.
7. Transfer the chicken to sauce mixture and toss to coat. Garnish with sesame to serve.

597. Delicious strawberry turkey
Servings: 2
Prep & Cooking Time: 50 Minutes
Ingredients:
- 2 lbs. turkey breast
- 1 tbsp. olive oil
- Salt & pepper
- 1 cup fresh strawberries

Directions:
1. Pre-heat your fryer to 375°F.
2. Massage the turkey breast with olive oil, before seasoning with a generous amount of salt and pepper.
3. Cook the turkey in the fryer for fifteen minutes. Flip the turkey and cook for a further fifteen minutes.
4. During these last fifteen minutes, blend the strawberries in a food processor until a smooth consistency has been achieved.
5. Heap the strawberries over the turkey, then cook for a final seven minutes and enjoy.

598. Chicken breasts in marinara sauce
Servings: 2
Prep & Cooking Time: 25 Minutes
Ingredients:
- 1 egg, beaten
- 1/2 cup chicken breasts
- 1/2 cup breadcrumbs

- A pinch of salt and black pepper
- 2 tbsps. marinara sauce
- 2 tbsps. Grana Padano cheese, shredded
- 2 slices mozzarella cheese

Directions:
1. Dip the chicken breasts in the egg, then into the crumbs and arrange in the fryer; cook for 5 minutes at 400°F.
2. Then, turn over and drizzle with marinara sauce, Grana Padano and mozzarella.
3. Cook for 5 minutes.

599. Chicken burgers with onion and garlic
Servings: 4
Prep & Cooking Time: 25 Minutes
Ingredients:
- 1/2 onion, minced
- 2 garlic cloves, minced
- 1 egg, beaten
- 1/2 cup breadcrumbs
- 1/2 tbsp ground cumin
- 1/2 tbsp paprika
- 1/2 tbsp cilantro seeds, crushed
- Salt & pepper to taste

Directions:
1. In a bowl, mix chicken, onion, garlic, egg, breadcrumbs, cumin, paprika, cilantro, salt, and black pepper, with hands; shape into 4 patties.
2. Grease the air fryer with oil, and arrange the patties inside. Do not layer them.
3. Cook in batches if needed.
4. Cook for 20 minutes at 380°F, turning once halfway through.

600. Juicy herbed drumsticks with mustard
Servings: 4
Prep & Cooking Time: 22 Minutes
Ingredients:
- 1/2 tbsp. fresh rosemary, minced
- 1 tbsp. fresh thyme, minced
- 4 boneless chicken drumsticks
- 1/4 cup Dijon mustard
- 1 tbsp. honey
- 2 tbsp. olive oil
- Salt & ground black pepper, to taste

Directions:
1. Preheat the air fryer to 320°F and grease an air fryer basket.
2. Combine all of the ingredients in a bowl except the drumsticks until well combined.
3. Stir in the drumsticks and coat generously with the mixture.
4. Cover and refrigerate to marinate for about 30 minutes.
5. Cook it into the air fryer basket and cook for about 12 minutes.
6. Set the air fryer to 355°F and cook for about 10 minutes.
7. Serve warm.

601. Chicken breasts with spinach
Servings: 4
Prep & Cooking Time: 15 Minutes
Ingredients:
- 4 tbsps. cottage cheese
- 2 boneless, skinless chicken breasts
- Juice of 1/2 lime
- 2 tbsps. Italian seasoning
- 2 tbsps. olive oil

Directions:
1. Warm your fryer to 400°F.
2. Grease the fryer basket with cooking spray.
3. Mix the spinach with the cottage cheese in a bowl.
4. Halve the chicken breasts with a knife and flatten them with a meat mallet. Season with Italian seasoning. Divide the spinach/cheese mixture between the four chicken pieces. Roll up to form cylinders and use toothpicks to secure them.
5. Brush with olive oil and transfer to the air fryer basket. Cook for 6 minutes, flip, and cook for another 6 minutes. Serve with salad.

602. Chicken wings with maple syrup
Servings: 4
Prep & Cooking Time: 25 Minutes
Ingredients:
- 2 tbsps. sesame oil
- 2 tbsps. maple syrup
- Salt & black pepper
- 3 tbsps. sesame seeds

Directions:
1. In a mixing bowl, add wings, oil, maple syrup, salt and pepper, and stir to coat well.
2. In another bowl, add the sesame seeds and roll the wings in the seeds to coat thoroughly.
3. Set the wings in an even layer inside your air fryer and cook for 20 minutes on 360°F, turning once halfway through.

603. Chicken breasts with cheddar and cream
Servings: 2
Prep & Cooking Time: 25 Minutes
Ingredients:
- 2 oz. full-fat cream cheese, softened
- 4 slices sugar-free bacon, cooked and crumbled
- 1/4 cup pickled jalapenos, sliced
- 1/2 cup sharp cheddar cheese, shredded and divided
- 2 x 6-oz. boneless skinless chicken breasts

Directions:
1. In a mixing bowl, combine the jalapeno slices, bacon, cream cheese, and half of the cheddar cheese until well-combined.
2. Cut parallel slits in the chicken breasts of about 3/4 the length – make sure not to cut all the way down. You should be able to make between six and eight slices, depending on the size of the chicken breast.
3. Insert evenly sized dollops of the cheese mixture into the slits of the chicken breasts. Top the chicken with sprinkles of the rest of the cheddar cheese. Place the chicken in the basket of your air fryer.
4. Set the fryer to 350°F and cook the chicken breasts for twenty minutes.
5. Test with a meat thermometer. The chicken should be at 15°F when fully cooked. Serve hot and enjoy!

604. Simple chicken sliders
Servings: 3
Prep & Cooking Time: 30 Minutes
Ingredients:
- 1/2 cup all-purpose flour
- 1 tsp. garlic salt
- 1/2 tsp. black pepper, preferably freshly ground
- 1 tsp. celery seeds
- 1/2 tsp. mustard seeds
- 1/2 tsp. dried basil
- 1 egg
- 2 chicken breasts, cut in thirds
- 6 small-sized dinner rolls

Directions:
1. In mixing bowl, thoroughly combine the flour and seasonings.

2. In a separate shallow bowl, beat the egg until frothy.
3. Coat the chicken in the flour mixture, then in the egg mixture; Afterwards, roll them over the flour mixture again.
4. Spritz the chicken pieces with a cooking spray on all sides. Transfer them to the cooking basket.
5. Cook in the preheated air fryer at 380°F for 1minute; turn them over and cook an additional 10 to 12 minutes.
6. Test for doneness and adjust the seasonings. Serve immediately on dinner rolls.

605. Rice and veggies with chicken
Servings: 3
Prep & Cooking Time: 20 Minutes
Ingredients:
- 3 cups cold boiled white rice
- 1 cup cooked chicken, diced
- 1/2 cup frozen carrots
- 1/2 cup frozen peas
- 1/2 cup onion, minced
- 6 tbsps. soy sauce
- 1 tbsp. vegetable oil

Directions:
1. Preheat the air fryer to 360°F and grease a 7" nonstick pan.
2. Mix the rice, soy sauce, and vegetable oil in a bowl.
3. Stir in the other ingredients until thoroughly blended.
4. Transfer the rice mixture into the pan and place in the Air fryer.
5. Cook for about 20 minutes and dish out to serve immediately.

606. Special maple-glazed chicken
Servings: 4
Prep & Cooking Time: 20 Minutes
Ingredients:
- 2 1/2 tbsps. maple syrup
- 1 tbsp. tamari soy sauce
- 1 tbsp. oyster sauce
- 1 tsp. fresh lemon juice
- 1 tsp. minced fresh ginger
- 1 tsp. garlic puree
- Salt and freshly ground pepper, to taste
- 2 boneless, skinless chicken breasts

Directions:
1. In a mixing bowl, combine the maple syrup, tamari sauce, oyster sauce, lemon juice, fresh ginger and garlic puree. This is your marinade.
2. Sprinkle the chicken breasts with salt and pepper.
3. Coat the chicken breasts with the marinade. Place some foil over the bowl and refrigerate for hours, or overnight if possible.
4. Remove the chicken from the marinade. Place it in the air fryer and fry for 15 minutes at 365°F, flipping each one once or twice throughout.
5. In the meantime, add the remaining marinade to a pan over medium heat. Allow the marinade to simmer for 3 - minutes until it has reduced by half.
6. Pour over the cooked chicken and serve.

607. Chicken wings with soy sauce and honey
Servings: 2
Prep & Cooking Time: 25 Minutes
Ingredients:
- 2 lemongrass stalks (white portion), minced
- 1 onion, finely minced
- 1 tbsp. soy sauce
- 1 1/2 tbsp. honey
- Salt and ground white pepper, as required
- 1 lb. chicken wings, rinsed and trimmed
- 1/2 cup cornstarch

Directions:
1. In a bowl, mix together the lemongrass, onion, soy sauce, honey, salt, and white pepper.
2. Add the wings and generously coat with marinade.
3. Cover and refrigerate to marinate overnight.
4. Set the temperature of air fryer to 355°F. Grease an air fryer basket.
5. Remove the chicken wings from marinade and coat with the cornstarch.
6. Arrange chicken wings into the prepared air fryer basket in a single layer.
7. Air fry for about 25 minutes, flipping once halfway through.
8. Remove from air fryer and transfer the chicken wings onto a platter.
9. Serve hot.

608. Manchego cheese and turkey meatballs
Servings: 4
Prep & Cooking Time: 15 Minutes
Ingredients:
- 1 lb. ground turkey
- 1/2 lb. ground pork
- 1 egg, well beaten
- 1 tsp. dried basil
- 1 tsp. dried rosemary
- 1/4 cup Manchego cheese, shredded
- 2 tbsps. yellow onions, finely minced
- 1 tsp. fresh garlic, finely minced
- Sea salt & ground black pepper, to taste

Directions:
1. In a wide bowl, whisk all the ingredients until every element is well incorporated.
2. Shape the mixture into 1-inch balls.
3. Cook the meatballs in the preheated air fryer at 390°F for 7 minutes. Shake halfway through the cooking time. Work in batches.
4. Serve with your favorite pasta. Bon appétit!

609. Chili chicken barbecue with sweet lime
Servings: 2
Prep & Cooking Time: 1 hour and 15 minutes
Ingredients:
- 1/4 cup soy sauce
- 1 cup sweet chili sauce
- 1-lb. chicken breasts
- Juice from 2 limes, freshly squeezed

Directions:
1. Combine all items in a Ziploc bag and shake well.
2. Marinate it for 30 minutes in the refrigerator.
3. Preheat the air fryer to 355°F.
4. Insert the air fryer's grill pan attachment.
5. Place chicken on the grill and cook for 30 minutes. Flip the chicken every 10 minutes to cook evenly.
6. Meanwhile, use the remaining marinade and put it in a saucepan. Simmer until the sauce thickens.
7. Once the chicken is cooked, brush with the thickened marinade.

610. Chinese-style turkey thighs sticks
Servings: 6
Prep & Cooking Time: 35 Minutes
Ingredients:
- 1 tbsp. sesame oil

- 2 lbs. turkey thighs
- 1 tsp. Chinese Five-spice powder
- 1 tsp. pink Himalayan salt
- 1/4 tsp. Sichuan pepper
- 6 tbsps. honey
- 1 tbsp. Chinese rice vinegar
- 2 tbsps. soy sauce
- 1 tbsp. sweet chili sauce
- 1 tbsp. mustard

Directions:
1. Heat up your fryer to 380°F.
2. Brush the sesame oil all over the turkey thighs. Season them with spices.
3. Cook for 2minutes, turning over once or twice. Make sure to work in batches to ensure even cooking
4. In the meantime, combine the remaining ingredients in a wok (or similar type pan that is preheated over medium-high heat. Cook and stir until the sauce reduces by about a third.
5. Add the fried turkey thighs to the wok; gently stir to coat with the sauce.
6. Let the turkey rest for 10 minutes before slicing and serving. Enjoy!

611. Spicy turkey meatloaf
Servings: 6
Prep & Cooking Time: 55 Minutes
Ingredients:
- 2 lbs. turkey breasts, ground
- 1/2 lb. Cheddar cheese, cubed
- 1/2 cup turkey stock
- 1/3 tsp. hot paprika
- 3 eggs, lightly beaten
- 1 1/2 tbsps. olive oil
- 2 cloves garlic, pressed
- 1 1/2 tsps. dried rosemary
- 1/2 cup yellow onion, minced
- 1/3 cup ground almonds
- 1/2 tsp. black pepper
- A few dashes of Tabasco sauce
- 1 tsp. seasoned salt
- 1/2 cup tomato sauce

Directions:
1. Heat the olive oil in a saucepan over a moderate flame; now, sauté the onions, garlic, and dried rosemary until just tender, or about 3 to 4 minutes.
2. In the meantime, set the air fryer to cook at 385°F.
3. Place all the ingredients, minus the tomato sauce, in a mixing dish together with the sautéed mixture; thoroughly mix to combine.
4. Shape into meatloaf and top with the tomato sauce. Air-fry for minutes. Bon appétit!

612. The finest pizza chicken
Servings: 4
Prep & Cooking Time: 20 Minutes
Ingredients:
- 4 small-sized chicken breasts, boneless and skinless
- 1/4 cup pizza sauce
- 1/2 cup Colby cheese, shredded
- 16 slices pepperoni
- Salt and pepper, to savor
- 1 1/2 tbsps. olive oil
- 1 1/2 tbsps. dried oregano

Directions:
1. Carefully flatten out the chicken breast using a rolling pin.
2. Divide the ingredients among four chicken fillets. Roll the chicken fillets with the stuffing and seal them using a small skewer or two toothpicks.
3. Roast in the preheated air fryer grill pan for 1to 15 minutes at 370°F. Bon appétit!

613. Supreme creole chicken tenders
Servings: 4
Prep & Cooking Time: 25 Minutes
Ingredients:
- 3 eggs
- 4 cup chicken tenders
- 2 1/4 cup flour, divided
- 1 tbsp olive oil
- 1/2 tbsp plus
- 1/2 tbsp garlic powder, divided
- 1 tbsp salt
- 3 tbsp Creole seasoning, divided
- 1/4 cup milk

Directions:
1. Season the chicken with salt, pepper, 1/2 tbsp garlic powder and 2 tbsp Creole seasoning.
2. Combine 2 cups flour, the rest of the Creole seasoning and the rest of the garlic powder, in a bowl.
3. In another bowl, whisk the eggs, milk, olive oil, and quarter cup flour.
4. Preheat the air fryer to 370°F
5. Line a baking sheet with parchment paper.
6. Dip the chicken into the egg mixture, and then into the flour mixture. Arrange on the sheet. If there isn't enough room, work in two batches. Cook for 1minutes.

614. Coconut chicken fritters t dill
Servings: 8
Prep & Cooking Time: 16 Minutes
Ingredients:
- 1-lb. chicken breast, skinless, boneless
- 3 ounces shredded coconut
- 1 tbsp. ricotta cheese
- 1 tsp. mascarpone
- 1 tsp. dried dill
- 1/2 tsp. salt
- 1 egg yolk
- 1 tsp. avocado oil

Directions:
1. Cut the chicken breast into the tiny pieces and put them in the bowl. Add shredded coconut, ricotta cheese, mascarpone, dried dill, salt, and egg yolk.
2. Make the chicken fritters with the help of the fingertips. Preheat the air fryer to 360°F.
3. Line the air fryer basket with baking paper and put the chicken cakes in the air fryer.
4. Sprinkle the chicken fritters with avocado oil and cook for 8 minutes. Then flip the chicken fritters on another side and cook them for 8 minutes more.

615. Coconut meatballs with chicken
Servings: 4
Prep & Cooking Time: 10 Minutes
Ingredients:

- 1 lb. ground chicken
- 1 1/2 tsps. sriracha
- 1/2 tbsp. soy sauce
- 1/2 tbsp. hoisin sauce
- 1/4 cup shredded coconut
- 1 tsp. grapeseed oil
- 1/2 cup fresh cilantro, minced
- 2 green onions, minced
- Pepper
- Salt

Directions:
1. Spray air fryer basket with cooking spray.
2. Add all ingredients into the large bowl and mix until well combined.
3. Make small balls from meat mixture and place into the air fryer basket.
4. Cook at 350°F for 10 minutes. Turn halfway through.
5. Serve and enjoy.

616. Turnip with paprika chicken legs
Servings: 3
Prep & Cooking Time: 30 Minutes
Ingredients:
- 1 lb. chicken legs
- 1 tsp. Pink Himalayan salt
- 1 tsp. paprika
- 1/2 tsp. ground black pepper
- 1 tsp. butter, melted
- 1 turnip, trimmed and sliced

Directions:
1. Spritz the sides and bottom of the cooking basket with a nonstick cooking spray.
2. Season the chicken legs with salt, paprika, and ground black pepper.
3. Cook at 360°F for 10 minutes. Increase the temperature to 380°F.
4. Drizzle turnip slices with melted butter and transfer them to the cooking basket with the chicken. Cook the turnips and chicken for 15 minutes more, flipping them halfway through the cooking time.
5. Serve and enjoy!

617. Cheese, black bean and baked rice
Servings: 4
Prep & Cooking Time: 55 Minutes
Ingredients:
- 1 cooked skinless boneless chicken breast halves, minced
- 1 cup shredded Swiss cheese
- 1/2 (15 ounce) can black beans, drained
- 1/2 (4 ounces) can diced green chili peppers, drained
- 1/2 cup vegetable broth
- 1/2 medium zucchini, slimly sliced
- 1/4 cup sliced mushrooms
- 1/4 tsp. cumin
- 1-1/2 tsp. olive oil
- 2 tbsp. and 2 tsp. diced onion
- 3 tbsp. brown rice
- 3 tbsp. shredded carrots
- Ground cayenne pepper to taste
- Salt to taste

Directions:
1. Grease you air fryer pan with cooking spray. Add rice and broth, and cover the pan with foil.
2. Let it cook for 10 minutes at 390°F.
3. Lower heat to 300°F and fluff rice. Cook for another 10 minutes and then let it stand for 10 minutes more. Transfer to a bowl and set aside.
4. Add oil to same baking pan. Stir in onion and cook for 5 minutes at 330°F.
5. Stir in mushrooms, chicken, and zucchini. Mix well and cook for 5 minutes.
6. Stir in cayenne pepper, salt, and cumin. Whisk well and cook for 2 minutes more.
7. Stir in 1/2 of the Swiss cheese, carrots, chiles, beans, and rice. Toss well to mix. Evenly spread in pan. Top with remaining cheese.
8. Cover pan with foil.
9. Cook for 15 minutes at 390°F and then remove foil and cook for another 5 to 10 minutes or until tops are lightly browned.
10. Serve and enjoy.

618. Honey glazed turkey breast
Servings: 6
Prep & Cooking Time: 55 Minutes
Ingredients:
- 2 tsps. butter, softened
- 1 tsp. dried sage
- 2 sprigs rosemary, minced
- 1 tsp. salt
- 1/4 tsp. ground black pepper
- 1 whole turkey breast
- 2 tbsps. turkey broth
- 1/4 cup honey
- 2 tbsps. whole-grain mustard
- 1 tbsp. butter

Directions:
1. Pre-heat your air fryer to 360°F.
2. Mix together the tbsp. of butter, sage, rosemary, salt, and pepper.
3. Rub the turkey breast with this mixture.
4. Place the turkey in your fryer's cooking basket and roast for 20 minutes. Turn the turkey breast over and allow to cook for another 15 - 16 minutes.
5. Finally turn it once more and roast for another 12 minutes.
6. In the meantime, mix together the remaining ingredients in a saucepan using a whisk.
7. Coat the turkey breast with the glaze.
8. Place the turkey back in the air fryer and cook for an additional 5 minutes. Remove it from the fryer, let it rest, and carve before serving.

619. King buffalo chicken
Servings: 4
Prep & Cooking Time: 25 Minutes
Ingredients:
- 1/2 cup yogurt
- 1 lb. chicken breasts cut into strips
- 1 tbsp ground cayenne
- 1 tbsp. hot sauce
- 2 beaten eggs
- 1 tbsp. sweet paprika
- 1 tbsp. garlic powder

Directions:
1. Preheat air fryer to 390°F. Whisk eggs along with the hot sauce and yogurt.
2. In a wide bowl, combine the breadcrumbs, paprika, pepper, and garlic powder. Line a baking dish with parchment paper.

3. Dip the chicken in the egg/yogurt mixture first, and then coat with breadcrumbs. Arrange on the sheet and bake in the air fryer for 8 minutes.
4. Flip the chicken over and bake for 8 more minutes. Serve.

620. Lemon sauce with ginger chicken
Servings: 4
Prep & Cooking Time: 25 Minutes
Ingredients:
- 2 tbsps. spring onions, minced
- 1 tbsp. ginger, shredded
- 4 garlic cloves, minced
- 2 tbsp. coconut aminos
- 8 chicken drumsticks
- 1/2 cup chicken stock
- Salt & black pepper to the taste
- 1 tsp. olive oil
- 1/4 cup cilantro, minced
- 1 tbsp. lemon juice

Directions:
1. Heat up the oil in a pan over medium-high heat, add the chicken drumsticks, brown them for 2 minutes on each side and transfer to a pan that fits the fryer.
2. Add all the other ingredients, toss every element, put the pan in the fryer and cook at 370°F for 20 minutes.
3. Divide the chicken and lemon sauce between plates and serve.

621. Shallot sauce with paprika turkey
Servings: 4
Prep & Cooking Time: 30 Minutes
Ingredients:
- 1 big turkey breast, skinless, boneless and cubed
- 1 tbsp. olive oil
- 1/4 tsp. sweet paprika
- Salt & black pepper to the taste
- 1 cup chicken stock
- 3 tbsps. butter, melted
- 4 shallots, minced

Directions:
1. Heat up a pan that fits the air fryer with the olive oil and the butter over medium high heat, add the turkey cubes, and brown for 3 minutes on each side.
2. Add the shallots, stir and sauté for 5 minutes more.
3. Add the paprika, stock, salt and pepper, toss, put the pan in the air fryer and cook at 370°F for 20 minutes.
4. Divide into bowls and serve.

622. Coconut broccoli and turkey
Servings: 4
Prep & Cooking Time: 25 Minutes
Ingredients:
- 1 lb. turkey meat, ground
- 2 garlic cloves, minced
- 1 tsp. ginger, shredded
- 2 tsps. coconut aminos
- 3 tbsps. olive oil
- 2 broccoli heads, florets separated and then halved
- A pinch of salt and black pepper
- 1 tsp. chili paste

Directions:
1. Heat up a pan that fits the air fryer with the oil over medium heat, add the meat and brown for 5 minutes.
2. Add the rest of the ingredients, toss, put the pan in the fryer and cook at 380°F for 20 minutes.
3. Divide every element between plates and serve.

623. Italian seasoned whole chicken
Servings: 4
Prep & Cooking Time: 50 Minutes
Ingredients:
- 3 lbs. whole chicken, remove giblets and pat dry chicken
- 1 tsp. Italian seasoning
- 1/2 tsp. garlic powder
- 1/2 tsp. onion powder
- 1/4 tsp. paprika
- 1/4 tsp. pepper
- 1 1/2 tsp. salt

Directions:
1. In a medium size bowl, mix together onion powder, garlic powder, Italian seasoning, paprika, pepper, and salt.
2. Rub spice mixture from inside and outside of the chicken.
3. Place chicken breast side down in air fryer basket.
4. Roast chicken for 30 minutes at 360°F.
5. Turn chicken and roast for 20 minutes more or internal temperature of chicken reaches at 165°F.
6. Serve and enjoy.

624. Maple mustard with turkey
Servings: 6
Prep & Cooking Time: 70 Minutes
Ingredients:
- 5 lbs. whole turkey breast
- 1 tbsp. olive oil
- 1 tsp. dried oregano
- 1/2 tsp. smoked paprika
- 1/2 tsp. dried sage
- 1 tsp. sea salt
- 1/2 tsp. black pepper
- 1 tbsp. unsalted butter, melted
- 2 tbsps. Dijon mustard
- 1/4 cup maple syrup

Directions:
1. Preheat the fryer to 350°F.
2. Brush the olive oil over the turkey breast.
3. Mix together the thyme, paprika, sage, salt, and pepper. Coat the turkey breast all over with this mixture.
4. Put the turkey breast in the air fryer basket and allow to cook for 25 minutes.
5. Flip it over and cook on the other side for a further 12 minutes.
6. Turn it once again and cook for another 12 minutes.
7. Check the temperature with a meat thermometer and ensure it has reached 165°F before removing it from the fryer.
8. In the meantime, combine the maple syrup, mustard, and melted butter in a saucepan over a medium heat.
9. Stir continuously until a smooth consistency is achieved.
10. Pour the sauce over the cooked turkey in the fryer.
11. Cook for a final 5 minutes, ensuring the turkey turns brown and crispy.
12. Allow the turkey to rest, under a layer of aluminum foil, before carving up and serving.

625. Middle eastern tzatziki sauce and chicken bbq
Servings: 6
Prep & Cooking Time: 24 Minutes
Ingredients:
- 1 1/2 lbs. skinless, boneless chicken breast halves - cut into bite-sized pieces

- 1 tsp. dried oregano
- 1/2 tsp. salt
- 1/4 cup olive oil
- 2 cloves garlic, minced
- 2 tbsps. lemon juice
- Tzatziki Dip Ingredients
- 1 (6 ounces) container plain Greek-style yogurt
- 1 tbsp. olive oil
- 2 tsps. white vinegar
- 1 clove garlic, minced
- 1 pinch salt
- 1/2 cucumber - peeled, seeded, and shredded

Directions:
1. In a medium bowl mix well, all Tzatziki dip Ingredients. Refrigerate for at least 2 hours to allow flavors to blend.
2. In a resealable bag, mix well salt, oregano, garlic, lemon juice, and olive oil. Add chicken, squeeze excess air, seal, and marinate for at least hours.
3. Thread chicken into skewers and place on skewer rack. Cook in batches.
4. For 12 minutes, cook on 360°F. Halfway through cooking time, turnover skewers and baste with marinade from resealable bag.
5. Serve and enjoy with Tzatziki dip.

626. Chicken tenders with worcestershire sauce
Servings: 3
Prep & Cooking Time: 30 Minutes
Ingredients:
- 2 (6-ounces) boneless, skinless chicken breasts, lbed into 1/2-inch thickness and cut into tenders
- 1/2 cup all-purpose flour
- 1 1/2 cups panko breadcrumbs
- 1/4 cup Parmesan cheese, finely shredded
- 2 large eggs
- 1 1/2 tsps. Worcestershire sauce, divided
- 3/4 cup buttermilk
- 1/2 tsp. smoked paprika, divided
- Salt & ground black pepper, as required

Directions:
1. Preheat the air fryer to 400°F and grease an air fryer basket.
2. Mix buttermilk, 3/4 tsp. of Worcestershire sauce, 1/4 tsp. of paprika, salt, and black pepper in a bowl.
3. Combine the flour, remaining paprika, salt, and black pepper in another bowl.
4. Whisk the egg and remaining Worcestershire sauce in a third bowl.
5. Blend the Parmesan cheese and breadcrumbs in a deep plate.
6. Put the chicken tenders into the buttermilk mixture and refrigerate overnight.
7. Remove the chicken tenders from the buttermilk mixture and dredge into the flour mixture.
8. Dip into the egg and coat with the breadcrumb mixture.
9. Arrange half of the chicken tenders into the air fryer basket and cook for about 15 minutes, flipping once in between.
10. Repeat with the remaining mixture and dish out to serve warm.

627. Pecorino parmesan and cauliflower chicken
Servings: 4
Prep & Cooking Time: 30 Minutes
Ingredients:
- 2 lbs. chicken legs
- 2 tbsps. olive oil
- 1 tsp. sea salt
- 1/2 tsp. ground black pepper
- 1 tsp. smoked paprika
- 1 tsp. dried marjoram
- 1 (1-lb.) head cauliflower, broken into small florets
- 2 garlic cloves, minced
- 1/3 cup Parmesan cheese, freshly shredded
- 1/2 tsp. dried oregano
- Salt, to taste

Directions:
1. Toss the chicken legs with the olive oil, salt, black pepper, paprika, and marjoram.
2. Cook in the preheated air fryer at 380°F for 11 minutes. Flip the chicken legs and cook for a further 5 minutes.
3. Toss the cauliflower florets with garlic, cheese, thyme, and salt.
4. Increase the temperature to 380°F; add the cauliflower florets and cook for 12 more minutes. Serve warm.

628. Coconut milk casserole and spinach-egg
Servings: 6
Prep & Cooking Time: 20 Minutes
Ingredients:
- 1/4 cup coconut milk
- 1 onion, minced
- 1 tsp. garlic powder
- 12 large eggs, beaten
- 2 tbsps. coconut oil
- 3 cups spinach, minced
- Salt & pepper to taste

Directions:
1. Preheat the air fryer for 5 minutes.
2. In a bowl, mix all ingredients except for the spinach.
3. Whisk until well-incorporated.
4. Place the spinach in a baking dish and transfer over the egg mixture
5. Drop into the air fryer chamber and cook for 20 minutes at 310°F.

629. Carrots and chicken
Servings: 2
Prep & Cooking Time: 25 Minutes
Ingredients:
- 1 carrot, peeled and slimly sliced
- 2 tbsps. butter
- 2 (4-ounces) chicken breast halves
- 1 tbsp. fresh rosemary, minced
- Salt & black pepper, as required
- 2 tbsps. fresh lemon juice

Directions:
1. Preheat the air fryer to 375°F and grease an air fryer basket.
2. Place square-shaped parchment papers onto a smooth surface and arrange carrot slices evenly in the center of each parchment paper.
3. Drizzle 1/2 tbsp. of butter over carrot slices and season with salt and black pepper.
4. Layer with chicken breasts and top with rosemary, lemon juice and remaining butter.
5. Fold the parchment paper on all sides and transfer into the Air fryer.
6. Cook for about 25 minutes and dish out in a platter to serve.

630. Pesto chicken with ginger
Servings: 2
Prep & Cooking Time: 20 Minutes
Ingredients:
- 4 chicken drumsticks
- 6 garlic cloves
- 1/2 jalapeno pepper
- 2 tbsps. lemon juice

- 2 tbsps. olive oil
- 1 tbsps. ginger, sliced
- 1/2 cup cilantro
- 1 tsp. salt

Directions:
1. Add all the ingredients except chicken into the blender and blend until smooth.
2. Pour blended mixture into the large bowl.
3. Add chicken and stir well to coat. Place in refrigerator for 2 hours.
4. Spray air fryer basket with cooking spray.
5. Place marinated chicken into the air fryer basket and cook at 390°F for 20 minutes. Turn halfway through.
6. Serve and enjoy.

631. Chicken wings with cheese
Servings: 2
Prep & Cooking Time: 25 Minutes
Ingredients:
- 1 lb. chicken wings
- 1 garlic clove, minced
- 2 tbsps. butter
- 2 tbsps. parmesan cheese, shredded
- tsp. paprika
- 1/2 tsp. oregano
- 1/2 tsp. rosemary
- 1/4 tsp. salt

Directions:
1. Preheat the air fryer to 390°F.
2. Place the chicken wings into the air fryer basket. Cook for about 20 minutes.
3. Shake basket 2-3 times while cooking.
4. Meanwhile, for sauce melt butter in a pan over medium heat. Add garlic and sauté for seconds.
5. Mix together herb and spices and add to the pan.
6. Toss chicken wings with pan sauce and top with cheese.
7. Serve and enjoy.

632. Casserole with pizza spaghetti
Servings: 4
Prep & Cooking Time: 30 Minutes
Ingredients:
- 8 ounces spaghetti
- 1 lb. smoked chicken sausage, sliced
- 2 tomatoes, pureed
- 1/2 cup Asiago cheese, shredded
- 1 tbsp. Italian seasoning mix
- 3 tbsps. Parmesan cheese, shredded
- 1 tbsp. fresh basil leaves, chiffonade

Directions:
1. Boil a large pot of salted water.
2. Cook your spaghetti for 7-8minutes or until al dente; drain and reserve.
3. Mix the chicken sausage, tomato puree, Asiago cheese, and Italian seasoning with the spaghetti.
4. Then, spritz a baking pan with cooking spray; add the spaghetti mixture to the pan. Bake in the preheated air fryer at 500°F for 11 minutes.
5. Top with the shredded Parmesan cheese. Turn the temperature to 390°F and cook an additional 5 minutes or until every element is thoroughly heated and the cheese is melted.
6. Garnish with fresh basil leaves. Bon appétit!

633. Smart chicken wings
Servings: 2
Prep & Cooking Time: 25 Minutes
Ingredients:
- 1 lb. chicken wings
- Salt & black pepper, to taste

Directions:
1. Heat up your air fryer to 380°F and grease an air fryer basket.
2. Season the chicken wings evenly with salt and black pepper.
3. Set the drumsticks into the air fryer basket and cook for about 25 minutes.
4. Serve the chicken drumsticks onto a platter and serve warm.

634. Dill chicken and parmesan
Servings: 6
Prep & Cooking Time: 20 Minutes
Ingredients:
- 18 ounces chicken breast, skinless, boneless
- 5 ounces pork rinds
- 3 ounces Parmesan, shredded
- 3 eggs, beaten
- 1 tsp. chili flakes
- 1 tsp. ground paprika
- 2 tbsps. avocado oil
- 1 tsp. stevia
- 1/4 tsp. onion powder
- 1 tsp. cayenne pepper
- 1 chili pepper, minced
- 1/2 tsp. dried dill

Directions:
1. In the shallow bowl mix up chili flakes, ground paprika, Erythritol. onion powder, and cayenne pepper. Add dried dill and stir the mixture gently.
2. Rub the chicken breast in the spice mixture, and then in the minced chili pepper.
3. Dip the chicken breast in the beaten eggs. After this, coat it in the Parmesan and dip in the eggs again. Then coat the chicken in the pork rinds and sprinkle with avocado oil.
4. Preheat the air fryer to 380°F.
5. Put the chicken breast in the air fryer and cook it for 15 minutes. Then flip the chicken breast on another side and cook it for 4 minutes more.

635. Lemon-chicken breast with pepper flavor
Servings: 1
Prep & Cooking Time:
Ingredients:
- 1 chicken breast
- 1 tsp. minced garlic
- 2 lemons, rinds and juice reserved
- Salt & pepper to taste

Directions:
1. Preheat the air fryer.
2. Place all ingredients in a baking dish that will fit in the air fryer.
3. Drop into the air fryer basket.
4. Close and cook for 20 minutes at 350°F.

636. Battered thighs with lemon-butter
Servings: 8
Prep & Cooking Time: 35 Minutes
Ingredients:
- 1/2 cup chicken stock

- 1 cup almond flour
- 1 egg, beaten
- 1 onion, diced
- 2 lbs. chicken thighs
- 2 tbsps. capers
- 3 tbsps. olive oil
- 4 tbsps. butter
- Juice from 2 lemons, freshly squeezed
- Salt & pepper to taste

Directions:
1. Preheat the air fryer for 5 minutes.
2. Combine all ingredients in a baking dish. Make sure that all lumps are removed.
3. Place the baking dish in the air fryer chamber.
4. Cook for 35 minutes at 325°F.

637. Fried cheesy chicken
Servings: 6
Prep & Cooking Time: 15 Minutes
Ingredients:
- 6 tbsps. seasoned breadcrumbs
- 1 lb. chicken breasts, skinless, boneless, and cut into slim strips
- 2 tbsps. Parmesan cheese, shredded
- 1 tbsp. melted butter
- 1/2 cup mozzarella cheese, shredded
- 1 tbsp. marinara sauce
- Cooking spray as needed

Directions:
1. Preheat your air fryer to 390°F.
2. Grease the cooking basket with cooking spray.
3. In a small bowl, mix breadcrumbs and Parmesan cheese.
4. Brush the chicken pieces with butter and dredge into the breadcrumbs.
5. Add chicken to the cooking basket and cook for 6 minutes.
6. Turn over and top with marinara sauce and shredded mozzarella; cook for 3 more minutes.

638. Crunchy chicken legs
Servings: 3
Prep & Cooking Time: 25 Minutes
Ingredients:
- 3 (8-ounces) chicken legs
- 1 cup buttermilk
- 2 cups white flour
- 1 tsp. garlic powder
- 1 tsp. onion powder
- 1 tsp. ground cumin
- 1 tsp. paprika
- Salt & ground black pepper, as required
- 1 tbsp. olive oil

Directions:
1. Preheat the air fryer to 360°F and grease an air fryer basket.
2. Mix the chicken legs, and buttermilk in a bowl and refrigerate for about hours.
3. Combine the flour and spices in another bowl and dredge the chicken legs into this mixture.
4. Now, dip the chicken into the buttermilk and coat again with the flour mixture.
5. Set the chicken legs into the air fryer basket and drizzle with the oil
6. Cook for about 25 minutes and dish out in a platter to serve warm.

639. Chinese style duck
Servings: 6
Prep & Cooking Time: 30 Minutes + Marinating Time
Ingredients:
- 2 lbs. duck breast, boneless
- 2 green onions, minced
- 1 tbsp. light soy sauce
- 1 tsp. Chinese 5-spice powder
- 1 tsp. Szechuan peppercorns
- 3 tbsps. Shaoxing rice wine
- 1 tsp. coarse salt
- 1/2 tsp. ground black pepper

Glaze:
- 1/4 cup molasses
- 3 tbsps. orange juice
- 1 tbsp. soy sauce

Directions:
1. In a ceramic bowl, place the duck breasts, green onions, light soy sauce, Chinese 5-spice powder, Szechuan peppercorns, and Shaoxing rice wine. Let it marinate for hour in your refrigerator.
2. Heat up the air fryer to 400°F for 5 minutes.
3. Now, discard the marinade and season the duck breasts with salt and pepper. Cook the duck breasts for 12 to 15 minutes or until they are golden brown. Repeat with the other ingredients.
4. In the meantime, add the reserved marinade to the saucepan that is preheated over medium-high heat. Add the molasses, orange juice, and 1 tbsp. of soy sauce.
5. Bring to a simmer and then, whisk constantly until it gets syrupy. Brush the surface of duck breasts with glaze so they are completely covered.
6. Place duck breasts back in the air fryer basket; cook an additional 5 minutes. Enjoy!

640. Paprika liver spread
Servings: 6
Prep & Cooking Time: 8 Minutes
Ingredients:
- 1-lb. chicken liver
- 2 tbsps. ghee
- 1 tsp. salt
- 1 tsp. smoked paprika
- 1/4 cup hot water

Directions:
1. Preheat the air fryer to 400°F.
2. Wash and trim the chicken liver and arrange it in the air fryer basket. Cook the ingredients for 5 minutes. Then flip them on another side and cook for 3 minutes more.
3. When the chicken liver is cooked, transfer it in the blender. Add ghee, salt, and smoked paprika. Add hot water and blend the mixture until smooth.
4. Transfer the cooked chicken pâté in the bowl and store it in the fridge for up to 3 days.

641. Spicy chicken in tomato sauce
Servings: 8
Prep & Cooking Time: 18 Minutes
Ingredients:
- 8 chicken drumsticks
- 1/2 tsp. cayenne pepper
- 1/2 tsp. chili powder
- 1/4 tsp. jalapeno pepper, minced
- 1/2 tsp. ground cumin
- 1 tsp. dried oregano
- 1 tsp. keto tomato sauce

- 1 tbsp. nut oil
- 1/2 tsp. salt

Directions:
1. In the mixing bowl mix up tomato sauce and nut oil. Then add minced jalapeno pepper and stir the mixture until homogenous.
2. Rub the chicken drumsticks with chili powder, cayenne pepper, dried cumin, thyme, and sprinkle with salt.
3. Brush the chicken with tomato sauce mixture and leave to marinate for overnight or for at least 8 hours.
4. Preheat the air fryer to 375°F.
5. Put the marinated chicken drumsticks in the air fryer and cook them for 15 minutes.

642. Roasted tomatoes with mediterranean chicken breasts
Servings: 8
Prep & Cooking Time: 1 Hour
Ingredients:
- 2 tsps. olive oil, melted
- 3 lbs. chicken breasts, bone-in
- 1/2 tsp. black pepper, freshly ground
- 1/2 tsp. salt
- 1 tsp. cayenne pepper
- 2 tbsps. fresh parsley, minced
- 1 tsp. fresh basil, minced
- 1 tsp. fresh rosemary, minced
- 4 medium-sized Roma tomatoes, halved

Directions:
1. Preheat your air fryer to 370°F.
2. Brush the cooking basket with tsp. of olive oil.
3. Sprinkle the chicken breasts with all seasonings listed above.
4. Cook for 25 minutes or until chicken breasts are slightly browned. Work in batches.
5. Set the tomatoes in the cooking basket and brush them with the remaining tsp. of olive oil. Season with sea salt.
6. Cook the tomatoes at 370°F for 10 minutes, shaking halfway through the cooking time. Serve with chicken breasts. Bon appétit!

643. English muffins and eggs benedict
Servings: 5
Prep & Cooking Time: 40 Minutes
Ingredients:
- 1/2 tsp. onion powder
- 1 cup milk
- 1 stalk green onions, minced
- 1/2 (.9 ounce) package hollandaise sauce mix
- 1/2 cup milk
- 1/2 tsp. salt
- 1/4 tsp. paprika
- 2 tbsps. margarine
- 3 English muffins, cut into 1/2-inch dice
- 4 large eggs
- 6-ounces Canadian bacon, cut into 1/2-inch dice

Directions:
1. Grease a fryer baking pan with cooking spray.
2. Place half of the bacon on bottom of pan, evenly spread died English muffins on top. Evenly spread remaining bacon on top.
3. In a large bowl, whisk well eggs, 1 cup milk, green onions, onion powder, and salt. Pour over English muffin mixture. Sprinkle top with paprika. Cover with foil and refrigerate overnight.
4. Preheat air fryer to 390°F.
5. Cook in air fryer covered in foil for 2 minutes.
6. Remove foil and continue cooking for another 15 minutes or until set.
7. Meanwhile, make the hollandaise sauce by melting margarine in a sauce pan. Mix remaining milk and hollandaise sauce in a small bowl and whisk into melted margarine. Simmer until thickened while continuously stirring.
8. Serve and enjoy with sauce.

644. Sweet curried chicken cutlets
Servings: 3
Prep & Cooking Time: 35 Minutes
Ingredients:
- 1 tbsp. mayonnaise
- 2 eggs
- 1 tbsp. chili pepper
- 1 tbsp. curry powder
- 1 tbsp. sugar
- 1 tbsp. soy sauce

Directions:
1. Put the chicken cutlets on a clean flat surface and use a knife to slice in diagonal pieces. Gently lb. them to become slimmer using a rolling pin. Place them in a bowl and add soy sauce, sugar, curry powder, and chili pepper.
2. Mix well and refrigerate for 1 hour; preheat the air fryer to 350°F.
3. Remove the chicken and crack the eggs on.
4. Add the mayonnaise and mix. Remove each chicken piece and shake well to remove as much liquid as possible.
5. Place them in the fryer basket and cook for 8 minutes.
6. Flip and cook further for 6 minutes. Remove onto a platter and continue to cook with the remaining chicken. Serve.

645. Black olives and chicken sauce recipe
Servings: 2
Prep & Cooking Time: 18 Minutes
Ingredients:
- 1 chicken breast cut into 4 pieces
- 2 tbsps. olive oil
- 3 garlic cloves; minced

For the sauce:
- 1 cup black olives; pitted
- 2 tbsps. olive oil
- 1/4 cup parsley; minced
- 1 tbsp. lemon juice
- Salt & black pepper to the taste

Directions:
1. In a food processor, combine olives, salt, pepper, 2 tablespoons olive oil, lemon juice, and parsley; process until smooth and transfer to a basin.
2. Season chicken with salt and pepper, rub with the oil and garlic, place in your preheated air fryer and cook at 370 °F, for 8 minutes.
3. Divide chicken on plates, top with olives sauce and serve.

646. Chicken enchiladas
Servings: 6
Prep & Cooking Time: 65 Minutes
Ingredients:
- 2 cups cheese, shredded
- 1/2 cup salsa
- 1 can green chilies, minced
- 12 flour tortillas
- 2 cans enchilada sauce

Directions:
1. Preheat your Fryer to 400°F.

2. In a bowl, mix salsa and enchilada sauce. Toss in the minced chicken to coat. Place the chicken on the tortillas and roll; top with cheese. Place the prepared tortillas in the air fryer cooking basket and cook for 60 minutes. Serve with guacamole

647. Asian chicken fillets with cheese and ginger
Servings: 2
Prep & Cooking Time: 50 Minutes
Ingredients:
- 4 rashers smoked bacon
- 2 chicken fillets
- 1/2 tsp. coarse sea salt
- 1/4 tsp. black pepper, preferably freshly ground
- 1 tsp. garlic, minced
- 1 (2-inch) piece ginger, peeled and minced
- 1 tsp. black mustard seeds
- 1 tsp. mild curry powder
- 1/2 cup coconut milk
- 1/3 cup tortilla chips, crushed
- 1/2 cup Parmesan cheese, freshly shredded

Directions:
1. Preheat your air fryer to 400°F.
2. Add the smoked bacon and cook in the preheated air fryer for 5 to 7 minutes. Reserve.
3. In a mixing bowl, place the chicken fillets, salt, black pepper, garlic, ginger, mustard seeds, curry powder, and milk. Let it marinate in your refrigerator about 30 minutes.
4. In another bowl, mix the crushed chips and shredded Parmesan cheese.
5. Dredge the chicken fillets through the chips mixture and transfer them to the cooking basket. Reduce the temperature to 380°F and cook the chicken for 6 minutes.
6. Turn them over and cook for a further 6 minutes.
7. Repeat the process until you have run out of ingredients.
8. Serve with reserved bacon. Enjoy!

648. Veggie breakfast frittata
Servings: 6
Prep & Cooking Time: 45 Minutes
Ingredients:
- 1/2-lb. breakfast sausage
- 1 cup cheddar cheese shredded
- 1 tsp. kosher salt
- 1/2 cup milk or cream
- 1/2 tsp. black pepper
- 6 eggs
- 8-ounces frozen mixed vegetables (bell peppers, broccoli, etc.), thawed

Directions:
1. Slightly grease your baking pan cooking spray.
2. Cook for about 10 minutes to 365°F the breakfast sausage and crumble. Halfway through cooking time, crumble sausage some more until it looks like ground meat. Once done cooking, discard excess fat.
3. Stir in thawed mixed vegetables and cook for 7 minutes or until heated through, stirring halfway through cooking time.
4. Meanwhile, in a bowl, whisk well eggs, cream, salt, and pepper.
5. Remove basket, evenly spread vegetable mixture, and transfer in egg mixture. Cover pan with foil.
6. Cook for another 1 minute, remove foil and continue cooking for another 5-10 minutes or until eggs are set to desired doneness.
7. Serve and enjoy.

649. Old-fashioned chicken drumettes
Servings: 3
Prep & Cooking Time: 30 Minutes
Ingredients:
- 1/3 cup all-purpose flour
- 1/2 tsp. ground white pepper
- 1 tsp. seasoning salt
- 1 tsp. garlic paste
- 1 tsp. rosemary
- 1 whole egg + 1 egg white
- 6 chicken drumettes
- 1 heaping tbsp. fresh chives, minced

Directions:
1. Heat up your air fryer to 390°F.
2. Mix the flour with white pepper, salt, garlic paste, and rosemary in a small-sized bowl.
3. In another bowl, beat the eggs until frothy.
4. Dip the chicken into the flour mixture, then into the beaten eggs; coat with the flour mixture one more time.
5. Cook the chicken drumettes for 22 minutes. Serve warm, garnished with chives.

650. Garlic and herbs chicken
Servings: 4
Prep & Cooking Time: 32 Minutes
Ingredients:
- 2 lbs. chicken drumsticks
- 1 fresh lemon juice
- 9 garlic cloves, sliced
- 4 tbsps. butter, melted
- 2 tbsps. parsley, minced
- 2 tbsps. olive oil
- Pepper
- Salt

Directions:
1. Preheat the air fryer to 400°F.
2. Add all ingredients into the large size mixing bowl and toss well.
3. Transfer chicken wings into the air fryer basket and cook for 15 minutes. Toss halfway through.
4. Serve and enjoy.

651. Leftover turkey in mushroom sauce
Servings: 4
Prep & Cooking Time: 25 Minutes
Ingredients:
- 6 cups leftover turkey meat, skinless, boneless and shredded
- A pinch of salt and black pepper
- 1 tbsp. parsley, minced
- 1 cup chicken stock
- 3 tbsps. butter, melted
- 1 lb. mushrooms, sliced
- 2 spring onions, minced

Directions:
1. Heat up a pan that fits the air fryer with the butter over medium-high heat, add the mushrooms and sauté for 5 minutes.
2. Add the rest of the ingredients, toss, put the pan in the machine and cook at 370°F for 20 minutes.
3. Divide every element between plates and serve.

652. Easy to cook turkey wings
Servings: 4
Prep & Cooking Time: 26 Minutes
Ingredients:
- 2 lbs. turkey wings

- 4 tbsps. chicken rub
- 3 tbsps. olive oil

Directions:
1. Warm the air fryer to 380°F and grease an air fryer basket.
2. Mix the turkey wings, chicken rub, and olive oil in a bowl until well combined.
3. Set the turkey wings into the air fryer basket and cook for about 26 minutes, flipping once in between.
4. Serve the turkey wings in a platter and serve warm.

653. The finest chicken burgers
Servings: 4
Prep & Cooking Time: 20 Minutes
Ingredients:
- 1 tbsp. olive oil
- 1 onion, peeled and finely minced
- 2 garlic cloves, minced
- Sea salt & ground black pepper, to taste
- 1/2 tsp. paprika
- 1/2 tsp. ground cumin
- 1 lb. chicken breast, ground
- 4 soft rolls
- 4 tbsps. ketchup
- 4 tbsps. mayonnaise
- 2 tsps. Dijon mustard
- 4 tbsps. green onions, minced
- 4 pickles, sliced

Directions:
1. Preheat your fryer to 365°F
2. In a pan over high heat, heat the olive oil. Then, sauté the onion until golden and translucent, about 4 minutes.
3. Add the garlic and cook an additional 30 seconds or until it is aromatic. Season with salt, pepper, paprika, and cumin; reserve.
4. Add the chicken and let it cook for 2 minutes, stirring and crumbling with a fork.
5. Add the onion mixture and combine well.
6. Form patties with the mixture and transfer them to the cooking basket.
7. Cook in the preheated fryer for 6 minutes. Turn them over and cook an additional 5 minutes. Work in batches.
8. Smear the base of the roll with ketchup, mayo, and mustard. Top with the chicken, green onions, and pickles. Enjoy!

654. Coconut milk with chicken pot pie
Servings: 8
Prep & Cooking Time: 30 Minutes
Ingredients:
- 1/4 small onion, minced
- 1/2 cup broccoli, minced
- 3/4 cup coconut milk
- 1 cup chicken broth
- 1/3 cup coconut flour
- 1-lb. ground chicken
- 2 cloves of garlic, minced
- 2 tbsps. butter
- 4 1/2 tbsps. butter, melted
- 4 eggs
- Salt & pepper to taste

Directions:
1. Preheat the air fryer for 5 minutes.
2. Place tbsp. butter, broccoli, onion, garlic, coconut milk, chicken broth, and ground chicken in a baking dish that will fit in the air fryer. Season with salt and pepper to taste.
3. Mix the butter, coconut flour, and eggs in a deep plate.
4. Sprinkle evenly the top of the chicken and broccoli mixture with the coconut flour dough.
5. Place the dish in the air fryer.
6. Cook for 30 minutes at 325°F.

655. Battered chicken with almond flour coco-milk
Servings: 4
Prep & Cooking Time: 30 Minutes
Ingredients:
- 1/4 cup coconut milk
- 1/2 cup almond flour
- 1 1/2 tbsp. old bay Creole seasoning
- 1 egg, beaten
- 4 small chicken thighs
- Salt & pepper to taste

Directions:
1. Preheat the air fryer for 5 minutes.
2. Whisk the egg and coconut milk in a bowl.
3. Soak the chicken thighs in the beaten egg mixture.
4. In another bowl, combine salt & pepper, the almond flour, and Creole seasoning.
5. Dredge the chicken thighs in the almond flour mixture.
6. Drop into the air fryer basket.
7. Cook for 30 minutes at 350°F.

656. Chicken casserole with broccoli-rice
Servings: 4
Prep & Cooking Time: 28 Minutes
Ingredients:
- 1 (10 ounce) can chunk chicken, drained
- 1 cup uncooked instant rice
- 1 cup water
- 1/2 (1 1/3 cup) can condensed cream of chicken soup
- 1/2 (1 1/3 cup) can condensed cream of mushroom soup
- 1/2 cup milk
- 1/2 small white onion, minced
- 1/2-lb. processed cheese food
- 2 tbsps. butter
- 8-ounce frozen minced broccoli

Directions:
1. Grease your air fryer baking pan with cooking spray.
2. Drop in some water and bring it to a boil at 390°F.
3. Stir in rice and cook for 3 minutes.
4. Stir in processed cheese, onion, broccoli, milk, butter, chicken soup, mushroom soup, and chicken. Mix well.
5. Cook for 15 minutes at 380°F, fluff mixture and continue cooking for another 10 minutes until tops are browned.
6. Serve and enjoy.

657. Zaatar chicken
Servings: 4
Prep & Cooking Time: 35 Minutes
Ingredients:
- 4 chicken thighs
- 2 sprigs thyme
- 1 onion, cut into chunks
- 2 1/2 tbsps. zaatar
- 1/2 tsp. cinnamon
- 2 garlic cloves, smashed
- 1 lemon juice
- 1 lemon zest
- 1/4 cup olive oil

- 1/4 tsp. pepper
- 1 tsp. salt

Directions:
1. Add oil, lemon juice, lemon zest, cinnamon, garlic, pepper, 2 tbsps. zaatar, and salt in a large zip-lock bag and shake well.
2. Add chicken, thyme, and onion to bag and shake well to coat. Place in refrigerator for overnight.
3. Preheat the air fryer to 365°F.
4. Add marinated chicken in air fryer basket and cook at 380°F for 15 minutes.
5. Turn chicken to another side and sprinkle with remaining za'atar spice and cook at 380°F for 118 minutes more.
6. Serve and enjoy.

658. Quick and easy chicken drumsticks
Servings: 4
Prep & Cooking Time: 35 Minutes
Ingredients:
- 8 chicken drumsticks
- 1 tsp. cayenne pepper
- 2 tbsp. mustard powder
- 2 tbsp. oregano
- 2 tbsp. thyme
- 3 tbsp. coconut milk
- 1 large egg, lightly beaten
- 1/3 cup cauliflower
- 1/3 cup oats
- Pepper and salt to taste

Directions:
1. Pre-heat the air fryer to 350°F.
2. Sprinkle salt and pepper over the chicken drumsticks and massage the coconut milk into them.
3. Put all the ingredients except the egg into the food processor and pulse to create a bread crumb-like mixture.
4. Transfer to a bowl.
5. In a separate bowl, put the beaten egg. Coat each chicken drumstick in the bread crumb mixture before dredging it in the egg. Roll it in the bread crumbs once more.
6. Put the coated chicken drumsticks in air fryer basket and cook for 20 minutes. Serve hot.

659. Peanut sauce with malaysian chicken satay
Servings: 4
Prep & Cooking Time: 25 Minutes
Ingredients:
- 1 tbsp. fish sauce
- 1 tbsp. lime juice
- 1 tbsp. white sugar
- 1 tbsp. yellow curry powder
- 1 tsp. fish sauce
- 1 tsp. white sugar
- 1/2 cup chicken broth
- 1/2 cup unsweetened almond milk
- 1/2 tsp. granulated garlic
- 1/4 cup creamy peanut butter
- 1-lb. skinless, boneless chicken breasts, cut into strips
- 2 tbsps. olive oil
- 2 tsps. yellow curry powder
- 3/4 cup unsweetened almond milk

Directions:
1. In resealable bag, mix well garlic, tsp. fish sauce, 1 tsp. sugar, 2 tsps. curry powder, and 1/2 cup almond milk. Add chicken and toss well to coat. Remove excess air and seal bag. Marinate for 2 hours.
2. Thread chicken into skewer and place on skewer rack.
3. For 10 minutes, cook on 390°F. Halfway through cooking time, turnover skewers.
4. Meanwhile, make the peanut sauce by bringing remaining almond milk to a simmer in a medium saucepan. Stir in curry powder and cook for minutes. Add 1 tbsp fish sauce, lime juice, 1 tbsp sugar, peanut butter, and chicken broth. Mix well and cook until heated through. Transfer to a small bowl.
5. Serve and enjoy with the peanut sauce.

660. Veggie kabobs, pineapple and jerk chicken
Servings: 8
Prep & Cooking Time: 20 Minutes
Ingredients:
- 8 (4-ounces) boneless, skinless chicken thigh fillets, trimmed and cut into cubes
- 1 tbsp. jerk seasoning
- 2 large zucchinis, sliced
- 8 ounces white mushrooms, stems removed
- Salt & ground black pepper, as required
- 1 (20-ounces) can pineapple chunks, drained
- 1 tbsp. jerk sauce

Directions:
1. In a bowl, mix together the chicken cubes and jerk seasoning.
2. Cover the bowl and refrigerate overnight.
3. Sprinkle the zucchini slices, and mushrooms evenly with salt and black pepper.
4. Thread the chicken, vegetables and pineapple onto greased metal skewers.
5. Set the temperature of air fryer to 370°F. Grease an air fryer basket.
6. Arrange skewers into the prepared air fryer basket in 2 batches.
7. air fry for about 8-9 minutes, flipping and coating with jerk sauce once halfway through.
8. Remove from air fryer and transfer the chicken skewers onto a platter.
9. Serve hot.

Chapter 4
Fish Recipes

661. Tilapia fillet, spicy and salty
Servings: 2
Prep & Cooking Time: 15 Minutes
Ingredients:
- 1 chili pepper, minced
- 1 tsp. chili flakes
- 1 tbsp. sesame oil
- 1/2 tsp. salt
- 10 ounces tilapia fillet
- 1/4 tsp. onion powder

Directions:
1. In the shallow bowl mix up chili pepper, chili flakes, salt, and onion powder. Gently churn the mixture and add sesame oil.
2. Slice the tilapia fillet and sprinkle with chili mixture. Massage the fish with the help of the fingertips gently and leave for 8 minutes to marinate.
3. Preheat the air fryer to 390°F.
4. Put the tilapia fillets in the air fryer basket and cook for 5 minutes. Flip the fish on another side and cook for 4 minutes more.

662. Smooth salmon
Servings: 2
Prep & Cooking Time: 20 Minutes
Ingredients:
- 3/4 lb. salmon, cut into 6 pieces
- 1/4 cup yogurt
- 1 tbsp. olive oil
- 1 tbsp. dill, minced
- 3 tbsps. kefir
- Salt to taste

Directions:
1. Sprinkle some salt on the salmon.
2. Put the salmon slices in the air fryer basket and add in a drizzle of olive oil.
3. Air fry the salmon at 285°F for 10 minutes.
4. In the meantime, combine together the cream, dill, yogurt, and salt.
5. Plate up the salmon and transfer the creamy sauce over it. Serve hot.

663. Trout with shallots
Servings: 4
Prep & Cooking Time: 15 Minutes
Ingredients:
- 4 trout fillets, boneless
- Juice of 1 lime
- 1/2 cup butter, melted
- 1/2 cup olive oil
- 3 garlic cloves, minced
- 6 shallots, minced
- A pinch of salt and black pepper

Directions:
1. In a pan that fits the air fryer, combine the fish with the shallots and the rest of the ingredients, toss gently, put the pan in the machine and cook at 390°F for 10 minutes, flipping the fish halfway.
2. Divide between plates and serve with a side salad.

664. Creamy breaded shrimp
Servings: 3
Prep & Cooking Time: 20 Minutes
Ingredients:
- 1/4 cup all-purpose flour
- 1 cup panko breadcrumbs
- 1 lb. shrimp, peeled and emptied
- 1/2 cup mayonnaise
- 1/4 cup sweet chili sauce
- 1 tbsp. Sriracha sauce

Directions:
1. Preheat the air fryer to 400°F and grease an air fryer basket.
2. Place flour in a shallow bowl and mix the mayonnaise, chili sauce, and Sriracha sauce in another bowl.
3. Place the breadcrumbs in a third bowl.
4. Coat each shrimp with the flour, dip into mayonnaise mixture and finally, dredge in the breadcrumbs.
5. Arrange half of the coated shrimps into the air fryer basket and cook for about 10 minutes.
6. Serve the coated shrimps onto serving plates and repeat with the remaining mixture.

665. Creole lemon salmon
Servings: 1
Prep & Cooking Time: 15 Minutes
Ingredients:
- 1 salmon fillet
- 1 tsp. Creole seasoning
- 1/2 lemon, squeezed
- 1/4 tsp. sugar
- 2 lemon wedges, for serving

Directions:
1. Pre-heat the air fryer to 350°F.
2. Combine the lemon juice and sugar.
3. Cover the salmon with the sugar mixture.
4. Coat the salmon with the Creole seasoning.
5. Line the base of your fryer with a sheet of parchment paper.
6. Transfer the salmon to the fryer and allow to cook for 7 minutes.

666. Catfish nibbles
Servings: 4
Prep & Cooking Time: 10 Minutes
Ingredients:
- 1/4 cup shredded coconut
- 3 tbsps. coconut flour
- 1 tsp. salt
- 3 eggs, beaten
- 10 ounces catfish fillet
- Cooking spray

Directions:
1. Cut the catfish fillet on the small pieces (nuggets) and sprinkle with salt. After this, dip the catfish pieces in the egg and coat in the coconut flour. Then dip the fish pieces in the egg again and coat in the shredded coconut.
2. Preheat the air fryer to 385°F.
3. Place the catfish nuggets in the air fryer basket and cook them for 6 minutes.
4. Flip the nuggets on another side and cook them for 4 minutes more.

667. Superb shrimps with goat cheese
Servings: 2
Prep & Cooking Time: 10 Minutes
Ingredients:
- 1/2 tbsp. fresh parsley, roughly minced
- 1 1/2 tbsps. balsamic vinegar
- Sea salt flakes, to taste
- 1 lb. shrimp, emptied
- 1 tbsp. coconut aminos
- 1 tsp. Dijon mustard
- 1/2 tsp. garlic powder
- 1 1/2 tbsp. olive oil
- 1/2 tsp. smoked cayenne pepper
- Salt & ground black peppercorns, to savor
- 1 cup goat cheese, shredded

Directions:
1. Set the air fryer to cook at 385°F.
2. In a medium size mixing bowl, thoroughly blend all the ingredients, except for cheese.
3. Dump the shrimp into the cooking basket; air-fry for 7 to 8 minutes. Bon appétit!

668. Buttery chives trout
Servings: 4
Prep & Cooking Time: 12 Minutes
Ingredients:
- 4 trout fillets, boneless
- 4 tbsps. butter, melted
- Salt & black pepper to the taste
- Juice of 1 lime
- 1 tbsp. chives, minced
- 1 tbsp. parsley, minced

Directions:
1. Mix the fish fillets with the melted butter, salt and pepper, rub gently, put the fish in your air fryer's basket and cook at 390°F for 6 minutes on each side.
2. Divide between plates and serve with lime juice drizzled on top and with parsley and chives sprinkled at the end.

669. Salmon fillets with broccoli
Servings: 2
Prep & Cooking Time: 12 Minutes
Ingredients:
- 1 1/2 cups small broccoli florets
- 1/4 tsp. cornstarch
- 2 (6-ounces) salmon fillets, skin-on
- 1 scallion, slimly sliced
- 2 tbsps. vegetable oil, divided
- Salt & black pepper, as required
- 1 (1/2-inch) piece fresh ginger, shredded
- 1 tbsp. soy sauce
- 1 tsp. rice vinegar
- 1 tsp. light brown sugar

Directions:
1. Preheat the air fryer to 375°F and grease an air fryer basket.
2. Mix the broccoli, 1 tbsp. of vegetable oil, salt, and black pepper.
3. Combine ginger, soy sauce, rice vinegar, sugar and cornstarch in another bowl.
4. Rub the salmon fillets evenly with remaining olive oil and the ginger mixture.
5. Place the broccoli florets into the air fryer basket and top with salmon fillets.
6. Cook for about 12 minutes and dish out in serving plates.

670. Saporous herbed trout
Servings: 4
Prep & Cooking Time: 20 Minutes
Ingredients:
- 4 trout fillets, boneless and skinless
- 1 tbsp. lemon juice
- 2 tbsps. olive oil
- A pinch of salt and black pepper
- 1 bunch asparagus, trimmed
- 2 tbsps. ghee, melted
- 1/4 cup mixed chives and tarragon

Directions:
1. Mix the asparagus with half of the oil, salt and pepper, put it in your air fryer's basket, cook at 380°F for 6 minutes and divide between plates.
2. In a bowl, mix the trout with salt, pepper, lemon juice, the rest of the oil and the herbs and toss,
3. Put the fillets in your air fryer's basket and cook at 380°F for 7 minutes on each side.
4. Divide the fish next to the asparagus, drizzle the melted ghee all over and serve.

671. Lemony branzino with creole
Servings: 4
Prep & Cooking Time: 8 Minutes
Ingredients:
- 1-lb. branzino, trimmed, washed
- 1 tsp. Creole seasoning
- 1 tbsp. sesame oil
- 1 tbsp. lemon juice
- 1 tsp. salt

Directions:
1. Rub the branzino with salt and Creole seasoning carefully. Then sprinkle the fish with the lemon juice and sesame oil.
2. Preheat the air fryer to 380°F. Place the fish in the air fryer and cook it for 8 minutes.

672. Bacalao portuguese style
Servings: 4
Prep & Cooking Time: 25 Minutes
Ingredients:
- 1 clove garlic, minced, divided
- 1 yellow onions, slimly sliced
- 1/4 cup minced fresh parsley, divided
- 1/4 cup olive oil
- 1-lb. cod fish filet, minced
- 2 hard cooked eggs, minced
- 2 tbsps. butter
- 2 Yukon Gold potatoes, peeled and diced
- 3/4 tsp. dried peppers
- 5 pitted black olives

- 5 pitted green olives
- Freshly ground pepper to taste

Directions:
1. Grease your air frier baking pan with oil and heat up your fryer to 365°F
2. Add the melt butter into the baking pan and stir in onions. cook for 6 minutes until caramelized.
3. Stir in black pepper, dried peppers, half of parsley, garlic, olive oil, diced potatoes and minced fish. Cook for 10 minutes. Halfway through cooking time, stir well to mix.
4. Garnish with remaining parsley, eggs, black and green olives.
5. Serve and enjoy with chips.

673. Garlicky salmon
Servings: 4
Prep & Cooking Time: 15 Minutes
Ingredients:
- 3 tbsps. parsley, minced
- 4 salmon fillets, boneless
- 1/4 cup ghee, melted
- 2 garlic cloves, minced
- 4 shallots, minced
- Salt & black pepper to the taste

Directions:
1. Heat up a pan that fits the air fryer with the ghee over medium-high heat, add the garlic, shallots, salt, pepper and the parsley, stir and cook for 5 minutes.
2. Add the salmon fillets, toss gently, introduce the pan in the air fryer and cook at 380°F for 10 minutes.
3. Divide between plates and serve.

674. Pollock with a mix of kalamata olives and herbs
Servings: 3
Prep & Cooking Time: 20 Minutes
Ingredients:
- 2 tbsps. olive oil
- 1 red onion, sliced
- 2 cloves garlic, minced
- 1 Florina pepper, emptied and minced
- 3 pollock fillets, skinless
- 2 ripe tomatoes, diced
- 12 Kalamata olives, pitted and minced
- 2 tbsps. capers
- 1 tsp. oregano
- 1 tsp. rosemary
- Sea salt, to taste
- 1/2 cup white wine

Directions:
1. Heat up your air fryer to 360°F.
2. Warm the oil in a baking pan. Once hot, sauté the onion, garlic, and pepper for 2 to 3 minutes or until fragrant.
3. Add the fish fillets to the baking pan. Top with the tomatoes, olives, and capers. Sprinkle with the oregano, rosemary, and salt. Pour in white wine and transfer to the cooking basket.
4. Turn the temperature to 500°F and bake for 10 minutes.
5. Taste for seasoning and serve on individual plates, garnished with some extra Mediterranean herbs if desired. Enjoy!

675. Summertime shrimp skewers
Servings: 4
Prep & Cooking Time: 15 Minutes + Marinating Time
Ingredients:
- 1 1/2 lbs. shrimp
- 1/4 cup vermouth
- 2 cloves garlic, crushed
- Kosher salt, to taste
- 2 tbsp. olive oil
- 1/4 tsp. black pepper, freshly ground
- 8 skewers
- 1 lemon, cut in wedges

Directions:
1. Preheat the fryer to 400°F
2. Add the shrimp, vermouth, garlic, salt, black pepper, and olive oil in a ceramic bowl; let it sit for hour in your refrigerator.
3. Discard the marinade and toss the shrimp with flour.
4. Thread on to skewers and transfer to the lightly greased cooking basket.
5. Cook for 5 minutes, tossing halfway through.
6. Serve with lemon wedges. Bon appétit!

676. Slightly acid branzini fillets
Servings: 2
Prep & Cooking Time: 15 Minutes
Ingredients:
- 2 branzini fillets
- Salt & pepper to taste
- 3 lemons, juice freshly squeezed
- 2 oranges, juice freshly squeezed

Directions:
1. Preheat the air fryer at 395°F
2. Place all ingredients in a Ziploc bag.
3. Allow to marinate in the fridge for 30 minutes.
4. Place the fish on the fryer grill pan and cook for 15 minutes until the fish is flaky.

677. Spiced coco-lime skewered shrimp
Servings: 6
Prep & Cooking Time: 12 Minutes
Ingredients:
- 1 lime, zested and squeezed
- 1/3 cup minced fresh cilantro
- 1/3 cup shredded coconut
- 1/4 cup olive oil
- 1/4 cup soy sauce
- 1-lb. uncooked medium shrimp, peeled and emptied
- 2 garlic cloves
- 2 jalapeno peppers, seeded

Directions:
1. In food processor, process until smooth the soy sauce, olive oil, coconut oil, cilantro, garlic, lime juice, lime zest, and jalapeno.
2. In a shallow dish, mix well shrimp and processed marinade. Toss well to coat and marinate in the ref for 3 hours.
3. Thread shrimps in skewers. Place on skewer rack in air fryer.
4. For 6 minutes, cook on 360°F. If needed, cook in batches.
5. Serve and enjoy.

678. Flaky crab croquettes
Servings: 4
Prep & Cooking Time: 30 Minutes
Ingredients:
- 1 1/2 lbs. lump crab meat
- 3 egg whites, beaten
- 1/3 cup kefir
- 1/3 cup mayonnaise
- 1 1/2 tbsps. olive oil
- 1 red pepper, minced finely
- 1/3 cup minced red onion

- 2 1/2 tbsps. minced celery
- 1/2 tsp. minced tarragon
- 1/2 tsp. minced chives
- 1 tsp. minced parsley
- 1 tsp. cayenne pepper

Breading:
- 1 1/2 cups breadcrumbs
- 2 tsps. olive oil
- 1 cup flour
- 4 eggs, beaten
- Salt to taste

Directions:
1. Place a skillet over medium heat on a stovetop, add 1/2 tbsp olive oil, red pepper, onion, and celery. Sauté for 5 minutes or until sweaty and translucent. Turn off heat. Add the breadcrumbs, the remaining olive oil, and salt to a food processor. Blend to mix evenly; set aside. In 2 separate bowls, add the flour and 4 eggs respectively, set aside.
2. In a separate bowl, add crabmeat, mayo, egg whites, kefir, tarragon, chives, parsley, cayenne pepper, and celery sauté and mix evenly. Form bite-sized balls from the mixture and place onto a plate.
3. Preheat the air fryer to 360°F. Dip each crab meatball (croquettes) in the egg mixture and press them in the breadcrumb mixture. Place the croquettes in the fryer basket, avoid overcrowding.
4. Close the air fryer and cook for 10 minutes or until golden brown. Remove them and plate them. Serve the crab croquettes with tomato dipping sauce and a side of vegetable fries.

679. Crab cakes in dijon seasoning
Servings: 2
Prep & Cooking Time: 10 Minutes
Ingredients:
- 1/4 cup minced green onion
- 1/2 cup panko
- 1 1/2 tsps. old bay seasoning
- 1 tsp. Dijon mustard
- 1 tsp. Worcestershire sauce
- 1-lb. lump crab meat
- 2 large eggs
- Salt & pepper to taste

Directions:
1. Heat up the air fryer to 380°F.
2. In a mixing bowl, combine all ingredients until every element is well-incorporated.
3. Form small patties of crab cakes, an put them in the grill pan. Cook for about 10 minutes.
4. Flip the crab cakes halfway through the cooking time for even browning.

680. Salmon in chili sauce
Servings: 4
Prep & Cooking Time: 17 Minutes
Ingredients:
- 2 lbs. salmon fillet, skinless and boneless
- 2 lemon juice
- 1 orange juice
- 1 tbsp. olive oil
- 1 bunch fresh dill
- 1 chili, sliced
- Pepper
- Salt

Directions:
1. Preheat the air fryer to 325°F.
2. Place salmon fillets in air fryer baking pan and drizzle with olive oil, lemon juice, and orange juice.
3. Sprinkle chili slices over salmon and season with pepper and salt.
4. Place pan in the air fryer and cook for 15-17 minutes.
5. Garnish with dill and serve.

681. Burned halibut in brioche
Servings: 4
Prep & Cooking Time: 25 Minutes
Ingredients:
- 4 brioche rolls
- 1 lb. smoked halibut, minced
- 4 eggs
- 1 tsp. dried oregano
- 1 tsp. dried basil
- Salt & black pepper, to taste

Directions:
1. Cut off the top of each brioche; then, scoop out the insides to make the shells.
2. Lay the prepared brioche shells in the lightly greased cooking basket.
3. Spritz with cooking oil; add the halibut. Crack an egg into each brioche shell; sprinkle with thyme, basil, salt, and black pepper.
4. Bake in the preheated air fryer at 325°F for 20 minutes. Bon appétit!

682. Trouble-free salmon fillets
Servings: 2
Prep & Cooking Time: 7 Minutes
Ingredients:
- 2 salmon fillets
- 2 tsps. olive oil
- 2 tsps. paprika
- Pepper
- Salt

Directions:
1. Rub salmon fillet with oil, paprika, pepper, and salt.
2. Drop the salmon fillets onto the air fryer basket and cook at 390°F for 7 minutes.
3. Serve and enjoy.

683. Creole cod fillets with avocado sauce
Servings: 2
Prep & Cooking Time: 20 Minutes
Ingredients:
- 2 cod fish fillets
- 1 egg
- Sea salt, to taste
- 1/2 cup tortilla chips, crushed
- 2 tsps. olive oil
- 1/2 avocado, peeled, pitted, and mashed
- 1 tbsp. mayonnaise
- 3 tbsps. kefir
- 1/2 tsp. yellow mustard
- 1 tsp. lemon juice
- 1 garlic clove, minced
- 1/4 tsp. black pepper
- 1/4 tsp. salt
- 1/4 tsp. hot pepper sauce

Directions:
1. Start by preheating your air fryer to 360°F. Spritz the air fryer basket with cooking oil.
2. Pat dry the fish fillets with a kitchen towel. Beat the egg in a shallow bowl.

3. In a separate bowl, thoroughly combine the salt, crushed tortilla chips, and olive oil.
4. Dip the fish into the egg, then, into the crumb mixture, making sure to coat thoroughly. Cook in the preheated air fryer approximately 12 minutes.
5. Meanwhile, make the avocado sauce by mixing the remaining ingredients in a bowl. Place in your refrigerator until ready to serve.
6. Serve the fish fillets with chilled avocado sauce on the side. Bon appétit!

684. Fish packets
Servings: 2
Prep & Cooking Time: 15 Minutes
Ingredients:
- 2 cod fish fillets
- 1/2 tsp. dried tarragon
- 1/2 cup bell peppers, sliced
- 1/4 cup celery, cut into julienne
- 1/2 cup carrots, cut into julienne
- 1 tbsp. olive oil
- 1 tbsp. lemon juice
- 2 pats butter, melted
- Salt & pepper, to taste

Directions:
1. In a deep platter, mix together lemon juice, salt, butter, and tarragon.
2. Add vegetables and toss well. Set aside.
3. Take two parchments paper pieces to fold vegetables and fish.
4. Spray fish with cooking spray and season with pepper and salt.
5. Place a fish fillet on each parchment paper piece and top with vegetables.
6. Fold parchment paper around the fish and vegetables.
7. Place veggie fish packets into the air fryer basket and cook at 350°F for 15 minutes.
8. Serve and enjoy.

685. Creamed trout salad with mayonnaise
Servings: 2
Prep & Cooking Time: 20 Minutes
Ingredients:
- 1/2 lb. trout fillets, skinless
- 2 tbsps. horseradish, prepared, drained
- 1/4 cup mayonnaise
- 1 tbsp. fresh lemon juice
- 1 tsp. mustard
- Salt and ground white pepper, to taste
- 6 ounces chickpeas, canned and drained
- 1 red onion, slimly sliced
- 1 cup Iceberg lettuce, torn into pieces

Directions:
1. Grease your fryer basket with cooking spray or oil.
2. Cook the trout fillets in the preheated air fryer at 395°F for 10 minutes or until opaque. Make sure to turn them halfway through the cooking time.
3. Break the fish into bite-sized chunks and place in the refrigerator to cool. Toss your fish with the remaining ingredients. Bon appétit!

686. Peppery halibut fillets
Servings: 4
Prep & Cooking Time: 20 Minutes
Ingredients:
- 2 medium-sized halibut fillets
- 1 tsp. curry powder
- 1/2 tsp. ground coriander
- Kosher salt and freshly grounded mixed peppercorns, to taste
- 1 1/2 tbsp. olive oil
- 1/2 cup Parmesan cheese, shredded
- 2 eggs
- 1/2 tsp. hot paprika
- A few drizzles of tabasco sauce

Directions:
1. Set your air fryer to cook at 365°F.
2. Then, grab two mixing bowls. In the first bowl, combine the parmesan cheese with olive oil.
3. In another shallow bowl, thoroughly whisk the egg. Next step, evenly drizzle the halibut fillets with Tabasco sauce; add hot paprika, curry, coriander, salt, and grounded mixed peppercorns.
4. Dip each fish fillet into the whisked egg; now, roll it over the parmesan mix.
5. Place (without overlapping) in the air fryer cooking basket.
6. Cook for 10 minutes, working in batches.
7. Serve over creamed salad if desired. Bon appétit!

687. Flaky cod fish nuggets
Servings: 4
Prep & Cooking Time: 20 Minutes
Ingredients:
- 2 tbsps. olive oil
- 2 eggs, beaten
- 1 cup breadcrumbs
- A pinch of salt
- 1 cup flour

Directions:
1. Preheat air fryer to 390°F.
2. Mix breadcrumbs, olive oil, and salt in a bowl until combined. In another bowl, place the eggs, and the flour into a third bowl.
3. Toss the cod fillets in the flour, then in the eggs, and then in the breadcrumb mixture.
4. Drop into the fryer basket and cook for 9 minutes. At the 5-minute mark, quickly turn the chicken nuggets over.
5. Once done, remove to a plate to serve.

688. Cool breaded flounder
Servings: 3
Prep & Cooking Time: 12 Minutes
Ingredients:
- 1 egg
- 1 cup dry breadcrumbs
- 3 (6-ounces) flounder fillets
- 1 lemon, sliced
- 1/4 cup vegetable oil

Directions:
1. Preheat the air fryer to 360°F and grease an air fryer basket.
2. Whisk the egg in a shallow bowl and mix breadcrumbs and oil in another bowl.
3. Dip flounder fillets into the whisked egg and coat with the breadcrumb mixture.
4. Arrange flounder fillets into the air fryer basket and cook for about 12 minutes.
5. Serve the flounder fillets onto serving plates and garnish with the lemon slices to serve.

689. Pistachio incrusted salmon
Servings: 1
Prep & Cooking Time: 15 Minutes

Ingredients:
- 1 tsp. mustard
- 3 tbsps. pistachios
- A pinch of sea salt
- A pinch of garlic powder
- A pinch of black pepper
- 1 tsp. lemon juice
- 1 tsp. shredded Parmesan cheese
- 1 tsp. olive oil

Directions:
1. Heat up the air fryer to 350°F, and whisk mustard and lemon juice together.
2. Season the salmon with salt, pepper, and garlic powder.
3. Brush the olive oil on all sides. Brush the mustard mixture onto salmon.
4. Chop the pistachios finely and combine them with the Parmesan cheese; sprinkle on top of the salmon.
5. Transfer the salmon in the air fryer basket with the skin side down.
6. Cook for 1minute, or at your convenience.

690. Ham tilapia fillets
Servings: 4
Prep & Cooking Time: 10 Minutes
Ingredients:
- 16 ounces tilapia fillet
- 4 ham slices
- 1 tsp. sunflower oil
- 1/2 tsp. salt
- 1 tsp. dried rosemary

Directions:
1. Cut the tilapia on 4 servings.
2. Sprinkle every fish serving with salt, dried rosemary, and sunflower oil. Then carefully wrap the fish fillets in the ham slices and secure with toothpicks.
3. Preheat the air fryer to 400°F.
4. Put the wrapped tilapia in the air fryer basket in one layer and cook them for 10 minutes.
5. Gently flip the fish on another side after 5 minutes of cooking.

691. Greek-style roast fish
Servings: 3
Prep & Cooking Time: 20 Minutes
Ingredients:
- 2 tbsps. olive oil
- 1 red onion, sliced
- 2 cloves garlic, minced
- 1°Florina pepper, emptied and minced
- 3 pollock fillets, skinless
- 2 ripe tomatoes, diced
- 12 Kalamata olives, pitted and minced
- 2 tbsps. capers
- 1 tsp. oregano
- 1 tsp. rosemary
- Sea salt, to taste
- 1/2 cup white wine

Directions:
1. Warm your air fryer to 365°F.
2. Heat the oil in a baking pan. Once hot, sauté the onion, garlic, and pepper for 2-3 minutes or until fragrant.
3. Add the fish fillets to the baking pan. Top with the tomatoes, olives, and capers. Sprinkle with the oregano, rosemary, and salt. Pour in white wine and transfer to the cooking basket.
4. Turn the temperature to 500°F and bake for 10 minutes. Taste for seasoning and serve on individual plates, garnished with some extra Mediterranean herbs if desired. Enjoy!

692. Herbed salmon
Servings: 4
Prep & Cooking Time: 20 Minutes
Ingredients:
- 1/2 tsp. dried rosemary
- 1/2 tsp. dried oregano
- 1/2 tsp. dried basil
- 1/2 tsp. ground coriander
- 1/2 tsp. ground cumin
- 1/2 tsp. ground paprika
- 1/2 tsp. salt
- 1-lb. salmon
- 1 tbsp. olive oil

Directions:
1. In the bowl mix up spices: dried rosemary, thyme, basil, coriander, cumin, paprika, and salt. After this, gently rub the salmon with the spice mixture and sprinkle with olive oil.
2. Preheat the air fryer to 375°F. Line the air fryer with baking paper and put the prepared salmon inside.
3. Cook the fish for 15 minutes or until you get the light crunchy crust.

693. Tender tuna with herbs
Servings: 4
Prep & Cooking Time: 20 Minutes
Ingredients:
- 1 tbsp. butter, melted
- 1 medium-sized leek, slimly sliced
- 1 tbsp. chicken stock
- 1 tbsp. dry white wine
- 1 lb. tuna
- 1/2 tsp. dried Peppers, crushed
- Sea salt & ground black pepper, to taste
- 1/2 tsp. dried rosemary
- 1/2 tsp. dried basil
- 1/2 tsp. dried oregano
- 2 small ripe tomatoes, pureed
- 1 cup Parmesan cheese, shredded

Directions:
1. Heat up your air fryer to 370°F.
2. Melt 2 tbsp. of butter in a pan over medium-high heat.
3. Now, cook the leek and garlic until tender and aromatic. Add the stock and wine to deglaze the pan.
4. Grease a casserole dish with the remaining 1/2 tbsp. of melted butter. Place the fish in the casserole dish. Add the seasonings. Top with the sautéed leek mixture.
5. Add the tomato puree and cook for 10 minutes in the preheated air fryer.
6. Top with shredded Parmesan cheese; cook an additional 7 minutes until the crumbs are golden. Bon appétit!

694. Basil and paprika cod
Servings: 4
Prep & Cooking Time: 15 Minutes
Ingredients:
- 4 cod fillets, boneless
- 1 tsp. red pepper flakes
- 1/2 tsp. hot paprika
- 2 tbsps. olive oil
- 1 tsp. basil, dried

- Salt & black pepper to the taste

Directions:
1. Toss the fish with the other ingredients in a mixing basin. Place the fish in the basket of your air fryer and cook for 15 minutes at 380°F.
2. Divide the cod between plates and serve.

695. Saucy catfish with ginger and garam masala
Servings: 2
Prep & Cooking Time: 25 Minutes
Ingredients:
- 2 tsps. olive oil
- 1/4 cup coconut milk
- 1/2 tsp. cayenne pepper
- 1 tsp. Garam masala
- 1/4 tsp. Kala namak (Indian black salt)
- 1/2 tsp. fresh ginger, shredded
- 1 garlic clove, minced
- 2 catfish fillets
- 1/4 cup coriander, roughly minced

Directions:
1. Heat up your fryer to 390°F.
2. Spritz the baking dish with a nonstick cooking spray.
3. In a mixing bowl, whisk the olive oil, milk, cayenne pepper, Garam masala, Kala namak, ginger, and garlic.
4. Coat the catfish fillets with the Garam masala mixture. Cook the catfish fillets in the preheated air fryer approximately 18 minutes, turning over halfway through the cooking time.
5. Garnish with fresh coriander and serve over hot noodles if desired.

696. Halibut with lemony capers mix
Servings: 4
Prep & Cooking Time: 18 Minutes
Ingredients:
- 4 halibut fillets, boneless
- A pinch of salt and black pepper
- 1 shallot, minced
- 2 garlic cloves, minced
- 1 cup parsley, minced
- 1 tbsp. chives, minced
- 1 tbsp. lemon zest, shredded
- 1 tbsp. capers, drained and minced
- 1 tbsp. lemon juice
- 1 tbsp. olive oil
- 1 tbsp. butter, melted

Directions:
1. Warm the oil and the butter in a pan (large enough to suit your air fryer) over medium heat; add the shallot and the garlic and sauté for 2 minutes.
2. Add the rest of the ingredients except the fish, toss and sauté for 3 minutes more.
3. Add the fish, sear for minute on each side, toss it gently with the herbed mix, place the pan in the air fryer and cook at 380°F for 12 minutes.
4. Divide every element between plates and serve.

697. Creole fish cakes with swiss cheese
Servings: 4
Prep & Cooking Time: 30 Minutes
Ingredients:
- 2 catfish fillets
- 1 cup all-purpose flour
- 3 ounces butter
- 1 tsp. baking powder
- 1 tsp. baking powder
- 1/2 cup buttermilk
- 1 tsp. Creole seasoning
- 1 cup Swiss cheese, shredded

Directions:
1. Boil a saucepan of water (salted) over high heat.
2. Boil the fish fillets for 5 minutes or until it is opaque. Flake the fish into small pieces.
3. Blend the remaining ingredients in a mixing bowl; add the fish and mix until well combined. Shape the fish mixture into 1patties.
4. Cook in the preheated air fryer at 300°F for 15 minutes. Work in batches. Enjoy!

698. Strong cod fillets
Servings: 4
Prep & Cooking Time: 14 Minutes
Ingredients:
- 1 lb. cod fillets
- 1 egg
- 1/3 cup coconut, shredded and divided
- 1 scallion, minced finely
- 2 tbsps. fresh parsley, minced
- 1 tsp. fresh lime zest, shredded finely
- 1 tsp. red chili paste
- Salt, to taste
- 1 tbsp. fresh lime juice

Directions:
1. Preheat the air fryer to 375°F and grease an air fryer basket.
2. Put cod filets, lime zest, egg, chili paste, salt and lime juice in a food processor and pulse until smooth.
3. Transfer the cod mixture to a bowl and add 2 tbsps. coconut, scallion and parsley.
4. Make 12 equal sized round cakes from the mixture.
5. Put the remaining coconut in a shallow dish and coat the cod cakes in it.
6. Arrange cakes in the air fryer basket and cook for about 7 minutes.
7. Repeat with the remaining cod cakes and serve warm.

699. Tasty and smooth fish fillets
Servings: 4
Prep & Cooking Time: 25 Minutes
Ingredients:
- 4 fish fillets
- 1 egg, beaten
- 1 cup bread crumbs
- 4 tbsps. olive oil
- Pepper and salt to taste

Directions:
1. Pre-heat the air fryer at 350°F.
2. In a shallow dish, combine together the bread crumbs, oil, pepper, and salt.
3. Pour the beaten egg into a second dish.
4. Dredge each fish fillet in the egg before rolling them in the bread crumbs. Drop into the air fryer basket.
5. Allow to cook in the air fryer for 12 minutes.

700. Snapper fillets with nutty sauce
Servings: 4
Prep & Cooking Time: 20 Minutes
Ingredients:
- 4 skin-on snapper fillets
- Sea salt and ground pepper, to taste
- 1/2 cup parmesan cheese, shredded

- 2 tbsps. fresh cilantro, minced
- 1/2 cup coconut flour
- 2 tbsps. flaxseed meal
- 2 medium-sized eggs
- For the Almond sauce:
- 1/4 cup almonds
- 2 garlic cloves, pressed
- 1 cup tomato paste
- 1 tsp. dried dill weed
- 1/2 tsp. salt
- 1/4 tsp. freshly ground mixed peppercorns
- 1/4 cup olive oil

Directions:
1. Heat up your fryer to 390°F
2. Using pepper and salt, proceed to season the fish fillets.
3. In a shallow plate, thoroughly combine the Parmesan cheese and fresh minced cilantro.
4. In another shallow plate, whisk the eggs until frothy. Place the coconut flour and flaxseed meal in a third plate.
5. Dip the fish fillets in the flour, then in the egg; afterward, coat them with the parmesan mixture; cook for 16 minutes or until crisp.
6. To make the sauce, chop the almonds in a food processor. Add the remaining sauce ingredients, but not the olive oil.
7. Blitz for 30 seconds; then, slowly and gradually pour in the oil; process until smooth and even. Serve the sauce with the prepared snapper fillets. Bon appétit!

701. Browned branzino
Servings: 4
Prep & Cooking Time: 20 Minutes
Ingredients:
- 4 medium branzino fillets; boneless
- 1/2 cup parsley; minced
- 2 tbsps. olive oil
- A pinch of red pepper flakes; crushed
- Zest from 1 lemon; shredded
- Zest from 1 orange; shredded
- Juice from 1/2 lemon
- Juice from 1/2 orange
- Salt & black pepper to the taste

Directions:
1. Toss fish fillets with lemon zest, orange zest, lemon juice, orange juice, salt, pepper, oil, and pepper flakes in a large mixing dish.
2. Place fillets in a 350°F preheated air fryer and bake for 20 minutes, turning once.
3. Arrange the fish on plates, garnish with parsley, and serve immediately.

702. Cod fillets hong kong style
Servings: 2
Prep & Cooking Time: 15 Minutes
Ingredients:
- 2 cod fish fillets
- 250 mL water
- 3 tbsps. coconut aminos
- 3 tbsps. coconut oil
- 5 slices of ginger
- A dash of sesame oil
- Green onions for garnish

Directions:
1. Preheat the air fryer for 5 minutes
2. Place all ingredients except for the green onions in a baking dish.
3. Drop into the air fryer and cook for 15 minutes at 400°F.
4. Garnish with green onions.

703. Grilled shrimp
Servings: 4
Prep & Cooking Time: 35 Minutes
Ingredients:
- 18 shrimps, shelled and emptied
- 2 tbsp. freshly squeezed lemon juice
- 1/2 tsp. hot paprika
- 1/2 tsp. salt
- 1 tsp. lemon-pepper seasoning
- 2 tbsp. extra-virgin olive oil
- 2 garlic cloves, peeled and minced
- 1 tsp. onion powder
- 1/4 tsp. cumin powder
- 1/2 cup fresh parsley, coarsely minced

Directions:
1. Whisk all the ingredients in a wide bowl, making sure to coat the shrimp well. Refrigerate for 30 minutes.
2. Preheat the air fryer at 400°F
3. Air-fry the shrimp for 5 minutes, ensuring that the shrimps turn pink.
4. Serve with pasta or rice.

704. Yummy sockeye salmon fillets
Servings: 2
Prep & Cooking Time: 25 Minutes
Ingredients:
- 1/2 bulb fennel, slimly sliced
- 4 tbsps. melted butter
- Salt & pepper to taste
- 1-2 tsp. fresh dill
- 2 sockeye salmon fillets
- 8 cherry tomatoes, halved
- 1/4 cup fish stock

Directions:
1. Preheat air fryer to 400°F.
2. Bring to a boil salted water over medium heat. Add the potatoes and cook for about 2 minutes; then drain.
3. Cut 2 large-sized rectangles of parchment paper of x15 inch size.
4. In a large bowl, mix potatoes, fennel, pepper, and salt.
5. Divide the mixture between parchment paper pieces and sprinkle with dill. Top with fillets. Add cherry tomatoes on top and drizzle with butter; pour fish stock on top. Fold the squares and seal them.
6. Cook the packets in the air fryer for 10 minutes.

705. Shrimp in rice flour coating
Servings: 3
Prep & Cooking Time: 20 Minutes
Ingredients:
- 3 tbsps. rice flour
- 1 lb. shrimp, peeled and emptied
- 2 tbsps. olive oil
- 1 tsp. powdered sugar
- Salt & black pepper, as required

Directions:
1. Preheat the air fryer to 325°F and grease an air fryer basket.
2. Mix rice flour, olive oil, sugar, salt, and black pepper in a bowl.
3. Stir in the shrimp and transfer half of the shrimp to the air fryer basket.
4. Cook for about 10 minutes, flipping once in between.

5. Serve the mixture onto serving plates and repeat with the remaining mixture.

706. Definitive parmesan fish fillets
Servings: 4
Prep & Cooking Time: 15 Minutes
Ingredients:
- 1 cup Parmesan, shredded
- 1 tsp. garlic powder
- 1/2 tsp. shallot powder
- 1 egg, well whisked
- 4 white fish fillets
- Salt & ground black pepper, to taste
- Fresh Italian parsley, to serve

Directions:
1. Put the Parmesan cheese in a wide mixing bowl.
2. In another bowl, combine the garlic powder, shallot powder, and the beaten egg.
3. Generously season the fish fillets with salt and pepper. Dip each fillet into the beaten egg.
4. Then, roll the fillets over the parmesan mixture. Set your air fryer to cook at 370°F. Air-fry for 10 to 12 minutes.
5. Serve garnished with fresh parsley and enjoy!

707. Mustard and parmesan cod
Servings: 4
Prep & Cooking Time: 14 Minutes
Ingredients:
- 1 cup Parmesan, shredded
- 4 cod fillets, boneless
- Salt & black pepper to the taste
- 1 tbsp. mustard

Directions:
1. In a bowl, mix the Parmesan with salt, pepper and the mustard and stir. Spread this over the cod, arrange the fish in the air fryer's basket and cook at 370°F for 7 minutes on each side.
2. Divide between plates and serve with a side salad.

708. Shrimps with monterey jack cheese
Servings: 4
Prep & Cooking Time: 5 Minutes
Ingredients:
- 14 ounces shrimps, peeled
- 2 eggs, beaten
- 1/4 cup heavy cream
- 1 tsp. salt
- 1 tsp. ground black pepper
- 4 ounces Monterey jack cheese, shredded
- 5 tbsps. coconut flour
- 1 tbsp. lemon juice, for garnish

Directions:
3. In the mixing bowl mix up heavy cream, salt, and ground black pepper. Add eggs and whisk the mixture until homogenous.
4. Mix up coconut flour and Monterey jack cheese. Dip the shrimps in the heavy cream mixture and coat in the coconut flour mixture.
5. Dip the shrimps in the egg mixture again and coat in the coconut flour.
6. Preheat the air fryer to 400°F. Set the shrimps in the air fryer in one layer and cook them for 5 minutes.
7. Repeat the same step with remaining shrimps. Sprinkle the bang-bang shrimps with lemon juice.

709. Sunlight pollock fish
Servings: 2
Prep & Cooking Time: 20 Minutes
Ingredients:
- 2 pollock fillets
- Salt & black pepper, to taste
- 1 tbsp. olive oil
- 1 cup chicken broth
- 2 tbsps. light soy sauce
- 1 tbsp. brown sugar
- 1 tsp. fresh garlic, minced
- 2 tbsps. butter, melted
- 1 tsp. fresh ginger, minced
- 2 tortillas (corn)

Directions:
1. Pat dry the pollock fillets and season with salt and black pepper; sprinkle with sesame oil.
2. Heat up your air fryer to 380°F and cook the fish for 11 minutes. Cut into bite-size pieces.
3. Meanwhile, make the sauce. Bring the broth to a boil in a large saucepan. Combine the soy sauce, sugar, butter, ginger, and garlic in a mixing bowl. Reduce the heat to a low simmer and cook until the liquid is somewhat reduced.
4. Toss the fish into the heated sauce, and serve with corn tortillas and eat up!

710. Glazed halibut steak
Servings: 3
Prep & Cooking Time: 15 Minutes
Ingredients:
- 1 garlic clove, minced
- 1/4 tsp. fresh ginger, finely shredded
- 1/2 cup cooking wine
- 1/2 cup low-sodium soy sauce
- 1/4 cup fresh orange juice
- 2 tbsps. lime juice
- 1/4 cup sugar
- 1/4 tsp. red pepper flakes, crushed
- 1 lb. halibut steak

Directions:
1. In a medium pan, add the garlic, ginger, wine, soy sauce, juices, sugar, and red pepper flakes and bring to a boil.
2. Cook for about 3-4 minutes, stirring continuously.
3. Remove the pan of marinade from heat and let it cool.
4. In a small bowl, add half of the marinade and reserve in a refrigerator.
5. In a resealable bag, add the remaining marinade and halibut steak.
6. Seal the bag and shake vigorously to coat.
7. Chill for roughly 30 minutes.
8. Heat up your fryer to 400°F and grease an air fryer basket with cooking spray.
9. Place halibut steak into the prepared air fryer basket.
10. Air fry for about 9-11 minutes.
11. Remove from air fryer and place the halibut steak onto a platter.
12. Cut the steak into 3 equal-sized pieces and coat with the remaining glaze.
13. Serve immediately.

711. Lime-garlic shrimps
Servings: 1
Prep & Cooking Time: 6 Minutes
Ingredients:
- 1 clove of garlic, minced
- 1 cup raw shrimps

- 1 lime, squeezed and zested
- Salt & pepper to taste

Directions:
1. In a mixing bowl, combine all ingredients and give a good stir.
2. Preheat the air fryer to 390°F.
3. Skewer the shrimps onto the metal skewers that come with the double layer rack accessory.
4. Place on the rack and cook for 6 minutes.

712. Basil paprika calamari
Servings: 2
Prep & Cooking Time: 10 Minutes
Ingredients:
- 8 ounces calamari, peeled, trimmed
- 1 tsp. ghee, melted
- 1 tsp. fresh basil, minced
- 1/2 tsp. smoked paprika
- 1/2 tsp. white pepper
- 1 tbsp. white wine vinegar

Directions:
1. In the shallow bowl mix up melted ghee, basil, smoked paprika, white pepper, and white wine vinegar.
2. Sprinkle the calamari with ghee mixture and leave for 5 minutes to marinate. After this, roughly slice the calamari.
3. Preheat the air fryer to 400°F. Put the sliced calamari in the air fryer and cook for 2 minutes.
4. Shake the seafood well and cook for 2 minutes more.

713. Delightful crab cakes
Servings: 4
Prep & Cooking Time: 20 Minutes
Ingredients:
- 8 ounces crab meat
- 2 tbsps. butter, melted
- 2 tsp. Dijon mustard
- 1 tbsp mayonnaise
- 1 egg, lightly beaten
- 1/2 tsp. old bay seasoning
- 1 green onion, sliced
- 2 tbsps. parsley, minced
- 1/4 cup almond flour
- 1/4 tsp. pepper
- 1/2 tsp. salt

Directions:
1. Add all ingredients except butter in a mixing bowl and mix until well combined.
2. Make four equal shapes of patties from mixture and place on parchment lined plate.
3. Place plate in the fridge for 5 minutes.
4. Spray air fryer basket with cooking spray.
5. Brush melted butter on both sides of crab patties.
6. Place crab patties in air fryer basket and cook for 10 minutes at 350°F.
7. Turn patties halfway through.
8. Serve and enjoy.

714. Butter paprika swordfish
Servings: 4
Prep & Cooking Time: 12 Minutes
Ingredients:
- 4 swordfish fillets, boneless
- 1 tbsp. olive oil
- 3/4 tsp. sweet paprika
- 2 tsp. basil, dried

- Juice of 1 lemon
- 2 tbsps. butter, melted

Directions:
1. In a bowl, mix the oil with the other ingredients except the fish fillets and whisk.
2. Brush the fish with this mix, place it in your air fryer's basket and cook for 6 minutes on each side.
3. Divide between plates and serve with a side salad.

715. Rosemary garlic prawns
Servings: 2
Prep & Cooking Time: 15 Minutes
Ingredients:
- 3 garlic cloves, minced
- 1 rosemary sprig, minced
- 1/2 tbsps. melted butter
- Salt and pepper, to taste

Directions:
1. Preheat the air fryer to 355°F.
2. Combine garlic, butter, rosemary, salt and pepper, in a bowl.
3. Pour the prawns into the bowl and mix to coat them well. Cover the bowl and refrigerate for an hour.
4. Cook for 6 minutes. Increase the temperature to 390°F, and cook for one more minute.

716. Air fried fresh broiled tilapia
Servings: 4
Prep & Cooking Time: 15 Minutes
Ingredients:
- 1 tbsp. old bay seasoning
- 2 tbsps. canola oil
- 2 tbsps. lemon pepper
- Salt to taste
- 2-3 butter buds

Directions:
1. Preheat fryer to 400°F.
2. Drizzle oil over tilapia. In a bowl, mix salt, lemon pepper, butter buds, and seasoning; spread on the fish.
3. Transfer the fillets in the air fryer and cook for 15 minutes until crispy.

717. Mouthwatering tuna cakes
Servings: 6
Prep & Cooking Time: 10 Minutes
Ingredients:
- 2 (6-ounces) cans tuna, drained
- 1/2 cup panko bread crumbs
- 1 egg
- 2 tbsps. fresh parsley, minced
- 2 tsps. Dijon mustard
- Dash of Tabasco sauce
- Salt & black pepper, to taste
- 1 tbsp. fresh lemon juice
- 1 tbsp. olive oil

Directions:
1. Preheat the air fryer to 355°F and line a baking tray with foil paper.
2. Mix all the ingredients in a large bowl until well combined.
3. Make equal sized patties from the mixture and refrigerate overnight.
4. Set the patties on the baking tray and transfer to an air fryer basket.
5. Cook for about 10 minutes and dish out to serve warm.

718. No-stress cat fish recipe
Servings: 4
Prep & Cooking Time: 25 Minutes
Ingredients:
- 1/4 cup seasoned fish fry
- 1 tbsp. olive oil
- 1 tbsp. parsley, minced

Directions:
1. Preheat your air fryer to 400°F, and add seasoned fish fry, and fillets in a large Ziploc bag; massage well to coat. Place the fillets in your air fryer's cooking basket and cook for 20 minutes.
2. Flip the fish and cook for 2-3 more minutes.
3. Top with parsley and serve.

719. Cumin, thyme 'n oregano herbed shrimps
Servings: 4
Prep & Cooking Time: 6 Minutes
Ingredients:
- 1/4 tsp. cayenne pepper
- 1/4 tsp. red chili flakes
- 1 tsp. cumin
- 1 tsp. oregano
- 1 tsp. salt
- 1 tsp. thyme
- 2 tbsps. coconut oil
- 2 tsps. cilantro
- 2 tsps. onion powder
- 2 tsps. smoked paprika
- 20 jumbo shrimps, peeled and emptied

Directions:
1. Preheat the air fryer to 390°F.
2. Season the shrimps with all the Ingredients.
3. Place the seasoned shrimps in the double layer rack.
4. Cook for 6 minutes.

720. Fresh lobster tails with green olives
Servings: 5
Prep & Cooking Time: 20 Minutes
Ingredients:
- 2 lbs. fresh lobster tails, cleaned and halved, in shells
- 2 tbsps. butter, melted
- 1 tsp. onion powder
- 1 tsp. cayenne pepper
- Salt & ground black pepper, to taste
- 2 garlic cloves, minced
- 1 cup green olives

Directions:
1. In a plastic closeable bag, thoroughly combine all ingredients; shake to combine well.
2. Transfer the coated lobster tails to the greased cooking basket.
3. Cook in the preheated air fryer at 360°F for 6 to 7 minutes, shaking the basket halfway through. Work in batches.
4. Serve with green olives and enjoy!

721. Zesty salmon fillet
Servings: 2
Prep & Cooking Time: 15 Minutes
Ingredients:
- 1 tbsp. butter, melted
- 1 tbsp. minced fresh thyme or 1 tsp. dried oregano
- 1 tsp. shredded lemon zest
- 1/2 tsp. salt
- 1/4 tsp. lemon-pepper seasoning
- 1/4 tsp. paprika
- 1-1/2 cups soft bread crumbs
- 2 garlic cloves, minced
- 2 salmon fillets (6 ounces each)
- 2 tbsps. minced fresh parsley

Directions:
1. In a medium bowl mix well bread crumbs, fresh parsley thyme, garlic, lemon zest, salt, lemon-pepper seasoning, and paprika.
2. Grease your air frier baking pan with oil. Add salmon filet with skin side down. Evenly sprinkle crumbs on tops of salmon.
3. For 10 minutes, cook on 380°F. Let it rest for 5 minutes.
4. Serve and enjoy.

722. Fantastic calamari
Servings: 2
Prep & Cooking Time: 25 Minutes
Ingredients:
- 1 cup club soda
- 1/2 lb. calamari tubes [or tentacles], about 1/4 inch wide, rinsed and dried
- 1/2 cup honey
- 1 – 2 tbsps. sriracha
- 1 cup flour
- Sea salt to taste
- Red pepper and black pepper to taste
- Red pepper flakes to taste

Directions:
1. In a bowl, cover the calamari rings with club soda and mix well. Leave to sit for 10 minutes.
2. In another bowl, combine the flour, salt, red and black pepper.
3. In a third bowl mix together the honey, pepper flakes, and Sriracha to create the sauce.
4. Remove any excess liquid from the calamari and coat each one with the flour mixture.
5. Spritz the fryer basket with the cooking spray.
6. Set the calamari in the basket, well-spaced out and in a single layer.
7. Cook at 380°F for 11 minutes, shaking the basket at least two times during the cooking time.
8. Take the calamari out of the fryer, coat it with half of the sauce and return to the fryer. Cook for an additional 2 minutes.
9. Plate up the calamari and pour the rest of the sauce over it.

723. Lively calamari salad
Servings: 3
Prep & Cooking Time: 15 Minutes
Ingredients:
- 1 lb. squid, cleaned, sliced into rings
- 2 tbsps. sherry wine
- 1/2 tsp. granulated garlic
- Salt, to taste
- 1/2 cup mayonnaise
- 1/2 tsp. ground black pepper
- 1/2 tsp. basil
- 1/4 cup olives, pitted and sliced
- 1/2 tsp. dried rosemary
- 1 cup grape tomatoes
- 1 small red onion, minced
- 1 tsp. yellow mustard
- 1/2 cup fresh parsley leaves, minced

Directions:
1. Warm your air fryer to 400°F.
2. Grease your air frier baking pan with oil.

143

3. Combine the squid rings, sherry wine, garlic, salt, pepper, basil, and rosemary in a mixing bowl. Cook for 5 minutes in a hot air fryer, shaking the basket halfway through.
4. Work in batches and allow the mixture to cool to room temperature. When the squid has cooled enough, add the other ingredients.
5. Gently whisk everything together and serve well chilled. Good appetite!

724. Salmon with honey blackberry sauce
Servings: 2
Prep & Cooking Time: 12 Minutes
Ingredients:
- 2 salmon fillets, boneless
- 1 tbsp. honey
- 1/2 cup blackberries
- 1 tbsp. olive oil
- Juice of 1/2 lemon
- Salt & black pepper to taste

Directions:
1. In a blender, mix the blackberries with the honey, oil, lemon juice, salt, and pepper; pulse well.
2. Spread the blackberry mixture over the salmon, and then place the fish in your air fryer's basket.
3. Cook at 380°F for 12 minutes, flipping the fish halfway.
4. Serve hot, and enjoy!

725. Cod fennel platter
Servings: 4
Prep & Cooking Time: 15 Minutes
Ingredients:
- Salt & pepper to taste
- 1 cup grapes, halved
- 1 small fennel bulb, sliced
- 1/2 cup pecans
- 2 tsps. white balsamic vinegar
- 2 tbsps. extra virgin olive oil

Directions:
1. Preheat air fryer to 400°F. Season fillets with salt and pepper; drizzle oil on top.
2. Drop into the air fryer basket and cook for 10 minutes.
3. In a mixing bowl, add grapes, pecans, and fennels. Drizzle oil over the grape mixture, and season with salt and pepper. Add the mixture to the basket and cook for 3 minutes. Add balsamic vinegar and oil to the mixture, season with salt and pepper.
4. Pour over the fish, and serve.

726. Shrimps with black olives
Servings: 4
Prep & Cooking Time: 15 Minutes
Ingredients:
- 1 lb. shrimp, peeled and emptied
- 4 garlic clove, minced
- 1 cup black olives, pitted and minced
- 3 tbsps. parsley
- 1 tbsp. olive oil

Directions:
1. In a pan that fits the air fryer, stir all the ingredients, toss, put the pan in the machine and cook at 380°F for 10 minutes.
2. Divide between plates and serve.

727. Fish fillets with sesame
Servings: 5
Prep & Cooking Time: 20 Minutes
Ingredients:
- 5 white fish fillets
- 5 biscuits, crumbled
- 3 tbsps. flour
- 1 egg, beaten
- A pinch of salt
- A pinch of black pepper
- 1/4 tsp. rosemary
- 3 tbsp olive oil divided
- A handful of sesame seeds

Directions:
1. Let the air fryer to heat up to 400°F.
2. In a wide bowl, mix the flour, pepper and salt. In another shallow bowl, combine the sesame seeds, crumbled biscuits, oil, and rosemary.
3. Dip the fish fillets into the flour mixture first, then into the beaten egg, and finally, coat them with the sesame mixture.
4. Arrange them in the air fryer on a sheet of aluminum foil; cook the fish for 8 minutes.
5. Flip the fillets over and cook for an additional 4 minutes. Serve and enjoy.

728. Zesty briny prawns
Servings: 4
Prep & Cooking Time: 10 Minutes
Ingredients:
- 12 prawns, cleaned and emptied
- Salt & ground black pepper, to taste
- 1/2 tsp. cumin powder
- 1 tsp. fresh lemon juice
- 1 medium egg, whisked
- 1/2 cup flour
- 1 tsp. baking powder
- 1 tbsp. curry powder
- 1/2 tsp. shredded fresh ginger
- 1 cup flaked coconut

Directions:
1. Coat the prawns in the salt, pepper, cumin powder, and lemon juice.
2. In a mixing bowl, combine together the whisked egg, a quarter-cup of the flour, baking powder, curry, and ginger.
3. In a second bowl, put the remaining quarter-cup of flour, and in a third bowl, the flaked coconut.
4. Dredge the prawns in the flour, before coating them in the beer mixture. Finally, coat your prawns in the flaked coconut.
5. Air-fry at 360°F for minutes. Flip them and allow to cook on the other side for another 2 to 3 minutes before serving.

729. White fish fillets
Servings: 4
Prep & Cooking Time: 15 Minutes
Ingredients:
- 1 cup crushed saltines
- 1/4 cup extra-virgin olive oil
- 1 tsp. garlic powder
- 1/2 tsp. shallot powder
- 1 egg, well whisked
- 4 white fish fillets
- Salt & ground black pepper to taste
- Fresh Italian parsley to serve

Directions:
1. In a shallow bowl, combine the crushed saltines and olive oil.
2. In a separate bowl, mix together the garlic powder, shallot powder, and the beaten egg.

3. Sprinkle a good amount of salt and pepper over the fish, before dipping each fillet into the egg mixture.
4. Coat the fillets with the crumb mixture.
5. Air fry the fish at 370°F for 10 - 12 minutes.
6. Serve with fresh parsley.

730. Italian style shrimp
Servings: 4
Prep & Cooking Time: 12 Minutes
Ingredients:
- 1 lb. shrimp, peeled and emptied
- A pinch of salt and black pepper
- 1 tbsp. sesame seeds, toasted
- 1/2 tsp. Italian seasoning
- 1 tbsp. olive oil

Directions:
1. Into a wide mixing bowl, combine the shrimp with the rest of the ingredients and toss well.
2. Put the shrimp in the air fryer's basket, cook at 370°F for 10 minutes, divide into bowls and serve,

731. Peppery shrimps
Servings: 2
Prep & Cooking Time: 6 Minutes
Ingredients:
- 1/2 lb. shrimp, peeled and emptied
- 1/2 tsp. old bay seasoning
- 1 tsp. cayenne pepper
- 1 tbsp. olive oil
- 1/4 tsp. paprika
- tsp. salt

Directions:
1. Preheat the air fryer to 390°F.
2. Add all ingredients into the bowl and toss well.
3. Transfer shrimp into the air fryer basket and cook for 6 minutes.
4. Serve and enjoy.

732. Sea scallops mediterranean style
Servings: 3
Prep & Cooking Time: 10 Minutes
Ingredients:
- 1-lb. sea scallops, meat only
- 3 tbsps. olive oil, divided
- 1 tsp. dried sage
- Salt & pepper to taste
- 1 cup grape tomatoes, halved
- 1/3 cup basil leaves, shredded

Directions:
1. Preheat the air fryer at 390°F
2. Season the scallops with half of the olive oil, sage, salt and pepper.
3. Toss into the air fryer, using the grill tray, and grill for 10 minutes.
4. Once cooked, serve with tomatoes and basil leaves.
5. Drizzle the remaining olive oil and season with more salt and pepper to taste.

733. White fish tots
Servings: 4
Prep & Cooking Time: 1 Hr. 20 Minutes
Ingredients:
- 1 1/2 cups whitefish fillets, minced
- 1 1/2 cups green beans, finely minced
- 1/2 cup chives, minced
- 1 chili pepper, emptied and minced
- 1 tbsp. red curry paste
- 1 tsp. sugar
- 1 tbsp. fish sauce
- 2 tbsps. white wine vinegar
- 1 tsp. water
- Sea salt flakes, to taste
- 1/2 tsp. grounded black peppercorns
- 1 1/2 tsp. butter, at room temperature
- 1 lemon

Directions:
1. Place all of the ingredients a bowl, following the order in which they are listed.
2. Combine well with a spatula or your hands.
3. Mold the mixture into several small cakes and refrigerate for 1 hour.
4. Put a piece of aluminum foil in the cooking basket and lay the cakes on top.
5. Cook at 390°F for 10 minutes. Turn each fish cake over before air-frying for another minutes.
6. Serve the fish cakes with a side of cucumber relish.

734. Superb fried cod fish
Servings: 4
Prep & Cooking Time: 20 Minutes
Ingredients:
- 4 tbsp minced cilantro
- Salt to taste
- A handful of green onions, minced
- 1 cup water
- 5 slices of ginger
- 5 tbsps. light soy sauce
- 3 tbsp oil
- 1 tsp. dark soy sauce
- 5 cubes rock sugar

Directions:
1. Warm your fryer to 360°F, and cover codfish with salt and coriander; drizzle with oil. Place the fish fillet in your air fryer's cooking basket and cook for 15 minutes.
2. Place the remaining ingredients in a frying pan over medium heat; cook for 5 minutes. Serve the fish with the sauce, and enjoy.

735. Flounder in mascarpone sauce
Servings: 3
Prep & Cooking Time: 12 Minutes
Ingredients:
- 9 ounces flounder fillets
- 4 ounces crab meat, minced
- 1 tbsp. mascarpone
- 1/2 tsp. ground nutmeg
- 2 spring onions, diced
- 1/2 tsp. dried oregano
- 2 ounces Parmesan, shredded
- 1 egg, beaten

Directions:
1. Line the air fryer baking pan with baking paper.
2. After this, cut the flounder fillet on servings and transfer them in the baking pan in one layer.
3. Sprinkle the fish fillets with ground nutmeg and dried oregano. Then top them with minced crab meat, spring onions, and Parmesan.
4. In the mixing bowl, mix up mascarpone and egg.
5. Pour the liquid over the cheese.
6. Preheat the air fryer to 385°F.
7. Place the baking pan with fish in the air fryer and cook the meal for minutes.

736. Italian-style mackerel
Servings: 2
Prep & Cooking Time: 25 Minutes
Ingredients:
- 8 ounces mackerel, trimmed
- 1 tbsp. Italian seasonings
- 1 tsp. keto tomato sauce
- 2 tbsps. ghee, melted
- 1/2 tsp. salt

Directions:
1. Rub the mackerel with Italian seasonings, and tomato sauce.
2. After this, rub the fish with salt and leave for 5 minutes in the fridge to marinate.
3. Meanwhile, preheat the air fryer to 390°F.
4. When the time of marinating is finished, brush the fish with ghee and wrap in the baking paper.
5. Place the wrapped fish in the air fryer and cook it for 15 minutes.

737. Boneless paprika tilapia
Servings: 4
Prep & Cooking Time: 20 Minutes
Ingredients:
- 4 tilapia fillets, boneless
- 3 tbsps. ghee, melted
- A pinch of salt and black pepper
- 2 tbsps. capers
- 1 tsp. garlic powder
- 1/2 tsp. smoked paprika
- 1/2 tsp. oregano, dried
- 2 tbsps. lemon juice

Directions:
1. In an empty bowl, combine all the ingredients without the fish and toss.
2. Set the fish in a pan that fits the air fryer, pour the capers mix all over, put the pan in the air fryer and cook 360°F for 20 minutes, shaking halfway.
3. Serve in plates equally and serve warm.

738. Garlic shrimps combination
Servings: 3
Prep & Cooking Time: 5 Minutes
Ingredients:
- 1-lb. shrimps, peeled
- 1/2 tsp. garlic powder
- 1/4 tsp. minced garlic
- 1 tsp. ground cumin
- 1/4 tsp. lemon zest, shredded
- 1/2 tbsp. avocado oil
- 1/2 tsp. dried parsley

Directions:
1. In the mixing bowl mix up shrimps, garlic powder, minced garlic, ground cumin, lemon zest, and dried parsley.
2. Then add avocado oil and mix up the shrimps well.
3. Preheat the air fryer to 400°F.
4. Put the shrimps in the preheated air fryer basket and cook for 5 minutes.

739. Haddock with rosemary and sesame seeds
Servings: 4
Prep & Cooking Time: 14 Minutes
Ingredients:
- 4 tbsps. plain flour
- 2 eggs
- 1/2 cup sesame seeds, toasted
- 1/2 cup breadcrumbs
- 4 (6-ounces) frozen haddock fillets
- and tsp. dried rosemary, crushed
- Salt & ground black pepper, as required
- 3 tbsps. olive oil

Directions:
1. Preheat the air fryer to 390°F and grease an air fryer basket.
2. Place the flour in a shallow bowl and whisk the eggs in a second bowl.
3. Mix sesame seeds, breadcrumbs, rosemary, salt, black pepper and olive oil in a third bowl until a crumbly mixture is formed.
4. Coat each fillet with flour, dip into whisked eggs and finally, dredge into the breadcrumb mixture.
5. Arrange haddock fillets into the air fryer basket in a single layer and cook for about 14 minutes, flipping once in between.
6. Serve the haddock fillets onto serving plates and serve warm.

740. Milkfish bellies, filipino-style
Servings: 4
Prep & Cooking Time: 10 Minutes + Marinating Time
Ingredients:
- 2 milkfish bellies, deboned and sliced into 4 portions
- 3/4 tsp. salt
- 1/4 tsp. ground black pepper
- 1/4 tsp. cumin powder
- 2 tbsps. calamansi juice
- 2 lemon grass, trimmed and cut crosswise into small pieces
- 1/2 cup tamari sauce
- 2 tbsps. fish sauce [Patis]
- 2 tbsps. sugar
- 1 tsp. garlic powder
- 1/2 cup chicken broth
- 2 tbsps. olive oil

Directions:
1. Dry the fish using some paper towels.
2. Put the fish in a large bowl and coat with the rest of the ingredients; let marinate it for at least, 30 minutes, in the refrigerator.
3. Cook the fish steaks on an air fryer grill basket at 280°F for 5 minutes.
4. Turn the steaks over and allow to grill for 2 additional minutes. Cook until medium brown.
5. Serve with steamed white rice.

741. Marinated salmon
Servings: 4
Prep & Cooking Time: 45 Minutes
Ingredients:
- 2 cloves garlic, minced
- 4 tbsps. butter, melted
- Sea salt & ground black pepper, to taste
- 1 tsp. smoked paprika
- 1/2 tsp. onion powder
- 1 tbsp. lime juice
- 1/4 cup dry white wine
- 4 salmon steaks

Directions:
1. Place all ingredients in a large ceramic dish. Cover and let it marinate for 30 minutes in the refrigerator.
2. Set the salmon steaks on the grill pan. Bake at 390°F
3. for 5 minutes, or until the salmon steaks are easily flaked with a fork.

4. Flip the fish steaks, baste with the reserved marinade, and cook another 5 minutes. Bon appétit!

742. Salmon with spinach
Servings: 4
Prep & Cooking Time: 16 Minutes
Ingredients:
- 25 ounces salmon fillet
- 1 tbsp. green pesto
- 1 cup mayonnaise
- 1/2 ounce olive oil
- 1 lb. fresh spinach
- 2 ounces Parmesan cheese, shredded
- Pepper
- Salt

Directions:
1. Preheat the air fryer to 370°F.
2. Spray air fryer basket with cooking spray.
3. Season salmon fillet with pepper and salt and place into the air fryer basket.
4. In a mixing bowl, mix together mayonnaise, parmesan cheese, and pesto and spread over the salmon fillet.
5. Cook salmon for 14-16 minutes.
6. Meanwhile, in a pan sauté spinach with olive oil until spinach is wilted, about 2-3 minutes. Season with pepper and salt.
7. Transfer spinach in serving plate and top with cooked salmon.
8. Serve and enjoy.

743. 7 creole shrimps
Servings: 4
Prep & Cooking Time: 6 Minutes
Ingredients:
- 8 ounces shrimps, peeled
- 1 tsp. Cajun spices
- 1 tsp. cream cheese
- 1 egg, beaten
- 1/2 tsp. salt
- 1 tsp. avocado oil

Directions:
1. Sprinkle the shrimps with Cajun spices and salt. In the mixing bowl mix up cream cheese and egg,
2. Dip every shrimp in the egg mixture.
3. Preheat the air fryer to 400°F.
4. Place the shrimps in the air fryer and sprinkle with avocado oil.
5. Cook the popcorn shrimps for 6 minutes.
6. Shake them well after 3 minutes of cooking.

744. Shrimps with lemon flavor
Servings: 3
Prep & Cooking Time: 14 Minutes
Ingredients:
- 1/2 cup plain flour
- 2 egg whites
- 1 cup breadcrumbs
- 1 lb. large shrimp, peeled and emptied
- Salt & ground black pepper, as required
- 1/4 tsp. lemon zest
- 1/4 tsp. cayenne pepper
- 1/4 tsp. dried Peppers, crushed
- 2 tbsps. vegetable oil

Directions:
1. Preheat the air fryer to 400°F and grease an air fryer basket.
2. Mix flour, salt, and black pepper in a shallow bowl.
3. Whisk the egg whites in a second bowl and mix the breadcrumbs, lime zest and spices in a third bowl.
4. Coat each shrimp with the flour, dip into egg whites and finally, dredge in the breadcrumbs.
5. Drizzle the shrimp evenly with olive oil and arrange half of the coated shrimps into the air fryer basket.
6. Cook for about 7 minutes and dish out the coated shrimps onto serving plates.
7. Repeat with the remaining mixture and serve warm.

745. Flounder fillets with worcestershire sauce
Servings: 2
Prep & Cooking Time: 20 Minutes
Ingredients:
- 2 flounder fillets
- 1 egg
- 1/2 tsp. Worcestershire sauce
- 1/4 cup coconut flour
- 1/4 cup almond flour
- 1/2 tsp. lemon pepper
- 1/2 tsp. coarse sea salt
- 1/4 tsp. chili powder

Directions:
1. Rinse and pat dry the flounder fillets.
2. Whisk the egg and Worcestershire sauce in a shallow bowl. In a separate bowl, mix the coconut flour, almond flour, lemon pepper, salt, and chili powder.
3. Then, dip the fillets into the egg mixture. Lastly, coat the fish fillets with the coconut flour mixture until they are coated on all sides.
4. Transfer them to the greased air fryer basket. Cook at 390°F for 7 minutes.
5. Turn them over, spritz with cooking spray on the other side, and cook another minutes. Bon appétit!

746. Char and fennel
Servings: 4
Prep & Cooking Time: 18 Minutes
Ingredients:
- 4 char fillets, boneless
- 3 tbsps. olive oil
- 1 fennel bulb, sliced with a mandolin
- A pinch of salt and black pepper
- 5 garlic cloves, minced
- 1 tsp. caraway seeds
- 2 tbsps. balsamic vinegar
- 1 tbsp. lemon juice
- 1 tbsp. lemon peel, shredded
- 1/2 cup dill, minced

Directions:
1. Mix the fish with all the other ingredients in a pan (large enough to suit your air fryer), toss, and put into the air fryer. Cook at 390°F 4 minutes.
2. Divide the fish between plates and serve with a side salad.

747. Easy cod fillets with garlic and herbs
Servings: 4
Prep & Cooking Time: 15 Minutes
Ingredients:
- 4 cod fillets
- 1/4 tsp. fine sea salt
- 1/4 tsp. ground black pepper, or more to taste
- 1 tsp. cayenne pepper
- 1/2 cup non-dairy milk
- 1/2 cup fresh Italian parsley, coarsely minced

- 1 tsp. dried basil
- 1/2 tsp. dried oregano
- 1 Italian pepper, minced
- 4 garlic cloves, minced

Directions:
1. Grease your air frier baking dish with cooking spray or oil.
2. Season the cod fillets with salt, pepper, and cayenne pepper.
3. Next, puree the remaining ingredients in your food processor.
4. Toss the fish fillets with this mixture.
5. Set the air fryer to cook at 380°F. Cook for 10 to 12 minutes or until the cod flakes easily. Bon appétit!

748. Quick and easy salmon
Servings: 2
Prep & Cooking Time: 20 Minutes
Ingredients:
- Olive oil
- 2 cup asparagus, steamed
- Salt, to taste
- Zest of a lemon

Directions:
1. Spray the fillets with olive oil and rub them with salt and lemon zest.
2. Line baking paper in your air fryer's basket to avoid sticking.
3. Cook the fillets for 10 minutes at 360°F, turning once halfway through.
4. Serve with steamed asparagus and a drizzle of lemon juice.

749. Haddock with herbs
Servings: 2
Prep & Cooking Time: 8 Minutes
Ingredients:
- 2 (6-ounce) haddock fillets
- 2 tbsps. pine nuts
- 3 tbsps. fresh basil, minced
- 1 tbsp. Parmesan cheese, shredded
- 1/2 cup extra-virgin olive oil
- Salt & black pepper, to taste

Directions:
1. Preheat the air fryer to 355°F and grease an air fryer basket.
2. Coat the haddock fillets evenly with olive oil and season with salt and black pepper.
3. Place the haddock fillets in the air fryer basket and cook for about 8 minutes.
4. Serve the haddock fillets in serving plates.
5. In the meanwhile, combine the other ingredients in a food processor and pulse until smooth.
6. Top this cheese sauce over the haddock fillets and serve warm.

750. Fisherman's fish fingers
Servings: 4
Prep & Cooking Time: 40 Minutes
Ingredients:
- 3/4 lb. fish, cut into fingers
- 1 cup friendly bread crumbs
- 2 tsp. mixed herbs
- 1 tsp. baking powder
- 2 eggs, beaten
- 3 tsps. flour
- 2 tbsps. Maida
- 1 tsp. garlic ginger puree
- 1/2 tsp. black pepper
- 2 tsps. garlic powder
- 1/2 tsp. red chili flakes
- 1/2 tsp. turmeric powder
- 2 tbsps. lemon juice
- 1/2 tsp. salt

Directions:
1. Put the fish, garlic ginger puree, garlic powder, red chili flakes, turmeric powder, lemon juice, tsp. of the mixed herbs, and salt in a bowl and combine well.
2. In a separate bowl, combine the flour, Maida, and baking soda.
3. In a third bowl pour in the beaten eggs.
4. In a fourth bowl, stir together the bread crumbs, black pepper, and another tsp. of mixed herbs.
5. Pre-heat the air fryer to 300°F.
6. Coat the fish fingers in the flour.
7. Pour in the eggs, then roll in the breadcrumb mixture.
8. Put the fish fingers in the fryer's basket and allow to cook for 10 minutes, ensuring they crisp up nicely.

751. Coconut crusted shrimps
Servings: 3
Prep & Cooking Time: 40 Minutes
Ingredients:
- 8 ounces coconut milk
- 1/2 cup sweetened coconut, shredded
- 1/2 cup panko breadcrumbs
- 1 lb. large shrimp, peeled and emptied
- Salt & black pepper, to taste

Directions:
1. Preheat the air fryer to 350°F and grease an air fryer basket.
2. Place the coconut milk in a shallow bowl.
3. Mix coconut, breadcrumbs, salt, and black pepper in another bowl.
4. Dip each shrimp into coconut milk and finally, dredge in the coconut mixture.
5. Arrange half of the shrimps into the air fryer basket and cook for about 20 minutes.
6. Serve the shrimps onto serving plates and repeat with the remaining mixture to serve.

752. Crunchy cod sticks
Servings: 2
Prep & Cooking Time: 7 Minutes
Ingredients:
- 3 (4-ounces) skinless cod fillets, cut into rectangular pieces
- 3/4 cup flour
- 4 eggs
- 1 green chili, finely minced
- 2 garlic cloves, minced
- 2 tsps. light soy sauce
- Salt & ground black pepper, to taste

Directions:
1. Preheat the air fryer to 375°F and grease an air fryer basket.
2. Place flour in a shallow dish and whisk the eggs, garlic, green chili, soy sauce, salt, and black pepper in a second dish.
3. Coat the cod fillets evenly in flour and dip in the egg mixture.
4. Set the cod pieces in an air fryer basket and cook for about 7 minutes.
5. Serve and serve warm.

753. Chinese-style garlicky shrimp
Servings: 5
Prep & Cooking Time: 15 Minutes
Ingredients:
- Juice of 1 lemon
- 1 tsp. sugar
- 3 tbsps. peanut oil

- 2 tbsps. cornstarch
- 2 chives, minced
- 1/4 tsp. Chinese powder
- Chopped chili to taste
- Salt & black pepper to taste
- 4 garlic cloves

Directions:
1. Preheat air fryer to 370°F. In a Ziploc bag, mix lemon juice, sugar, pepper, half of oil, cornstarch, powder, Chinese powder and salt. Add in the shrimp and massage to coat evenly. Let sit for 5 minutes.
2. Add the remaining peanut oil, garlic, chives, and chili to a pan, and fry for 5 minutes over medium heat.
3. Place the marinated shrimp in your air fryer's basket and cover with the sauce. Cook for 10 minutes, until nice and crispy. Serve.

754. Buttery scallops with rosemary
Servings: 4
Prep & Cooking Time: 1 Hour 10 Minutes
Ingredients:
- 2 lbs. sea scallops
- 1/2 cup beer
- 4 tbsps. butter
- 2 sprigs rosemary, only leaves
- Sea salt and grounded black pepper, to taste

Directions:
1. In a ceramic dish, mix the sea scallops with beer; let it marinate for hour.
2. In the meanwhile, combine the other ingredients in a food processor and pulse until smooth.
3. Melt the butter and add the rosemary leaves. Stir for a few minutes.
4. Discard the marinade and transfer the sea scallops to the air fryer basket. Season with salt and black pepper.
5. Cook the scallops in the preheated air fryer for 7 minutes, shaking the basket halfway through the cooking time. Work in batches.
6. Bon appétit!

755. Japanese-style flounder with chives
Servings: 4
Prep & Cooking Time: 15 Minutes + Marinating Time
Ingredients:
- 4 flounder fillets
- Sea salt and freshly grounded mixed peppercorns, to taste
- 1 1/2 tbsps. dark sesame oil
- 2 tbsps. sake
- 1/4 cup soy sauce
- 1 tbsp. shredded lemon rind
- 2 garlic cloves, minced
- 2 tbsps. minced chives, to serve

Directions:
1. Place all the ingredients, without the chives, in a large-sized mixing dish. Cover and allow it to marinate for about 2 hours in your fridge.
2. Remove the fish from the marinade and cook in the air fryer cooking basket at 360°F for 10 to 1minutes; flip once during cooking.
3. Pour the remaining marinade into a pan that is preheated over a medium-low heat; let it simmer, stirring continuously, until it has thickened.
4. Pour the prepared glaze over flounder and serve garnished with fresh chives.

756. Fish fillets in pesto sauce
Servings: 3
Prep & Cooking Time: 20 Minutes
Ingredients:
- 1 bunch fresh basil
- 1 cup olive oil
- 1 tbsp. parmesan cheese, shredded
- 2 cloves of garlic,
- 2 tbsp. pine nuts
- 3 white fish fillets
- Salt & pepper to taste

Directions:
1. Whisk all the ingredients, except for the fish fillets, in a food processor, and pulse until smooth.
2. Place the fish in a baking dish and pour over the pesto sauce.
3. Drop into the air fryer and cook for 20 minutes at 380°F.

757. Shrimps with pine nuts fusion
Servings: 4
Prep & Cooking Time: 12 Minutes
Ingredients:
- 1/2 cup parsley leaves
- 1/2 cup basil leaves
- 2 tbsps. lemon juice
- 1/3 cup pine nuts
- 1/4 cup parmesan, shredded
- A pinch of salt and black pepper
- 1/2 cup olive oil
- 1 and 1/2 lbs. shrimp, peeled and emptied
- 1/4 tsp. lemon zest, shredded

Directions:
1. In a blender, stir all the ingredients except the shrimp and pulse well. In a bowl, mix the shrimp with the pesto and toss.
2. Put the shrimp in your air fryer's basket and cook at 360°F for 15 minutes, flipping the shrimp halfway.
3. Divide the shrimp into bowls and serve.

758. Mouth-watering shrimps skewers
Servings: 5
Prep & Cooking Time: 15 Minutes
Ingredients:
- 4-lbs. shrimps, peeled
- 2 tbsps. fresh cilantro, minced
- 2 tbsps. white wine vinegar
- 1 tsp. ground coriander
- 1 tbsp. avocado oil
- Cooking spray

Directions:
1. In the shallow bowl mix up avocado oil, ground coriander, white wine vinegar, and fresh cilantro.
2. Then put the shrimps in the big bowl and sprinkle with avocado oil mixture. Mix them well and leave for 5 minutes to marinate.
3. String the shrimps on the skewers.
4. Preheat the air fryer to 400°F.
5. Set the shrimp skewers in the air fryer and cook them for 5 minutes.

759. Mahi mahi fillets with green beans
Servings: 4
Prep & Cooking Time: 12 Minutes
Ingredients:
- 5 cups green beans
- 2 tbsps. fresh dill, minced

- 4 (6-ounces) Mahi Mahi fillets
- 1 tbsp. avocado oil
- Salt, as required
- 2 garlic cloves, minced
- 2 tbsps. fresh lemon juice
- 1 tbsp. olive oil

Directions:
1. Preheat the air fryer to 375°F and grease an air fryer basket.
2. Mix the green beans, avocado oil and salt in a large bowl.
3. Arrange green beans into the air fryer basket and cook for about 6 minutes.
4. Combine garlic, dill, lemon juice, salt and olive oil in a bowl.
5. Coat Mahi Mahi in this garlic mixture and place on the top of green beans.
6. Cook for more minutes and dish out to serve warm.

760. Trout in nutty butter sauce

Servings: 5
Prep & Cooking Time: 15 Minutes
Ingredients:

- 4 trout fillets, boneless
- Cooking spray
- Salt & black pepper to taste
- For the sauce:
- 1 cup almond butter
- 4 tsps. soy sauce
- 1/4 cup lemon juice
- 1 tsp. almond oil
- 1/4 cup water

Directions:
1. Put the fish fillets in your air fryer, season with salt and pepper, and grease with the cooking spray.
2. Cook at 380°F for 5 minutes on each side and divide between plates.
3. Heat up a pan with the almond butter over medium heat; then add the soy sauce, lemon juice, almond oil, and the water.
4. Whisk the sauce well and cook for 2-3 minutes.
5. Drizzle the almond butter sauce over the fish and serve.

761. Jumbo shrimp

Servings: 4
Prep & Cooking Time: 10 Minutes
Ingredients:

- 12 jumbo shrimps
- 1/2 tsp. garlic salt
- 1/4 tsp. freshly grounded mixed peppercorns

For the Sauce:

- 1 tsp. Dijon mustard
- 4 tbsps. mayonnaise
- 1 tsp. lemon zest
- 1 tsp. chipotle powder
- 1/2 tsp. cumin powder

Directions:
1. Sprinkle the garlic salt over the shrimp and coat with the grounded peppercorns.
2. Fry the shrimp in the cooking basket at 395°F for 5 minutes.
3. Turn the shrimp over and allow to cook for a further 2 minutes.
4. In the meantime, mix together all ingredients for the sauce with a whisk.
5. Serve over the shrimp.

762. Amazing ginger cod

Servings: 2
Prep & Cooking Time: 8 Minutes

Ingredients:

- 10 ounces cod fillet
- 1/2 tsp. cayenne pepper
- 1/4 tsp. ground coriander
- 1/2 tsp. ground ginger
- 1/2 tsp. ground black pepper
- 1 tbsp. sunflower oil
- 1/2 tsp. salt
- 1/2 tsp. dried rosemary
- 1/2 tsp. ground paprika

Directions:
1. In the shallow bowl mix up cayenne pepper, ground coriander, ginger, ground black pepper, salt, dried rosemary, and ground paprika. Then rub the cod fillet with the spice mixture.
2. After this, sprinkle it with sunflower oil.
3. Preheat the air fryer to 390°F.
4. Place the cod fillet in the air fryer and cook it for 4 minutes. Then carefully flip the fish on another side and cook for 4 minutes more.

763. Shrimps with parmesan

Servings: 4
Prep & Cooking Time: 20 Minutes
Ingredients:

- 2/3 cup Parmesan cheese, shredded
- 2 lbs. shrimp, peeled and emptied
- 4 garlic cloves, minced
- 2 tbsps. olive oil
- 1 tsp. dried basil
- 1/2 tsp. dried oregano
- 1 tsp. onion powder
- 1/2 tsp. dried Peppers, crushed
- Ground black pepper, as required
- 2 tbsps. fresh lemon juice

Directions:
1. Preheat the air fryer to 350°F and grease an air fryer basket.
2. Mix Parmesan cheese, garlic, olive oil, herbs, and spices in a large bowl.
3. Arrange half of the shrimp into the air fryer basket in a single layer and cook for about 10 minutes.
4. Serve the shrimps onto serving plates and drizzle with lemon juice to serve warm.

764. Sesame seeds coated tuna

Servings: 2
Prep & Cooking Time: 6 Minutes
Ingredients:

- 1/4 cup white sesame seeds
- 1 tbsp. black sesame seeds
- 1 egg white
- 2 (6-ounces) tuna steaks
- Salt & black pepper, as required

Directions:
1. Preheat the air fryer to 400°F and grease an air fryer basket.
2. Whisk the egg white in a shallow bowl.
3. Mix the sesame seeds, salt, and black pepper in another bowl.
4. Dip the tuna steaks into the whisked egg white and dredge into the sesame seeds mixture.
5. Set the tuna steaks into the air fryer basket in a single layer and cook for about 6 minutes, flipping once in between.
6. Serve the tuna steaks onto serving plates and serve warm.

765. Hake fillets with garlic sauce
Servings: 3
Prep & Cooking Time: 20 Minutes
Ingredients:
- 3 hake fillets
- 6 tbsps. mayonnaise
- 1 tsp. Dijon mustard
- 1 tbsp. fresh lime juice
- 1 cup parmesan cheese, shredded
- Salt, to taste
- 1/4 tsp. ground black pepper, or more to taste
- Garlic Sauce
- 1/4 cup Greek-style yogurt
- 2 tbsps. olive oil
- 2 cloves garlic, minced
- 1/2 tsp. tarragon leaves, minced

Directions:
1. Pat dry the hake fillets with a kitchen towel.
2. In a shallow bowl, whisk together the mayonnaise, mustard, and lime juice. In another shallow bowl, thoroughly combine the parmesan cheese with salt, and black pepper.
3. Dip the fish fillets in the mayo mixture; then, press them over the parmesan mixture.
4. Spritz the air fryer grill pan with non-stick cooking spray. Grill in the preheated air fry at 395°F for 10 minutes, flipping halfway through the cooking time.
5. In the meanwhile, create the sauce by mixing together all of the ingredients.
6. Serve warm fish fillets with the sauce on the side. Bon appétit!

766. Fried shrimps with chili
Servings: 1
Prep & Cooking Time: 6 Minutes
Ingredients:
- 1/2 cup flour
- 1/2 cup sweet chili sauce
- 1/2 lb. raw shrimps, peeled and emptied
- 1 egg, beaten
- 1 tsp. chili powder
- Salt & pepper to taste

Directions:
1. Mix together the shrimps and eggs in a bowl. Season with salt and pepper to taste.
2. In a second mixing bowl, mix the chili powder and flour.
3. Dredge the shrimps in the flour mixture.
4. Preheat the air fryer to 330°F.
5. Place the shrimps on the double layer rack.
6. Cook for minutes.
7. Serve with chili sauce.

767. Indian famed fish curry
Servings: 4
Prep & Cooking Time: 25 Minutes
Ingredients:
- 2 tbsps. sunflower oil
- 1/2 lb. fish, minced
- 2 red chilies, minced
- 1 tbsp. coriander powder
- 1 tsp. curry paste
- 1 cup coconut milk
- Salt and white pepper, to taste
- 1/2 tsp. fenugreek seeds
- 1 shallot, minced
- 1 garlic clove, minced
- 1 ripe tomato, pureed

Directions:
1. Heat up your air fryer to 380°F; brush the cooking basket with tbsp. of sunflower oil.
2. Cook your fish for 10 minutes on both sides. Transfer to the baking pan that is previously greased with the remaining tbsp. of sunflower oil.
3. Add the remaining ingredients and reduce the heat to 380°F.
4. Continue to cook an additional 10 to 12 minutes or until every slimg is heated through. Enjoy!

768. Pleasant thyme catfish
Servings: 4
Prep & Cooking Time: 12 Minutes
Ingredients:
- 20 ounces catfish fillet (4 ounces each fillet)
- 2 eggs, beaten
- 1 tsp. dried oregano
- 1/2 tsp. salt
- 1 tsp. white wine vinegar
- 1 tsp. avocado oil
- 1/4 tsp. cayenne pepper
- 1/3 cup coconut flour

Directions:
1. Sprinkle the catfish fillets with dried oregano, salt, white wine vinegar, cayenne pepper, and coconut flour. Then sprinkle the fish fillets with avocado oil.
2. Preheat the air fryer to 385°F. Put the catfish fillets in the air fryer basket and cook them for 8 minutes. Then flip the fish on another side and cook for 4 minutes more.

769. Sweety sea bass with lentils
Servings: 2
Prep & Cooking Time: 20 Minutes
Ingredients:
- 2 sea bass fillets
- Zest from 1/2 orange; shredded
- Juice from 1/2 orange
- 2 tbsps. mustard
- 2 tsps. honey
- 2 tbsps. olive oil
- 1/2 lb. canned lentils, drained
- A small bunch of dill, minced
- A pinch of salt & black grounded pepper
- 2 oz. watercress
- A small bunch of parsley, minced
- Salt & black grounded pepper, to taste

Directions:
1. Heat up your fryer to 360°F
2. Using pepper and salt, proceed to season the sea bass; add orange zest and juice.
3. Rub the fish with a mixture of oil, honey, and mustard.
4. Transfer to your air fryer and cook for 10 minutes; flipping halfway.
5. Meanwhile; put lentils in a small pot, warm it up over medium heat, add the rest of the oil, watercress, dill and parsley; stir well and divide among plates.
6. Add fish fillets and serve right away.

770. Beer cod filet
Servings: 2
Prep & Cooking Time: 15 Minutes
Ingredients:

- 1/2 cup all-purpose flour
- 3/4 tsp. baking powder
- 1 1/4 cups lager beer
- 2 cod fillets
- 2 eggs, beaten
- Salt & pepper to taste

Directions:
1. Preheat the air fryer to 390°F.
2. Pat the fish fillets dry then set aside.
3. In a mixing bowl, combine the rest of the Ingredients to create a batter.
4. Dip the fillets on the batter and place on the double layer rack.
5. Cook for 1minute.

771. Quick and easy scallops
Servings: 2
Prep & Cooking Time: 4 Minutes
Ingredients:
- 3/4 lb. sea scallops
- 1 tbsp. butter, melted
- 1/2 tbsp. fresh thyme, minced
- Salt & black pepper, to taste

Directions:
1. Preheat the air fryer to 390°F and grease an air fryer basket.
2. Mix all the ingredients in a bowl and toss to coat well.
3. Set the scallops in the air fryer basket and cook for about 4 minutes.
4. Serve and serve warm.

772. Linguine with grilled tuna
Servings: 2
Prep & Cooking Time: 20 Minutes
Ingredients:
- 1 tbsp. capers, minced
- 1 tbsp. olive oil
- 12 ounces linguine, cooked according to package directions
- 1-lb. fresh tuna fillets
- 2 cups parsley leaves, minced
- Juice from 1 lemon
- Salt & pepper to taste

Directions:
1. Heat up the air fryer to 390°F.
2. Season the tuna with salt and pepper. Brush with oil.
3. Grill for 20 minutes.
4. Once the tuna is cooked, shared using forks and place on top of cooked linguine. Add parsley and capers.
5. Using pepper and salt, proceed to season the fillets.

773. Turmeric salmon with soy sauce
Servings: 4
Prep & Cooking Time: 12 Minutes
Ingredients:
- 1/2 tbsp. sugar
- 1/2 tbsp. turmeric powder
- 1 cup cherry tomatoes
- 1 slab of salmon fillets, sliced into cubes
- 1 tbsp. soy sauce
- A dash of black pepper
- Chopped coriander for garnish

Directions:
1. Season the salmon fillets with turmeric powder, sugar, soy sauce, and black pepper. Allow to marinate for 30 minutes in the fridge.
2. Preheat the air fryer to 330°F.
3. Skewer the salmon cubes alternating with tomatoes

4. Place on the double layer rack.
5. Cook for 10 to 12 minutes.

774. Succulent crab cake burgers
Servings: 3
Prep & Cooking Time: 2 Hours 20 Minutes
Ingredients:
- 2 eggs, beaten
- 1 shallot, minced
- 2 garlic cloves, crushed
- 1 tbsp. olive oil
- 1 tsp. yellow mustard
- 1 tsp. fresh cilantro, minced
- 10 ounces crab meat
- 1 cup tortilla chips, crushed
- 1/2 tsp. cayenne pepper
- 1/2 tsp. ground black pepper
- Sea salt, to taste
- 3/4 cup fresh bread crumbs

Directions:
1. In a mixing bowl, thoroughly combine the eggs, shallot, garlic, olive oil, mustard, cilantro, crab meat, tortilla chips, cayenne pepper, black pepper, and salt. Mix until well combined.
2. Shape the mixture into 6 patties. Dip the crab patties into the fresh breadcrumbs, coating well on all sides. Place in your refrigerator for hours.
3. Spritz the crab patties with cooking oil on both sides. Cook in the preheated air fryer at 390°F for 14 minutes. Serve on dinner rolls if desired. Bon appétit!

775. Pleasant baby octopus salad
Servings: 3
Prep & Cooking Time: 50 Minutes
Ingredients:
- 1 1/2 tbsps. olive oil
- 2 cloves garlic, minced
- 1 1/2 tbsps. capers
- 1 1/4 tbsps. balsamic glaze
- 1 bunch parsley, minced roughly
- 1 bunch baby fennel, minced
- 1 cup semi-dried tomatoes, minced
- 1 red onion, sliced
- A handful of arugula
- Salt & pepper to taste
- 1/4 cup minced grilled Halloumi
- 1 long red chili, minced
- 1 1/2 cups water

Directions:
1. Boil a saucepan of water (salted) over high heat.
2. Cut the octopus into bite sizes and add it to the boiling water for 45 seconds; drain the water.
3. Add the garlic, olive oil, and octopus in a bowl. Coat the octopus with garlic and olive oil. Leave to marinate for 15 minutes.
4. Preheat the air fryer to 380°F. Place the octopus in the fryer basket and grill for 5 minutes. In a salad mixing bowl, add the capers, halloumi, chili, tomatoes, olives, parsley, red onion, fennel, octopus, arugula, and balsamic glaze. Season with salt and pepper and mix. Serve with a side of toasts.

776. Sole fish and cauliflower nibbles
Servings: 2
Prep & Cooking Time: 30 Minutes
Ingredients:

- 1/2 lb. sole fillets
- 1/2 lb. mashed cauliflower
- 1 egg, well beaten
- 1/2 cup red onion, minced
- 2 garlic cloves, minced
- 2 tbsps. fresh parsley, minced
- 1 bell pepper, finely minced
- 1/2 tsp. scotch bonnet pepper, minced
- 1 tbsp. olive oil
- 1 tbsp. coconut aminos
- 1/2 tsp. paprika
- Salt and white pepper, to taste

Directions:
1. Start by preheating your air fryer to 395°F. Spritz the sides and bottom of the cooking basket with cooking spray.
2. Cook the sole fillets in the preheated air fryer for 10 minutes, flipping them halfway through the cooking time.
3. In a mixing bowl, mash the sole fillets into flakes. Stir in the remaining ingredients. Shape the fish mixture into patties.
4. Bake in the preheated air fryer at 390°F for 1 minute, flipping them halfway through the cooking time. Bon appétit!

777. Cod with spring onions
Servings: 2
Prep & Cooking Time: 15 Minutes
Ingredients:
- 2 cod fillets, boneless
- Salt & black pepper to the taste
- 1 bunch spring onions, minced
- 3 tbsps. ghee, melted

Directions:
1. In a pan that fits the air fryer, stir all the ingredients, toss gently, introduce in the air fryer and cook at 360°F for 10 minutes.
2. Divide the fish and sauce between plates and serve.

778. Grilled shrimp with butter
Servings: 4
Prep & Cooking Time: 15 Minutes
Ingredients:
- 6 tbsps. unsalted butter
- 1/2 cup red onion, minced
- 1 1/2 tsps. red pepper
- 1 tsp. shrimp paste or fish sauce
- 1 1/2 tsps. lime juice
- Salt & pepper to taste
- 24 large shrimps, shelled and emptied

Directions:
1. Preheat the air fryer at 395°F
2. Drop all ingredients in a Ziploc bag; shake well.
3. Skewer the shrimps through a bamboo skewer and place on the grill pan.
4. Cook for 1minutes.
5. Flip the shrimps halfway through the cooking time.

779. Tasty halibut steaks
Servings: 4
Prep & Cooking Time: 15 Minutes
Ingredients:
- 1 lb. halibut steaks
- Salt & pepper for better taste
- 1 tsp. dried basil
- 2 tbsps. honey
- 1/4 cup vegetable oil

- 2 1/2 tbsps. Worcester sauce
- 1 tbsp. freshly squeezed lemon juice
- 2 tbsps. vermouth
- 1 tbsp. fresh parsley leaves, coarsely minced

Directions:
1. In a large bowl, mix all of the ingredients. Make sure the fish is covered completely with the seasoning.
2. Move it to your air fryer and set it to 390°F. Cook it for 5 minutes.
3. Cook the other side of the fish for another 5 minutes as well.
4. Check if the fish is completely cooked, cook longer as needed.
5. Serve with a side of potato salad.

780. Crispy herbed calamari rings
Servings: 4
Prep & Cooking Time: 4 Minutes
Ingredients:
- 1 chili pepper, minced
- 1/4 tsp. salt
- 10 ounces calamari
- 1/2 tsp. dried cilantro
- 1/2 tsp. dried parsley
- 1 tsp. white wine vinegar
- 1 tsp. butter, melted
- 1/4 tsp. ground coriander
- 1 tsp. sesame oil

Directions:
1. Trimmed and wash the calamari. Then slice it into rings and sprinkle with salt, dried cilantro, ground coriander, and white wine vinegar. Add sesame oil and stir the calamari rings.
2. Preheat the air fryer to 400°F.
3. Put the calamari rings in the air fryer basket and cook them for 2 minutes.
4. When the time is finished, shake them well and cook for 2 minutes more.
5. Transfer the calamari rings in the big bowl and sprinkle with butter.

781. Haddock in creamy sauce
Servings: 4
Prep & Cooking Time: 8 Minutes
Ingredients:
- 12 ounces haddock fillet
- 1 egg, beaten
- 1 tsp. cream cheese
- 1 tsp. chili flakes
- 1/2 tsp. salt
- 1 tbsp. flax meal
- Cooking spray

Directions:
1. Cut the haddock on 4 pieces and sprinkle with chili flakes and salt. After this, in the small bowl mix up egg and cream cheese.
2. Dip the haddock pieces in the egg mixture and generously sprinkle with flax meal.
3. Preheat the air fryer to 400°F.
4. Put the prepared haddock pieces in the air fryer in one layer and cook them for 4 minutes from each side or until they are golden brown.

782. Prawns and salmon pasta
Servings: 4
Prep & Cooking Time: 18 Minutes
Ingredients:
- 14 ounces pasta (of your choice)
- 4 tbsp. pesto, divided

- 4 (4-ounces) salmon steaks
- 2 tbsps. olive oil
- 1/2 lb. cherry tomatoes, minced
- 8 large prawns, peeled and emptied
- 2 tbsps. fresh lemon juice
- 2 tbsps. fresh thyme, minced

Directions:
1. In a pan with salted boiling water, add the pasta and cook for about 8- minutes or until desired doneness.
2. Meanwhile, in the bottom of a baking dish, spread 1 tbsp. of pesto.
3. Place salmon steaks and tomatoes over pesto in a single layer and drizzle evenly with the oil.
4. Now, add the prawns on top in a single layer.
5. Drizzle with lemon juice and sprinkle with thyme.
6. Preheat your air fryer to 390°F
7. Set the baking dish in the air fryer and cook for about 8 minutes.
8. Once done, remove the salmon mixture from air fryer.
9. Drain the pasta and transfer into a large bowl.
10. Add the remaining pesto and toss to coat well.
11. Add the pasta evenly onto each serving plate and top with salmon mixture.
12. Serve immediately.

783. Grilled squids rings with kale
Servings: 3
Prep & Cooking Time: 15 Minutes
Ingredients:
- 1 2-lb. squid, cleaned and sliced into rings
- Salt & pepper to taste
- 3 cloves of garlic, minced
- 1 sprig rosemary, minced
- 1/4 cup red wine vinegar
- 3 lbs. kale, torn
- 3 tomatoes, minced

Directions:
1. Preheat the air fryer at 400°F.
2. Season the squid rings with salt, pepper, garlic, rosemary, and wine vinegar.
3. Transfer the, to the grill tray and cook for 15 minutes.
4. Serve octopus on a bed of kale leaves and garnish with tomatoes on top.

784. Classic fish and chips
Servings: 4
Prep & Cooking Time: 25 Minutes
Ingredients:
- Salt & pepper to taste
- 4 white fish fillets
- 2 tbsps. flour
- 1 egg, beaten
- 1 cup breadcrumbs
- Salt & black pepper

Directions:
1. Warm your fryer to 400°F
2. Season the fillets with olive oil, salt and black pepper.
3. Place them in the air fryer, and cook for 20 minutes.
4. Spread flour on a plate and coat the fish. Dip in the egg, then into the crumbs. and season with salt and black pepper. At the minutes' mark, add the fish to the fryer and cook with the chips. Cook until crispy.
5. Serve with lemon slices, mayo and ketchup.

785. Shrimps kebabs
Servings: 2
Prep & Cooking Time: 10 Minutes
Ingredients:
- 3/4 lb. shrimp, peeled and emptied
- 1 tbsp. fresh cilantro, minced
- Wooden skewers, presoaked
- 2 tbsps. fresh lemon juice
- 1 tsp. garlic, minced
- 1/2 tsp. paprika
- 1/2 tsp. ground cumin
- Salt & ground black pepper, as required

Directions:
1. Preheat the air fryer to 350°F and grease an air fryer basket.
2. Mix lemon juice, garlic, and spices in a bowl.
3. Stir in the shrimp and mix to coat well.
4. Thread the shrimp onto presoaked wooden skewers and transfer to the air fryer basket.
5. Cook for about 10 minutes, flipping once in between.
6. Serve the mixture onto serving plates and serve garnished with fresh cilantro.

786. Louisiana-style shrimps
Servings: 4
Prep & Cooking Time: 18 Minutes
Ingredients:
- 1 egg, beaten
- 1/4 cup flour
- 1/4 cup white breadcrumbs
- 2 tbsps. Creole seasoning
- Salt & black pepper to taste
- 1 lemon, cut into wedges

Directions:
1. Heat up your air fryer to 390°F.
2. Spray the air fryer basket with cooking spray.
3. Beat the eggs in a bowl and season with salt and black pepper. In a separate bowl, mix white breadcrumbs with Creole seasoning. In a third bowl, pour the flour.
4. Dip the shrimp in the flour and then in the eggs, and finally in the breadcrumb mixture. Spray with cooking spray and place in the cooking basket. Cook for 6 minutes, Slide out the fryer basket and flip; cook for 6 more minutes. Serve with lemon wedges.

787. Salmon with green beans
Servings: 4
Prep & Cooking Time: 12 Minutes
Ingredients:
- For Green Beans
- 5 cups green beans (I use frozen)
- 1 tbsp. avocado oil
- Salt, as required

For Salmon
- 2 garlic cloves, minced
- 2 tbsp. fresh dill, minced
- 2 tbsp. fresh lemon juice
- 1 tbsp. olive oil
- Salt, as required
- 4 (6-ounces) salmon fillets

Directions:
1. Set the temperature of air fryer to 375°F. Grease an air fryer basket.
2. In a large bowl, mix well the green beans, oil, and salt.
3. Arrange green beans into the prepared air fryer basket.
4. Air fry for about 6 minutes.

5. Meanwhile, for salmon: in a bowl, mix together the garlic, dill, lemon juice, and olive oil.
6. Remove the basket from air fryer.
7. Flip the green beans and top with salmon fillets.
8. Place the garlic mixture evenly on top of each salmon fillet and then, sprinkle with the salt.
9. Air fry for about 6 minutes.
10. Remove from air fryer and place the salmon fillets onto serving plates.
11. Serve hot alongside the green beans.

788. Sea bass and olives combination
Servings: 2
Prep & Cooking Time: 20 Minutes
Ingredients:
- 2 sea bass, fillets
- 1 fennel bulb, sliced
- Juice of 1 lemon
- 1/3 cup olives, pitted and sliced
- 1 tbsp. olive oil
- A pinch of salt and black pepper
- 1/4 cup basil, minced

Directions:
1. In a pan that fits the air fryer, stir all the ingredients, introduce the pan in the machine and cook at 380°F for 20 minutes, shaking the fryer halfway.
2. Divide between plates and serve.

789. Crispy pesto salmon fillets
Servings: 2
Prep & Cooking Time: 15 Minutes
Ingredients:
- 1/4 cup cereals, roughly minced
- 1/4 cup pesto
- 2 x 4-oz. salmon fillets
- 2 tbsps. unsalted butter, melted

Directions:
1. Mix the cereals and pesto together.
2. Place the salmon fillets in a round baking dish, roughly six inches in diameter.
3. Brush the fillets with butter, followed by the pesto mixture, ensuring to coat both the top and bottom. Put the baking dish inside the fryer.
4. Cook for twelve minutes at 390°F.
5. The salmon is ready when it flakes easily when prodded with a fork. Serve warm.

790. Shrimp and celery salad
Servings: 4
Prep & Cooking Time: 5 Minutes
Ingredients:
- 3 ounces chevre
- 1 tsp. avocado oil
- 1/2 tsp. dried oregano
- 8 ounces shrimps, peeled
- 1 tsp. butter, melted
- 1/2 tsp. salt
- 1/2 tsp. chili flakes
- 4 ounces celery stalk, minced

Directions:
1. Sprinkle the shrimps with dried oregano and melted butter and put in the air fryer.
2. Cook the seafood at 400°F for 5 minutes. Meanwhile, crumble the chevre.
3. Put the minced celery stalk in the salad bowl.
4. Add crumbled chevre, chili flakes, salt, and avocado oil.
5. Mix up the salad well and top it with cooked shrimps.

791. Lemony grilled halibut with tomatoes
Servings: 4
Prep & Cooking Time: 15 Minutes
Ingredients:
- 1/2 cup hearts of palm, rinse and drained
- 1 cup cherry tomatoes
- 2 tbsps. oil
- 4 halibut fillets
- Juice from 1 lemon
- Salt & pepper to taste

Directions:
1. Heat up the air fryer to 355°F.
2. Season the halibut fillets with lemon juice, salt and pepper. Brush with oil.
3. Place the fish on the fryer grill pan.
4. Set the hearts of palms and cherry tomatoes on the side and sprinkle with more salt and pepper.
5. Cook for about 15 minutes.

792. Ghee shrimps
Servings: 4
Prep & Cooking Time: 12 Minutes
Ingredients:
- 1 lb. shrimps, peeled and emptied
- 1 cup cherry tomatoes, halved
- 4 garlic cloves, minced
- Salt & black pepper to the taste
- 1 tbsp. rosemary, minced
- 2 tbsps. ghee, melted

Directions:
1. In a pan that fits the air fryer, mix all the ingredients, toss, put the pan in the fryer and cook at 380°F for 10 minutes.
2. Divide into bowls and serve warm.

793. Buttered scallops
Servings: 2
Prep & Cooking Time: 4 Minutes
Ingredients:
- 3/4 lb. sea scallops, cleaned and patted very dry
- 1 tbsp. butter, melted
- 1/2 tbsp. fresh thyme, minced
- Salt & black pepper, as required

Directions:
1. Preheat the air fryer to 390°F and grease an air fryer basket.
2. Mix scallops, butter, thyme, salt, and black pepper in a bowl.
3. Arrange scallops in the air fryer basket and cook for about 4 minutes.
4. Serve the scallops in a platter and serve warm.

794. Pecan crusted tilapia
Servings: 5
Prep & Cooking Time: 20 Minutes
Ingredients:
- 2 tbsps. ground flaxseeds
- 1 tsp. paprika
- Sea salt and white pepper for better taste
- 1 tsp. garlic paste
- 2 tbsps. extra-virgin olive oil
- 1/2 cup pecans, ground
- 5 tilapia fillets, slice into halves

Directions:
1. Combine the ground flaxseeds, paprika, salt, white pepper, garlic paste, olive oil, and ground pecans in a Ziploc bag.
2. Put in the fish fillets, coat it by shaking.
3. Grease your air frier basket with cooking spray or oil. Set the air fryer at 400°F and let it cook for 10 minutes; cook the other side for 6 more minutes. Do it in batches.
4. Serve with lemon wedges, if desired. Enjoy!

795. Pecan crusted tilapia
Servings: 5
Prep & Cooking Time: 20 Minutes
Ingredients:
- 2 tbsps. ground flaxseeds
- 1 tsp. paprika
- Sea salt and white pepper, to taste
- 1 tsp. garlic paste
- 2 tbsps. extra-virgin olive oil
- 1/2 cup pecans, ground
- 5 tilapia fillets, slice into halves

Directions:
1. Combine the ground flaxseeds, paprika, salt, white pepper, garlic paste, olive oil, and ground pecans in a Ziploc bag.
2. Add the fish fillets and shake to coat well.
3. Grease your air frier basket with cooking spray or oil. Cook in the preheated air fryer at 400°F for 10 minutes; turn them over and cook for 6 minutes more. Work in batches.
4. Serve with lemon wedges, if desired. Enjoy!

796. Avocado sauce on creole cod fillets
Servings: 2
Prep & Cooking Time: 20 Minutes
Ingredients:
- 2 cod fish fillets
- 1 egg
- Sea salt for better taste
- 1/2 cup tortilla chips, crushed
- 2 tsps. olive oil
- 1/2 avocado, peeled, pitted, and mashed
- 1 tbsp. mayonnaise
- 3 tbsps. kefir
- 1/2 tsp. yellow mustard
- 1 tsp. lemon juice
- 1 garlic clove, minced
- 1/4 tsp. black pepper
- 1/4 tsp. salt
- 1/4 tsp. hot pepper sauce

Directions:
1. First, heat up your air fryer. Set it to 360°F. Cover the air fryer basket with cooking oil.
2. Pat dry the fish fillets with a kitchen towel. Using a shallow bowl, whisk the egg lightly.
3. In a separate bowl, thoroughly combine the salt, crushed tortilla chips, and olive oil.
4. Dip the fish into the egg, then, into the crumb mixture, making sure to coat thoroughly. For approximately 12 minutes, let it cook in the preheated air fryer.
5. Meanwhile, make the avocado sauce by mixing the remaining ingredients in a bowl. Keep it cool in your refrigerator and serve it cold.
6. Serve the fish fillets with chilled avocado sauce on the side. Bon appétit!

797. Chives trout in butter
Servings: 4
Prep & Cooking Time: 12 Minutes
Ingredients:
- 4 trout fillets, boneless
- 4 tbsps. butter, melted
- Salt & black pepper to the taste
- Juice of 1 lime
- 1 tbsp. chives, minced
- 1 tbsp. parsley, minced

Directions:
1. Mix the fish fillets with the melted butter, salt and pepper, rub gently, put the fish in your air fryer's basket and cook at 390°F for 6 minutes on each side.
2. Serve in plates equally and serve with lime juice drizzled on top and with parsley and chives sprinkled at the end.

798. Yummy buttered scallops
Servings: 2
Prep & Cooking Time: 4 Minutes
Ingredients:
- 3/4 lb. sea scallops, cleaned and patted very dry
- 1 tbsp. butter, melted
- 1/2 tbsp. fresh thyme, minced
- Salt & black pepper, as required

Directions:
1. Preheat the air fryer to 390°F before greasing the fryer basket with oil.
2. Combine scallops, butter and thyme then add salt and black pepper in a bowl.
3. Position the scallops in the air fryer basket and cook for about 4 minutes.
4. Serve the scallops on a platter and serve warm.

799. Juicy jumbo shrimp
Servings: 4
Prep & Cooking Time: 10 Minutes
Ingredients:
- 12 jumbo shrimps
- 1/2 tsp. garlic salt
- 1/4 tsp. freshly grounded mixed peppercorns

For the Sauce:
- 1 tsp. Dijon mustard
- 4 tbsps. mayonnaise
- 1 tsp. lemon zest
- 1 tsp. chipotle powder
- 1/2 tsp. cumin powder

Directions:
1. Cover the shrimp with salt by lightly sprinkling on top of it and coat with the grounded peppercorns.
2. Fry the shrimp in the cooking basket at 395°F for 5 minutes.
3. Turn the shrimp over and allow to cook for a further 2 minutes.
4. In the meantime, mix together all ingredients for the sauce with a whisk.
5. Serve over the shrimp.

800. Butterflied prawns with garlic-sriracha
Servings: 2
Prep & Cooking Time: 15 Minutes
Ingredients:
- 1 tbsp. lime juice
- 1 tbsp. sriracha
- 1-lb. large prawns, shells removed and cut lengthwise or butterflied
- 1tsp. fish sauce

- 2 tbsps. melted butter
- 2 tbsps. minced garlic
- Salt & pepper to taste

Directions:
1. Arm your fryer to 390°F
2. Season the prawns with the rest of the ingredients.
3. Place on the grill pan, and cook into the fryer for 15 minutes. Make sure to flip the prawns halfway through the cooking time.

801. Paprika tilapia
Servings: 4
Prep & Cooking Time: 20 Minutes
Ingredients:
- 4 tilapia fillets, boneless
- 3 tbsps. ghee, melted
- A pinch of salt and black pepper
- 2 tbsps. capers
- 1 tsp. garlic powder
- 1/2 tsp. smoked paprika
- 1/2 tsp. oregano, dried
- 2 tbsps. lemon juice

Directions:
1. In a bowl, mix all the ingredients except the fish and toss.
2. Set the fish in a pan that fits the air fryer, pour the capers mix all over, put the pan in the air fryer and cook 360°F for 20 minutes, shaking halfway.
3. Divide between plates and serve warm.

802. Dijon mustard and parmesan crusted tilapia
Servings: 2
Prep & Cooking Time: 15 Minutes
Ingredients:
- 1 tbsp. lemon juice
- 1 tsp. prepared horseradish
- 1/4 cup dry bread crumbs
- 2 tbsps. shredded Parmesan cheese, divided
- 2 tsps. butter, melted
- 2 tsps. Dijon mustard
- 2 tilapia fillets (5 ounces each)
- 3 tbsps. reduced-fat mayonnaise

Directions:
1. Grease your air fryer baking pan with cooking spray.
2. Place tilapia in a single layer.
3. In a small bowl, whisk well mayo, lemon juice, mustard, 1 tbsp. cheese and horseradish. Spread on top of fish.
4. In another bowl, mix remaining cheese, melted butter, and bread crumbs. Sprinkle on top of fish.
5. For 15 minutes, cook on 390°F.
6. Serve and enjoy.

803. Summertime fish packets
Servings: 2
Prep & Cooking Time: 20 Minutes
Ingredients:
- 2 snapper fillets
- 1 shallot, peeled and sliced
- 2 garlic cloves, halved
- 1 bell pepper, sliced
- 1 small-sized serrano pepper, sliced
- 1 tomato, sliced
- 1 tbsp. olive oil
- 1/4 tsp. freshly ground black pepper
- 1/2 tsp. paprika
- Sea salt, to taste
- 2 bay leaves

Directions:
1. Arrange two sheets of parchment paper on a work surface. Place the fish in the middle of one of the parchment paper sheets.
2. Arrange the shallot, garlic, peppers, and tomato on top.
3. Drizzle the fish and veggies with olive oil. Season with salt, black pepper, and paprika. Mix in the bay leaves.
4. Fold the other side of the paper over. Fold the paper firmly around the edges to form a half moon shape, trapping the fish within.
5. Cook for 15 minutes in a 390°F preheated air fryer.
6. Serve hot.

804. Lovely seafood pie
Servings: 3
Prep & Cooking Time: 60 Minutes
Ingredients:
- 1 lb. russet potatoes, peeled and quartered
- 1 cup water
- 1 carrot, shredded
- 1/2 head baby fennel, shredded
- 1 bunch dill sprigs, minced
- 1 sprig parsley, minced
- A handful of baby spinach
- 1 small tomato, diced
- 1/2 celery sticks, shredded
- 2 tbsps. butter
- 1 tbsp. milk
- 1/2 cup shredded Cheddar cheese
- 1 small red chili, minced
- 1/2 lemon, squeezed
- Salt & pepper to taste

Directions:
1. Add the potatoes to a pan, pour the water, and bring to a boil over medium heat on a stovetop. Use a fork to check that if they are soft and mash-able, after about minutes.
2. Drain the water and use a potato masher to mash. Add the butter, milk, salt, and pepper. Mash until smooth; set aside.
3. In a mixing bowl, add the celery, carrots, cheese, chili, fennel, parsley, lemon juice, seafood mix, dill, tomato, spinach, salt, and pepper; mix well.
4. Preheat air fryer to 370°F. In a casserole dish, add half of the carrot mixture.
5. Top with half of the potato mixture and level.
6. Place the dish in the air fryer and bake for 20 minutes until golden brown and the seafood is properly cooked.
7. Remove the dish and add the remaining seafood mixture and level out.
8. Top with the remaining potato mash and level it too. Place the dish back to the fryer and cook at 330°F for 20 minutes.
9. Once ready, ensure that it's well cooked, and remove the dish. Slice the pie and serve.

805. Crab cakes
Servings: 4
Prep & Cooking Time: 55 Minutes
Ingredients:
- 1/4 cup minced red onion
- 1 tbsp. minced basil
- 1/4 cup minced celery
- 1/4 cup minced red pepper
- 3 tbsps. mayonnaise
- Zest of half a lemon

- 1/4 cup breadcrumbs
- 2 tbsps. minced parsley
- Old Bay seasoning, as desired
- Cooking spray

Directions:
1. Preheat the air fryer to 390°F.
2. Place all ingredients in a large bowl, and mix well.
3. Make 4 large crab cakes from the mixture and place them on a lined sheet. Refrigerate for 30 minutes. Spray air basket with cooking spray and arrange the crab cakes inside it.
4. Cook for 7 minutes on each side, until crispy.

806. Shrimps with celery salad
Servings: 4
Prep & Cooking Time: 5 Minutes
Ingredients:
- 3 ounce schevre
- 1 tsp. avocado oil
- 1/2 tsp. dried oregano
- 8 ounces shrimps, peeled
- 1 tsp. butter, melted
- 1/2 tsp. salt
- 1/2 tsp. chili flakes
- 4 ounces celery stalk, minced

Directions:
1. Sprinkle the shrimps with dried oregano and melted butter and put in the air fryer. Cook the seafood at 400°F for 5 minutes.
2. Meanwhile, crumble the chevre.
3. Put the minced celery stalk in the salad bowl.
4. Add crumbled chevre, chili flakes, salt, and avocado oil. Mix up the salad well and top it with cooked shrimps.

807. Halibut steaks
Servings: 4
Prep & Cooking Time: 15 Minutes
Ingredients:
- 1 lb. halibut steaks
- Salt & pepper to taste
- 1 tsp. dried basil
- 2 tbsps. honey
- 1/4 cup vegetable oil
- 2 1/2 tbsps. Worcester sauce
- 1 tbsp. freshly squeezed lemon juice
- 2 tbsps. vermouth
- 1 tbsp. fresh parsley leaves, coarsely minced

Directions:
1. Put all of the ingredients in a large bowl. Combine and cover the fish completely with the seasoning.
2. Transfer to your air fryer and cook at 390°F for 5 minutes.
3. Turn the fish over and allow to cook for a further 5 minutes.
4. Ensure the fish is cooked through, leaving it in the fryer for a few more minutes if necessary.
5. Serve with a side of potato salad.

808. Trout with zucchinis and tomato salad
Servings: 4
Prep & Cooking Time: 15 Minutes
Ingredients:
- 3 zucchinis, cut in medium chunks
- 4 trout fillets, boneless
- 2 tbsps. olive oil
- 1/4 cup keto tomato sauce
- Salt & black pepper to the taste
- 1 garlic clove, minced
- 1 tbsp. lemon juice
- 1/2 cup cilantro, minced

Directions:
1. In a pan, (large enough to suit your air fryer), mix the fish with the other ingredients, toss, introduce in the fryer and cook at 380°F for 10 minutes.
2. Divide everything between plates and serve right away.

809. Mouth-watering spiced coco-lime skewered shrimp
Servings: 6
Prep & Cooking Time: 12 Minutes
Ingredients:
- 1 lime, zested and squeezed
- 1/3 cup minced fresh cilantro
- 1/3 cup shredded coconut
- 1/4 cup olive oil
- 1/4 cup soy sauce
- 1-lb. uncooked medium shrimp, peeled and emptied
- 2 garlic cloves
- 2 jalapeno peppers, seeded

Directions:
1. In food processor, process until smooth the soy sauce, olive oil, coconut oil, cilantro, garlic, lime juice, lime zest, and jalapeno.
2. In a shallow dish, mix well shrimp and processed marinade. Toss well to coat and marinate in the ref for 3 hours.
3. Thread shrimps in skewers. In your air fryer, place it on skewer rack.
4. For 6 minutes, cook on 360°F. If needed, cook in batches.
5. Serve and enjoy.

810. Fish fillets with tarragon
Servings: 4
Prep & Cooking Time: 25 Minutes
Ingredients:
- 2 eggs, beaten
- 1/2 tsp. tarragon
- 4 fish fillets, halved
- 2 tbsp. dry white wine
- 1/3 cup parmesan cheese, shredded
- 1 tsp. seasoned salt
- 1/3 tsp. mixed peppercorns
- 1/2 tsp. fennel seed

Directions:
1. Add the parmesan cheese, salt, peppercorns, cumin seeds, and tarragon to your food processor; blitz for about 20 seconds.
2. Drizzle fish fillets with dry white wine. Dump the egg into a shallow dish.
3. Now, coat the fish fillets with the beaten egg on all sides; then, coat them with the seasoned cracker mix.
4. Air-fry at 3°F for about 17 minutes. Bon appétit!

811. Stuffed tuna with capers and greek yogurt
Servings: 4
Prep & Cooking Time: 16 Minutes
Ingredients:
- 4 starchy potatoes, soaked for about 30 minutes and drain
- 1 (6-ounces) can tuna, drained
- 2 tbsps. plain Greek yogurt
- 1 scallion, minced and divided
- 1 tbsp. capers
- 1/2 tbsp. olive oil

- 1 tsp. red chili powder
- Salt & black pepper, to taste

Directions:
1. Preheat the air fryer to 355°F and grease an air fryer basket.
2. Transfer your potatoes into the air fryer basket and cook for about 30 minutes.
3. Meanwhile, mix tuna, yogurt, red chili powder, salt, black pepper and half of scallions in a bowl and mash the mixture well.
4. Once the potatoes are done, halve them lengthwise carefully.
5. Stuff in the tuna mixture in the potatoes and top with capers and remaining scallion.
6. Put on a platter and serve immediately.

812. Lean salmon with cauliflower rice
Servings: 4
Prep & Cooking Time: 25 Minutes
Ingredients:
- 4 salmon fillets
- Salt & black pepper to the taste
- 1 cup cauliflower, riced
- 1/2 cup chicken stock
- 1 tsp. turmeric powder
- 1 tbsp. butter, melted

Directions:
1. In a pan (large enough to suit your air fryer) mix the cauliflower rice with the other ingredients except the salmon; toss well.
2. Set the salmon fillets over the cauliflower rice, put the pan in the fryer and cook at 360°F for 25 minutes, flipping the fish after several minutes.
3. Divide every element between plates and serve.

813. Grilled fish burgers
Servings: 4
Prep & Cooking Time: 10 Minutes + Chilling Time
Ingredients:
- 2 cans canned tuna fish
- 2 celery stalks, trimmed and finely minced
- 1 egg, whisked
- 1/2 cup parmesan cheese, shredded
- 1 tsp. whole-grain mustard
- 1/2 tsp. sea salt
- 1/4 tsp. freshly grounded black peppercorns
- 1 tsp. paprika

Directions:
1. Combine all the listed ingredients and mix well
2. Shape into four cakes; chill for 50 minutes.
3. Place on an air fryer grill pan. Spritz each cake with a non-stick cooking spray, covering all sides.
4. Grill at 400°F for 5 minutes; then, pause the machine, flip the cakes over and set the timer for another 3 minutes. Serve over mashed potatoes.

814. Boiled tilapia
Servings: 4
Prep & Cooking Time: 10 Minutes
Ingredients:
- 1 lb. tilapia fillets
- 1/2 tsp. lemon pepper
- Salt to taste

Directions:
1. Spritz the air fryer basket with some cooking spray.
2. Put the tilapia fillets in basket and sprinkle on the lemon pepper and salt.
3. Cook at 400°F for 7 minutes.
4. Serve with a side of vegetables.

815. Piquant shrimp kebab
Servings: 4
Prep & Cooking Time: 25 Minutes
Ingredients:
- 1 1/2 lbs. jumbo shrimp, cleaned, shelled and emptied
- 1 lb. cherry tomatoes
- 2 tbsps. butter, melted
- 1 tbsp. Sriracha sauce
- Sea salt & ground black pepper, to taste
- 1/2 tsp. dried oregano
- 1/2 tsp. dried basil
- 1 tsp. dried parsley flakes
- 1/2 tsp. marjoram
- 1/2 tsp. mustard seeds

Directions:
1. Preheat your air fryer at 400°F
2. In a medium size deep platter, combine all the ingredients in a mixing bowl until the shrimp and tomatoes are covered on all sides.
3. Soak the wooden skewers in water for 15 minutes.
4. Thread the jumbo shrimp and cherry tomatoes onto skewers.
5. Cook for 5 minutes, working with batches. Bon appétit!

816. Ginger cod
Servings: 2
Prep & Cooking Time: 8 Minutes
Ingredients:
- 10 ounces cod fillet
- 1/2 tsp. cayenne pepper
- 1/4 tsp. ground coriander
- 1/2 tsp. ground ginger
- 1/2 tsp. ground black pepper
- 1 tbsp. sunflower oil
- 1/2 tsp. salt
- 1/2 tsp. dried rosemary
- 1/2 tsp. ground paprika

Directions:
1. In the shallow bowl mix up cayenne pepper, ground coriander, ginger, ground black pepper, salt, dried rosemary, and ground paprika.
2. Rub the cod fillet with the spice mixture. sprinkle it with sunflower oil.
3. Preheat the air fryer to 390°F.
4. Place the cod fillet in the air fryer and cook it for 4 minutes. Then carefully flip the fish on another side and cook for 4 minutes more.

817. Grilled shrimps on pesto sauce
Servings: 4
Prep & Cooking Time: 16 Minutes
Ingredients:
- 1 cup pesto
- 1/4 cup minced fresh basil
- 1-lb. extra-large shrimp, peeled and emptied
- bamboo skewers, soaked in water
- Extra-virgin olive oil, for drizzling
- Freshly ground black pepper

Directions:
1. Thread shrimp into skewers and place on skewer rack. Drizzle with oil, season with pepper and salt.

2. For 8 minutes, cook on 360°F. Halfway through cooking time, turnover skewers and baste with pesto.
3. Serve and enjoy with a garnish of fresh basil.

818. Delicious crab cakes
Servings: 4
Prep & Cooking Time: 55 Minutes
Ingredients:
- 1/4 cup minced red onion
- 1 tbsp minced basil
- 1/4 cup minced celery
- 1/4 cup minced red pepper
- 3 tbsps. mayonnaise
- Zest of half a lemon
- 1/4 cup breadcrumbs
- 2 tbsps. minced parsley
- Old bay seasoning, as desired
- Cooking spray

Directions:
1. Preheat the air fryer to 390°F.
2. Add and mix all ingredients in a large bowl. Mix well. Make 4 large crab cakes from the mixture and place them on a lined sheet.
3. Refrigerate for 30 minutes.
4. Spray air basket with cooking spray and arrange the crab cakes inside it. Cook for 7 minutes on each side, until crispy.

819. Creole veggie-shrimp bake
Servings: 4
Prep & Cooking Time: 20 Minutes
Ingredients:
- 1 Bag of Frozen Mixed Vegetables
- 1 Tbsp. Gluten Free Creole Seasoning
- Olive Oil Spray
- Season with salt and pepper
- Small Shrimp Peeled and Emptied (Regular Size Bag about 50-80 Small Shrimp)

Directions:
1. Grease your air frier baking pan with oil or cooking spray.
2. Add all ingredients and toss well to coat. Season with pepper and salt, generously.
3. For 10 minutes, cook on 330°F. Halfway through cooking time, stir.
4. Cook for 10 minutes at 400°F.
5. Serve and enjoy.

820. Spring onions salmon with tarragon
Servings: 4
Prep & Cooking Time: 15 Minutes
Ingredients:
- 12 ounce salmon fillet
- 2 spring onions, minced
- 1 tbsp. ghee, melted
- 1 tsp. peppercorns
- 1/2 tsp. salt
- 1/2 tsp. ground black pepper
- 1 tsp. tarragon
- 1/2 tsp. dried cilantro

Directions:
1. Cut the salmon fillet on 4 servings. Then make the parchment pockets and place the fish fillets in the parchment pockets.
2. Sprinkle the salmon with salt, ground black pepper, tarragon, and dried cilantro.
3. After this, top the fish with spring onions, peppercorns, and ghee.
4. Preheat the air fryer to 385°F.
5. Set the salmon pockets in the air fryer in one layer and cook them for 10 minutes.

821. Tilapia with cottage cheese and caper sauce
Servings: 4
Prep & Cooking Time: 15 Minutes
Ingredients:
- 4 tilapia fillets
- 1 tbsp. extra-virgin olive oil
- Celery salt, to taste
- Freshly grounded pink peppercorns, to taste
- For the creamy caper sauce:
- 1/2 cup crème fraîche
- 2 tbsps. mayonnaise
- 1/4 cup Cottage cheese, at room temperature
- 1 tbsp. capers, finely minced

Directions:
1. Toss the tilapia fillets with olive oil, celery salt, and grounded peppercorns until they are well coated.
2. Place the fillets in a single layer at the bottom of the air fryer cooking basket. Air-fry at 360°F for about 1minutes; turn them over once during cooking.
3. Meanwhile, prepare the sauce by mixing the remaining items.
4. Lastly, garnish air-fried tilapia fillets with the sauce and serve immediately!

Chapter 5
Desserts Recipes

822. Almond flour crackers
Servings: 8
Prep & Cooking Time: 20 Minutes
Ingredients:
- 1 cup almond flour
- 1 tsp. cornstarch
- 1 tsp. flax meal
- 1/2 tsp. salt
- 1 tsp. baking powder
- 1 tsp. lemon juice
- 1/2 tsp. ground clove
- 2 tbsp. stevia
- 1 egg, beaten
- 3 tbsp. coconut oil, softened

Directions:
1. In the mixing bowl mix up almond flour, cornstarch, flax meal, salt, baking powder, and ground clove.
2. Add Erythritol, lemon juice, egg, and coconut oil.
3. Stir the mixture gently with the help of the fork. Then knead the mixture till you get a soft dough.
4. Line the chopping board with parchment.
5. Put the dough on the parchment and roll it up in a slim layer.
6. Cut the slim dough into squares (crackers). Preheat the air fryer to 360°F. Place some baking paper on the basket.
7. Put the prepared crackers in the air fryer basket in one layer and cook them for minutes or until the crackers are dry and light brown.
8. Repeat the same steps with remaining uncooked crackers.

823. Vanilla plum cake
Servings: 12
Prep & Cooking Time: 30 Minutes
Ingredients:
- 1/4 tsp. salt
- 1/2 cup erythritol powder
- 1 vanilla bean, scraped
- 1/3 cup water
- 2/3 cup butter, melted
- 4 large eggs

Directions:
1. Preheat the air fryer for 5 minutes.
2. Combine all ingredients in a mixing bowl.
3. Pour into a greased baking dish.
4. Cook for about 30 minutes at 355°F.

824. The quickest banana cake
Servings: 6
Prep & Cooking Time: 40 Minutes
Ingredients:
- 1 1/2 cups cake flour
- 1 tsp. baking soda
- 1/2 tsp. ground cinnamon
- Salt, to taste
- 1/2 cup vegetable oil
- 2 eggs
- 1/2 cup sugar
- 1/2 tsp. vanilla extract
- 3 medium bananas, peeled and mashed
- 1/4 cup walnuts, minced
- 1/4 cup raisins, minced

Directions:
1. In a large bowl, mix well flour, baking soda, cinnamon, and salt.
2. In another bowl, beat well eggs and oil.
3. Add the sugar, vanilla extract, and bananas. Whisk until well combined.
4. Add the flour mixture and stir until just combined.
5. Set the temperature of air fryer to 320°F. Grease a cake pan.
6. Place mixture evenly into the prepared cake pan and top with walnuts and raisins.
7. With a piece of foil, cover the pan.
8. Set the cake pan into an air fryer basket.
9. Now, set the temperature of air fryer to 300°F.
10. Air fry for about 30 minutes.
11. Remove the piece of foil and set the temperature to 285°F.
12. Cook it for about 7-8 minutes more.
13. Once it's cooked place the cake pan on a wire rack to cool for about 10 minutes.
14. Now, invert the cake onto wire rack to completely cool before slicing.
15. Cut the cake into desired size slices and serve.

825. Old style buttermilk biscuits
Servings: 4
Prep & Cooking Time: 8 Minutes
Ingredients:
- 1/2 cup cake flour
- 1 1/4 cups all-purpose flour
- 3/4 tsp. baking powder
- 1/4 cup + 2 tbsp. butter, cut into cubes
- 3/4 cup buttermilk
- 1 tsp. granulated sugar
- Salt, to taste

Directions:
1. Preheat the air fryer to 400°F and grease a pie pan lightly.
2. Sift together flours, baking soda, baking powder, sugar and salt in a large bowl.
3. Add cold butter and mix until a coarse crumb is formed.
4. Stir in the buttermilk slowly and mix until a dough is formed.
5. Press the dough into 1/2 inch thickness onto a floured surface and cut out circles with a 1 3/4-inch round cookie cutter.
6. Set the biscuits in a pie pan in a single layer and brush butter on them.
7. Transfer into the air fryer and cook for about 8 minutes until golden brown.

826. Peanut butter and chocolate fondants
Servings: 4
Prep & Cooking Time: 25 Minutes

Ingredients:
- 1/2 cup peanut butter, crunchy
- 2 tbsp butter, diced
- 1/4 cup + 1/4 cup sugar
- 4 eggs, room temperature
- 1/8 cup flour, sieved
- 1 tsp. salt
- 1/4 cup water
- Cooking spray

Directions:
1. Make a salted praline to top the chocolate fondant.
2. Add 1/4 cup of sugar, tsp. of salt and water into a saucepan.
3. Stir and bring it to a boil over low heat. Simmer until the desired color is achieved and reduced.
4. Pour it into a baking tray and leave to cool and harden.
5. Preheat the air fryer to 300°F.
6. Place a pot of water over medium heat and place a heatproof bowl over it. Add in chocolate, butter, and peanut butter. Stir continuously until fully melted, combined, and smooth.
7. Remove the bowl and allow to cool slightly. Add eggs to the chocolate and whisk. Add flour and remaining sugar; mix well.
8. Grease small loaf pans with cooking spray and divide the chocolate mixture between them.
9. Place 2 pans at a time in the basket and cook for 7 minutes.
10. Remove them and serve the fondants with a piece of salted praline.

827. Nutella pastries
Servings: 4
Prep & Cooking Time: 12 Minutes
Ingredients:
- 1 puff pastry sheet, cut into 4 equal squares
- 1/2 cup Nutella
- 2 bananas, sliced
- 2 tbsp. icing sugar

Directions:
1. Preheat the air fryer to 375°F and grease an air fryer basket.
2. Spread Nutella on each pastry square and top with banana slices and icing sugar.
3. Fold each square into a triangle and slightly press the edges with a fork.
4. Set the pastries in the air fryer basket and cook for about 12 minutes.
5. Serve immediately.

828. Speedy pound cake
Servings: 8
Prep & Cooking Time: 35 Minutes
Ingredients:
- 1 stick butter, at room temperature
- 1 cup swerve sweetener
- 4 eggs
- 1 1/2 cups coconut flour
- 1/2 tsp. baking powder
- 1/2 tsp. baking soda
- 1/4 tsp. salt
- A pinch of freshly shredded nutmeg
- A pinch of ground star anise
- 1/2 cup buttermilk
- 1 tsp. vanilla essence

Directions:
1. Begin by preheating your air fryer to 320°F. Spritz the bottom and sides of a baking pan with cooking spray.
2. Beat the butter and swerve sweetener with a hand mixer until creamy. Then, fold in the eggs, one at a time, and mix well until fluffy.
3. Stir in the flour along with the remaining ingredients. Mix to combine well.
4. Pour the batter into the prepared baking pan, and let it cook for about 15 minutes.
5. Rotate the pan and bake an additional 15 minutes, until the top of the cake springs back when gently pressed with your fingers. Bon appétit!

829. Mozzarella cheese cookies
Servings: 8
Prep & Cooking Time: 12 Minutes
Ingredients:
- 2 eggs
- 5 tbsps. Butter, melted
- 1/3 cup kefir
- 1/3 cup mozzarella cheese, shredded
- 1 ¼ cup almond flour
- ½ tsp. baking powder
- ½ tsp. salt

Directions:
1. Preheat the air fryer to 370°F.
2. Add all of the ingredients into a wide bowl and mix using a hand mixer.
3. Spoon batter into the mini silicone muffin molds and place into the air fryer and cook for 12 minutes.
4. Serve and enjoy.

830. Applesauce brownies
Servings: 4
Prep & Cooking Time: 10 Minutes
Ingredients:
- 2 tbsp cocoa powder
- 1 1/2 tsp. baking powder
- 2 tbsps. unsweetened applesauce
- 1 tsp. liquid stevia
- 1 tbsp. coconut oil, melted
- 3 tbsps. almond flour
- 1/2 tsp. vanilla
- 1 tbsp. unsweetened almond milk
- 1/2 cup almond butter
- 1/4 tsp. sea salt

Directions:
1. Preheat the air fryer to 350°F.
2. Grease air fryer baking dish with cooking spray and set aside.
3. In a small bowl, mix together almond flour, baking powder, cocoa powder, baking powder, and salt. Set aside.
4. In a small bowl, add coconut oil and almond butter and microwave until melted.
5. Add sweetener, vanilla, almond milk, and applesauce in the coconut oil mixture and stir well.
6. Mix wet and dry ingredients, and stir to combine.
7. Pour batter into prepared dish and place into the air fryer and cook for 10 minutes.
8. Slice and serve.

831. Apple-toffee with upside-down cake
Servings: 9
Prep & Cooking Time: 30 Minutes
Ingredients:
- 1/4 cup almond butter
- 1/4 cup grapeseed oil

- 1/2 cup walnuts, minced
- 3/4 cup + 3 tbsp. maple sugar
- 3/4 cup water
- 1 1/2 tsp. mixed spice
- 1 cup plain flour
- 1 lemon, zest
- 1 tsp. baking soda
- 1 tsp. vinegar
- 3 baking apples, cored and sliced

Directions:
1. Preheat the air fryer to 390°F.
2. In a skillet, melt the almond butter and 3 tbsp. sugar. Pour the mixture over a baking dish that will fit in the air fryer. Set the slices of apples on top. Set aside.
3. In a mixing bowl, combine flour, 3/4 cup sugar, and baking soda. Add the mixed spice.
4. In another bowl, mix the oil, water, vinegar, and lemon zest. Stir in the minced walnuts.
5. Combine the wet ingredients to the dry ingredients until well combined.
6. Pour over the tin with apple slices.
7. Bake for 30 minutes or until a toothpick inserted comes out clean.

832. Easy peach pie
Servings: 4
Prep & Cooking Time: 45 Minutes
Ingredients:
- 1 pie dough
- 2 1/4 lbs. peaches; pitted and minced.
- 2 tbsp. cornstarch
- 1 tbsp. lemon juice
- 1/2 cup sugar
- 2 tbsps. flour
- A pinch of nutmeg; ground
- 2 tbsps. butter

Directions:
1. Press pie dough into the air fryer pan
2. Combine peaches, cornstarch, sugar, flour, nutmeg, lemon juice, and butter.
3. Pour into a pie pan and bake at 180°F for 35 minutes. Warm or chilly.

833. Macadamia cookies
Servings: 6
Prep & Cooking Time: 10 Minutes
Ingredients:
- 1/2 cup butter, softened
- 1 cup coconut flour
- 3 ounces macadamia nuts, grinded
- 1/2 tsp. baking powder
- 3 tbsp. stevia
- Cooking spray

Directions:
1. In the mixing bowl mix up butter, coconut flour, grinded coconut nuts, baking powder, and Erythritol. Knead the non-sticky dough.
2. Cut the dough into small pieces and roll them into balls.
3. Press every cookie ball gently to get the shape of cookies.
4. Now a cooking spray should be used to oil the basket.
5. Preheat the air fryer to 365°F.
6. Put the uncooked cookies in the air fryer and cook them for 8 minutes.
7. Then cook for extra 2 minutes at 390°F to get the light brown crust.

834. Apple nutty pudding
Servings: 8
Prep & Cooking Time: 44 Minutes
Ingredients:
For Bread Pudding:
- 10 1/2 ounces bread, cubed
- 1/2 cup apples, peeled, cored and minced
- 1/2 cup raisins
- 1/4 cup walnuts, minced
- 1 1/2 cups milk
- 3/4 cup water
- 5 tbsp. honey
- 2 tsp. ground cinnamon
- 2 tsp. cornstarch
- 1 tsp. vanilla extract

For Topping:
- 1 1/3 cups plain flour
- 3/5 cup brown sugar
- 7 tbsp. butter

Directions:
1. In a big mixing bowl, mix the apple, bread, walnuts, and raisins.
2. In a separate dish, combine the other pudding ingredients and stir until completely blended.
3. Stir the milk mixture into the bread mixture until fully blended.
4. Refrigerate for about 15 minutes, tossing every now and then.
5. To make the topping, combine the flour and sugar in a mixing basin.
6. Add the butter (cubed) until a crumbly mixture forms.
7. Preheat the air fryer to 355°F.
8. Place the mixture evenly into 2 baking pans and spread the topping mixture on top of each.
9. Place 1 pan into an air fryer basket.
10. Air fry for about 22 minutes.
11. Repeat with the remaining pan. Serve and enjoy.

835. Peanut crumble
Servings: 4
Prep & Cooking Time: 25 Minutes
Ingredients:
- 1/2 cup coconut flour
- 2 tbsp. butter, softened
- 2 tbsp. stevia
- 3 ounces peanuts, crushed
- 1 tbsp. cream cheese
- 1 tsp. baking powder
- 1/2 tsp. lemon juice

Directions:
1. In the mixing bowl mix up coconut flour, butter, Erythritol, baking powder, and lemon juice. Stir the mixture until homogenous. Then place it in the freezer for 15 minutes.
2. Meanwhile, mix up peanuts and cream cheese.
3. Grate the frozen dough.
4. Line the air fryer mold with baking paper.
5. Put 1/2 of shredded dough in the mold and flatten it. Top it with cream cheese mixture. Then put remaining shredded dough over the cream cheese mixture.
6. Place the mold with the crumble in the air fryer and cook it for 25 minutes at 330°F.

836. Custard with a hint of nutmeg
Servings: 6
Prep & Cooking Time: 32 Minutes

Ingredients:
- 2 egg yolks
- 3 eggs
- 1/2 cup erythritol
- 2 cups heavy whipping cream
- 1/2 tsp. vanilla
- 1 tsp. nutmeg

Directions:
1. Preheat the air fryer to 325°F.
2. Combine all ingredients in a large size bowl and beat until well combined.
3. Pour custard mixture into the greased baking dish and place into the air fryer.
4. Cook for 32 minutes.
5. Let it cool completely then place in the refrigerator for 1-2 hours.
6. Serve and enjoy.

837. Lemon muffins

Servings: 6
Prep & Cooking Time: 30 Minutes
Ingredients:
- 1/2 cup sugar
- 1 small egg
- 1 tsp. lemon zest
- 3/4 tsp. baking powder
- 1/4 tsp. baking soda
- 1/2 tsp. salt
- 2 tbsp vegetable oil
- 1/2 cup milk
- 1/2 tsp. vanilla extract

Glaze:
- 1/2 cup powdered sugar
- 2 tsp. lemon juice

Directions:
1. Preheat the air fryer to 350°F. In a mixing bowl, whisk all of the dry ingredients (not the glaze ones).
2. Whisk, until well combined, the wet ingredients in a separate bowl.
3. Divide the batter into 6 greased muffin cups.
4. Cook the muffin pans in the air fryer for 1 to 14 minutes.
5. Combine the lemon juice and the powdered sugar in a mixing bowl.
6. Spread the glaze on top of the muffins.

838. Ginger and cinnamon pear fritters

Servings: 4
Prep & Cooking Time: 20 Minutes
Ingredients:
- 2 pears, peeled, cored and sliced
- 1 tbsp. coconut oil, melted
- 1 1/2 cups all-purpose flour
- 1 tsp. baking powder
- A pinch of fine sea salt
- A pinch of freshly shredded nutmeg
- 1/2 tsp. ginger
- 1 tsp. cinnamon
- 2 eggs
- 4 tbsp. milk

Directions:
1. Preheat your air fryer to 360°F
2. Mix all ingredients, except for the pears, in a shallow bowl. Dip each slice of the pears in the batter until well coated.
3. Cook the slices for about 4 minutes, flipping them halfway through the cooking time. Repeat with the remaining ingredients.
4. Dust with powdered sugar if desired. Bon appétit!

839. Fiery dark chocolate cake

Servings: 4
Prep & Cooking Time: 20 Minutes
Ingredients:
- 3 1/2 tbsps. sugar
- 1 1/2 tbsps. self-rising flour
- 3 1/2 ounces dark chocolate, melted
- 2 eggs

Directions:
1. Grease 4 ramekins with butter.
2. Preheat the air fryer to 375°F and beat the eggs and sugar until frothy.
3. Stir in the butter and chocolate; gently fold in the flour.
4. Divide the mixture between the ramekins and bake in the air fryer for 10 minutes.
5. Let cool for 2 minutes before turning the lava cakes upside down onto serving plates.

840. Vanilla-scented custard

Servings: 6
Prep & Cooking Time: 35 Minutes + Chilling Time
Ingredients:
- 6 eggs
- 7 ounces cream cheese, at room temperature
- 2 1/2 cans condensed milk, sweetened
- 1/2 cup swerve sweetener
- 1/2 tsp. orange rind, shredded
- 1 1/2 cardamom pods, bruised
- 2 tsp. vanilla paste
- 1/4 cup fresh orange juice

Directions:
1. In a saucepan, melt swerve sweetener over a moderate flame; it takes about to 12 minutes. Immediately but carefully pour the melted sugar into six ramekins, tilting to coat their bottoms; allow them to cool slightly.
2. In a mixing dish, beat the cheese until smooth; now, fold in the eggs, one at a time, and continue to beat until pale and creamy.
3. Add the orange rind, cardamom, vanilla, orange juice, and the milk; mix again. Pour the mixture over the caramelized sugar.
4. Air-fry, covered, at 385°F for 28 minutes or until it has thickened.
5. Refrigerate overnight; garnish with berries or other fruits and serve.

841. Hazelnuts cobbler

Servings: 4
Prep & Cooking Time: 30 Minutes
Ingredients:
- 1/4 cup heavy cream
- 1 egg, beaten
- 1/2 cup almond flour
- 1 tsp. vanilla extract
- 2 tbsp. butter, softened
- 1/4 cup hazelnuts, minced

Directions:
1. Mix up heavy cream, egg, almond flour, vanilla extract, and butter. Then whisk the mixture gently.
2. Preheat the air fryer to 325°F. Line the air fryer pan with baking paper.
3. Pour 1/2 part of the batter in the baking pan, flatten it gently and top with hazelnuts. Then pour the remaining batter over the hazelnuts and place the pan in the air fryer.
4. Cook the cobbler for 30 minutes.

842. Cake of other times
Servings: 8
Prep & Cooking Time: 35 Minutes
Ingredients:
- 1 stick butter, at room temperature
- 1 cup sugar
- 2 eggs
- 1 cup all-purpose flour
- 1 tsp. baking powder
- 1/2 tsp. baking soda
- 1/4 tsp. salt
- A pinch of freshly shredded nutmeg
- A pinch of ground star anise
- 1/4 cup buttermilk
- 1 tsp. vanilla essence

Directions:
1. Begin by preheating your air fryer to 320°F. Spritz the bottom and sides of a baking pan with cooking spray.
2. Beat the butter and sugar with a hand mixer until creamy. Then, fold in the eggs, one at a time, and mix well until fluffy.
3. Stir in the flour along with the remaining ingredients. Mix to combine well.
4. Scrape the batter into the prepared baking pan.
5. Bake for about 15 minutes; rotate the pan and bake an additional 15 minutes, until the top of the cake springs back when gently pressed with your fingers. Bon appétit!

843. Coconut vanilla cookies
Servings: 30
Prep & Cooking Time: 12 Minutes
Ingredients:
- 8 ounce cream cheese
- 1 tsp. vanilla
- 1 tbsp baking powder
- 3/4 cup shredded coconut
- 1 cup swerve sweetener
- 3/4 cup butter, softened
- 1 1/4 cup coconut flour
- Pinch of salt

Directions:
1. Preheat the air fryer to 325°F.
2. Combine the butter, cream cheese, and sweetener in a bowl using a hand mixer until fluffy.
3. Add vanilla and stir well.
4. Add baking powder, coconut flour, and salt. Whisk well until combined.
5. Add shredded coconut and mix to combine.
6. Make cookies from mixture and place on a plate.
7. Place cookies in batches in the air fryer and cook for 12 minutes.
8. Serve and enjoy.

844. Strawberry and philadelphia pop tarts
Servings: 6
Prep & Cooking Time: 25 Minutes
Ingredients:
- 1 ounce reduced-fat Philadelphia cream cheese
- 1 tsp. cornstarch
- 1 tsp. stevia
- 1 tsp. sugar sprinkles
- 1/2 cup plain, non-fat vanilla Greek yogurt
- 1/3 cup low-sugar strawberry preserves
- 2 refrigerated pie crusts
- Olive oil or coconut oil spray

Directions:
1. Cut pie crusts into 6 equal rectangles.
2. In a bowl, mix cornstarch and preserves, and add preserves in middle of crust. Fold over crust. Crimp edges with fork to seal.
3. Repeat process for remaining crusts.
4. Grease the baking pan with cooking spray.
5. Add pop tarts in a single layer. Cook in batches for 8 minutes at 380°F.
6. Meanwhile, make the frosting by mixing stevia, cream cheese, and yogurt in a bowl. Spread on top of cooked pop tart and add sugar sprinkles.
7. Serve and enjoy.

845. Tasty plum bars
Servings: 8
Prep & Cooking Time: 26 Minutes
Ingredients:
- 2 cups dried plums
- 6 tbsp. water
- 2 tbsp. butter; melted
- 1 egg; whisked
- 2 cup rolled oats
- 1 cup brown sugar
- 1/2 tsp. baking soda
- 1 tsp. cinnamon powder
- Cooking spray

Directions:
1. In your food processor, mix plums with water and blend until you obtain a sticky spread.
2. In a mixing bowl stir oats with cinnamon, baking soda, sugar, egg and butter and whisk really well.
3. Press half of the oats mix in a baking pan that fits your air fryer sprayed with cooking oil, spread plums mix and top with the other half of the oats mix.
4. Put it in the air fryer and let it cook at 350°F, for 16 about minutes.
5. Leave mix aside to cool down, cut into medium bars and serve.

846. Cheesecake with white chocolate and berries
Servings: 4
Prep & Cooking Time: 5-10 Minutes
Ingredients:
- 8 ounces cream cheese, softened
- 2 ounces heavy cream
- 1/2 tsp. Splenda
- 1 tsp. raspberries
- 1 tbsp. Da Vinci Sugar-Free syrup, white chocolate flavor

Directions:
6. Whip together the ingredients to a thick consistency.
7. Divide in cups.
8. Refrigerate.
9. Serve!

847. Hazelnut brownies
Servings: 12
Prep & Cooking Time: 30 Minutes
Ingredients:
- 6 oz. semisweet chocolate chips
- 1 stick butter, at room temperature
- 1 cup sugar
- 2 large eggs
- 1/4 cup red wine
- 1/4 tsp. hazelnut extract
- 1 tsp. pure vanilla extract

- 3/4 cup flour
- 2 tbsp. cocoa powder
- 1/2 cup ground hazelnuts
- Pinch of kosher salt

Directions:
1. Melt the butter and chocolate chips in the microwave.
2. In a large bowl, combine the sugar, eggs, red wine, hazelnut and vanilla extract with a whisk. Pour in the chocolate mix.
3. Add in the flour, cocoa powder, ground hazelnuts, and a pinch of kosher salt, continuing to stir until a creamy, smooth consistency is achieved.
4. Take a muffin tin and place a cupcake liner in each cup. Spoon an equal amount of the batter into each one.
5. Air bake at 360°F for 28 - 30 minutes, cooking in batches if necessary.
6. Serve with a topping of ganache if desired.

848. Peanut butter cookies
Servings: 4
Prep & Cooking Time: 5 Minutes
Ingredients:
- 4 tbsp. peanut butter
- 4 tsp. stevia
- 1 egg, beaten
- 1/4 tsp. vanilla extract

Directions:
1. In the mixing bowl mix up peanut butter, Erythritol, egg, and vanilla extract. Blend well the mixture with the help of the fork. Then make 4 cookies.
2. Preheat the air fryer to 355°F.
3. Place the cookies in the air fryer and cook them for 5 minutes.

849. Soft rice pudding
Servings: 6
Prep & Cooking Time: 20 Minutes
Ingredients:
- 1 tbsp. butter, melted
- 7 ounces white rice
- 16 ounces milk
- 1/3 cup sugar
- 1 tbsp. heavy cream
- 1 tsp. vanilla extract

Directions:
1. Place all ingredients in a pan that fits your air fryer and stir well.
2. Put the pan in the fryer and cook at 360°F for 15 minutes.
3. Stir the pudding, divide it into bowls, refrigerate, and serve cold.

850. Fritters with strawberries
Servings: 8
Prep & Cooking Time: 15 Minutes
Ingredients:
- 3 tbsp. coconut oil
- 3/4 lb. strawberries
- 1/3 cup demerara sugar
- 1/4 tsp. salt
- 1 1/4 cups soy milk
- 1/2 tsp. coconut extract
- 1/2 tsp. baking powder
- 3/4 cup all-purpose flour

Directions:
1. Thoroughly combine all ingredients in a mixing dish.
2. Next step, drop tsp. full amounts of the mix into the air fryer cooking basket; air-fry for 4 minutes at 345°F.
3. Dust with ginger sugar if desired. Bon appétit!

851. Classic lemon curd
Servings: 2
Prep & Cooking Time: 30 Minutes
Ingredients:
- 3 tbsps. sugar
- 1 egg
- 1 egg yolk
- 3/4 lemon, squeezed

Directions:
1. Add sugar and butter in a medium ramekin and beat evenly. Add egg and yolk slowly while still whisking the fresh yellow color will be attained. Add the lemon juice and mix.
2. Place the bowl in the fryer basket and cook at 250°F for 6 minutes. Increase the temperature again to 320°F and cook for 15 minutes.
3. Remove the bowl onto a flat surface; use a spoon to check for any lumps and remove. Cover the ramekin with a plastic wrap and refrigerate overnight or serve immediately.

852. Cherries bars
Servings: 12
Prep & Cooking Time: 35 Minutes
Ingredients:
- 2 eggs, lightly beaten
- 1 cup erythritol
- 1/2 tsp. vanilla
- 1/4 cup water
- 1/2 cup butter, softened
- 3/4 cup cherries, pitted
- 1 1/2 cup almond flour
- 1 tbsp cornstarch
- 1/2 tsp. salt

Directions:
1. In a bowl, mix together almond flour, erythritol, eggs, vanilla, butter, and salt until dough is formed.
2. Press dough in air fryer baking dish.
3. Drop into the air fryer and cook at 385°F for 10 minutes.
4. Meanwhile, mix together cherries, cornstarch, and water.
5. Pour cherry mixture over cooked dough and cook for 2 minutes more.
6. Slice and serve.

853. Chocolate cashew cake
Servings: 8
Prep & Cooking Time: 18 Minutes
Ingredients:
- 1 egg
- 2 ounce cashews, crushed
- 1/2 tsp. baking soda
- 1/3 cup heavy cream
- 1 ounce dark chocolate, melted
- 1 tbsp. butter
- 1 tsp. vinegar
- 1 cup coconut flour

Directions:
1. Add egg in a bowl and beat using a hand mixer. Add coconut flour and stir well.
2. Add butter, vinegar, baking soda, heavy cream, and melted chocolate and stir well.
3. Add cashews and mix well.
4. Preheat the air fryer to 350°F.
5. Add prepared dough in air fryer baking dish and flatten it into a pie shape.

6. Cook for 18 minutes.
7. Slice and serve.

854. Classic banana split
Servings: 8
Prep & Cooking Time: 10 Minutes
Ingredients:
- 1 cup panko bread crumbs
- 4 bananas, peeled and halved lengthwise
- 1/2 cup corn flour
- 2 eggs
- 2 tbsp. walnuts, minced
- 3 tbsp. coconut oil
- 3 tbsp. sugar
- 1/4 tsp. ground cinnamon

Directions:
1. Preheat the air fryer to 280°F and grease an air fryer basket lightly.
2. Heat coconut oil in a skillet on medium heat and add bread crumbs. Cook it for about 4 minutes or until golden brown.
3. Transfer into a bowl.
4. Pour the flour in a bowl and whisk the eggs in another one.
5. Coat banana slices evenly with flour and dip in eggs and dredge again in the bread crumbs.
6. Combine cinnamon and sugar in a small bowl and sprinkle over the banana slices.
7. Set the banana slices in the air fryer basket and cook for about 10 minutes.
8. Top with walnuts and serve.

855. Lemon cake
Servings: 8
Prep & Cooking Time: 2 Hours 20 Minutes
Ingredients:
- 1 stick softened butter
- 1 cup sugar
- 1 medium egg
- 1 1/4 cups flour
- 1 tsp. butter flavoring
- 1 tsp. vanilla essence
- Pinch of salt
- 3/4 cup milk
- Grated zest of 1 medium-sized lemon

For the Glaze:
- 2 tbsp. freshly squeezed lemon juice

Directions:
1. In a large bowl, use a creamer to mix together the butter and sugar. Fold in the egg and continue to stir.
2. Add in the flour, butter flavoring, vanilla essence, and salt, combining every element well.
3. Pour in the milk, followed by the lemon zest, and continue to mix.
4. Lightly brush the inside of a cake pan with the melted butter.
5. Pour the cake batter into the cake pan.
6. Place the pan in the air fryer and bake at 350°F for 15 minutes.
7. After removing it from the fryer, run a knife around the edges of the cake to loosen it from the pan to transfer it to a serving plate.
8. Leave it to cool completely.
9. Meanwhile, create the glaze by cooling lemon juice in the refrigerator for about 30 to 45 minutes.
10. Glaze the cake and let it sit for a further 2 hours before serving.

856. Quick and easy cheesecake
Servings: 6
Prep & Cooking Time: 28 Minutes
Ingredients:
For crust:
- 2 tbsps. butter, melted
- 1/4 tsp. cinnamon
- 1 tbsp. swerve sweetener
- 1/2 cup almond flour
- Pinch of salt

For Cheesecake:
- 1 egg
- 1/2 tsp. vanilla
- 1/2 cup swerve sweetener
- 8 ounces cream cheese

Directions:
1. Preheat the air fryer to 280°F
2. Grease the fryer baking pan with cooking spray.
3. Add all crust ingredients into the bowl and mix until combined.
4. Transfer crust mixture into the prepared baking dish and press down into the bottom of the dish.
5. Let it cook in the air fryer for 12 minutes.
6. In a large bowl, beat cream cheese using a hand mixer until smooth.
7. Add vanilla, egg, and salt. Stir to combine.
8. Pour cream cheese mixture over cooked crust and cook for 16 minutes.
9. Allow to cool completely.
10. Slice and serve.

857. Rhubarb pie with nutmeg flavor
Servings: 6
Prep & Cooking Time: 1 Hour 15 Minutes
Ingredients:
- 1 1/4 cups almond flour
- 5 tbsp. cold water
- 8 tbsp. butter
- 1 tsp. sugar

For the filling:
- 3 cups rhubarb; minced.
- 1/2 tsp. nutmeg; ground
- 1 tbsp. butter
- 3 tbsp. flour
- 1 1/2 cups sugar
- 2 eggs
- 2 tbsp. low fat milk

Directions:
1. In a mixing bowl stir 1/4 cups flour with 1 tsp. sugar, 8 tbsp. butter and cold water; stir and knead until you obtain a dough
2. Transfer dough to a floured working surface, shape a disk, flatten, wrap in plastic, keep in the fridge for about 30 minutes; roll and press on the bottom of a pie pan that fits your air fryer
3. In a mixing bowl stir rhubarb with 1 1/2 cups sugar, nutmeg, tbsp. flour and whisk.
4. In another bowl, whisk eggs with milk, add to rhubarb mix, transfer the whole mix into the pie crust, introduce in your air fryer and cook at 390 °F, for 10 minutes. Cut and serve it cold

858. Quick apple wedges with apricots
Servings: 4
Prep & Cooking Time: 25 Minutes
Ingredients:
- 4 large apples
- 2 tbsps. olive oil
- 1/2 cup dried apricots, minced
- 1 – 2 tbsps. sugar
- 1/2 tsp. ground cinnamon

Directions:
1. Peel the apples and slice them into eight wedges. Throw away the cores.
2. Coat the apple wedges with the oil.
3. Place each wedge in the air fryer and cook for 12 - 15 minutes at 380°F.
4. Add in the apricots and allow to cook for a further 3 minutes.
5. Stir together the sugar and cinnamon. Sprinkle this mixture over the cooked apples before serving.

859. Cream cheese cookies
Servings: 15
Prep & Cooking Time: 12 Minutes
Ingredients:
- 1 egg
- 1/2 tsp. baking powder
- 1 tsp. vanilla
- 1/2 cup swerve sweetener
- 1/2 cup butter, softened
- 3 tbsps. cream cheese, softened
- 1/2 cup coconut flour
- Pinch of salt

Directions:
1. In a mixing bowl, beat together butter, sweetener, and cream cheese.
2. Add egg and vanilla and beat until smooth and creamy.
3. Add coconut flour, salt, and baking powder and beat until combined. Cover and place in the fridge for 1 hour.
4. Preheat the air fryer to 325°F.
5. Make cookies from dough and place into the air fryer and cook for 12 minutes.
6. Serve and enjoy.

860. Best fudgy brownies with ricotta cheese
Servings: 8
Prep & Cooking Time: 35 Minutes
Ingredients:
- 1 cup granulated swerve sweetener
- 2 tbsp. unsweetened cocoa powder, sifted
- 1/2 cup almond flour
- 1/2 cup coconut flour
- 1/4 tsp. salt
- 1/4 tsp. baking powder
- 1/2 cup butter, melted then cooled
- 2 eggs room temperature
- 1 tsp. vanilla
- 2 ounces unsweetened chocolate chips
- 1/2 cup sour cream
- 1/3 cup powdered erythritol
- 3 ounces Ricotta cheese, room temperature

Directions:
1. In a mixing bowl, thoroughly combine granulated swerve sweetener, cocoa powder, flour, salt, and baking powder.
2. Mix in butter, eggs, and vanilla. Add the batter to a lightly-greased baking pan.
3. Air-fry for 25 minutes at 500°F. Allow them to cool slightly on a wire rack.
4. Microwave the chocolate chips until every element's melted; allow the mixture to cool at room temperature.
5. After that, add Ricotta cheese, sour cream, and powdered erythritol; mix until every element is blended.
6. Spread this mixture onto the top of your brownie. Serve well chilled.

861. Nutty sweety muffins
Servings: 10
Prep & Cooking Time: 10 Minutes
Ingredients:
- 1 package fudge brownie mix
- 1 egg
- 2 tsp. water
- 1/4 cup walnuts, minced
- 1/3 cup vegetable oil

Directions:
1. Preheat the air fryer to 300°F and grease muffin tins lightly.
2. Mix brownie mix, egg, oil and water in a bowl.
3. Fold in the walnuts and transfer the mixture in the muffin cups.
4. Transfer the muffin tins in the air fryer basket and cook for about 10 minutes.
5. Serve and serve immediately.

862. Griddle cakes with greek yogurt
Servings: 4
Prep & Cooking Time: 15 Minutes
Ingredients:
- 3/4 cup self-rising flour
- 1/4 tsp. fine sea salt
- 2 tbsp. sugar
- 1/2 cup milk
- 2 eggs, lightly beaten
- 1 tbsp. butter
- Topping:
- 1 cup Greek-style yogurt
- 1 banana, mashed
- 2 tbsp. honey

Directions:
1. Mix in a medium bowl the sugar, flour, and salt, then, stir in the milk, eggs, and butter. Mix until smooth and uniform.
2. Drop tbsp. of the batter into the air fryer pan.
3. Cook at 300°F for 4 to 5 minutes or until bubbles form on top of the griddle cakes. Repeat with the remaining batter.
4. Meanwhile, mix all ingredients for the topping. Let them cool down in your refrigerator until ready to serve.
5. Serve the griddle cakes with the chilled topping. Enjoy!

863. Chocolate cake
Servings: 4
Prep & Cooking Time: 25 Minutes
Ingredients:
- 3 1/2 oz. butter, melted
- 3 1/2 tbsp. sugar
- 3 1/2 oz. chocolate, melted
- 1 1/2 tbsp. flour
- 2 eggs

Directions:
1. Pre-heat the air fryer to 375°F.
2. Grease four ramekins with a little butter.
3. Rigorously combine the eggs and butter before stirring in the melted chocolate.
4. Slowly fold in the flour.
5. Drop an equal amount of the mixture into each ramekin.
6. Put them in the air fryer and cook for 10 minutes
7. Place the ramekins upside-down on plates and let the cakes fall out. Serve hot.

864. Honey and blueberry pancakes
Servings: 4
Prep & Cooking Time: 20 Minutes

Ingredients:
- 1/2 tsp. vanilla extract
- 2 tbsp. honey
- 1/2 cup blueberries
- 1/2 cup sugar
- 2 cups + 2 tbsp. flour
- 3 eggs, beaten
- 1 cup milk
- 1 tsp. baking powder
- Pinch of salt

Directions:
1. Pre-heat the air fryer to 390°F.
2. In a medium size bowl, combine all of the dry ingredients.
3. Pour in the wet ingredients and combine with a whisk, ensuring the mixture becomes smooth.
4. Roll each blueberry in some flour to lightly coat it before folding it into the mixture. This is to ensure they do not change the color of the batter.
5. Grease the baking dish with some oil or butter.
6. Spoon several equal amounts of the batter onto the baking dish, spreading them into pancake-shapes and ensuring to space them out well. This may have to be completed in two batches.
7. Place the dish in the fryer and bake for about 10 minutes.

865. Lemony ricotta cake
Servings: 4
Prep & Cooking Time: 50 Minutes
Ingredients:
- 8 eggs; whisked
- 3 lbs. ricotta cheese
- Zest from 1 lemon; shredded
- Zest from 1 orange; shredded
- 1/2 lb. sugar
- Butter for the pan

Directions:
1. In a mixing bowl stir eggs with sugar, cheese, lemon and orange zest and stir very well
2. Grease a baking pan that fits your air fryer with some batter, spread ricotta mixture, introduce in the fryer at 390 °F and bake for 30 minutes
3. Reduce heat at 280 °F and bake for 40 more minutes. Take out of the oven, leave cake to cool down and serve!

866. Dark chocolate cupcakes
Servings: 6
Prep & Cooking Time: 20 Minutes
Ingredients:
- 3/4 cup self-rising flour
- 1 cup powdered sugar
- 1/4 tsp. salt
- 1/4 tsp. nutmeg, preferably freshly shredded
- 1 tbsp. cocoa powder
- 2 ounces butter, softened
- 1 egg, whisked
- 2 tbsp. almond milk
- 1/2 tsp. vanilla extract
- 1 1/2 ounces dark chocolate chunks
- 1/2 cup almonds, minced

Directions:
1. Combine the sugar, flour, nutmeg, salt, and cocoa powder into a large mixing bowl. Mix to combine well.
2. In another bowl, whisk the butter, egg, almond milk, and vanilla.
3. Now, add the wet egg mixture to the dry ingredients. Then, carefully fold in the chocolate chunks and almonds; gently stir to combine.
4. Scrape the batter mixture into muffin cups.
5. Bake your cupcakes at 355°F for about 12 minutes or until a toothpick comes out dry and clean.
6. Decorate with chocolate sprinkles if desired. Serve and enjoy!

867. Walnuts and dark chocolate brownies
Servings: 10
Prep & Cooking Time: 35 Minutes
Ingredients:
- 6 ounce butter
- 3/4 cup white sugar
- 3 eggs
- 2 tsp. vanilla extract
- 3/4 cup flour
- 1/4 cup cocoa powder
- 1 cup minced walnuts
- 1 cup white chocolate chips

Directions:
1. Line a pan inside your air fryer with baking paper.
2. Melt chocolate and butter in a saucepan over low heat.
3. Do not stop stirring until you obtain a smooth mixture.
4. Let cool slightly, and then whisk in eggs and vanilla.
5. Sift flour and cocoa and stir to mix well. Sprinkle the walnuts over and add the white chocolate into the batter.
6. Drop the mixture in the pan and cook for 20 minutes at 340°F.
7. Serve with raspberry syrup and ice cream.

868. Raspberries and avocado cake
Servings: 4
Prep & Cooking Time: 30 Minutes
Ingredients:
- 4 ounces raspberries
- 2 avocados, peeled, pitted and mashed
- 1 cup almonds flour
- 3 tsp. baking powder
- 1 cup swerve sweetener
- 4 tbsp. butter, melted
- 4 eggs, whisked

Directions:
1. In a mixing bowl, whisk all the ingredients, until well combined.
2. Transfer this into a cake pan that fits the air fryer after you've lined it with parchment paper, put the pan in the fryer and cook at 340°F for 30 minutes.
3. Let the cake cool down.
4. Slice and serve.

869. Delicious coconut cream pie
Servings: 4
Prep & Cooking Time: 25 Minutes
Ingredients:
- 4 tbsp. coconut cream
- 1 tsp. baking powder
- 1 tsp. white wine vinegar
- 1 egg, beaten
- 1/4 cup shredded coconut
- 1 tsp. vanilla extract
- 1/2 cup coconut flour
- 4 tsp. Splenda
- 1 tsp. cornstarch
- Cooking spray

Directions:
1. Put all liquid ingredients in the bowl: coconut cream, white wine vinegar, egg, and vanilla extract.
2. Stir the liquid until homogenous and add baking powder, shredded coconut, coconut flour, Splenda, and cornstarch. Stir the ingredients until you get the smooth texture of the batter.
3. Spray the air fryer cake mold with cooking spray. Pour the batter in the cake mold.
4. Preheat the air fryer to 330°F.
5. Put the cake mold in the air fryer basket and cook it for 25 minutes. Then cool the cooked pie completely and remove it from the cake mold.
6. Cut the cooked pie into servings.

870. Cinnamon cake with cranberries
Servings: 6
Prep & Cooking Time: 16 Minutes
Ingredients:
- 4 eggs
- 1 tsp. orange zest
- 2 tsp. mixed spice
- 2 tsp. cinnamon
- 1/4 cup swerve sweetener
- 1 cup butter, softened
- 2/3 cup dried cranberries
- 1 1/2 cups almond flour
- 1 tsp. vanilla

Directions:
1. Preheat the air fryer to 325°F.
2. In a mixing bowl, add sweetener and melted butter and beat until fluffy.
3. Add cinnamon, vanilla, and mixed spice and stir well.
4. Add eggs stir until well combined.
5. Add almond flour, orange zest, and cranberries and stir to combine.
6. Pour batter in a greased air fryer cake pan and place into the air fryer.
7. Cook cake for 16 minutes.
8. Slice and serve.

871. Lemon cake for beginners
Servings: 10
Prep & Cooking Time: 30 Minutes
Ingredients:
- 4 eggs
- 2 tbsps. lemon zest
- 1/2 cup butter softened
- 2 tsp. baking powder
- 1/4 cup coconut flour
- 2 cups almond flour
- 1/2 cup fresh lemon juice
- 1/4 cup swerve sweetener
- 1 tbsp. vanilla

Directions:
1. Preheat the air fryer to 280°F, and grease the air fryer baking pan with cooking spray. Set aside.
2. In a large bowl, beat all ingredients using a hand mixer until a smooth.
3. Pour batter into the prepared dish and place into the air fryer and cook for 25 minutes.
4. Slice and serve.

872. Coconutty bars with lemon flavor
Servings: 12
Prep & Cooking Time: 25 Minutes
Ingredients:
- 1/4 cup cashews
- 1/4 cup lemon juice, fresh
- 3/4 cup oat milk
- 3/4 cup erythritol
- 1 cup desiccated coconut
- 1 tsp. baking powder
- 2 eggs, beaten
- 2 tbsp. coconut oil
- A dash of salt

Directions:
1. Preheat the air fryer for 5 minutes.
2. In a mixing bowl, combine all ingredients.
3. Use a hand mixer to mix every element.
4. Drop it in an air fryer baking pan.
5. Bake for 2minutes at 355°F or until a toothpick inserted in the middle comes out dried and clean.

873. Superb chocolate and meringue cake
Servings: 4
Prep & Cooking Time: 40 Minutes
Ingredients:
For Cake:
- 1/3 cup plain flour
- 1/4 tsp. baking powder
- 1 1/2 tbsp. unsweetened cocoa powder
- 2 egg yolks
- 1/2 ounce caster sugar
- 2 tbsp. vegetable oil
- 3 3/4 tbsp. milk
- 1 tsp. vanilla extract

For Meringue:
- 2 egg whites
- 1 ounce caster sugar
- 1/8 tsp. cream of tartar

Directions:
1. For cake: in a bowl, sift together the flour, baking powder, and cocoa powder.
2. In another bowl, add the remaining ingredients and whisk until well combined.
3. Add the flour mixture and whisk until well combined.
4. For meringue: in a clean glass bowl, add all the ingredients and with an electric whisker, whisk on high speed until stiff peaks form.
5. Place 1/3 of the meringue into flour mixture and with a hand whisker, whisk well.
6. Fold in the remaining meringue.
7. Preheat the fryer to 355°F.
8. Place the mixture into an ungreased chiffon pan.
9. With a piece of foil, cover the pan tightly and poke some holes using a fork.
10. Set the cake pan into an air fryer basket.
11. Now, set the temperature of air fryer to 320°F.
12. Air fry for about 30-35 minutes.
13. Remove the piece of foil and set the temperature to 285°F.
14. Air fry for another 5 minutes or until a toothpick inserted in the center comes out clean.
15. Remove the cake pan from air fryer and place onto a wire rack to cool for about 10 minutes.
16. Now, invert the cake onto wire rack to completely cool before slicing.
17. Cut the cake into desired size slices and serve.

874. Vanilla and coconut oat cookies
Servings: 12
Prep & Cooking Time: 20 Minutes
Ingredients:
- 1 cup butter, melted
- 1 3/4 cups granulated sugar
- 3 eggs
- 2 tbsp. oat milk
- 1 tsp. coconut extract
- 1 tsp. vanilla extract
- 2 1/4 cups all-purpose flour
- 1/2 tsp. baking powder
- 1/2 tsp. baking soda
- 1/2 tsp. fine table salt
- 2 cups coconut chips

Directions:
1. Preheat your fryer to 350°F
2. With an electric mixer, whisk the butter and sugar until well combined. Now, add the eggs one at a time, and mix well; add the oat milk, coconut extract, and vanilla; beat until creamy and uniform.
3. Combine the baking powder with flour, salt, and baking soda.
4. Pour the flour mixture into the butter mixture and stir until every element is well incorporated.
5. Finally, fold in the coconut chips and mix again. Scoop out 1 tbsp. size balls of the batter on a cookie pan, leaving 2 inches between each cookie.
6. Bake for about 8 to 10 minutes or until golden brown, rotating the pan once or twice through the cooking time.
7. Let your cookies cool on wire racks. Bon appétit!

875. Coconut and white chocolate cookies
Servings: 10
Prep & Cooking Time: 40 Minutes
Ingredients:
- 3/4 cup butter
- 2 1/2 cups coconut flour
- 2 tbsps. coconut oil
- 3/4 cup granulated swerve sweetener
- 1/3 tsp. ground anise star
- 1/3 tsp. ground allspice
- 1/3 tsp. shredded nutmeg
- 1/4 tsp. fine sea salt
- 8 ounces white chocolate, unsweetened
- 2 eggs, well beaten

Directions:
1. Put all of the above ingredients, minus egg, into a mixing dish. Then, knead with hand until a soft dough is formed. Place in the refrigerator for 20 minutes.
2. Roll the chilled dough into small balls; flatten your balls and preheat the air fryer to 350°F.
3. Make an egg wash by using the remaining egg. Then, glaze the cookies with the egg wash; bake about 11 minutes. Bon appétit!

876. Apples stuffed with oats, mielke and walnuts
Servings: 4
Prep & Cooking Time: 25 Minutes
Ingredients:
- 4 apples
- 1/4 cup rolled oats
- 1/4 cup sugar
- 2 tbsp. honey
- 1/3 cup walnuts, minced
- 1 tsp. cinnamon powder
- 1/2 tsp. ground cardamom
- 1/2 tsp. ground cloves
- 2/3 cup water

Directions:
1. Peel the apples and remove the seeds.
2. In a mixing bowl, combine together the rolled oats, sugar, honey, walnuts, cinnamon, cardamom, and cloves.
3. Fill the apples with the mixture.
4. Pour the water into an air fryer safe dish.
5. Place the apples in the dish.
6. Bake at 3°F for 17 minutes.
7. Serve at room temperature. Bon appétit!

877. Sweety peach skewers
Servings: 4
Prep & Cooking Time: 40 Minutes
Ingredients:
- 4 cups peaches, sliced
- 2 – 3 tbsp. sugar
- 2 tbsp. flour
- 1/3 cup oats
- 2 tbsp. unsalted butter
- 1/4 tsp. vanilla extract
- 1 tsp. cinnamon

Directions:
1. In a medium size bowl, mix the vanilla extract, peach slices, cinnamon, and sugar.
2. Pour the mixture into a baking tin and place it in the air fryer.
3. Cook for minutes on 290°F.
4. In the meantime, combine the oats, flour, and unsalted butter in a separate bowl.
5. Once the peach slices cooked, transfer the butter mixture on top of them.
6. Cook for an additional 10 minutes at 300 - 310°F.
7. Remove from the fryer and allow to crisp up for 5 – Serve with ice cream if desired.

878. Easy ghee cake
Servings: 6
Prep & Cooking Time: 40 Minutes
Ingredients:
- 2 tbsp. ghee, melted
- 1 cup coconut, shredded
- 1 cup mashed avocado
- 3 tbsp. stevia
- 1 tsp. cinnamon powder
- 2 tsp. cinnamon powder

Directions:
1. Mix in a medium size bowl all the ingredients and stir well.
2. Pour this into a cake pan lined with parchment paper, place the pan in the fryer and cook at 340°F for 40 minutes.
3. Cool the cake down, slice and serve.

879. Succulent chocolate cake
Servings: 9
Prep & Cooking Time: 40 Minutes
Ingredients:
- 1/3 cup plain flour
- 1/4 tsp. baking powder
- 1 1/2 tbsp. unsweetened cocoa powder
- 2 eggs, yolks and whites separated
- 3 3/4 tbsp. milk
- 1 1/2-ounce castor sugar, divided
- 2 tbsp. vegetable oil

- 1 tsp. vanilla extract
- 1 tsp. cream of tartar

Directions:
1. Preheat the air fryer to 330°F and grease a chiffon pan lightly.
2. Mix flour, baking powder and cocoa powder in a bowl.
3. Combine the remaining ingredients in another bowl until well combined.
4. Stir in the flour mixture slowly and transfer this mixture into the chiffon pan.
5. Cover with the foil paper and poke some holes in the foil paper.
6. Transfer the baking pan into the air fryer basket and cook for about 30 minutes.
7. Remove the foil and set the air fryer to 285°F.
8. Cook for 10 more minutes and cut into slices to serve.

880. Vanilla custard peaches
Servings: 2
Prep & Cooking Time: 15 Minutes
Ingredients:
- 1 peach, peeled, cored and halved
- 1 cup prepared vanilla custard
- 2 puff pastry sheets
- 1 egg, beaten lightly
- 1 tbsp. sugar
- Pinch of ground cinnamon
- 1 tbsp. whipped cream

Directions:
1. Preheat the air fryer to 340°F and grease an air fryer basket.
2. Place a spoonful of vanilla custard and a peach half in the center of each pastry sheet.
3. Mix sugar and cinnamon in a bowl and sprinkle on the peach halves.
4. Pinch the corners of sheets together to shape into a parcel and transfer into the air fryer basket.
5. Cook for about 1minute and top with whipped cream.
6. Serve and serve with remaining custard.

881. Lava chocolate cake
Servings: 4
Prep & Cooking Time: 20 Minutes
Ingredients:
- 1 cup dark cocoa candy melts
- 1 stick butter
- 2 eggs
- 4 tbsp. sugar
- 1 tbsp. honey
- 4 tbsp. flour
- Pinch of kosher salt
- Pinch of ground cloves
- 1/4 tsp. shredded nutmeg
- 1/4 tsp. cinnamon powder

Directions:
1. Spritz the insides of four custard cups with cooking spray.
2. Melt the cocoa candy melts and butter in the microwave for 30 seconds to 1 minute.
3. In a wide bowl, combine the sugar, the eggs, and honey. Whisk until frothy, and then pour it in the melted chocolate mix.
4. Drop in the rest of the ingredients and combine well with an electric mixer or a manual whisk.
5. Transfer equal portions of the mixture into the prepared custard cups.
6. Drop them into the air fryer and air bake at 350°F for 12 minutes.
7. Once they are cooked let them to cool for 5 to 6 minutes.
8. Place each cup upside-down on a dessert plate and let the cake slide out. Serve with fruits and chocolate syrup if desired.

882. Coconut and vanilla cookies
Servings: 8
Prep & Cooking Time: 10 Minutes
Ingredients:
- 5 ounces sunflower seed butter
- 6 tbsp coconut flour
- 1 tsp. vanilla
- 1/4 tsp. olive oil
- 2 tbsps. swerve sweetener
- Pinch of salt

Directions:
1. Add all ingredients into a deep plate and mix well until dough is formed.
2. Preheat the air fryer to 360°F.
3. Make cookies from mixture and place into the air fryer and cook for 10 minutes.
4. Serve and enjoy.

883. Old fashion crème brulee
Servings: 3
Prep & Cooking Time: 60 Minutes
Ingredients:
- 1 cup milk
- 2 vanilla pods
- 10 egg yolks
- 4 tbsp sugar + extra for topping

Directions:
1. In a pan, add the milk and cream. Cut the vanilla pods open and scrape the seeds into the pan with the vanilla pods also.
2. Over a medium heat on a stovetop, bring the ingredients into the pan to boiling while stirring regularly.
3. Turn off the heat. Add the egg yolks to a bowl and beat it.
4. Add the sugar and mix well but not too bubbly.
5. Remove the vanilla pods from the milk mixture; transfer the mixture onto the eggs mixture while stirring constantly. Let it sit for 10 minutes.
6. Fill 2 to 3 ramekins with the mixture.
7. Put the ramekins in your fryer basket and cook them at 190°F for 50 minutes. Once ready, remove the ramekins and let sit to cool.
8. Drizzle with the remaining sugar and use a torch to melt the sugar, so it browns at the top.

884. Buttery doughnuts
Servings: 12
Prep & Cooking Time: 24 Minutes
Ingredients:
For Doughnuts:
- 1 cup all-purpose flour
- 1 cup whole wheat flour
- 2 tsp. baking powder
- Salt, to taste
- 3/4 cup sugar
- 1 egg
- 1 tbsp. butter, softened
- 1/2 cup milk
- 2 tsp. vanilla extract

For Glaze:
- 2 tbsp. icing sugar
- 2 tbsp. condensed milk
- 1 tbsp. cocoa powder

Directions:
1. In a large bowl, mix well flours, baking powder, and salt.
2. In another bowl, add the sugar and egg. Whisk until fluffy and light.

3. Add the flour mixture and stir until well combined.
4. Add the butter, milk, and vanilla extract and mix until a soft dough forms.
5. Refrigerate the dough for at least 1 hour.
6. Now, put the dough onto a lightly floured surface and roll into 1/2-inch thickness.
7. With a small doughnut cutter, cut 24 small doughnuts from the rolled dough.
8. Preheat your air fryer to 380°F and then grease an air fryer basket.
9. Place doughnuts into the prepared air fryer basket in 3 batches.
10. Air fry for about 6-8 minutes.
11. Remove from air fryer and transfer the doughnuts onto a platter to cool completely.
12. In a deep plate, combine the cocoa powder and condensed milk.
13. Spread the glaze over doughnuts and sprinkle with icing sugar.
14. Serve.

885. Almond and coconut bars
Servings: 6
Prep & Cooking Time: 25 Minutes
Ingredients:
- 1/4 cup almond butter
- 1 tbsp. unsweetened almond milk
- 1/2 cup coconut flour
- 3/4 tsp. baking soda
- 1/2 cup dark sugar free chocolate chips, divided
- 1 cup canned sugar free pumpkin puree
- 1/4 cup swerve sweetener
- 1 tsp. cinnamon
- 1 tsp. vanilla extract
- 1/4 tsp. nutmeg
- 1/2 tsp. ginger
- 1 tsp. salt
- 1 tsp. ground cloves

Directions:
1. Preheat the air fryer to 360°F and layer a baking pan with wax paper.
2. Mix pumpkin puree, swerve sweetener, vanilla extract, milk, and butter in a bowl.
3. Combine coconut flour, spices, salt, and baking soda in another bowl.
4. Combine the two mixtures and mix well until smooth.
5. Add about 1/3 cup of the sugar free chocolate chips.
6. Transfer this mixture into the baking pan, and place it into the air fryer basket. Let it cook for about 25 minutes.
7. Microwave sugar free chocolate bits on low heat and dish out the baked cake from the pan.
8. Top with melted chocolate and slice to serve.

886. Soft biscuits with buttermilk
Servings: 4
Prep & Cooking Time: 25 Minutes
Ingredients:
- 1/2 tsp. baking soda
- 1/2 cup cake flour
- 3/4 tsp. salt
- 1/2 tsp. baking powder
- 4 tbsp butter, minced
- 1 tsp. sugar
- 3/4 cup buttermilk

Directions:
1. Preheat your air fryer to 400°F.
2. Combine all dry ingredients, in a mixing bowl.
3. Place the minced butter in the bowl, and rub it into the flour mixture, until crumbed. Stir in the buttermilk.
4. Flour a flat and dry surface and roll out until half-inch thick. Cut out 10 rounds with a small cookie cutter. Set the biscuits on a lined baking sheet. Cook for 8 minutes.

887. Orange nuggets
Servings: 6
Prep & Cooking Time: 1 Hour 20 Minutes
Ingredients:
- 1/2 cup milk
- 1/4 cup granulated sugar
- 1 tbsp. yeast
- 1/2 stick butter, at room temperature
- 1 egg, at room temperature
- 1/4 tsp. salt
- 2 cups all-purpose flour
- 2 tbsp. fresh orange juice

Filling:
- 2 tbsp. butter
- 4 tbsp. white sugar
- 1 tsp. ground star anise
- 1/4 tsp. ground cinnamon
- 1 tsp. vanilla paste
- 1/2 cup confectioners' sugar

Directions:
1. In a microwave-safe dish, heat the milk, and transfer the warm milk to the bowl of a stand electric mixer. Add the granulated sugar and yeast, and mix to combine well. Cover and let it sit until the yeast is foamy.
2. Then, beat the butter on low speed. Fold in the egg and mix again. Add salt and flour. Add the orange juice and mix on medium speed until a soft dough forms.
3. On a slightly floured surface, work the dough. Cover it loosely and let it sit in a warm place about 1 hour or until doubled in size. Then, spritz the bottom and sides of a baking pan with cooking oil (butter flavored).
4. Roll your dough out into a rectangle.
5. Spread 2 tbsp. of butter all over the dough. In a mixing dish, combine the white sugar, ground star anise, cinnamon, and vanilla; sprinkle evenly over the dough.
6. Then, roll up your dough to form a log. Cut into equal rolls and place them in the parchment-lined air fryer basket.
7. Bake at 350°F for 12 minutes, turning them halfway through the cooking time. Dust with confectioners' sugar and enjoy!

888. Mascarpone cake with peppermint flavor
Servings: 6
Prep & Cooking Time: 40 Minutes
Ingredients:
- 2 tbsp. stevia
- 1/2 cup coconut flour
- 1/2 cup butter
- 1 cup mascarpone cheese, at room temperature
- 4 ounces baker's chocolate, unsweetened
- 1 tsp. vanilla extract
- 2 drops peppermint extract

Directions:
1. Beat the sugar, coconut flour, and butter in a mixing bowl.
2. Press the mixture into baking pan, previously greased.
3. Bake at 350°F for 18 minutes.
4. Place it in your freezer for 10 minutes.
5. Then, make the cheesecake topping by mixing the remaining ingredients.
6. Place this topping over the crust and allow it to cool in your freezer for a further 15 minutes.
7. Serve well chilled.

889. Pears clafouti

Servings: 6
Prep & Cooking Time: 30 Minutes
Ingredients:
- 3/4 cup extra-fine flour
- 1 1/2 cups plums, pitted and
- 4 medium-sized pears, cored and sliced
- 1/2 cup coconut cream
- 3/4 cup coconut milk
- 3 eggs, whisked
- 1/2 cup powdered sugar, for dusting
- 3/4 cup white sugar
- 1/2 tsp. baking soda
- 1/2 tsp. baking powder
- 1/3 tsp. ground cinnamon
- 1/2 tsp. crystalized ginger
- 1/4 tsp. shredded nutmeg

Directions:
1. Lightly grease 2 mini pie pans using a nonstick cooking spray. Lay the plums and pears on the bottom of the pie pans.
2. In a saucepan that is preheated over a moderate flame, warm the cream along with coconut milk until thoroughly heated.
3. Remove the pan from the heat; mix in the flour along with baking soda and baking powder.
4. In a medium-sized mixing bowl, whip the eggs, white sugar, and spices; whip until the mixture is creamy.
5. Add the creamy milk mixture. Carefully spread this mixture over the fruits.
6. Bake at 320°F for about 20-25 minutes.
7. To serve, dust with powdered sugar.

890. Vanilla cookies

Servings: 15
Prep & Cooking Time: 25 Minutes
Ingredients:
- 1/2 cup salted butter, softened
- 2 cups almond meal
- 1 organic egg
- 1 tsp. ground cinnamon
- 2 tsp. sugar
- 1 tsp. organic vanilla extract

Directions:
1. Preheat the air fryer to 370°F and grease an air fryer basket.
2. Mix all the ingredients in a bowl until well combined.
3. Make equal sized balls from the mixture and transfer in the air fryer basket.
4. Cook for about 5 minutes and press down each ball with fork.
5. Cook for about 20 minutes and allow the cookies to cool to serve with tea.

891. Sweety coconut flour rolls

Servings: 6
Prep & Cooking Time: 1 Hour 20 Minutes
Ingredients:
- 1/2 cup milk
- 1/4 cup swerve sweetener
- 1 tbsp. yeast
- 1/2 stick butter, at room temperature
- 1 egg, at room temperature
- 1/4 tsp. salt
- 2 cups coconut flour
- 2 tbsp. fresh orange juice

Filling:
- 2 tbsp. butter
- 4 tbsp. swerve sweetener
- 1 tsp. ground star anise
- 1/4 tsp. ground cinnamon
- 1 tsp. vanilla paste
- 1/2 cup confectioners' swerve sweetener

Directions:
1. Warm the milk in a microwave safe bowl and transfer the warm milk to the bowl of a stand electric mixer.
2. Add the 4 cup of swerve sweetener and yeast, and mix to combine well. Cover and let it sit until the yeast is foamy.
3. Then, beat the butter on low speed. Fold in the egg and mix again. Add salt and flour. Add the orange juice and mix on medium speed until a soft dough forms.
4. Knead the dough on a lightly floured surface. Cover it loosely and let it sit in a warm place about 1 hour or until doubled in size. Then, spritz the bottom and sides of a baking pan with cooking oil (butter flavored).
5. Roll your dough out into a rectangle.
6. Spread 2 tbsp. of butter all over the dough. In a mixing dish, combine 4 tbsp. of swerve sweetener, ground star anise, cinnamon, and vanilla; sprinkle evenly over the dough.
7. Then, roll up your dough to form a log. Cut into equal rolls and place them in the parchment-lined air fryer basket.
8. Bake at 350°F for 12 minutes, turning them halfway through the cooking time. Dust with confectioners' swerve sweetener and enjoy!

892. Coconut and cacao pudding

Servings: 1
Prep & Cooking Time: 65 Minutes
Ingredients:
- 1 cup coconut milk
- 2 tbsps. cacao powder or organic cocoa
- 1/2 tsp. Sugar powder extract or 2 tbsp honey/maple syrup
- 1/2 tbsps. quality gelatin
- 1 tbsp. water

Directions:
1. On a medium heat, combine the coconut milk, cocoa and sweetener.
2. In a separate bowl, mix in the gelatin and water.
3. Add to the pan and stir until fully dissolved.
4. Pour into small dishes and refrigerate for 1 hour.
5. Serve!

893. Sweet potato and heavy cream pie

Servings: 4
Prep & Cooking Time: 45 Minutes
Ingredients:
- 6-ounces sweet potatoes
- 1 (9-inch) prepared frozen pie dough, thawed
- 2 large eggs
- 1 tbsp. butter, melted
- 1 tsp. olive oil
- 1/4 cup heavy cream
- 2 tbsp. maple syrup
- 1 tbsp. light brown sugar
- 1/2 tsp. ground cinnamon
- 1 tsp. ground nutmeg
- Salt, to taste
- 3/4 tsp. vanilla extract

Directions:
1. Preheat the air fryer to 400°F and grease a pie pan.
2. Rub the sweet potato with oil and arrange in the air fryer basket.
3. Cook for about 30 minutes and dish out in a bowl.
4. Allow to cool and mash it completely.
5. Add rest of the ingredients and mix until well combined.
6. Set the shell into a pie pan and place the mixture over the pie shell.
7. Transfer the pie pan in the air fryer basket and cook for about 30 minutes.
8. Serve and serve warm.

894. Pecan streusel with mixed berries
Servings: 3
Prep & Cooking Time: 20 Minutes
Ingredients:
- 3 tbsp. pecans, minced
- 3 tbsp. almonds, slivered
- 2 tbsp. walnuts, minced
- 3 tbsp. granulated swerve sweetener
- 1/2 tsp. ground cinnamon
- 1 egg
- 2 tbsp. cold salted butter, cut into pieces
- 1/2 cup mixed berries

Directions:
1. Mix your nuts, swerve sweetener, cinnamon, egg, and butter until well combined.
2. Place mixed berries on the bottom of a lightly greased air fryer-safe dish. Top with the prepared topping.
3. Bake at 370°F for 17 minutes. Serve at room temperature. Bon appétit!

895. Vanilla-scented mozzarella bombs
Servings: 8
Prep & Cooking Time: 4 Minutes
Ingredients:
- 2 eggs, beaten
- 1 tsp. almond butter, melted
- 7 ounces coconut flour
- 2 ounces almond flour
- 5 ounces Mozzarella, shredded
- 1 tbsp. butter
- 2 tbsp. swerve sweetener
- 1 tsp. baking powder
- 1/2 tsp. vanilla extract
- Cooking spray

Directions:
1. In the mixing bowl mix up butter and Mozzarella. Microwave the mixture for -15 minutes or until it is melted.
2. Then add almond flour and coconut flour. Add swerve sweetener and baking powder.
3. Add vanilla extract and stir the mixture. Knead the soft dough. Microwave the mixture for 2-5 seconds more if it is not melted enough.
4. In the bowl mix up almond butter and eggs. Make 8 balls from the almond flour mixture and coat them in the egg mixture.
5. Preheat the air fryer to 400°F.
6. Grease the fryer basket with cooking spray from inside and place the bread rolls in one layer.
7. Cook the dessert for 4 minutes or until the bread roll is golden brown.
8. Cool the cooked dessert completely and sprinkle with Splenda if desired.

896. Nutmeg churros
Servings: 4
Prep & Cooking Time: 20 Minutes
Ingredients:
- 3/4 cup water
- 1 tbsp. swerve sweetener
- 1/4 tsp. sea salt
- 1/4 tsp. shredded nutmeg
- 1/4 tsp. ground cloves
- 6 tbsp. butter
- 3/4 cup almond flour
- 2 eggs

Directions:
1. To make the dough, boil the water in a pan over medium-high heat; now, add the swerve sweetener, salt, nutmeg, and cloves; cook until dissolved.
2. Pour in the butter and turn the heat to low.
3. Gradually stir in the almond flour, whisking continuously, until the mixture forms a ball.
4. Remove from the heat; fold in the eggs one at a time, stirring to combine well.
5. Pour the mixture into a piping bag with a large star tip. Squeeze inch strips of dough into the greased air fryer pan.
6. Cook at 410°F for 6 minutes, working in batches. Bon appétit!

897. 900. Coconut berry pudding
Servings: 6
Prep & Cooking Time: 15 Minutes
Ingredients:
- 2 cups coconut cream
- 1/3 cup blackberries
- 1/3 cup blueberries
- 3 tbsp. swerve sweetener
- Zest of 1 lime, shredded

Directions:
1. In a blender, stir all the ingredients and pulse well. Divide this into 6 small ramekins, put them in your air fryer and cook at 340°F for 10 minutes. Serve cold.

898. Ricotta dessert
Servings: 8
Prep & Cooking Time: 30 Minutes
Ingredients:
- 3 eggs, lightly beaten
- 1 tsp. baking powder
- 1/2 cup ghee, melted
- 1 cup almond flour
- 1/3 cup erythritol
- 1 cup ricotta cheese, soft

Directions:
1. Mix all the ingredients into a bowl until well combined.
2. Pour batter into the greased air fryer baking dish and place into the air fryer.
3. Cook at 355°F for 30 minutes.
4. Slice and serve.

899. Lemon and tangerine cake
Servings: 8
Prep & Cooking Time: 30 Minutes
Ingredients:
- ¾ cup sugar
- 2 cups flour
- ½ tsp. vanilla extract
- ¼ cup olive oil

- ½ cup milk
- 1 tsp. cider vinegar
- Juice and zest from 2 lemons
- Juice and zest from 1 tangerine
- Tangerine segments; for serving

Directions:
1. In a mixing bowl stir flour with sugar and stir
2. Combine the oil with vinegar, milk, lemon juice, vanilla extract, zest and tangerine zest into a large mixing bowl. Whisk very well.
3. Add flour and stir well.
4. Transfer this into a cake pan that fits your air fryer, introduce in the fryer and cook at 390 °F, for 20 minutes.
5. Serve right away with tangerine segments on top.

900. Banana and chocolate brownie
Servings: 4
Prep & Cooking Time: 16 Minutes
Ingredients:
- 1 cup bananas, overripe
- 1 scoop protein powder
- 2 tbsps. unsweetened cocoa powder
- 1/2 cup almond butter, melted

Directions:
1. Preheat the air fryer to 325°F.
2. Grease your air fryer baking tray with cooking spray.
3. Combine all the ingredients with a blender until smooth.
4. Pour batter into the prepared pan and place in the air fryer basket.
5. Cook brownies for 16 minutes.
6. Serve and enjoy.

901. Dark chocolate and cream cheese cheesecake
Servings: 6
Prep & Cooking Time: 34 Minutes
Ingredients:
- 3 eggs, whites and yolks separated
- 1 cup dark chocolate, minced
- 1/2 cup cream cheese, softened
- 2 tbsp. cocoa powder
- 1/4 cup dates jam
- 2 tbsp. powdered sugar

Directions:
1. Preheat the air fryer to 285°F and grease a cake pan lightly.
2. Refrigerate egg whites in a bowl to chill before using.
3. Microwave chocolate and cream cheese on high for about minutes.
4. Remove from microwave and whisk in the egg yolks.
5. Whisk together egg whites until firm peaks form and combine with the chocolate mixture.
6. Drop the batter in a cake pan and place it in your air fryer basket.
7. Cook for about 30 minutes and dish out.
8. Dust with powdered sugar and spread dates jam on top to serve.

902. Old style churros
Servings: 1
Prep & Cooking Time: 15 Minutes
Ingredients:
- 1/2 cup water
- 1/4 cup butter
- 1/2 cup flour
- 3 eggs
- 2 1/2 tsp. sugar

Directions:
1. In a saucepan, bring the butter and the oil to a boil.
2. Once it is bubbling, add the flour and mix to create a doughy consistency.
3. Remove from the heat, allow to cool, and crack the eggs into the saucepan. Blend with a hand mixer until the dough turns fluffy.
4. Transfer the dough into a piping bag.
5. Pre-heat the fryer at 380°F.
6. Pipe the dough into the fryer in several three-inch-long segments. Cook for ten minutes before removing from the fryer and coating in the sugar.
7. Serve with the low-carb chocolate sauce of your choice.

903. Cheat apple pie
Servings: 8
Prep & Cooking Time: 30 Minutes
Ingredients:
- 2 ounces butter, melted
- 2 ounces sugar
- 1 ounce brown sugar
- 2 tsp. cinnamon
- 1 egg, beaten
- 1/4 tsp. salt
- 3 large puff pastry sheets

Directions:
1. Combine white sugar, brown sugar, cinnamon, salt, and butter in a mixing bowl. Coat the apples in the mixture and place them in a baking dish. Cook the baking dish in the air fryer for minutes at 350°F.
2. Meanwhile, on a floured flat surface, spread out the dough and cut each sheet into 6 equal pieces. Divide the apple filling evenly among the slices.
3. Brush the egg along the edges of the pastry pieces.
4. Fold them in half and use a fork to seal the edges. Cook for 8 minutes in the fryer at 370°F on a prepared baking sheet. Cook for 2 minutes more after flipping, increasing the temperature to 390°F.

904. Chocolate custard with heavy cream
Servings: 4
Prep & Cooking Time: 32 Minutes
Ingredients:
- 2 eggs
- 1 tsp. vanilla
- 1 cup heavy whipping cream
- 1 cup unsweetened almond milk
- 2 tbsps. unsweetened cocoa powder
- 1/4 cup Swerve
- Pinch of salt

Directions:
1. Preheat the air fryer to 305°F.
2. Using a blender, whisk all ingredients until smooth.
3. Pour mixture into the ramekins and place into the air fryer.
4. Cook for 32 minutes.
5. Serve and enjoy.

905. Pecan cookies and puffy coconut
Servings: 10
Prep & Cooking Time: 30 Minutes
Ingredients:
- 3/4 cup coconut oil, room temperature
- 1 1/2 cups coconut flour
- 1 cup pecan nuts, unsalted and roughly minced
- 3 eggs plus an egg yolk, whisked
- 1 1/2 cups extra-fine almond flour
- 3/4 cup monk fruit

- 1/4 tsp. freshly shredded nutmeg
- 1/3 tsp. ground cloves
- 1/2 tsp. baking powder
- 1/3 tsp. baking soda
- 1/2 tsp. pure vanilla extract
- 1/2 tsp. pure coconut extract
- 1 tsp. fine sea salt

Directions:
1. Into a large bowl, combine both types of flour, baking soda and baking powder. In a separate bowl, beat the eggs with coconut oil. Combine egg mixture with the flour mixture.
2. Throw in the other ingredients, mixing well. Shape the mixture into cookies.
3. Bake at 350°F for about 25 minutes. Bon appétit!

906. Strawberries and lemon stew
Servings: 4
Prep & Cooking Time: 20 Minutes
Ingredients:
- 1 lb. strawberries, halved
- 4 tbsps. stevia
- 1 tbsp. lemon juice
- 1 and 1/2 cups water

Directions:
1. Mix all the ingredients in a deep plate.
2. Transfer the mixture in the air fryer pan and cook it 340°F for about 20 minutes. Divide the stew into cups and serve cold.

907. Cranberry bread pudding
Servings: 4
Prep & Cooking Time: 45 Minutes
Ingredients:
- 1-1/2 cups milk
- 2-1/2 eggs
- 1/2 cup cranberries1 tsp. butter
- 1/4 cup and 2 tbsp. white sugar
- 1/4 cup golden raisins
- 1 tsp. ground cinnamon
- 3/4 cup heavy whipping cream
- 3/4 tsp. lemon zest
- 3/4 tsp. kosher salt
- 3/4°French baguettes, cut into 2-inch slices
- 3/8 vanilla bean, split and seeds scraped away

Directions:
1. Grease the air fryer baking pan with cooking spray.
2. On the baking pan, spread baguette slices, cranberries, and raisins.
3. In blender, blend well vanilla bean, cinnamon, salt, lemon zest, eggs, sugar, and cream.
4. Pour over baguette slices, and let it soak for an hour.
5. Cover pan with foil.
6. For 35 minutes, cook on 330°F.
7. Let it rest for 10 minutes.
8. Serve and enjoy.

908. 9 almond cheese cake with strawberries
Servings: 6
Prep & Cooking Time: 35 Minutes
Ingredients:
- 1 cup almond flour
- 3 tbsp coconut oil, melted
- 1/2 tsp. vanilla
- 1 egg, lightly beaten
- 1 tbsp fresh lime juice
- 1/4 cup erythritol
- 1 cup cream cheese, softened
- 1 lb. strawberries, minced
- 2 tsps. baking powder

Directions:
1. Combine all the ingredients into the large bowl and mix well.
2. Spray air fryer cake pan with cooking spray.
3. Pour batter into the prepared pan and place into the air fryer and cook at 350°F for 35 minutes.
4. Allow to cool completely.
5. Slice and serve.

909. Almond and coconut cookies with butter rum flavor
Servings: 6
Prep & Cooking Time: 35 Minutes
Ingredients:
- 1/2 cup almond flour
- 1/2 cup coconut flour
- 1/2 tsp. baking powder
- 1/4 tsp. fine sea salt
- 1 stick butter, unsalted and softened
- 1/2 cup swerve sweetener
- 1 egg
- 1/2 tsp. vanilla
- 1 tsp. butter rum flavor
- 3 ounces walnuts, finely minced

Directions:
1. Begin by preheating the air fryer to 360°F.
2. In a mixing dish, thoroughly combine the flour with baking powder and salt.
3. Beat the butter and swerve sweetener with a hand mixer until pale and fluffy; add the whisked egg, vanilla, and butter rum flavoring; mix again to combine well. Now, stir in the dry ingredients.
4. Fold in the minced walnuts and mix to combine. Divide the mixture into small balls; flatten each ball with a fork and transfer them to a foil-lined baking pan.
5. Bake in the preheated air fryer for 14 minutes.
6. Work in a few batches and transfer to wire racks to cool completely. Bon appétit!

910. Dark chocolate and zucchini brownies
Servings: 12
Prep & Cooking Time: 35 Minutes
Ingredients:
- 1 cup butter
- 1 cup dark chocolate chips
- 1 1/2 cups zucchini, shredded
- 1/4 tsp. baking soda
- 1 egg
- 1 tsp. vanilla extract
- 1/3 cup applesauce, unsweetened
- 1 tsp. ground cinnamon
- 1/2 tsp. ground nutmeg

Directions:
1. Preheat the air fryer to 345°F and grease 3 large ramekins.
2. Mix all the ingredients in a large bowl until well combined.
3. Pour evenly into the prepared ramekins and smooth the top surface with the back of the spatula.
4. Transfer the ramekin in the air fryer basket and cook for about 35 minutes.
5. Serve and cut into slices to serve.

911. Simple angel food cake
Servings: 12
Prep & Cooking Time: 30 Minutes
Ingredients:
- 1/4 cup butter, melted
- 1 cup powdered erythritol
- 1 tsp. strawberry extract
- 12 egg whites
- 2 tsp. cream of tartar
- A pinch of salt

Directions:
1. Preheat the air fryer for 5 minutes.
2. Combine, in a deep plate, the eggs whites and cream of tartar.
3. Use a hand mixer and whisk until white and fluffy.
4. Add the rest of the ingredients except for the butter and whisk for another minute.
5. Pour into a baking dish.
6. Drop into the air fryer basket and cook for 30 minutes at 400°F or if a toothpick inserted in the middle comes out clean.
7. Drizzle with melted butter once cooled.

912. Fast dark chocolate hot drink
Servings: 2
Prep & Cooking Time: 7 Minutes
Ingredients:
- 1/4 tsp. vanilla extract
- 1/3 cup coconut milk
- 1 tsp. butter
- 1 tbsp. cocoa powder
- 1/2 ounce dark chocolate
- 1 tsp. Monk fruit

Directions:
1. In the big cup whisk together coconut milk and cocoa powder. When the liquid is smooth, add vanilla extract and Monk fruit. Stir it gently. Then add dark chocolate and butter.
2. Put the cup with chocolate mixture in the air fryer and cook it at 375°F for 3 minutes.
3. Then stir the liquid and cook it for 4 minutes more.
4. Carefully remove the cups with hot chocolate from the air fryer.
5. Stir the hot chocolate gently with the help of the tsp.

913. Pecans cake
Servings: 6
Prep & Cooking Time: 30 Minutes
Ingredients:
- 1/2 cup butter, melted
- 1/2 cup swerve sweetener
- 1 tsp. vanilla essence
- 1 egg
- 1/2 cup almond flour
- 1/2 tsp. baking powder
- 1/4 cup cocoa powder
- 1/2 tsp. ground cinnamon
- 1/4 tsp. fine sea salt
- 1 ounce bakers' chocolate, unsweetened
- 1/4 cup pecans, finely minced

Directions:
1. Preheat your air fryer to 355°F.
2. Lightly grease six silicone molds.
3. In a mixing dish, beat the melted butter with the swerve sweetener until fluffy. Next, stir in the vanilla and egg and beat again.
4. After that, add the almond flour, baking powder, cocoa powder, cinnamon, and salt. Mix until every element is well combined.
5. Fold in the chocolate and pecans; mix to combine. Bake in the preheated air fryer for 20 to 22 minutes. Enjoy!

914. Dark chocolate brownies with avocado dough
Servings: 12
Prep & Cooking Time: 30 Minutes
Ingredients:
- 1 cup avocado, peeled and mashed
- 1/2 tsp. vanilla extract
- 4 tbsp. cocoa powder
- 3 tbsp. coconut oil, melted
- 2 eggs, whisked
- 1/2 cup dark chocolate, unsweetened and melted
- 3/4 cup almond flour
- 1 tsp. baking powder
- 1/4 tsp. baking soda
- 1 tsp. stevia

Directions:
1. In a mixing bowl combine the flour with stevia, baking powder and soda, and stir well.
2. Add the rest of the ingredients gradually, whisk and transfer into a cake pan that fits the air fryer after you lined it with parchment paper.
3. Put the pan in your air fryer and cook at 355°F for 30 minutes.
4. Cut into squares and serve cold.

915. Tejeringos spanish-style doughnut
Servings: 4
Prep & Cooking Time: 20 Minutes
Ingredients:
- 3/4 cup water
- 1 tbsp. sugar
- 1/4 tsp. sea salt
- 1/4 tsp. shredded nutmeg
- 1/4 tsp. ground cloves
- 6 tbsp. butter
- 3/4 cup all-purpose flour
- 2 eggs

Directions:
1. To make the dough, boil the water in a pan over medium-high heat.
2. Now, add the sugar, salt, nutmeg, and cloves; cook until dissolved.
3. Pour in the butter and turn the heat to low.
4. Gradually stir in the flour, whisking continuously, until the mixture forms a ball.
5. Remove from the heat; fold in the eggs one at a time, stirring to combine well.
6. Pour the mixture into a piping bag with a large star tip. Squeeze inch strips of dough into the greased air fryer pan.
7. Cook at 410°F for 6 minutes, working in batches. Bon appétit!

916. Peaches and honey cake
Servings: 6
Prep & Cooking Time: 40 Minutes
Ingredients:
- 1/2 lb. peaches, pitted and mashed
- 3 tbsps. honey
- 1/2 tsp. baking powder
- 1 1/4 cups cake flour
- 1/2 tsp. orange extract
- 1 tsp. pure vanilla extract
- 1/4 tsp. ground cinnamon

- 1/3 cup ghee
- 1 tsp. salt
- 1/2 cup caster sugar
- 2 eggs
- 1/4 tsp. freshly shredded nutmeg

Directions:
1. Firstly, preheat the air fryer to 3°F. Spritz the cake pan with a nonstick cooking spray.
2. In a mixing bowl, beat the ghee with caster sugar until creamy. Fold in the egg, mashed peaches and honey.
3. Then, make the cake batter by mixing the remaining ingredients; now, stir in the peach/honey mixture.
4. Now, transfer the prepared batter to the cake pan; level the surface with a spoon.
5. Bake for 3 minutes or until a tester inserted in the center of your cake comes out completely dry. Enjoy!

917. Vanilla sauce apples
Servings: 4
Prep & Cooking Time: 13 Minutes
Ingredients:
- 4 small firm apples, cored
- 1/2 cup golden raisins
- 1/2 cup blanched almonds
- 4 tbsp. sugar, divided
- 1/2 cup whipped cream
- 1/2 tsp. vanilla extract

Directions:
1. Preheat the air fryer to 355°F and grease a baking dish lightly.
2. Put raisins, almond and half of sugar in a food processor and pulse until minced.
3. Stuff the raisin mixture inside each apple and arrange the apples in the prepared baking dish.
4. Transfer the baking dish in the air fryer basket and cook for about 10 minutes.
5. Put cream, remaining sugar and vanilla extract on medium heat in a pan and cook for about 3 minutes, continuously stirring.
6. Remove from the heat and serve apples with vanilla sauce.

918. Buttery fritters
Servings: 16
Prep & Cooking Time: 30 Minutes
Ingredients:
For the dough:
- 4 cups flour
- 1 tsp. kosher salt
- 1 tsp. sugar
- 3 tbsp. butter, at room temperature
- 1 packet instant yeast
- 1 1/4 cups lukewarm water

For the topping:
- 1 cup sugar
- Pinch of cardamom
- 1 tsp. cinnamon powder
- 1 stick butter, melted

Directions:
1. Pour all the ingredients in a big mixing bowl and combine well.
2. Add in the lukewarm water and mix until a soft, elastic dough forms.
3. Place the dough on a lightly floured surface and lay a greased sheet of aluminum foil on top of the dough. Refrigerate for 5 to 10 minutes.
4. After removing it from the refrigerator, divide it in two.
5. Mold each half into a log and slice it into 20 pieces.
6. In a shallow bowl, combine the sugar, cardamom and cinnamon.
7. Coat the slices with a light brushing of melted butter and the sugar.
8. Spritz air fryer basket with cooking spray.
9. Transfer the slices to the fryer and air fry at 360°F for roughly 10 minutes. Turn each slice once during the baking time.
10. Dust each slice with the sugar before serving.

919. Cranberry brownies for°father's day
Servings: 10
Prep & Cooking Time: 40 Minutes
Ingredients:
- 1/3 cup cranberries
- 8 ounces white chocolate
- 3/4 cup self-rising flour
- 3 tbsps. shredded coconut
- 1/2 cup coconut oil
- 2 eggs plus an egg yolk, whisked
- 3/4 cup white sugar
- 1/4 tsp. ground cardamom
- 1 tsp. pure rum extract

Directions:
1. Microwave white chocolate and coconut oil until every element's melted; allow the mixture to cool at room temperature.
2. After that, thoroughly whisk the eggs, sugar, rum extract, and cardamom.
3. Next step, add the rum/egg mixture to the chocolate mixture. Stir in the flour and shredded coconut; mix to combine.
4. Fold the cranberries into the batter. Press the batter into a lightly buttered cake pan.
5. Air-fry for 3minutes at 340°F. Allow them to cool slightly on a wire rack before slicing and serving.

920. Lemon glazed pop-tarts
Servings: 6
Prep & Cooking Time: 1 Hour
Ingredients:
For the Pop-tarts:
- 1 cup coconut flour
- 1 cup almond flour
- 1/2 cup of ice-cold water

Pop-tarts:
- 1/4 tsp. salt
- 2 tbsp. swerve sweetener
- 2/3 cup very cold coconut oil
- 1/2 tsp. vanilla extract

For the Lemon Glaze:
- 1 1/4 cups powdered swerve sweetener
- 2 tbsp. lemon juice
- Zest of 1 lemon
- 1 tsp. coconut oil, melted
- 1/4 tsp. vanilla extract

Directions:
Pop-tarts:
1. Preheat the air fryer to 375°F and grease an air fryer basket.
2. Mix all the flours, swerve sweetener, and salt in a bowl and stir in the coconut oil.
3. Mix well with a fork until an almond meal mixture is formed.
4. Stir in vanilla and 1 tbsp. of cold water and mix until a firm dough is formed.

5. Cut the dough into two equal pieces and spread in a slim sheet.
6. Cut each sheet into 12 equal sized rectangles and transfer 4 rectangles into the air fryer basket.
7. Cook for about 10 minutes and repeat with the remaining rectangles.
8. Lemon Glaze:
9. Meanwhile, mix all the ingredients for the lemon glaze and pour over the cooked tarts.
10. Top with sprinkles and serve.

Chapter 6
More recipes

921. Ham and baked eggs on a veggie casserole
Servings: 4
Prep & Cooking Time: 30 Minutes
Ingredients:
- 2 tbsps. butter, melted
- 1 zucchini, diced
- 1 bell pepper, seeded and sliced
- 1 red chili pepper, seeded and minced
- 1 medium-sized leek, sliced
- 3/4 lb. ham, cooked and diced
- 5 eggs
- 1 tsp. cayenne pepper
- Sea salt, to taste
- 1/2 tsp. ground black pepper
- 1 tbsp. fresh cilantro, minced

Directions:
1. Set the air fryer to 380°F. Grease the sides and bottom of a baking pan with the melted butter.
2. Place the zucchini, peppers, leeks and ham in the baking pan. Bake in the preheated air fryer for 6 minutes.
3. Crack the eggs on top of ham and vegetables; season with the cayenne pepper, salt, and black pepper. Make sure that the whites are all set before taking it off the air fryer.
4. Garnish with fresh cilantro and serve. Bon appétit!

922. Spinach and eggs florentine
Servings: 2
Prep & Cooking Time: 20 Minutes
Ingredients:
- 2 tbsps. ghee, melted
- 2 cups baby spinach, torn into small pieces
- 2 tbsps. shallots, minced
- 1/4 tsp. red pepper flakes
- Salt, to taste
- 1 tbsp. fresh thyme leaves, roughly minced
- 4 eggs

Directions:
1. First, heat up your air fryer to 350°F. Brush the sides and bottom of a gratin dish with the melted ghee.
2. Put the spinach and shallots into the bottom of the gratin dish. Season with red pepper, salt, and fresh thyme.
3. Make four indents for the eggs; crack one egg into each indent. Set the bake time to 12 minutes. Rotate it from time to time for even cooking result. Enjoy!

923. Chicken frittata, chive, and feta
Servings: 4
Prep & Cooking Time: 10 Minutes
Ingredients:
- 1/3 cup Feta cheese, crumbled
- 1 tsp. dried rosemary
- 1/2 tsp. brown sugar
- 2 tbsps. fish sauce
- 1 1/2 cup cooked chicken breasts, boneless and shredded
- 1/2 tsp. coriander sprig, finely minced
- 3 medium-sized whisked eggs
- 1/3 tsp. ground white pepper
- 1 cup fresh chives, minced
- 1/2 tsp. garlic paste
- Fine sea salt, to taste
- Nonstick cooking spray

Directions:
1. Grab a baking dish that fit in your air fryer.
2. Coat the baking dish with a non-stick oil of your choice. Stir in all ingredients, minus Feta cheese. Stir to combine well.
3. Set your machine to cook at 365°F for 8 minutes; check for doneness. Scatter crumbled Feta over the top and eat immediately!

924. Delicious and healthy celery and bacon cakes
Servings: 4
Prep & Cooking Time: 25 Minutes
Ingredients:
- 2 eggs, lightly beaten
- 1/3 tsp. freshly grounded black pepper
- 1 cup Colby cheese, shredded
- 1/2 tbsp. fresh dill, finely minced
- 1/2 tbsp. garlic paste
- 1/3 cup onion, finely minced
- 1/3 cup bacon, minced
- 2 tsps. fine sea salt
- 2 medium-sized celery stalks, trimmed and shredded
- 1/3 tsp. baking powder

Directions:
1. Place the celery on a paper towel and squeeze them to remove the excess liquid.
2. Combine the vegetables with the other ingredients in the order listed above. Shape the balls using 1 tbsp. of the vegetable mixture.
3. Then, gently flatten each ball with your palm or a wide spatula. Spritz the croquettes with a nonstick cooking oil.
4. Bake the vegetable cakes in a single layer for 17 minutes at 318°F. Serve warm with sour cream.

925. Delicious chicken with tomato sauce
Servings: 4
Prep & Cooking Time: 20 Minutes + Marinating Time
Ingredients:
- 1 tbsp. balsamic vinegar
- 1/2 tsp. red pepper flakes, crushed
- 1 fresh garlic, roughly minced
- 2 1/2 large-sized chicken breasts, divide into halves
- 1/3 handful fresh cilantro, roughly minced
- 2 tbsps. olive oil
- 4 Roma tomatoes, diced
- 1 1/2 tbsps. butter
- 1/3 handful fresh basil, loosely packed, sniped
- 1 tsp. kosher salt

- 2 cloves garlic, minced
- Cooked bucatini, to serve

Directions:
1. Mix ingredients 1-7 in a medium-sized dish; let it marinate for a couple of hours.
2. Preheat the air fryer to 3°F. Air-fry your chicken for 32 minutes and serve warm.
3. In the meantime, prepare the tomato sauce by preheating a deep saucepan. Simmer the tomatoes until you make a chunky mixture. Throw in the garlic, basil, and butter; give it a good stir.
4. Serve the cooked chicken breasts with the tomato sauce and the cooked bucatini. Bon appétit!

926. Western eggs recipe
Servings: 6
Prep & Cooking Time: 20 Minutes
Ingredients:
- 6 eggs
- 3/4 cup milk
- 1 ounce cream cheese, softened
- Sea salt, at your convenience
- 1/4 tsp. ground black pepper
- 1/4 tsp. paprika
- 6 ounces cooked ham, diced
- 1 onion, minced
- 1/3 cup cheddar cheese, shredded

Directions:
1. Begin by preheating the air fryer to 360°F. Shower the sides of the baking pan with cooking oil plus the bottom as well.
2. In a mixing dish, whisk the eggs, milk, and cream cheese until pale. Add the spices, ham, and onion; stir until every element is well incorporated.
3. Arrange the mixture on the baking pan and top it with cheese *cheddar for better taste) .
4. Bake in the preheated air fryer for 12 minutes. Serve warm and enjoy!

927. Stuffed chicken rolls with cheese and chive
Servings: 6
Prep & Cooking Time: 20 Minutes
Ingredients:
- 2 eggs, well-whisked
- Tortilla chips, crushed
- 1 1/2 tbsps. extra-virgin olive oil
- 1 1/2 tbsps. fresh chives, minced
- 3 chicken breasts, halved lengthwise
- 1 1/2 cup soft cheese
- 2 tsps. sweet paprika
- 1/2 tsp. whole grain mustard
- 1/2 tsp. cumin powder
- 1/3 tsp. fine sea salt
- 1/3 cup fresh cilantro, minced
- 1/3 tsp. freshly ground black pepper for added taste (add more depending on your palette)

Directions:
1. Flatten out each piece of the chicken breast using a rolling pin. Then, grab three mixing dishes.
2. In the first one, combine the soft cheese with the cilantro, fresh chives, cumin, and mustard.
3. In another mixing dish, whisk the eggs together with the sweet paprika. In the third dish, combine the salt, black pepper, and crushed tortilla chips.
4. Cover each chicken piece with cheese mixture. Repeat with the remaining pieces of the chicken breasts; now, roll them up.
5. Coat each chicken roll with the whisked egg; dredge each chicken roll into the tortilla chips mixture. Lower the rolls onto the air fryer cooking basket. Drizzle extra-virgin olive oil over all rolls.
6. Air fry at 345°F for 28 minutes, working in batches. Serve warm, garnished with sour cream if desired.

928. Fruit skewers greek style
Servings: 2
Prep & Cooking Time: 10 Minutes
Ingredients:
- 6 strawberries, halved
- 1 banana, peeled and sliced
- 1/4 pineapple, peeled and cubed
- 1 tsp. fresh lemon juice
- 1/4 cup Greek-Style yoghurt, optional
- 2 tbsps. honey
- 1 tsp. vanilla

Directions:
1. Toss the fruits with lemon juice in a mixing dish. Tread the fruit pieces on skewers.
2. Cook at 340°F for 5 minutes.
3. Meanwhile, whisk the Greek yogurt with the honey and vanilla. Serve the fruit skewers with the Greek sauce on the side. Bon appétit!

929. Stuffed chicken with double cheese
Servings: 6
Prep & Cooking Time: 30 Minutes
Ingredients:
- 2 eggs, well-whisked
- 1 cup shredded parmesan cheese
- 1 1/2 tbsps. extra-virgin olive oil
- 1 1/2 tbsps. fresh chives, minced
- 3 chicken breasts, halved lengthwise
- 1 1/2 cups mozzarella cheese
- 2 tsps. sweet paprika
- 1/2 tsp. whole grain mustard
- 1/2 tsp. cumin powder
- 1/3 tsp. fine sea salt
- 1/3 cup fresh cilantro, minced
- 1/3 tsp. of freshly ground black pepper (or more) to taste

Directions:
1. Flatten out each piece of the chicken breast using a rolling pin. Then, grab three mixing dishes.
2. In the first one, combine mozzarella cheese with the cilantro, fresh chives, cumin, and mustard.
3. In another mixing dish, whisk the eggs together with the sweet paprika. In the third dish, combine the salt, black pepper, and parmesan cheese.
4. Cover each chicken with cheese mixture. Repeat with the remaining pieces of the chicken breasts; now, roll them up.
5. Coat each chicken roll with the whisked egg; dredge each chicken roll into the parmesan mixture. Lower the rolls onto the air fryer cooking basket. Drizzle extra-virgin olive oil over all rolls.
6. Air fry at 345°F for 28 minutes, working in batches. Serve warm, garnished with sour cream if desired.

930. Special potato and kale croquettes
Servings: 6
Prep & Cooking Time: 9 Minutes
Ingredients:
- 4 eggs, slightly beaten
- 1/3 cup flour
- 1/3 cup goat cheese, crumbled

- 1 1/2 tsps. fine sea salt
- 4 garlic cloves, minced
- 1 cup kale, steamed
- 1/3 cup breadcrumbs
- 1/3 tsps. dried peppers, crushed
- 3 potatoes, peeled and quartered
- 1/3 tsp. dried dill weed

Directions:
1. Firstly, boil the potatoes in salted water. Mash the potato once cooked. Introduce kale and goat cheese to the mashed potato then season it with minced garlic, sea salt and dried peppers. Add dill and egg and stir it to mix well.
2. Now, roll the mixture to form small croquettes.
3. Grab three shallow bowls. Position the flour in the first empty bowl.
4. Beat the remaining 3 eggs in the second bowl. Position the breadcrumbs into the third empty bowl.
5. Dip each croquette in the flour; then, dip them in the eggs bowl; lastly, roll each croquette in the breadcrumbs.
6. Air fry at 335°F for 7 minutes or until golden. Check the taste, add salt as needed, serve it.

931. Beef and tomato with baked eggs
Servings: 4
Prep & Cooking Time: 20 Minutes
Ingredients:
- Non-stick cooking spray
- 1/2 lb. leftover beef, coarsely minced
- 2 garlic cloves, pressed
- 1 cup kale, torn into pieces and wilted
- 1 tomato, minced
- 4 eggs, beaten
- 4 tbsps. heavy cream
- 1/2 tsp. turmeric powder
- Salt & ground black pepper, at your convenience
- and tsp. ground allspice

Directions:
1. Spritz the inside of four ramekins with a cooking spray.
2. Divide all of the above ingredients among the prepared ramekins. Stir until every element is well combined.
3. Air-fry at 390°F for 16 minutes; check with a wooden stick and return the eggs to the air fryer for a few more minutes as needed. Serve immediately.

932. Original pork rinds
Prep & Cooking Time: 50 Minutes
Ingredients:
- 1 lb. pork rind raw, scored by the butcher
- 1 tbsps. sea salt
- 2 tbsps. smoked paprika

Directions:
1. Rub salt and sprinkle it on the skin. Allow it to sit for 30 minutes.
2. Roast at 380°F for 8 minutes; turn them over and cook for a further 8 minutes or until blistered.
3. Sprinkle the smoked paprika all over the pork rinds and serve. Bon appétit!

933. Fontina, frittata and sausage, pepper
Servings: 5
Prep & Cooking Time: 14 Minutes
Ingredients:
- 3 pork sausages, minced
- 5 well-beaten eggs
- 1 1/2 bell peppers, seeded and minced
- 1 tsp. smoked cayenne pepper
- 2 tbsps. Fontina cheese
- 1/2 tsp. tarragon
- 1/2 tsp. ground black pepper
- 1 tsp. salt

Directions:
1. In a cast-iron skillet, sweat the bell peppers together with the minced pork sausages until the peppers are fragrant and the sausage begins to release liquid.
2. Lightly grease the inside of a baking dish with pan spray.
3. Throw all of the above ingredients into the prepared baking dish, including the sautéed mixture; stir to combine.
4. Bake at 380°F approximately 9 minutes. Serve right away with the salad of choice.

934. Deviled eggs farmer's breakfast
Servings: 3
Prep & Cooking Time: 25 Minutes
Ingredients:
- 6 eggs
- 6 slices bacon
- 2 tbsps. mayonnaise
- 1 tsp. hot sauce
- 1/2 tsp. Worcestershire sauce
- 2 tbsps. green onions, minced
- 1 tbsp. pickle relish
- Salt & ground black pepper for added taste
- 1 tsp. smoked paprika

Directions:
1. Position the wire rack inside the fryer; use it to hold the eggs.
2. Cook at 350°F for 15 minutes.
3. Once done, place it in a cold water to stop it getting overcooked. Peel the eggs under cold running water; slice them into halves.
4. Cook the bacon at 400°F for 3 minutes; flip the bacon over and cook an additional 3 minutes; chop the bacon and reserve.
5. Mash the egg yolks with the mayo, hot sauce, Worcestershire sauce, green onions, pickle relish, salt, and black pepper; add the reserved bacon and spoon the yolk mixture into the egg whites.
6. Garnish with smoked paprika. Bon appétit!

935. Cheesy and yummy broccoli
Servings: 4
Prep & Cooking Time: 25 Minutes
Ingredients:
- 1/3 cup shredded yellow cheese
- 1 large-sized head broccoli, stemmed and cut small florets
- 2 1/2 tbsps. canola oil
- 2 tsps. dried rosemary
- 2 tsps. dried basil
- Ground black pepper and salt for a more flavorful taste

Directions:
1. Bring a medium pan filled with a lightly salted water to a boil. Then, boil the broccoli florets for about 3 minutes.
2. Then, drain the broccoli florets well; toss them with the canola oil, rosemary, basil, salt and black pepper.
3. Set your air fryer to 390°F; arrange the seasoned broccoli in the cooking basket; set the timer for 17 minutes. Toss the broccoli halfway through the cooking process.
4. Serve warm topped with shredded cheese and enjoy!

936. Manchego and cauliflower croquettes
Servings: 4
Prep & Cooking Time: 15 Minutes
Ingredients:

- 1 cup Manchego cheese, shredded
- 1 tsp. paprika
- 1 tsp. freshly ground black pepper
- 1/2 tbsp. fine sea salt
- 1/2 cup chives, finely minced
- 1 lb. cauliflower florets
- 2 tbsps. canola oil
- 2 tsps. dried basil

Directions:
1. Crumble the cauliflower florets in a food processor. Then, combine the broccoli with the rest of the above ingredients.
2. Then, shape the balls using your hands. Now, flatten the balls to make the patties.
3. Next, cook your patties at 380°F approximately 10 minutes. Bon appétit!

937. Halibut and eggs keto rolls
Servings: 4
Prep & Cooking Time: 25 Minutes
Ingredients:
- 4 keto rolls
- 1 lb. smoked halibut, minced
- 4 eggs
- 1 tsp. dried oregano
- 1 tsp. dried basil
- Black pepper and salt for taste

Directions:
1. Cut off the top of each keto roll; then, scoop out the insides to make the shells.
2. Lay the prepared keto roll shells in the lightly greased cooking basket.
3. Spritz with cooking oil; add the halibut. Crack an egg into each keto roll shell; sprinkle with thyme, basil, salt, and black pepper.
4. Bake in the preheated air fryer at 325°F for 20 minutes. Bon appétit!

938. Delicious roasted cherries
Servings: 3
Prep & Cooking Time: 40 Minutes
Ingredients:
- 9 ounces dark sweet cherries
- 2 tbsps. brown sugar
- 1 tbsp. honey
- A pinch of shredded nutmeg
- 1/4 tsp. ground cloves
- 1/4 tsp. ground cardamom
- 1 tsp. vanilla

Directions:
1. Place the cherries in a lightly greased baking dish.
2. Whisk the remaining ingredients until every element is well combined; add this mixture to the baking dish and gently stir to combine.
3. Bake in the preheated air fryer at 350°F for 35 minutes. Serve at room temperature. Bon appétit!

939. Apple fries country-style
Servings: 4
Prep & Cooking Time: 20 Minutes
Ingredients:
- 1/2 cup milk
- 1 egg
- 1/2 all-purpose flour
- 1 tsp. baking powder
- 4 tbsps. brown sugar
- 1 tsp. vanilla extract
- 1/2 tsp. ground cloves
- A pinch of kosher salt
- A pinch of shredded nutmeg
- 1 tbsp. coconut oil, melted
- 2 Pink Lady apples, cored, peeled, slice into pieces (shape and size of French fries
- 1/3 cup granulated sugar
- 1 tsp. ground cinnamon

Directions:
1. In a mixing bowl, whisk the milk and eggs; gradually stir in the flour; add the baking powder, brown sugar, vanilla, cloves, salt, nutmeg, and melted coconut oil. Mix to combine well.
2. Dip each apple slice into the batter, coating on all sides. Spritz the bottom of the cooking basket with cooking oil.
3. Cook the apple fries in the preheated air fryer at 375°F approximately 8 minutes, turning them over halfway through the cooking time.
4. Divide in small batches then cook slowly for even cooking.
5. In the meantime, mix the granulated sugar with the ground cinnamon; sprinkle the cinnamon sugar over the apple fries. Serve warm.

940. Tasty paprika chicken
Servings: 4
Prep & Cooking Time: 30 Minutes
Ingredients:
- 1 1/2 tbsps. freshly squeezed lemon juice
- 2 small-sized chicken breasts, boneless
- 1/2 tsp. ground cumin
- 1 tsp. dry mustard powder
- 1 tsp. paprika
- 2 tsps. cup pear cider vinegar
- 1 tbsp. olive oil
- 2 garlic cloves, minced
- Kosher salt and freshly ground mixed peppercorns, to savor

Directions:
1. Warm the olive oil in a nonstick pan over a moderate flame. Sauté the garlic for just a few minutes.
2. Remove your pan from the heat; add cider vinegar, lemon juice, paprika, cumin, mustard powder, kosher salt, and black pepper. Place this paprika sauce into a baking dish.
3. Pat the chicken breasts dry; transfer them to the prepared sauce. Bake in the preheated air fryer for about 28 minutes at 395°F; check for doneness using a thermometer or a fork.
4. Allow to rest for 8 to 9 minutes before slicing and serving. Serve with dressing.

941. Melting bagel 'n' egg
Servings: 3
Prep & Cooking Time: 25 Minutes
Ingredients:
- 3 eggs
- 3 slices smoked ham, minced
- 1 tsp. Dijon mustard
- 1/4 cup mayonnaise
- Salt and white pepper, to taste
- 3 bagels
- 3 ounces Colby cheese, shredded

Directions:
1. Position the wire rack inside the air fryer; lower the eggs onto the wire rack.
2. Cook at 370°F for 15 minutes.

3. Once done, place it in a cold water to stop it getting overcooked. Peel the eggs under cold running water; coarsely chop them and set aside.
4. Combine the minced eggs, ham, mustard, mayonnaise, salt, and pepper in a mixing bowl.
5. Slice the bagels in half. Spread the egg mixture on top and sprinkle with the shredded cheese.
6. Grill in the preheated air fryer at 3°F for 7 minutes or until cheese is melted. Bon appétit!

942. Finger sage and lime wings
Servings: 4
Prep & Cooking Time: 30 Minutes
Ingredients:
- 1 tsp. onion powder
- 1/3 cup fresh lime juice
- 1/2 tbsp. corn flour
- 1/2 heaping tbsp. fresh minced parsley
- 1/3 tsp. mustard powder
- 1/2 lb. turkey wings, cut into smaller pieces
- 2 heaping tbsp. fresh minced sage
- 1/2 tsp. garlic powder
- 1/2 tsp. seasoned salt
- 1 tsp. freshly grounded black or white peppercorns

Directions:
1. Simply dump all of the above ingredients into a mixing dish; cover and let it marinate for about hours in your refrigerator.
2. Air-fry turkey wings for 20 minutes at 355°F. Bon appétit!

943. Baked eggs and bacon with quinoa
Servings: 4
Prep & Cooking Time: 40 Minutes
Ingredients:
- 1/2 cup quinoa
- 1/2 lb. potatoes, diced
- 1 onion, diced
- 6 slices bacon, precooked
- 1 tbsp. butter, melted
- Ground black pepper and sea salt for better taste
- 6 eggs

Directions:
1. Rinse the quinoa under cold running water. Place the rinsed quinoa in a pan and add cup of water.
2. Bring it to the boil. Turn the heat down and let it simmer for 13 to 15 minutes or until tender; reserve.
3. Place the diced potatoes and onion in a lightly greased casserole dish. Add the bacon and the reserved quinoa. Drizzle the melted butter over the quinoa and sprinkle with salt and pepper.
4. Bake in the preheated air fryer at 390°F for 10 minutes.
5. Turn the temperature down to 350°F.
6. Make six indents for the eggs; crack one egg into each indent. Allow even cooking by rotating pan from time to time. Cook for 12 minutes. Enjoy!

944. Eggs, swiss chard and ham
Servings: 2
Prep & Cooking Time: 20 Minutes
Ingredients:
- 2 eggs
- 1/4 tsp. dried or fresh marjoram
- 2 tsp. chili powder
- 1/3 tsp. kosher salt
- 1/2 cup steamed Swiss Chard
- 1/4 tsp. dried or fresh rosemary
- 4 pork ham slices
- 1/3 tsp. of ground black pepper (or more) for added taste

Directions:
1. Divide the Swiss Chard and ham among 2 ramekins; crack an egg into each ramekin. Sprinkle with seasonings.
2. Cook for 15 minutes at 335°F or until your eggs reach desired texture.
3. Serve warm with spicy tomato ketchup and pickles. Bon appétit!

945. Cheesy mozzarella stick nachos
Servings: 4
Prep & Cooking Time: 40 Minutes
Ingredients:
- 1 (16-ounce) package mozzarella cheese sticks
- 2 eggs
- 1/2 cup flour
- 1/2 (7 12-ounce bag multigrain tortilla chips, crushed
- 1 tsp. garlic powder
- 1 tsp. dried oregano
- 1/2 cup salsa, preferably homemade

Directions:
1. Set up your breading station. Put the flour into a shallow bowl; beat the eggs in another shallow bowl; in a third bowl, mix the crushed tortilla chips, garlic powder, and oregano.
2. Coat the mozzarella sticks lightly with flour, followed by the egg, and then the tortilla chips mixture. Place in your freezer for 30 minutes.
3. Place the breaded cheese sticks in the lightly greased air fryer basket. Cook at 400°F for 6 minutes.
4. Serve with salsa on the side and enjoy!

946. Parsley yogurt dip for green pea fritters
Servings: 4
Prep & Cooking Time: 20 Minutes
Ingredients:
Pea Fritters:
- 1 1/2 cups frozen green peas
- 1 tbsp. sesame oil
- 1/2 cup chives, minced
- 2 garlic cloves, minced
- 1 cup chickpea flour
- 1 tsp. baking powder
- 1/2 tsp. sea salt
- 1/2 tsp. ground black pepper
- 1/4 tsp. dried dill
- 1/2 tsp. dried basil

Parsley Yogurt Dip:
- 1/2 cup Greek-Style yoghurt
- 2 tbsps. mayonnaise
- 2 tbsps. fresh parsley, minced
- 1 tbsp. fresh lemon juice
- 1/2 tsp. garlic, smashed

Directions:
1. Place the thawed green peas in a mixing dish; pour in hot water. Drain and rinse well.
2. Mash the green peas; add the remaining ingredients for the pea fritters and mix to combine well. Make a patties-shaped mixture then cook it in the greased cooking basket of your air fryer.
3. Bake at 380°F for 14 minutes or until thoroughly heated.
4. Meanwhile, make your dipping sauce by whisking the remaining ingredients. Place in your refrigerator until ready to serve.
5. Serve the green pea fritters with the chilled dip on the side. Enjoy!

947. Avocado chicken sliders for dinner
Servings: 4
Prep & Cooking Time: 10 Minutes
Ingredients:
- 1/2 lb. ground chicken meat
- 4 burger buns
- 1/2 cup Romaine lettuce, loosely packed
- 1/2 tsp. dried parsley flakes
- 1/3 tsp. mustard seeds
- 1 tsp. onion powder
- 1 ripe fresh avocado, mashed
- 1 tsp. garlic powder
- 1 1/2 tbsps. extra-virgin olive oil
- 1 cloves garlic, minced
- Nonstick cooking spray
- Grounded black pepper and salt (peppercorns to taste)

Directions:
1. Firstly, spritz an air fryer cooking basket with a nonstick cooking spray.
2. Mix ground chicken meat, mustard seeds, garlic powder, onion powder, parsley, salt, and black pepper until every element is thoroughly combined. Make sure not to overwork the meat to avoid tough chicken burgers.
3. Shape the meat mixture into patties and roll them in breadcrumbs; transfer your burgers to the prepared cooking basket. Brush the patties with the cooking spray.
4. Air-fry at 355°F for 9 minutes, working in batches. Slice burger buns into halves. In the meantime, combine olive oil with mashed avocado and pressed garlic.
5. To finish, lay Romaine lettuce and avocado spread on bun bottoms; now, add burgers and bun tops. Bon appétit!

948. Crispy wontons with asian-style sauce
Servings: 4
Prep & Cooking Time: 20 Minutes
Ingredients:
- 1 tsp. sesame oil
- 3/4 lb. ground beef
- Sea salt, to taste
- 1/4 tsp. Sichuan pepper
- 20 wonton wrappers

Dipping Sauce:
- 2 tbsps. low-sodium soy sauce
- 1 tbsp. honey
- 1 tsp. Gochujang
- 1 tsp. rice wine vinegar
- 1/2 tsp. sesame oil

Directions:
1. Warm tsp. of sesame oil in a wok over medium-high heat. Cook the ground beef until no longer pink. Season with salt and Sichuan pepper.
2. Lay a piece of the wonton wrapper on your palm; add the beef mixture in the middle of the wrapper. Then, fold it up to form a triangle; pinch the edges to seal tightly.
3. Place your wontons in the lightly greased air fryer basket. Cook in the preheated air fryer at 380°F for 10 minutes. Work in batches.
4. Meanwhile, mix all ingredients for the sauce. Serve warm.

949. Super sweet potato fries
Servings: 4
Prep & Cooking Time: 20 Minutes
Ingredients:
- 1 1/2 tbsps. olive oil
- 1/2 tsp. smoked cayenne pepper
- 3 sweet potatoes, peeled and cut into 1/4-inch long slices
- 1/2 tsp. shallot powder
- 1/3 tsp. of freshly ground black pepper (or more) to taste
- 3/4 tsp. garlic salt

Directions:
1. First, heat up your air fryer to 360°F.
2. Then, add the sweet potatoes to a mixing dish; toss them with the other ingredients.
3. Cook the sweet potatoes approximately 14 minutes. Serve with a dipping sauce of choice.

950. Asparagus and spinach egg salad
Servings: 4
Prep & Cooking Time: 25 Minutes + Chilling Time
Ingredients:
- 4 eggs
- 1 lb. asparagus, minced
- 2 cups baby spinach
- 1/2 cup mayonnaise
- 1 tsp. mustard
- 1 tsp. fresh lemon juice
- Ground black pepper and sea salt for added taste

Directions:
1. Position the wire rack in the air fryer basket; put the eggs in it.
2. Cook at 370°F for 15 minutes.
3. Once done, put it in cold water to stop cooking it. Remove shells while under cold running water, cut it and leave it aside.
4. Increase the temperature to 400°F. Position the asparagus in the lightly greased air fryer basket.
5. Cook for minutes or until tender. Place in a nice salad bowl. Add the baby spinach.
6. In a mixing dish, thoroughly combine the remaining ingredients. Drizzle this dressing over the asparagus in the salad bowl and top with the minced eggs. Bon appétit!

951. Sweet chocolate doughnuts
Servings: 6
Prep & Cooking Time: 20 Minutes
Ingredients:
- 1 can (16-ounce can buttermilk biscuits
- Chocolate Glaze:
- 1 cup powdered sugar
- 4 tbsps. unsweetened baking cocoa
- 2 tbsps. butter, melted
- 2 tbsps. milk

Directions:
1. Bake your biscuits in the preheated air fryer at 350°F for 8 minutes, flipping them halfway through the cooking time.
2. While the biscuits are baking, make the glaze.
3. Beat the ingredients with whisk until smooth, adding enough milk for the desired consistency; set aside.
4. Dip your doughnuts into the chocolate glaze and transfer to a cooling rack to set. Bon appétit!

952. Roasted garlic and sausage and decadent frittata
Servings: 6
Prep & Cooking Time: 20 Minutes
Ingredients:
- 6 large-sized eggs
- 2 tbsps. butter, melted
- 3 tbsps. cream
- 1 cup chicken sausage, minced
- 2 tbsps. roasted garlic, pressed

- 1/3 cup goat cheese such as Caprino, crumbled
- 1 tsp. smoked cayenne pepper
- 1 tsp. freshly ground black pepper
- 1/2 red onion, peeled and minced
- 1 tsp. fine sea salt

Directions:
1. First of all, grease six oven safe ramekins with melted butter. Then, divide roasted garlic and red onion among your ramekins. Add chicken sausage and toss to combine.
2. Beat the eggs with cream until well combined and pale; sprinkle with cayenne pepper, salt, and black pepper; beat again.
3. Scrape the mixture into your ramekins and air-fry for about 1minutes at 355°F.
4. Top with crumbled cheese and serve immediately.

953. Peppery egg salad with a twist
Servings: 3
Prep & Cooking Time: 20 Minutes + Chilling Time
Ingredients:
- 6 eggs
- 1 tsp. mustard
- 1/2 cup mayonnaise
- 1 tbsp. white vinegar
- 1 habanero pepper, minced
- 1 red bell pepper, remove the seed and sliced
- 1 red bell pepper, remove the seed and sliced
- 1 shallot, sliced
- Ground black pepper and sea salt for added taste

Directions:
1. Position the wire rack inside the air fryer; use the wire rack to hold the eggs.
2. Cook at 380°F for 15 minutes.
3. Once done, place it in a cold water to stop it getting overcooked. Remove shells while under cold running water, cut it and leave it aside.
4. Toss with the remaining ingredients and serve well chilled. Bon appétit!

954. Chicken and provolone cheese and za'atar eggs
Servings: 2
Prep & Cooking Time: 20 Minutes
Ingredients:
- 1/3 cup milk
- 1 1/2 Roma tomato, minced
- 1/3 cup Provolone cheese, shredded
- 1 tsp. freshly grounded pink peppercorns
- 3 eggs
- 1 tsp. Za'atar
- 1/2 chicken breast, cooked
- 1 tsp. fine sea salt
- 1 tsp. freshly grounded pink peppercorns

Directions:
1. First, heat up your air fryer to cook at 365°F. In a medium-sized mixing dish, whisk the eggs together with the milk, Za'atar, sea salt, and grounded pink peppercorns.
2. Spritz the ramekins with cooking oil; divide the prepared egg mixture among the greased ramekins.
3. Shred the chicken with two forks or a stand mixer. Add the shredded chicken to the ramekins, followed by the tomato and the cheese.
4. To finish, air-fry for 18 minutes or until it is done. Bon appétit!

955. Blueberries and honey with french toast
Servings: 6
Prep & Cooking Time: 20 Minutes
Ingredients:
- 1/4 cup milk
- 2 eggs
- 2 tbsps. butter, melted
- 1/2 tsp. ground cinnamon
- 1/4 tsp. ground cloves
- 1 tsp. vanilla extract
- 6 slices day-old French baguette
- 2 tbsps. honey
- 1/2 cup blueberries

Directions:
1. In a mixing bowl, whisk the milk eggs, butter, cinnamon, cloves, and vanilla extract.
2. Dip each piece of the baguette into the egg mixture and place in the parchment-lined air fryer basket.
3. Cook in the preheated air fryer at 360°F for 6 to 7 minutes, turning them over halfway through the cooking time to ensure even cooking.
4. Serve garnished with honey and blueberries. Enjoy!

956. Goat cheese in a roasted green bean salad
Servings: 4
Prep & Cooking Time: 10 Minutes + Chilling Time
Ingredients:
- 1 lb. trimmed green beans, cut into bite-sized pieces
- Salt and freshly grounded mixed pepper for added taste
- 1 shallot, slimly sliced
- 1 tbsp. lime juice
- 1 tbsp. champagne vinegar
- 1/4 cup extra-virgin olive oil
- 1/2 tsp. mustard seeds
- 1/2 tsp. celery seeds
- 1 tbsp. fresh basil leaves, minced
- 1 tbsp. fresh parsley leaves
- 1 cup goat cheese, crumbled

Directions:
1. In a greased air fryer basket, position the green beans and add salt and pepper.
2. Set the air fryer to 400°F. Leave it for 5 minutes to cook or longer as needed.
3. Add the shallots and gently stir to combine.
4. In a mixing bowl, whisk the lime juice, vinegar, olive oil, and spices. Dress the salad and top with the goat cheese. Serve at room temperature or chilled. Enjoy!

957. Mushroom omelet philadelphia style
Servings: 2
Prep & Cooking Time: 20 Minutes
Ingredients:
- 1 tbsp. olive oil
- 1/2 cup chives, minced
- 1 bell pepper, seeded and slimly sliced
- 6 ounces button mushrooms, slimly sliced
- 4 eggs
- 2 tbsps. milk
- Sea Salt & freshly ground black pepper for added taste
- 1 tbsp. fresh chives, for serving

Directions:
1. Warm the olive oil in a skillet over medium-high heat. Now, sauté the chives and peppers until aromatic.

2. Add the mushrooms and continue to cook an additional 3 minutes or until tender. Reserve.
3. Generously grease a baking pan with nonstick cooking spray.
4. Then, whisk the eggs, milk, salt, and black pepper. Spoon into the prepared baking pan.
5. Cook in the preheated air fryer at 360°F for 4 minutes. Flip and cook for a further 3 minutes.
6. Place the reserved mushroom filling on one side of the omelet. Fold your omelet in half and slide onto a serving plate. Serve immediately garnished with fresh chives. Bon appétit!

958. Stuffed chicken breasts with cheese and garlic
Servings: 2
Prep & Cooking Time: 20 Minutes
Ingredients:
- 1/2 cup Cottage cheese
- 2 eggs, beaten
- 2 medium-sized chicken breasts, halved
- 2 tbsps. fresh coriander, minced
- 1tsp. fine sea salt
- Seasoned breadcrumbs
- 1/3 tsp. freshly ground black pepper, to savor
- 3 cloves garlic, finely minced

Directions:
1. Firstly, flatten out the chicken breast using a meat tenderizer.
2. In a medium-sized mixing dish, combine the Cottage cheese with the garlic, coriander, salt, and black pepper.
3. Spread 1/of the mixture over the first chicken breast. Repeat with the remaining ingredients. Roll the chicken around the filling; make sure to secure with toothpicks.
4. Now, whisk the egg in a shallow bowl. In another shallow bowl, combine the salt, ground black pepper, and seasoned breadcrumbs.
5. Coat the chicken breasts with the whisked egg; now, roll them in the breadcrumbs.
6. Cook in the air fryer cooking basket at 370°F for 22 minutes. Serve immediately.

959. Tasty omelet with beef
Servings: 4
Prep & Cooking Time: 20 Minutes
Ingredients:
- Non-stick cooking spray
- 1/2 lb. leftover beef, coarsely minced
- 2 garlic cloves, pressed
- 1 cup kale, torn into pieces and wilted
- 1 bell pepper, minced
- 6 eggs, beaten
- 6 tbsp. sour cream
- 1/2 tsp. turmeric powder
- 1 tsp. red pepper flakes
- Salt & ground black pepper, at your convenience

Directions:
1. With a cooking spray, spritz the inside of four ramekins.
2. Divide all of the above ingredients among the prepared ramekins. Stir until every element is well combined.
3. Air-fry at 400°F for 16 minutes; check with a wooden stick and return the eggs to the air fryer for a few more minutes as needed. Serve immediately.

960. Super cheesy mushroom balls
Servings: 4
Prep & Cooking Time: 30 Minutes
Ingredients:
- 1 1/2 tbsps. olive oil
- 4 ounces cauliflower florets
- 3 garlic cloves, peeled and minced
- 1/2 yellow onion, finely minced
- 1 small-sized red chili pepper, seeded and minced
- 1/2 cup roasted vegetable stock
- 2 cups white mushrooms, finely minced
- Ground black pepper and sea salt (or more) for added taste
- 1/2 cup Swiss cheese, shredded
- 1/4 cup pork rinds
- 1 egg, beaten
- 1/4 cup Parmesan cheese, shredded

Directions:
1. Crumble the cauliflower florets by blitzing it in your food processor (it should be the size of rice).
2. Warm a saucepan over a moderate heat; now, heat the oil and sweat the cauliflower. garlic, onions, and chili pepper until tender.
3. Fry the mushrooms until it start to smell and the liquid has evaporated.
4. Add the vegetable stock and boil for 18 minutes. Now, add the salt, black pepper, Swiss cheese pork rinds, and beaten egg; mix to combine.
5. Allow the mixture to cool completely. Shape the mixture into balls. Dip the balls in the shredded Parmesan cheese. Air-fry the balls for 7 minutes at 400°F. Bon appétit!

961. Egg muffins for breakfast
Servings: 4
Prep & Cooking Time: 20 Minutes
Ingredients:
- 1/2 cup almond flour
- 1 tsp. baking powder
- 1 tbsp. granulated sweetener of choice
- 4 eggs
- 1 tsp. cinnamon powder
- 1 tsp. vanilla paste
- 1/4 cup coconut oil
- 4 tbsps. peanut butter

Directions:
1. First, heat up your air fryer to 330°F. Now, in slow but quick succession, spray cooking oil to the silicone muffin tins.
2. Thoroughly combine all ingredients in a mixing dish. Fill the muffin cups with batter.
3. Cook in the preheated air fryer approximately 1minutes. Check with a toothpick; when the toothpick comes out clean, your muffins are done.
4. Leave it to cool down or cold enough for you to remove it from the muffin tins.
5. Serve immediately.

962. Curry turkey and dijon cutlets
Servings: 4
Prep & Cooking Time: 30 Minutes
Ingredients:
- 1/2 tbsp. Dijon mustard
- 1/2 tsp. curry powder
- Sea salt flakes and freshly grounded black peppercorns, to savor
- 1/3lb. turkey cutlets
- 1/2 cup fresh lemon juice
- 1/2 tbsps. tamari sauce

Directions:
1. Set the air fryer to cook at 375°F. Then, on a mixing dish, place the turkey cutlets; add freshly squeezed lemon juice, tamari, and mustard; leave it for at least 2 hours.

2. Coat each turkey cutlet with the curry powder, salt, and freshly grounded black peppercorns; roast for 25 minutes; work in batches. Bon appétit!

963. Sausage in a scrambled eggs

Servings: 6
Prep & Cooking Time: 25 Minutes
Ingredients:
- 1 tsp. lard
- 1/2 lb. turkey sausage
- 6 eggs
- 1 scallion, minced
- 1 garlic clove, minced
- 1 sweet pepper, seeded and minced
- 1 chili pepper, seeded and minced
- Sea salt & ground black pepper for added taste
- 1/2 cup Swiss cheese, shredded

Directions:
1. First, heat up your air fryer to 330°F. Now, spritz 6 silicone molds with cooking spray.
2. Melt the lard in a saucepan over medium-high heat. Now, cook the sausage for 5 minutes or until no longer pink.
3. Coarsely chop the sausage; add the eggs, chives, garlic, peppers, salt, and black pepper. Divide the egg mixture between the silicone molds. Top with the shredded cheese.
4. Bake in the preheated air fryer at 380°F for 15 minutes, checking halfway through the cooking time to ensure even cooking. Enjoy!

964. Cheesy parmesan broccoli fritters

Servings: 6
Prep & Cooking Time: 30 Minutes
Ingredients:
- 1 1/2 cups Monterey Jack cheese
- 1 tsp. dried dill weed
- 1/3 tsp. ground black pepper
- 3 eggs, whisked
- 1 tsp. cayenne pepper
- 1/2 tsp. kosher salt
- 2 1/2 cups broccoli florets
- 1/2 cup Parmesan cheese

Directions:
1. Crumble the broccoli florets in the food processor. Then, combine the broccoli with the rest of the above ingredients.
2. Roll the mixture into small balls; place the balls in the fridge for approximately half an hour.
3. Then, heat up your air fryer to 385°F and set the timer to 14 minutes; cook until broccoli croquettes are browned and serve warm.

965. Cheesy cheese and shrimp dip

Servings: 8
Prep & Cooking Time: 25 Minutes
Ingredients:
- 2 tsps. butter, melted
- 8 ounces shrimp, peeled and emptied
- 2 garlic cloves, minced
- 1/4 cup chicken stock
- 2 tbsp. fresh lemon juice
- Salt & ground black pepper for added taste
- 1/2 tsp. red pepper flakes
- 4 ounces cream cheese, at room temperature
- 1/2 cup sour cream
- 4 tbsp. mayonnaise
- 1/4 cup mozzarella cheese, shredded

Directions:
1. Set the fryer to 395°F. Grease the sides and bottom of a baking dish with the melted butter.
2. Place the shrimp, garlic, chicken stock, lemon juice, salt, black pepper, and red pepper flakes in the baking dish.
3. Transfer the baking dish to the cooking basket and bake for 10 minutes. Add the mixture to your food processor; pulse until the coarsely is minced.
4. Add the cream cheese, sour cream, and mayonnaise. Top with the mozzarella cheese and bake in the preheated air fryer at 360°F for 6 to 7 minutes or until the cheese is bubbling.
5. Serve immediately with breadsticks if desired. Bon appétit!

966. Chicken creamed creole

Servings: 6
Prep & Cooking Time: 10 Minutes
Ingredients:
- 3 green onions, slimly sliced
- 1/2 tbsps. Creole seasoning
- 1 1/2 cups buttermilk
- 2 large-sized chicken breasts, divided in strips
- 1/2 tsp. garlic powder
- 1 tsp. salt
- 1 cup cornmeal mix
- 1 tsp. shallot powder
- 1 1/2 cups flour
- 1 tsp. ground black pepper for added taste (add more depending on your palette)

Directions:
1. Prepare three mixing bowls. Combine 2 cup of the plain flour together with the cornmeal and Creole seasoning in your bowl. In another bowl, place the buttermilk.
2. Pour the remaining 1 cup of flour into the third bowl.
3. Sprinkle the chicken strips with all the seasonings. Then, dip each chicken strip in the 1 cup of flour, then in the buttermilk; finally, dredge them in the cornmeal mixture.
4. Cook the chicken strips in the air fryer baking pan for 16 minutes at 365°F. Serve garnished with green onions. Bon appétit!

967. Healthy vegetable burrito

Servings: 6
Prep & Cooking Time: 35 Minutes
Ingredients:
- 2 tbsp. olive oil
- 1 small onion, minced
- 2 sweet peppers, seeded and minced
- 1 chili pepper, seeded and minced
- Sea salt & ground black pepper for added taste
- 1 tsp. red pepper flakes, crushed
- 1 tsp. dried parsley flakes
- 10 ounces cooked pinto beans
- 12 ounces canned sweet corn, drained
- 6 large corn tortillas
- 1/2 cup vegan sour cream

Directions:
1. First, heat up your air fryer to 400°F.
2. Warm the olive oil in a baking pan. Once hot, cook the onion and peppers until they are tender and fragrant, about 15 minutes.
3. Stir in the salt, black pepper, red pepper, parsley, beans, and sweet corn; stir to combine well.
4. Divide the bean mixture between the corn tortillas. Roll up your tortillas and place them on the parchment-lined air fryer basket.

5. Bake in the preheated air fryer at 400°F for 15 minutes. Serve garnished with sour cream. Bon appétit!

968. Sausage and swiss cheese with spicy eggs
Servings: 6
Prep & Cooking Time: 25 Minutes
Ingredients:
- 1 tsp. lard
- 1/2 lb. turkey sausage
- 6 eggs
- 1 scallion, minced
- 1 garlic clove, minced
- 1 bell pepper, seeded and minced
- 1 chili pepper, seeded and minced
- Sea salt & ground black pepper for added taste
- 1/2 cup Swiss cheese, shredded

Directions:
1. First, heat up your air fryer to 330°F. Now, spritz 4 silicone molds with cooking spray.
2. Melt the lard in a saucepan over medium-high heat. Now, cook the sausage for 5 minutes or until no longer pink.
3. Coarsely chop the sausage; add the eggs, chives, garlic, peppers, salt, and black pepper. Divide the egg mixture between the silicone molds. Top with the shredded cheese.
4. Bake in the preheated air fryer at 3°F for 15 minutes, checking halfway through the cooking time to ensure even cooking. Enjoy!

969. Delicious baked hot fruit
Servings: 4
Prep & Cooking Time: 40 Minutes
Ingredients:
- 2 cups blueberries
- 2 cups raspberries
- 1 tbsp. cornstarch
- 3 tbsps. maple syrup
- 2 tbsps. coconut oil, melted
- A pinch of freshly shredded nutmeg
- A pinch of salt
- 1 cinnamon stick
- 1 vanilla bean

Directions:
1. Place your berries in a lightly greased baking dish. Sprinkle the cornstarch onto the fruit.
2. Whisk the maple syrup, coconut oil, nutmeg, and salt in a mixing dish; add this mixture to the berries and gently stir to combine.
3. Add the cinnamon and vanilla. Bake in the preheated air fryer at 390°F for 35 minutes. Serve warm or at room temperature. Enjoy!

970. Omelet with sausage, baked
Servings: 5
Prep & Cooking Time: 14 Minutes
Ingredients:
- 3 pork sausages, minced
- 8 well-beaten eggs
- 1 1/2 bell peppers, seeded and minced
- 1 tsp. smoked cayenne pepper
- 2 tbsps. Fontina cheese
- 1/2 tsp. tarragon
- 1/2 tsp. ground black pepper
- 1 tsp. salt

Directions:
1. In a cast-iron skillet, sweat the bell peppers together with the minced pork sausages until the peppers are fragrant and the sausage begins to release liquid.
2. Lightly grease the inside of a baking dish with pan spray.
3. Throw all of the above ingredients into the prepared baking dish, including the sautéed mixture; stir to combine.
4. Bake at 3°F approximately 9 minutes. Serve right away with the salad of choice.

971. Cheesy bacon rolls
Servings: 6
Prep & Cooking Time: 10 Minutes
Ingredients:
- 1/3 cup Swiss cheese, shredded
- 10 slices of bacon
- 10 ounces canned crescent rolls
- 2 tbsps. yellow mustard 6

Directions:
1. First, heat up your air fryer to 325°F.
2. Then, form the crescent rolls into "sheets". Spread mustard over the sheets. Place the minced Swiss cheese and bacon in the middle of each dough sheet.
3. Create the rolls and bake them for about 9 minutes.
4. Then, set the machine to 385°F; bake for an additional minutes in the preheated air fryer. Eat warm with some extra yellow mustard.

972. Baked eggs masala-style
Servings: 6
Prep & Cooking Time: 25 Minutes
Ingredients:
- 6 medium-sized eggs, beaten
- 1 tsp. garam masala
- 1 cup chives, finely minced
- 3 cloves garlic, finely minced
- 2 cups leftover chicken, shredded
- 2 tbsps. sesame oil
- Hot sauce, for drizzling
- 1 tsp. turmeric
- 1 tsp. mixed peppercorns, freshly grounded
- 1 tsp. kosher salt
- 1/3 tsp. smoked paprika

Directions:
1. Warm sesame oil in a sauté pan over a moderate flame; then, sauté the chives together with garlic until just fragrant; it takes about 5 minutes. Now, throw in leftover chicken and stir until thoroughly warmed.
2. In a medium-sized bowl or a measuring cup, thoroughly combine the eggs with all seasonings.
3. Then, coat the inside of six oven safe ramekins with a nonstick cooking spray. Divide the egg/chicken mixture among your ramekins.
4. Air-fry approximately 18 minutes at 355°F. Drizzle with hot sauce and eat warm.

973. Pork meatloaf country-style
Servings: 4
Prep & Cooking Time: 25 Minutes
Ingredients:
- 1/2 lb. lean minced pork
- 1/3 cup breadcrumbs
- 1/2 tbsp. minced green garlic
- 1 1/2 tbsps. fresh cilantro, minced
- 1/2 tbsp. fish sauce
- 1/3 tsp. dried basil
- 2 leeks, minced
- 2 tbsps. tomato puree

- 1/2 tsp. dried oregano
- Salt & ground black pepper for added taste

Directions:
1. Add all ingredients, except for breadcrumbs, to a large-sized mixing dish and combine every element using your hands.
2. Lastly, add the breadcrumbs to form a meatloaf.
3. Bake for 2 minutes at 365°F. Afterward, allow your meatloaf to rest for 10 minutes before slicing and serving. Bon appétit!

974. Italian sausage and winter baked eggs
Servings: 4
Prep & Cooking Time: 30 Minutes
Ingredients:
- 1 lb. Italian sausage
- 2 sprigs rosemary
- 1 celery, sliced
- 1/2 lb. broccoli, divided into small parts
- 2 sprigs thyme
- 1 bell pepper, trimmed and cut into matchsticks
- 2 garlic cloves, smashed
- 2 tbsps. extra-virgin olive oil
- 1 leek, divide into halves lengthwise
- A pinch of shredded nutmeg
- Salt & black pepper for added taste
- 4 whole eggs

Directions:
1. Arrange vegetables on the bottom of the air fryer baking dish.
2. Sprinkle with the seasonings and top with the sausage.
3. Roast approximately 20 minutes at 5°F, stirring occasionally. Top with eggs and reduce the temperature to 330°F.
4. Bake an additional 5 to 6 minutes. Bon appétit!

975. Cornmeal pudding jamaican style
Servings: 6
Prep & Cooking Time: 1 Hour + Chilling Time
Ingredients:
- 3 cups almond milk
- 2 ounces butter, softened
- 1 tsp. cinnamon
- 1/2 tsp. shredded nutmeg
- 1 cup sugar
- 1/2 tsp. fine sea salt
- 1 1/2 cups yellow cornmeal
- 1/4 cup all-purpose flour
- 1/2 cup water
- 1/2 cup raisins
- 1 tsp. rum extract
- 1 tsp. vanilla extract

Custard:
- 1/2 cup almond milk
- 1 ounce butter
- 1/4 cup honey
- 1 dash vanilla

Directions:
1. Place the almond milk, butter, cinnamon, nutmeg, sugar, and salt in a large saucepan; bring to a rapid boil. Warm off.
2. In a mixing dish, combine the cornmeal and flour then add water; combine evenly.
3. Add the milk/butter mixture to the cornmeal mixture; mix to combine. Bring the cornmeal mixture to boil; then, reduce the heat and simmer approximately 7 minutes, whisking continuously.
4. Remove from the heat. Now, add the raisins, rum extract, and vanilla.
5. Put the mixture into a lightly greased baking pan and set air fryer to 320°F, Bake for 12 minutes.
6. In a saucepan, whisk the almond milk, butter, honey, and vanilla; let it simmer for 2 to 3 minutes. Now, prick your pudding with a fork and top with the prepared custard.
7. Return to your air fryer and bake for about 35 minutes more or until a toothpick inserted comes out dry and clean. Place in your refrigerator until ready to serve. Bon appétit!

976. Seafood casserole and breakfast eggs
Servings: 2
Prep & Cooking Time: 30 Minutes
Ingredients:
- 1 tbsp. olive oil
- 2 garlic cloves, minced
- 1 small yellow onion, minced
- 1/4 lb. tilapia pieces
- 1/4 lb. rockfish pieces
- 1/2 tsp. dried basil
- Salt and white pepper for added taste
- 4 eggs, lightly beaten
- 1 tbsp. dry sherry
- 4 tbsps. cheese, shredded

Directions:
1. First, heat up your air fryer to 350°F; add the olive oil to a baking pan. Once hot, cook the garlic and onion for 2 minutes or until fragrant.
2. Add the fish, basil, salt, and pepper. In a mixing dish, thoroughly combine the eggs with sherry and cheese. Pour the mixture into the baking pan.
3. Cook at 390°F approximately 20 minutes. Bon appétit!

977. Florentine baked eggs
Servings: 2
Prep & Cooking Time: 20 Minutes
Ingredients:
- 1 tbsp. ghee, melted
- 2 cups baby spinach, torn into small pieces
- 2 tbsps. shallots, minced
- 1/4 tsp. red pepper flakes
- Salt, to taste
- 1 tbsp. fresh thyme leaves, roughly minced
- 4 eggs

Directions:
1. First, heat up your air fryer to 350°F. Brush the sides and bottom of a gratin dish with the melted ghee.
2. Put the spinach and shallots into the bottom of the gratin dish. Season with red pepper, salt, and fresh thyme.
3. Make four indents for the eggs; crack one egg into each indent. Rotate the pan as needed to ensure even cooking. Cook for at least 12 minutes. Enjoy!

978. Grilled pork chops with lemon
Servings: 5
Prep & Cooking Time: 35 Minutes
Ingredients:
- 5 pork chops
- 1/3 cup vermouth
- 1/2 tsp. paprika
- 2 sprigs thyme, only leaves, crushed
- 1/2 tsp. dried oregano
- Fresh parsley, to serve
- 1 tsp. garlic salt
- 1/2 lemon, cut into wedges

- 1 tsp. freshly grounded black pepper
- 3 tbsps. lemon juice
- 3 cloves garlic, minced
- 2 tbsps. canola oil

Directions:
1. Firstly, heat the canola oil in a sauté pan over a moderate heat. Now, sweat the garlic until just fragrant.
2. Take the pan off the heat and pour vermouth and lemon juice. Now, throw in the seasonings. Dump the sauce into a baking dish, along with the pork chops.
3. Tuck the lemon wedges among the pork chops and air-fry for 25 minutes at 385°F. Bon appétit!

979. Meatloaf a la creole turkey
Servings: 6
Prep & Cooking Time: 45 Minutes
Ingredients:
- 1 1/3 lbs. turkey breasts, ground
- 1/2 cup vegetable stock
- 2 eggs, lightly beaten
- 1/2 sprig thyme, minced
- 1/2 tsp. Creole seasonings
- 1/2 sprig coriander, minced
- 1/2 cup seasoned breadcrumbs
- 2 tbsps. butter, room temperature
- 1/2 cup chives, minced
- 1/3 tsp. ground nutmeg
- 1/3 cup tomato ketchup
- 1/2 tsp. table salt
- 2 tsps. whole grain mustard
- 1/3 tsp. mixed peppercorns, freshly grounded

Directions:
1. Firstly, warm the butter in a medium-sized saucepan that is placed over a moderate heat; sauté the chives together with the minced thyme and coriander leaves until just tender.
2. While the chives are sautéing, set your air fryer to cook at 365°F.
3. Combine all the ingredients, minus the ketchup, in a mixing dish; fold in the sautéed mixture and mix again.
4. Shape into a meatloaf and top with the tomato ketchup. Air-fry for 50 minutes. Bon appétit!

980. Bacon wrapped onion rings
Servings: 4
Prep & Cooking Time: 25 Minutes
Ingredients:
- 12 rashers back bacon
- 1/2 tsp. ground black pepper
- Chopped fresh parsley, to taste
- 1/2 tsp. paprika
- 1/2 tsp. chili powder
- 1/2 tbsp. soy sauce
- 1/2 tsp. salt

Directions:
1. First, heat up your air fryer to 355°F.
2. Season the onion rings with paprika, salt, black pepper, and chili powder. Simply wrap the bacon around the onion rings; drizzle with soy sauce.
3. Bake for 17 minutes, garnish with fresh parsley and serve. Bon appétit!

981. Linguica sausage and baked eggs
Servings: 2
Prep & Cooking Time: 18 Minutes
Ingredients:
- 1/2 cup Cheddar cheese, shredded
- 4 eggs
- 2 ounces Linguica (Portuguese pork sausage), minced
- 1/2 onion, peeled and minced
- 2 tbsps. olive oil
- 1/2 tsp. rosemary, minced
- 1/2 tsp. marjoram
- 1/4 cup sour cream
- Sea Salt & freshly ground black pepper for added taste
- 1/2 tsp. fresh sage, minced

Directions:
1. Lightly grease 2 oven safe ramekins with olive oil. Now, divide the sausage and onions among these ramekins.
2. Crack an egg into each ramekin; add the remaining items, minus the cheese. Air-fry at 355°F approximately 13 minutes.
3. Immediately top with Cheddar cheese, serve, and enjoy.

982. Super english muffins
Servings: 4
Prep & Cooking Time: 15 Minutes
Ingredients:
- 4 English muffins, split in half
- 2 eggs
- 1/3 cup milk
- 1/4 cup heavy cream
- 2 tbsps. honey
- 1 tsp. pure vanilla extract
- 1/4 cup confectioners' sugar

Directions:
1. Cut the muffins crosswise into strips.
2. In a mixing dish, add the eggs and milk with the heavy cream. Pour honey and vanilla extract.
3. Dip each piece of muffins into the egg mixture and place in the parchment-lined air fryer basket.
4. Cook in the preheated air fryer at 360°F for 6 to 7 minutes, turning them over halfway through the cooking time to ensure even cooking.
5. Dust with confectioners' sugar and serve warm.

983. Savory crespelle italian style
Servings: 3
Prep & Cooking Time: 25 Minutes
Ingredients:
- 3/4 cup all-purpose flour
- 2 eggs, beaten
- 1/4 tsp. allspice
- 1/2 tsp. salt
- 3/4 cup milk
- 1 cup ricotta cheese
- 1/2 cup Parmigiano-Reggiano cheese, preferably freshly shredded
- 1 cup marinara sauce

Directions:
1. Mix the flour, eggs, allspice, and salt in a large bowl. Gradually add the milk, whisking continuously, until well combined.
2. Let it stand for 10 minutes.
3. Spritz the air fryer baking pan with cooking spray. Pour the batter into the prepared pan.
4. Cook at 230°F for 3 minutes. Flip and cook until browned in spots, 2 to 3 minutes longer.
5. Repeat with the remaining batter. Serve with the cheese and marinara sauce. Bon appétit!

984. Sweet small monkey rolls
Servings: 6
Prep & Cooking Time: 25 Minutes
Ingredients:
- 3/4 cup brown sugar
- 1 stick butter, melted
- 1/4 cup granulated sugar
- 1 tsp. ground cinnamon
- 1/4 tsp. ground cardamom
- 1 (16-ounces) can refrigerated buttermilk biscuit dough

Directions:
1. Spritz 6 standard-size muffin cups with nonstick spray. Mix the brown sugar and butter; divide the mixture between muffin cups.
2. Mix the granulated sugar with cinnamon and cardamom. Separate the dough into 16 biscuits; cut each in 6 pieces. Roll the pieces over the cinnamon sugar mixture to coat. Divide between muffin cups.
3. Bake at 380°F for about 20 minutes or until golden brown. Turn upside down and serve.

985. Original pork chops
Servings: 6
Prep & Cooking Time: 22 Minutes
Ingredients:
- 1/3 cup Italian breadcrumbs
- Roughly minced fresh cilantro, to taste
- 2 tsps. Creole seasonings
- Nonstick cooking spray
- 2 eggs, beaten
- 3 tbsps. white flour
- 1 tsp. seasoned salt
- Garlic and onion spice blend, to taste
- 6 pork chops
- 1/3 tsp. freshly grounded black pepper

Directions:
1. Coat the pork chops with Creole seasonings, salt, pepper, and the spice blend on all sides.
2. Then, add the flour to a plate. In a shallow dish, whisk the egg until pale and smooth. Position the Italian breadcrumbs in another empty bowl.
3. Dredge each pork piece in the flour; then, coat them with the egg; finally, coat them with the breadcrumbs. Spritz them with cooking spray on both sides.
4. Now, air-fry pork chops for about 18 minutes at 380°F; make sure to taste for doneness after first 12 minutes of cooking.
5. Lastly, garnish with fresh cilantro. Bon appétit!

986. Omelet with special mushrooms and peppers
Servings: 2
Prep & Cooking Time: 20 Minutes
Ingredients:
- 1 tbsp. olive oil
- 1/2 cup chives, minced
- 1 bell pepper, seeded and slimly sliced
- 6 ounces button mushrooms, slimly sliced
- 4 eggs
- 2 tbsps. milk
- Sea Salt & freshly ground black pepper for added taste
- 1 tbsp. fresh chives, for serving

Directions:
1. Warm the olive oil in a skillet over medium-high heat. Now, sauté the chives and peppers until aromatic.
2. Add the mushrooms and continue to cook an additional 3 minutes or until tender. Reserve.
3. Generously grease a baking pan with nonstick cooking spray.
4. Then, whisk the eggs, milk, salt, and black pepper. Spoon into the prepared baking pan.
5. Cook in the preheated air fryer at 360°F for 4 minutes. Flip and cook for a further 3 minutes.
6. Place the reserved mushroom filling on one side of the omelet. Fold your omelet in half and slide onto a serving plate. Serve immediately garnished with fresh chives. Bon appétit!

987. Healthy and zesty broccoli bites with hot dip
Servings: 6
Prep & Cooking Time: 20 Minutes
Ingredients:
For the Broccoli Bites:
- 1 medium-sized head broccoli, broken into florets
- 1/2 tsp. lemon zest, freshly shredded
- 1/3 tsp. fine sea salt
- 1/2 tsp. hot paprika
- 1 tsp. shallot powder
- 1 tsp. porcini powder
- 1/2 tsp. granulated garlic
- 1/3 tsp. celery seeds
- 1 1/2 tbsps. olive oil

For the Hot Sauce:
- 1/2 cup tomato sauce
- 3 tbsps. brown sugar
- 1 tbsp. balsamic vinegar
- 1/2 tsp. ground allspice

Directions:
1. Toss all the ingredients for the broccoli bites in a mixing bowl, covering the broccoli florets on all sides.
2. Cook them in the preheated air fryer at 360°F for 13 to 15 minutes. In the meantime, mix all ingredients for the hot sauce.
3. Pause your air fryer, mix the broccoli with the prepared sauce and cook for further minutes. Bon appétit!

988. Kernel and sweet corn fritters
Servings: 4
Prep & Cooking Time: 20 Minutes
Ingredients:
- 1 medium-sized carrot, shredded
- 1 yellow onion, finely minced
- 4 ounces canned sweet corn kernels, dried
- 1 tsp. sea salt flakes
- 1 heaping tbsp. fresh cilantro, minced
- 1 medium-sized egg, whisked
- 2 tbsps. plain milk
- 1 cup of Parmesan cheese, shredded
- 1/4 cup of self-rising flour
- 1 tsp. baking powder
- 1/3 tsp. brown sugar

Directions:
1. Press down the shredded carrot in the colander to remove excess liquid. Then, spread the shredded carrot between several sheets of kitchen towels and pat it dry.
2. Then, mix the carrots with the remaining ingredients in the order listed above.
3. Make a roll of ball from the mixture. Use your hand to flatten it. Now, repeat with the remaining ingredients.
4. Spitz the balls with a nonstick cooking oil. Cook in a single layer at 350°F for 8 to 11 minutes or until they're firm to touch in the center. Serve warm and enjoy!

989. Chicken sausage with delectable frittata
Servings: 2
Prep & Cooking Time: 15 Minutes
Ingredients:
- 1 tbsp. olive oil
- 2 chicken sausages, sliced
- 4 eggs
- 1 garlic clove, minced
- 1/2 yellow onion, minced
- Sea salt & ground black pepper for added taste
- 4 tbsps. Monterey-Jack cheese
- 1 tbsp. fresh parsley leaves, minced

Directions:
1. Grease the sides and bottom of a baking pan with olive oil.
2. Add the sausages and cook in the preheated air fryer at 360°F for 4 to 5 minutes.
3. In a mixing dish, whisk the eggs with garlic and onion. Season with salt and black pepper.
4. Pour the mixture over sausages. Top with cheese. Cook in the preheated air fryer at 360°F for another 6 minutes.
5. Serve immediately with fresh parsley leaves. Bon appétit!

990. Kale omelet with beef
Servings: 4
Prep & Cooking Time: 20 Minutes
Ingredients:
- Non-stick cooking spray
- 1/2 lb. leftover beef, coarsely minced
- 2 garlic cloves, pressed
- 1 cup kale, torn into pieces and wilted
- 1 tomato, minced
- 1/4 tsp. brown sugar
- 4 eggs, beaten
- 4 tbsps. heavy cream
- 1/2 tsp. turmeric powder
- Salt & ground black pepper, at your convenience
- and tsp. ground allspice

Directions:
1. Spritz the inside of four ramekins with a cooking spray.
2. Divide all of the above ingredients among the prepared ramekins. Stir until every element is well combined.
3. Air-fry at 400°F for 16 minutes; check with a wooden stick and return the eggs to the air fryer for a few more minutes as needed. Serve immediately.

991. Fried mushrooms for all
Servings: 4
Prep & Cooking Time: 15 Minutes
Ingredients:
- 1 lb. button mushrooms
- 1 cup cornstarch
- 1 cup all-purpose flour
- 1 tsp. baking powder
- 2 eggs, whisked
- 2 cups seasoned breadcrumbs
- 1/2 tsp. salt
- 2 tbsps. fresh parsley leaves, roughly minced

Directions:
1. Use paper towel to dry the mushrooms.
2. To begin, set up your breading station. Mix the cornstarch, flour, and baking powder in a shallow dish. In another empty dish, prepare the eggs.
3. Finally, place your breadcrumbs and salt in a third dish.
4. Start by dredging the mushrooms in the flour mixture; then, dip them into the eggs. Press your mushrooms into the breadcrumbs, coating evenly.
5. Cover the air fryer basket with cooking oil. Add the mushrooms and cook at 400°F for 6 minutes, flipping them halfway through the cooking time.
6. Serve garnished with fresh parsley leaves. Bon appétit!

992. Delicious chicken with tamari sauce
Servings: 4
Prep & Cooking Time: 10 Minutes + Marinating Time
Ingredients:
For the Marinade:
- 1 1/2 tsp. olive oil
- 1 tsp. red pepper flakes, crushed
- 1/3 tsp. chicken bouillon granules
- 1/3 tsp. shallot powder
- 1 1/2 tbsps. tamari soy sauce
- 1/3 tsp. cumin powder
- 1 1/2 tbsps. mayo
- 1 tsp. kosher salt

For the chicken:
- 2 beaten eggs
- Breadcrumbs
- 1 1/2 boneless and skinless chicken breasts
- 1 1/2 tbsps. plain flour

Directions:
1. Butterfly the chicken breasts, and then, marinate them for at least 55 minutes.
2. Coat the chicken with plain flour; then, coat with the beaten eggs; finally, roll them in the breadcrumbs.
3. Lightly grease the cooking basket. Air-fry the breaded chicken at 385°F for 12 minutes, flipping them halfway.

993. Cheese and cauli rice with baked eggs
Servings: 4
Prep & Cooking Time: 30 Minutes
Ingredients:
- 1 lb. cauliflower rice
- 1 onion, diced
- 6 slices bacon, precooked
- 1 tbsp. butter, melted
- Sea salt & ground black pepper for added taste
- 6 eggs
- 1 cup cheddar cheese, shredded

Directions:
1. Place the cauliflower rice and onion in a lightly greased casserole dish. Add the bacon and the reserved quinoa. Drizzle the melted butter over cauliflower rice and sprinkle with salt and pepper.
2. Bake in the preheated air fryer at 390°F for 10 minutes.
3. Turn the temperature down to 390°F.
4. Make six indents for the eggs; crack one egg into each indent. Bake for 10 minutes, rotating the pan once or twice to ensure even cooking.
5. Top with cheese and bake for a further minutes. Enjoy!

994. Creamy frittata with kale italian-style
Servings: 3
Prep & Cooking Time: 20 Minutes
Ingredients:
- 1 yellow onion, finely minced
- 6 ounces wild mushrooms, sliced
- 6 eggs
- 1/4 cup double cream

- 1/2 tsp. cayenne pepper
- Ground black pepper and sea salt for added taste
- 1 tbsp. butter, melted
- 2 tbsps. fresh Italian parsley, minced
- 2 cups kale, minced
- 1/2 cup mozzarella, shredded

Directions:
1. Begin by preheating the air fryer to 360°F. Spritz the sides and bottom of a baking pan with cooking oil.
2. Add the onions and wild mushrooms, and cook in the preheated air fryer at 360°F for 4 to 5 minutes.
3. In a mixing dish, whisk the eggs and double cream until pale. Add the spices, butter, parsley, and kale; stir until every element is well incorporated.
4. Pour the mixture into the baking pan with the mushrooms.
5. Top with the cheese. Cook in the air fryer for 10 minutes. Serve immediately and enjoy!

995. Caci cavallo with keto brioche

Servings: 6
Prep & Cooking Time: 15 Minutes
Ingredients:
- 1/2 cup ricotta cheese, crumbled
- 1 cup part skim mozzarella cheese, shredded
- 1 egg
- 1/2 cup coconut flour
- 1/2 cup almond flour
- 1 tsp. baking powder
- 2 tbsps. plain whey protein isolate
- 3 tbsps. sesame oil
- 2 tsps. dried oregano
- 1 1/2 cups CACI cavallo, shredded
- 1 cup leftover chicken, shredded
- 3 eggs
- 1 tsp. kosher salt
- 1 tsp. of freshly grounded black pepper, or more for added taste
- 1/3 tsp. gremolata

Directions:
1. To make the keto brioche, microwave the cheese for minute 30 seconds, stirring twice. Add the cheese to the bowl of a food processor and blend well. Fold in the egg and mix again.
2. Add in the flour, baking powder, and plain whey protein isolate; blend again. Scrape the batter onto the center of a lightly greased cling film.
3. Form the dough into a disk and transfer to your freezer to cool; cut into 6 pieces and transfer to a parchment-lined baking pan (make sure to grease your hands).
4. Firstly, slice off the top of each brioche; then, scoop out the insides.
5. Brush each brioche with sesame oil. Add the remaining ingredients in the order listed above.
6. Place the prepared brioche onto the bottom of the cooking basket. Bake for 7 minutes at 345°F. Bon appétit!

996. Turkey bacon, green onions and eggs

Servings: 4
Prep & Cooking Time: 25 Minutes
Ingredients:
- 1/2 lb. turkey bacon
- 4 eggs
- 1/3 cup milk
- 2 tbsp. yogurt
- 1/2 tsp. sea salt
- 1 bell pepper, finely minced
- 2 green onions, finely minced
- 1/2 cup Colby cheese, shredded

Directions:
1. Place the turkey bacon in the cooking basket.
2. Cook at 360°F for 9 to 11 minutes. Work in batches. Reserve the fried bacon.
3. In a mixing bowl, thoroughly whisk the eggs with milk and yogurt. Add salt, bell pepper, and green onions.
4. Brush the sides and bottom of the baking pan with the reserved 1 tsp. of bacon grease.
5. In the baking pan, add the egg mixture. Cook at 3°F about 5 minutes. Top with shredded Colby cheese and cook for 5 to 6 minutes more.
6. Serve the scrambled eggs with the reserved bacon and enjoy!

997. Cauliflower balls with cheese

Servings: 4
Prep & Cooking Time: 26 Minutes
Ingredients:
- 4 ounces cauliflower florets
- 1/2 cup roasted vegetable stock
- 1 egg, beaten
- 1 cup white mushrooms, finely minced
- 1/2 cup parmesan cheese, shredded
- 3 garlic cloves, peeled and minced
- 1/2 yellow onion, finely minced
- 1/3 tsp. ground black pepper, or more for added taste
- 1 1/2 bell peppers, seeded minced
- 1/2 chipotle pepper, seeded and minced
- 1/2 cup Colby cheese, shredded
- 1 1/2 tbsps. canola oil
- Sea salt, to savor

Directions:
1. Crumble the cauliflower florets in your food processor until it is the size of a rice.
2. Warm a saucepan over a moderate heat; now, heat the oil and sweat the garlic, onions, bell pepper, cauli rice, and chipotle pepper until tender.
3. Fry the mushroom until it starts to smell and dry up.
4. Add in the stock; boil for 18 minutes. Now, add the cheese and spices; mix to combine.
5. Allow the mixture to cool completely. Shape the mixture into balls. Dip the balls in the beaten egg; then, roll them over the shredded parmesan.
6. Air-fry these balls for minutes at 400°F. Serve with marinara sauce and enjoy!

998. Yummy omelet with smoked veggies and tofu

Servings: 2
Prep & Cooking Time: 20 Minutes
Ingredients:
- 2 eggs, beaten
- 1/3 cup cherry tomatoes, minced
- 1 bell pepper, seeded and minced
- 1/3 tsp. freshly ground black pepper
- 1/2 purple onion, peeled and sliced
- 1 tsp. smoked cayenne pepper
- 5 medium-sized eggs, well-beaten
- 1/3 cup smoked tofu, crumbled
- 1 tsp. seasoned salt
- 1 1/2 tbsp. fresh chives, minced

Directions:
1. Brush a baking dish with a spray coating.
2. Throw all ingredients, minus fresh chives, into the baking dish; give it a good stir.
3. Cook about 15 minutes at 5°F. Garnish with fresh minced chives. Bon appétit!

999. Fried rice with eggs japanese style
Servings: 2
Prep & Cooking Time: 30 Minutes
Ingredients:
- 2 cups cauliflower rice
- 2 tsps. sesame oil
- Sea Salt & freshly ground black pepper, at your convenience
- 2 eggs, beaten
- 2 chives, white and green parts separated, minced
- 1 tbsp. Shoyu sauce
- 1 tbsp. sake
- 2 tbsps. Kewpie Japanese mayonnaise

Directions:
1. Thoroughly combine the cauliflower rice, sesame oil, salt, and pepper in a baking dish.
2. Cook at 340°F about 13 minutes, stirring halfway through the cooking time.
3. Pour the eggs over the cauliflower rice and continue to cook about 5 minutes. Next, add the chives and stir to combine. Continue to cook 2 to minutes longer or until every element is heated through.
4. Meanwhile, make the sauce by whisking the Shoyu sauce, sake, and Japanese mayonnaise in a mixing bowl.
5. Divide the fried cauliflower rice between individual bowls and serve with the prepared sauce. Enjoy!

1000. Cheesy risotto balls with a spicy twist
Servings: 4
Prep & Cooking Time: 26 Minutes
Ingredients:
- 3 ounces cooked rice
- 1 /2 cup roasted vegetable stock
- 1 egg, beaten
- 1 cup white mushrooms, finely minced
- 1/2 cup seasoned breadcrumbs
- 3 garlic cloves, peeled and minced
- 1/2 yellow onion, finely minced
- 1/3 tsp. ground black pepper, or more for added taste
- 1 1/2 bell peppers, seeded minced
- 1/2 chipotle pepper, seeded and minced
- 1/2 tbsp. Colby cheese, shredded
- 1 1/2 tbsps. canola oil
- Sea salt, to savor

Directions:
1. Warm a saucepan over a moderate heat; now, heat the oil and sweat the garlic, onions, bell pepper and chipotle pepper until tender. Fry the mushrooms until tender and it starts to smell. Make sure it becomes dry and the liquid has evaporated.
2. Throw in the cooked rice and stock; boil for 18 minutes. Now, add the cheese and spices; mix to combine.
3. Allow the mixture to cool completely. Shape the risotto mixture into balls. Dip the risotto balls in the beaten egg; then, roll them over the breadcrumbs.
4. Air-fry risotto balls for 6 minutes at 390°F. Serve with marinara sauce and enjoy!

1001. Garlic-mayo sauce for potato
Servings: 4
Prep & Cooking Time: 19 Minutes
Ingredients:
- 2 tbsps. vegetable oil of choice
- Kosher Salt & freshly ground black pepper for added taste
- 3 Russet potatoes, cut into wedges
- For the Dipping Sauce:
- 2 tsps. dried rosemary, crushed
- 3 garlic cloves, minced
- 1/3 tsp. dried marjoram, crushed
- 1/4 cup sour cream
- 1/3 cup mayonnaise

Directions:
1. Lightly grease your potatoes with a slim layer of vegetable oil. Season with salt and ground black pepper.
2. Set the seasoned potato wedges in an air fryer cooking basket. Bake at 395°F for 15 minutes, shaking once or twice.
3. In the meantime, prepare the dipping sauce by mixing all the sauce ingredients. Serve the potatoes with the dipping sauce and enjoy!

1002. Creamy asparagus and egg salad
Servings: 4
Prep & Cooking Time: 25 Minutes + Chilling Time
Ingredients:
- 2 eggs
- 1 lb. asparagus, minced
- 2 cup baby spinach
- 1/2 cup mayonnaise
- 1 tsp. mustard
- 1 tsp. fresh lemon juice
- Sea salt & ground black pepper for added taste

Directions:
1. Position the wire rack inside the air fryer; lower the eggs onto the wire rack.
2. Cook at 390°F for 15 minutes.
3. Once done, place it in a cold water to stop it getting overcooked. Remove shells while under cold running water, cut it and leave it aside.
4. Increase the temperature to 390°F. Place your asparagus in the lightly greased air fryer basket.
5. Cook for minutes or until tender. Place in a nice salad bowl. Add the baby spinach.
6. In a mixing dish, thoroughly combine the remaining ingredients. Drizzle this dressing over the asparagus in the salad bowl and top with the minced eggs. Bon appétit!

1003. Cheesy carrot fries
Servings: 3
Prep & Cooking Time: 20 Minutes
Ingredients:
- 3 carrots, sliced into sticks
- 1 tbsp. coconut oil
- 1/3 cup Parmesan cheese, preferably freshly shredded
- 2 tsp. granulated garlic
- Sea salt & ground black pepper for added taste

Directions:
1. Toss all ingredients in a mixing bowl until the carrots are coated on all sides.
2. Cook at 380°F for 15 minutes, shaking the basket halfway through the cooking time.
3. Serve with your favorite dipping sauce. Bon appétit!

1004. Original onion rings with mayo dip

Servings: 3
Prep & Cooking Time: 25 Minutes
Ingredients:
- 1 large onion
- 1/2 cup almond flour
- 1 tsp. salt
- 1/2 tsp. ground black pepper
- 1 tsp. cayenne pepper
- 1/2 tsp. dried oregano
- 1/2 tsp. dried oregano
- 1/2 tsp. ground cumin
- 2 eggs
- 4 tbsps. milk
- Mayo Dip:
- 3 tbsps. mayonnaise
- 3 tbsps. sour cream
- 1 tbsp. horseradish, drained
- Kosher Salt & freshly ground black pepper for added taste

Directions:
1. Cut off the top 2 inch of the Vidalia onion; peel your onion and place it cut-side down. Starting 1/2 inch from the root, cut the onion in half. Make a second cut that splits each half in two. You will have 4 quarters held together by the root.
2. Repeat these cuts, splitting the 4 quarters to yield eighths; then, you should split them again until you have 16 evenly spaced cuts. Peel the onion parts with your fingers or separate outer parts.
3. In a mixing bowl, thoroughly combine the almond flour and spices. In a separate bowl, whisk the eggs and milk. Dip the onion into the egg mixture, followed by the almond flour mixture.
4. Spritz the onion with cooking spray and transfer to the lightly greased cooking basket. Cook for 370°F for 12 to 15 minutes.
5. Meanwhile, make the mayo dip by whisking the remaining ingredients. Serve and enjoy!

1005. Amazing greek revithokeftedes

Servings: 3
Prep & Cooking Time: 30 Minutes
Ingredients:
- 12 ounces canned chickpeas, drained
- 1 red onion, sliced
- 2 cloves garlic
- 1 chili pepper
- 1 tbsp. fresh coriander
- 2 tbsps. all-purpose flour
- 1/2 tsp. cayenne pepper
- Sea salt and freshly ground pepper for added taste
- 3 large (6 1/2 -inch pita bread

Directions:
1. Pulse the chickpeas, onion, garlic, chili pepper and coriander in your food processor until the chickpeas are ground.
2. Add the all-purpose flour, cayenne pepper, salt, and black pepper; stir to combine well.
3. Make balls from the chickpea mixture and cook it in a slightly greased air fryer.
4. Cook at 380°F for about 15 minutes, shaking the basket occasionally to ensure even cooking.
5. Warm the pita bread in your air fryer at 390°F for around 6 minutes.
6. Serve the revithokeftedes in pita bread with tzatziki or your favorite Greek topping. Enjoy!

1006. Potato wedges with a spicy twist

Servings: 4
Prep & Cooking Time: 23 Minutes
Ingredients:
- 1 1/2 tbsps. melted butter
- 1 tsp. dried parsley flakes
- 1 tsp. ground coriander
- 1 tsp. seasoned salt
- 3 large-sized red potatoes, cut into wedges
- 1/2 tsp. chili powder
- 1/3 tsp. garlic pepper

Directions:
1. Dump the potato wedges into the air fryer cooking basket. Drizzle with melted butter and cook for 20 minutes at 380°F. Make sure to shake them a couple of times during the cooking process.
2. Add the remaining ingredients; toss to coat potato wedges on all sides. Bon appétit!

1007. Chicken and goat cheese in a spring frittata

Servings: 4
Prep & Cooking Time: 10 Minutes
Ingredients:
- 1 cup goat cheese, crumbled
- 1 tsp. dried rosemary
- 2 cups cooked chicken breasts, boneless and shredded
- 1/4 tsp. mustard seeds
- 1 tsp. red pepper flakes, crushed
- 5 medium-sized whisked eggs
- 1/3 tsp. ground white pepper
- 1/2 cup green onions, minced
- 1 green garlic stalk, minced
- Fine sea salt, to taste
- Nonstick cooking spray

Directions:
1. Grab a baking dish that fit in your air fryer.
2. Add and sprinkle non-stick oil to the baking dish. Stir in all ingredients, minus cheese. Stir to combine well.
3. Set your machine to cook at 5°F for 8 minutes; check for doneness. Scatter crumbled goat cheese over the top and eat immediately!

1008. Cheesy cheese sticks with ketchup dip

Servings: 4
Prep & Cooking Time: 15 Minutes
Ingredients:
- 1/4 cup coconut flour
- 1/4 cup almond flour
- 2 eggs
- 1/2 cup parmesan cheese, shredded
- 1 tbsp. Creole seasonings
- 8 cheese sticks, kid-friendly
- 1/4 cup ketchup, low-carb

Directions:
1. To begin, set up your breading station. Place the flour in a shallow dish. In another empty dish, prepare the eggs.
2. Finally, mix the parmesan cheese and Creole seasoning in a third dish.
3. Start by dredging the cheese sticks in the flour; then, dip them into the egg. Press the cheese sticks into the parmesan mixture, coating evenly.
4. Place the breaded cheese sticks in the lightly greased air fryer basket. Leave it to cook for 6 minutes at 380°F.
5. Serve with ketchup and enjoy!

1009. Ground meat omelet filipino-style
Servings: 3
Prep & Cooking Time: 20 Minutes
Ingredients:
- 1 tsp. lard
- 2/3 lb. ground beef
- 1/4 tsp. chili powder
- 1/2 tsp. ground bay leaf
- 1/2 tsp. ground pepper
- Sea salt, to taste
- 1 red bell pepper, seeded and minced
- 1 red bell pepper, seeded and minced
- 6 eggs
- 1/3 cup double cream
- 1/2 cup Colby cheese, shredded
- 1 tomato, sliced

Directions:
1. Melt the lard in a cast-iron skillet over medium-high heat. Add the ground beef and cook for 4 minutes until no longer pink, crumbling with a spatula.
2. Add the ground beef mixture, along with the spices to the baking pan. Now, add the bell peppers.
3. In a mixing bowl, whisk the eggs with double cream. Spoon the mixture over the meat and peppers in the pan.
4. Cook in the preheated air fryer at 355°F for 10 minutes.
5. Top with the cheese and tomato slices. Continue to cook for minutes more or until the eggs are golden and the cheese has melted.

1010. Cashew sauce for fingerling potatoes
Servings: 4
Prep & Cooking Time: 20 Minutes
Ingredients:
- 1 lb. fingerling potatoes
- 1 tbsp. butter, melted
- Sea salt & ground black pepper, at your convenience
- 1 tsp. shallot powder
- 1 tsp. garlic powder

Cashew Sauce:
- 1/2 cup raw cashews
- 1 tsp. cayenne pepper
- 3 tbsps. nutritional yeast
- 2 tsps. white vinegar
- 4 tbsps. water
- 1/4 tsp. dried rosemary
- 1/4 tsp. dried dill

Directions:
1. Toss the potatoes with the butter, salt, black pepper, shallot powder, and garlic powder.
2. Place the fingerling potatoes in the lightly greased air fryer basket and cook at 400°F for 6 minutes; shake the basket and cook for a further 6 minutes.
3. Meanwhile, make the sauce by mixing all ingredients in your food processor or high-speed blender.
4. Drizzle the cashew sauce over the potato wedges. Bake at 400°F for 2 more minutes or until every element is heated through. Enjoy!

1011. Salty pretzel crescents
Servings: 4
Prep & Cooking Time: 20 Minutes
Ingredients:
- 1 can crescent rolls
- 10 cups water
- 1/2 cup baking powder
- 1 egg, whisked with 1 tbsp. water
- 1 tbsp. poppy seeds
- 2 tbsps. sesame seed
- 1 tsp. coarse sea salt

Directions:
1. Unroll the dough onto your work surface; separate into 8 triangles.
2. In a large saucepan, bring the water and baking powder to a boil over high heat.
3. Cook each roll for a few seconds. Remove from the water using a slotted spoon; place on a kitchen towel to drain.
4. Repeat with the remaining rolls. Use brush to apply egg wash at the top; sprinkle each roll with the poppy seeds, sesame seed and coarse sea salt. Cover and let rest for 10 minutes.
5. Set the pretzels in the lightly greased air fryer basket.
6. Bake in the preheated air fryer at 340°F for 7 minutes or until golden brown. Bon appétit!

Chapter 7
Cooking Measurements & Kitchen Conversion Chart

U.S. Measurements

U.S. Liquid Volume Measurements

Cups	Fluid Ounces	Tablespoons	Teaspoons
1	8	16	48
3/4	6	12	36
1/2	4	8	24
1/3	2 2/3	5 tbsp + 1 tsp	16
1/4	2	4	12
1/16	.5	1	3

U.S. to Metric Conversions

Weight Conversions

Imperial	Metric
1/2 oz.	14 g
1 oz.	28 g
2 oz.	57 g
3 oz.	85 g
4 oz.	113 g
5 oz.	142 g
6 oz.	170 g
7 oz.	199 g
8 oz.	227 g
9 oz.	255 g
10 oz.	284 g
12 oz	340 g
1 lb.	454 g
1 ½ lb.	680 g
2 lb.	907 g
2.2 lb.	1 kg

U.S. to Metric Conversions

Liquid Volume Conversions

Fluid Ounces	Cups	Mililiters	Liters
2	1/4	59	.059
4	1/2	118	.118
8	1	237	.237
16	2	473	.473
24	3	710	.71
32	4	946	.946
33.6	4.22	1000	1

Temperature Conversions

Fahrenheit	Celsius	Gas Mark	Description
225	107	1/4	Very Low
250	121	1/2	Very Low
275	135	1	Low
300	149	2	Low
325	163	3	Moderate
350	177	4	Moderate
375	190	5	Moderately Hot
400	204	6	Moderately Hot
425	218	7	Hot
450	238	8	Hot
475	246	9	Very Hot

Chapter 8
Air fryer Cooking Chart

VEGETABLES

FOOD	TEMP	TIME	FOOD	TEMP	TIME
Asparagus	400	5	Onions (pearl)	400	10
Beets (whole)	400	40	Parsnips (cubes)	380	15
Broccoli	400	6	Peppers (1 inch chunks)	400	15
Brussel sprouts	380	15-20	Potatoes (baby)	400	15
Carrots (sliced)	380	15	Potatoes (1 inch chunks)	400	12
Cauliflower florets	400	12	Potatoes (baked whole)	400	40
Corn on the cob	400	9-10	Squash (1/2 inch chunks)	400	12
Eggplant	370	20	Squash (cut in half)	360	25-30
Green beans	400	8	Sweet potato (baked)	380	35
Kale leaves	250	12	Tomatoes (cherry)	400	4
Mushrooms (sliced)	400	5	Tomatoes (halves)	350	10
Mushrooms (whole)	380	10-12	Zucchini (1/2 inch sticks)	400	12

MEAT

FOOD	TEMP	TIME	FOOD	TEMP	TIME
Chicken breasts	380	12	Meatballs	380	7-10
Chicken drumsticks	370	20	Ribeye (bone in)	400	10-18
Chicken thighs (bone in)	380	22	Sirloin steaks	400	9-14
Chicken thighs (boneless)	380	20	Beef eye round roast	390	45-55
Chicken legs (bone in)	380	30	Pork loin	360	55
Chicken wings	400	12	Pork chops (bone in)	400	12
Whole chicken	360	75	Pork tenderloin	370	15
Tenders / chicken strips	360	10	Bacon	400	5-10
Burger	370	16	Sausages	380	15
Filet mignon	400	18	Lamb loin chops	400	8-12
Flank steak	400	12	Rack of lamb	380	22

FISH & SEAFOOD

FOOD	TEMP	TIME	FOOD	TEMP	TIME
Calamari	400	4-8	Swordfish steak	400	10
Fish fillet	400	8-12	Tuna steak	400	7-10
Lobster tails	375	7-10	Scallops	400	5-7
Salmon fillet	380	10-12	Shrimp	350	5-8

FROZEN FOODS

FOOD	TEMP	TIME	FOOD	TEMP	TIME
Onion rings	400	8	Pot stickers	400	8
Potato wedges	350	25-30	Fish sticks	400	10
Thin french fries	400	14	Fish fillets	400	14
Thick french fries	400	18	Chicken nuggets	400	10
Mozzarellla sticks	400	8	Chicken tenders	400	15
Sausage rolls	400	15	Breaded shrimp	400	9
Egg rolls /spring rolls	400	8-10	Hot pockets	370	11-13

BAKED SWEETS & SNACKS

FOOD	TEMP	TIME	FOOD	TEMP	TIME
Muffins	300	15	Cookies	360	10
Cake	300	30	Personal pizza	360	8
Cupcakes	300	15	Tortilla chips/taco shells	350	3-8
Brownies	320	30	Roasted nuts	350	5-8
Banana bread	360	25	Chickpeas	400	15
Mug cakes	360	15	Baked apples	400	15

Printed in Great Britain
by Amazon